Praise for *The Othe*

"The result of eight years of reportir ... the story of Bobby. . . . [Nicholas] Da... presents portraits of the individuals involved, juxtaposed with research on segregation, the Great Migration, and mass incarceration." —*The New Yorker*

"A powerful, poignant and profound account of deindustrialization, racial discrimination, inequality and mass incarceration."
—Glenn Altschuler, *Florida Courier*

"Nicholas Dawidoff's *The Other Side of Prospect* might well be the best book on race in America in the past decade."
—Larry Matthews, *Washington Independent Review of Books*

"At the tender core of Dawidoff's remarkable book is his portrait of Bobby, a boy from the 'other side' who came of age while incarcerated, and although he was exonerated, he reentered society from prison branded with an invisible 'scarlet *P*.'"
—*National Book Review*

"Gripping. . . . [B]y brilliantly documenting in the most compelling personal terms the broader challenges of economic racism, criminal injustice, and urban neglect, [Dawidoff] is challenging New Haven and America to pay attention." —Paul Bass, *New Haven Independent*

"A monumental, wrenching account of urban inequity."
—*Harvard Magazine*

"A rich, sweeping tale of interlocking lives and tragic history. . . . [U]ltimately, Dawidoff, a New Haven native, is taking aim at economics and weapons as the worst villains."
—James Ledbetter, *Yale Alumni Magazine*

"A searing portrait of injustice in America." —*Publishers Weekly*

"[A] rigorously reported, urgent book." —*Kirkus Reviews*

"*The Other Side of Prospect* isn't just a necessary American book, it's an essential American book. By unraveling the long, profound story across generations that leads to one teenager twice confessing to a crime that he didn't commit, Nicholas Dawidoff reveals just how pervasive the failures of our time can be. A child of intelligence and personal promise becomes a killer; an elderly grandfather is murdered; and an innocent boy suffers under the brutal weight of nearly a decade in prison with memories no exoneration can erase. This is beyond the best book about the crisis of incarceration in America. It is also a book that reminds us indelibly that the Great Migration has tragically ended for many in not just the closing of factories and opportunities, but also the filling of graves and prison cells."

—Reginald Dwayne Betts, author of *Felon*

"*The Other Side of Prospect* illuminates complex social issues—the Great Migration, mass incarceration, wrongful conviction, prisoner reentry—in deeply personal terms. This is a haunting, devastating, magnificent work of narrative nonfiction."

—James Forman Jr., Pulitzer Prize–winning author of *Locking Up Our Own*

"This intricate book continues to grow like a tree in me—Bobby's tender, persistent yearnings bound by the generations of contaminated soil that fear creates. Nicholas Dawidoff's huge accomplishment is that he does the meticulous forensics of the crime of our fearing those in peril, and *The Other Side of Prospect* portrays the ongoing consequences of what we all continue to lose—all the knowledge lost, all the joy that's stilled—when fear predominates. I finished reading his book with heartbreak and great gratitude. Its quest for broader justice pushes forward."

—Adrian Nicole LeBlanc, author of *Random Family*

"*The Other Side of Prospect* is an intimate and haunting recovery of lives both lost and found, potential both squandered and realized, and struggles both failed and furthered. It forces us to face the brutal injustice and inequality that defines our nation's justice system as well as one of its richest and most prestigious cities, and to take a hard look at the deeper roots and wider resonances of that ugliness. The true gift of Nicholas Dawidoff's powerful recovery of this wrongful conviction and the fight to have it overturned, however, is its ability to help us to see what is still irrevocably beautiful about this country, and thus what still may be possible for its future."

—Heather Ann Thompson, Pulitzer Prize–winning author of *Blood in the Water*

"*The Other Side of Prospect* is a riveting narrative that shows and tells the story of a deeply distressed Black ghetto neighborhood severely challenged by the ills of deindustrialization, racialized poverty, and random street crime and violence—a must-read for anyone wishing to understand."

—Elijah Anderson, Sterling Professor of Sociology and of African American Studies, Yale University, and author of *Black in White Space*

THE OTHER SIDE OF PROSPECT

ALSO BY NICHOLAS DAWIDOFF

Collision Low Crossers

The Crowd Sounds Happy

The Fly Swatter

In the Country of No Country

The Catcher Was a Spy

THE OTHER SIDE OF PROSPECT

A STORY OF VIOLENCE, INJUSTICE, AND THE AMERICAN CITY

NICHOLAS DAWIDOFF

W. W. NORTON & COMPANY
Celebrating a Century of Independent Publishing

Printed in the United States of America
First published as a Norton paperback 2023

For information about permission to reproduce selections from this book, write to
Permissions, W. W. Norton & Company, Inc., 500 Fifth Avenue, New York, NY 10110

For information about special discounts for bulk purchases, please contact
W. W. Norton Special Sales at specialsales@wwnorton.com or 800-233-4830

Manufacturing by Lakeside Book Company
Book design by Chris Welch Design
Production manager: Julia Druskin

Library of Congress Cataloging-in-Publication Data

Names: Dawidoff, Nicholas, author.
Title: The other side of prospect : a story of violence, injustice, and the American city /
Nicholas Dawidoff.
Description: First edition. | New York, NY : W. W. Norton & Company, Inc, [2022] |
Includes bibliographical references.
Identifiers: LCCN 2022036538 | ISBN 9781324002024 (hardcover) |
ISBN 9781324002031 (epub)
Subjects: LCSH: Discrimination in justice administration—Connecticut—New Haven. |
Race discrimination—Connecticut—New Haven. | African Americans—Civil rights—
Connecticut—New Haven. | Income distribution—Connecticut—New Haven. | Equality—
Connecticut—New Haven. | Deindustrialization—Connecticut—New Haven.
Classification: LCC HV9956.N48 D38 2022 | DDC 364.9746/8—dc23/eng/20220916
LC record available at https://lccn.loc.gov/2022036538

ISBN 978-1-324-06602-6 pbk.

W. W. Norton & Company, Inc., 500 Fifth Avenue, New York, N.Y. 10110
www.wwnorton.com

W. W. Norton & Company Ltd., 15 Carlisle Street, London W1D 3BS

1 2 3 4 5 6 7 8 9 0

For Larry Harris, Greg Lyss, and Jamie Wright, old times

and for Dwayne Betts, new haven

these too are your children this too is your child

—Lucille Clifton, "the times"

Every crime, as soon as it actually occurs, turns at once into a completely particular case, sir; and sometimes, just think, really completely unlike all the previous ones.

—Fyodor Dostoyevsky, *Crime and Punishment*

If one really wishes to know how justice is administered in a country, one does not question the policemen, the lawyers, the judges, or the protected members of the middle class. One goes to the unprotected.

—James Baldwin, *No Name in the Street*

CONTENTS

Prologue: **Prospect Street** 1

PART I: POP-POP 13

PART II: JUST AROUND 85

PART III: THE STICKUP KID AND THE INNOCENT BOY 187

PART IV: TRUE BELIEVER 245

PART V: REENTRY 281

PART VI: AMERICAN DREAMS 353

Epilogue: **Prospects** 399

Acknowledgments 405
A Note on Sources 407
Bibliography 415

AUTHOR'S NOTE

All spoken words in this book were either said in my presence, were recounted by people who were there, or appear printed in legal documents such as police reports, court transcripts, or depositions. Certain names of individuals have been changed, but no facts have been altered.

THE OTHER SIDE OF PROSPECT

PROLOGUE

Prospect Street

Early on the summer evening of August 1, 2006, on a mournful New Haven side street, an elderly man from another town who'd just cashed checks worth nearly $2,000 was sitting in his cream-colored luxury car. A young stranger appeared at his window and killed the man with a single, point-blank gunshot to the neck from a .45 caliber pistol. A .45 is a weapon so powerful it's a handheld artillery piece. Few people are murderers. Fewer still kill strangers. Far fewer again are capable of such an intimate execution. Another stranger, a sixteen-year-old boy who was blocks away, inside a pharmacy, went to prison for the shooting. Whatever muted outcry that followed in the city was soon undercut by the settled belief that these were the things that happened. The conditioned insignificance of the crime carried its significance. In three men, inextricably bound by violence, was the gone grandeur of cities, the end of new beginnings, and old, unresolved American history.

RUNNING OUT NORTH from the campus of Yale University at the center of New Haven, a small American city with big-city problems, is a shady boulevard called Prospect Street. The flat roadway is flanked by steep hillsides, making driving the length of Prospect Street somewhat like crossing a mesa. Most of Prospect Street is residential, a line of rambling old mansions and villas, privet hedges, gardens, courtyards, and statuary that lend it the aura of times past, when carriages rolled along rather than SUVs. True to its name, Prospect was conceived as a promontory from which "the socially acceptable," as a local guide once described its residents, could stand at their high windows and take in the city. Sloping downward, to the southeast, were the gables of handsome houses and church spires, giving way to the shimmering amplitude of the harbor, the Long Island Sound, and, on a clear day, the Gold Coast of Long Island. But to turn about and look to the west offered no vista. The leafage remained so dense that the view resembled a vast sweep of open green parasols, with all that lay below impossible to see. What could be heard, however, with alarming frequency, was the sound of gunfire.

The neighborhood over the hill is called Newhallville. For well over a century it was inhabited by waves of immigrants—Irish, Germans, Poles, Italians—who found nearby industrial jobs that paid for first houses, until each moved up and out, giving way, in turn, to the African Americans who arrived from the Carolinas and other Southern states during the later stages of the Great Migration. They lived much as their European forebears had done, and in the early 1960s, Newhallville became, as one resident from the time remembered, "the most risen, solid Black neighborhood." Then the factories closed, creating the persistent American postindustrial problem of a fully formed working-class neighborhood without any work. New Haven had always been a city of contrasts, a lunch-bucket company town and an Ivy League college town. Postindustrial lack of opportunity deepened local division, and in the new millennium New Haven became the United States city with the fastest growing ratio for inequality. Yet what set New Haven apart made it also representative: in a country riven by concentrated peaks and depths of wealth and poverty, Jed Kolko's study found that New Haven residents' age, education level, race, and ethnicity gave it the demographic distinction of being America's most "normal" city. While Yale's endowment soared beyond $42 billion, the adjacent community of Newhallville, said a woman who'd lived there through it all, was "fallen to the depths."

For recent generations of young people in Newhallville, who referred to their home as "the Ville," Prospect Street was the invisible railroad track, the boundary that cleaved their New Haven into two unequal cities, one affluent and white, the other poor and Black. Those on each slope of the hill spoke of the community up and over as the other side. The word "other" communicated the distance and unfamiliarity of close neighbors, and plenty of people on the Newhallville side felt also that there was disregard, an assumption that their circumstances existed because they were different rather than differently treated.

This was a longstanding American class phenomenon. As the wealthy white New York reformer and co-founder of the NAACP, Mary White Ovington, wrote of her later nineteenth-century childhood in fashionable Brooklyn Heights near a worker's district, "No place was more remote than that section of the city in which persons of a different caste lived." Ovington marveled at how indifferent she had become in her youth to such divergent conditions, how she simply "accepted" the poverty and segregation that existed right across the way as the inevitability of things as opposed to a "problem in my city" that people worried about. That it was willful unawareness, never personal or urgent, was exactly the problem.

When, in 1968, Martin Luther King Jr. gave a speech in suburban Detroit he called "The Other America," he explained that a geographic "dualism" persisted in "every city in our country." What differentiated New Haven then, and still now, from the similar American race-class juxtapositions in New York, New Orleans, Baltimore, St. Louis, Los Angeles, and Chicago was that New Haven's was an extreme version of these unequal frontiers, with generations of neighbors living side by side, so close, right there, yet each unknown to the other. That you couldn't take public transportation from Newhallville through Prospect Hill enhanced "an artificial sense of separation and distance," said one Black Newhallville native. Another Black man from Newhallville, Ned Moundsman, grew up with parents working the first and third shifts at munitions, packaging, and bagel factories that all would go out of business or leave town. "Prospect Street is the divide," he said. "That's always been there. There's an imaginary line for us. One New Haven over that side of the hill. This side is a whole 'nother New Haven. Chocolate Hill. You don't cross over. Unwritten rule. Our parents told us, *You don't go over there. Something might happen to you.*"

The entire Newhallville neighborhood spans less than a mile. It is compact and self-contained, like a galvanized pail without a handle. All streets but the former commercial corridors were built on a narrow, horse-drawn scale offering significant challenges to minivans, especially in snow. Among younger people, many streets are referenced in shorthand—D-Side for Division Street, the R and the W mean Read and Willis Streets—and other streets are described in a patter everybody knows: "It's hard on Harding." The grid of streets was reorganized by city planners during the 1990s to form a confusing sequence of one-way signs, some of them, including on Read Street, requiring abrupt block-to-block directional switches, done to frustrate car thieves and out-of-town drug purchasers.

Single mothers headed most households. But in the pale fog of child poverty, the family structure was less fundamental than the lack of resources. Low salaries and corresponding grocery budgets were often why, in 2021, as in 2006, 4 in 10 families were hungry on a regular basis; 6 in 10 residents got by on means deep below the federal poverty line. Life expectancy was fifteen years less than in the nearby mostly white suburban town of Orange. Something else that Newhallville had in scarce supply was middle-aged men, a deficit that could be explained, in part, by health, limited chances for gainful employment, and prison sentences. The relationship between Connecticut prisons and Newhallville had long been entwined. By 2015, only three streets in the neighborhood did not have a formerly incarcerated person living on them.

As recently as the 1960s, Newhall Street and Shelton Avenue pulsed with customers walking into the neighborhood's hardware stores, record shops, bakeries, and workingmen's taverns, but by the 2000s its 6,500 residents were well accustomed to having no grocery store, no bank, no laundry, no gas station, nowhere to get a money order. There was a basketball court near Lincoln-Bassett Elementary School, but most kids avoided it because of what they called "the violence."

As both the director of Ice the Beef, an anti-violence organization, and an employee at the board of education, a Black New Haven native named Chaz Carmon daily confronted what living in one city with "two different worlds" meant. Tranquil Prospect Street, for instance, was lined with blue "panic phones," while Newhallville had none. But it was Newhallville where panic pressed. In Connecticut, as across the larger country, homicide rates had subsided in the pre-COVID years, with one caveat. Homicide was the leading American cause of death for Black men age forty-five and younger. In Connecticut, Blacks were twenty-two times more likely than whites to be shot to death.

The killings of Black men, most of them undereducated and from poor city neighborhoods, carried an intimacy. Since the early 1990s, Carmon guessed that he had personally known one hundred people murdered in New Haven. During his teens, he said, "Living in poverty to us was normal. Shooting people is normal now." Gunfire was to Carmon an expression of the times, of a city with "communities right together but right apart," of the humiliation of being less cared about and cared for. Doctors who spent their lives studying trauma in children, like Bessel van der Kolk, said that shooters often wanted others to suffer as they suffered, and that gun violence brought "a certain amount of power in a powerless world. Gives you a sense of self-worth: I can take action. I can do things. Respect and humiliation are central."

ONE PERSON FROM Newhallville whose life followed in the grooves of such explanations was a boy known as Major. Major was the most compelling student in whatever classroom he entered. His pre-algebra teacher noticed that variables and probabilities just made sense to Major, while in social studies, if a concept relating to pre-Jamestown history was taught in September, he stored it away, and when the industrial revolution was discussed in late spring, Major alone retrieved the old era to explain the new. "Major had natural abilities," his social studies teacher said. "Real potential. I left teaching because watching kids like Major hurt my heart."

As a teenager, Major had ventured alone over Prospect Hill for the purpose of committing street robberies. Pointing guns at strangers and telling them to "run it" landed Major in juvenile detention. There, a man who counseled him took in both Major's intelligence and his emptiness of spirit—his twilit feeling, even at age fifteen, that the city held no hope for somebody like him. After Major was released, he soon moved on from being a stickup kid to being thought to have committed so many street murders in the summer of 2006, he became neighborhood-famous for violence. As another young Newhallville shooter said, Major was "brief-full-fledged." After Major was murdered himself, there was a gust of public grief for him, a church overfilled with mourners. Nobody wanted a child to follow this course, but Major, too, was an extreme variation on a common American calamity.

Major's tragedy was interwoven with the tragedies of his victims—those who died, and also young people uninvolved in street violence becoming enmeshed because they were from the neighborhood. Such was the case with Bobby. In 2006, to those young Newhallville men in the neighborhood drug game, sixteen-year-old Bobby was "just around." He wasn't deep into the streets, was instead a still-growing teenage face in the crowd of corner standers who described spending their time "politicking" outside an all-night market known as "the 2-4"—another boy who cared about basketball, girls, and Air Jordan sneakers; a "corny" stoner who hung out watching *Space Jam* over and over with a kid two years younger whose nickname was Regular. Bobby himself didn't have a nickname. Coming of age in this neighborhood, which local elders sometimes referred to as "a forgotten community," meant that it was easy to look past what distinguished someone like Bobby.

Bobby's just-around reputation spoke to one of his abilities, which was fitting in wherever he went, to his instinct for being there. "I feel I was the type of kid who adapted," he said. "That came natural to me and I did it." Seated on outside couches, playing basketball at the park, chilling at house parties, he listened to others with attentive interest while maintaining nonchalant scrutiny of what went on. Bobby's conversation was efficient to the point of being epigrammatic, and yet when he described his block, it came alive, like a watercolor: "Crazy foot traffic. People on porches. Jumping out of cars. Walk around." Not yet fully grown at five-foot-six, with an induction buzzcut for summertime that emphasized protruding ears, dark skin, a trusting pre-adolescence in his eyes, Bobby was skilled at being watchful without seeming watchful, an alert, accurate close observer who saw blurry life with clarity, and remembered what he saw. "I pay attention to everything," he said, thinking back on his boyhood self. "I knew who was who. I knew everything. It's not hard. You notice my eyes are always moving. Taking everything in. That's different about me."

Bobby had been up close to abundant hardship all his young life, and he understood the unrelenting avalanche of crises and strife that defined the days of many people around him. It was never just someone's heart failure. Even when it came to the things people were most ashamed of, like an addict who stole her grandmother's rent money to get high, Bobby could see the way difficult conditions drove actions that then brought humiliation. So his usual first impulse was to consider rather than condemn. With that compassionate sensitivity came a boundaried discretion. As a result, vulnerable people often confided in Bobby. "To me it's always easy to separate things I know," he said. "I'm a big secret holder for other people. That's how I was as a kid. People tell me their vicious secrets."

Bobby was also a kid who craved worldly experience, and so, on his own, he went off in search. Over time, Bobby came to think of himself as "a traveler." A traveler, he said, was not the typical boy who stayed stuck in his neighborhood but someone who ventured out and beyond. By age nine, Bobby was riding his red BMX bike with the low seat and high handlebars "everywhere" across New Haven, including up Prospect Hill. Traveling the city, Bobby himself often felt anonymous, invisible to others, making him the unseen person who sees.

Astride his BMX bike, Bobby could traverse Newhallville in less than three minutes. Moving from the marshy, cattailed "Beaver Pond" to the west out by Sherman Parkway, he'd cross the busy Dixwell Avenue strip by the 2-4 and pedal several blocks through the forlorn, used-dishwater everydayness of the Flats. Streets named for flowers (Lilac) and shrubs (Hazel) were lined with small, close-to-the-curb wood-frame Victorian homes, often split up into multifamily units. The sidewalk meridians had rows of tree trunks sized out of proportion to the narrow roads and buildings, the branches creating such a thick canopy that even on bright summer days, they contributed, in Bobby's mind, to "the dark energy of Newhallville." At Winchester Avenue, he'd pedal more vigorously, climbing the steep residential escarpment of Up-Top, passing red traffic signs that were sometimes amended in white spray paint to read STOP SNITCHING. At the hill's crest he came bursting over the lip onto Prospect Street, where, abruptly, America changed.

On the hilltop, Bobby had parallax views of his parallax city. "It's wicked," was his assessment of the stark Prospect Street divide. "These people literally in your backyard, your next-door neighbors." Because people, as Bobby put it, "stay in their own zone," there was insufficient sense outside Newhallville of the way old problems became new problems. Most of those, for instance, who relied on food stamps traced their histories back to Reconstruction-era formerly enslaved Southern rural Black families who never received the promised forty acres of farmland. Black ministers then had proposed land redistribution so "we can best take care of ourselves."

When he was up around Prospect Street, Bobby sensed wary eyes on him, that he was being sized up as an interloper lacking a passport. Still, to him there was agency in being a traveler, and he enjoyed the quality of the air, the sight lines—even the substance of the rainwater seemed superior. "That's this city," he said. "Come over that hill, it's a whole different reality. You can feel peacefulness." By contrast in Newhallville, he said, "You feel the harm. It's dirty. No maintenance of properties. The liquor stores. Little corner bodegas. No fresh. No healthy. You look around—why's it not healthy?"

Down in the Ville, every kid Bobby knew, whether just around or in the game, had to reckon with the possibility of violence. The nature of gun violence was that aggressors one day were victims the next, and the silent uninvolved majority in the neighborhood were damaged by proximity. By age sixteen, Bobby had lived vicarious mayhem enough that, "It's impossible to run out of stories. If I had a recorder to follow me across my life, stuff I seen, people killed in front of me, shot, stabbed, beat up . . ." He estimated that twenty young people he knew had died. It was more when he actually began counting.

If Bobby needed to get away and feel safer, he took out his bike and rode up to Prospect Hill. Bobby believed there was apathy for Newhallville among those living in New Haven's prosperous areas, and probably scorn. To Bobby it seemed taken for granted by those over the hill that Black people on his side should be poor and reside in a less-desirable place to live, and that likewise nobody up there had any idea of what the day-to-day was for a person like Bobby. Prospect Street functioned as one-way reflective glass: Bobby could see them, but they couldn't see him.

The police could. The police were thought by young people in Newhallville to be instantly responsive to crimes committed on Prospect Hill, which made potential culprits from over the hill stay away. "The consequences are more severe when you're in good communities," Bobby said. It was a very small Newhallville cohort who were the feared neighborhood stickup kids, and most-everyone knew who they were. But Bobby said even his impeccably law-abiding peers from the neighborhood would never spend time near Prospect Street, afraid of being roughed up or arrested for being where they didn't live. This led Bobby to relax up there in a way he never did down in Newhallville. "On Prospect Street, you don't have to go eye-surfing," he said. "Newhallville, you can't park and sit there. On Prospect, nothing happens."

In his own heavily policed neighborhood, Bobby sensed a different law-enforcement calculus. "Move on to the other side of Prospect," he said, "they don't give a damn about Newhallville murders as long as they arrest someone."

PEOPLE AROUND BOBBY were bothered when their neighborhood was reduced to its problems. For many who lived there, such as Bobby's close friend and teenage crush, a slightly older honor student named Shay, Newhallville was the old neighborhood. Shay's maternal grandmother had come up from Georgia, to work at the Winchester gun factory, and owned the house Shay grew up in, down the block from Bobby on Willis Street. Wherever she went, just about everybody who happened to be there would greet her, "Shay! What up, Shay!" Even those Shay hadn't met were bound to be familiar—"If you don't know that one, they know two of your three. And then if I don't know two of their three, they know at least my one. So, everybody is some way connected."

That the Ville was "all family-knit" also came over Shay after school when she'd walked down Newhall Street, past the house decorated with figurines, colored bottles, and other Southern-style yard art, perhaps stopping in at Mr. Eddie's Barber Shop, where, for schoolchildren in this neighborhood with no library, the owner kept a dictionary and other reference books. (Waiting customers could peruse magazines and a copy of *A Black Man's Guide to Law Enforcement in America*.) Moving along, Shay might encounter a local pastor staging a spontaneous sidewalk gathering. "He'll walk out and sing and have a church service right there on the corner," she said. Street preachers were commonly seen in Shay's family's part of the South, and while Shay thought "people up North are very for themselves," these neighbors were "trying to do community stuff, and that's what I like." To her, the richly textured neighborhood itself was family.

Throughout Newhallville, there were plenty of older homeowners, like Shay's grandmother, who had decided they would never leave. It wasn't just the houses they owned; it was the serious work of life they'd put into the neighborhood. There was an animating feeling to these narrow streets where arrivals from far away had remade their existences, an underground entrepreneurial spirit that went back to the "side hustles" and "bootlegger houses" born out of Jim Crow privation in the South. For fulfilling life's small, spontaneous staples and pleasures, said Shay, "the Ville is the spot. You can get anything you need at one in the morning. Like, you know, you can get a potato, and you can get a bag of sugar, or you can get a dollar soda at one in the morning. No other neighborhood has it like this." The situation corresponded to the Newhallville trees. Those large branches brought somber shadows to the sidewalks, and they also conveyed light, health, and beauty.

People who'd grown up in Newhallville and then long since departed often returned for haircuts, for church, for socializing. One contingent of older African American men routinely parked their Mercedes and Cadillacs on Shelton Avenue and went into a clubhouse they called the Mudhole for a Saturday drink and a game of poker. Many had come to New Haven's factories fifty years ago as young men from the rural Carolinas, and even now might refer to themselves as "country boys." Among them was a former Wolfton, South Carolina, farming kid, Herbert Fields Jr., known as Pete.

In 1960, when Fields's parents bought a house on Read Street, that was still the time of a prevalent rising Black middle class in Newhallville, and the Fields kids walked up and over Prospect Hill without thinking anything about it. By 1964, Pete Fields had a career and a mortgage of his own out in

West Haven. Then, in the late 1970s, came a larger house in West Haven, where Fields remained.

Not only was his property immaculate, he also maintained the neighborhood. In a time when Keep America Beautiful was still a recently conceived civic campaign, Pete took it upon himself to collect litter during long daily walks. If he spotted someone in the driveway making car repairs, he'd stroll up to help. Later, a foil-covered plate might be left at their door. Pete's pastime was grilling spiced, seasoned meats brushed with vinegar-based South Carolina–style barbecue sauce. That his relationships were born of considerate gestures, his son Peter said, made his father an unelected local official—"The Patriarch of our street. Black kids. White kids. Cops' kids. Mail carriers' kids. They all looked at him as their father. We didn't want to hear, 'Wait till your daddy gets home.' My friends' [single] moms would say, 'Don't let me call Mr. Fields down here.'" The warning had purchase because, as Pete's daughter, Susan, said, "My dad had the street smarts. He was a tough guy."

In 2006, not far from the Mudhole clubhouse, it was Fields who was sitting in his car when a teenager who didn't know him appeared and pointed a .45. The .45 was Major's weapon of choice. Killing up close was another signature.

The slaughter of an elderly Black man on the single block of a gloomy street was yet another homicide in a neighborhood where distressing incidents of violence were common enough that everybody knew somebody. All the more reason to draw a line, keep a distance, stay away, leave it to the two detectives—who arrested Bobby.

TO TRULY UNDERSTAND how all this had come to pass required going back in time to Pete Fields's post-Depression-era South Carolina childhood, required seeing Bobby with the care with which he saw you. Bicycling through his city, Bobby could tell that place in America matters, especially for boys, and that being born into a segregated slum all but predicts your lack of a good future. "New Haven," he said, "it's nothing here to look forward to."

There was a limit to how much you could learn from a bike seat. Bobby grew up within walking distance of one of the best universities in the world, but it took going away to prison for him to become educated, and for him to surmise the importance of experience, how "people aspire to be what they know." Only in prison would Bobby take in how much he didn't know. Inexperience all but defines being young, but in prison Bobby looked around and grasped that very different were the stakes of inexperience for kids like him.

To understand about Bobby's childhood was to understand something about the nature of how young people lived during the age of inequality in a largely poor, segregated neighborhood that felt rejected by its wealthier neighbors. For even the toughest people, to be rejected is rarely benign; mostly it just hurts. "It has to do something to the psyche of a town," said a former teacher at one of Bobby's schools. "Kids living in one section, and within a stone's throw is another world, and knowing you can't be part of that other world."

PART I

\\\\\\\\\\\\\\\\\\\\\\\\

POP-POP

Chapter One

Herbert Fields Jr., known to all as Pete, raised a daughter, Susan, and two sons in Connecticut, and from them he kept his childhood a mystery of another time and place. "My dad didn't tell us a lot about South Carolina," Susan said. "We'd miss the bus and he'd tell us he walked six miles to school. And that after sixth grade he had to stop school and work on the farm." Pete Fields himself had thirteen brothers and sisters, the youngest Katie-Jean Fields, a retired schoolteacher in the mid-South. When Katie-Jean began organizing *My Time Has Come and Gone*, a book of family memory, from some of her siblings she encountered a reluctance to go back there similar to what Susan felt from her father. Nobody wanted to be portrayed in any way as a victim. For them, past consequential events were so much about loss that they seemed better left between the family and God, which perhaps enabled an acceptance of what might otherwise have been too painful to reconcile.

THE AMERICAN DREAM has always been about property. Across generations, there's been no more reliable way of accumulating wealth than through the increasing value of land and a home. Ownership, in turn, has meant both individual and community self-possession, because people naturally have most wanted to care for and improve what belonged to them. For those who were kept close to the land before it could be theirs, the desire to own was profound. Historian Steven Hahn describes Civil War interactions in Southern states when Northerners encountered formerly enslaved people who made clear their attachment to where they lived, and the yearning to have, as one South Carolina elder put it, "land that is rich with the sweat of we face and the blood of we back. We born here, we parents' graves here; this here our home."

The post–Civil War Reconstruction-era failure to redistribute land among formerly enslaved Black Southerners effectively meant that African Americans were, said Frederick Douglass, "sent away empty-handed, without money, without friends, and without a foot of land to stand upon." The predictable result was Black Southerners were positioned as inferiors outside the system, for whom there was still no justice, no generational accumulation of net worth, their self-sufficient subsistence a challenge on plots of low-grade soil.

Yet after Reconstruction, Black families owning larger farms "was rare, but more common than you would think," said Kenneth Middleton, whose father, Earl, in the 1950s founded Orangeburg, South Carolina's first Black-owned real estate firm out of his barber shop. Land in much of the post–Civil War South had been relatively inexpensive, and motivated Black farmers bought large, fertile swaths, usually off the main roads, places they'd be less likely to attract white people's envy.

Pete Fields's grandfather David Fields, a prudent businessman farmer, in the first part of the twentieth century amassed 192 acres of sandy-loam soil in the fertile central South Carolina countryside watered by the North fork of the Edisto River, outside the crossroads "area" of Wolfton. Locals pronounce Wolfton as "Woof-ton" and like to say it was more thought up than founded. Named for a local Swiss-German farming family called Wolfe, Wolfton center is remote, eleven country miles outside Orangeburg. David Fields's cotton and corn fields were down unpaved roads in a backwoods thick with sweet gum, white oak, old pines, vines, waterways, and snapping turtles that could bite off a human arm. The Fields farm was so secluded that no doctors would come. The property had fishing ponds, cattle barns, horse and mule stables, henhouses, hog pens, outbuildings for storing equipment, a vegetable garden, and a spacious single-story eight-room homeplace the color of natural lumber.

In the 1920s, David's son, Herbert Lee Fields (Herbert Sr.), Herbert Sr.'s wife, Susie, and their growing family were part of a rising middle-class Black community in Philadelphia. There, Herbert Sr. had a job as an elevator operator, a city home with plumbing and electricity, and the relief of no longer having to defer to white people everywhere he walked. Then David fell ill. Having acquired what his daughter, Katie-Jean, calls "a taste of a better life," Herbert Sr. and his family left it to help the ailing David back in Wolfton. Trouble soon found them there.

Writer Edward Ball found that among white Americans, 40 percent have ancestors who first came into North America through New York's Ellis Island. Among Black Americans, 40 percent have ancestors who arrived on slave ships that docked in Charleston, South Carolina. South Carolina, writes historian Tiya Miles, was "an exaggerated version of the undemocratic slaveholding South." It was the first state to secede, the state where the South's highest percentage (half) of the white population were enslavers, the state which invented the plantation patrols that enforced subjugation. A prominent governor and plantation owner, James Henry Hammond, called slavery "the greatest of all the great blessings which Providence has bestowed upon our glorious region." The system Hammond extolled depended upon the inflicting of sadistic plantation punishments, like whipping and wound-salting, atrocities that made Frederick Douglass among the many who would come to understand how exposure to violence begat violence, among everybody, Black and white people, during slavery and after.

When the Fields family lived near Orangeburg, white swimmers in the Edisto River were required to swim upstream and black people to swim downstream to avoid contamination. The Black section in the balcony of a movie theater was known by white people as the "buzzard's roost." A granite column soaring thirty feet high with a bronze rifle-carrying Confederate soldier on top honoring "the brave defenders of our rights" complemented a well-earned local reputation for lynching through the first world war, and ongoing organized bigotry. After integration, private segregated academies for white students would emerge like mushrooms on a damp lawn. In 1968, at historically Black South Carolina State University, three unarmed student demonstrators were killed and twenty-eight wounded, half shot in the back or the soles of their feet. The "Orangeburg Massacre" more than doubled the casualties at Kent State.

According to Eric Powell, an Orangeburg historian, the area's racial hierarchy was enforced by whites "railroading" noncompliant Black people out of their homes or throwing them in jail: "People were vehement about it, everybody needing to stay in their place. If somebody got out of their place, there would be trouble. If a family was told to get out of a community, that would be a really good idea." Every Black family had stories of enraged white responses to perceptions of "uppity" Black behavior. Beyond the prohibitions against shaking hands, sharing Bibles and sinks, eating or going to church or school together, Black people knew not to publicly express displeasure with their predicament or any ambition to rise above it. Those who did prosper concealed their success. To accumulate and flaunt property and possessions beyond the so-called Dixie Limit was to borrow danger.

The Dixie Limit was the ceiling for Black wealth. Because how much was too much remained undefined, impulses toward self- and material improvement meant a perpetual discretion. Successful Black cotton farmers still kept their heads low as they drove their mule-pulled wooden wagons into town, asked white farmers for "furnish" loans they no longer needed, and distributed their crop among different brokers to disguise how many bales they produced. Black farmers who drove a more expensive car than a weathered Ford took to keeping a chauffeur's cap with them to ward off trouble and refrained from accelerating past cars driven by whites. The Fieldses left their backwoods home unpainted because restrictions about house painting allowed Black families only to use dark red, which the Fieldses did not favor. "Lynchings have occurred," wrote Ralph Ellison, "because Negroes painted their homes."

Land confiscation was common. Randy McAllister, a retired Black police officer of Pete Fields's generation in Florence, South Carolina, said both his great-great-grandfather and great-grandfather owned substantial farms not far from Wolfton that were stolen for "trickery," in the local phrasing, because of the Dixie Limit. "The Dixie Limit was a common conversation, a common thing when I was coming up," McAllister said. "You know you can't be too showy. They'll take your stuff. You got that fine car, you might not have a job for long. If you were educated, you couldn't go around talking educated. You had to live a dual role."

David Fields had understated mannerisms, didn't assert his financial ingenuity or make enemies. But after David died, Herbert Sr. took over the farm. Although he had only three years of schooling, Herbert Sr. taught himself to read and to play several instruments, including the guitar and accordion, and he had a gift for measurement, could spread his arms and reckon far distances with uncanny accuracy. He was a strong baseball player and liked both talking politics and crossing the creek to dance with some of his grandmother's local Cherokee relatives. While courting Susie in his buggy, he always brought along small, thoughtful gifts. For his children Herbert Sr. made from scratch batches of ice cream, peanut butter, and peanut brittle. He could also be personally mild to the point of diffidence.

People worried that because his father had done so well, Herbert Sr. was "spoiled" and did not engage challenges with sufficient rigor. It was from his mother, Susie, that Pete Fields acquired his way of carrying himself. Pete was a neighborly person who, until the day he died, took no stuff from anybody.

Susie stood only four feet, eleven inches. She was attracted to order and beauty, collected small, pretty objects: a cobalt-blue sugar basin and creamer set embossed with little flowers; a pair of decorative elephants—one pink, one green. She wore dresses and skirts, never pants or lipstick and, said her youngest child, Katie-Jean, had a practical way of overcoming things she'd never been taught: "My mother didn't go to college, but she was a doctor of circumstances. She learned to understand preventive medicine. How to induce labor in a pregnant woman, how to diagnose why someone was suddenly falling a lot, how to dress a wound with webs of a particular spider." Another quality Susie handed down to Pete was her toughness. Raising many children had long been the way of farm families the world over, but only after the last of her fourteen births did Susie take any rest. With four sons, Katie-Jean said her parents were "always so worried my brothers would be found hung in the woods somewhere. My brothers had to be home before dark for fear of Klansmen roaming around looking for whom they can devour."

ONE EVENING IN the late 1930s, a uniformed local highway patrolman named Bill Wolfe drove through the Wolfton countryside to the Fields homeplace. As Katie-Jean, in her written recollections, and others in the family, including Pete and Katie-Jean's cousin Hubert Fields (who was there), describe what ensued, Herbert Sr. walked out into the yard to talk with Bill Wolfe. Wolfe told Herbert Sr. there was a problem at the bank regarding his farm. The word "audit" was used. Wolfe asked Herbert Sr. for the property deed and his bank book. Nothing to worry about; it would all be returned after everything was cleared up. When Herbert Sr. spoke to Bill Wolfe, he always kept one foot back, his head averted sideways, and his eyes to the ground. He hated assuming a submissive posture, but he did not rebel, said Katie-Jean, because that was to be "uppity" or "insolent," and "it would not have been beneficial for him to do so." But Herbert Sr. declined to give Bill Wolfe his documents. The lawman kept returning. "Every time he came," said Hubert Fields, "he asked for the deed and bank book. He kept asking him. He'd tell him, 'No. No.' All his concern was the deed."

Then one day, Wolfe returned, words were spoken, and something changed. Herbert Sr. went inside, came back out, and handed his documents to Wolfe. "I was there when he gave it to him," said Hubert. "He told my uncle he was going to keep the title. He gave him the title and the bank book too. One hundred and ninety-two acres of land. I was just looking. He was a trooper. He was by himself. It was Bill Wolfe. He was in uniform. It was out in the yard. My uncle went back into the house. Bill Wolfe was standing by the car."

After the lawman left, Susie was upset. She asked her husband why he'd given in. "They talked," said Hubert. "She told him he was wrong." Susie always remained angry that, when facing Bill Wolfe, her husband hadn't prepared ahead for such a moment, that he hadn't said he was unsure where the land documents were. "You never tell white people everything," she'd rebuke him as the children listened. But Katie-Jean was understanding—"My father was afraid of white men. He had a right to be."

Bill Wolfe had a reputation among Black families for roughness and cruelty. A Black man who knew him said that Black people who stood up for themselves with Wolfe did so at their peril: "If you didn't take any junk, were outspoke, bad things could happen to you." Once, when Wolfe's children were sick, he insulted a young Black man in a local store. Without thinking, the young man retorted that maybe the lawman's kids were "afflicted" because he was "always mistreating people." That night, three truckloads of white men were organized to come looking for the young man, who'd already left the area and would stay away for years.

The Fieldses' deeds disappeared, never to be seen again, and suddenly the cash crops the Fields family grew belonged to someone else and they were sharecroppers on their own land. Sharecropping was a notoriously rigged system, one that made a family's finances dependent upon the self-interested whims of a landowner whose decisions about what was "furnished," what was deducted, what was kept, and what was paid were supported not by reliable ink columns in a notation ledger but by the implicit threat of armed truckloads. The Fieldses now did all the plowing, planting, and harvesting in service of a short-tempered man who gave Herbert Sr. occasional ten-dollar allotments to support his family, and handed him a small sum after the harvest, at settling-up time.

There are now no records of the Fields family's ownership in the extant chain of title. This isn't uncommon. Many Black landowners never even held their deeds. One common style of property fraud in the Deep South during the time was the "selling" of land to Black farmers at exorbitant rates during times of flourishing "boom" profits, so that when the economy reversed toward "bust," the land was abruptly seized. Another scam was pretending to sell land, but then either providing "spurious titles" or completing the transaction without the exchange of any official documentation. Eventually, a Black Mississippian told Northern researchers, "Negroes have got wary, and won't try to buy land."

The Fields land confiscation took place so long ago, even the people who were there have difficulty remembering finer details. Katie-Jean says it "happened in the late 1930s." The local courthouse records do not mention the name Fields. They do, however, say that in 1938, the property deed was transferred to the name of Bill Wolfe, and there it remained for decades. Bill Wolfe's father was a leading Orangeburg lawyer, who died early in 1938. Court records reveal that, in his will, the lawyer chose to leave his own extensive property holdings to two of Bill's brothers, described as "my beloved sons," excluding Bill without mention.

THE LOST LAND was the defining shadow across Pete Fields's childhood. Born in 1936, according to his daughter Susan, Herbert Fields Jr. was called Pete because a Klansman from around Wolfton "liked my dad. He gave him that nickname when he was young." Others remember that the nickname came to Pete because he was mischievous, a little "Peter Rabbit." Katie-Jean said, "My brother was my mother's heart, her heartstring. She had a brother named Peter. He was the baby boy." Pete tormented his sisters with frogs in the swimming hole; even underwater they could hear him laughing. But if anybody else bothered them, Pete was their scourge. He was a fisherman, a hunter, and when he played Cowboys and Indians, he was a cowboy because, he said, the cowboys won.

Another member of the extended Fields family growing up in the 1930s, in a tiny settlement about two miles from their Wolfton farm, was the future performer Eartha Kitt. Kitt was the daughter of a Black mother and white father, neither of whom raised her. She was brought up by unwilling guardians who dressed her in rags and croker sacks, made her pick cotton by age six, and fed her clabber milk and scraps of fatback and greens. Kitt later said she survived by adopting a policy of remaining mute. All her celebrated life, Kitt would remember back to white children taunting her: "N—r, n—r is a fool. N—r, n—r need no school." Everybody knew school was the key to the highway of life opportunity. Pete Fields and his siblings went to a Black-only one-room schoolhouse, a five-and-a-half-mile walk from home, across creeks, streams, and marsh. The Fields daughters received more schooling than their brothers, both because the boys were needed for plowing and, as Herbert Sr. pointed out, the local jobs available to educated young Black men were so few.

Pete Fields grew up regarding schools, courts, police, and prisons as buttresses of a system of tyranny that the tyrannized people could never benefit from. "A white man can steal from or maltreat a Negro in almost any way without fear of reprisal, because the Negro cannot claim the protection of the police or courts," wrote the scholar of midcentury race relations, Gunnar Myrdal. That the Fields family had no documents at the courthouse or at government offices to prove Herbert Sr. "was bamboozled, lost the land" as one of Pete Fields's cousins put it, was a family bitterness without recourse. Each Black family in Wolfton knew these double-dealings happened. All were also aware that what permitted every unfairness was the crude possibility of violence. From the home where Pete Fields grew up, there was sometimes a swarm of vultures above a stand of trees in the near distance. The Fields children heard older Black people say that was the place where white night riders buried the Black people they'd killed in a shallow grave.

When Eartha Kitt listened to an account of a Black man stabbing his romantic rival to death, she heard it explained that nothing would happen to the murderer because "no white law made for black people killing each other." That the system actively encouraged Black people to turn their rage upon one another was affirmed by a Southern chief of detectives, who told the police historian Raymond Fosdick that his city had three classes of homicide: "If a n—r kills a white man, that's murder. If a white man kills a n—r, that's justifiable homicide. If a n—r kills another n—r, that's one less n—r." After the first Black Atlanta police officers were appointed, in 1948, the African American historian W. Marvin Dulaney discovered that they were obligated to take an oath pledging, "I do solemnly swear as a n—r policeman that I will uphold the segregation laws of the city of Atlanta." In Wolfton, the Fields family joined with neighbors to enforce their own legal standard. When word spread of a wife batterer, Susie Fields's father and some of her brothers and friends stuffed the abuser into a barrel and floated him on the Edisto River. Pete Fields's mother always included those incarcerated by the state in her prayers.

HERBERT SR. BROODED, disconsolate, over his land. Homeplaces were the center of family ties, considered, as anthropologist Carol Stack wrote, "a haven of safety." The teenage Pete Fields's secure place, however, was inside a car. Pete came of age at a time when automobile prices were falling low enough that working-class African Americans of modest means were increasingly able to buy them. By the 1930s, better than 1 in 5 Black farmers owned cars. And if they were often put to practical tractor-like tasks, the liberating pleasure was that behind the wheel, where you went was your choice, up to you.

Yet no good time went unpunished. In the 1930s, General Motors had a policy of not selling Cadillacs to Blacks. In the South, the practice of selling rickety vehicles to Black farmers during successful crop years led to collections of abandoned cars in woods and swamps. If you didn't have new-car money, you might buy a "hooptie"—a worn, broken-down jalopy. Hooptie is a corruption of Coupe D—from Coupe de Ville, the prestige-model sedan Cadillac began making in 1949. A 1949 article in *Ebony* described the Cadillac as "an instrument of aggression, a solid and substantial symbol for many a Negro that he is as good as any white man."

As car ownership in the United States during the 1950s reached 60 million, long-range personal mobility not only broadened the lived experience of the country, it also charged the national inner life. This was perhaps especially true for African Americans. The Black novelist Ann Petry wrote that for a Black man "the act of driving the car made him feel he was a powerful being who could conquer the world." By the 1950s, the white Georgia novelist Flannery O'Connor told Robert Lowell, her mother was grousing that every Black man she knew "has a better-looking car than she does." Such innuendo was common, and obtuse. Car choices frequently were a result of housing and property-related chicanery, like blockbusting. As a Black man named Leon Price explained to sociologist Mary Barr, "A lot of people look around and ask why so many Negroes are driving fancy cars. I'll tell you why. Because after saving twenty-five hundred dollars for a home, they found that wasn't enough for a down payment. So they did the next best thing."

From the day he first got behind a steering wheel, as a teenager around 1950, Pete Fields liked driving attractive, powerful cars at speed. Pete's daughter, Susan, said her father's lifelong desire to own luxury automobiles had to do with both enjoyment and self-esteem: "He loved cars. Always did. They made him feel better as a man."

As an adult, Fields would own a succession of fast and stylish automobiles: a Datsun 280Z, a Mazda RX7, a Pontiac Firebird, and the one he died in, a Chrysler 300. But as a teenager in Wolfton, Pete Fields first used the family vehicle, a black 1939 Chevrolet. Owning a car lessened the reliance of families like the Fieldses on local merchants, and it gave them an improved means of measuring the world beyond Wolfton. Pete's father didn't drive, so when the Fieldses needed to visit Orangeburg on a "going-to-town day," to attend church, or travel over to the curiously named North, South Carolina, behind the wheel was Pete. Out his window as the 1950s began, he could see that all around him people were leaving.

THE GREAT MIGRATION of Black Southerners to the North is the largest population relocation by choice in American history. When it began, during World War I, 9 in 10 African Americans lived in the South. Six decades and 6 million transits later, in 1970, the distribution was nearly even. Millions of Americans on the move was an enormously complex event. At various stages, reasons for leaving included the crop depredations of the boll weevil, mechanization that left mule-driving dirt farmers "tractored out," and factories in need of wartime labor. It was a wave of departures, a Northern fever passed on by word of mouth from railroad men, from older brothers and cousins, from factory agents, through words on newsprint or personal stationery, via the enticements of "Justice's Tickets," and $8 spots in the back of northbound trucks. The photographs of Great Migration Black families packed into old cars with their luggage tied to the roof resemble Dorothea Lange images of Dust Bowl refugees driving to California. A truth of the Great Migration was that the first generation self-selected for ambition and initiative. They tended to be young, strong, better-educated, often married people who had the backing of other family members who sometimes pooled their money to help them go. It was a chain migration, where each family that went north was a fillip for other families to pick up and do the same. By economists Bryan Stuart's and Evan Taylor's calculation, each person who left inspired four further decampments for what was commonly called Glory Land.

Many Black migrants had been, like the Fieldses, farm workers, doing intensive field labor bent over with a hoe, chopping for little pay at dirt, grass, and weeds in summer heat so area-extreme it seemed to have an oscillating drone. There weren't crowds of people dying of sunstroke inside factories. Industrial jobs doubled earnings, creating a path toward the economic mainstream from which Black people had been so pointedly excluded that the creation of Social Security had not included any benefits for agricultural or domestic workers. Northern schools were regarded as lighthouses that would guide the children of uneducated parents to better lives. There was also the lure of property ownership. The early African American historian of the Great Migration (and future co-founder of the National Urban League) George Edmund Haynes wrote in his Columbia University doctoral dissertation in 1912, "A number of youths have expressed their conviction that since their fathers and mothers have accumulated nothing after years on the land, they did not intend to stay on the plantation to repeat the process."

Seeking economic opportunity was also escaping white supremacy. On every Newhallville block among the Fields family's future neighbors would be a dozen people who'd each lived a different final indignity that made them seek a new haven. At a rural Georgia store, a young woman trying to buy her father a sandwich was presented with two sandwiches, one of which had been spit in. She was given a choice: eat it immediately or be raped. Her brother heard about what had happened, went to the store, and delivered a beating. Then he was gone. Another Newhallville man left the South after a white woman made a pass at him. A third escaped an attempted lynching. A woman who laundered clothes was told by her employer that she'd now be paid in eggs rather than money, and so the woman washed her hands of that life, began anew.

The largest percentage of Black residents to leave a state were from South Carolina. In Orangeburg County, the day after high school graduation, the lines at the bus and train stations were long like flipped tassels. There were less than one hundred people in Ernest Shaw's Williamsburg County, South Carolina, high school graduating class, and six of them later met their future husband or wife in New Haven. When local historian Eric Powell consulted with Black families about people's reasons for going, they all gave him the same explanation: "Everybody left because of the oppression here." Randy McAllister, the retired Black police officer, remembered of the exodus, "people lived back to the edge of the woods lines. The Migration meant those houses started getting vacant. They were leaving and weren't saying a word." The Equal Justice Initiative in Montgomery today considers those who left states like South Carolina during the Great Migration to have been refugees fleeing the terrorism of a police state.

A SEVERE STORM that ruined the Fields family's crop was the inciting event for Susie, yet the deeper reason for leaving Wolfton in 1951 was she didn't want her family to live under Jim Crow anymore. Four years after the Fieldses left, a local church would burn because the preacher supported *Brown v. Board of Education*. Susie believed her children were intelligent, interesting people and they deserved much better than separate and unequal.

Susie had been hearing about New Haven for years. Before World War II there were few industrial jobs in New England for Blacks, and those typically offered roles avoided by whites. The need to fill massive orders during World War II led the Winchester arms and ammunition factory to dispatch job recruiters south, pitching New Haven's housing and safety, the freedom to vote, the city's good schools. Young Isaiah Hooks, who lived near Wolfton, was convinced, and up north on a one-way ticket he went. Then, after Hooks was gainfully established, on a visit home he met his wife, Rebecca Fields, one of Pete and Katie-Jean's older sisters. The couple's ensuing letters to Wolfton said, "Things are good." Convincing evidence of this were the gifts they enclosed, such as a fancy dress with crinolines for Nina Fields. When she wore it to a school dance, everybody gathered around the finery. Gradually, all the older Fields children followed Rebecca to New Haven. Then Susie herself went up, came back, went again, and finally decided. She collected seven children and an infant grandchild, and headed for the Seaboard Coastline train depot in North. Only Herbert Sr. stayed behind. He had a heart condition, but his reluctance wasn't medical. He found it too painful to leave the land.

The Black diaspora from the South, like every diaspora, was a deep-breath endeavor. Eartha Kitt had been told, "You don't wanna go up North, Eartha Mae," because New York houses were stacked like firewood one home atop the next, trains rode along through the air and sometimes fell down, and the weather was so cold "you ain't never gonna get warm." But Kitt hoped for more than living mute in a cotton patch. Clifton Watson, whose family came to Newhallville in the 1950s, said that what prevailed in the New Haven migrants they knew was "the enormous optimism of people who left the South."

Pete Fields was fifteen when he stood with his mother and siblings at the North depot. The station platform was long, with roofing over an area where local cotton farmers stored their bales, awaiting transport to textile mills. By then, there was a daily crowd of African American families. Stories circulated about white landowners, irate at losing cheap labor, confronting

Black people at the station, boarding trains and making scenes. None of this happened to the Fieldses.

The Fieldses rode a train nicknamed the Silver Meteor, which many called the Silver Meter. Until Washington, DC, northbound trains were segregated. Black people typically sat directly behind the engine, with the mail car also separating them from white passengers. Most of the Fields family's possessions had been given away, and aside from Susie's sugar basin, creamer, and twin elephants, they carried necessities, no heirlooms of what was about to be their past. Black people couldn't order food on board—which is why Louis Armstrong said "colored persons going North crammed their baskets full of everything but the kitchen stove." The fare was either fried or baked with butter so it wouldn't spoil. Susie packed fried chicken, pound cake, biscuits, and sweet-potato pie. Every Newhallville family could recall exactly what they ate, taste becoming a souvenir, carrying the lasting significance of the new-life moment.

The Fieldses arrived in New Haven after the school year had begun. Several weeks later, Herbert Sr. did join his family, becoming a farming man with heart disease living on the third floor of a cramped four-story tenement in a busy city. He missed the countryside, was often depressed. Those who came north died younger on average than those who stayed back, such fatalities the sum of the sufferings and deprivations of the past, the anxiety of departure, the weight of starting again. Not that this was discussed. Secrecy became a family habit. Susie believed them to be vulnerable, and the more you revealed, the more vulnerable you became. For self-preservation, it was better to seem blandly content than to disclose—or to admit—any pain.

Pete Fields was a little boy standing near his father when a man, whose job description began with serve and protect, came through the woods to steal his family's land. Pete saw everything and, like his father, he never got over it. "It's horrible, some of the things that were done to Black people," said Katie-Jean. "Sometimes I don't want to think about it, the killings, the disappearance of people you'd never see again."

The reason she did think about it, did write down her family recollections, had to do with Katie-Jean's instinct that the Fields family's history was specific to their own experiences of America, both tragic and triumphant, and yet also representative. Newhallville was a community re-formed by migrants from fifty dozen rural Southern places not so different from Wolfton, a Northern neighborhood that remains home to people only a few generations removed from living under state-mandated segregation, an American apartheid.

In Newhallville, the Fieldses would live among many people from a South Carolina farm belt stretching from the rice-growing wetlands near Georgetown across the Pee Dee River watershed to Florence, down to Orangeburg and over to Columbia. Even now, three generations later, on the narrow Newhallville streets are cars with Carolina license plates, and riding along I-95 through the Carolinas are more cars with Connecticut plates. African American funerals in South Carolina are often delayed, to give the people in Connecticut time to drive down. Those holding jobs that don't offer ample vacation benefits have made New Haven's rental-car agencies accustomed to a Friday-afternoon rush, and then to cars brought back late Sunday with two thousand miles more on the odometer. At the beginning of summer, school lets out in New Haven and families still go South for the annual visit. Connection to the South for Great Migration people from Newhallville, said Clifton Watson, "is very complex. It's a complex tension in your roles as a Northerner, a Southerner, an African American, an American. When our fathers don't talk about the past, they are saying something without speaking, through the act of their going back."

Year after year, the adult Pete Fields would get behind the wheel of his latest handsome automobile and point it south. In those days, before troopers wore body cameras, Pete's version of a chauffeur's cap was to place five new hundred-dollar bills with his license and registration in the glove compartment. Driving in a sleek sedan with Connecticut plates at speed past the big billboards telling him to "Repent and Believe Jesus Is Coming Soon," the little country signs urging him to buy turnips and black-eyed peas, the five new bills were what experience had taught Pete was the cost of making it safely to Wolfton. Once there, he'd always stay with his cousin Lillie and visit with relatives who considered him to be "a real nice-going fella."

Pete was a walking man, and a favorite foray took him through some dense woods off a grassy cow path, where, if you knew what you were looking for, in among the foliage, hanging vines, and fragrant purple wisteria, it was possible to make out a chimney and the residuum of a house foundation that the forest had all but reclaimed. The property had such a peaceful beauty that, looking at the ruined homeplace, for religious people it was easy to think of it as the fallen Paradise they'd cast themselves out of. The one time Pete brought his daughter with him, all he told her was "I used to live there" before they were back in the car, returning to the secure life he'd given her in Connecticut.

Chapter Two

New Haven was founded in 1638, by English Puritans seeking freedom to worship, an exodus religious scholars named the Great Migration. The fantastical spectacle of two iron-red, sunset-hued peaks glowing above a lush riverine plain had led passing Dutch tradesmen to refer to the area with practical restraint as Rodenberghen (Red Hills). According to historian Rollin Osterweis, when the ecstatic English settlers sailed into the estuary forming the city's natural harbor, its congruity to biblical descriptions made them think "this was the Promised Land." In the Bible, the Promised Land was Canaan, containing the city of Jerusalem, and there were prophetic visions detailing its configurations with specificity. The pious settlers sought to bring scripture to life. As they went ahead and built it, their city formed a perfect square that subdivided into nine equal squares, a Sudoku puzzle sub-grid. Many architectural historians consider those original squares to mark the seminal American planned community, the representative American city. Right away, the land was understood in terms of value, a means of earning and accumulating wealth. It was purchased from indigenous Quinnipiacs who were promised protection; some would later describe them as the first occupants of a reservation. But for arriving generations, this remained fundamentally the new haven.

The Fields family arrived there as cotton farmers with little schooling or vocational skills, only a vague, unspecific sense of beckoning opportunity. As Susan said of her grandparents, her parents, and their siblings, "They came to Connecticut for jobs, to have a better life." That was the country's history, and that of the Great Migration, people unmooring from the familiar, traveling a long distance on the conviction they could improve themselves by going somewhere unknown, to try their best at something new. Merely by leaving the Jim Crow South, the Fields family had gained. The reduction in impediment was their advantage; they were now hopeful seekers.

Dating back to the city founders, some of whom were enslavers, New Haven had offered Black men such little chance to be more than servants and janitors that the city reinforced the abolitionist William Lloyd Garrison's description of Connecticut as "The Georgia of New England." At the time of the American Revolution, Connecticut had 6,400 enslaved people, the most in New England. By 1800, when there were 951 enslaved people in the state, New Haven's 220 Blacks included 60 enslaved people. The last enslaved person sold on the city's Green, in 1825, was then immediately set free by one of New Haven's many abolitionists. A large party of those local abolitionists traveled to "bleeding" Kansas territory in the 1850s, to support the "free-stater" anti-slavery cause. Only in 1848 did Connecticut abolish slavery.

New Haven's first Black church was organized in 1818, when the city was home to six hundred free people of color. In 1915, there was one Black dentist in town and one Black-owned business, a tavern. As of 1920, there still had not been a single white-collar African American worker in New Haven, not even a clerk. If your name in a city directory was followed by *Col'd*, you were many times more likely than a white person to be jobless or to have been convicted or to be living in the candle-lit shanties in the New Liberia section or the hovels of Poverty Square or Negro Lane. (New Haven's penchant for on-the-nose geographical nomenclature was itself indicative of the city's attitudes; a genteel part of town was called Quality Row.) As the white Yale scholar Robert Austin Warner explained in *New Haven Negroes*, published in 1940, white employers were candid in their preference for hiring "my own kind," for "white men's jobs." Warner reflected that "most New Haven Negroes lack the stimulus of a job which tests their powers and opens avenues of promise to their aspirations . . . interests are blunted and enthusiasm dulled by the impossibility of fulfillment." The lack of opportunity led to frequent cases of depression. Warner was succinct in describing the final tragic dimension: "most die penniless."

When, in 1951, the Fieldses arrived from Wolfton, African Americans then numbered around 10,000 in a city reaching its all-time peak population of nearly 165,000. More Black people came to Connecticut than any other New England state. The Fieldses settled in Dixwell, by then considered New Haven's traditional Black neighborhood, which was 62 percent "non-white" and home to historical congregations and prominent professionals. Those prosperous exceptions belied the poverty most New Haven Black families experienced in Dixwell, and in other neighborhoods, like Oak Street. Writer Ta-Nehisi Coates might as well have been thinking of Dixwell when he wrote, "It is common today to become misty-eyed about the old black ghetto, where doctors and lawyers lived next door to meatpackers and steelworkers, who themselves lived next door to prostitutes and the unemployed. This segregationist nostalgia ignores . . . the fact that the old ghetto was premised on denying black people privileges enjoyed by white Americans."

The Fieldses were part of a postwar African American onrush so substantial that, coinciding as it did with the millions of demobilized GIs and a downsized construction industry, created a housing crisis in Black communities across the country, as happened in Dixwell. Part of this also had to do with urban planning—the denial of housing to Black families, a structural practice that is evident in the 1937 Federal Home Owner's Loan Corporation map of New Haven. This was the infamous "red-lining," and Dixwell was indeed red-lined with a lowest-level D-rating (for Hazardous), which the accompanying neatly typed area description blamed on Dixwell's congestion, old buildings, and "character of development and inhabitant." Dixwell was pronounced a neighborhood "given over largely to Negros employed as domestics," who were faulted for propensities to "vandalism." The general purpose of the maps was guiding mortgage lenders' assessment of risk, and by habitually discouraging investment in Black communities like Dixwell, they engineered isolated, overpopulated Black slums and undermined Black home-ownership equity for generations.

As renters, the issue for the Fieldses more than red-lining was limited neighborhood choices imposed on Black families by segregation. Few options meant realtors could charge a premium. "Doubling up" was the way new arrivals from the South afforded the inflated Dixwell tenement rents, and that's what the Fields family did. They moved into a third-floor Charles Street apartment already occupied by the family's eldest daughter, Bertha, and her three children, making a dozen people for three bedrooms. Once Herbert Sr. arrived, he and Susie took one room. In each of the other two bedrooms, four people slept. The boys, Pete and Thomas, were out on the living-room sofa.

There, on Charles Street, they lived as immigrants from their own country, adjusting to life without those they'd left in Wolfton, without their teacher, their church, the closeness of a community where everyone was near to kin. Susie and Herbert Sr. had no influential connections, no savings or property, no winter coats. There wasn't any newcomer orientation guide to Northern cities explaining about indoor plumbing or garbage collection. The Fieldses missed the familiar farmhouse meals of what Katie-Jean called "slavery country food"—collard and spring greens, sausage rice pudding, dishes made from the head, ears, feet, tails, and intestines of hogs. "I'm a poor ol' boy, a long ways from home," went the classic blues, and that was them, that was the neighborhood.

Dixwell had a raffish quality, a half-rural, half-urban feeling of transitional times. All around were other people up from places like Wolfton who were finding it difficult to relinquish the rhythms of rural life—telling time by the sun, the company of the livestock. One Fields neighbor was a "Watkins Man," who sold relief door-to-door: liniments, syrups, extracts, and tonics. Others found succor from their upheaval in religion, in superstition, in liquor. The expectation of Glory Land and then the discovery of abundant bigotry in Northern life capsized some people. Drunken men were always loitering on the corner near the Fieldses' apartment, and three homeless alcoholics slept in the stairwell of their building. The men answered to vivid nicknames. One was known as Get Out the Car, a second went by Vernow Cow, the third was Everyday. Susie would feed them meals, tell them to straighten up. When the men wanted to sleep, they loosened the naked hallway lightbulb and spread out in a resting geometry to which the entire Fields family became so accustomed that everybody could step over the sleeping men without looking down or breaking stride. That was fortuitous the night a man chased a terrified Katie-Jean down the street. The pursuer was close behind as she made it into her building hallway. She was sure she would have been attacked had not the man tripped over Everyday, who then awakened and launched him back down the stairs.

All were apprehensive about the winter weather. When it finally snowed, the younger Fields children walked to school in just-acquired wool snowsuits, holding hands along sidewalks with drifts of air-light snow banked so high on either side, it seemed to them they were feeling their way through a fluffy cotton tunnel. Near the corner, they removed their mittens and muffs, flung their fingers up above the drift line, and shook them. Small and fearful of being unseen, they believed that if they didn't wave, something might come along and obliterate them.

Katie-Jean would remember, "We adjusted rather quickly to life in New Haven. We worked all the time. There wasn't a lot of playing going on." The variety of legislations limiting immigration had thinned the country's ranks of unskilled labor, and young men around Charles Street said you could quit one job in the morning, close your eyes, spin, point, and hold a new full-time position in that direction by afternoon. Joe Fields was hired by the Sargent locks and hardware factory. Thomas Fields reported to Majestic, a commercial laundry. The daughters in the family did "day's work," scrubbing, polishing, and cleaning. Some Black women who held regular domestic jobs for wealthy white New Haven families found themselves confronted with challenges beyond the labor. They might discover coins scattered under the mattress they'd been told to flip—a virtue test. An employer of three Fields sisters once offered them chicken crawling with maggots for lunch. That the Fields sisters did not sleep in maid's quarters but instead were "living out" and had their own home to return to was, as historian Jacqueline Jones explained, crucial to self-esteem, given the menial, low-paying work most Black women were limited to. Only blocks away from the Fields home was Shelton Avenue, and the Fields children learned, "You don't go there or they'll whoop you." This white, mostly Irish working-class enclave where Blacks were not welcome was a primary "living out" place: Newhallville.

While others were stunned in delayed comprehension of how much Northern racism there was, sometimes Susie invited hungry street people to come upstairs to join her family for supper. Herbert Sr. warned her that one of these days she'd let someone walk through that door who'd kill them all, but Susie was undeterred, as was Pete. Clear to the others was that Susie's self-assurance and her desire to help the destitute were being passed on to her favorite child. Pete seemed older than he was, a short teenager projecting nervy optimism—a certainty that things would work out for the best, the uncommon conviction in a boy still so young that he himself had the family's back.

Pete Fields would manage a soul band as a young adult, and as a grown-up he listened to many kinds of American popular music, including a lot of country. Part of that was coming up in Dixwell, where music emanated. Local doo-wop groups like the Nutmegs rehearsed in building hallways and on Dixwell street corners. Another group, the Five Satins, began work on their songs as local high school boys, singing on the sidewalks, not for money but to impress young women. When Fred Parris, the group's leader, began to perform something new he'd written, "In the Still of the Night," he found, "that song, the girls, they'd be there, we could depend on that!" The Fieldses knew all about the Satins. Parris's mother was heavily involved in the music at their church, St. Paul's UAME, located off Dixwell Avenue.

Around the neighborhood there were record shops selling rhythm & blues, bars and clubs like the Playback, the Sound Track II, the Golden Gate, where Black musicians played on a stage set into the front window. As the neighborhood grew through the postwar years, the Monterey attracted Billie Holiday, Charlie Parker, and John Coltrane as they worked their way north toward the larger jazz venues of Boston. At the bus stop one day, teenage Katie-Jean was engaged in conversation by an urbane man who requested a date. She turned him down. A telephone number? Not that either. The answer was the same even after he identified himself as the influential hard-bop pianist Horace Silver, who, as a teenager, had played two nights a week at the Monterey. A few years later, Katie-Jean would marry a cousin of another pianist, Thelonious Monk.

It was the postwar, a notable time of American aspiration, and not just among the white city-dwelling veterans now petitioning the FHA for mortgages on the new ranch houses out along the crabgrass frontier. A Black woman who grew up near Charles Street said, "Buying the one-family house, that was always pushed. The American dream: a lawn, a driveway, near a good school." In Southern Black families who'd come to New England to work unskilled or semi-skilled jobs explicitly as investments in their children's future, their high expectations for the young were typically unambiguous. If a boy was "going bad," he might be put on the southbound train. For Black children who'd attended segregated schools in the South, sitting in classrooms with whites could be intimidating at first, which then made their parents' strict ambitions for them only more stressful. Ralph Ellison described this dislocation as feeling like a jack-in-the box broken loose from its springs. Katie-Jean went to school with an especially talented girl who pushed herself so hard to succeed she had a breakdown.

Susie believed her children had not completed a journey so much as begun one. She and Herbert Sr. used the verb "socialize" to explain taking children who'd come to Dixwell from a culture of "Dixie Limits" and "buzzard's roosts" beyond the neighborhood to recreations and amusements across Connecticut. Susie thought of this as revealing a great America out there, which needed to be known if you were going places in this real-going country.

Pete went the farthest. In January 1955, he quit high school and joined the army. The very qualities that led him away from the family were what they most missed when he'd gone. He was so up for it in life.

It was the neighborhood that improved ambition and purpose. Before school, sitting on her building stoop, Katie-Jean watched well-dressed Black women pass by on their way to nursing and office jobs. Katie-Jean's favorite was a tall, slender woman who wore red lipstick and colorful, beautifully cut professional clothes. Katie-Jean never spoke to any of the women, but she was there with them every day—deciding that she too would one day have a good job, dress well, and wear red lipstick. She did. That was what an encouraging family and upwardly mobile neighbors could do for a determined person.

At Fort Dix, Pete, who'd grown up hunting game in the Carolina woods, was issued a rifle and trained as a sharpshooter. He competed in lightweight army boxing matches, had good times that included watching Big Joe Williams play his nine-string guitar while singing the Mississippi Delta blues. He was posted to Germany, where he met a local woman he thought about marrying, but didn't. In 1957, Pete was assigned to Arkansas, where President Eisenhower had sent in federal troops to protect nine Black school students whose efforts to integrate Little Rock Central High School had met with enraged protests. News footage of nine young people keeping their composure as they were tormented daily by a livid segregationist mob gave their ordeal its national moment. But beyond describing how upsetting he'd found the "hate sneers" on the faces of white protesters, Pete was one of those soldiers who came back from a troubling experience, changed out of uniform, and afterward did not talk about what he'd seen. Nick Pastore, who would become chief of police in New Haven, also served that year in Little Rock. Pastore didn't know Pete Fields, but he guessed that for a young Black soldier who'd lived in South Carolina and New Haven, watching those teenagers facing down bigots screaming about killing them would have been a formative experience that made him decide never to retreat from anybody who threatened his door.

AFTER NINE YEARS of renting apartments, in 1960 the Fields family bought a house at 156 Read Street in Newhallville previously inhabited by a railroad-car inspector named William Killeen. They had down-payment help from a New York uncle who traveled the country as a professional gambler. Read Street became a move up for all of the Fieldses, excepting Herbert Sr. He slept the first night there, and never awakened. He'd never really recovered from Wolfton. "My father died at fifty-nine, hurt and worried," Katie-Jean said. "He felt he gave it all away."

The man of the house became Pete, and the building itself was put in his name. Now in the army reserves, he worked as an assembler at the Seamless Rubber Company, making surgical gloves by dipping molds into liquid. He was well enough regarded that he could help fellow South Carolinians get hired, like Melvin Wearing and Jim Ponteau, who'd wanted something better than the paper mill and rice fields of Plantersville. At Seamless, "nothing he wouldn't do for you," Ponteau said of Pete. "Very nice, hardworking family man." In 1968, Wearing joined New Haven's police department, one of only 31 Black officers out of 446, and the future first Black chief. Ponteau was hired, too, and became an exceptional detective.

Both Ponteau and Wearing continued to see Fields informally, bumped into him inside Newhallville bars, went to the parties he threw when somebody was headed off for Vietnam. "Pete was always the same guy," Ponteau said. "Always had good conversations." That's what being "just around" meant in the 1960s.

Pete cut a figure. He favored thin silk shirts, walking suits, carried his father's pocket watch. The Ford Thunderbird convertible in the Read Street driveway was his. With men he bellied up in bucket-of-blood bars, and he went to the more upscale nightclubs like the Cotton Club and the Monterey for the young women to dance with. "Women loved him," Katie-Jean said. "Women were everywhere." If women telephoned looking for Pete, Susie was curt, always made a point of saying she'd never heard of them. "No women were worthy of her boys," said Katie-Jean. Then one night out, Pete met a younger woman named Charlene Tilley.

Charlene was from Durham, North Carolina, where her father, Daniel, was known in the family as "a country entrepreneur." Daniel made his own whiskey, which he sold out of the house, also providing music and food—a dew drop inn. Daniel was doing well at this, but Charlene's brother-in-law, Joe Pullen, said that in the 1940s and 1950s "you had to pay the man off in the South if you operated a business. He was paying off one cop, and the cop started bringing his friends around. [Daniel] said 'I'm not doing this.' He was shot by the police in the stomach. They claimed he had a gun. It was a flashlight. You know how that goes. The kids were really young."

Charlene's widowed mother, Mary, did field labor on tobacco farms, as did Charlene's brothers. In 1956 and 1957, once the children finished high school, the family "came up," to New Haven, where Mary found a job as a housekeeper at Yale. Charlene first went to work at the Sikorsky helicopter factory. Later, she moved to a position with the post office. She was a young person others considered "beautiful inside and out," "magnetic," and "fun-loving." She enjoyed jazz and dancing, was good at card games and baking, had a "groovy" big-city sense of style that included knee-high boots, hoop earrings, paisley minidresses, and several different ways of wearing her hair. "My mom was beautiful," Susan said. "She always changed it up, and that's what my father liked best about her, such a beautiful woman on his arm." Pete wasn't so much handsome, his daughter thought, as "a very alive presence. You see him, you feel him."

On their dates Pete began wearing high-heeled shoes because Charlene in her boots was taller. She bought him a black leather suit, and long after they were married, in 1961, that buttery garment was a small legend among Charlene and Pete's three children.

Eventually, Pete got his GED, but he was living for his children's future even before Susan, Jeffrey, and Peter were born. Pete and Charlene aspired to a house in a good school district, saved for college tuition, sought to position the kids for professions more fulfilling than their own. The couple felt lifted by their ambition, did not speak of any of this as personal sacrifice. So forward would be the focus, it took time for Susan to realize she and her brothers didn't know their New Haven past at all because "they kept it from us." Her father was devoted to Newhallville, and visited often, but he never took Susan. All she could say about the old neighborhood was that it had given Pete what New Haven itself had offered since its beginning, a home and the hand of opportunity to people with difficult histories. It was the new frontier.

Chapter Three

From the first, New Haven was a template of American urban test runs and rough drafts, remarkably varied given its compact population, a city-scaled laboratory sufficiently receptive to the new that it achieved influential urban innovations such as early sewers and electrical lighting, the first commercial telephone exchange (and the very first telephone book), and a computerized system for fire departments to predict likely locations for arson. Another progressive idea was the industrial-era conception of one's place of employment as a location discrete from a person's residence. That people left home and went to work meant the development of neighborhoods made up of homes for workers. Before Newhallville there was Whitneyville.

Eli Whitney believed his cotton-gin invention would end slavery by reducing the need for labor. Instead his ideas were lifted, he earned little, the number of slave states increased from eight to fifteen, and he turned to guns. Whitney was not a gunsmith; he had an artistic mechanical imagination and could improvise nimble solutions to mass-production dilemmas. To fulfill a 1798 government order for 10,000 muskets, Whitney conceived a series of jigs and machine tools that workers could use for turning out parts with near-standardized assembly. The task required laborers from as far off as Massachusetts to work at Whitney's riverside armory on the unsettled edge of New Haven. With nowhere convenient for his employees to live, Whitney constructed a row of white stone houses at the far northeast corner of what is now Prospect Hill. Industrial historians describe these accommodations, along with the boardinghouse he built for bachelors (and a schoolroom for children), as possibly the first American mill village, and credit Whitney's blueprinting the use of housing to attract a workforce.

Going forward, the new shape of the city included working-class districts of recently relocated, similarly employed people who kept in place all day for the experience of achieving mobility after hours. A family like the Fieldses might begin in less than salubrious confines on Charles Street, but one day they could buy a home in the more rarefied city air of Newhallville.

At first Newhallville was Plainfield, a bucolic area of farmland and beaver ponds spreading toward West Rock. You could hear croaking bullfrogs, gather wild chestnuts. It was out there, rather than in New Haven's downtown carriage district, that, in 1849, George Newhall situated his carriage emporium, on acres where there had been an old mill, a corn patch, a cow pasture, and a defunct canal. The former towpath was covered over with what drew Newhall to the spot—railroad tracks. Trains meant expanded distribution to the biggest carriage market, the South, and a steady supply of hoppers filled with coal. Newhall was the first New Haven carriage baron to convert his entire operation to steam power, and in an industry where boosting flourished, there he led the way as well, blowing smoke that his was "the largest carriage manufacturing factory in the world."

Newhall eventually employed over two hundred people and needed to provide places for them to live. He responded as Whitney had. Typical was the square-frame, double-decker, Italian villa–style single men's boardinghouse built on Thompson Street in 1860. Soon there would be an emerging community, with churches, a school, and a horse-drawn trolley to the city center. Yet Newhall, like the industry itself, was about to be surpassed by time. A former New Haven carriage mechanic would recall of the workers he'd known: "Most of them, when the automobile came in, followed the trade to Detroit." Newhall retired to the countryside, his legacy the creation of a singular working-class city neighborhood, a peaceful community that thrived because of guns.

Between the end of the Civil War and 1900, New Haven became a city of more than one hundred thousand people and seven hundred factories, internationally renowned for building bicycles, fishhooks, eyeglasses, clocks, street-paving materials, and more birdcages and corsets than anywhere else. The emblematic figure of the city's reputation for innovative manufacturing was a thick-shouldered entrepreneur determined to "remedy [an] evil." The wickedness in question was the uncomfortable pull of a shirt collar into a suspender-wearing man's neck, and Oliver Winchester's solution was to patent a tapered collar. By making the improved shirt, and in bulk by using sewing machines instead of seamstresses, Winchester accumulated significant capital, which he invested in a new business. Like Whitney, Winchester knew little about guns beyond sensing potential demand. With partners, Winchester bought concepts for repeating long-barrel firearms from a pair of designers, Horace Smith and Daniel Wesson, who were turning their attention to handguns.

By the 1860s, Winchester had fully traded out shirts for breeches. In a still largely single-shot era, the New Haven Arms Company's lever-action rifles could transfer cartridges from a magazine and fire them continuously and accurately. In 1871, Winchester moved his company, now called the Winchester Repeating Arms Company, onto farmland below his Prospect Street mansion, close to the site of Newhall's carriage works. There were still surrounding pastures, and Winchester employees at the factory windows sometimes took aim at grazing cattle.

After Winchester's death, in 1880, the business was bequeathed to his son, William, who died within months. William's devastated widow, Sarah, left the top of Prospect Hill for San Jose, California, and spent the next four decades compulsively adding on to her house, until she died in a home with 161 rooms. Among the most popular theories for why has to do with Sarah's stricken conscience, her belief that only her own ceaseless chambering would protect her from the avenging spirits of all those killed by Winchester guns.

On the edge of Newhallville, Winchester became the world's biggest producer of guns and bullets, with thousands of employees and a terrible reputation among labor advocates. When writer Theodore Dreiser toured the factory in 1898, preparing an article on the country's "master armorer" for *Ainslee's* magazine, he described 2,300 grimy-faced, bare-armed men and women working in shadowy rooms amid a cacophony: "the air is thick and choking with the heat, and the smell of iron and the sound of hammers and revolving, grunting machines become unbearable." A man with a bugle blew alerts so, during testing, drivers outside would be prepared to rein in their startled horses. Skilled as workmen might be, they typically only understood their own role in the mass assembly. They were gunmakers who could not make a gun. Indisputable is that during all the years of high Winchester employment in Newhallville, the neighborhood was notably safe from gun violence.

During World War I, enormous military ordnance contracts meant Winchester's physical plant doubled in size, as many as 22,000 employees making hundreds of thousands of Enfields and Brownings. By 1917, Winchester employees were most of New Haven's workforce, and Winchester families represented a full third of the population.

After the war, Winchester would attempt to diversify into sporting goods, kitchen appliances, tools, and hardware, all of it promised to be "As Good as the Gun." When the skates and lawn mowers were sometimes far from that, the company would be acquired, in 1931, by the Olin family's Western Cartridge Company, whose East Alton, Illinois, executives better understood modern munitions. During World War II, Winchesters, as the company came to be known around workingman's New Haven, hired 45,413 different people—13,667 of them on the job at peak employment, an astonishing population to be housed, fed, and clothed by the paychecks from one local concern.

When the United States was at peace, Winchester shipped to a global arms market and increasingly sought to sell guns to American consumers. This was done by building quality firearms in counterpoint with the manufacture of a spectacular aura. The coastal New England city where the guns actually came from was less important than the Great Plains association the company created for them. The famed Winchester Model 1873 became the emblem of a primary triumphalist narrative, renowned as "The Gun That Won the West." But, as writer Pamela Haag explains, no such victory took place. This was an advertising slogan dreamed up back in 1919 after the European armistice by the company's expert consigliere, Edwin Pugsley, cultivating a modern American worry that the virtues of frontier resilience were being lost and the country was going soft. His sales line lasted far longer than the gun, which disappeared from the Winchester catalogue by 1924.

Winchester was promoted as the eponym for a sharpshooting rifle, inducing other people to desire one; the company could draw on history alive with stories, some true, of scouts, gunslingers, and celebrities whose collective association with the product made the rifle itself a winning character on the American scene. Among those who'd shot sure with their Winchesters were trick markswoman Annie Oakley, Teddy Roosevelt, Ernest Hemingway, and Buffalo Bill Cody, both in his Wild West Show and in dime novels—"Make the old scoundrel supply you with a Winchester and a partner!" James Stewart starred in the 1950 film *Winchester '73*. John Wayne carried Winchesters in *The Searchers*, *The Man Who Shot Liberty Valance*, and also *Stagecoach*:

"You may need me and this Winchester, Curly!" A bronze statue of Wayne would be installed at the main entrance lobby to the factory, with a worker assigned to keep it at high polish.

Winchester promoted the idea that customers were one with their "trusty" companion, which gave them recourse to handle trouble, a message to dangerous people that the average person could be dangerous right back. A member of Billy the Kid's gang's dying instructions for his wife: Sell everything but keep the Winchester. The word's deadly impact as an equalizer was well understood by post-Reconstruction civil rights activists like Ida B. Wells, who recommended, for protection against lynch mobs, Winchesters to have "a place of honor in every black home." Likewise, Timothy Thomas Fortune bluntly assessed guns from New Haven as fallback justice for Americans unsupported by laws and lawmen: "It's the bad 'n—r' with the Winchester who can defend his home and children and wife." During fluctuations of demand, the need for a gun was nourished in city residents, women, and also children.

The company was well aware that the desires of youth formed adult expenditure. Twelve was the age the company's sales division once identified as the threshold for children becoming "prospects." A company publication, the *Winchester Herald*, would eventually trumpet, "There isn't a boy in your town who doesn't want to own a Winchester Rifle." Later, there would be mordant irony in the outrage at the popularity of guns among Black teenage boys in segregated neighborhoods like Newhallville, as though the desire to hold a ratchet had come from some perverse quality unique to them.

As grew Winchester, so grew Newhallville, and both did so because of immigrants. New Haven's stages of immigration parallel those of larger American cities like Philadelphia, New York, and Boston, each new misery of elsewhere creating the latest Irish, then Italian, then Russo-Polish wave willing to endure grinding labor and crowded, inexpensive conditions as the newcomer's dues. Close behind pioneers were cousins and second cousins. At one time, within Newhallville was Germantown; at another, Irish lived on one side of the tracks and Italians on the other. By the early twentieth century, more than two-thirds of New Haven's 133,605 residents were from recent immigrant families. It was a human torrent that gave a city of ethnic hamlets its distinctly American vitality. Newhallville was the quintessential interior village, and since so many Winchester employees lived there, the neighborhood was the ur factory town.

Winchester's effect on Newhallville after 1880 can be seen on the large annual Sanborn Fire Insurance street maps on which white paper expanses of empty lots began to fill with colorful squares and rectangles denoting new structures; such a rapid building-up, map surfaces reviewed one after the next approximate the look of someone winning at a popular board game conceived during the period—Monopoly. After 1890, modest single-family Colonial and Victorian revivals and airier Italianate double-decker wood-frame homes lined the streets. Despite the pace of growth, many of Newhallville's homes were given features that, later on, to others would imply character and fine craftsmanship, from art glass windows to sliding "pocket" doors. Flooring materials in these two-family houses represented both the aspirations and the financial limitations of working people. On the level where owners lived, the surfaces were typically made of hardwoods like oak; rental tenants walked on cheaper pine. The riptide energy with which the neighborhood grew explains Newhallville's outward continuity of form and style. Between 1894 and 1896, the same developer constructed houses with front-facing gables down the entire south side of the Willis Street block that Bobby would bike past more than one hundred years later. When, in the 1970s, the architecture critic Elizabeth Mills Brown surveyed the two-family houses of Newhallville, she said they "exemplified the American dream."

Winchester employees arriving in the main entrance lobby confronted a sign: THROUGH THESE GATES PASS THE GREATEST CRAFTSMEN WHO MAKE THE WORLD FAMOUS WINCHESTER FIREARMS. Winchester sought to instill a community spirit with a car-repair service, theatrical productions, and company bowling and baseball leagues. Newspapers were read aloud to employees on the job in foreign languages like Italian and Polish. When the apple tree on the company grounds near Division Street was ready for harvest, security staff opened the gates and allowed people from Newhallville to come in and pick the branches clean. Even so, it was factory work, and most considered the nobility of manual labor done in hot rooms to be overstated because of the unrelenting monotony. "Most of us were clock watchers," admitted Craig Gauthier, who worked there for more than twenty years, mostly in the barrel shop. Yet Winchester could offer an increasingly remunerative career as broom pushers became skilled machinists or in-house carpenters, electricians, or plumbers. "Every part of history is humanizing and dehumanizing," said Connecticut historian William Brown. "Factories had dreary, exploitative jobs, but guys I knew were transformed by their lives at Winchester."

The first Black workers had come to Winchester in numbers only when surging labor demand during World War II made Winchester relent in its prejudicial hiring policies. (Western Cartridge, located in the sundown community of East Alton, refused to do so.) In the Carolinas, railroad employees brought word when Winchester had openings, as did newspapers and employment agents who sometimes were given large trucks to drive around the South with instructions to fill them up with strong men. As Blacks were belatedly hired, they arrived at a company that featured blackface images in house publications. They'd be offered only low-skill, low-pay positions, the dirtiest, most dangerous jobs. Deep-hole barrel drilling, for instance, the first step in building a gun, used a toxic oil lubricant. A thick mist clouded the spray booths where stain and lacquer were applied to gun stock. Back at home, wives refused to sleep in the same bed with husbands because they smelled so bad.

When some few Black workers were given increased responsibilities, they encountered pushback from Winchester's skilled white workers, who, according to Matthew Bloom, "were violent and discriminatory towards black workers as they sought to protect their jobs against the encroaching black population." In 1943, Lawrence Young, who'd come to Connecticut from Arkansas, became one of Winchester's first two Black woodworkers. White woodworkers refused to tell him anything, but Young was a gifted craftsman and made his way. Young would work at Winchester for forty-three years, a job he valued except, as he told the Greater New Haven Labor History Association, "You always had to do more than anyone else to do the job, because I am Black." Black men believed they were paid far less than whites—the way of the Union since the Civil War, when the 200,000 Black men who fought for the Northern army were paid $7 a month, while white solders received $13. Still, as another Black employee said, Winchester was better than picking cotton and peas in Lake City, South Carolina. Racist restrictions on promotion had always meant no matter what a Black American's qualifications, there was no chance at a career, at a "lifework," as W.E.B. Du Bois said. Here, at least, you could begin as a gunstock shaper, sanding and polishing wood until your hands blistered, but if you displayed promise doing menial assignments, Winchester would teach you a trade, like checkering—carving the ornamental scrimshaw patterned on stocks to improve grip.

NEWHALLVILLE HADN'T BEEN redlined. In 1937, it was instead awarded the second-lowest classification, a yellow C (for "Definitely Declining"). The

Newhallville area description noted that many inhabitants worked at Winchester and cautioned that "pride of ownership is decidedly spotty." Implied was the writer's real source of complaint, that the neighborhood then was 50 percent foreign-born, apparently a mark of irredeemable moral deficiency. As each Newhallville generation grew established, some would leave for the sun and light of elsewhere, and others would remain at the bottom of the back of the hill to share the old neighborhood with—and sometimes detest—whomever came next. It wasn't the same neighborhood anymore because of *those* people, because "I smell an Irishman." A New Haven real estate agent's view of Italian immigrants in the 1930s was "They come here and live like animals . . . eight or ten in a room, and breed like pigs." It was possible to rise above Newhallville, as did Anna Boselli and Camillo Borgnino's son, actor Ernest Borgnine, who would win a 1956 Academy Award for playing the lonely Bronx butcher Marty Piletti.

In a white house on Shelton Avenue near Read Street, with well-tended rosebushes and a low fence at the sidewalk edge, lived the mayor. Back when Richard Lee was six, in the 1920s, his father was blackballed at Winchester after trying to organize a union. Lee's daughter Sally says that as a result, Frederick Lee lapsed into depression, never worked again, and died of heart failure. Lee's mother, the last of a County Armagh farmer's thirteen children, carried a large cast-iron pot across the ocean to Newhallville. After her husband fell ill, she ended each weekend making enough meat-and-potato stew that she wouldn't have to cook again all week. She worked an assembly-line shift at Winchester, and afterward, for reduced rent, scrubbed and swept the staircases and hallways of their Starr Street apartment building. Through childhood, Richard Lee made money cleaning out saloon spittoons, carrying coffins, setting pins at a bowling alley. He'd have given all to attend Yale, but the necessity of helping his family meant Lee never went to college. Yet as he came of age, his mesmerizing eyebrows added physical dimension to a way of speaking that made people feel Lee was for them—he had "the gift," his mother would say. After he became mayor, in 1954, Lee attended every funeral, distributed potted lilies at Easter and poinsettia at Christmas. At home he pruned and watered his roses, living alongside a Polish family, known to the Lees as "the Communists." There were also the Italian construction workers across the street, the nurse down the block, the bakery around the corner that Lee visited every weekend, extolling its jelly doughnut as the finest ever sold.

Newhallville was the place that made Lee's political career, the out-and-up neighborhood that launched white working-class children to college educations, professions, middle-class neighborhoods. Everybody knew of families where the grandparents from Ireland met in Newhallville at a County Kerry party, worked at Winchester, bought a house on Shelton Avenue, had kids who lived in a Hamden ranch house, who, in turn, had kids who earned graduate degrees, ended up commuters out on the tony shoreline. Lee would always think of Newhallville as a place to lift people, a neighborhood to overcome.

White postwar Newhallville was guided by the assumption that life should be good for you, and better for your children. Winchester made providers of working people, and they spent their wages along Newhallville's commercial strips, where, over the years, there was a furrier, a record shop, a watch repair, more than one beauty salon. A network of tramps had a system for marking homes receptive to strangers requesting a meal.

In October 1956, an artful headline in the New Haven *Journal Courier* reported, "Newhall Street Holdup Attempt Leaves Neighbors Bored." The proprietor of Ben's Liquor Shop, Benjamin Gurewitz, told two would-be robbers, "Get out, you bums," and they did. There were many witnesses, all glad to describe the pair to the police, including the owner of the Sav-A-Day Laundromat. A newspaper photographer captured a child yawning in the aftermath, leaving the impression of a neighborhood that could not be intimidated. Arthur Pope, a Congregational minister who grew up in Newhallville, remembers that day. "For crime," he said, "this was it. This was the event of the century."

One Christmas Eve, Mayor Lee heard about a Black mother just up from Alabama with five children and nowhere to live. By that afternoon, he'd found them a home and delivered a Christmas tree. When a Black family from the Carolinas moved into the two-family house across the street, Lee's daughter Sally was enraptured watching the children run outside to touch snow for the first time. Other white people in the neighborhood, however, wrote frostily in their journals, "Negroes moved next door today."

Out in the suburbs there was high-production new home-building. In Newhallville, every year there were more Black neighbors and, on photograph day at school, more young Black faces. Arthur Pope said he felt a free-floating dread consuming the white community—"They had many fears. All kinds of fears." Some of this mimicked the reflexive bigotry confronting each generation of uneducated poor people from distant provinces. Blacks were the new Italians, the new Irish—unclean, bug-infested, ate only potato chips. Some of it was fear of property values and schools declining. Another neighborhood terror was that Black people carried grudges over slavery, had it in for white people.

THE THREE-STORY WHITE Colonial-revival home the Fields family bought in 1960 had been constructed on Read Street during a 1908 Newhallville building boom, by an enterprising carpenter named Reid. There was crown molding, stained glass above the front door, a stately interior staircase. These would give a churchly effect when Fields family brides descended during their wedding ceremonies. The yard had space for both Susie's garden and a rose arbor. That garden, Susie's cooking, and her sugar bowl, creamer, and elephants were the only outward evidence of Wolfton. To support the house, the family both rented out the first floor and everyone worked jobs except four-foot-eleven Susie, who ran the household like a field marshal. "My mother was Napoleon," Katie-Jean said.

In the normal course, no American neighborhood stays the way it was, because people are always moving on for better jobs, bigger or smaller homes, warmer climates, to be closer to family. In the 1950s, when Newhallville went from 97 percent white to 42 percent Black, all those reasons were true. There were also new reasons. "It was gradual," said Edmund Funaro, who began working at Visels Pharmacy in the 1950s, and then bought it in 1965. "You would never notice until one day you said, 'Gee, what happened to . . .' and it was 'Well, they moved.' Nobody came out and said I'm getting out of here because I can't stand it." The German bakeshop, well known for European-style eclairs, one day just began selling sweet-potato pie.

Around the neighborhood, there was performative white door locking, weapon-display, and stage whispering about "the invasion." One white man responded to the arrival of Black people next door by building a garage. On the wall facing the home of his white neighbors, the man placed two windows. On the side looking out on the new Black neighbor's property, there was no window. That Black neighbor was philosophical: "He had issues—and a beautiful '63 Cadillac!" Another white man would get drunk, stand on his Lilac Street porch, and yell, "I can't wait to get away from you . . ." followed by a stream of slurs. When Stacy Spell's family bought a house on Starr Street, in 1964, he said, "With our Southern upbringing, we'd say to them *Good Morning! Good Afternoon! Good Evening!* But they never said a word to us. They moved out in a month."

The Fieldses were the second Black family on their Read Street block. Up and down Read Street, their neighbors worked as braziers, steamfitters, were employed at Winchester and the electric company. Most were Irish, others German, Polish, and Italian. Not for long. "Change happened rapidly," said one man who arrived in Newhallville from South Carolina in 1961. "Read Street was one of the first Black streets."

A few houses down from the Fieldses lived a white boy who took the school bus and had classes with Katie-Jean but never acknowledged her. No Fields ever got used to living among such people. The implication was the neighbors thought the Fieldses didn't deserve a nice home in a good neighborhood. But her Black family, Katie-Jean thought, had come to Newhallville, not for anything to do with the white people but for the same reasons of opportunity as they had. By moving to Newhallville, families like the Fieldses were letting it be known race wasn't going to be a part of decisions about where and how they lived, and the message sent in response was that race mattered very much.

But not always. After a snowfall, prompted by their parents, Black children hurried out to clear the walks of their elderly neighbors, at first mostly white. A white man who drove a produce truck gave his neighbors apples so large a pie could be made from just one. Next door to the Fieldses on Read Street lived an older white woman and her adult daughter, whom the Fields children all called Miss Rose. "She and my mom were always good talking buddies," Katie-Jean said. In 1967, when an engraved vellum invitation summoned guests to watch Katie-Jean descend the Read Street stairs in her wedding dress, Miss Rose was still next door. After her mother died, Miss Rose eventually left, and then a Black family moved in.

That was the rigid pattern. By 1970, Ernest Shaw noticed the only whites left in Newhallville were elderly homeowners who locked up their doors at dusk. In thirty years, New Haven lost half of its white population. Though everybody blamed white flight for what was happening in Newhallville, the truer instrument of segregation isn't flight, which is visible, so much as something unseen, avoidance. "Segregation of the neighborhood wasn't overt," said Bill Dyson, a Black teacher who became Newhallville's state representative. "Nobody wrote anything down. I know this shit's going on. But you can't convince anyone, and it steeps your anger. Is something wrong with me?" The American immigration pattern had always begun with the latest migrant group inhabiting "ethnic" neighborhoods. Immigration quotas shrunk the number of first-generation Europeans moving to American cities, but white declines were more severe in integrating neighborhoods. As demographers discovered in the 1960s, the difference between white ethnic communities and those where Black migrants settled was that Black neighborhoods were, from the first, more segregated than white neighborhoods ever had been. While whites moved to diversifying communities, poor Black neighborhoods grew intensely segregated. White Newhallville landlords, like Adolph Konopacke, the owner of three-family houses on Newhall Street, could attest that Newhallville became almost all-Black because no whites were choosing to replace departing whites.

The role of realtors was significant in creating housing discrimination and reinforcing these racial attitudes. For his 1955 Yale doctoral dissertation on real estate agents, Stuart Palmer interviewed 29 New Haven realtors and all but two told him they "would do anything legally possible to avoid selling a house to a Negro unless the area already contained a number of Negro residents." Barbara B. Tower, a New Haven realtor, in the 1980s told an employee what it had been like earlier in her career, when a leading realtor was an intimidating woman named Mabel Benton. "Mabel ran real estate in New Haven," Tower said. "She'd say, 'Black people don't want to live among white people. So show them homes on this side [of Prospect Hill].'" A great feature of real estate steering was plausible deniability. Nobody could prove what properties realtors were choosing not to show to which people, the true reasons mortgages were granted or denied. Cynthia Teixeira, a longtime mediator at New Haven's Eviction Court, said, "People were unaware. They didn't know the agent taking you to see a lovely little house was only taking Black people to see it. You're just happy with the lovely little house."

Across three decades beginning in 1950, Newhallville's Black population increased from 3 percent to 92 percent as it became the neighborhood with the largest Black housing ownership in the state. An intense kinship existed there among Blacks sharing a feeling of having traveled a difficult path to reach the immigrant's paired sense of identity. Pete Fields was a "Carolina homeboy," and now, because of the house, he was Newhallville.

This was the first time in the country's history that a majority of Black people lived outside the South, and in Newhallville, the recent past was present. "We said we lived up North, but we lived like we were down South," said a local woman. Children addressed women neighbors as Auntie and Miss, and neighbors were deputized to correct children, telling them to "straighten up and fly right." Read Street was to one Black resident, Edward Cherry, the image of a Southern town: "Neighbors you could talk to. Cars coming down the street. No shooting. No fighting. People walk down the sidewalk, everybody speaks, 'How do! How do! How you?'"

In backyards some people harvested peaches, beans, and okra. For others, dusty pickups with Carolina plates and beds full of greens drove the wider streets, the driver yelling, "Come get your vegetables!" People canned for winter, made jellies and preserves, slaughtered a hen on Sunday for a fried-chicken dinner, used the yellow eggs for baking, and anything left went into the garden for fertilizer. At the Country Market, people bought sweet potatoes and the hog parts they called Down South meat. On the bar in taverns were pickled pigs' knuckles, vinegar and deviled eggs, ham hocks and pork cracklings. The "Hot Peanut Man" sold brown bags full outside Staten's pool hall. Holes in the yard were covered by metal grates, and above them the smoky aroma of grilling ribs. From house to house was the oven smell of pineapple upside-down cake. "The air made you hungry," said a woman.

Life then for Black Newhallville families unfolded much as it had for earlier generations of white arrivals. Winchester parents bought rifles for themselves and for their kids, some of whom went to nearby woods for small-game shooting. On Saturdays, hedges were trimmed, then starched shirts and fedoras replaced denim overalls. House parties were held up and down Read Street. Women made quilts and they made dresses, which they wore along with stockings and gloves even to go to the market and, of course, to attend church, though not always the same church since, with surprising frequency, disaffected members of congregations would split off and begin new churches. A former German social club became the Knickerbocker, a Black men's golf club. But it was a golf club with no golf course. Members played at public courses, gathering afterward for revelry at the small stone schloss.

People sent money "Back South," known as "kissing the envelope," and made regular visits bringing presents, these rituals of generosity also a gift to themselves, the declaration they were making it, living the dream. They returned North with ingredients and bottles of moonshine. Some families wanted their children born in the South, as if to establish a form of dual citizenship. It was not uncommon for these New Haven families to retain their membership in Southern churches. Fall was typically the time Southern family members came up to stay at an aunt's or older brother's home, known as "the stopping-off place," until they made their own way in the North.

AS BLACK PEOPLE in number had continued to arrive in New Haven from the South, plenty had difficulty. One day, Richard Lee visited the Oak Street neighborhood, across town from Newhallville, which Lee didn't know well. There he met an elderly one-legged Black man crutching home with a bucket of pump water for the four grandchildren he was raising. Lee accompanied the man inside his apartment, where noisome kerosene lighting provided dim cover for swarms of vermin. Lee hadn't known the other half still lived this way. Back outside, Lee recalled, "I was just as sick as a puppy." This was the origin story that Lee would say made him a social-reform politician, so outraged at New Haven's inequity that he set out to reimagine it as a "slumless" American city.

Urban renewal, sometimes referred to as "Negro removal," meant the mayor of an old harbor city to which immigrants had come by boat and train was responding to crowds of white residents leaving along new interstate highways for suburban split-levels with linoleum floors, family rooms, and swimming pools. The concentrated convenience of new shopping plazas outside the city made downtown seem obsolete. Lee's idea was using federal housing and transportation funds to reinvent the modern city in the suburban image, making New Haven attractive again to those with disposable income who were rejecting it.

Lee was a born storyteller whose most memorable tale became the revival of his "dying city." He told it well enough to secure three times more federal dollars per capita for New Haven than anywhere else got. As for how to spend it, Lee relied upon a staff of socially committed, highly educated workaholics, each surer of himself than the next, almost none from New Haven.

They would destroy much of the city in order to save it. By some estimates, 20,000 structures were eventually knocked down. The entire Oak Street neighborhood of 886 families and 350 businesses disappeared into splinters and dust. The downtown commercial district was relieved of nearly 800 small retail businesses, many of which had occupied "Second Empire" ornamented European-style buildings. The area was then reimagined with a new skyline in the rebar-and-concrete style, imposing structures designed by Brutalist architects, a two-story mall, and a high-speed Oak Street Connector to hurry cars in and out. The Macy's department store opening in 1964 swept up the *New York Times* into a headline of spectacular length and optimism: "New Department Store to Aid New Haven in War Against Urban Blight; Macy's and New Haven Hoping to Revive Downtown Business; $5 Million Store Opening Today Is on Site Once Blighted by Poolrooms and Bars—Shift to Suburbs Reversed."

Not true. During Lee's years as mayor, when New Haven became known as the Model City for urban renewal, the city would lose half of its 500 factories and two-thirds of its 26,180 manufacturing positions, as employers followed the interstates—and the tax breaks—to industrial parks across the country. The true disaster of that time for New Haven and its neighborhoods was the lack of a postindustrial solution, the abandonment without reconstitution of energetic neighborhoods whose reason for being had been work. And the nadir was the fall of the factory neighborhood where Lee's parents had worked and lived. In the 1950s, Mayor Lee and Winchester's parent Olin Corporation had disputes over taxes and requests for favors, like closing off a street to neighborhood access. After one such discussion, John Olin became so angry, he boarded his airplane back to Illinois and told his staff, "I want everything out of New Haven in a year." That didn't happen, but what began was a long goodbye.

Lee left office in 1970 and lived out in Westville. As Newhallville declined, his daughters listened to his outrage at how Winchester was "Shutting the door on the neighborhood, how extreme it was." Not that he absolved himself. "If New Haven is a model city," he sorrowed, "then God help urban America." Lee had misread what made people like living in cities. Perplexing about him, a man from Newhallville, was how his best civic intentions went astray because he undervalued what presumably he knew best, the intimate experience of city life. Oak Street had the vitality of intermingled cultures; the disappeared neighborhood had been home to Italians, Irish, Blacks, Jews, Poles, Turks, and Greeks, and people had come from all over New Haven for Oak Street's robust commercial culture of jewelers, butchers, and a baker whose bread smelled like fresh flowers.

There was also the solace of the pleasing familiar as a bulwark against the inevitability of something new. Lee would have seemed a likely preservationist, a born reviver of careworn communities. Late in life, he told his daughter Sally, "If I had to do it again, I'd never knock those buildings down." He had, she said, "a dream. He thought he could make lives better." In emphasizing new buildings rather than new jobs, Lee's daughter Tara thought his vulnerability was lack of education. Lee revered Yale, and had he gone to a college like it, Tara believed he might have pushed back against expert advisers who "had no emotional attachment" to New Haven's neighborhoods, might have seen his own advantages as a person who "was from the neighborhood, knew the people, was immersed in it—never forgot where he came from."

Back in Lee's old neighborhood was a Black man named Harry Perkins. His parents had worked in North Carolina chicken plants and tobacco fields. By contrast, New Haven in the 1960s, Perkins said, "felt like the Promised Land. I felt that I had a job forever." But ten years later, Perkins was seeing the advent of postindustrial America from inside a Northern factory. "When people lost jobs, a large proportion was Black," he said. "Whites lost their jobs, too, but it wasn't as many. I didn't put myself equal with a white person. I felt I could get fired a lot easier than they could. So, I watched my steps." Growth industries wanted educated employees, and that Black people had typically received less was an important reason, after 1972, Black unemployment was at Depression levels, and consistently twice the white level.

By then, Pete Fields was long gone from Read Street. On the same day, in 1962, Fields received his honorable discharge from military service, his daughter Susan was born. Two years later, Fields moved out to the Allingtown section of neighboring West Haven. His detective friend, Jim Ponteau, would remember him then as "one of the first homeboys to own a house."

Chapter Four

In the 1960s, when a dilapidated (and red-lined), largely Black area near West Haven's oceanfront was chosen for redevelopment, displaced residents were redirected to a new tract in an old section of West Haven. Dating back to a seventeenth-century blacksmith named Alling, Allingtown had attracted working people who wanted out of New Haven. Now these freshly surveyed Allingtown lanes and circles brought to mind the subdivisions that, since the end of World War II, had been shifting the composition of the country. After word spread that mortgages could be had by Black families, Pete Fields used a VA loan to cover the entire $15,000 cost of a new modest, blue-gray ranch house on Norfolk Street.

By 1970, per capita income for Blacks in West Haven was more than 50 percent higher than in New Haven. Pete worked briefly at West Haven's Armstrong Rubber Company and at a hospital. Many transplanted Southerners had several employers before settling in with one, and for Pete, that would be the large Stop & Shop warehouse in North Haven, which had been built off the new I-91 highway in 1962, to position trucks for midway distribution between New York and Boston. The warehouse was a unionized job site, offering high pay and benefits, and Pete was among the first Black employees on the job. Pete, known among his colleagues as Popeye because of his muscular forearms and powerful chest, drove a forklift, and while he was a stalwart member of company softball and bowling teams, in the Norfolk Street years his priority was family.

The Fieldses stopped having children after their third, Peter, was born. They had the means to give Susan, Jeffrey, and Peter childhoods that Susan considered "sheltered." There was basketball in the driveway, frequent cookouts. Although West Haven wouldn't have its first full-time Black police officers until 1976, Allingtown was an integrated neighborhood where the Italian vegetable man, Irish kids noticed, would cry, "Tomatoes, lettuce, watermalones." Pete wouldn't have stood for such slurs. When he learned the candy-shop owner was serving white kids from the back of the line before his son, Pete paid the store a call. As a teenager Peter Fields was known among younger kids as someone who'd listen to your troubles without making you feel bad about them, but behind the wheel of his father's "nice" cars, Peter said he himself too often "fit the description." So Pete went to the police station to discuss why officers kept pulling his son over. "My dad didn't take no mess," said Susan. "Nothing. Off nobody. He had a full-grown beard. He was a little husky. My boyfriends who came to the door would run away. He was scary. I was the only girl. He didn't want nobody messing with me, and they were scared of him. He was a sweetheart and he was tough. Two sides."

Susan said she and her brothers knew that their parents "always worked hard, and they wanted us to be in decent neighborhoods so we wouldn't have to deal with the issues Black kids deal with in neighborhoods like Newhallville. When he got married, he put us in the suburbs. That's why we're so clueless of the streets." And yet, she said, frequent fatherly admonitions were that they needed to toughen up. "If somebody was picking on you," Susan said, "he'd say don't let them. If my brothers didn't fight, my dad didn't like that." Whenever somebody hit Jeffrey, he refused to hit back. "He got teased and picked on," said Susan. "I fought his battles. My dad tried to make a hard boy out of him and he couldn't." Jeffrey was closest to his mother, but then they all were attached foremost to Charlene, including Pete.

Up and down Norfolk Street, the factory workers, VA nurses, and mail carriers got used to Pete picking up litter, helping someone change a tire, and then retreating to his grill, him listening to soul singers like Al Green, Otis Redding, and James Brown and then switching over to country music as he added wood chips and charcoal, brushed more sauce on a pork shoulder, and turned the meat with his bare hands. That, as a brother-in-law exclaimed, "he didn't use the spatula!" was Pete's chefly habit. He claimed this was the best way to detect how well the meat was absorbing flavor. Pete and Charlene were also always inviting people over to eat what he'd made and play cards.

Susan believed that in their racially mixed community, where white people paid a lot of skeptical attention to how Black people behaved, Pete Fields was the exemplar of shared neighborhood values. White people didn't tend to ask Black people what their days were like or what they hoped life would bring, but Susan felt anybody could see Pete and Charlene worked hard, took care of their possessions, were saving up for college tuitions, placed their children before themselves. Because Pete treated the neighborhood with such generosity, others did the same for his family, and there was concord.

Susan believed that her father found again on Norfolk Street what he'd liked best about Read Street. And also true was that when he stood grilling in his West Haven yard, the ritual went further back in him, the Southern music and the flavorful smells a sentient experience of his lost South Carolina home. In 1976, when the Fields family moved from densely settled Norfolk Street to a more commodious home on Alden Road in West Haven, Pete and Charlene chose the house mostly because its enormous living room and patio made it ideal for entertaining.

Compared with the noise of Newhallville, on Alden Road every day had a Sunday stillness. Out back, Pete increased his grilling output. He cooked pans and pans of South Carolina barbecue for his children's boyfriends and girlfriends, for the neighbors, for coworkers, for his car dealer. When the Fieldses had parties, besides barbecue, also on offer was Charlene's baking, wine Pete made from grapes supplied by his sister in Hamden, top-shelf spirits, tables for poker, spades, bid whist, and a nickel-ante children's game in the basement. Pete hosted the card-game nights wearing plush jogging suits, keeping up a witty, teasing line of repartee. "Drink my liquor and talk to me!" he'd call as he won another hand. Yet even in these sociable games, if Pete lost, Susan knew her father was seething: "My dad's a gambler and he didn't want to give up his money."

Before the Fieldses moved in, there were no Black families on Alden Road. Susan said once the seller learned they were Black, completing the sale had suddenly been difficult. When they moved in, Pete found Klan literature left behind. Those were experiences with property no data points about race and real estate could reveal. To their many guests at the handsome house, the Fieldses seemed confident, thriving members of the risen Black middle class. Yet when Susan and Peter later thought about why there had been almost relentless social activity, they recalled parents who seemed vulnerable. "Black people did a lot of things to cover up the feeling of the pain and stress and depression of feeling not good enough," said Susan. "My parents partied a lot. There was always alcohol and cards and loud music. That was their way of feeling better about life. Same as my dad with cars."

THAT PEOPLE LIKE the Fieldses were living well in West Haven obscured how much of a struggle the city and suburbs were for most Black people. Property was the enduring American source of wealth, and that far fewer Black families owned homes, and that the houses Black people did possess were, on the average, worth less, had a lot to do with where in the city, and outside, people could buy. Between 1934 and 1968, all but 2 percent of government-approved mortgages in Connecticut were given to whites. New Haven bank mortgagers told Stuart Palmer, for his 1955 dissertation, their steering practice was to, without explanation, "simply refuse to grant the mortgage. We're not answerable to anyone." For her undergraduate Yale thesis about the "segregationist spirit" of the same period, Sarah Donaldson found that agreements among neighboring white homeowners, "wherein they agreed not to sell to African Americans, were in full effect in New Haven." When real estate companies advertised "restricted" developments, they alluded to racial covenants deep within deeds like this 1950 document from Hamden, three miles from Newhallville: "That no persons of any race other than the white race shall use or occupy any building on any lot." Darien was not the state's only sundown town. Bill Fisher, a local Black realtor who worked mostly with Black clients, between 1972 and 1995 never sold a home in such New Haven suburbs as Orange, Woodbridge, and Milford. This created housing scarcity in neighborhoods like Newhallville, raising rents to the extent that numbers of poor Blacks were enticed into buying houses beyond their means. When they foreclosed, the house could be sold again. One Newhallville cleaning woman had three mortgages on one home, all through the same realtor. "He set her up for failure," Fisher said.

Outside New Haven was also where the jobs were going. By the late 1970s, only 1,400 people still worked in the ever-smaller Winchester complex. Winchester Avenue had now been closed off on the Newhallville side, despite much community opposition to the high gates. The present company bywords and phrases were those of recession times: subcontractor, downsize, layoff, union-concession, division shutdown. By 1981, when Winchester was bought out and reconstituted as the U.S. Repeating Arms Company, New Haven had become the country's seventh poorest city. Things were such that historian Joe Dobrow would publish an elegy in 1993, thirteen years before the company actually left for good. Winchester "was not just another factory," Dobrow wrote. "In few other cities had a single enterprise ever employed such a large percentage of the citizens for such a long period of time."

In Newhallville, everybody knew several men who used to work at Winchester. The reaction around the neighborhood was crushing. Women were more likely to find other employment, in the health and service industries, leaving men alone with their humiliation. "I remember my father and his friends talking," said Thaddeus Reddish, who grew up in Newhallville and became a police officer. "My father knew guys who worked at Winchester. These guys all came up from down South. It was weird—the men were shamed. Couldn't work. Laid-off. Some never went back to work." The listing factory meant there was nobody to support the neighborhood's breakfast counters and taverns, barber and dress shops, the doctor's and dentist's offices. Some men traversed the city looking for scrap metal to haul away and sell. Others tried to make it doing freelance car repair or by hosting after-hours house parties. None of that paid anything approaching a factory check. "Unskilled labor," Jack London wrote, "is the first to feel the slackness of hard times." Many men continued to exit their houses every day, but now made it only as far as the corners, where they hoped to be chosen by passing contractors for pickup construction or landscaping labor. This is how corners became the redoubts of working-class pain.

Harry Perkins still had his factory position and his home in Newhallville, but he saw how "after the jobs left, a lot of guys took to the street. You'd see them begging on the corners or outside the bar. People were desperate. Eventually, most of the bars along Newhall Street and Winchester Avenue left. People had nowhere to go. They'd hang around the liquor stores, day drinking while sitting in cars. A lot became drunks, alcoholics. It's bad when you run into a friend or an old work acquaintance and they're drunk. Eventually, you won't see them anymore." Winchester union leaders began to hear about suicides. In the Black churches of Newhallville, discouraged men confided their misery to pastors like Donald Morris, a former community activist. "You been on one job for thirty years and all of a sudden it's gone," Morris said. "It was a devastating feeling for a lot of men. I have no other skills, so I start drinking, start hanging around, go visiting, and that's where babies come from. It's a terrible thing. Man can't bring in groceries, he becomes belittled, feels useless. They start medicating themselves."

Addiction costs money. In the late 1970s and 1980s, Black Newhallville family men were chaining their front hoods closed because so many car batteries were being stolen. Black parents were teaching their kids to ask, "Who is it?" before turning the front door lock. The grocer put word out that he'd got a gun to protect himself. A young Newhallville woman named Dorothy Johnson did as Katie-Jean Fields had, earning pocket money by babysitting, doing day's work, getting summer jobs at local businesses. But gradually the Newhallville sidewalks became something to ponder before heading outside. Abruptly, the family house was sold and "my father moved us to Hamden for safety."

When Thaddeus Reddish's family moved to North Haven, they left because of maternal misgivings. "My family made it and we got out," Reddish said. "So many people were able to leave. My mother could see it coming. 'We have to go.' My father was, 'This is our neighborhood!' But she saw the bigger picture."

Some who remained, like Susie Fields, didn't want to give up the houses they'd invested so much in. The white landlord Adolph Konopacke was also that way. He intended never to leave the neighborhood. But eventually one of his children took him to see a house in North Haven. Did he agree that it was a nice house? It was indeed a very fine house. "This is it," she told him, writing a check. "You're out of Newhallville." That happened in 1983. The purchaser of the three-family home Konopacke had lived in for sixty years on Newhall Street immediately took out his stained-glass windows for use where people paid higher rents.

Others were choiceless—stuck in Newhallville. If you didn't have a car and depended upon public transportation (or your feet) to get to work, you couldn't follow your job, and if you didn't have expertise, you couldn't find a new one. Even if you had a ride, white suburban employers were notoriously opposed to hiring Black city men, claiming their commutes would make them late. (White laboring Southerners, who came to the North in number after World War II, had it easier finding homes near jobs.) The kind of vocational tutorials that factories had once provided to willing-but-uneducated European immigrants and rural Black Southerners were now rare, and skilled employees took years to train. The timing of the Great Migration's second wave had coincided with shifts in the nature of employment that could not quickly be adjusted to. How to suddenly prevail over generations of Jim Crow schoolhouses was a catastrophic problem, and one that government did not really address. A Newhallville man named Rodney Williams said uneducated Black parents felt shame at their personal inability to "help their kids coming up," and as a result, "We never got a first chance."

In the early 1980s, there was a surge in heroin use, and then a few years later crack cocaine created a third manufacturing boom in Newhallville, a predatory successor to carriages and rifles. A man who lived on Newhallville's Lilac Street in those years said, "Lilac and Winchester would rival anywhere I've been, and I've been around a lot of places where drugs were being sold. It was *busy*. I never saw so many people selling drugs so brazenly in the open and so much traffic." Lucrative corners that provided dealers with BMWs, bedizened designer clothes, and $100 bills enough to make it rain in the clubs had to be defended from rivals. Heroin addicts nodded peaceably; crack addicts came down aggressive. The result of all this was that if guns had once sustained Newhallville, now they made corners so dangerous for those in the game a dealer named Sere said, "I saw three or four people shot in a day. I watched somebody die right in front of my eyes. I been shot seven times." In 1989, 320 people were wounded in New Haven shootings.

Another popular crack concession operated out of a jungled-up empty lot with several large rocks over by what had once been an offload for oil along the railroad track—the Mudhole. Bulk trash of the kind that elsewhere landed at the bottom of gullies was strewn. In the daytime, the Mudhole was used as a cut-through to Dixwell Avenue. But after dark, few but cocaine dealers, cocaine buyers, prostitutes, and their clients ventured into the gloom, where business was conducted behind the big rocks and under a large tree. But only twenty steps beyond the cut, busy at cards inside a red-and-yellow converted cinder-block building that had once been an appliance repair shop, were those poker-playing men who'd come up from Carolina poverty and now drove Mercedes and Cadillacs. Among them on weekends might be Pete Fields.

The new life Pete had begun on Alden Road continued in consistent outline from the 1970s through the 1990s. Both he and Charlene held the same jobs, they never missed a Valentine's Day dance, they took cruises, had reliable pleasures. Pete was a follower of the New York Yankees—especially the muscular, flexing outfielder Reggie Jackson: Susan said, "Put a baseball cap on [my father] when he had his little afro, it was about like looking in a mirror." Pete liked Anita Baker's music so well he once listened to an album of hers for fourteen hours straight. He watched Spencer Tracy and Katherine Hepburn movies, *The Andy Griffith Show*, and as many westerns as possible. Clint Eastwood, John Wayne, Johnny Cash, Reba McEntire, and Charlie Pride made him happy, as did wearing cowboy boots and a black cowboy hat. "Embarrassing! Embarrassing!" said Peter. "I'm on the West Haven High basketball team. My mom's looking good. My dad comes in—cowboy hat!"

Behind his house, Pete had a country vegetable garden, and for his daughter-in-law's yard he made, and kept up, a second patch. He remained the son of a farming family that valued frugality. Pete and his siblings had an emergency sibling kitty into which for many years everyone placed $10 every month—money available on credit, interest-free to those who needed it. Nobody ever took out any. On his daily walks, Pete continued to collect litter. For all of it, Pete's greatest enthusiasm remained cars. Over time, the speedy Firebirds and Datsuns of his young manhood gave way to Cadillacs and Acuras. When his teenage children drove them, he encouraged all three to do so with confidence. He said the road was theirs.

Having raised them in what Susan said her father considered "the best neighborhoods," what Pete desired most for his children was higher education. He had nieces and nephews taking graduate degrees, becoming doctors and professors. "He wanted us to turn out that way," Susan said. "We didn't. I wish I would have. All my cousins on my dad's side, everybody's educated. Coming where they came from, being dirt poor as they were, it's surprising his family is so educated. Surprising, only because they were Black." Susan began college at Morgan State in Baltimore and then became ill enough that her father had to bring her home. Neither she nor Peter finished college, taking positions instead at the post office. "We're working people," Susan said. "We pay our bills. We have good paychecks. We had good role models who told us you got to take care of yourself, you got to work."

The youngest, Jeffrey Fields, was an excellent student and a dancer, so good-looking and good-natured he was inevitably surrounded by girls. While Jeffrey and Charlene were very close, into his teens Jeffrey and his father had continuing conflict because Pete fretted Jeffrey was soft. After high school, Jeffrey went to City College in New York, and then he took a well-paying job in finance. "My brother was gay," said Susan. "In the mid-'80s, in that time, homosexuality was tougher. They always leave home to live the lifestyle. He went first to New York, and ended up outside Washington, DC." When Jeffrey visited Connecticut, he was accompanied by his boyfriend, a flight attendant. It took Pete time, but he became accepting of both. Jeffrey was twenty-four years old in 1988, when his boyfriend brought him back to West Haven. Jeffrey was quiet, thin, weakened, and sad. He went up to his room and didn't want to come out. The family knew what they were seeing. AIDS had become a second modern epidemic in New Haven, the leading cause of death among young adults, many of them impoverished drug users, and increasingly women of color. Susan said to her mother, "Jeffrey's dying. He wanted to come home to die." When it was decided Jeffrey needed full-time medical care, Pete had to carry him down the stairs and out to the car.

After he died, said Susan, Charlene "couldn't handle" the loss of her child. Joe Pullen thought his sister-in-law "went to pieces. When her son died, Charlene died with him." She became more than a social drinker. Pete began to attend church services regularly, at St. Paul UAME, where he'd last gone as a teenager with his mother. After a brief period of religion, Pete turned to different consolations. At times gambling seemed to consume him. To most, he and Charlene remained a model couple. "They stayed together for the kids," said Susan. "My mother told me this on her death bed. She didn't want to break up the family. She loved him, he loved her, but they had their problems."

Susie Fields remained in Newhallville but always intended to move back to South Carolina, and eventually bought a plot of land in Orangeburg. Every year, Pete would drive his mother down to Wolfton, journeying straight through without stopping. During one South Carolina visit, Susie discovered the retirement land no longer belonged to her, the cost of a missed tax payment for which she'd never received a bill. Susie and two of her daughters, Katie-Jean and Nina, bought the land back, at a much higher price than Susie had first paid. And this time on the property deed Susie placed the name of her son Pete, the owner of a big home outside New Haven, and a man who took no stuff.

Susie never did leave Read Street, remaining until she died in 1986, at age eighty-four. Every time Katie-Jean visited her mother, she'd seen the way white flight fulfilled what it feared. With people, businesses, and the taxes they paid abandoning the neighborhood, schools lost funding and houses were devalued as assets. When the Read Street house was eventually sold, in 1993, Katie-Jean could get for it only a pittance. Of her family's experience in Newhallville she said, "It was a wonderful time. It was a wonderful place to live. We were very happy there. Now what it was is just a memory."

PETE FIELDS CONTINUED to visit Newhallville. For a drink he'd go by the Seven-Eleven Club or the Knickerbocker, but he liked the Mudhole best, formed as it had been by his fellow Carolina farm people come to the city as tradesmen and factory mechanics. Over the years, weekend activities during the good times had included fielding a Mudhole softball team and holding Mudhole family cookouts. The name had come about after a water pipe ruptured over by the empty lot. Led by a man known as Junkyard, the club members seized the opportunity, digging out a fishing hole and stocking it with perch. For a while they called this the Fish Pond, and then, with its soft bottom, it became the Mudhole. After the water company filled it all in, the name remained.

Benjamin Butler owned a liquor store on the block as well as the Mudhole clubhouse, and it was his observation that in postindustrial times, for some of the laid-off men who came to the club, "being there was what they did." Others were middle-class former Newhallville residents, like Pete, who'd moved on to bigger homes in the nearby suburbs yet still felt emotionally attached enough to the old neighborhood that on weekends you'd see them parking their shiny sedans in front of the Mudhole. A couple of times, Pete brought relatives with him, but one considered the "juke joint" ambiance too rough, and after the other had his pockets cleaned out playing stud poker, it wasn't his crowd either.

For Pete, some of the attraction was the past-present feel of the place. The musty clubhouse had a bar, chairs and tables that didn't match, beer signs, a TV with the game on, veteran stereos and rustic appliances in the kitchen, and out back a charcoal grill amid a tangle of old patio furniture. There were photographs of Mudhole holiday gatherings of yore, "beautiful Black family" pride posters, and a prominent list of house rules: "Absolutely no drugs permitted." "Absolutely no weapons permitted." "No gambling permitted." "Arguing and fighting will not be tolerated." Once his liquor store closed for the night, Benjamin Butler sold after-hours beer out of the club; many Mudhole regulars tippled Carolina corn liquor. Butler, like Fields, was from a Great Migration family in which what had gone on in towns like Wolfton wasn't discussed in the house around the children. Butler's son Tony said, "They shielded us, didn't want us to see it." Those feelings were taken instead to private places, like the Mudhole.

Even as cocaine and gunfire had come to the Mudhole in the 1980s and 1990s, the card games went on. At the end of Saturday afternoons, the men ambled in and kept studiously to their cards, staying away from the cut, which was alive with dangers. The drug dealers, in turn, gave them distance. Word had it that "the old men in there don't play," but really, said one man who was in the drug game for a few years, it was "The older people in there don't bother nobody. It's our fathers and uncles. They were the known caring people." As time went on, those drug dealers, operating just steps away from the club, like most young people in the neighborhood, had fewer and fewer sources of connection to all the optimistic miles their families had traveled. Many in the neighborhood came to think of the clubhouse scene with pleasure—as one woman said, "like the olden days down South."

That the club was a comforting place to be, and timeless across the decades, was what the prominent Black artist Winfred Rembert wanted to express in a painting of drinking and gambling pleasure-seekers he called *The Mud Hole*. A native of Cuthbert, Georgia, who settled in Newhallville, Rembert's "idea," said his wife, Patsy, "was to let you know the same things people did in the South, they did in the North. It was just a place where Black men hang out and tell lies about their big fish and best women. They also let off what they held in all week long. That was the outlet where they felt safe to talk about what happened to them down South. Nobody over their shoulder, memories of old times would come up. What happened there, why they left."

Pete never took his children to Newhallville. "He wanted to give us a good childhood, keeping us out of the streets in the suburbs," said Susan. "But where was *he*? In the streets! He used to go to the hood in New Haven all the time. He just didn't want to live there. He wanted to socialize there on weekends." What attracted her elusive father to the Mudhole wasn't just nostalgia. Susan thought it also spoke to a steady provider who liked the action: "He had a little hustle in him."

Chapter Five

Pete Fields retired from driving forklifts at the Stop & Shop warehouse in 1998, after working there for half of his life. At age sixty-two, he could look forward to a good pension, Social Security, and a first-of-the-month morning financial ritual. Pete would bring his checks to his bank in West Haven, request from the teller enough cash back to pay his bills and fund his days, and then he'd drive from creditor to creditor, meeting obligations. "He always paid old-school," Susan said. "My dad didn't go to the ATM. No computer. No direct deposit." Only a fraction of Pete's checks ever went into his savings account, meaning that as he started out from the bank on the first, he might be carrying upward of $2,000 in cash wedged up against his hip. He enjoyed the feeling. Sometimes he'd remove the bills just to enjoy the crisp parchment touch. "He loved money," Susan said. "I never saw anybody love money like he did. Could be because they were very, very poor in South Carolina."

Not only poor. There was the sense in the family that Pete felt the loss of the family's stolen land more acutely than anybody else, that he felt caught up in his father's shame, and that there was compensatory pleasure in displaying wealth. When Pete was flush, he might offer friends like his former Stop & Shop colleague John Sylvia a long look into his billfold. Which didn't concern Sylvia. "He liked to carry a lot of money and to show it," Sylvia said. "Pete was strong and physical. He used to go to rough places. I think he carried a gun. A lot of people did. They had permits." Since his days as an army marksman, Pete always owned pistols, but he had other means of defending himself. Once, he walked into a corner store, and three young men followed him inside. When they tried to hold him up, Pete used his feet, kicking his way out to his car. Afterwards, telling family about it, he said "When you're trained in the military, your body is a weapon."

Pete's morning walks might take him out of West Haven, on into New Haven, across the busy Boulevard, through the shabby West River and Dwight-Kensington neighborhoods, past the buildings of Yale and downtown, around the city's original sixteen-acre Green, and looping back toward home. He covered a distance of at least seven miles, and all along Pete picked up trash. Deep in him was the civic importance of upkeep, helping out, expressing care for those around you. Because he spent so much time outside every day, Pete knew people's patterns, could tell at a glance when something was amiss. On one walk, he spotted his white neighbor in her parked car having what he guessed was a stroke. Acting quickly, he saved her life.

Pete was a vigorous older man whose age was telling in one significant way. After all the years of turning ribs, beef, and pork shoulder on the grill with his bare hands, he had hardly any feeling left in his fingers. He'd been working hard since he was a kid on a farm, plowing, chopping, lifting. Now it had got to the point where some days he couldn't twist open a bottle.

In retirement Pete's gambling increased. He'd play pitty-pat, but poker was his game, and he was always especially available for hands the week Social Security checks arrived in mailboxes. At a round card table, his ball-cap brim tilted to two o'clock, Pete had the stare-down self-assurance that on good days forced others to fold their better cards when the money got real. Immersed in the tactics and the rush of chance, he was free from his dead son, his inconsolable wife, all the old sadnesses.

Nobody's always lucky, and if Pete lost, he paid his debts right away, even if that meant borrowing from his children or his sister. When a friend was short on what he owed, Pete might give that man the money. Then would come a call to Susan or Peter. They referred to these moments as their father "robbing Peter to pay Paul."

Wherever he went during the week, Pete was always home before dark, removing his shoes, settling into his black velvet recliner, watching black-and-white films or the pinstriped Yankees, eating vanilla ice cream, listening to country music. At exactly ten o'clock, the recliner's footrest would noisily clank into closed position, and Pete would say, "Oh, boy!" as he hoisted to his feet, then put away the ice-cream dish, checked the door locks, and padded off to bed.

After retiring from his job, Pete made more road trips, most happily when accompanied by his nephew Floyd Hooks. Pete had lost a son, and to Floyd, "my uncle was a second father." As they both aged, the traveling companions began to share a striking facial resemblance, a similar build and temperament. "Floyd, he's just like my father," Susan said. "Two big Black cats. The same. Floyd is very sensitive. And he's very, very close. I don't know anybody closer to my father."

Wolfton was the place Pete and Floyd visited most, the plumb line that kept the family to its South Carolina axis. Around Wolfton, Pete was known as "a giver." That he was arriving in a fine automobile, so obviously living comfortably in Connecticut, provided a measure of satisfaction for those who'd remained around Wolfton and, of course, for Pete. Black families who'd left during segregation times and done well were said to have "punished the South."

To Floyd, his uncle seemed both a confident man, and yet a person filled with irresolution. Pete was engaged in trying to know who he was, where he truly came from. He'd done well, and yet there was sometimes the nothing-to-live-for, nothing-more-coming-my-way feeling he heard in Otis Redding songs. Why, Floyd himself wanted to understand, after a life of pushing forward in Connecticut, should going back to Wolfton matter so much to his uncle? It had begun to feel crucial to Pete to have a home there. Katie-Jean and Nina continued to pay taxes on the Orangeburg plot, but Pete wasn't interested in that. He wanted his grandfather's land, the old family property that had been taken from his father. He spent a lot of time thinking about how to get it back.

In the ten years since the death of her son, Charlene had been drinking enough clandestine vodka it was no secret to anyone. She was gaunt and her lovely complexion had grown sallow and blotchy. "When my mother started drinking, the gorgeousness started going," Susan said. "It was so sad." Doctors consider liver failure among the most miserable forms of disease. By 2004, with both her liver and kidneys losing function, Charlene did not look well, she did not feel well, and because of that, neither did Pete. The difficulties of life had led to tension between them, but in their long marriage they always cared about each other, and for Pete, a man who depended on routines, it was Charlene who made it possible for him to live as he liked.

In the fall of 2004, Charlene's liver began shutting down and she was admitted to the hospital, where a family meeting was arranged to discuss how to proceed after her death. The appointed time was 1:00 p.m., but Pete arrived at noon, gave Charlene a long kiss, and then left. In the end, only

Susan was there to hear her mother say, "I'm ready. I raised three good kids. I'm tired of suffering. I'm ready to go." Then Charlene asked Susan to move with her husband and son into the large Alden Road home "so your father won't be by himself." Susan promised.

A few nights later, Pete couldn't sleep, got out of bed, dressed himself, and walked across half of New Haven to the hospital, where Charlene was writhing in pain. When she died, Pete was filled with self-loathing, worried he'd been insufficiently loving, blamed himself for her death.

WITH SUSAN, HER husband, and their six-year-old son, Xavier, joining him on Alden Road, Pete's household was livelier. So was the telephone; he began calling two or more sisters every morning. One day, the mail brought him a Bible and an encouraging note from his sister Nina promising if he read it, "you will receive more than a college education." Another day, Pete received a surprise check, the payout from a life-insurance policy Charlene had owned for years and told nobody about. Pete spent it on the down payment for a 2004 cream-colored Chrysler 300. The Chrysler had a pouting grille, a cabin upholstered in leather, the latest in headlamps, and a high-end sound system—a purring automotive object of desire. Senator Barack Obama drove one; it was soon to be the acclaimed ride of such cultural ministers as Ice Cube, Dr. Dre, and Snoop Dogg. Pete left the dealer's lot and drove to the cemetery, where he thanked Charlene for everything he'd ever wanted in a car.

Pete also had a new passenger, his grandson. To Xavier, Pete was Pop-Pop, and while Xavier's parents were at work, Pete would meet the school bus and take him out for hamburgers or haircuts, visits to friends and family, and even, Susan learned to her horror, to the Mudhole.

Among the men Pete referred to as "my Carolina homeboys," Pete was known as a "latecomer." He had dropped by the place for years on weekends, but only in retirement had he become a daytime regular. He'd park his new Chrysler out on Shelton Avenue, walk down the driveway, and disappear into the dank little building. Kids in the neighborhood were always curious about what all those old guys were doing in there. The answer was the same as they'd always been doing: drinking, watching TV, playing cards in a smoke-filled room, and bantering the days away with exchanges about politics, sports, women, the state of the neighborhood, the world-weary, about nothing at all.

The clubhouse was fustier by the year, and additions to the decor, such as the pinup poster of Lil' Kim, were infrequent. Most of the membership now were senior citizens. Quite a few were struggling with drink and other problems; people who lived nearby described the bedraggled older figures as "innocents." Pete got into the habit of taking over the grill out back and cooking up meat he brought to feed the most precarious men. He'd serve a meal and fill a Tupperware container for later. Over time, Pete handed out so much food that his son Peter, concerned about the sums Pete was spending on Tupperware alone, bought his father a bulk supply of Styrofoam takeaway containers.

One observant person who noticed Pete at the Mudhole was Otha Buffaloe, who'd arrived as a boy from North Carolina to become one of the first Black detectives in New Haven. In retirement Buffaloe maintained his Newhallville connections. Buffaloe knew Pete as "Herbie" and thought, "He was a decent man. Herbie, he'd say, 'Look, man, you're all right, but you got a family. Here's a couple hundred bucks. See you later.' " Likewise, if Pete got word that a young single Newhallville mother didn't have anything for her three children at Christmas, Pete took her with her kids out shopping for presents. "People talked about it," Buffaloe said. "Thought they were his relatives. Wasn't anybody related to him." To Katie-Jean, "He was Robin Hood. He'd take from his family and he'd give it to people in the Mudhole—a lot of alcoholics and people who were hungry he'd cook for. He'd never let Peter or Susan in that environment. I don't know why he started hanging out there."

Pete had become a Mudhole regular during the most unstable time of his adult life. Helping troubled men of his generation made Pete feel more like his orderly, good-neighbor self. He did have boundaries. He stopped by the Mudhole on outings with Xavier, but he never took Xavier inside, remaining out front, protecting both the child and the dignity of the men who, even at their lowest, would frown at a boy brought into a place like that.

Otha Buffaloe did have a concern about Pete Fields. He saw how many scratch-off lottery tickets he was buying, how hard he was playing the daily numbers, and decided "He had a gambling problem. No doubt that was the only problem he had."

IN FEBRUARY 2006, Pete and Katie-Jean met up down in Orangeburg. They had decided to try to reclaim the stolen Wolfton acres and to build back a family homeplace on the land. The principal absconder had been Bill Wolfe.

Years back, when he was dying, Bill Wolfe had heard that Susie Fields was visiting Orangeburg and sent word that he'd like to see her. When Susie arrived, with Katie-Jean, Bill Wolfe had been frail, near death, and he told Susie and Katie-Jean that he was sorry for any wrong he might have done the family. Now, in Orangeburg, Pete and Katie-Jean sought to find deeds, land records, witnesses—anything or anybody who could help them prove their ownership. Katie-Jean considered it "a worthless and depressing endeavor," but throughout the year, she and Floyd Hooks could see that recovering the land had become Pete's mission. He would drive fourteen hours from West Haven to Orangeburg just to spend a little time visiting Bill Wolfe's son, also called Bill, forging a relationship, getting to know him, measuring. This was edgework. Pete's plan was that once he and Bill the son knew each other well enough, Pete would bring up the land. On one trip to South Carolina with Floyd that summer of 2006, Pete won $20,000 playing the state lottery. He described this victory to many people, instructing each, in turn, not to tell anybody else. This boasting made Katie-Jean wince. It seemed unworthy of her brother. She also thought he was asking for trouble.

In the year and a half since Charlene's death, more and more money slipped through Pete's numbed fingers. There were weeks when every day Pete asked Susan for $20 or $40. Sometimes the entreaty was "$100 to feed the poor." Which poor? she wondered. She had her family to support, but she felt her father's expectation that she should take care of his needs and gave him what he requested. Also true was she and her husband had rented out their own house and were paying Pete a nominal sum to live on Alden Road. But Pete's behavior was distressing. The man behind the counter at the gas station near their home let Susan know her father was buying too many scratch-off tickets. The proprietor of a West Haven convenience store volunteered the same to Peter. On a trip South, Pete made several stops in one state to buy lottery tickets. He told Floyd he knew he had a problem but that he couldn't stop. Then he'd ask Floyd for money. Floyd didn't object. Pete always paid all their travel expenses. But for Susan and Peter, it stung seeing unswept paths of disorder in such an otherwise disciplined man.

During the February 2006 trip, Katie-Jean discovered Pete had sold his mother's Orangeburg land. When his sisters asked, "How could you?" he explained he'd needed the money to pay Charlene's medical and funeral expenses. Katie-Jean closed her eyes and thought, "Things happen in families." After his lottery strike in South Carolina, Pete told his sister he planned to use some of those winnings to open a bank account for Katie-Jean's grandson's future. She didn't take it seriously. In the past, Pete had asked her for loans, which he had yet to repay. Lately, he had also been requesting infusions from the sibling kitty.

Susan was grinding her teeth in her sleep. She loved her father, and it was difficult to watch as he refinanced his house and sold Peter's car. What did it mean that Pete had monthly payments on his Chrysler approaching $500? When Susan did the laundry, she'd find dead lottery tickets in Xavier's pants pockets. So Susan would ask Xavier how he and his grandfather were spending their days together, and the answer would come: "Pop-Pop gave me scratch-offs." Then one day, it was "Pop-Pop told me not to tell you something." To that, Susan, heart in her mouth, asked, "Well, what did he tell you not to tell me?" The answer was gleeful: "Pop-Pop and all the cousins were fighting!"

Susan thought the death of Charlene had triggered unresolved losses in Pete, going all the way back to the day he'd been at his father's side as he was stripped of the land. There was in her father, it seemed to Susan, an infinite grief over that moment, and the gambling met an infinite need. The gambling hurt everybody in Pete's life, most of all Pete himself, because he knew all the pain he was causing and was helpless to stop. Loss, too, is an addiction. Across the world people bought long-shot lottery tickets, little prayers for a change in life that came with a paper receipt. One afternoon, Pete visited a doctor, began to speak about himself, talked and talked with tears streaming down his face until, at eight o'clock, the doctor gently said it was time for them both to go home.

ON THE FINAL day of March 2006, the last 198 jobs at U.S. Repeating Arms were eliminated, and the production of Winchester rifles and shotguns ceased in New Haven. A few experienced employees remained until June, one of them an electrician named David Roy. When it was time for the last few to go, Roy gave a farewell polish to the John Wayne statue by the front entrance. Then everybody gathered around the Duke to say goodbye, and Winchester chained its gates.

The factory had not been a significant supplier of jobs to New Haven in years, and most products embossed with the Winchester name had long since been made in distant places. That Winchester's empty buildings were now an industrial ruin was an extended irony, given the rifle's legacy as the avatar of western expansion, and then, as frontier outposts became ghost towns, of western obsolescence.

With American wage and employment growth both at post–World War II lows, and with federal aid to cities reduced to almost nothing, by 2006, greater New Haven had become its own desolation row. Among the closed businesses was the Stop & Shop warehouse where Pete Fields had worked until his retirement. Stop & Shop explained that "efficiencies" had led it to give notice to 850 workers. The warehouse, along with shuttered industrial printing shops and mills, had all been receptive to giving jobs to people who had not been to college, and also to hiring those with prison records.

That summer, work grew more urgent for the directors of the New Haven Family Alliance, a social services organization near Winchester Avenue dedicated to improving the health and safety of some of the city's most at-risk children. Said one of the directors, "2006 was the year we started getting scared again about the violence." There would be twenty-four New Haven killings in 2006, the most in the small city since the drug-related mayhem of 1994. Perhaps a truer measure of how dangerous parts of New Haven became in 2006 were the 120 non-fatal shootings. American violence by then was in decline, although in concentrated areas, generally poor and Black, the terror of gunfire remained part of daily life for young people.

Newhallville had become a treacherous place. "By 2006," said an African American high school sophomore in New Haven, "everybody was staying away. It was so dangerous." Likewise, police officers such as Thaddeus Reddish, who'd grown up in Newhallville and had returned there to live, considered it to be unsafe for children because "gun battles could erupt at any point. In 2006, it was off-the-chain bad." A call would come in about a shooting, and when detectives responded, they'd encounter a house, its front stippled with bullet holes. The detectives would begin digging out spent projectiles, and the homeowner might come out and tell them they were gathering evidence from the wrong shooting: "This one over here's from last night."

Katie-Jean came up from the South and visited New Haven in June 2006, accompanied by a friend to whom she wanted to show the city of her youth. How far Read Street had come down since the 1960s was upsetting for older people who, as the singer Fred Parris said, had considered it "the model street in a model neighborhood. My aunt would be so disappointed to see it destroyed."

Susan thought her own aunt "so sophisticated and classy. The way she dresses. She's a woman from the old days." When Katie-Jean told Pete she was going down to see Read Street, he discouraged her, saying it was nothing like the place where they'd grown up. When Katie-Jean insisted, Pete said she couldn't walk around Newhallville wearing her diamond wedding ring and costly clothes. At the old house on Read Street, the front door's stained glazing was knocked out. Looking through where it had been, Katie-Jean saw that the interior staircase was also wrecked. "It was devastating," she said. "The staircase I came down on my wedding day was so beautiful and elegant. When I came back, I stared at it through broken glass."

Another day, Pete took Katie-Jean and her friend to a beach Katie-Jean had last gone to with her family as a girl. Then they got in Pete's Chrysler, and he began driving fast. He had the car radio on loud and was still moving at high speed as they turned onto Winchester Avenue, in Newhallville. Abruptly he slowed and began sauntering the car along the very middle of the street as people on corners and porches called out "Hey, Pete!" to him. "Like he was a celebrity," Katie-Jean thought. When a driver behind them grew impatient and attempted to pass, Pete weaved the Chrysler. "People don't do that," Katie-Jean told her brother. She was "worried sick," afraid there'd be road rage, that they would be shot. Pete patted the console and told her, "Don't worry about it." Was he telling her he had a gun in there? They reached Shelton Avenue, drew up behind a gold Cadillac, and parked. Pete said, "That's the Rev's car. His congregation bought it for him." Then he explained they were at the Mudhole social club, where he'd scheduled his sister to talk with members about their troubles. This turn of events confused Katie-Jean; she was an elementary school teacher, hadn't ever given personal counseling to adults she didn't know. But because it was her brother asking, she agreed to do her best.

They walked inside, and Katie-Jean's eyes went from the No Gambling sign on the wall to a table spread with money around which a card game was in process. Pete introduced the sixty-one-year-old Katie-Jean to the room as "an educator from the South" who had come to help them. A chair had been set up for Katie-Jean. She sat, and confronted downtrodden men who had dressed up in their best jackets and ties to meet Pete Fields's sister. Taking in the "defeated" pallor of the faces, Katie-Jean recognized someone she'd gone to high school with. He'd been nice-looking then, but now, with his misbuttoned jacket and disheveled hair, he reminded her of Everyday and the other homeless foyer-dwellers she'd known as a child. All those life-blasted generations, Katie-Jean thought. It didn't reflect well on New Haven. As the people at the Mudhole took turns sitting down next to her and describing their absent parents, lack of education and training, their poverty, how they'd fallen into drink, fallen into prostitution, Katie-Jean saw what her brother had done. These were people who, it seemed, had never experienced what she was to Pete on the telephone every morning: a sympathetic listener committed to hearing about serious problems without judgment. She took her brother's unspoken point, that people were more than the debts they carried.

Afterward, Pete drove Katie-Jean on over to Martin Luther King Elementary School on Dixwell Avenue, where Pete had again volunteered her as a guest speaker. They went from classroom to classroom, Katie-Jean doing her spontaneous best to inspire the children by talking with them about the uses of an education. That evening, Pete was supposed to meet up with Katie-Jean and her friend and take them for an anticipated dinner at a casino and resort an hour and a half from New Haven, but at the last minute he called and canceled, saying he had to drive his new girlfriend to the airport. It was, he said, probably for the best he wasn't going to the casino because, "I'd just walk in and lose."

Katie-Jean was upset. Her brother was buying too many lottery tickets, and then his reckless driving, and his pessimistic tone as he'd canceled their last night's plans for some woman he hadn't even introduced her to. After Charlene's death, Kate-Jean knew Pete had dated a woman he'd met at Susan's wedding who'd gone to high school with Charlene. His children had liked that woman because she was steady and mature, but the relationship didn't take. Now Katie-Jean worried Pete was behaving like "a teenager." She got back home, called her sister Nina, and told her, "He's going to die. I can see him in the casket. There's an aura of death around him."

When Katie-Jean next spoke with Pete, he said the people from the Mudhole had showed him renewed respect ever since she'd gone there with him. Then some money arrived from Pete for Katie-Jean to open the bank account for her grandson. In late July 2006, Katie-Jean went on vacation to Florida. Pete telephoned her there and said he was at a restaurant near the ocean in West Haven with his girlfriend. He asked Katie-Jean to say hello and handed over the phone. As Katie-Jean listened, she thought the woman's voice was coarse.

Her name was Ella, and as Susan understood it, she'd met her father through someone at the Mudhole. Ella had a job at a chain home-accessories store outside New Haven, but she lived in a Newhallville rooming house on West Ivy Street near the corner of Dixwell Avenue. West Ivy Street was a single residential block of mostly multifamily houses, just three blocks from the Mudhole, but in the "suburbs," as the west side of Dixwell was sometimes known. A young Newhallville nurse said of West Ivy, "The street doesn't have a good name. Drugs. Fights. People hanging out." In city neighborhoods, it took only one or two houses to give an entire street a reputation.

Katie-Jean began hearing on the telephone every morning about how "revitalizing" Ella was for her seventy-year-old brother. Ella was some twenty years younger, but said Floyd Hooks, "to him she was a young girl. A teenager." Pete's children could see that she had given their father a hopeful feeling of starting over, and so, as Susan said, they were "trying not to be a snob." Yet both were increasingly bothered, said Peter, that Ella was "too street. Too ghetto. We were used to our mother." They'd heard rumors about Ella's struggles, heard that their father was giving Ella money. For Susan, living at her father's house with her husband and young son, the presence of her father's new girlfriend made her resentful. "I didn't like her," Susan said. "Never did. She was very strange-acting towards me. I got this vibe off her. We didn't hit it off, me and Ella. I grew up in this home. My mom just passed. Here she comes, just walking in." Trying to spare everyone the awkwardness of his girlfriend entering what had been their mother's bedroom, Pete would "hide" Ella in the darkened living room until Susan and her family were in bed. One night, Susan was visited by her brother, and they discussed their concerns about Ella in the kitchen. They didn't know Ella was sitting a few feet away, hearing it all. From then on, Ella walked into the house, went straight up to the bedroom, and closed the door.

In late July, Pete told family members about a loan he was going to make to Spikes, a grandson of Ella's. In recent years, Pete had become very outspoken against drug use, and Spikes had received police attention on drug charges, but eventually Pete agreed to give him some cash. "I could see him doing it for her," Susan said. "He liked her a lot." Katie-Jean was unsettled when Pete mentioned that Ella wanted to send her grandson out to Alden Road on the first to borrow the money. Pete explained that he'd refused because, "I don't deal with drug people and I don't let thugs come to my house. He's not gonna come near my family."

ON AUGUST 1, 2006, John DeStefano, the son of a New Haven police officer and the city's mayor since 1994, gave a press conference in which he promoted two officers to assistant chief, and spoke of feeling "encouraged" about the safety of the city's neighborhoods, because of the police department's successful dialogue with citizens.

As the mayor spoke, the day was unfolding at the Fields home. Ella had spent the night with Pete, and then in the morning he'd driven her to work. Afterward, because it was the first of the month, he'd gone on to the bank, where he handed the teller checks for $2,500, of which he took back $1,900 in cash. Then he thought again, retrieved fifty dollars from his wallet, and added to his deposit. After leaving, Pete didn't seem to have paid any bills as was usual. Instead, he bought some (losing) lottery tickets and went home to watch a western. Susan returned from work, dressed for a wake, and departed again. It was a warm summer late afternoon, and Pete, the old soldier, walked out of his house wearing fatigues: a double extra-large short-sleeve crewneck camouflage T-shirt, camouflage cargo shorts, and sandals. He picked up Ella, and they went for a walk along the beach in West Haven. When rain clouds scudded in off the water, Pete left a message for Susan to close the windows at home. Then Pete took Ella out for an early dinner at the Greek Olive, a restaurant on New Haven's Long Wharf that was popular with police officers. At the bar happened to be Pete's old friend Jim Ponteau. They embraced. Pete said he was going take his girlfriend by her house, and then he'd be back to have a drink with Ponteau. The retired detective found himself thinking about the contradictions in Pete Fields, a man who couldn't control his gambling, yet was otherwise the most reliable of men in his habits.

Pete and Ella drove into Newhallville to make the loan to Ella's grandson, Spikes. According to Ella, the plan was to meet at the Mudhole. But the young man wasn't there when they arrived and, after a wait, Spikes changed the rendezvous to out in front of Ella's building. (Spikes would later claim that they were to meet there all along.) So Pete left the Mudhole and circled around to West Ivy Street, probably by passing another old haunt of his, the Knickerbocker golf club, and then making a right and coming down West Ivy Street, which traveled one way, east toward Dixwell.

The two-and-a-half-story rooming house at 241 West Ivy, where Ella lived, had been built in 1895 by a blacksmith named Joseph Boisvert. It was now divided into ten apartments; Ella's was up on the third floor. The building spread five windows wide and had rust-colored shingling, with an extended front porch protected by a rusting metal rail fence. There was said then to be late-night gambling and liquor sales inside. The home next door, closer to the busy Dixwell corner, had a large black meat smoker in the yard. Between the two buildings ran the driveway for Number 241, now occupied by a broken-down car, meaning Pete couldn't pull in. He parked his cream-colored Chrysler at the curb in front of the driveway, just beyond the rooming house.

Ella went upstairs while Pete remained in his car, sitting by for Spikes. The air was warm and dry, and Pete had the windows down, the sunroof open. Ella later said when she got inside the house, she'd discovered a note from her landlord, which she brought down and discussed with Pete. Then she said she went back to talk with the landlord who was on hand, fixing something with power tools. It was dusk.

Sitting there in the gleaming Chrysler on this pleasant, still, late summer Tuesday evening, Pete's seat belt was fastened, the motor running. He expected to leave at any moment. But ten minutes passed. Spikes still hadn't appeared and Ella remained inside. Down toward the opposite end of the block, there was movement. Had Pete looked into his mirror, he would have seen two Black teenage boys in the near distance. One was stocky with dark skin and short hair, dressed in a T-shirt and shorts. The other was taller and slimmer, with lighter skin and braids, wearing pants and a long-sleeved white shirt. They came together, clasping their arms around one another's shoulders, hugging up. Then they broke apart and sprinted down the street, passing several people out on their porches enjoying the sultry weather, passing men in a car who were there to pick up a friend on the block, passing a trio of voter-registration organizers knocking on doors across the street from Ella's building. The two teenagers appeared suddenly at Pete's two front side windows, bracketing the car. The boy with braids held a large pistol. There was a demand for money, and then a struggle as Pete, trapped in his seat belt, put up strong resistance. "That man and the love of money he had?" said Susan. "Forget about it. I never saw anybody love money like he did." The love of the farm, the love of his father, the love of the neighborhood, the love of Jeffrey, the love of his mother, the love of Charlene. The pistol was a .45, such a powerful weapon, when fired it explodes like a hand cannon. "They didn't know Pete Fields," said Joe Pullen, Charlene's brother-in-law.

A witness down the block on West Ivy Street described the report from the .45 as sounding like the pop of a loud firecracker. A full metal case bullet has a tip that induces heavy bleeding, tears away at skin. Had a surgeon been stationed right there, the hole this bullet opened in Pete Fields's neck would still not have been easily sutured. The bullet built for deep penetration went hurrying through Pete's spinal column like a speeding drill bit, went in and out of his right lung, exiting his armpit and lodging in the metal car seat frame. Smoke poured out of the driver's-side window.

Immediately, the two young men were running around the car, plunging inside the Chrysler. A witness reported, "They was just moving crazy like." That this was happening in plain view of so many people could have made everything easy to document. But uninvolved bystanders to murder are looking on in astonishment, and some, like the community organizers, were terrified. "We left that damn street," said one. The young men's furious riffling movements were confusing to witnesses, who would later place each teenager at both sides of the car as the shooting took place, offer inconsistent descriptions. Such transposing is common among people witnessing flurried motion. This rummaging through the car lasted many seconds, two minutes by one exaggerated estimate, until the pair found what they had come for. Street robberies often are staged near intersections, to ease escape. The two young men ran to the nearby corner, turned right (south) down Dixwell Avenue, and disappeared. It was nearly eight o'clock in the evening.

Emergency calls were placed. Ella came outside, discovered Pete blown back in his seat with a gaping hollow in his neck, and began crying. She would later explain that because her landlord was using power tools, she didn't hear the gunshot. She also said she had no idea Pete was carrying well over $1,500 in his pocket. Spikes never arrived. He later told police that he'd been on his bicycle, riding up Dixwell Avenue to meet Pete, when, still three blocks away, he heard the gunshot, became afraid, and took cover behind a rear dumpster at the Martin Luther King Elementary School, where Katie-Jean had so recently been giving encouragement to children. Spikes lived to the north of West Ivy Street, and that he was now coming from the south, placing him directly in the flight path of the murderers, did not capture the attention of investigators.

Ella telephoned Peter, who was at his father's house. "It was her," he said, "so I didn't answer." When she kept calling, he picked up. To Peter, Ella sounded hysterical as she told him, "Your dad was shot." Susan had just returned home from the wake. She was changing out of her funeral clothes when she heard her brother yelling from downstairs, "Sue! Dad just got shot!" To Susan, it "seemed like the world stopped."

Peter drove his car to West Ivy Street while Susan took Xavier and sped as fast as she could to Yale–New Haven Hospital. She arrived just as paramedics were removing her father from an ambulance. A blood-drenched sheet covered him on a gurney. "Get that kid away. You don't want him to see this," they screamed at her. Nothing that was happening was unimaginable to anyone who'd watched a police television drama. It was all unimaginable. After he died, Pete's body was washed of blood, and Susan, Peter, and other family members spent a final half an hour in a hospital room with him. To Susan, "it was like he was sleeping."

Floyd Hooks had just got off work in Massachusetts and was in his driveway when Susan reached him. He immediately reversed course, thinking through the news as he pointed the car for New Haven. It hadn't occurred to Floyd that going into Newhallville might be risky for his uncle because "that there was his old home. He went all the time. He had friends. I had a cousin who lived across from Ella. I had an aunt who lived down the street. I wouldn't think that block to be that bad." What had concerned Floyd were kids in groups around the neighborhood. "They were basically strays," he said. "Strays in the sense I originally thought it was a gang—kids hanging out who didn't have a home, hanging around harassing people." Floyd knew who these kids were from growing up with their parents and grandparents, and his mind's aperture went wide and generous, comparing those children's circumstances with that of his cousins when they had been Newhallville teenagers. "The city's evolved," he said. "Lot of people come and go. The opportunity's gone. Those kids are basically the victims."

Susan's suspicions about Ella grew as she absorbed the details. Pete had died on a quiet residential street Ella had brought him to, on the one day he was carrying a large sum of money, which Susan was certain Ella knew about, because of the first-of-the-month loan Pete had agreed in advance to Ella's grandson.

On West Ivy Street, police investigators converged. The Chrysler's front seat was soaked in blood. The seat belt had been cut by paramedics to remove Pete from behind the steering wheel. There were bank receipts from his transactions, and deep within his pocket, $47.33. The car held also the souvenir features of how a man lived his ordinary day-to-day moments: a drinking cup from McDonald's, an out-of-date flip phone fallen between the driver's seat and door. In the Chrysler's closed center console was Pete's wallet; it was empty of cash and a credit card had been removed but then left behind. There were two untouched checkbooks in the map pouch on the back of the driver's seat. Spent lotto tickets littered the car floor. It was impossible to say exactly how much of Pete's money had been stolen, because nobody could know what cash he'd spent during the day on his girlfriend, and elsewhere.

Police cordoned off the crime scene and began gathering evidence.

Among the responding officers was Holly Wasilewski, who found the fatal bullet lodged in the framed undergirding of the front seat, which, along with other traces of the crime, including four separate hand- and fingerprints lifted from the exterior car surface, were packaged for transport to the state's bureau of investigation for scientific evaluation. One of the prints was a clear, latent right-palm impression from the front passenger door, below the window. The angle of positioning and the clarity suggested it had been made by somebody either opening the door or pressing for balance as he leaned forward through the window into the car. Uncovering a single fingerprint is uncommon in murder cases. A nearly full palm print was an extraordinary discovery, the forensic equivalent of a rare coin.

HERBERT FIELDS JR.'s funeral was held at the Bethel AME Church in New Haven, which had been Charlene's mother's church. All six hundred places were filled with people, with more mourners overflowing outside, unable to get in. There were messages from several politicians, police patrolling on motorcycles. Ella arrived late, in the company of a teenage boy. Because there was no more space in the pews, the pair sat in the choir loft, where everybody could see them.

The ceremony led Susan to think, "He was just my dad, and now all this. People felt bad a seventy-year-old man was murdered by some kids. But it was more." History was rushing into the moment. There was grief over the death of a decent man, the collective grief of a community that could see its losses in him, could see the pangs of generations. Among the speakers were family members, friends, and the West Haven neighbor whose life Pete had saved. While his death was tragic, likewise nobody wanted to remember Pete as a passive victim. If there was faulting to be done, the blame belonged to society, which was not supposed to make choices about who could feel protected.

What those who really knew Pete considered him to be was the epitome of that plainspoken commendation—a good guy. People rose to say that when they didn't have a place to go, when they were down, Pete Fields took care of them. He was described as an unassuming person who lived as he wanted to, and in his actions and enthusiasms, in the way he felt about neighborhoods and music and property and region and family, people saw a man whose life embraced the lived experiences of many. He'd come to New Haven as an aspirant, hoping to better his prospects, and he'd died there as a man of qualities others could aspire to. Representatives from the Mudhole approached Susan afterward, and handed her a card, with a gift of money enclosed, and told her with great formality how much they'd "loved him."

In Newhallville, everyone in the streets was discussing the murder, how a seventeen-year-old kid called Major and his slightly younger cousin BlackJack had taken $2,000 (from block to block the total kept rising) off an elderly man they'd ambushed while he was sitting parked in his fancy car. "It's all because of how mad-weird everything is," said one kid. "You know who did it. It's crazy. Everybody's all connected. It's a small network. They all converse." Word of the crime hurried through the city and out into the prisons, where inmates and guards alike discussed the murder. Fields's old friend John Sylvia was now working as a corrections officer, and Sylvia heard inmate speculation that his friend "got set up by that lady when she went upstairs and left him there for those guys." Even though such conjecture was based on rumors that came fluttering inside from out and around New Haven, the theory made sense to Sylvia, because "how'd they know he had the money?" A truck driver from Newhallville, who was known as "Officer" because of his spare-time penchant for listening to his police scanner, was also out and about, and heard that the "word on the street was Major killed that guy. Stuff comes up in conversation, and if you've had five conversations . . ." Major's name was likewise whispered in the just-between-us, behind-the-hand conversations a few Newhallville residents were having with police officers who worked the neighborhood. Those officers would have gladly passed on the name, but the detectives chosen to work the case were in the habit of gathering their own information, a hierarchy of sourcing indulged by their superiors. "We were treated as redheaded stepchildren by the department," said one street officer from the time.

From the first, the Fields murder investigation had more than street talk going for it. This was an unusual daylit public event, with a line of witnesses. One of them, a teenage girl sitting on her porch reading a book, had looked up as a pair of boys ran by, and she watched the crime unfold. That girl, as well as a woman in her fifties and several people elsewhere on the street, had all seen who'd done it, and some of them knew who the killers were. Not to tell the police what they'd observed could enable the boys to get away with murder, a form of Russian roulette, because if Major and his cousin were not arrested, then others in the community, including the witnesses themselves, might be in danger. None of them would tell.

"There's a code in the Ville that no one snitches on anyone," said Charlie

Gargano, a police officer who patrolled the neighborhood for years. "It's your life. If you did, you'd have to move. And if they can't get you, they'd get your family's life." Because of the no-snitching code, Newhallville was known as "Death Valley" among investigators. Al Vazquez, a New Haven detective for many years who was appreciatively known to some as "Gumshoe," said, "It's always been a struggling battle to get the community to help you solving murder cases. They happen right in front of many people, and if you get one or two people to help you, you're doing good."

Almost all people in Newhallville, like almost all people everywhere, craved justice. Most neighborhood murders involved men in a network of criminal subculture, and most every resident of the neighborhood preferred that the police arrest the murderers. The hitch was that Newhallville was full of law-abiding people from families, like the Fieldses, who did not trust police. The legacy of traffic stops just because you were Black and driving a nice car—and all the other humiliating police assumptions, police accusations, and police misdeeds from South to North—led to such ongoing alienation, one Newhallville pastor didn't even like to be seen in the company of an officer because "I don't want people thinking I'm police."

Clifton Watson, who wrote his doctoral dissertation on his family's migrations from the South to Newhallville, said his first ancestor to arrive in the neighborhood from the South was a man who fled after defending himself when a white coworker started a fight at a sawmill. Decades later, most family elders would still not discuss what had happened, even with Watson. Newhallville was filled, he said, with people who were well aware that it's been only two full lifetimes since the end of slavery, and who believed that personal information yielded to anyone outside the close community "will get you done in." When a "citizen" like Pete Fields was killed, not holding the perpetrators responsible made the no-snitching code a form of injustice itself. But one consistent truth about snitching anywhere is the difficulty of persuading even justice-loving people to cooperate with a police murder investigation when they do not trust the authorities to care enough to protect them from their fear of becoming the next victim.

In contrast were the city's mostly white middle-class neighborhoods like East Rock, where, said Thomas Ullmann, who was New Haven's chief public defender in 2006, he could count on witnesses who saw crimes happen: "They go to the police station and give statements."

After a murder happens in a community with a no-snitching code, a wide net is quietly cast by detectives. Reliable sources of information are contacted in confidence, and some are paid. People from the neighborhood where the crime happened who have pending criminal accusations against them may be consulted and presented with the opportunity to position themselves for leniency by passing along the lowdown on this more serious neighborhood crime. An aversion to speaking up and informing may seem like human nature—beginning in childhood, nobody likes squealers and tattletales—yet the hard truth about snitching is that those who most benefit from the taboo against informing are the least inhibited by it. As the retired New Haven detective Jo Schaller explained, the no-snitching code may be "deeply embedded, but it's also one of the biggest lies told in the ghetto. Everybody snitches if it's in their interest to snitch. Some of the people who are most vocal about no snitching are more than happy to snitch on someone else when they get arrested. Cops solve cases because people talk." The unruly possibility was that a criminal with compelling interests might give someone up, yes, but not always the right someone.

PART II

\\\\\\\\\\\\\\\\\\\\\\\\\\

JUST AROUND

Chapter Six

That summer of 2006, sixteen-year-old Bobby seemed both young and old for his age, and unfinished enough as a person that older relatives thought of him as both unworldly and over-trusting. More calculating people also took in those qualities of Bobby's. With the formal investigation into the murder of Pete Fields showing no progress after more than a week, Bobby's name dropped into the streets like a plump bread-crumb, and winging down for him came the police.

Bobby's feeling about the neighborhood no-snitching code was public acceptance and private misgivings. "Every day I see a murderer in the Ville," he said of those he shared the sidewalks with. His neighborhood was to him "like a secret society" where everybody knew the rules: "If you're shot, you can't tell who shot you. You witness a shooting, you can't tell who did it." If many young people didn't necessarily respect these customs, most went along out of fear. Bobby's thoughts on the very confusing ethical conditions under which he and other children were growing up in Newhallville sometimes coursed, like his lengthy bike rides, in far-flung directions, but always ended up back where he'd been raised. "You can put yourself, your family, in harm's way," he said. "That's how critical it is to keep your mouth shut. People don't care. They will harm you. Just walking around, shoot a person in the head, say 'A'ight, who's next?' You can't change it. It's too deep." If some people, he said, claimed the code protected the community's honor, to him, following the code was simply a practical necessity, even as remaining tight-lipped about violence further empowered violent people, and also created opportunities for retaliation. Violent people could afford to snitch. Those, like Bobby, who were just around, could not.

Older members of Bobby's family described him as a teenage boy who "blended in with the crowd. Not below the bar, not above the bar." Bobby's mother's father thought of him similarly, as "just an average kid." If he seemed indifferent to school, Bobby's pleasures were movies, hip-hop, video games, basketball, girls, Air Jordans, and Reese's Peanut Butter Cups. These not-unusual teenage preferences made him seem the person his family appeared to describe. But enthusiasm set Bobby apart. It was how much he cared about basketball, that he memorized every line of his favorite films and songs, and that he placed his sneakers back in their original boxes after each use, lining them up against the wall of his bedroom so looking over from his bed he could know that the full regiment was there, standing by, at attention.

Bobby had no airs, no need to be highly regarded by others, and because of that he was. An aunt described him as "a roundabout person. He'll tell you the good and bad no matter what it is." That he could be timorous in academic settings made it easy to overlook how perceptive he was in noticing other people's fine-drawn features.

One more aspect of Bobby's life was the inability of people from outside the neighborhood to regard him as "an average kid." Older men in his family believed this was "because he's a Black kid." Which meant a double predicament. Bobby was average only insomuch as his existence as another face in the crowd obscured that he was not average at all. Someone who came to know him well described Bobby as "an extraordinary ordinary person." He took getting to know, had subtle virtues. And if Pete Fields's tragedy was to have unwittingly made himself too conspicuous in the neighborhood where he'd grown up, on so many levels Bobby's misfortune was to be another boy just around in the Ville.

Bobby's maternal grandparents were central figures in his childhood, and these respected family elders, one with a dignified demeanor that felt formal, the other open with fullhearted warmth, were addressed as Granddad and Grandma. They left Columbia, South Carolina, in the early 1960s, with Bobby's future aunts Faith and Joy, the first two of five daughters. These grandparents came a decade later than the Fieldses had, carried by similar optimism. "They said you can get a better life, get ahead," Faith recalled. "This was the Place to Go." Granddad was, much like Pete Fields, glad to drive back down South for reunion visits, but otherwise reluctant to reengage the details of his earlier times with younger generations. "When we have past dark evil, we tend to bottle it up," Bobby said. "I ask him questions about his upbringing and he won't talk about those things. I have no clue what happened. I think he talks to nobody about it."

As a boy, Bobby made occasional summertime trips to visit South Carolina, where people seemed to him to be existing out of time, which he described with characteristic supple detail: "Nothing but grass. Mad land. Trees. So spaced out, house to house. Huge difference from Connecticut. Much less going on. The majority down there live out in the country. All desperate. They still live in old times. Stuck in the phase."

In New Haven, Granddad found a career as a tool- and diemaker at Sargent & Company, manufacturers since 1810 of locks and hardware. His unusual grasp of how complicated machines worked made Granddad resemble the chosen men at Winchester who had their own workshop, building custom-order rifles for the company's high-end customers. Diemakers are artisanal engineers, the designers of machines used to make machines. Granddad considered the work to be the essence of industrial production and said he regretted that, in the digital age, computerized robotics had rendered the tool-and-die man's work "a dying art."

Granddad's personal passion was taking apart and reassembling Chevrolet models from his young manhood. The barn out behind his Newhallville home contained three, including a 1966 Chevy II Super Sport. What most appealed to Granddad about this upgrade model, he said, was that "I guess Black folks wasn't supposed to have a car like that." Although he was scrupulously law-abiding, Granddad was pulled over by police in his Chevrolets "for no reason." It annoyed him that he was never recognized as an exemplary citizen in a pristine car, that no police officers in his neighborhood "ever took the time to know me." Instead, he, too, was just around. Granddad wanted to trust the police, but said, "I just don't."

Granddad was a quiet, firm person whose decisions were alloyed bonds. In contrast, Grandma was very social. A tiny woman with a youthful, loving face, she enjoyed cooking for others. Like Granddad, Grandma was committed to a job that well suited her, nursing. She worked lengthy shifts, even as the couple had five daughters, the fifth of them Grace, Bobby's mother.

After nearly fifteen years of marriage, Grandma and Granddad divorced in 1976, when Grace was two. When Granddad remarried Aretha, one of his daughters, Joy, believed her father was that fortunate man who'd discovered "his soul mate." In 1986, Granddad and Aretha bought a Newhallville house and together renovated every detail, right down to the gleaming finials. Bobby noticed his grandfather had devised "his own atmosphere."

Granddad was the orderly patriarch who built locks, and when it came to looking out across life, long-term security was what he thought about. As one of Faith's daughters said, "He had a vision for how he could see his family." In fact, what Granddad hoped for was nothing very different from the ambitions of generations of Newhallville parents who'd come from far-off to launch an upwardly mobile life. Granddad had succeeded, and he wanted that for the young people in his family, which he believed was only possible if they, too, took life seriously. "My grandfather doesn't play," said Bobby's older sister Tonya. "He's always been strict. He wants everybody to make something of themselves."

But children's lives are what happens when parents are busy making other plans for them. Granddad and Grandma had all come of age in such a ripe time for Black employment in American history. Granddad's daughters, however, were growing up in an era of downward American fortunes. Blacks had it worst, with only a third of Black children growing up to maintain their parents' occupational status. Meanwhile, the crack epidemic was devastating New Haven's poor and working-class neighborhoods. Bobby cared about nothing more than family, and as a boy he spent a lot of time "trying to piece out what happened" to his relatives when they were girls. He found explanations in the torments a famous singer-songwriter described in her lyrics. "The females in my family," he said, "were going through the same things as Mary J. Blige. I seen women sit there listening to her and start crying listening to her songs."

AS GRANDDAD'S CHILDREN grew up, there was an abundance of struggle, including addiction and eviction—that family members assumed Granddad found almost unbearably discouraging. "He'll be there at the end of the day," a granddaughter said. "He'll be there for you. But his hurt and his pain will mean he's quiet."

One morning, Bobby's aunt Faith woke up and decided to do something astonishing with her life. By herself, on a nurse's salary, Faith brought up not only her four children, she took in five sons and daughters of three of her sisters, and raised them as her own. Her father's daughter, Faith approached parenting in an increasingly dangerous neighborhood as a problem of domestic engineering. Bobby's sister Shavonne remembered,

"She didn't play. Whole bunch of structure." The children were given bicycles but allotted limited range. "If we rode our bikes," said Bobby's cousin Hank, "we were allowed to go three houses down and three houses up. If your tire was an inch past the fence, you had to go inside. She had binocular eyeballs!" A child Faith raised said, "My house felt like a safe house. Outside was a danger zone."

Bobby's mother, Grace, the youngest daughter, was outgoing, smart, would ride wing with you to a party or meet you out for ice cream. Then, at fourteen, Grace's childhood abruptly changed when she became pregnant with Tonya. Faith would take in and raise Tonya, but a year later, Grace was pregnant again, and Bobby was born to a fifteen-year-old mother. Grace said the reaction of both her parents was "disappointed." Yet, she added, "I always wanted a slew of kids." In time, she had them.

Grace eventually gave birth to ten children, including twins, from nine different fathers, none of whom helped her in any significant way to raise the children. That she was creating such a large family on her own led relatives to worry, "It's crazy! Really crazy!" And to ask more calmly, "Why so many?" Tonya considered her mother's choices to be an insoluble puzzle: "To me, I think she didn't want to be alone."

To others, so much about Grace's life as a single mother just seemed daunting, the hour-to-hour, day-after-day necessity of responding to little kids, the dismal science of household economics, endless logistics, your time never fully your own. If it had been 1930, in County Armagh, Ireland, or Richland County, South Carolina, having ten kids would have been a common thing—the building of a farm labor force. Someone who knew Bobby thought Grace needed "a labor force of love." Grace said she had no expectations of men: "I was never into my relationships. I would almost sabotage my relationships. I'd have it in my head they're gonna leave, so I'd sabotage it." There was hope in a young life. "People," Grace said, "search for love in all kinds of ways." Grace was smart, creative, and capable, and Grace's children brought her happiness, insulated her from the discouragement around her, gave her a higher purpose—the opportunity to express the complexity of who she was.

For some kids who grow up in single-parent families, it's not a problem to have only a mom or dad there if you have the right single parent—which in many ways Grace's children thought she was. To support Bobby and his siblings, Grace worked as a certified nursing assistant, first as a special-duty nurse, performing home care, before getting a clinical technician job at a hospital when Bobby was fifteen. "I'd go in the morning," she recalled, "come home, sleep three hours, then out to do more hours." She was pleased when patients told her that her name suited her. As her children grew in number, Grace also received public assistance. Thinking back on the lives of his childhood friends, Bobby would say, "My mother gave us more than anybody's mom."

On weekends, Grace's way of cleaning the house was to turn up the music and get everyone dancing together to R&B songs as mother and children swept, mopped, and dusted. On Sundays, she used many pans and pots for large Southern-style family meals of fried and baked chicken, mac 'n' cheese, and greens. Bobby was then a small, thin boy with a heart-shaped face, jug-handle ears, and full lips, and he'd watch the meal preparation carefully with eyes that weren't large but seemed it because they were such a deep, pure color. Grace explained ingredients and timing to him, just as her mother had explained to her, and Bobby developed an ability for cooking.

For children's birthdays, Grace did not just give parties, she curated them. New photographs of the birthday child were framed and set out with elaborate table lamps and decorative centerpieces of Grace's own design that featured the enthusiasms of the young celebrant—ponies, say, or basketball players. In the neighborhoods where Bobby grew up, the after-dark dangers of the streets turned Halloween into an inside holiday. Grace made her children candy apples, chocolate-covered strawberries, and she screened scary movies for them. At Christmas, there would be cairns of wrapped gifts rising all over the house. "We had everything we asked for," Bobby's sister Stephanie said. "I asked my mom to do my room in SpongeBob on Christmas. I wake up and I had SpongeBob TV. SpongeBob games. I had SpongeBob pajamas. I had a SpongeBob comforter. I had a SpongeBob robe. I had a SpongeBob trash can. SpongeBob curtains, SpongeBob hamper. I was twelve then."

Grace had a lot to give, yet the family moved often and Bobby attended more schools than he can recall. "I can't tell you how many places I lived," he said. "So hard. We never got explanations why we moved." There were also meal shortages. "We ran out of food plenty of times," he said. "We just had to eat hot dogs. Usually didn't have to wait too long."

Grace drained herself with work and with getting to work. She had no car, and the inconvenient patterns of bus routes and bus schedules meant the children spent a lot of unsupervised time watching TV. "She had to go to work," Bobby said, "so she'd go to sleep. We'd wait, then turn on the TV. We'd stay up all night, be tired out of our minds, fall asleep in classes."

As a little boy, Bobby was also a family man. "He'd always try to get me to cook dinners so the whole family would come over," Grace said. "He'd try to organize events, check up on everybody, and for him to be that young, it was surprising."

Nobody was ever bored with Bobby around. He was good at both mimicry and teasing; you didn't want to find yourself losing to him at *Jeopardy!* or visiting him wearing an ugly shirt. His sister Stephanie, who was especially close to him, thought that, within the lined demarcations of a basketball court, Bobby was most fully himself. The game's rules and structure seemed to allow him the freedom to be expressive. He had a swaying way of advancing his dribble that flustered opponents, and an idiosyncratic laid-back unfurling of his jump shot. "Everything to him is basketball," Stephanie said. "When he plays, it's his person out on the court. He's happy, very determined, very open, secure in what he does, and he jokes around a lot."

Among the various cousins, Bobby had a best friend in solid, good-natured Hank with whom he competed on basketball courts, had dance contests, listened to music, and rewatched their favorite movies—always a mixed blessing with Bobby, who could remember the entire dialogue of *Like Mike* and *Major Payne* well enough to recite every line right through to the credits, at volume, as everyone begged him, "Please, dude! Stop talking for two minutes so we can watch it!" Whatever the children were doing, there was a way in which Bobby's guttural laugh and big, contagious "cheesin'" smile lit everybody up. "A happy typical kid's all he was," Hank thought. "When he smiled at you, you'd smile. He was that funny. If he made you mad, he'd smile and you'd laugh! That's how he was." Bobby's effect upon his mother was similarly restorative. "If I was having a bad day," said Grace, "I'd see that smile and it'd change my whole attitude."

Bobby's mother was the primary figure in his life, and he had the emotionally aware child's acute feeling for her: "The struggles with bills and men. Men was the main thing. With each individual, you kind of saw the lost hope and the lost pride. Used to be so sad. We'd be, 'Mommy's downstairs crying.'" Some of Bobby's favorite childhood moments at home came when his mother sang Sunshine Anderson's female-empowerment anthem "Heard It All Before," in which the singer tells a sweet-talking, two-timing man that she's shutting him down and, Bobby said, expresses the courage "to stand up," to say "I'm done with all that." Bobby said, "My mother used to kill that song!" He wanted Grace to always be that person.

At times, Bobby felt bursting affection for the bighearted Grace, who adored her smart, interesting flock of kids: "My mom was a great mom. I don't even know how she did it. Every day she showed us the love of a single mom. She provided us everything a mom's supposed to, the love and understanding. She spent a lot of quality time." Other days, he was exasperated by how Grace was placing herself under duress having more children. "When I think about the situation," he said, "I think my mom's lonely. Or she's got something absent. She failed with us and wants to try over."

Grace and Bobby were only fifteen years apart, and even before Bobby was ten, there was a sense they were mother and son and also older sister and younger brother—growing up together. Grace was eager to take on extra hours at work to supplement her paycheck, and as a result, at an early age, Bobby was responsible for taking care of the five sisters who were then living at home with him. "I was eight or nine," he said. "I changed a lot of diapers."

Over the years, as Grace's schedule fluctuated, Bobby might have to prepare a pancake breakfast and get everyone off to school, meet the yellow bus in the afternoon, make use of the cooking lessons by preparing a dinner of chicken or baked ziti for six people. Dessert was his specialty—cakes, cookies, pudding. Cousin Hank looked on with admiration: "I watched him fry chicken. He said, 'You're home by yourself all the time, you can't just eat noodles and hot dogs.' He put flour in the bag. Seasoning. Shook it for four minutes. It was actually pretty good."

Some mornings, Bobby was aglow, teasing his sisters about how unpresentable they were for school: "You're a mess! Take that off! Your hair's a mess too!" Stephanie found him to be "a very funny character," and enjoyed how "you're always laughing until your stomach hurts. He should be a comedian." That his face hadn't yet grown into proportion with his lips and ears was a further source of amusement, though these sisterly jabs were offered with tact. They depended upon him too much to risk really hurting his feelings. By the time Bobby was ten, Bobby's sister Kenya said, "He'd tuck us into bed every night. Wake us up. Make sure we made the school bus." Stephanie said, "He was our protector. We had to ask him as our father figure, 'Bobby, can I go outside? Can you help us with our homework?' He'd look in our books with us."

As Bobby was parentified, gradually he grew attuned to the rhythms of children, the way "when someone gets sick then everybody gets sick." He saw how siblings relate, show one another their worst selves, so that when they leave the house, they can put on a positive face—and how when parents are under severe stress, the dynamic reverses, with consequences for kids in their classrooms. Bobby felt responsibility for including Tonya when she came by, "because she grew up at my aunt's house. I felt like I needed to provide her love." All of the sisters understood that Bobby wasn't just at home with them, he was as fully there for them as an adolescent boy could be—from teaching them the "Harlem Shake" to wanting them to see the roundabout truths of the world. When they were very little girls, it was important to him that they know there was no Santa Claus, that gifts came because of their mother. But they were reluctant to accept this. So, he made them stay up all night on Christmas Eve.

Although the family had such limited resources that a child was half-acting as a parent, Bobby thought of himself as privileged. He was going to school with children who were wearing the same clothes every day, living without heat and meals, with absent or addicted parents. His mother attempted to compensate him for all he was doing, meaning, Grace said, "Anything he asked for, he had it." Bobby's room was filled with sneakers, video games, and fashionable clothes. What Grace was providing led other kids from the neighborhood to later tell Bobby, "I used to hate you because you was spoiled. Like, I used to think about robbing you and taking everything from you."

It was, of course, all relative; Grace bought Bobby multipack bags of peanut butter cups because it was a gesture she could make. When Bobby couldn't have the newest Air Jordans, he'd rebuke himself for coveting them: "I'd think, I'm not the kid who has no shoes. I can't be depressed about sneakers." Grace's circumstances meant, Bobby said, he did not have regular dental or medical checkups, he was not read to or taken to the library or to music lessons, his mother did not often attend parent-teacher conferences, and at home, "I didn't ask my mother for help with stuff." Bobby couldn't say what Grace's favorite color was, what her childhood ambitions had been, how she met his father. "I don't know my mom's history, even my sisters' history," he said. "I know them, but I really don't *know* them." Because poverty collapses time, the family lived moment to moment, without reflection or advance preparation—with no soft landing set up against disaster. "Our parents are so caught up in their own things, they never talk to us about our future," Bobby said.

FOR BOBBY, SCHOOL became the place where he exhaled. "I never went to school to learn," he said. "A lot of times when the teacher gave us problems, I'd sit there and know the answer, but I'd rather goof off." He was, by his own description, the "class clown," who became expert in such arts as squirting out glue, covering it in decorative glitter, and throwing it at girls. He took particular pleasure in leaning back in his chair and balancing himself on two legs. When confronted by annoyed teachers, "I just get an attitude and people don't like dealing with me when I'm mad."

His fourth-grade teacher was Teasie Blassingame, whose husband, John, taught history at Yale and helped establish the university's program in African American studies. Blassingame was a formidable educator, and her way of letting Bobby know that she didn't appreciate his disruptions was asking him to help her carry some boxes out to her car after class. In the relative privacy of the parking lot, she upbraided him: "She told me, 'You're the smartest one in the class and you don't listen.'" The admonition he found memorable because "at that moment I understood a teacher's love for a student. She fought me more than anybody. Once, we went to the parking lot three times in one day!" When Blassingame forbade him from playing basketball in the gym until his behavior improved, his behavior did improve because "I always liked people who'd tell me no."

Blassingame was one of Bobby's few Black teachers, and fourth grade, Bobby said, was the only year he sat in classes with white children. Analysis by scholars like Rucker Johnson has found that school segregation leads to lower graduation rates, as well as lower adult incomes and worse health, while integrated schools foreshadow having more of life's favors. Bobby's personal experience of an integrated classroom told him the same. "It's way better than all-Black schools," he said. "Teachers were pushing us forward. In other schools I never saw homework, was never forced to do it. I was never corrected. When we were with white kids, everybody was getting along very well."

Bobby's school records and the accompanying teacher comments reveal an erratic performer whose poor remedial skills, especially reading, left him "extremely frustrated and dissatisfied." His teachers found Bobby to be a sensitive person, with high standards that he was galled not to be meeting. An IQ test he took around age eleven rated him at 69, such a low classification, it suggested he might be intellectually impaired. But the test was unable to capture a sensitive listener with unusual insight, an intelligence about emotion that led him to grasp what others were like, how the everyday looked and felt to them. Bobby's teachers saw in him a lack of academic confidence, a yearning for close relationships. There was the sense that Bobby talked back and argued in class because he was a stressed-out kid who craved adult attention. It was noted how well he did during individual sessions with teachers, and how good he was at organizational tasks in the classroom—aspects of life he knew a lot about from home. "He's really, really smart," his sister Shavonne said. "We all were in different schools constantly. We all acted out. Everybody. It was emotions. We didn't know how to be oriented, we moved so much." Shavonne noticed something about her brother that mystified her. When he read aloud, he had no difficulty with polysyllables. What he stumbled over were short words, the most basic vocabulary. It was as though he'd missed an early stage. She saw him as "a child," who only during school felt the license to be a kid.

Poverty suffused Bobby's classrooms. Students had holes in their shoes, took cold showers all winter and gathered at home by the open oven door. On the way to and from school, Bobby and his grammar-school classmates passed discarded needles and condoms and liquor bottles. There were days when Grace wouldn't let Bobby go to school because she'd heard that kids with guns were shooting up the bus stop.

Some children with much to endure in their childhoods soothe the pain by making up a world out of life around them. Bobby didn't do that. Clear-eyed Bobby noticed how often kids he went to school with were diagnosed with learning disabilities. To him, there was so much unfairness in an institutional view that whatever was going wrong in the classroom, the fault lay with flaws in the children. "Always something wrong with somebody in the class," he said. "Never evaluating what's going on in the home to make kids come and act like this." The most common true affliction he identified at his schools was fear of failure. "You're supposed to be learning something," he said of school, "but kids couldn't handle rejection, and they didn't want to be put down. So, they shut down in class. Wouldn't participate in school. That started early."

As someone who didn't have any close family members whose academic experiences connected to a blossoming career, school's value was something for Bobby to take on faith. But as he headed for junior high school, his clear sense was the boys he was going to school with were more likely to end up in prison than college. In Newhallville, the high dropout rate was a collective way of saying, "What's the point?" "In our environment, it's hard to be responsible," he said. "Lack of jobs. Men don't know how to be. That's the tragedy of our world."

Growing up with a single mother and so many sisters, Bobby said, "meant I always been on women's side." Bobby grew preoccupied with lurking dangers to women, and became, Grace said, "overprotective of his sisters and me. Anywhere I went, 'Where you going? What time you coming back?' I'm gone too long, 'Where are you now?'" When it came to supervising his sisters, even before most reached puberty, Bobby's prevailing concern became boys who were out to get young girls pregnant. "Dealing with boyfriends, I didn't tolerate it," he said. "If I see [them] with a male, I go crazy. Grab them. Walk them home. I didn't want my sisters or cousins to have a bad reputation." Playing the no-nonsense father to a houseful of girls, he said, "at times it would be stressful. I'd think of things I wanted to do I couldn't do. Go outside and play with my friends." Stephanie said of her brother, "He was the man of the house."

Because of that, as he got older, when he could Bobby began spending more and more time away from the house—especially at his grandmother's in Hamden. "Bobby was basically back and forth," Tonya remembered. "My mom would tell him those days he had to work. If my mom was home with the kids, he'd be over there."

Grandma's grandchildren described her as the ebullient, engaged, straightforward family mainstay, "the glue that held everything together." It redounded to Grandma that so many of her relatives followed her into nursing, work which was defined as caring.

Grandma lived with a man known as Chubby, a partnership that lasted the rest of her life, with him always referring to her as his "fiancée." Chubby was a genial, easygoing small-town North Carolinian with a muddy drawl. He'd come to New Haven in 1968, "to better myself," he said, working at Winchester shaping gun stocks, and then as a truck driver. "I was real close to Chubby," Bobby said. "Chubby treated me like his grandson." Chubby liked Bobby to come by so much he bought Bobby a minibike to ease his transits.

At Grandma's house, Bobby might also encounter Chubby's three sons, whom he called the Uncles. Bobby looked up to these older figures for the confident way they carried themselves, how "fresh" they dressed, the fast cars they drove. Uncle Mikey's room had vintage posters of Magic Johnson and Larry Bird, free weights, and a computer, which Bobby was welcome to use if he was careful and kept the room neat. Hank and other cousins who lived nearby were also always showing up for games of basketball and sleepovers, a line of boys under blankets across the living-room rug. Hank could tell how much being in a house with grown men meant to Bobby: "He could just be a guy. Didn't have to scream out of frustration at anybody for not cleaning up."

The best part of visiting Grandma for Bobby was time alone with Grandma, whose large smile was a mirroring reflection of his. She said with open affection that the boy was "my heart." It was from her that he learned some basic plumbing and house wiring. Often Bobby and his grandmother would tour around in her large silver Ford, Grandma raised up on a booster seat. As they drove, years before he was sixteen, Grandma would impress upon Bobby he should be planning on having his driver's license, his own car, that he should not indiscriminately give people rides in that car, and that it should be kept neat.

Like so many sons of absent fathers, Bobby wondered what deficiencies there might be in him as a result of only growing up with women. Fathers preoccupied Bobby. He'd watch TV and "see commercials. The guy's putting on a tie going to work. The kid's behind him in the mirror, emulating him putting on a tie. I was fascinated." Bobby believed he lacked "principles of living," that even things he knew how to do, like play basketball and ride a bike, seemed diminished because he hadn't learned them from the person who was supposed to teach him. Without a father, "you're really not sure what you're good at. Your father's absent, you kind of lose respect for yourself."

He did have Granddad, whom he admired "as a man who'd sit there and listen and tell you what he thinks and let us make our own choices." Bobby would have liked to have conversations about life with Granddad, to go deep, but Granddad's way of spending time with his grandsons was teaching them to change the oil, adjust brakes, fix headlights. Bobby said, "I was very nonreceptive when he tried to teach me about cars."

At twelve, Bobby had become a free-range child, walking out the door when he felt like it, catching the city bus, or biking off into the day. For years, even when he lived in other New Haven neighborhoods, he'd been playing basketball and getting haircuts in Newhallville, and now, he said, "I always found my way to the Ville."

Bobby was young, but it was difficult to restrict the movements of someone on whom so much responsibility was imposed. If he came in after bedtime at his grandmother's house, in Hamden, she locked the door and made him sleep on the porch. Back at his mother's, after Bobby began getting home at one and two o'clock in the morning, Grace established a curfew. "My mother tried," he said. "Sometimes it was futile. I kind of made my own curfew." Grace responded by locking the doors and windows and going to bed, forcing

Bobby to bang on the door until she woke up and let him in. Even so, he believed, "I always had control. My mom, she'd be yelling at me, 'Stop coming in so late!'" He was, he said, "a hardheaded-ass kid. Tell me how to live my life, I'd go crazy. That's when they brought my father into my life."

Bobby had always been under the assumption he shared a father with one of his sisters. But one day after a youth baseball game on a field near Newhallville, Grace introduced him to an older couple, the Renfroes, whom Grace told, "This is your grandson." Grandfather Renfroe's reaction was "I thought it was crazy." He and his wife soon confirmed that their son hadn't known about Bobby. Ever after, Grace's shorthand way was to say simply that Bobby's father belatedly "had come into his life." As for Bobby, "I didn't know how to respond to it. Accepted it. When something bad happens, I don't question it." Bobby's real father was a man known as Tim-Buck II, whom Bobby knew only by his intimidating Read Street reputation.

In Newhallville, assorted people's views of Tim-Buck II taken as a whole revealed a compelling person who was: "*Respected and sort of popular. Lot of heart. Down to earth. Very intelligent. Very political. Very good fisherman. Angler. Con artist. Gift of gab. A hustler and a runner. Out there robbing. Whatever you had that was not locked down, Tim-Buck II get it.*" There was a neighborhood saying, "Put your money in your shoe, here come Tim-Buck II."

People who knew him thought that with Tim-Buck II's charisma and ability, he should have been having a great life in America. But as one younger person said, "Nobody knows what he's been through, why he acts out." James Baldwin noticed that in poor, segregated communities, many young Black men's frustration led them to fairly ring with malice and alienation. "And there they go," Baldwin wrote, "with an overwhelming bitterness . . . which completes their ruin. They become the menial or the criminal or the shiftless, the Negroes whom segregation has produced."

Bobby was quite sure once his father learned of him, he genuinely wanted "to be there for me," but Bobby never grew close to Tim-Buck II. He did spend nights at his new grandparents' house, helped the Renfroes with chores and errands. When an aunt's son died, Bobby appeared to rake and neaten her yard. The Renfroes sensed of Bobby that "his living situation was not easy," and to help Bobby, they might slip him a little pocket money or take him out to an arcade. "I always used to tell him, 'Don't get in any trouble out there,'" Grandfather Renfroe said. "He said, 'No, Grandpa. I'm not.'"

AFTER BOBBY TURNED fourteen, in late 2003, he said he "took on a whole different identity. You start to install your own values, the values of negative peers. Start to learn by that creed." Clothing and music began to matter even more, he wanted to walk girls home from school, meet them at a party, test if he could jam a basketball over somebody older. "At fourteen," he said, "it was the moments when I used to do stupid stuff just because I could do it and see if I could get away with it."

Bobby spent half that year living at his aunt Joy's house on Read Street, the Fieldses' former street, of which a young man called Elbow said, "We took pride in Read Street being one of the most violent streets in New Haven." The reputation grew so glorified Bobby said every young man in Newhallville "wants to be from Read Street. They're feared the most. Everybody claiming Read Street. Never been there a day in their lives." But for Bobby, who'd been in and out of Newhallville his whole childhood, it was no big thing to spend time with Read Street kids he'd played basketball and baseball with since he could remember—"I'd just chill with the boys on the porches."

Aunt Faith also moved. Her family had helped rebuild several houses for Habitat for Humanity. When the latest home was completed, the organization surprised Faith by presenting it to her. It was in Newhallville, and for the other cousins, this meant "You see Bobby, you see Hank." Hank found it difficult to fall asleep in his new home. Newhallville at night juddered with noises, and the occasional gunshots seemed almost designed to keep every kid on alert. In his bed, Hank would think about the people over on Lilac Street resting supine on the floor because "They don't want to catch bullets sleeping," and then he'd imagine doors someone had possibly forgotten to lock, so "I creeped around a lot making sure everything was okay."

Along the sidewalk, the threat of being robbed at gunpoint by another kid was real. Police and public-safety officials could tell you the most dangerous blocks to avoid, but as one of them said, "Ville's so damn small, everything's a hot spot." One of Bobby's acquaintances from the neighborhood was a baby-faced kid called Jerome. Jerome had moved from the dreary East New York section of Brooklyn, and he considered Newhallville more dangerous: "Newhallville's big for robbing people. Can happen anytime."

Violent crime is statistically rare, even in the most dangerous neighborhoods. But it doesn't take much to make dread pervasive. Bobby's mother, his aunt Faith, and his sister Tonya hadn't once been victims, but were preoccupied with the possibility. Even when she lived a block from her job, Grace never walked alone to work, and "after dark I'm in the house." Aunt Faith once watched teenagers with guns sprinting past her house at such speed one kid ran right out of his shoe. Looking at that lonely sneaker, she shook her head and thought, "No value for life." When Bobby's friends parted, they bid one another farewell by saying "Be safe."

The looming everyday possibility that trouble would find you existed in part because kids in the streets and those who were not all lived pressed up against one another, everybody right there, every day. "If I live in that environment, no choice but to be friends with killers, drug dealers," Bobby said. The fear was so potent, he said, that it disrupted everything else, made it challenging to concentrate in class and "people doing great in school become dark overnight." Kids like Jerome took up shooting as a matter of safety, so others would fear them, and also for self-respect. "Most of us get in the streets, we want to take power over our life," Jerome said. "But we have no sovereignty. That's why we get in the streets."

Days were spent on constant alert, assessing how people carried themselves, responding to cues, reading what was danger and what was bravado. Should you give way and walk close to the curb, or did that mark you as a victim? A kid called Crossover said, "You never look down and away, but you don't want to keep eye contact too long and seem like a threat. You keep it fifty-fifty, make eye contact, nod, keep moving." A kid from Lilac Street who knew Bobby growing up explained, "Violence became necessary in the Ville for survival. You learned how not to be in a position where you had the choice of either escalating or not, and thus putting your own reputation at risk, which invites more violence. You had to be savvy enough to defuse. A stressful way to grow up. Stares, insults, any violation of the norm had to be responded to."

In middle school Bobby began chafing at authority and became "a rebellious young man. I didn't like the principal, always telling people what to do, so I told him he was fat." Bobby was expelled and sent to Urban Youth, a small "transitional" New Haven middle school in a former church building near the Hamden line in Newhallville. The name Urban Youth was itself a stereotype. People referred to "the troublemaker school," and the destination for "bad kids." It was a depository filled with poor Black and Latino students, most of whom had terrible records, both academic and disciplinary. One man who worked there said, "You can't go to jail until you're out of eighth grade, so you go to Urban Youth."

Urban Youth's mission was to help struggling children successfully return to the regular city schools that had been unable to handle them and did not want them. The morning began with students checked for weapons with security wands as they entered the building, and then fed a prepackaged breakfast. Why was it that American public school meals were invariably not nutritious? Classroom sizes were small, but the composition was ominous, because placed in one classroom would be kids from the Tribe, Tre, Ville, and Hill neighborhoods, who had grown up despising one another, inherited territorial beefs that were of lethal magnitude even though they now existed purely on geographic pretext. In addition to the teacher, classrooms were staffed by a behavioral technician. When students couldn't control themselves, the tech led them out to the "refocus room." People from juvenile probation regularly came through.

The school building had broken windows, warped hardwood floors, erratic heating seeping from old radiators, moldy rugs, peeling ceiling plaster, damaged chalkboards, and secondhand books. "That school's kind of like a prison," one boy said. "Had an old Gothic look. You resist, they put you in a little room like solitary."

The principal was a gentle Black man with a neat mustache named Milton Brown. During special assemblies, when Brown threw back his head and led a chorus of "Lift Every Voice and Sing," everybody could see how filled up he was with the spirit of creating a loving, protective place for one hundred vulnerable children. Many of them, Brown said, didn't know where they would sleep at night, when or if they would eat. "They lived in the streets. Anybody who prevented them from getting what they needed to survive could be a problem with them. All of them were looking for someone to care for them and provide for the empty space in their lives."

Bobby hated how "nasty" and "dirty" the building was, how "disrespected" it made students feel. Everybody, he said, understood that successfully earning one's "spot" again at their former school was never going to happen. Their predicament made the kids he went to Urban Youth with "uncivilized," and Bobby said he himself "definitely was that kid. I wanted to get suspended so I didn't have to go there."

But Bobby's teachers saw him at such variance from the way he described himself, it was as though they knew another person. Milton Brown said he considered Bobby to be notably "honest," and "had a loving spirit and wanted to be cared for. A lot of kids gravitated towards him. They wanted him to be more streetwise. He never challenged the administration, never went too far." To survive, Brown believed Bobby had to put on a tough front, but, he said, "I wished he thought more of himself. He viewed himself lower than what he was."

The disciplinary techs called Bobby "The Original," and one tech said they all thought he was a "great kid." This was an opinion shared by the basketball coaches who helped Bobby to channel the anger they saw into becoming a tenacious defensive player. That, along with a mature strategic understanding of the sport, and Bobby's bravery at taking on bigger boys and going through them to rise and finish drives at the rim, all made the coaches sure he had college potential. Teachers like Cindy Burns noticed what the coaches noticed, that Bobby "was so responsive when people nurtured him. All the kids were looking for strong, positive attention. With Bobby, we thought, 'How did he end up here? He doesn't belong here.'"

Or perhaps it was that Bobby exemplified the reasons that landed students in Urban Youth, and how much more they could be than their troubles. A new white member of the faculty, Dyane Rizzo, was intimidated by aggressive boys in her classroom. "If I didn't hear 'Fuck you' one hundred times by seven thirty in the morning, something was wrong," she said. Rizzo herself was repeatedly called "bitch" by her students, and one morning "there was a lot of rough talk about rape." She began to cry. That's when, she said, Bobby "stood up and told them to cut it out. He said to me, 'Don't worry, Miss.'" After that, Bobby was for her the protective presence he was for the women in his family. "Bobby, I never had an issue with a kid in my classroom when he was with me," Rizzo said. "It was, 'Hey, don't talk to my teacher like that.' He had a charisma about him and a toughness. And he had the respect of other kids. He was one of those good people."

Bobby himself made a distinction between his individual relationships and how the system at large thought of him. "School records say I was a bad kid," he said, "but I had sympathy for my teachers. Miss Rizzo! That was my girl! I love that lady with passion. She was a white lady going to teach a bunch of Black kids she wanted to help, all the bad kids from all the schools going there. She was my world. She'd get me something to eat. She'd play music for me if the music pertained to what I was working on. She listened to me. We had the greatest relationship I ever had with a teacher." At home, Rizzo mended her students' clothing and cooked them pasta and chicken dishes she then warmed on a classroom hot plate. It pleased Bobby that she'd tell him to avoid the streets. "I'd be like, 'Nah, Miss. I'm chillin', staying out of other people's business.'"

He was just as appreciative of Zanniece Smith, an experienced Black teacher. Not only did Smith explain the particulars of body and oral hygiene to Bobby's class, she used her own money to buy the children clothing, toothbrushes, washcloths, and deodorant, took students to her house so they could shower. Noticing how hungry they all were even after the school-provided breakfast, Smith set up a classroom kitchen and cooked pancakes and bacon every morning. On Fridays, if they'd been well behaved all week, she made the class fried chicken and potato salad for lunch. "Some of the kids had been in juvenile detention centers," Smith said. "Some had bracelets on their ankle. One had been stealing cars left and right. He'd drive it to school. I had kids who'd hang out all night and come to school tired. It was an easy classroom. They just wanted to have somebody who cared."

WHEN THE SECTION 8 program of supplemental government payments to landlords made it possible for Grace to move into a single-family Newhallville house, white with black shutters and a chain-link fence at the end of the first block of Willis Street, Bobby joined them. There were individual bedrooms for the three eldest family members, a second bathroom, and a washing machine and clothes dryer, significant conveniences since there was no laundromat in Newhallville and the family had no car. The washing machine meant, Bobby said, "My mom's life got crazy because the whole neighborhood came over to wash clothes." Grace, he said, also felt like "a grocery store," because so many kids appeared at mealtimes—"Every day you see dudes starving because [their] mom got high." Newhallville, where some kids made meals of a bag of hot fries and blue juice (25-cent sugar-water), got Bobby "sad." He had friends living in homes with no furniture, coming to school from surfing the latest couch, coming to school from the homeless shelter. Precarity, he said, was everywhere: "I hear people crying, 'I need somebody to watch the kids.' Somebody always needs somebody to watch the kids. Always they need a ride. People don't have lives." In Newhallville, Bobby knew of kids whose mothers were so desperate to buy groceries for their children, the mothers slept with government officials to keep their EBT card benefits.

On Willis Street, Bobby was still responsible for a lot of the childcare, which brought him both frustration and sartorial compensations from Grace. In Bobby's first-floor bedroom at the back of the house, the closet made clear "he was swag," as his aunt Joy said. "He had to match, from the drawers to the socks. If there was a speck of dirt on his shirt, he was hurt!"

Bobby had also a TV set, a DVD player, and wall décor suggesting enthusiasm for football and women—at least until Aunt Faith visited, and down came the pinup posters. If Bobby's sisters sneaked in to watch cartoons on the TV while he was out, no matter how neat they were, afterward Bobby could always tell.

Although he was far from full-grown, Bobby's sisters saw that Bobby had going what Stephanie called "his wannabe charm! He thinks he's so good-looking. He's not obviously handsome, but he's so confident, he *seems* so handsome." While Bobby cooked dinner for his sisters, Kenya said "the whole downstairs was full of girls. They love Bobby!" The attention concerned Grace: "I'd tell him, 'Don't bring no babies home.'"

Most afternoons, Bobby and Hank played basketball, sometimes with other cousins. As to which court they'd use, Hank deferred to Bobby, because Bobby knew "more areas where there wasn't violence. He knew where to go." Playing point guard was, Bobby said, the one place where he had control, where "everything else doesn't matter."

In Grandma's Hamden neighborhood, there was a lightness to being. The cousins made friends with kids whose houses had kempt lawns and two newish cars in the driveway; whose young professional mothers and fathers walked their children to school before they went to work with "business attire on," Bobby said with approval; who came home for supper where they talked at the dinner table in front of Bobby "about college and being somebody." On December nights around Hamden, the porches flickered with Christmas lights and decorations. Behind first-floor windows were trees silvery with tinsel. "At Christmas it glows," Bobby said. "Why can't the Ville glow? When we were younger, our grandparents would tell us stories: 'We used to leave the door wide open!' How?! It's so hateful now. But you could tell how peaceful it was then. The world is shaped crazy."

The one community informed his questions about the other. He'd return to Newhallville and notice "people stagnated. Nothing to do. Stuck. Compliant. I don't see enough lawyers, doctors, where I am. How come? Why are they not in my neighborhood? It's an invisible concept being a lawyer or a doctor unless somebody gets a bullet and needs a doctor or catches a case and needs a lawyer. Then people say, 'I should have been a lawyer—I could represent myself!' Or, 'I should have been a doctor, I could have delivered my own baby.'"

In 2004, Grandma began losing weight. Her energy flagged. Her memory began to lapse. For a long, terrible year this went on until, in late summer 2005, when Bobby was fifteen, Grandma was admitted to the hospital in great pain. There was confusion among the grandchildren about what was wrong. Some thought she had cancer of the brain, others that it was her stomach. Uncle Mikey believed, in addition to cancer, she'd been stuck at work by an HIV-infected needle. If her large family represented one metaphorical house, Grandma was both foundation and front door—supportive and welcoming to all. It wasn't only that a tiny woman possessed warm energy enough to convince two generations she was there for everybody, Grandma's benevolent way of being felt exemplary, them all at their generous best. Many family members were there, weeping at her bedside, in August of 2005, when she died.

Afterward, everyone was devastated and nobody talked about it. Plain to see was that Grace was taking the death of her mother hardest. As Shavonne explained, "My mother and my grandmother were peanut butter and jelly. She died, and my mother felt like she had nobody and shut down." Grace herself said, "Once my mom passed away, I stopped wanting things."

The family cleaved. Tonya, an A-student and state-champion high school track star, who'd walked through the streets of the Ville head-down, reading books, stopped going to class, lost her college scholarship. What was it about grief that those who were most experienced in it didn't master the condition but were instead reduced?

Bobby didn't betray his feelings, and because his face was impassive, his eyes dry, people in the family deemed him cold. He was trying to follow the wishes of Grandma. She'd reassured him she was leaving for a better place, that Bobby must let her go, needn't mourn, should be happy. He did his best for her. But his head grew tight, a throbbing he could not relax away. He worked to become numb.

Looking back on those days of traveling back and forth between Newhallville and Hamden, Bobby would say, "When I do some introspection, I realize I was brought up in two different worlds. I now see the outcome of both."

Chapter Seven

Losing his grandmother and watching his mother fall into depression led Bobby to seek comfort elsewhere. At fifteen, he began regularly hanging out at the 2-4, the open-all-night corner store by the bus stop at the intersection of Bassett Street and Dixwell Avenue. The 2-4 was one of several small groceries on corners around Newhallville, and each had the bustling social junction feel of crossroads stores in farming communities. A police officer who grew up with the TV comedy *Happy Days* thought that for Newhallville young people, the 2-4 was also "their little Arnold's," referring to the show's drive-in where high school students met up for milk shakes. Except that at the 2-4, there were many corner-standers well beyond their teens, and some were deep into the streets.

One such person was Bobby's older cousin Lion, a charismatic drug dealer who was so identified with the 2-4, he had the numerals tattooed on his arm. "I didn't really want him to be out there," Lion said of Bobby. But "I know how it is growing up in that neighborhood. The Dixwell and Bassett area is the limelight. Constant traffic. Lots of females. It was exciting. Day and night, everybody stopped at that corner."

Evening became dark and the sidewalk lit up as more and more people came out to join with the crowd, creating a din, gesticulating, flashing "V" hand signs (for the Ville) to drivers sunk low in passing cars who beeped in solidarity. There were dice games, especially Cee-lo, people sidling by with their dogs, hip-hop. For kids from D-Side, from Read Street, from Dip-Set, even those with inter-Ville beefs, the 2-4 was neutral territory. Bobby liked that "Everybody's there, all posted."

To him, being in front of the 2-4 felt like the gift of new light. "The summertimes were special," he said. "My cousin Lion was playing music out of his car and dancing all the time. There were a lot of drug transactions going on out there, but I was never susceptible to that lifestyle." Lion said that older people enjoyed talking with his young cousin because "Bobby's funny and outspoken and quiet at the same time. Once he opens up, he's kindhearted." Out there, amid the flirting, smack talk, and politicking, Bobby was once again a traveler, attentive to the Christmas-tree-light tangle of neighborhood relationships, to people's old feelings and antagonisms, to the new events that erupted as a consequence, the roles all the local characters played in the daily drama of the Avenue.

As the 2-4 opened up a bigger world to Bobby, he found everything about it interesting. The physical reality of the 2-4 was dingy and cramped, the exterior sign—Dix Deli—itself an attenuation. The 2-4 sold iced tea and soda, sandwiches, packaged cakes and pies, salty snacks like pork rinds and off-brand chips, and Bobby's favorite item, honeybuns. Shelves held a jumble of staples—pancake mix, instant ramen noodles, stockings, African shea butter, loosies (individual cigarettes). "People don't want to come in and buy whole boxes of crackers," Bobby noticed, "so they sell them one sleeve. They made more money breaking product up." The front entrance was narrow enough that someone standing in the doorway eating the egg-and-cheese sandwich he'd just purchased could effectively block a police field investigator from seeing the drug transaction taking place down the aisle. Behind the counter there was a slushy machine, and deli items that were ordered by the dollar, not by the pound, from the Middle-Eastern cashier. (In this Black neighborhood, where proprietors often shifted, the corner stores were very rarely Black-owned.) The chugging coolers faded in and out of function, as did the security cameras. Collectively, what corner stores stocked wasn't so far afield from the options at prison commissaries, though they also might have such telling items as animal traps, glassine envelopes, marijuana grinders, and the votive candles placed at sidewalk shrines honoring those who'd died there.

Out in front of the 2-4 was a wide concrete apron leading down to the bus stop, where neighborhood people waited for transit downtown. There were, at times, a throng of panhandlers. In the morning, people just out of prison who'd been dropped off nearby might take a pause, deciding where to go. Across Bassett Street, at Visels Pharmacy, elders picked up their prescriptions. Down the block was the state social services office. The bus stop offered drug dealers both a draw for attracting customers and also a plausible excuse: they weren't loitering but waiting. In turn, there were police officers who, when in the mood for caprice, would fold their arms until the next bus hissed to a halt. Then a group of young men would reluctantly get on board and take a seat, muttering, "He crazy," about the cop sending them on a ride to nowhere.

During the day, Bobby and his male 2-4 friends played versions of capture the flag. There were water-balloon fights and conversation with the girls who came around. If no girls were there, the boys talked about girls. Across the street at Visels, several young women around Bobby's age held jobs, and so he made regular pilgrimages. "He never bothered nobody," said Bounce, one of Bobby's best friends, who worked there. "Everybody used to say, 'Why y'all be out there?' That's the move. Girls, pretty much."

But the corner reverberated with the stresses boys went there to get away from, and it didn't take much for some to act out. In the winter, one of Bobby's friends sailed a snowball through the window of a small white passing car, striking the driver, who hit the brakes, sprung from behind the wheel, and confronted Bobby's friend. Allies swarmed to the friend's defense, as the car driver's young son sobbed in the backseat, until Bobby interceded, began pulling everybody apart. Moments like that, and Bobby's aversion to shoplifting, won Bobby trust behind the counter of the 2-4 with his favorite clerk, a large man everyone called Fat Daddy. Soon, a credit sheet was created by Fat Daddy for Bobby, and Bobby was permitted to freely help himself to snacks, with the only downside that "they allow my sisters to do the same and I would have to pay for it." He was also sometimes enlisted to shovel snow and restock the shelves. Bobby's sense was "they thought I was special. They trusted me, made sure I stay out of trouble."

Plenty of kids were, like Bobby, only there at the 2-4 because Newhallville was almost rural in its aridity, didn't offer them near enough to do. "They leave us nothing, nothing but street corners," Bobby said. Elsewhere in Newhallville there remained vestiges of the spirit of ambition the migrants brought to New Haven: church groups, sports and other activities centered on the high schools, youth dance and drum corps. But Bobby had no afterschool activities in his neighborhood, no tutoring sessions, no open gyms, no library. Even cheerful Hank found that getting older made it "hard to be optimistic in Newhallville. We had sports. Different programs. But at a certain point it all vanished." For most of Bobby's 2-4 friends, afternoons following the last bell at school offered either an empty house or the streets.

In the streets. The phrase itself so seductive, elevating the lack of obligations, the bleakness of hanging out, selling drugs and carrying a gun to a noir existence of hard-boiled gravity. "If you're in the streets," Lion said, "you're in it. It's survival." The streets was "the life," and a way of life, and within the game everyone did assume a role. To be a lookout, a runner, or a shooter was known as "playing your position."

"On the road" was searching for meaning in the America out there. "In the streets" implied finding the intensity of pure experience within the interior limits, unfiltered action, an immediacy that left no time for reflection. "The saying about Newhallville," Bobby said, "is whoever is born to it is doomed. You grow up in the Ville, you got to get accustomed to the streets." As Bobby saw it, nobody was actually born violent. But if you remained sealed off from the rest of the city, "isolation means you don't become fascinated with the finer things in life. You become fascinated by what's around you." Violence might then seem, if not exactly appealing, alluring for the power and even prestige it could bring. "If you grow up in Newhallville," said Bobby, "people doing violent stuff get the most attention. Praised by women, dress the freshest, drive the best cars. You don't see your parents having those things. What does it take to have nice things? You think about it, no other jobs can pay like that, that they can get."

What the rest of the neighborhood did with its time people in the game didn't pay much mind. To them the streets was the neighborhood. As Bobby's schoolmate Jerome explained it, "I'm pretty sure in every state you have a Newhallville somewhere. An area where there's shootings, fights, drugs, robbers. Something is always going down. Speaking from a person in the streets, the outside world doesn't matter. Doesn't involve where you're from. You find meaning what you're lacking at home." Violence in support of the drug game held an appeal that might begin with cash but also had to do with exhibiting power in a community that had lost its agency.

It was more than women that attracted Bobby to the corner. It was also the company of men. Bobby coveted the lessons about manhood that he worried he'd missed out on by growing up in a fatherless home, and he wasn't alone in this. A boy Bobby's age said, "People might think it's women on the corner, but it's a father figure." The high number of missing men in New Haven's poor, Black communities had created a void such that Bobby's drug dealer friend Little Blue said, "I never saw a kid who knew his dad." Many had no idea why their father left the family. A phrase Bobby thought "so true" held that "a son has a hole in his heart the size of his father." One older man at the 2-4, whom Bobby said he considered a "father figure," was in his early twenties, "a nice, uplifting" person whom Bobby venerated because he would point out to Bobby, "Look at this guy. Don't be like him."

It sometimes seemed that all Bobby had ever wanted was someone to be proud of him. Proud of him for keeping out of trouble, for remaining a stand-up guy while standing among those who were sometimes low-down, for not judging people who felt life was giving them only bad choices. The attentions of those men Bobby met outside the 2-4 who encouraged his desire to be a good person he wore like a moral vestment.

Selling drugs attracted uneducated, untrained, but resourceful people who wanted to support themselves. Hustlers were young people trying to make it happen on their own, were by nature bootstrappers, providers. Such was their resistance to relying on anybody, even a taxi driver, that kids in the game would trade drugs for the use of a customer's car. The cars were referred to as "crack-head rentals." For a while, this could mean driving around someone's Mercedes or BMW, but automotive tastes shifted to Hondas because the luxury cars attracted the police. Kids worked other subterfuges. One took a low-paying job as a cover so he could use his drug money to help his struggling mother. She believed his claim that everything he gave her came from his wages. "Diaper money," Bobby said. "Formula money. When you gotta depend on other people for it, you know how that makes you feel? Starts as a kickstart by people living through hardship. Then it's 'All this money! Let's see how much money I can get.' "

Everybody was on some level well aware that standing in front of the 2-4 was not making it in America. But other than that diminished sense, Bobby said "we had no view on the outside world." Living in an effective cul-de-sac, without ready access to other realms, the 2-4 was the default option. People represented their neighborhood, "repped" even their corner store, said, "That's where I'm from, Moe's Market." With the neighborhoods not fully functional, the city was sectionalized in conflict, the enmity based upon honor, turf, and tradition in the absence of property, assets, or ideology. Everybody Bobby knew was aware the longstanding beef between the Tre and the Ville was so backwoods violent, for kids from one neighborhood to enter the other was risking your health. Being born into this hatred was a fact of life, even as kids had no idea of its causes. As one of Bobby's cousins said, "Nobody knows why."

IN ARMED YOUNG people was the ready potential for bedlam, but Bobby noticed that gun violence "added structure for a lot of left out people who felt empty inside." He meant that no matter the level of chaos, the disorder of things not working, blighted buildings, empty lots, mother and father not around, nothing on time or functional, the life-threatening object stood up and commanded attention. People found meaning in guns that alluded to many kinds of vulnerability. If you felt unheard, you had only to bring out a gun and then everybody was listening. If you were scared, this was reassurance. There was also, Bobby said, the "fashion" component of holding a "cool machine." Kids said if you had a gun, you wanted to show it off. It was the commodification Winchester's advertising men had encouraged, making a gun like carrying the keys to an Audi—you held in your pocket a striking object that earned you instant recognition, a source of prestige and pride. Gun possession also brought self-possession. Getting guns, talking guns, stashing guns, there, too, was structure. Nas writing the inner life of gun-as-man in his song "I Gave You Power" wasn't far afield from the lives of a gun in Newhallville.

Acquiring a gun in the neighborhood, Bobby said, "That's the easiest thing." There were gun rentals, group-owned "community" guns, time-share guns, and even loaners that went out with a warning, "Don't have a body come back to me." A Newhallville backyard once had a deep-shoveled hole in which ten guns were buried, wrapped in plastic and stored for use by those in the know. Often, after a gun was fired in a crime, it left town or went into a storm drain or off a bridge, depending how effectively it was used, and by whom. Ballistics reports told of guns fired from city to city, a road atlas of discharges making bad news travel fast.

Guns got to New Haven when high school students took the bus to states with less stringent gun-control laws, like Georgia, bought duffel bags full of guns, returned, and sold them. Others did this kind of bulk shopping at Southern gun shows. Interstate 95 North was known as "The Iron Pipeline." Another kind of conduit was the New York police officer whose practice was to notice the telltale lurch of a man walking along with something heavy at the waist, the man touching to be sure his unholstered piece wasn't about to fall down his pants. That cop would move in, confiscate the gun, and then let the person go. The cop forwarded the guns up from New York to his New Haven relatives, who did steady trade selling them out of the house. Girlfriends and other young women without criminal records legally purchased guns as proxy buyers for their boyfriends. Drug addicts from middle-class towns raided their parents' collections or they went to gun shops as straw buyers. It was more difficult to acquire the appropriate ammunition for a gun than the weapon itself, so there were kids who tried shooting pebbles, tried to melt down their own bullets.

In the 1980s and 1990s, guns had primarily been used in Newhallville to protect drug territory. But by Bobby's time, cell phones had changed the business and the 2-4 was an exception in corner trade. Instead, dealers took calls and met up at a fast-food parking lot or at IKEA. Guns were now most often used either for robbery or self-defense. Kids carried guns so as not to use them, deterrents making it so nobody with a gun messed with you. (This was the same reason people often gave for joining gangs and sets.) Yet the ubiquity of guns reduced the inhibitions against squeezing the trigger. A common impetus for shooting someone was self-defending an injured street reputation, and some police officers were astonished at how "frivolous" the grounds for such a beef might be. To say someone's girlfriend wasn't pretty could be your final opinion.

This was, after all, youth. Gaining competence with a gun, practicing accuracy, learning to take care of it, these were generally not considerations of those in the Newhallville streets who owned guns. "A lot of time it's a threat to bystanders," one teenage shooter said. "People don't have much aim." Stray bullets could not lose their own way, but the pinball type interaction of guns and kids and boredom and slights and revenge meant the wayward bullets were also not quite wayward. Neglected kids didn't know how to shoot and shot anyway, and other people paid for their aimlessness. In the summer of 2006, five armed young men from Newhallville, including Jerome, were in a car, searching for some kids from the Tribe area who'd previously shot at them. The kids from Newhallville came upon their foes at a party. They fired. The bullets lit up the evening, and a radiant thirteen-year-old girl bystander was killed.

When he was fifteen, Bobby owned a gun for a week. That week was a long one, both heady and taxing. Showing off the black-and-chrome .380 to his friends felt to him, he said, like having the best new toy: "It was a thrill. Everybody looked at you differently. Seemed like you were part of something instead of being something." Mostly, Bobby kept it in his backyard, hidden behind the trash cans. "I left it," he said. "You can't carry that stuff around." Nor did he ever have any bullets. "One of the things about the streets," he said, "is you get something, somebody out there will want it more." Sure enough, he'd paid $100 for the gun. After a week he sold it for twice that. The whole experience left him exhausted.

Most residents in Newhallville didn't carry guns, much less fire them at others, and wanted nothing to do with shooting. But the violence held everyone unfairly to account. It didn't take many grizzly-bear or white-shark attacks to terrorize a community, and in Newhallville, sporadic gunfire had ramifications well beyond the per capita. Shooting eroded social cohesion and quickly reduced a neighborhood that was so much more than shooting to shooting. And to grief.

Newhallville was a close enough place that whenever something happened, it was to a relative or a neighbor or a schoolmate or a friend or someone's child or once removed. The scale of Bobby's city also meant that as he walked down the street, there was no buffer between him and the dead, and memories of violence came bearing down upon him. In that house, this friend was shot. Over there, that girl killed her boyfriend. On one block, "Guy jumped out his car naked and killed himself." On another, Bobby had been a passenger, waiting for the light to change, when people he didn't know "just pulled out guns and started shooting at the car." The "craziest thing" Bobby ever saw was chancing upon a man as he first shot a woman in her driveway, then went to a nearby elementary schoolyard and put the gun to his own head, in front of children.

Bobby estimated by age sixteen he'd attended fifty funerals and one school graduation. The truth was Bobby felt "close to" so many people who'd died violent deaths, every time he calculated how many there were, he arrived at a different number. Young people he knew didn't assure others they meant it by saying "I swear to God." Their sacred emphasis invoked martyrs from the Ville: "On the dead Villains." At the 2-4, when a regular died, there was a memorial ritual involving stereos in parked cars turned up high. "People played sad songs," Bobby said. "They'd open all four doors. Hundred-and-change people out there. Happened too often. One of the sad songs was the Boyz II Men song 'It's So Hard to Say Goodbye.'"

Bobby's own ritual was striving to act as though death was just another dip in the road. At age fifteen, he decided that he'd become inured: "I've been to so many different funerals, I'm numb to death." This would turn out to be untrue. He and other kids were actively resistant to processing the events they knew were traumatic, creating separation from what might flatten them. One day someone doused the 2-4 with gunfire. Bobby and his friends ducked for cover. "You'd have thought everybody would stay away," he said, "but seconds later we were back out there."

Standing at the 2-4, Bobby seemed to be having it both ways. Drug dealers would offer Bobby a place on their "team," but he never joined up, and was proud of it. Yet these days near the fallen-wire-electricity of heightened experience, he considered "thrilling. It's fascinating. It's like being in the NBA, the NFL, the excitement. You're always on the threshold of something."

A kid from Shelton Avenue warned, "If you stand there, you usually get caught up. Nobody who wants to go somewhere in life hangs out at the 2-4." Bobby didn't disagree. The lifestyle, he saw, was "addictive." When a group of kids led by a guy named Jolt began robbing and bullying friends of Bobby's, "I got sick and tired of it, so I beat him. They had to pull me off. His contacts came out. I hate fighting. I was known as a guy who'd break up fights."

Then came another day at the 2-4, when the father of a nice girl Bobby knew spotted Bobby on the corner and admonished Bobby in front of everyone for spending his time this way. In response, Bobby said, "I knocked him out." Later, Bobby rebuked himself: "I swear, I thought I was being a leader. I was just a follower."

THE MEN AND women responsible for keeping people safe from gun violence in the Ville were police officers. To be Bobby's age coming up in the Ville was to have the police as a daily part of your life. As one of his friends who wasn't in the game said, even for just-around kids, so much energy went into police awareness that a kid had to "learn to scope, to survey the land before you even get there, the cops doing some bull crap sometimes, so you have to look out for the cops." The kids believed the cops saw every Black boy as a "perp" and a "target," and girls from Newhallville agreed there was a different standard for boys. Boys walking in a group were scattered by police, just because they were Black boys, the police not understanding that boys kept to groups in Newhallville because they were too frightened to go it alone. Boys on bicycles were pulled over if they wore hoodies on cold days.

Carl Suddler's lengthy study of midcentury Harlem children and their interactions with the criminal justice system found that poor Black city kids were seen by police as older and less innocent than they were. In a good kid/bad kid binary, the police wrote off poor Black children as incorrigible as soon as they were found to have deviated in any way from perceived social norms. As Suddler explained, for some police, delinquent white kids from better neighborhoods were troubled teens who needed a little help; Black kids from Harlem (or Newhallville) were hoodlums and "presumed criminal." Black boys from Newhallville believed that by being so scrutinized, they paid for their small sins as nobody else in the city did. It was a syllogism: more police contact meant young people engaging in random, transgressive adolescent behavior were more likely to be arrested than young people growing up elsewhere.

The longstanding quandary in Newhallville was being simultaneously over- and under-policed. The problem walked the continuously rising and descending staircase of what was intended to remove you from danger becoming itself dangerous, making safety impossible. It was the constant reinforcing that you were in somebody else's control, and that the control was so often subjective and arbitrary.

But just as all kids weren't the same, neither were all police. The Black detective Donald Harrison said that in Newhallville, it all came down to familiarity: "People would talk to you if they knew you. But if you only came out there when something bad happened, you'd have a harder time." Harrison himself was a genuine person who delivered get-well cards when he heard someone in the neighborhoods he'd patrolled as a street cop had fallen ill. What Harrison noticed about Newhallville was that residents could seem "more concerned with property crimes than shootings." Harrison supposed this was because "burglaries were more personal." Most shootings happened within a small street network. It was also judged one thing for a stickup kid to rob a drug dealer but quite another to take a TV set from a hardworking older woman.

White police officers who were assigned to Newhallville during Bobby's time tended to divide over how they felt about working the largely poor, Black neighborhood. Some had condescending "those people" views. Then there were officers whose approach was not inconsistent with a view of policing as a self-sacrificial form of public service that had enveloped the country after September 11, 2001. These men and women felt fortunate to work in Newhallville, both because of professional fulfillment and because they considered it the most interesting neighborhood in the city. They said things like "You can't arrest away poverty," spoke of their "love" for Newhallville, and developed an attachment to the neighborhood. Jason Minardi said he "admired" that "each block had its own family network. In the white suburbs there's not that type of thing. There [in Newhallville], things are more knitted together." As older people got to know Minardi, and how he felt about them, they would tell him if they'd seen where handguns were stashed.

And when Charlie Gargano dressed up in his blue uniform, with his slab of a mustache and short, plump-bellied build, kids called him Mario, for the Italian plumber video game character in Super Mario. Twelve- and thirteen-year-old boys would ask Gargano, "Mario, you working last night?" He'd say, "No." They'd tell him, "That guy got shot. Blood all over the place. You know how it is over here." It bothered Gargano that murder was a regional expectation for Newhallville kids; bothered him that "there really isn't anything to do."

Police officers were the male authority figures kids in the streets saw most frequently, and some police officers grew to love the kids. In the way of Urban Youth teachers, these police officers used their own money to buy children Christmas gifts and school supplies; they initiated coat, Thanksgiving turkey, and food drives; organized basketball games; sought to offer optimistic fatherly and motherly counsel. The kids gave the police nicknames—Mr. Goodbar, Daddy-Yo, Maniac, Psycho, White Shirt—and they navigated the duality of someone who hoped you'd have a good life even as he was not your father, was instead the person who might send you to prison if you messed up. The rub for a compassionate cop: he was a representative of the system that leaned on him because of underlying ailments in a society that had no design for offering the neighborhood a resolution to its larger problems.

That was how Sgt. Marc Calafiore saw it. He would "routinely go into a house and look at five or six kids eating out of a crock pot three days old, and so many cockroaches on the wall it looked like the wall was moving." Standing there, Calafiore's mind went to children growing up in palatial homes on the other side of Prospect Hill, how in the space of "two minutes, you're worlds apart. It's kind of amazing in America. You have these drastic demarcations."

Bobby never met a police officer who tried to know him. Yet he always felt treated with respect by police officers, even by those who cuffed him, put him on a wall, and patted him down. Bobby blamed himself for the police becoming a presence in his life at the 2-4. "You surround yourself with those kinds of people, you have to expect that," he said.

All around Bobby were kids who expected to be locked up. With the churn of people leaving and returning, everybody in the streets who stood in front of the 2-4 knew it might next be them. Stories drifted back of prison baseball teams entirely made up of players from Newhallville. People talked of prison years as bullets, said "a bullet ain't shit," considered a bid almost inevitable, a stage of life. "A criminal record is the normal," Bobby's mother, Grace, said. "They think it's normal. It's not normal." On the corner, Bobby said, there was no prison stigma: "You wouldn't ever be embarrassed. It's sad but true."

Bobby's family was not pleased about his new fealty to the 2-4, were fretful over what would become of him. When Aunt Faith stopped her green minivan at the 2-4 and called to Bobby, "What are you doing out here?" he'd respond, "Auntie, I'm not doing nothing." She'd tell her nephew to leave the corner, and each time Bobby's response was "I don't have to listen to you." Faith would drive off thinking, "He's always wanted to be somebody. But he doesn't know how." So, Faith forbade him from entering her house to visit Hank and the other cousins.

One day, a person from Faith's church asked Bobby if he was living God's purpose. He replied, "What's the purpose?" The woman told him that was up to him to discover. Bobby was now a limit tester. He was feeling himself. He told her, "I only live God's purpose if it intersects my purpose." The woman, he said, "went crazy!" But to Bobby it made no sense that God would withhold such necessary information for an eventual surprise reveal.

Among the Hamden uncles, there was incredulity about Bobby. "My brothers and I couldn't believe he was hanging out at the twenty-four-hour store," said Uncle June. "We thought Bobby was not built for this. We thought no way." Uncle Mikey was driving tractor trailers, and every time he returned from the road, there was something different about his young nephew, new sneakers, a new ballcap worn at a jauntier angle, a new way of talking that didn't sound like eager-to-please Bobby.

People faulted Grace for allowing her son to stand at the 2-4, but Letitia Charles, the social services coordinator for Project Longevity, an anti-gun-violence organization, said Grace's dilemma was familiar to her. "With no strong man in the family, the streets become a different kind of family," Charles said. "The moms I know, they had a lot of guilt. They made their sons the men of the family. They'd tell me, 'I can't tell him when to come in.'"

Bobby might be obnoxious with churchy women, might be glib with the uncles, but they understood he was raw and unformed, a teenager excited about creating worry in them. At sixteen, Bobby was growing into his big ears, scrutinizing and adjusting himself, looking outward, fitting in, absorbing more than gangster moves. He was living several teenage lives at once, behaving differently around different people, trying on various selves and not quite knowing it. That itself was a form of teenage innocence, such a challenge to retain in a community where the stakes were so high. There was in Bobby a quality common in people who've experienced disturbing things, of both living his life and simultaneously observing it.

With his younger sisters and cousins, it was Bobby who was playing the part of Aunt Faith, warning off any of them who came near the 2-4, ordering them, "Get out of here. Go home." If they had problems around the neighborhood, as Tonya did with an aggressive young woman who took a mysterious dislike to her, Bobby "brought us together. He resolved the issue."

When Bobby's sister Shavonne had a conflict with another girl on Read Street, again Bobby intervened. The police arrived, the girl's family accused Bobby of hitting their daughter, and although Bobby and Shavonne swore this wasn't true, Bobby was charged with breach of peace. At court, he was ordered to do community service at a soup kitchen. Then, in May 2006, a boy kept bothering Bobby's sisters, "So," Bobby said, "he and I got into it. I hit him in his eye." A police officer was right across the street, with the result that Bobby was cited again for breach of peace and given another court date. Toward the end of the month, he and a younger friend who lived across Willis Street, Kwame, were on their block after midnight on a Friday, and a police officer asked what they were doing out so late. The cop patted them down, ran their names, and told Bobby there was an arrest warrant for him due to his failure to appear in court on the breach-of-peace charge. Bobby was taken to the police department lockup. Despite the time of year, the cell was so cold he couldn't sleep. On Monday, it was discovered it had all been a mistake, and Bobby was sent home. As he left, he had premonitions—"I worried that once you go there it becomes going again and again, a cycle." He resolved to be more careful.

When he wasn't standing at the 2-4 or taking care of his sisters, Bobby was often with women. Friends named Bumpy and Boo and Sunshine liked how deeply he saw and felt, that he took genuine interest in them. "My women friends," he said, "the person they talk to is not their family but me. I come in the room, they cry. They say, 'My dude be dogging me out.' 'My mom puts her friends before me.' Simple life stuff."

Halfway down his block, Bobby got to know a woman a bit older, and a lot wilder, named Melanie. Sitting on the flower-patterned couch out on her screened-in porch, Melanie told lively stories about her adventures around the city, which Bobby listened to with interest. Melanie's studious sixteen-year-old "church girl" sister was Shay, who participated in after-school music programs, sang in gospel choirs, and was otherwise "chained to the porch" by Nana, her strict maternal grandmother and guardian. Shay wasn't allowed to go buy a carton of milk at the 2-4, only two blocks away, because, Shay said, "Too much going on, on the corner."

Before Melanie got to know Bobby, when he'd go past, the two sisters watched his sidewalk strut and thought him ludicrous, "a comedy clown." After Bobby began visiting their porch to talk to Melanie, it was soon nothing to tell that everything he said was really for Shay to hear, that out on the sidewalk it had all been for Shay, that he would have done anything to impress her. Shay had flashing brown eyes, vivid lashes, and after swooning Bobby said something foolish, a sly, appraising way of looking him over before she burst into laughter. What "a skinny little thing" she thought he was! Yet he kept returning for more teasing, and she began to notice how, in small, revealing, everyday ways, Bobby was his own person. Bobby didn't swear, and he wore a belt instead of "sagging" his pants down under his butt, even when other boys mocked him for it. "I loved that he kept his pants up," Shay said. "I hated those boys with their booty out. My sister and I would commend him."

Shay joked about being "barren to the porch," but the phrase suggested how original was her way of expressing whatever she observed, how even on the porch she was out in America. Her favorite musician was Otis Redding because, she said, every time you heard him singing a sad old soul ballad about loss, she was convinced Otis was himself going through it. She and Bobby had talks about faith and belief. Bobby hated superstition, declared that he made a point of stepping on sidewalk cracks. Shay said Nana was superstitious about everything. Nana believed if you bought a man shoes, he'd walk right out of your life. A hat on a bed was bad luck, and so was anything to do with the number 666. If the cash register at Dunkin' Donuts showed $6.66, you better add on a Munchkin, fast. Playing basketball, Bobby admitted, he'd tell himself if he made this next shot, it foretold he'd do well on the test tomorrow at school. But Shay, too, was a magical thinker! She'd watch the cars pass by on Willis Street and decide, "If I see three Acuras, I'm gonna get one! It's a happy thought. A self-boost."

Nana had been born in 1936, and Nana's grandmother had been enslaved. Nana's grandfather and father were the first Black plumbers in Augusta, Georgia. Her father could install an entire bathroom on his own. The risk, Nana said, was "if he got caught, he'd go to jail because he didn't have a license. But they wouldn't give Black man a license. Didn't want to." Superstition was, Shay thought, the consolation of people who had been deprived of security. "It comes from back then. We started jumping the broom [after] they took away our history."

Bobby preferred hip-hop music to Otis Redding. Bobby had no interest in church. The only history Bobby knew was that of the Black Panthers in

New Haven, and not that they created programs to feed and uplift poor children, only "how violent they were." But Bobby was enchanted with the studious, churchgoing Shay. He'd never met anybody like her. He wanted to have known her longer than he had known her. When his sisters talked about his smart, well-educated "girlfriend" who wasn't "ratchet," who wasn't "over the top or careless about life," he was proud, and proud that Nana thought well of him. "He was a nice little fellow" was Nana's verdict. "He was mannerable. I have to give it to him. He was always a good kid. No loud talking when he came on the porch chewing his big lip."

Since Shay wasn't allowed to walk anywhere with Bobby, Bobby would go to the 2-4 and buy her gifts of hot fries. Shay could tell how hard Bobby was crushing on her, and this was a problem. Shay had an older carpenter boyfriend. But then Bobby would cuddle up next to her on the couch and rub her feet, and she felt she could tell him anything that was bothering her, that she didn't have to hold back with Bobby, that he would do his best to help her find solutions, that he really cared about her. Bobby had, she thought, a crowded houseful of people to contend with. She, too, had a houseful. The neighborhood teemed with pitfalls and misfortune. Her porch was their refuge. Yes, he was just a kid, but he had the empathy of a much older person, natural compassion. "He was sweet to me," she said. "He made me feel I was the only girl in the world. He was special for me. I didn't plan to give no other guy the time of day. But I used to let Bobby come between me and my boyfriend."

Shay knew that "Bobby's hopes and dreams were he wanted to be my boyfriend." But Shay's plan was college. She'd long understood that the way to make it out of the neighborhood was to avoid it, so she'd done her part, spent her youth in the choir and on the porch. Just around the corner was what she'd been missing. It had never seemed like much of a sacrifice, especially the claims of 2-4 brotherhood. "I thought it was just ridiculous," Shay said. "Like [the 2-4 saying] 'everybody out there for everybody.' I didn't know what the hype was."

But how people went to college, Shay wasn't sure. She had nobody around her who'd been to college and could show her how to rig her sails. At eighteen, there wasn't even anybody to help her get a driver's license. "For us it was very rare to get a license," she said, "because it was extra stuff. If you want to do extra stuff, you got to do it yourself. You know the way you push off the wall when you start to swim? We don't have anything to push off to get us started." What Shay did possess was intelligence and will. Forgoing a driver's license was one thing, but, she said, "Not going to school was not an option for me. I had to go to school. It was my way off Willis Street. I had to get out of the hood. Everybody I knew was getting pregnant or getting shot. So, I was like, I don't want to be either. I have to get out of here."

ACROSS WILLIS STREET from Bobby's house lived Kwame, who was being raised by his aunt Julia Sykes, a preschool teacher and dance instructor. Kwame's mother died of a heart attack when he was six. Sykes was loving and devoted to Kwame, and to the several foster children she would bring up by herself. She took him to dance and drum lessons, and to church, enrolled him in sports leagues, but, said Kwame, "Can't nobody take your mother's spot."

Bobby and fourteen-year-old Kwame became, to Bobby, "Like brothers. That was my boy. He was up for everything. Truthful about everything. He played basketball. Liked the same music." Shay and Bobby began referring to Kwame as "our little bro." Kwame was a peaceful kid, and, said Bobby, "I wouldn't allow people to hurt him." They played Scrabble and Sorry!, went dancing with girls, had sleepovers at Bobby's, staying up late with movies and video games like Grand Theft Auto. "I basically lived with Bobby," Kwame said. "My aunt didn't want me to come back in late. I wanted to be outside." Outside meant the 2-4, which Kwame and Bobby enjoyed similarly. "It was the place in the neighborhood to go meet your friends," Kwame said.

Kwame's aunt gave her nephew a nickname. "I called him Blankman," Sykes said. "He's very quiet. You look at him, he's very closed." Sykes liked Bobby, and admired how responsible he was. He'd come to visit Kwame, and "then he'd leave and have to go get things for his sisters. Go fix things. He was treated as the father. I knew he had a lot on his plate. I think that's why he hung around Kwame. Kwame listens to you. Level-headed. He used to listen to Bobby."

It was natural for two sensitive boys in tough surroundings to notice what gave the other pain, and to confide things they otherwise tamped down. "You grow up in a neighborhood together," Bobby said, explaining their friendship. "We never questioned it when the cops jump out. Somebody dies. It's not adversity like normal people feel it." The relief of now having Kwame to share and navigate his adolescence was immense. "You never know people are feuding until an incident occurs," Bobby said. "We survive in this so-called jungle. We do our best to stay away so we're not forced to choose sides and incur a beef too."

One way the boys coped that spring and summer of 2006 was by smoking weed together. Bobby liked it because, he said, the weed "alleviated my pain." In Bobby's room, they'd "throw on an instrumental, start bugging! We'd rap freestyle. Sometimes we sounded awesome! We played PS2. Madden." In a city filled with stoner college kids, Kwame and Bobby were a high school version. When they got hungry, they'd walk up to the 2-4 and buy a honeybun or a beef patty. Then they'd cross the street to Visels Pharmacy, visit the girls there—one became Kwame's girlfriend—page through a magazine, and wait for their friend Bounce to finish his shift, so they could walk back across the street with him to the 2-4, stand and watch the world go by.

Shay, too, was watching. She had acquired an application to the University of Connecticut, filled out it and the financial-aid forms by herself, sent them in. But now her feelings about where she'd come from were shifting. Passing by the 2-4 after dark on warm, early summer nights, from the car window the corner glistened with light and youth, looked suddenly appealing to Shay, and she thought she could better understand its pull. Because the 2-4 stayed open longer than any store in Newhallville, when it got late, anybody from the neighborhood who needed something came through. "It was just the spot," Shay said. "You could see everybody coming and going. The crossroads. Meet me at the crossroads." She began to want to be outside after the streetlamps came on, to be part of it all instead of always holding herself apart. She wanted to go there, joining in, going rounds, getting lit. "The nighttime," she said, "everybody used to have the most fun. Just, you know, in the summertime, everybody will be still out on the street smoking, drinking, listening to music, flirting, flirting, dancing, dancing. I was like, 'Oh. So this is why.'"

Shay was admitted to UConn. That summer she left to immerse herself in sociology, a singing group, and a college boyfriend. Bobby's locus remained the 2-4, where without her he felt the increasing "thrill" of street life. But to kids in the game, Bobby was still only just around. Jerome was loyal to Moe's Market, not the 2-4, but he saw Bobby out in the neighborhood. "Bobby and his friends were stoners," he said. "Bobby just stayed out of trouble." Little Blue considered Bobby "Honest, real, loyal, fun, funny. We got high. Walked around doing dumb stuff, tossing rocks at taxis. Snatch-and-run out of stores. He was with us, but he just watched. He was too scared to get in trouble. He ate beef patties and honeybuns every day. He loved them. Me, the Big E, and Fizzy were the bad ones." Someone who was even deeper in the streets than Little Blue explained, "Bobby always brushed waves, licked his lips, wanted to be a pretty boy. Good dude. Play basketball. Bobby was around. Wasn't selling drugs. Wasn't carrying guns. Group of dudes. Some carry guns, some are selling drugs, some are just around because they live there. But if you're around, you're held to the same standards, schooled by the same standards as me."

To be a just-around kid, in Bobby's case, meant that he hit a grown-up who was publicly humiliating him, and beat up a boy who bullied his sister. On the other hand, it meant when other kids played Knockout (confronting strangers on the sidewalk and punching them in the face full-force), Bobby refused to join. It meant that Bobby didn't want to carry a gun. When Bobby walked into a store on Dixwell, ordered an after-school egg-and-cheese sandwich, and Little Blue and some others burst in to snatch and grab chips, candy, and cookies, Bobby just watched as they ran out. Then he paid for his sandwich. To be just around meant that, despite pressure, Bobby didn't sell drugs. He said that was partly because he was afraid of his older female cousins, who "would have snapped my neck. I never wanted to disappoint them."

At sixteen, Bobby was half out on his own, going along, trying to manage the risks of growing up in a neighborhood that was itself just around. Poverty left everybody on the ledge, and when trouble came, there was no net. The kinds of predicaments confronting people Bobby knew were a seized engine that had to be fixed with the rent money or there was no getting to work, but which, in turn, meant you had to figure out how to store the table and mattresses by tomorrow when the landlord would change the locks; and what to do with the baby while you dealt with yet another eviction. Then someone got sick. People blamed themselves for the insecure way they lived, and felt hopeless watching their sons, deprived of stability, become exposed to the streets and succumb.

For boys like Bobby, the peril around them made extremes seem routine. They expected to navigate enormous problems themselves. But they were children and, said New Haven police detective Michael Wuchek, "You need a protector to make it out." Bobby's grandmother had been his. "I loved my grandmother with all my heart," Bobby said. "She raised me. After she died, I didn't listen. If she'd been healthy, it wouldn't have happened."

Chapter Eight

August 1, 2006, was for Bobby a long, lazing summer afternoon of teenage back and forth, standing with his friends outside the 2-4, and then crossing Bassett Street to Visels Pharmacy to buy and drink a kiwi-strawberry juice while browsing magazines and conversing with the young women who worked the counter. Even though Bobby and his friend Kwame were distracting his employees, the store owner, Edmund Funaro, enjoyed the pair. "Always good kids," the pharmacist said. "We had a good time together. We'd talk, I'd get to know some of their problems. They could come in whenever they wanted." It was now the midst of a heat wave, over ninety degrees outside, and Visels was one of the only public places in the neighborhood that had air conditioning.

As Bobby and Kwame would remember the early evening of August 1, Kwame was over at the 2-4 while Bobby stood inside Visels, talking with his friend Bounce. Bounce worked his daily shift at the front counter from midafternoon until closing time, at eight p.m. Bobby and Kwame were in the habit of accompanying him across the street afterward to the 2-4. A few minutes before eight, Bobby heard "lots of commotion" outside, emergency vehicles speeding past. Telling Bounce, "I'll be back," Bobby left the store and walked alone the two blocks down to West Ivy Street, where he came upon "cops. Ambulances. People. Cops had it blocked off. Couldn't go down the street." It was therefore impossible for Bobby to view the crime scene. But he met Sharice, a young woman he knew from school, and "she briefed me on what's going on. All we heard was somebody got shot and killed." He returned to the 2-4.

Kwame stopped by Visels after Bobby left, then pedaled his bike down to check out the commotion on West Ivy, before eventually retracing to the 2-4. Bobby and Kwame were such reliable presences at the two stores, weeks and months later it would be challenging for others to think back and confirm their movements. Had the boys done or even worn something out of character, it might have been noticed. Instead, the consistency of their routines and their familiar presence in the neighborhood made them recede into the landscape. As ever, they were just around. The fateful implications of the bind weren't lost on their friend Bounce, at Visels, who thought, "That shit was crazy. If I wasn't working here, I could have been caught up myself."

That morning, New Haven mayor John DeStefano had given his optimistic city hall press conference in which he'd spoken of how "encouraged" he was about the progress in improving neighborhood safety. Now it was a day later and a different time. DeStefano called a second press conference to proclaim the Fields murder "intolerable." DeStefano's takeaway was the need to "reestablish relationships between police and neighborhoods." For the killers he promised "consequences." Up on the third floor at police headquarters, the members of the detective bureau, known internally as "The Floor," took notice.

As did the *New York Times*. In a 2002 editorial, the newspaper had described a state that "was rapidly dividing into two separate economies and worlds," and now, at the end of 2006, it connected a "level of violent crimes in [New Haven that] has everyone worried," as the physical expression of inequity in one of the country's poorest cities, where so much of the most valuable property was tax-exempt. By the following March, DeStefano's chastened evaluation would be that homicides were "way up" due to young, alienated repeat offenders, especially in Newhallville. Newhallville, the mayor had come to believe, "is like Beirut. A terrible challenge."

Newhallville did not compare to a foreign city subjected to years of shelling and bombardment. Even in a year of many homicides, murders in American cities are statistically rare. And yet the police understood shark and grizzly attacks—how little carnage it took for the residents of a neighborhood to feel in danger. The nationwide average murder clearance rate since the 1960s, when it was over 90 percent, by 2005 had dropped to a devastating 62 percent. In New Haven, between 2000 and 2005, only 52 percent of murders were solved. The majority of the victims in those years were young, male, and Black. When their killers weren't arrested, it undermined the public sense of well-being and fortified those who committed violence. A detective's professional standing always depended upon the ability to close murder cases.

Unlike robberies, all murders are investigated. Yet murders reflect the biases of larger society, and some homicides are accorded more resources by police than others. The mayor didn't call press conferences after every shooting. Kids in Newhallville believed that their murdered Black friends mattered less, that detectives assigned to cases involving young, poor Black men had cynical thoughts about "guilty victims." Yet when Pete Fields was shot, Fields's son Peter was assured by Det. Donald Harrison, "We're gonna get 'em, don't worry." Fields was what street cops and street kids both called "a citizen," a hardworking, law-abiding grandfather and widower, and one who had come up in New Haven with prominent members of the department, Melvin Wearing and Jim Ponteau. Crime solving was inevitably personal, detectives were inevitably human, and the more a victim's biography had in common with that of the detective assigned to a case, the more sympathetically invested the detective might be. All of it made Fields a red-ball murder, alluding to the old railroad practice of signaling track right-of-way priority with a bright semaphore. The situation was alive with pressure, impatience, and also the potential for an emboldened investigator to commit what some in the police department had begun referring to as "underhanded shit."

New cases were assigned in rotation to investigators, and when the Fields murder came to the Floor, it was Michael Quinn's turn to lead the inquiry. Quinn was the son of a police officer, a former high school football lineman, broad-chested and thick at the jib, with a big, open face, warm, friendly eyes that narrowed to a hooded squint when he was displeased, and, as one prosecutor observed, a "rough-and-tumble" way about him. He was a husky cross between the coach Mike Ditka and the actor Billy Baldwin. Another prosecutor thought of him as "mild-mannered and upstanding." Fellow police officers, too, were fond of Quinn, considered him affable and endearing, and when those who hadn't seen him in a while spotted Quinn, they'd come in for a hug. He worked first patrolling low-income housing projects, then spent years in narcotics, and moved on to major crimes. The 1998 murder of a Yale undergraduate, Suzanne Jovin, was national news, and after mishandling by the initial investigators embarrassed the department, it became a high-profile cold case, which Quinn was assigned to. Superiors generally thought well enough of Quinn, except for his habit of not creating a written record of his case progress, leaving everything to a final report. Whether strategy or laziness, that was not showing your work. If there were personal reservations among people who knew him professionally, one was that Quinn got along so well with those he worked with it made him deferential to more assertive colleagues.

QUINN COULD BEGIN the Fields investigation with known data about shootings in cities like New Haven. Most involve poor, not-highly educated young men who have already been exposed to violence, either as a shooter or a victim. In the years around 2006, a morbid coincidence was that, like the Fields homicide, murders happened most often on Tuesdays, because, according to historian of violence Roger Lane, "It's kids who are unemployed." Personal disputes over old slights, women, or a trodden sneaker far more often lead to murder than robberies do. People who commit armed street robberies typically display a convincer to quicken the victim's decision to hand over valuables. If the targets of street robberies are frequently unknown to the perpetrator, that doesn't make them randomly chosen. Robberies take place on terrain, and under conditions, that are familiar to the stickup person, circumstances that offer a sense of control.

And then sometimes a victim resists, the interaction escalates, there's alarm, rushing emotion, panic, an impulsive decision. When street robbers do suddenly shoot, a common explanation is that someone whose primary social connection is to the streets is protecting their street status, which is crucial to success and safety. The decisive factor can be the so-called audience effect: another person known to the armed robber watches the unfolding event, and so the robber feels backing down would display weakness. To be thwarted by an unarmed elderly man seat-belted into his car—that could get around.

Killing under any circumstances is difficult for most people, and firing a gun at someone up close is most challenging because it makes murder so intimate and personal. Drive-by shootings aren't just committed with getaway in mind; it's that taking shots from a passing car has the advantage of distancing. Rare is the person who can hold up a gun to another person's neck and execute him point-blank. Atypical again is the person who can conquer the taboo against premeditated killing without the support of drugs or alcohol—a cup of courage. When Toni Morrison's murderous character Guitar says, "I hate doing it. I'm afraid to do it. It's hard to do it when you aren't angry or drunk or doped up or don't have a personal grudge against the person," she was writing fiction and telling the well-researched truth. In any neighborhood, few people could fit this description, and Newhallville was no different.

Such facts were important, because detection often involved unstable elements. Looking back on his career, a retired New York detective named Michael Race told journalist Jim Dwyer that of the 750 cases he'd been assigned, only one investigation was done "the correct way, from A to Z." True detective stories tended to remain elliptical narratives, made up of scraps, fragments, lacunae, and omissions, some of them contradictory, joined up at crazy angles, cases deemed decisive even if it was never explicable in the end what-all had happened.

In New Haven, the consistent explanation given by detectives for the department's declining solve rates was that few people would help them. Since nobody wanted to be seen talking with a detective, detectives learned to work unseen. Most would never hand their business card to someone in public or ask a source to come by the police station. Instead, statements were taken in kitchens and suburban diners, somewhere out by the highway. Whatever they were told inevitably led detectives to theories, so a quality prized in detectives was the disciplined resistance to forming firm early conclusions.

The Fields shooting took place in fading daylight before several eyewitnesses in cars and on porches, at least one of them a local teenage coeval of the two perpetrators. One or more witnesses almost certainly recognized Pete Fields's killer. But these terrified witnesses weren't going to tell Michael Quinn that. Instead, Quinn received what you typically got from startled witnesses—vague descriptions, sometimes in conflict with one another. It was agreed that two young Black men in casual clothing had committed the crime, one taller, leaner, and lighter, the other shorter, stockier, and darker. They'd sprinted down the street to Fields's car, appeared at the front windows, and after Fields resisted, the man at the driver's side fired one gunshot. The two young men then flurried around the car before fleeing to the corner and to the right down Dixwell. They left behind both the expelled bullet and the palm print on the passenger door, both available for crime-lab analysis.

Quinn never seemed intrigued by these evidentiary gifts he'd been given. Investigators typically met with a supervisor and the technician to decide what would be "sent up" to the lab for processing, and Quinn made no request for handprint analysis. Ballistics reports were mandatory in homicide cases, and while the crime lab was notoriously "backlogged forever," as one detective said, it was perfectly acceptable to ask your superiors to request fast-track testing. Quinn didn't do that either. This approach was so contrary to his own interests that to other detectives it seemed at best obtuse. Instead, Quinn put his ear to the streets.

Quinn lacked Donald Harrison's large, reliable network of Newhallville sources, and enough days passed that Quinn later said he felt the Fields investigation had grown "kind of cold." In such moments, some detectives turned to the murky entity known as the registered confidential informant. Confidential informants were, by definition, transactional people, and plenty of detectives from the Floor avoided "stoolies" because, as one said, "informants tell you what they think you want to hear." They were "criminals and junkies" who "wanted a deal or money. It was shortcuts, and it blows up in your face." Quinn would later say in sworn testimony that during his career he never recalled using them during a homicide or shooting investigation.

Here, he said he pursued a more casual variation of the practice, distributing what he called "throwing-around money." These were twenty-dollar bills he handed to alcoholics in front of Newhallville liquor stores, addicts who kept near the location where they bought drugs, "drug dealers hanging out," and prostitutes—the people, Quinn said, "who are around stuff, and they know that they can make, you know, a quick buck with some information." In other words, sources whose needs made them value money more than discretion. Quinn expected dishonesty from those he spoke with. "Everyone lies that talks to me at some point," he said.

Those twenty-dollar inducements left Quinn nowhere until, his report says, he suddenly "developed information that a B/M [Black male] named Bob . . . was responsible for the shooting of Fields." That Bobby was never referred to as Bob was the sort of detail good detectives noticed, because people were precise about names; if the name wasn't right, the person might not be either. Unmentioned in Quinn's report was who first told him "Bob" was "responsible." Skipping ahead, Quinn wrote that once he had this name, it led him to "Howard," who was "Bobby's grandfather," a resident of neighboring Hamden who'd made incriminating statements about his grandson. Years later, Quinn would broaden his explanation, saying that this "old gentleman" had been playing in a regular card game held at a local garage and was "running his mouth that his grandson may have been involved in the shooting." Quinn claimed, "That was really the tip that broke the case open." The "gentleman" was Grandma's fiancé, Chubby, who wasn't named Howard, wasn't Bobby's actual grandfather.

To his own sons, like Uncle Mikey, Chubby was the "handsome, no-hype," warm and funny father who cooked hams, turkeys, and cakes and pies with Grandma. But one of Grandma's granddaughters, who very much liked Chubby, said "if he was a straight-up guy with us in the family, with friends he performed. If he caught a goldfish, he'd say he caught a baby shark! He liked to elaborate."

Chubby did regularly play cards, as part of a group of older Black Southern-born men who met up after work at "the Shop," a garage near the Hamden–Newhallville line owned by a much-admired man named Walter McCain. The Shop was similar to the Mudhole—old photographs and vintage car parts on display, regulars playing poker, telling stories, others stopping in to sell pheasant or raccoon they'd shot or fresh-caught fish. It was, said the grandson of another Shop regular, "male-performative. It was almost a secret club with its own rules. Men displayed a more social and talkative side. My grandfather was that way. More talkative than with his family." The men of the Shop knew Bobby because he sometimes came by to see Chubby.

Police interest in Bobby, according to McCain, "all started with Chubby running his mouth" at the Shop, where some days after the Fields murder Chubby offered that he'd heard someone say "his step-grandson did it." McCain believed Chubby did this because of his way of talking for effect at the Shop: "You can't put a foot on what Chubby will say. Tell you a lie for no reason at all. He wanted to get into conversations!"

A couple of days later, when McCain himself casually passed on what Chubby had said to some others, in earshot was a short man who sometimes came around the Shop nicknamed Speed Limit. This was a paid police informant. Immediately, McCain said, "Speed Limit ran with it." Michael Quinn soon appeared at the Shop and talked with Speed Limit. A day or two passed, Quinn returned, went up to Speed Limit and, McCain said, "I was right there when he gave him $200. Speed Limit was bad." When Quinn returned a third time, with him was a Black detective McCain knew, Clarence Willoughby. While McCain said Quinn took Chubby out for a talk in his car, Willoughby looked at McCain, "shook his head," and then "Willoughby told me [Bobby] didn't do it. He said that boy didn't do that." McCain had considered Willoughby "well-respected" in Newhallville because "he knew the community." But Chubby said McCain later warned him about Willoughby: "Don't get close to him. He'll betray you." As for who had killed Fields, McCain recalled "so many rumors went around." One was that people who'd committed the murder were implicating Bobby. In time, said McCain, "other young guys," including his son, "told me that boy didn't do it. I heard the person that did it got killed."

Shop talk was loose by nature, but a detective needed to be relentless in how he confirmed information. Quinn would write that Chubby told him he had no firsthand knowledge, had only heard a "street" rumor Bobby "was with the shooter." And years later, Chubby insisted only McCain had spoken of Bobby: "I don't know who Quinn is. When cops came looking for me, I said, "No, no, you got the wrong one.' I wasn't involved. Never the source of it. Them cops, they lied on it." At the possibility of Bobby executing anyone point-blank, Chubby was always incredulous—"You kidding me!" Bobby, he would say, was then still a little boy, and incapable of harming a flea. If a mouse was in the house, he added, Bobby'd run away—"That's how scared he is. Scared of his own shadow."

The tip from Speed Limit was pursued. On the afternoon of August 15, Quinn and his white colleague Marc Calafiore went to Bobby's home. When a knock came at the front door, Bobby and Kwame were in Bobby's first-floor bedroom smoking weed and listening to hip-hop, and Bobby's mother and sisters were in their own rooms. According to Bobby, the detectives "didn't give me no option" about whether or not to go with them. At the time, Bobby believed that nobody in his family saw this, but Bobby's sister Shavonne recalls a detective taking her brother's arm, leading him outside. Calafiore claimed to remember none of these events, but said they likely happened because "I did it all the time, spoke to multiple people on the street formally and informally." As they left, watching Bobby walk away was Kwame, taller, slimmer and lighter-skinned than Bobby, with what Quinn called "a large, unkempt afro." This aroused the detective's curiosity, even though the witnesses had said the second participant in the murder wore his hair in braids.

The two white detectives drove the sixteen-year-old Black boy downtown to police headquarters and brought him through a back entrance upstairs to the third floor, where there were two interrogation rooms separated by a lounge area for detectives. Nobody was ever obligated to say a word during an interrogation, a truth so at odds with the detective's objectives that most never used the word "interrogation," preferring "interview." To others they referred to the interrogation room blandly as the statement room. Among themselves, however, it was the Box. Interrogations existed to pry information from people who were often reluctant to offer it. Some detectives first left a subject alone, allowing the sides of the Box to close in a little. Then the detective would enter and pleasantly seek to relieve anxiety. If the subject felt gratitude for the company, rapport could be built.

Interrogations were divided into a "pre-interview" session, which could last several hours. Successful pre-interviews led to trial runs that might culminate in formal "statements" from witnesses or suspects. These statements were "memorialized" on handheld audiotape recording machines controlled during the inquiry by a detective who was expected to announce every time the On or Off button was used. Statements tended to be brief.

Videotaping police confessions had begun in the early 1970s, and while police had many misgivings, including that the camera might inhibit subjects (or detectives), by 1992, a report submitted to the National Institute of Justice found that most surveyed police believed videotaping strengthened cases and increased legitimacy. As long as the camera was, in fact, running, interrogations were transparent, and offered the opportunity to study nonverbal behavior. New Haven's policy, in 2006, of using only audiotapes and not recording pre-interviews meant that recorded statements existed in the context of no context. As an experienced New Haven criminal defense lawyer explained, "Pre-interviews were to sanitize the [eventual] statement, and no notes were made. Zero. So there's nothing that will contradict the tape. Even if they did take notes, they never preserved them." Keeping notes was requisite policy, and so was logging them into evidence with a copy for the case file. Some detectives didn't do this, but kept them for reference when testifying in court. But for others, notes were risky documentation. One detective wondered, "Can you trust everybody with access to the files? Some people who work at the police department, can you trust their allegiances?"

Without notes, should a suspect later complain in court about a detective's unscrupulous interrogation methods, it would be the word of someone accused of murder against that of sworn police. Implicit was that what happened unrecorded in the Box stayed in the Box.

The detectives led Bobby through a door marked STATEMENT IN PROGRESS. The door was shut, and Bobby found himself alone. It was a small room, unadorned. Three mismatched chairs faced a table; the two for detectives had wheels, and the third, for subjects, could not be rolled. The carpet was dull gray, the walls a garish white, with the table off to the side, so detectives had no buffer protecting their subject from them. Within the drop ceiling, a fluorescent lamp burned. It was stuffy. The one window looked out on the railroad station across the street, and the subject's back was always kept to it for the same reason there was no clock: thoughts of leaving were not encouraged.

"I was so high," Bobby remembered, but he believed "it didn't affect the situation because I was so used to smoking." Eventually, Bobby was joined by the two detectives and also Donald Harrison. They gave Bobby an orange soda and asked about the murder on West Ivy Street. When he said he didn't know what had gone on, they asked "if I'd had anything to do with the incident. I said, 'Nothing to do with it.'" When the detectives persisted, saying "they heard rumors I did it," Bobby told them to ask people at Visels, ask Kwame or Sharice. All would vouch for him. The detectives promised to. They put in front of Bobby photographs of several other teenagers from the neighborhood, including Major and BlackJack. The detectives told Bobby that rumors of their involvement were all over Newhallville. Any thoughts? Whatever Bobby had heard, he wasn't going to say; Major, for one, terrified him. Soon the session ended without the detectives recording anything. If notes were made and placed in an evidence bag, as Quinn would claim, they never surfaced. Quinn's final report states Bobby changed his account of his whereabouts several times. Quinn had thought the boy with the unkempt afro Quinn had noticed at Bobby's house resembled witness descriptions of the other murderer. So Quinn asked Bobby his friend's name. This person Quinn had decided was a crafty story-changer, here readily said his friend's name was "Kwame."

As detectives were driving Bobby back to Willis Street, one began speaking on his phone. He finished and told Bobby that Pete Fields's "wife" was an eyewitness to the murder. They turned down West Ivy Street. "Look! She's right there!" said Quinn. It was Ella. "She was short, light-skinned, old," Bobby said. If they hoped Ella would identify Bobby as Pete's killer, it didn't happen. "She walked up to the car," Bobby said. "She had no idea who I was."

Back at home, Grace got the impression from Bobby that "he thought they were talking with people in the neighborhood to find out what happened." Bobby wasn't unsettled by the experience, he said, because Detective Harrison had reassured him, "You're a good kid. We investigate lots of people in such situations." Calafiore was convinced Bobby wasn't involved. As for Harrison, he had a vacation scheduled, and now left the case for Disney World.

Down in the police lockup that day was a handsome teenager who was about to be charged with riding his bike up on another kid and shooting him in the leg. This was Sway, whose photograph was also among those the police showed Bobby. According to Quinn's report, because Sway was from

Newhallville, Quinn asked him about the Fields murder. Whether Quinn proposed cooperation in exchange for concessions related to Sway's own legal troubles, Quinn never said. Sway told Quinn he'd ridden his bike to the West Ivy Street crime scene where he'd overheard someone named Tim say Bee had done it. Who was this Bee, Quinn asked? Sway told Quinn that Bee was from Willis Street, and often stood with Tim in front of the 2-4. Quinn said he showed Sway a photograph of Bobby, and Sway confirmed that was Bee. Then Quinn brought up Kwame, and Sway confirmed for Quinn that Kwame sometimes wore his hair in braids. Sway refused to tape a statement or provide any information about Tim.

Nobody called Bobby Bee, while people commonly used this shorthand for BlackJack. Plenty of officers and detectives were familiar with BlackJack and also Sway, as kids from the Moe's Market part of Newhallville, near West Ivy Street. Both were deep in the streets. "The problem," explained Archie Generoso, a retired police administrator and state investigator who would later return to lead the detective bureau, was that BlackJack was "very tight with Sway. When they ask him, he says, 'Bee did it.' Who was Bee? When they ask him, he says, 'Bobby,' because [Sway's] tight with BlackJack." A Connecticut criminal defense lawyer said police routinely underestimate the savvy of young men in the streets: "Their narrative, when it's the truth, is often far different from what the police think happened. They're sharp like wizards." A devious way to avoid being arrested for a daylight murder might be to spread word implicating kids who both resemble you and are afraid of you.

Kwame did wear braids sometimes, but so did BlackJack's lean, light-skinned cousin Major, who otherwise matched witness descriptions of Pete Fields's killer, and then had perhaps the most violent reputation in the neighborhood. He was currently being investigated for committing two other recent homicides, one a case Quinn had participated in. But Quinn later claimed Major "wasn't on my radar," and before he conferred with Sway, pretty clearly he was already fixed on Bobby and Kwame as his suspects. Bobby himself would speculate the reason Sway threw him to Quinn was "maybe he thought I was the weakest link, the least threat to anybody." Bobby had never heard of a Tim who frequented the 2-4—"I don't know who the heck that is"—and Quinn never reported locating Tim. Instead, he took Tim at Sway's word, went and found Kwame, and brought the fourteen-year-old boy downtown.

Because Kwame was an unaccompanied minor, Quinn could not interrogate him. So he misrepresented this session as questioning a witness rather than a suspect interview. Yet he asked Kwame what he'd worn back on August 1, whether his hair was ever in braids. The answers were that he had on shorts and a T-shirt, and sometimes had braids. Quinn left out whether Kwame said—or whether Quinn had even asked—if Kwame had worn braids on August 1. Instead, Quinn let the session nurture his theory: "As a result of this interview, the undersigned began to believe that Kwame may have been involved in the shooting." When Kwame returned home, he told his guardian aunt, Julia Sykes, that he'd been interviewed by police as a murder suspect. "Kwame had never been in trouble before," Sykes would remember. "He seemed upset. He didn't understand. He seemed scared. Nervous."

Quinn did not go show photo boards or images of Bobby and Kwame to the crime witnesses. Some witnesses, like the community organizers who'd been at a house directly across the street from Pete Fields, Quinn never even contacted. Nor did he visit the 2-4 or Visels to check alibis or search for August 1 video feeds. Quinn was now on a path, had begun, as he wrote, to believe.

University of Michigan law professor Samuel Gross, a former litigator as well as an expert on wrongful conviction, said Quinn's approach was "typical of places with heavy dockets. There's a homicide in the Black community. So you go round up people and interrogate them until one confesses or turns on somebody else. You get the impression they're throwing a lot against the wall, seeing what sticks. Happens in Detroit. Happens in Philadelphia. I've seen it many times." Quinn was working a dragnet of vague suspicion that led him to look warily at kids who were just around, Quinn making no real attempt to know them as individuals, even though he must have been aware that few people are capable of executing a stranger. If he'd asked Walter McCain or Edmund Funaro, Quinn would have heard how unlikely it was that Bobby and Kwame were killers. But to be just around in a neighborhood like Newhallville made it so much easier for police like Quinn to assume you were involved in a serious crime, and more difficult for you to prove you weren't there. Because you were always there.

It was now that Clarence Willoughby, the Black detective McCain knew, became all-involved. Willoughby's size and reputation were such he answered to nicknames like "Big Time." Beginning in 1990, Willoughby claimed to have a 100 percent career solve rate on the murder investigations he led, a perfect record he said he tabulated himself since individual career statistics weren't compiled by the department. Willoughby had achieved his perfect record by solving—here, he could only estimate—somewhere between one hundred and five hundred cases. Officially in those years, there were a total of 363 murder cases, with 261 of them solved. Willoughby attributed his success to what McCain had said, that Willoughby knew Newhallville.

To white law enforcement officials in New Haven, Willoughby had unrivaled access to what was, for them, a foreign land. A white former detective said that even with cases Willoughby wasn't working, if you let him know the job involved Newhallville, he was eager to join in: "Clarence knew everybody in the Ville. He'd say to me, I'll go talk to him because I know that boy's mama." Prosecutors considered Willoughby indispensable to their work. "You couldn't try a case without the involvement of Willoughby," one said. "He had all the confidential informants. He was in every case. We thought he was a real bright detective we could depend upon. 'What do you need?' he'd always ask us, and he could get it. It's difficult to get cases off the ground. He was great. We loved him."

Part of Willoughby's mystique was the mystery of his methods. "He used to go talk to people in the neighborhood," said Michael Dearington, then New Haven's presiding prosecutor. "We didn't fully understand his MO." This could be overlooked because Willoughby's difference from the rest of the detective staff seemed the essential point. He was not a technician committed to the slow accumulation of detail. Willoughby was a carnivore in the competitive game of case solving. "He was no joke," a Newhallville minister said of Willoughby in his prime. "Hunting all the guys. He knew the players. They knew him. He would try to make it happen. Any way he could, he was gonna do it."

When Pete Fields was murdered, Willoughby had been on his annual August summer holiday, resting in the blue ranch house he owned out in West Haven. He later explained that earlier in his vacation, Speed Limit, who was his former brother-in-law and a paid informant he regularly worked with, "came by my house. He said Bobby—he said Bobby did the job on Ivy Street." Willoughby explained he'd then checked to see who was the lead detective on the case, and told Speed Limit how to contact Quinn. No informant use at all is mentioned in police reports from the case. After Bobby was first questioned by Quinn and Calafiore and taken home, Willoughby said he'd heard from a detective down at police headquarters: "Big Man, you need to get in here. They said they couldn't crack him." Willoughby called his supervisor, explained that he'd supplied "the name of the guy . . . They couldn't get a confession." To the supervisor, Willoughby declared, "I will come in and do it."

On Sunday afternoon, September 3, Bobby was watching TV in his first-floor room when a knock came at the front door. Standing there again was Michael Quinn, and Bobby saw that with him this time was a "tall dark-skinned man. Aggressive look. He was in a suit. Black suit. Red tie." Despite Willoughby's reputation around Newhallville, Bobby had never heard of him. "You need to come with me," Willoughby said. Grace was at home. Bobby said, "She told me to see what they want. I never thought to ask if my mother could come. I didn't do this crime they were saying. I felt I didn't need my mom."

WILLOUGHBY'S PARENTS WERE from South Carolina, and part of his own childhood was lived in Newhallville—"Right in the heart of it." Willoughby considered Newhallville to be "a rough place. They don't let outsiders in. Newhallville is different than any place I ever worked. They stick together. Only place I ever seen where you're not from there, we'll jump on you, but as soon as you leave, we go back fighting each other. Violent people are everywhere in Newhallville. I loved it when I lived there, though. The sense of belonging." Willoughby spent time at Talladega College in Alabama, an institution founded by two former enslaved men, where, Willoughby said, two important lessons taught him were: "You cannot shoot a rabbit out of hunting season, but n—rs are always in season. And you can be eighty years old and still be a boy in Alabama." After two years, Willoughby left school and returned to New Haven, where a Black detective named Odell Cohens, who'd known him as a child, recommended him for the police department.

Back in 1967, New Haven's four-day version of the street uprisings happening then in Black communities from Newark to Watts took place in the Hill neighborhood. A chief catalyst was determined to be the abysmal relationship between the city's police and the Black community. Part of that problem, in turn, was the lack of Black police officers. Only after "the Hill riots" was a Black officer first promoted to sergeant in New Haven.

A dozen years later, when he now joined the police department, Willoughby was six-four and lithe-muscled like the high school small forward he'd once been, with such long, fast-moving legs, as a younger police officer they earned him a nickname, partly for how he looked as he ran down fleeing criminals—Horsy. "He hit the fences like a gazelle," said one appreciative colleague. Willoughby walked the beat, worked in narcotics, but from the start, he was watching the detectives. The early generations of Black investigators in the city were few in number, and mostly part of the Great Migration community like Buffaloe, Wearing, Ponteau, and Gil Burton. Donald Morris, the Newhallville minister, said, "those guys came up and became detectives. It was, You're detectives! That's *all right*! They were proud of them. When we came up, detectives were mostly white. We didn't think it would happen for Black men in the city of New Haven. Big thing."

To Willoughby, the detectives had irresistible glamour. They dressed well, and when they appeared at a crime scene, they arrived from stage right, brushing aside the uniformed cops as people exclaimed, "The Big Boys are here!" Willoughby recalled, "I used to watch the guys wear nice suits, and walking around with a [case] folder in their hand. I had one suit myself at that time. So, I said I could do that job. I could walk around with a folder. And I got the suit." With Buffaloe's, Wearing's, and Ponteau's support, in 1990 he made the grade. To Wearing, the future chief, Willoughby was "almost a son I tutored."

Detective work, Willoughby found, "was pretty easy for me because I'm from the neighborhood. The same thing I was doing for free, they were paying me to do. If something happens in your neighborhood, right? You went down there, the whole crowd runs down there, right? First thing you do is [ask] Who shot so and so? Jimmy. Jimmy who? Jimmy Brown. That's the same thing the detective does. People in the neighborhood knows who do the stuff. Will they tell you? That's the one thing you gotta get." Willoughby had charisma that made people want to tell him things, and to go with it, he said, was his capacity for "drinking, partying, beer, liquor, whatever," that allowed him to sit with them deep into the night at the bars and clubs around Newhallville until they were ready to reveal what they knew.

As Willoughby's mentors retired, the working conditions for police investigation were shifting. A Black assistant chief named Herb Sharp explained years later that what had made men like Buffaloe and Ponteau effective were "the relationships they had in the community. Them guys knew everybody and everybody knew them. They loved those guys, felt they could talk to them." Among the most respected of these older detectives was Gil Burton, a huge, gentle man who'd become a police officer in the 1960s, after coming to New Haven as a teenager from North Carolina. When Burton retired, in 1998, he took Willoughby aside and told him that with his contacts, if he wanted, Willoughby could run the city. But Burton warned him the job was perilous, because of the power it offered. "Some go bad when they become a detective," Burton observed. "They go bad because they think they're God.

They think they know everything. It boils down to the person himself. The guys who it goes bad for forget the people are human."

The handsome Willoughby now cut a large figure in a small city, a hard-boiled solver of murders who built his flamboyant image with the beautiful lines of what he wore and what he drove. "You had to dress," Willoughby said. "You gotta have a *car,* you know?" A tailor counseled him to buy inexpensive suits, which the tailor then rebuilt so that they molded to his frame, Willoughby thought, "like a glove." There were one hundred suits hanging in his closet, and resting below were one hundred pairs of shoes chosen to match. The preference with footwear was for alligator. Early on Willoughby drove a Camaro, and after that it was all Jaguars and Mercedes. A man who played cards with him said "he always had on a suit, even for poker. And he always had a lot of money. He'd pull a stack of bills out of his pocket."

A substantial portion of Willoughby's income came from overtime he earned as a finisher, solving cases that stymied other detectives. "I know the streets, and they didn't," he said. "The police department didn't understand the working of the streets." By 2006, up on the Floor, Willoughby was a divisive figure, celebrated by his superiors for his willingness to take on and solve homicides, and denounced by other detectives who were skeptical of his methods and disliked his unwillingness to share what he knew, claimed that instead of collaborating with colleagues he moved in on their cases. John Velleca, a white detective who would later serve as the department's acting chief, watched Willoughby proclaiming his successes and said, "We thought he was full of shit, would arrest anybody." It was Velleca's belief that Willoughby used "fictitious informants" and seemed to keep no records as he worked cases. "The culture of policing at the time," Velleca said, was "cutting corners." Because supervisors "put so much emphasis on clearing the numbers, they didn't care who you arrested."

Velleca was far from alone in his views. Many of the department's detectives, both Black and white, eventually considered Willoughby to be so shifty they refused to partner with him. It was a similar dynamic out in the neighborhood; some thought Willoughby a valiant community avenger, while others considered him to be absolutely ruthless.

HOMICIDE DETECTIVES HAVE all day, every day, for what is known as the "evidence focus" of an open investigation. Thorough detectives might informally canvass neighborhoods for new sources; examine cell-tower location data and telephone records; review closed-circuit and surveillance camera feeds; talk with bus and taxi drivers who might have either seen something useful as they passed by or picked up a significant passenger; show photo boards to witnesses; press for the expedited processing of physical evidence; pursue hunches, what-ifs, and speculations. Yet because Willoughby (and Quinn) in the end claimed all but one page of their notes were lost or buried in the police property room, what procedural work Willoughby had done since joining the case was unknown. Over at Visels, the owner, Edmund Funaro, said he had the capability to bring up video evidence of "anything internal" that had happened within his store. He couldn't recall any police officers coming in following the murder to check whether Bobby had been there, as Bobby told the police. After leaving Visels, Bobby said he encountered Sharice, but she, too, was never contacted by the detectives. There was this: Uncle Mikey, Chubby's son, was outside his father's house one day when Willoughby appeared, dressed in what looked to Mikey like a bespoke Italian suit. Willoughby asked to talk with Chubby. To Mikey it was apparent "he didn't know him." Chubby would later explain he did encounter Willoughby once at the Shop, but hadn't ever talked with him. Mysterious is why Willoughby pressed on as he did after telling Walter McCain at the Shop that Bobby wasn't the killer. McCain, however, did know Willoughby some. McCain remembered an emotional moment when "Willoughby told me one time he regretted some of the things he did when he was younger."

The evidence focus of an investigation ends when the suspect focus begins. Once Bobby became Willoughby's quarry, Willoughby looked upon Bobby with an impersonal eye as the latest opponent in what he conceived as a fundamental contest: his job is to get away, my job is to get him. Willoughby said later "my mindset was he did it. I'm gonna get him to tell me he did it."

Willoughby and Quinn drove Bobby downtown in an unmarked staff car, and Bobby was brought up to the same spare room where he'd been in August. His seventeenth birthday was over a month away. Left alone, he grew bored. There are criminal gangs that prepare younger members for how to handle a police interrogation. Innocent young people are inevitably more guileless with investigators.

After half an hour, the door opened, and Willoughby strode in. Quinn handed Bobby a can of grape soda and a bag of chips, and then Willoughby began addressing Bobby in a stern tone. "He *knows* I did it," Bobby later said. "He's not letting me leave." But Willoughby told him, because he "knew"

Chubby, "he'd help me get out of the situation. I told him I had nothing to do with it." Bobby said that each time he repeated that he hadn't killed anybody, Willoughby would "get more aggressive."

There were myriad ways to convince a murder suspect to confess. By law, anyone is free to leave an interrogation unless they are under arrest. With that in mind, New Haven detectives typically treated those they were interviewing with courtesy, offering them bathroom use or a beverage. If the subject was hungry, the detectives might take a McDonald's order. One detective who didn't smoke cigarettes always carried a pack of Kools into interviews, and if a man accepted the offer, the detective would light up with him. The better to bond under a mutual cloud of smoke. Interrogation was an intensely private interaction, and most who were "good in the Box" had a Box persona, conceiving of themselves there as ministers or fishing buddies. They confided truths of their own lives to create trust. Telephone books didn't extract honest confessions; agile, patient people did.

A standard interview technique was to ask questions and then wait, so the subject would feel compelled to fill the silent space with words. Other detectives were more convivial, chatty forward-leaners earnestly seeking help in understanding events they said they found confusing. Willoughby, however, regarded interrogation as a siege in which he exerted his will—and he expressed all compulsions legally available to him in making a brutal world a little less brutal. Willoughby felt confident Bobby was like every murderer. Eventually, he would feel the relief of unburdening himself. That made Willoughby an impatient man with all the time. "Everybody wants to talk," Willoughby once said. "You just got to drag it out of them sometimes."

Willoughby sought confessions with such single-minded determination because no evidence is more persuasive to a jury than a confession. In medieval times on the European continent, the Latin phrase *Confessio est regina probationum* asserted that a confession was the queen of proofs—such a desirable confirmation of guilt that when there was probable cause, but only partial evidence, torture was an acceptable means of extricating the full "proof." (If you had no idea where the murder weapon was, the thinking went, you'd emerge with wounds but would avoid the gallows.) Investigators have always been tempted to press too hard for confessions because, as Steven Drizin and Richard Leo found in their landmark study of 125 confessions later proven to be false, "Confessions (even if they are demonstrably false) almost always seal the defendant's fate."

Aggressive police interviewing tactics have historically been so common in the United States that among English police they became known as "The American Method." American police officers have used such confession encouragements as rubber hoses, the "water cure" of pouring liquid up a suspect's nose, the dental torture of drilling into the nerves of teeth, extreme heat or lighting or sound or lack of sleep. Nobody can say, of course, how common such methods have been across time, but they represent the belief among police that only the guilty will break. Samuel Gross said his study of all people exonerated since 1989 told him "coerced confessions are usually true! The problem is, not always." Judges have also long known this, and one of them, Jerome Frank, noticed "when a police official declares that he tortures no one but criminals, he unwittingly exposes the real menace of the third degree: he is asserting the police have a right, without trial, to determine the guilt of an arrested person." Frank said in *Not Guilty*, his study of wrongful conviction, that a consequence of such behavior was the notable American distrust of the police and lack of cooperation with investigators.

In his book *How the Police Generate False Confessions*, the former homicide detective James L. Trainum writes, "Innocent people get caught up in police investigations all the time . . . Because most people believe that they would never confess to a crime they did not do, they don't see how it is possible in others." Clarence Willoughby was very much that way. His operational policy was nobody sitting in an interrogation room would voluntarily say anything against their own significant interest. Embedded in that belief was freedom for a detective. It meant coercion, too, was impossible.

Interrogation was an ancient art, but there was no codex, no golden mean. Instead, Willoughby's method for interrogating suspects followed features of the Reid technique, a popular modern method of police interrogation developed in the 1950s by a former Chicago police officer named John E. Reid. The Reid technique guidelines called first for fact-finding and then initial nonaccusatory assessment interviews with people potentially involved in the crime. If these phases pointed to a suspect, next came an interrogation applying psychological pressure. In pursuing the grail of confession, interrogators were told to begin with what in New Haven was called the "pre-interview," the un-recorded portion of the interrogation. Pre-interview was a misnomer; it was all interrogation. The Reid recommendation was for using a folder as a prop, the detective perhaps even waving it as he explained that all the evidence within proved the suspect's guilt. Detectives were to emphatically reject the inevitable suspect denials, even while evaluating the quality of the denials for plausibility. Convincing criminals to confess was understood to be so challenging that the Reid technique sanctioned behavior by investigators which for civilians would be considered unethical—such as misleading or even outright lying to suspects. It was sometimes effective to propose to suspects a justification for committing the crime that, as presented, might seem exculpatory, when of course it was not. The Reid technique recommended that the investigator intimidate the suspect by gradually drawing physically closer, imposing a looming proximity. No suspect was ever to be a match for the interrogator's high energy and purpose. Protestations of innocence should be ignored. When the suspect gave up and confessed, the interrogator collaborated with the suspect in organizing a complete narrative of confession. This culmination of the process led to what the New Haven police referred to as "memorializing." Only this did they capture on tape.

The Reid technique could be very effective if used by an honorable interrogator, but it overstated a city detective's ability to decipher human guilt by scrutinizing behavior. Studies of law enforcement have found that only the Secret Service is significantly better than college students in reading guilt into personal expressions or mannerisms. There was the legitimate danger that after hours of relentless grilling, an innocent person would falsely confess to make it stop. John Reid himself had once induced a false confession from a murder suspect after nine hours in a windowless room. For obvious reasons, there is no ready supply of tapes or transcripts from coerced confessions. But lawyers always knew behind-the-scenes coercion was commonplace, as did many others, including novelist Richard Wright, whose lengthy account of an unsuspecting Black man being "sweated" into falsely confessing to murder by white police, in the short 1941 novel *The Man Who Lived Underground*, is uncannily consistent with what modern researchers have learned. "Well, boy," the police tell the man. "We're going to keep you right here until you tell us what you did." Then, as time plods on and the suspect becomes "hypnotized" by the endless unreality of the experience and his desire to return to his pregnant wife, the police ask, "Don't you want to see your wife, boy?" And then, "Just sign your name and we'll take you home."

American law held that duplicity by interrogating police was permissible, so long as the deception would not compel an innocent person to confess. What might cross the line was left to the judgment of police officers. By rule, to gain a confession Willoughby and Quinn could not use physical force, threaten long prison sentences, or promise leniency. But the reality was the two detectives had full discretionary powers in the Box and no neutral person or camera overseeing them. Unless Quinn should object, Willoughby was working unregulated.

Willoughby and Quinn's pre-interview of Bobby went on for hours and, said Bobby, "Willoughby did all the work. You barely heard Quinn." Willoughby led with finality. "We know you did this," he announced. When Bobby denied it, Willoughby (falsely) told Bobby that he'd gone over to West Ivy Street, where it had been easy for the detective to find people who told him they'd seen Bobby commit the crime. Bobby insisted he'd been at Visels. "We checked the cameras," came the reply. "You wasn't on the camera." Then Willoughby told him, "We know you did it." Told him, "Everybody says you did." Told him, "We have eyewitnesses." Told him, "Give up the shit, we can help you out."

It kept going this way. Willoughby falsely informed Bobby his fingerprints had been found on Fields's car. Bobby put out his hands, offered to have them rolled. Willoughby said they knew he'd done it, there was no need to take fingerprints. Whenever Bobby tried to explain himself or propose a way to prove his innocence, Willoughby refused to let him finish. "I asked, 'Can I take a lie detector,' bunch of times," Bobby said. "They always said no." When Bobby began to defend himself from an accusation coming in from the left, immediately he confronted something new veering toward him at starboard. Bobby decided he should ask for a lawyer. Willoughby's answer was "No. We're here trying help you." That refusal was against the law. The "help" Bobby said the detective proposed, ten years' probation in exchange for Bobby's confession, was illegal for him to offer. As Bobby remembered, Willoughby guaranteed his offer, invoking what had become a hip-hop creed of commitment: "My word is my bond. Ten years' probation. I'll make sure of it." Bobby declined.

For Willoughby, there seemed to be a flavor of sport in the proceedings. He told Bobby they had a test that would prove whether he'd fired the murder weapon. Bobby was willing to take it, he said, so "they stripped me to my boxers. They sprayed me with some spray while I was in my boxers. My body, my head and arms. It was supposed to show gun residue." The white spray can didn't have a label, looked unlikely to Bobby, seemed to him like some kind of gag novelty device, perhaps something "from Party City." Bobby's skin began to glow where they'd sprayed him. Willoughby grinned and told him, "You're in trouble now. We got you." Was this a prank?

Bobby never learned what the spray was, and other police later said they knew of nothing like it. The session went on. Bobby said "a white guy with a white forensic coat" was brought in to do a real gunshot residue test (GSR) where, typically, the hand of a suspect is swabbed to reveal trace particle elements of the propellant primer released from a fired weapon. But whoever the man was—other police said nobody at the department worked in a lab coat—he left without performing a GSR. The chair was uncomfortable. The room was warm. By now Bobby's palms were moist, and when they left a damp resting impression on the table, Willoughby noticed and said, "You touched the table. We got you." Then he walked out.

After a break, Willoughby returned and was, said Bobby, "aggressive, yelling in my face." Willoughby's own handsome face had a protean quality. If he wanted you to like him, the face held a sweetness. If he didn't care about you, there was raw lack of pity. The six-foot-four detective stood nearly a foot taller than Bobby. Bobby said, "Me, I'm small. He's a giant." Willoughby was now looming so close, when he raised his voice his saliva sprayed Bobby's eyes. Bobby decided he'd had enough. "I got up and tried to walk out the door. He blocked the door. Told me to sit down. He shoved me towards the seat. I'm sitting there. He says he can give me ten years' probation, and if I didn't take it I'd never see my family again. I was trying to tell him I had nothing to do with it. He wouldn't listen to me." When Bobby still didn't capitulate, the threats grew: "After I was stubborn they threw the death penalty in." Then the detectives left again.

Bobby felt panic. By this point he had no idea how many hours he'd spent in the room. "At the time my mind was all over the place," he said. "I didn't know how to deal with it. I became fearful. I tried to think, What can I do to get out of the situation? My nerves were going crazy. My body's shaking. I didn't know how to handle it." He sat at the table and wondered, "What the hell is gonna come through that door next?"

More pressure. Willoughby showed Bobby six photographs of people from the neighborhood, among them Major and BlackJack, and Willoughby told him that two of them had identified Bobby as the murderer. He declined to say which ones. Some part of Bobby still hadn't caught on to what the detectives were doing. He was too busy to think, trying to repel forms of danger he couldn't immediately identify. If what Willoughby said about neighborhood people was true, it explained why it was Bobby they'd settled on. That anonymous people in Newhallville were throwing him to the detectives filled Bobby with despair. "I thought I was from the hood, I'm tough," he would remember. "They broke me down. Especially the big Black guy."

Willoughby so unnerved him that onward through life Bobby developed a tic that made him unable to pronounce the detective's name. He always said "Willdebee."

Bobby thought of Quinn in contrast to his partner. If Quinn didn't quite fulfill the other half of the good-cop-bad-cop dynamic from old police manuals, the lead detective was to Bobby someone who was going along, following. "Quinn, I try to leave, he blocked me too," Bobby said. "He saying eyewitness said I did it. He said it's only a matter of time before we get you for the crime." Quinn later denied this, claiming his interrogation training had taught him "it's better to be nice to the person." Quinn would assess Willoughby's demeanor during the interview as mild. Willoughby himself said, "I never had to yell at nobody," and insisted that he treated Bobby (and later Kwame) "like gentlemen." He would deny threatening Bobby or Kwame, deny that they'd ever requested a lawyer. He'd reject the idea that he falsely told Bobby or Kwame he had incriminating information, though he agreed with Quinn's belief that "you can lie to them." This seemed reasonable to both because, as Quinn said, lying was a way "to get the truth from them." Willoughby couldn't afterward remember whether he'd threatened Bobby with the death penalty or offered him the leniency of probation. "I might have used that one before," he once said; another time he dismissed the idea. But such methods, he explained, were "allowed." The particular personalities of the detective and the boy were leading to a tragic injustice, but Willoughby noted, the system permitted him.

For Bobby, time with the detectives dragged on, time stood still, time was lost to him, such an enjambment of hours he had no idea how many hours he'd been across the table. That Willoughby was unbending in the face of any alibi Bobby offered made him feel futile—"It seemed so hard to be truthful." He wanted the detectives to believe him, but how? "They didn't care about the inconsistent parts," he would remember. "They clench on the consistent parts."

Bobby decided if he could only get free of this room and these detectives, someone elsewhere could save him. That after all the hours he still hoped for these things had parallels to true beliefs about the neighborhood. If you could only get out, then you'd be treated differently, better would happen for you. But if they let Bobby out, where would he be going but back to the neighborhood. And they wouldn't let him out. Nobody but them knew he was in this room.

It still wasn't clear to Bobby why Willoughby had fastened on him, but

Bobby was growing certain he would never convince him of anything other than what Willoughby already believed. Bobby was tired and terrified, a sparrow squeezed between the cat's paws of police and the neighborhood people he feared too much even to mention by name. Bobby wanted what was happening to stop, wanted more than anything to go home. A culture of accumulated moments had built fantasy-inducing temperature in the room, the desire to control violence, the law asking a boy to save himself while making that impossible, him small beneath all those big piled-up moments. In response, a tempting illusion overtook Bobby. If he was cooperative, the terrifying experience would end and the better one promised by the police could begin. Cognitive dissonance prevailed, things later almost impossible to explain. "So," Bobby said, "I gave them what they wanted. It felt crazy to say I killed a man I never saw in my life, never interacted with, a man I never crossed paths with." He said he would "help," and there it was.

THE DETECTIVES WERE pleased. They moved swiftly to memorialize what Bobby was going to tell them. Yet now that Bobby had agreed to "help," there was a problem. Bobby didn't know the details of the crime. So, he said, "I freestyled it." But not quite. The process turned out to be collaborative, like scriptwriters in a writers' room, two suited detectives and a kid in a T-shirt and shorts working up dialogue for what the detectives now told Bobby was a sidewalk altercation that had turned violent. "I'd start saying the story," Bobby said. "I'd say anything," and "it was like he was leading me towards a story. They'd correct me. It felt weird, but I'm basically giving him what he wanted." This, Bobby said, lasted for another hour, during which Willoughby told him the specifics of the Fields murder. "He was releasing a lot of details what happened to the guy," Bobby said. When Willoughby asked Bobby "who I was with," Bobby didn't know how to answer. So, he said, Willoughby "told me about Terry."

Terry was a teenage relative on Granddad's side of the family, and Bobby said the detectives explained that Terry had committed the crime with Bobby. Shay, who was familiar with all of Bobby's routines, had never heard of him. Bobby knew Terry lived in Newhallville, but, he said, "I wasn't close to Terry. We were just cousins. We didn't hang out. I don't know where he hung out. They were interested in him for the simple fact he's my cousin, we were similar in age. Some guy must have told them [of Terry] because once they decided I was a suspect, they locked in."

Eventually, there had been discussion enough that Willoughby could diagram an outline for Bobby to refer to while he recorded a confession. Willoughby rehearsed Bobby's account of the crime. It began with the boys meeting up at a baseball field on Sherman Parkway, a block west of Dixwell Avenue. They had a gun and both handled it. Then they crossed the Parkway onto West Ivy Street and, right away, came upon a man with whom Terry quarreled, to the fatal result. For the actual memorializing, Quinn took over the interview, back at the lead. "The recorder went on," Bobby said, "and Willoughby didn't exist. Silent bully in the background."

Willoughby would later observe of Bobby that "he wasn't no rocket scientist." Perhaps the detective was remembering Bobby's many factual errors as he described the crime. "I said I shot him standing up, out of his car," Bobby said. "Said I shot him multiple times, because I didn't know how many times the dude got shot. I got the color of the car wrong. Later I found out he had his seat belt on. He never got out of the car." Bobby was tired and also distracted by Willoughby "in my face, giving me that devilish grin." Richard Wright once explained that for a person to falsely confess to murder, "He must wrench his mind loose from his innocent way of thinking and begin thinking cunningly and craftily, begin to think in terms that he never dreamed of before, guilty terms." That also made the recording experience challenging for Bobby, who said, "I felt uncomfortable saying things that weren't true."

Every time Bobby forgot the script, he said, Willoughby would explode in rage. Then the detectives would eject the tape, toss it in the trash, insert a new one, and begin again. The detectives, Bobby said, threw away at least four cassettes before there was a keeper. On the twelve-minute confession Bobby finally did record, he sounds tentative and, even after all the prompting, the statement is filled with easily disproven errors. Bobby begins his account of murdering a man who was killed while sitting seat-belted in his car by saying, "The guy was walking." Then Bobby describes a sidewalk confrontation over a breach of respect, rather than any kind of robbery: "My cousin Terry came bouncing to him. Start arguing. So he grabbed him and I shot him." On the tape, Bobby is two people, a person who seems to have no details in response to most questions, and someone who suddenly can offer ample specifics. The detectives ask Bobby about the murder weapon, and he says, "I don't know my guns." A moment later, Bobby questions them, "Looked like .45?" Quinn confirms, "It looked like a .45." Soon Bobby is asked about Fields's appearance, and describes the short, burly Fields as a "big guy, saggy eyes, saggy face." Quinn then revisits the question, and this time Bobby tells him Fields was "not that big, but big."

Bobby would explain it became possible to belatedly provide facts he hadn't known a moment earlier because Willoughby "had mad paper. Notes. He'd point out things for me to say." Willoughby was also sliding reference materials across the table to Bobby as he spoke. "I said I didn't know what the guy looked like," Bobby said. "He showed me his license. I described a funny-looking guy because I was looking at the license, describing the license. Old guy. Scrunchy face. That's the first time I ever seen him." It was the same with Fields's Chrysler. "I told him I didn't know what car it was," Bobby said. "Those dudes were looking at me like, *Are you kidding me!* He showed me a picture." On tape, Quinn freely admitted offering Bobby information. "Earlier in the interview we showed you some photographs of a vehicle," he said. "I'm showing you that photograph right now," he continued. Then he asked Bobby the color of the car in the photograph and Bobby said "Cream." Quinn's feeling seemed to be Bobby was so slow-witted he needed Quinn's help to tell what he knew. The default justification was that only a guilty person would agree to repeat such things on tape.

Some of what Willoughby and Quinn were embedding within questions or sharing outright was called hold-back detail, privileged information unreleased to the public that a murderer alone would know. Only the murderer (and the police) were aware Fields had been killed with one shot from a .45 pistol to the neck while seat-belted in his car. For most of the taped session, Bobby continually described a crime that took place out on the sidewalk. Then Quinn redirected Bobby, so Bobby obligingly pivoted and told of seat-belted Fields arguing with Terry, then reaching out through his open driver's side window, pulling the teenaged Terry to him, a struggle that Bobby ended by shooting around Terry and hitting Fields in the neck. It was nearly impossible marksmanship, especially with a heavy .45. No witness observed any of this. Nor did they see what Bobby, in the audiotape recording, claimed happened next. He said he'd "passed" Terry "the gun and tried to help the old guy," as Terry ran off, turning to the left, up Dixwell. Bobby would explain giving such a farfetched story to Willoughby as "trying to please him. I was trying to get the tape over with and go home. I wanted to go back to my peaceful life."

That Bobby didn't know the details and was so pliably going wherever the detectives pointed him should have troubled them. Perhaps it did. When Quinn asked Bobby what clothes he'd been wearing back on August 1, over a month later Bobby couldn't remember, as most people wouldn't. So, Bobby said he looked down at his shorts and "I described what I had on that day." According to Bobby, Willoughby noticed and "he was frustrated." Bobby's face in photographs from the time belongs to a trustful boy. He'd really been convinced a detective could offer him probation for admitting to murder. He really hadn't thought how he'd explain afterward to his mother his taking responsibility for murdering a grandfather in cold blood. Bobby would have had a much better chance of saving himself if he were cynical about the system. Kids deep in the game never talked. But Bobby believed.

Once the detectives became convinced they had their man, they seemed to succumb to confirmation bias, interpreting anything about Bobby only in ways that supported his guilt. They were unbothered by his blatant prevarications, because to them he was a murderer, and deceitful people committed murders. What had Quinn said? Everybody lied to him. Who made up stuff more than kids? As for the detectives' own prevarications, if you were a detective, you were allowed to lie. They'd never even laid a hand on him.

Peter Neufeld, a lawyer and the co-founder of the Innocence Project, had spent nearly forty years immersed in wrongful-conviction criminal cases and, to him, Bobby's experience fit the pattern. "I think what happens," he said, "is police think they have the right guy, so they aggressively interrogate that person and wear down that person. When the police ask how he did it, how it happened, he doesn't have the details, because he didn't do it. But the police officer thinks he's holding back, playing dumb, being smart, so the overeager officer, thinking it's the right person, says, 'Don't tell me you didn't do it, you know you put two silver dollars over her eyes.' He says, 'Yes, I did.' In his report the policeman says he volunteered the information only the police know. It's easy for an overzealous police officer to cross the line in a moment of interrogation, and then to repress facts later as to how he got the information. They're not all intentionally framing innocent people." Neufeld emphasized that once some police believed a person guilty, they would break rules to enhance the likelihood of conviction. "Happens all the time," he said.

Beyond desperation to get out of the Box, the interrogation had aroused in Bobby an irrational feeling that he must have been guilty of something to unleash a force like Willoughby. Richard Wright describes an emotional turning point when a falsely accused person has "the feeling that, though he had done nothing wrong, he was condemned, lost, inescapably guilty of some nameless deed." It was a disconnected sense of shame, like that felt by some sexual-assault and abuse victims who blamed themselves, who said by wearing that short skirt and walking into a bar I made it happen, by not breaking up with him and leaving, I made him hit me. If you grew up like unworldly Bobby, how difficult it was to leave.

Once the tape recorder was shut off, Bobby felt relief, but the detectives gave him a warning. "I tell anybody about the interviews, I wouldn't get ten years' probation." In other words, he was now to trust the terms of a deal created by people who'd made him lie. Then, instead of arresting someone who had just confessed to murder, Willoughby and Quinn took Bobby home.

Back on Willis Street, Bobby kept to his agreement, mentioning nothing of what had happened to anybody, including his mother. "I didn't tell her afterwards," Bobby said. "Sounds crazy. I always had it in my head I didn't do it. Eventually they'll figure out I didn't do it. I always thought about justice."

Chapter Nine

When a suspect makes a confession, before there is an arrest, a detective is expected to possess independent confirmation of what he's been told. "Here's the key," said a former New Haven detective from the time, Edward Reynolds. "When I got you in that room, I knew the skill set I had could lead to false confessions. So, I had to be convinced by other information that you were the killer. It's called doing your homework."

To corroborate Bobby's account, Willoughby and Quinn went to talk with Terry. It remained forever unknown what made the detectives become convinced Terry had been involved. Terry said later he'd been at home babysitting when the detectives plucked him from the house, put him in a car, and took him downtown. There, he was told he could make himself a witness or a suspect, that "I don't tell them something, I'm going to get arrested for it." During his pre-interview, Terry signed a witness identification form on which he confirmed "number seven is my cousin who I was with on West Ivy Street when he shot the man." Number seven was Bobby. Then, in a fourteen-minute recorded statement, Terry said he'd been with a friend at the 2-4. He left to walk with Bobby and Kwame to Bobby's house, then back around Sherman Parkway and down West Ivy Street. Kwame hadn't met Terry, so why he was now introduced made for another mystery. That all the witnesses had seen two people commit the crime had somehow been set aside. Terry's friend's girlfriend lived on West Ivy, and she was among those who, from her porch, had witnessed the murder. Terry said he'd stopped to say hello to her. Then Terry described looking ahead down the block and seeing Bobby arguing with a man. When asked if the man was inside or outside his car, Terry settled on "halfway in and halfway out." Terry said he hurried to the car and told Bobby "Let's go." Whereupon, "the guy grabbed my arm, and then Bobby shot him." Terry claimed Kwame wore a ski mask during the shooting, meaning his braids weren't visible. But the witnesses saw no mask and did see braids.

Several times Detective Quinn repeated a question after Terry answered it, and just as Bobby had done, Terry treated repetitions as cues to alter his response. With the ski mask signaled as a problem, Terry straddled the issue, claiming Kwame was masked, but that the mask was rolled up on his head until the trio reached West Ivy Street. As he had with Bobby, on the recording Quinn acknowledged giving Terry details of the crime scene—"I showed you some photographs of a white vehicle." Terry confirmed the white vehicle was the car Fields had been half-inside when Bobby withdrew from his pocket a black .45 with a wooden handle and shot Fields. (Bobby had described receiving a black-and-chrome .45 from Terry.) Terry said Kwame, meanwhile, was around by the passenger door, "trying to get into the car." Terry explained he'd observed this later activity at a receding distance, because "I ran." His destination, like Bobby's, he said, was his home, which for both boys meant turning left on the corner at Dixwell. All the witnesses had seen the perpetrators go right.

A day later, in the early evening, Kwame's aunt Julia Sykes met up with Kwame after work, and brought her nephew to police headquarters. Sykes was uncomfortable in elevators, so Willoughby walked the pair up the stairs to the third floor, with the diminutive Sykes taking in the detective alongside her as a "statue type of guy." Joined by Quinn, the four all sat around a table in a glass-walled area looking out upon the detective bureau known to some detectives as "the bubble" but which Quinn called "the fishbowl." It was larger than a statement room and offered greater visual transparency. Using the fishbowl when interrogating a juvenile, who'd be accompanied, was also more comfortable. "They said it was an interview, not an interrogation," Sykes said. "So, it started off as a lie, and not one thing was true. All they said were lies." At first, Sykes found the detectives to be "really nice" to Kwame, "asking him to tell the truth, telling him they'd find out if he was really involved." Then Quinn produced a closed file folder, and as he held it aloft, he accused Kwame of joining in murder. Sykes was thinking that simply couldn't be possible, "I always knew he didn't do it," she said. "Kwame always has been honest. He ate something from the table, he told me. He broke something, he told me."

The detectives began to press Kwame, showing him photographs, interrupting and waving off his denials, telling him, "That's not what happened. It was you and Terry and Bobby." In Sykes's and Kwame's memories, the detectives offered Kwame probation if he'd agree to say he'd been on the passenger side of the car, opposite Bobby. Kwame refused. Sitting there, Sykes thought, "They're getting upset because they're not getting a rise out of him. I had the feeling they were going to take him from me." She asked for a lawyer and was told there was no need for that because Kwame was a witness not a suspect.

When Sykes and Kwame later described the interrogation experience, their account closely resembled Bobby's, right down to offers of probation if he confessed, and "if he didn't, he'd get life." When Willoughby told Kwame his handprint had been discovered on the car, Kwame extended his hands, invited Willoughby to test them, and warned, "When they come back you're going to feel cheap." Willoughby surged up in Kwame's face, told him, "Son, I'm not one of your homeboys out there. You might have your aunt fooled, but you ain't got us fooled."

After more of what Sykes considered "badgering," she suddenly heard herself telling Kwame, "Come on, we're leaving." Willoughby informed her the courts would always believe a police officer's word against that of a Black teenager and accept the police recommendations. "You know what, you don't have to tell me the truth," she remembered the detective saying. "We'll go to the judge, he'll sign arrest papers and put a two-million-dollar bond on him."

Quinn eventually did visit Terry's friend's girlfriend on West Ivy Street. In his reporting, Quinn made no mention of showing her photographs of the three boys he was investigating. She knew them all, and could have told Quinn they hadn't been on West Ivy Street during the murder. Instead, according to Quinn, she now claimed to have had her face in a book during the murder, had seen nothing, and because she had a young child, didn't wish to give him a taped interview.

When Quinn reinterviewed what he thought was his best witness, a man named Michael, Michael told Quinn essentially what he'd told street police at the crime scene, that he had been driving along West Ivy Street when he heard an explosion and saw a column of smoke go off at a parked "silver" car. Michael noticed two teenagers, "One was light, one was dark," by the front driver's and passenger's side of the car, but Michael couldn't say which was the shooter, because the two rooted through the car in a frenzy before running off to the right, toward Dixwell.

With the detectives' case entirely reliant on Bobby's confession, Bobby began to notice that wherever he went around Newhallville, he was encountering Quinn and Willoughby, keeping a weather eye on him. An irony was that Newhallville kids like Bobby were stuck in place, had nowhere but the neighborhood to be. "I started to get scared," Bobby said. "They'd drive by frequently. They'd stare at me. Every day I see these guys." Because he feared losing his probation deal, Bobby continued not to talk with anybody about what was happening. The people he would have liked to confide in were his closest Willis Street friends. But Shay was at college, and the other two were sisters whose mother had recently died, so Bobby didn't think it would be the right moment to bring up his own troubles with them.

Others around the 2-4 could see the police giving Bobby and Kwame a hard time, but because the police always seemed to have it in for somebody, to them it was unremarkable. "The older guys in the neighborhood told us they were just messing with us," Bobby said. Bobby and Kwame had never discussed their interrogations, with Bobby reluctant to because of the probation deal. But now, Bobby said, "We tried to figure out how to get them to stop bothering us." Confronting the impossibility, the boys fell back on what the older guys had said, with life in a heavily surveilled neighborhood mediating against alarm. "Everybody wasn't taking the situation seriously," Bobby said. "So, we didn't. The advice was, this is how it is. They do stuff like that." Willoughby had told Bobby "my word is my bond." The detective's commitment to him was Bobby's handhold, and he clung. Whenever he felt most upset, Bobby would tell himself that at worst, "It wasn't jail. It was ten years' probation."

ON SEPTEMBER 15, an overcast Friday, Bobby was busy with plans. Lion was soon to be married, and Bobby accompanied his older cousin to meet with the minister. Next, Bobby spent an hour with his sisters and then went over to the red porch behind the 2-4, where teenagers gathered when the weather was bad. A group of Bobby's friends were there, sitting in a circle talking about a back-to-school party to be held that evening. In the morning, Bobby was headed to Lion's house for the weekend. Lion lived out on the edge of the city and had a swimming pool.

Bobby's back was to the street, so he missed that an unmarked black

Chevrolet Lumina sedan had circled the block. The car stopped, four men emerged, Willoughby, Quinn, another detective, and the case supervisor, all of them hurrying. Bobby turned just before he was engulfed. "All I saw," he said, "was them coming at me four deep. They didn't arrest me. They didn't handcuff me. Just threw me in the car. Two jump in back with me." As the car pulled off from the curb and accelerated, Bobby said, "I'm sitting in the car. I'm bunched in the middle. Those guys were humongous. I'm 140 pounds. When bad stuff happens, my mind goes somewhere else. I'm not in reality. I don't know how to feel. The way people express themselves, I can't. Same way when my grandmother passed away."

On the red porch, the teenagers wondered if they "should tell his mother." But nobody knew how to reach Grace. At the end of the afternoon, Grace came home from work. She'd planned to do a big food shop outside the neighborhood but was too tired to go, and so instead she sent Shavonne and Kenya to the 2-4 for milk, juice, and bread. The sisters made the purchases, came outside, and encountered a girl who informed them, "They just took your brother." The two sisters hurried home and told Grace, who got dressed to go downtown. "Then," said Kenya, "we had to find a cousin to watch my sisters. Usually Bobby watched us."

There had been a development in the Fields case. Back on the night of August 30, a good-looking, light-skinned teenage boy with braided hair wearing a black sweatshirt had left Newhallville for the Hill neighborhood, across town. When he stepped out of a car onto a quiet back-street sidewalk, he was soon ambushed and shot in the face and head. First responders found the boy lying facedown, his feet pointing toward the curb. A Ruger semiautomatic .45 caliber pistol was tucked into the victim's waistband. In his right front pocket was a Smith and Wesson semiautomatic .45. The young man was Major.

Seventeen days later, the Connecticut Forensic Science Laboratory processed Major's two handguns, and ballistics tests proved the Smith and Wesson .45 had been used to shoot Pete Fields. This was the kind of hard, explicit evidence detectives typically lit prayer candles for. And it all followed case logic. Major, with his braids and light complexion, conformed with witness descriptions of one of the two boys who'd run up on Pete Fields in his car. Major lived to the right off West Ivy Street, a short walk down Dixwell Avenue, at his grandmother's apartment in the Carter, the street nickname for the Presidential Gardens apartments taken from the fictional apartment complex that is turned into a crack den in the film *New Jack City*. The Carter coincided with what witnesses agreed had been the perpetrators' line of flight. It was also across the street from the school where Spikes had hidden during the murder. Major had by then become so enmeshed in gun violence, he was about to be arrested for two other recent murders. But Willoughby and Quinn already had tapes of someone else confessing to murdering Pete Fields. They were down a path.

As the four police officers entered the department with Bobby, a supervisor asked Willoughby why Bobby hadn't been handcuffed, as people charged with murder usually were. Bobby was led to the interrogation room for the third time and pulled down into a chair. "It was worse when I was in the room," Bobby said. "It was intense." Willoughby came up close to Bobby's face and began yelling at him about Major and the gun, "Talking mad stuff—'You're lying to me, you fucking liar. I knew you were a fucking liar. Your life is doomed. You broke the agreement. Make it right or you'll never see your family again.'" Looking at the detective, Bobby thought, "Dude has got a wicked mind."

Eventually, Bobby said, Willoughby calmed himself and began to outline a new version of events for him: "They said I lied to them. Terry never had the gun. You got it from Major. It's not consistent with the statement you made. You got to tell me you got it from Major." But the statement was built of details the detectives themselves had supplied to Bobby and, he said, "I was looking at [Willoughby]. Crazy!" Willoughby said he now had information that Bobby had gone to see Major and explained he needed a gun so he could rob someone. Major was amenable, Willoughby claimed, because Major was Bobby's cousin. "He said," Bobby recalled, "we found it on your cousin." In a subsequent police report written by Quinn, there's reference to Bobby earlier confirming Major was his cousin. But Bobby hadn't, and Major wasn't.

Major did have a first cousin who resembled Bobby, who sometimes stayed with Major at their grandmother's apartment. "He really got me mixed up with BlackJack," Bobby thought. "He really thinks I'm BlackJack. That's what it is." Major and Bobby were close in age, from the same neighborhood, had played in the same youth sports leagues. When younger, Bobby had visited the apartment, to play there with his friend, a younger cousin of Major's. As for Major, Bobby said, "I never once been with him by myself."

Ever since the Fields murder, like everybody else he knew in the neighborhood, Bobby was aware of rumors that Major and BlackJack were responsible. They were among the most feared people in the Newhallville streets.

Bobby had believed from the first that if he breathed anything to the detectives implicating Major, "He was gonna try to kill me." After Major died, there was still BlackJack and their associates. "You got people out here that doesn't play for this," Bobby said. "So you not only putting yourself at risk, but you're putting everybody else." He meant his family. Bobby had already done what the detectives wanted once. It didn't seem as painful to keep going along. He never dared utter the other boys' names.

Bobby had the impression Willoughby's stratagems were becoming distasteful to his colleague. "Quinn was in conflict," Bobby said. "You could see in his face, he didn't like what his partner was doing. At the end of the day, I felt he feared Willoughby and he couldn't apply his authority. Quinn wasn't aggressive. It was Willoughby. He didn't insult me, call me a liar. He just played his part when the recorder went on."

In the new script, there was no argument between Terry and Fields. Instead, this time Bobby stated his, Kwame's, and Terry's motivation was "We needed some money. Our pockets was dry." So, they decided to rob someone, which necessitated a gun. This led Bobby to visit with Major at the Presidential Gardens, where Major agreed to let him "hold" a gun, no fee mentioned. Then, referencing the pre-interview, Quinn said, "Earlier in the interview I showed you a single photograph," and Bobby agreed he'd recognized Major. This was one of multiple times in the fifteen-minute statement where Quinn made no secret of having shared information during the pre-interview. With the recording on, Quinn rarely asked open-ended questions, and when he did, he was often dissatisfied with Bobby's answer, and guided him to, in Quinn's word, make it "correct."

The story Bobby now told was that once the three teenagers had the gun from Major, they walked to the ballfield on Sherman and spent ninety minutes planning "who we should rob." That was a long time for what he said they agreed on, "anybody that came by." The trio set off down West Ivy Street and the very first person they spotted on a side street in a poor neighborhood just happened to have nearly $2,000 cash in his pocket. This was Fields, who was, Bobby said, "by the car." Taking no chances now, Quinn interjected, "He's seated in the car. Is that correct?" Bobby agreed. Bobby placed all three boys on the driver's side of the car, but Quinn had him rearrange, with Kwame moved around to the passenger side, while Terry was backspaced, down the sidewalk. In this account, Kwame no longer had a face mask. Bobby said Fields wasn't wearing a seat belt, a mistake Quinn didn't bother fixing. Instead, the lead detective moved along to the shooting.

They'd spent so much time working up falsehoods about the murder, a clinical distance had been achieved from the chilling fact of its cruelty, and this latest retelling sounded rote. Bobby said he ordered Fields to "run the money," which meant hand over his cash. Fields refused and threatened to call the police, so Bobby said he grabbed him and "then I shot him." Terry ran off and Kwame grabbed the money. "Where was the money?" Quinn wanted to know. Bobby asked in reply, "Either in his pocket or on?" Somewhat wearily, Quinn said, "I don't know, the center console of the car?" and Bobby immediately agreed, the console. Then Quinn asked if the money was in a wallet. Bobby agreed, a wallet in Fields's pocket, claimed that Kwame took out the $400 it contained and then threw the wallet back into the car. This was confusing to follow, and much of it did not happen. The new account concluded with Kwame and Bobby turning left up Dixwell, running to Bobby's house, splitting the money, and returning Major's gun three days later.

To this point, both of Bobby's taped statements lacked basic features of confessions, including the moment when a guilty person takes crime ownership and examines his guilt. As the session ended, Quinn seemed to recognize this omission, and asked whether Bobby had "any feelings in regards to this?" Bobby replied, "I don't know what I was thinking." That sounds emotionally authentic, and yet it feels less true to Bobby than like something another person would expect him to say. In his everyday life, when Bobby didn't know what to answer, he said, "I have no clue." He often said he had no clue about information. But describing his experience of true events was among the personal strengths that made Bobby himself. Bobby would later explain he'd said he didn't know what he was thinking because, "Willdebee told me to say that."

This time only three replacement tapes were removed from the little box of blank cassettes before Bobby's completely revised confession, changing a street fight to a robbery gone bad, was acceptable to the detectives. Tapes could not recount the full narrative. Left out was Bobby's eagerness to please; his faith that following instructions would yield a reward; his trust that he had been seen as different from the older, prison-bound guys of the 2-4; his crumpling before the aggressive detective. When this second confession was placed side by side with the earlier confession, the pair were sloppy enough with internal inconsistency and illogic that either could have been as true as the other. That they were so fungible made the two tragedies they contained almost banal. One was the murder. The other was that Bobby was so out of his league, he had no clue he'd just destroyed himself.

With the tape finished, Bobby was "ready to go home." The detectives led him downstairs to the first floor, through a door into a dull, colorless area with corridors of cells. Bobby thought he was going "to see my probation officer." A man "patted me down. Put me in a cell." Then Willoughby mildly told Bobby, "Shouldn't be that long." The detective left. Bobby would never talk to him again. Time passed. Bobby grew tired of waiting and, "I asked the marshal when I would see my probation officer so I can get out. He said, 'Probation officer? You've been charged with murder.' I was blank."

THERE IS A history of marginalized Americans falsely confessing to crimes because they saw no possibility of due process or acquittal. Historian Douglas Blackmon found that Black men in the 1880s often falsely confessed because white lawmen were so predisposed to their guilt that bargaining for mercy was the best of bad options. "Every Negro knows that a frightful proportion of Negroes accused of crime are absolutely innocent," wrote W.E.B. Du Bois in 1932. "Nothing in the world is easier in the United States than to accuse a black man of crime." While Black Americans are just 13 percent of the country's population, beginning in 1989, the National Registry of Exonerations found Blacks represented half of all exonerees. Innocent Black people are seven times more likely to be convicted of murder than innocent white people.

The modern legal scholars who began in earnest to study false confessions, like Brandon Garrett and Richard Leo, found that young people were more susceptible. The growing body of papers on adolescent decision-making by cognitive neuroscientists like Catherine Hartley linked immature brain development to impulsivity and an inability to project future consequences. But none knew how common false confessions were because, as Garrett explained, "There's so much faith in confessions, nobody revisits confessions. Cases with confessions are considered closed."

In the well-publicized New York case involving five teenagers who falsely confessed to raping a jogger while supposedly out "wilding" in Central Park, DNA evidence later proved that someone else had committed the crime. The exonerated teenagers were asked why they'd confessed. Among their explanations was their desire to please authority figures, their fear of the interrogators, their belief that justice would prevail no matter what they said, and their willingness to say anything to make the interrogation session end so they could go home. (Issues of stamina were said to have led a hold-out juror to capitulate.) But the exculpatory DNA evidence that proved their innocence exists in only a small percentage of all murder investigations. (Of those Americans freed because of DNA evidence, 29 percent gave false confessions.) When Bobby was arrested for the murder of Pete Fields, there was no DNA evidence to examine, and nobody then could think of a case in Connecticut history where a murder conviction with confessions was overturned without DNA.

After the confessional moment had passed, Bobby was eventually mystified by what he'd done. He'd spend years working to understand why. "It's so complex for me to think about my thoughts at the time," he said. "I'd never experienced anything like it. You think it may work out. In that moment, you don't have options because you don't know nothing, and you don't have the options to make it work, so you say stupid stuff that ruins your life." What had most affected him, he said, was fear of Willoughby. Bobby used a telling word to describe the detective's behavior. "The cops *wildin'*. Crazy. Cops is extra. I just wanted them to leave me alone."

Policing is itself an erratically understood profession, with such areas as criminal investigation methods not well studied. But enough is known about wrongful conviction and interviewing to make clear this truth: getting a kid to confess to what he didn't do can be really easy. As former New Haven police sergeant Shafiq Abdussabur wrote in his book *A Black Man's Guide to Law Enforcement in America*, "There is a saying among officers, 'If a person talks long enough, they will eventually say something that will get them locked up.' "

A COUPLE OF weeks after Bobby's arrest, the Connecticut State Police's Bureau of Identification was running a training exercise with the Automated Fingerprint Identification System. For their practice session, the untested crime-scene evidence they randomly chose to analyze was the latent palm print found on the passenger-side door of Pete Fields's car. The crime lab had it for use because Quinn and Willoughby, while happy to tell Kwame it was his, had never requested processing. When the testing was now done, the print was found to belong to BlackJack.

Like Major's gun, this was rare and coveted forensic evidence. Since the day of the crime, the print had always been available for scrutiny, and why Quinn and Willoughby had never called for it, they could never successfully explain. Quinn was equally unable to account for his failure to read through the police records that would have told him BlackJack was commonly addressed as Bee, and that he was Major's actual cousin and sometime housemate. When the prosecutor who'd been assigned to the Fields case, James Clark, was informed about the palm print, he was concerned, and instructed Quinn to go talk with BlackJack.

BlackJack was easy for Quinn to find; according to Quinn's report he was at the police department (under arrest on a drug charge). There he told Quinn that back on August 1, as part of his community release from incarceration, he'd been staying at a New Haven halfway house. Why his palm print was on Fields's car he could not explain, but BlackJack said that how it got there didn't matter because he'd been more than twenty miles away that August 1, attending an all-day first-of-the-month party held monthly in Bridgeport. Fields was murdered only three blocks from where BlackJack lived, but BlackJack said he would never set foot on West Ivy Street because his neighborhood was beefing with people from that neighborhood. Quinn's report does not show he followed up on any of this, pressing BlackJack about the party and how he got there, did not pursue others who were there to confirm BlackJack's presence. Quinn could have sought video or cell-tower records, he could have talked with supervisors at the halfway house. He did none of this.

In 2006, BlackJack was on a short law-enforcement list of the young men in New Haven most at risk for causing or becoming a victim of gun violence. That didn't make him Pete Fields's murderer. Neither did his full handprint on the Chrysler 300. Automobiles move around, and BlackJack could have touched Fields's car when it was parked elsewhere. Presidential Gardens, after all, was also close to the Mudhole. But the palm print only added to the likelihood that it was BlackJack who'd pressed his hand to Fields's front passenger-side car door, either when opening it or bracing himself as leaned through the window, telling an elderly man to give up his money, bills BlackJack had then helped scoop up after his cousin put a pistol to the man's neck and squeezed. BlackJack matched every physical description of one of the two young men who'd run up on Fields's car. He also looked a lot like Bobby.

Why Quinn proceeded as he did is difficult to know, because he offered no clear record of how he gathered procedural details. He later refused to publicly discuss the case, except when legally subpoenaed. Another New Haven detective from the time said of the investigation, "It'll never clear up. It'll always be murky. That team, they operated without transparency." Quinn's failure to corroborate what BlackJack told him made Quinn appear at best indifferent, perfunctory, and incurious. Perhaps it was that belated enterprise by him now would have been disruptive to the goal of the solve and would have revealed Quinn's investigation as problematic enough that it might have been handed off, might have cost him his gold detective shield. By doing so little, Quinn was making an active decision about how he wanted things to be.

KWAME'S AUNT JULIA SYKES had moved her family from Willis Street to a home in Hamden, and November 9 was Kwame's first day of eighth grade at his new middle school. She hurried him to put on his back-to-school clothes and dropped him off. She went to work, where a call was waiting for her. It was the school principal with news Kwame had been led to a police car in handcuffs.

Sykes arrived at New Haven police headquarters, and she, Kwame, Willoughby, and Quinn were soon reunited in the fishbowl, all sitting in the same seats they'd used in September. In her haste, Sykes had forgotten to bring reading glasses, but she agreed to sign a document that was read to her, a waiver of Kwame's Miranda right to remain silent and not incriminate himself, and to have an attorney present. Why the detectives had delayed after arresting Bobby to collect Kwame wasn't clear. They had no new information about him. Still, the two friends who'd allegedly gone in together on an armed robbery might now be coaxed to blame each other. That was exactly why, Yale law professor James Forman Jr. explained to his criminal law students, successful criminals advised working alone.

Detective Willoughby began to speak to Kwame in a tone Sykes found menacing. "I don't want to hear that same bullshit story that you told us the last time," he said. After some back-and-forth, while Kwame cowered in his chair, Willoughby yelled, "Your friend gave you up!" The detectives played Kwame the tape of Bobby confessing and placing Kwame at the crime scene. Kwame began to cry. Quinn interpreted that as an expression of guilt. Sykes thought it was Kwame's despair at hearing his friend implicating him in a crime they hadn't committed. Sykes asked for a lawyer and, she said, Willoughby refused. Quinn later denied her request happened. Willoughby announced that he was going to bring in his "supervisor." When the supervisor appeared, Sykes recognized him as a silent man who'd also briefly joined the detectives during the previous interrogation. This time the man spoke, and told Sykes, "We already got his fingerprints. You might as well make it better on him." Later, when Sykes would see a photograph of New Haven's police chief at the time, Francisco Ortiz, she exclaimed, "That's him!" (Ortiz denied being there.) After the man departed, Kwame still refused to confess to anything. "I felt imprisoned," she recalled. "I couldn't leave. There was a gun laying on the table." The detectives asked Sykes to persuade Kwame simply to admit he'd been on West Ivy Street with Bobby. Then they took up the gun and left her alone with her nephew.

Jonathan Moore, a lawyer who represented four of the Central Park Five, said that police interrogators bred on the Reid technique are taught to make particularly stubborn suspects admit simply that they were present when the crime happened. "The Central Park case had five people," Moore said. "None confessed to the crime, but all put themselves at the scene. You have young kids, fourteen, fifteen. They tell them, 'All you need to say is this and you can go home—we know you're a good kid.' And eight years later, you're still in jail. In the Central Park case, they got the parents to say 'Just tell them what they want to hear or we'll be here all day.' They just wanted to go home."

Willoughby and Quinn were still claiming they had proof Kwame's fingerprints were on the car. There was cold winter in how helpless their certainty about everything made Sykes feel. As she sat alone with Kwame, desperation came over her. The police had all the time, but Sykes didn't. She was a single working mother, responsible for several children and then also for her job, her students. When Kwame said, "I didn't do it. I didn't do it," Sykes said she told him, "They arrested you. I don't know what to do."

A short walk away from where Sykes sat was Yale University, and when Sykes would think back on this evening, she imagined the difference between how the two detectives might have treated a Yale student from their way of dealing with kids like Kwame and Bobby. "They don't see them," she said. "They look at them as if they won't amount to anything anyway. The cops think since they won't amount to anything, why not get rid of them right now. They'll just be a problem later. So why give them a chance. I feel like Yale's a chance. Yale's for the big dogs. They look at Kwame and Bobby as a little mutt."

Sykes had a cousin who worked for the police department as a detective, and Sykes decided to call her for advice. But the cousin didn't answer. Sykes gazed at her nephew. "Kwame was scared because I was scared," she said. Kwame was also insistent he hadn't done anything wrong. Sykes decided there was nothing to do but give up. "I said, 'Just tell him you were there. We'll get a lawyer to get you out.'"

When Sykes informed the detectives what they'd decided, the police told

Kwame to write down his account of the murder. But, according to Sykes, "Kwame said, 'I wasn't with them so how can I write it?' So, they told him what to write. They told him the story of the crime. What shorts he had on and everything." The detectives provided a mix of photographs and diagrams to Kwame. "He fed us lots of details," Sykes said. "Chrysler 300. Glasses. How he sat. They told how they struggled to get the wallet. How the old man wouldn't give it up. How the gun mistakenly went off. They told Kwame how his palm print was there because he reached in for the wallet. They gave a lot of detail. Lottery tickets on his lap." Eventually, the recording machine was switched on.

The subsequent transcript is halting and, according to Sykes, that's because "they turned [the handheld recorder] on and off. They stopped it to tell Kwame what to say." Kwame says on tape he joined Bobby and Terry, and together they walked around to West Ivy Street, where Bobby showed him a gun tucked into his waistband. Terry and Bobby walked down the sidewalk and "I went in the street" ahead of them. There was an argument, Kwame didn't know what about, then "a shot went off," and all three boys bolted, Kwame speed-walking to a park, while the others, he said, ran "through backyards." Nothing was said about Major.

Kwame was taken downstairs. His bail recommended by the detectives was what they'd once threatened, $2 million. Murder cases often take over a year before they go to trial. Now Sykes reached her cousin. The first thing Sykes said was, "They just got my son's life away."

BACK IN SEPTEMBER, after Grace's daughters came home and told her detectives had taken Bobby off in a car, she'd hurried to the station, where she was told only that her son was charged with murder and that his police-recommended bail was a million dollars. Grace was then making $25,000 annually and supporting eight children. Grace had been under it with stress since her mother's death, just trying to keep everyone housed, fed, and clothed. The penalty now for her absence was so high. There was a fantasy of intention about what a mother should do when an emergency called upon her. This was a mother living in a community where the flight paths of random bullets meant one of her children leaving the window open at night was an act of risk. With all the possible emergencies, sometimes it was just too much to check every window. Grace didn't know what to do.

She went home and called her nephew Lion, who was equally at a loss. "I didn't believe he was going away," he said. "It happened so sudden." Grace said her view of the police had long been more skeptical than her son's: "I wouldn't call them even before Bobby." Eventually, she sat the children down and told them, "Your brother's gonna be away for a while." When the girls asked why, and where Bobby was, Grace became too upset to continue the meeting. After that, Stephanie said, the subject felt closed, and it took years before she learned what happened to him.

Most of Bobby's former teachers knew about the murder, and when they heard he'd confessed to it, they were disbelieving. "We all thought he must be getting railroaded, couldn't be him," a staff member named Jarred Beck said. "But given the setting, Urban Youth, Newhallville, nothing's unbelievable." Among street kids from the neighborhood who'd ended up in prison, like Rabbit, the feeling was that Bobby and Kwame had crossed paths with the wrong detectives: "Everybody knows he didn't do it. He never did anything besides stand in front of the 2-4." Adults who were aware of how Bobby had grown up thought that poverty was to blame. Being poor went beyond a lack of resources. There was also the poverty of experience, by which people meant that Bobby's innocence had cost him.

When Willoughby and Quinn received word of Major's gun and Black-Jack's handprint, perhaps one or both had pause. But a retired New Haven police officer explained that once detectives acted on a theory of a crime, some felt they couldn't go back without terminating their professional standing. "Detectives in homicides, your credibility's on the line. Name's on the line. You get new information, you have a choice. [Either] you are no longer credible because you made a mistake and you now run risk of not being assigned to high-profile cases again. Informant money has been spent. [Or] you are telling your boss this is the guy."

Nobody who knew Major could conceive of him loaning Bobby a gun. On August 1, 2006, Major was in the midst of a violent spree, pursued both by street rivals and hunted by law enforcement, making him probably the least likely person in Newhallville to relinquish free of charge the weapon he would die with to dry-pocketed kids he didn't really know. But Willoughby's public commitment to his case never wavered, and he would cheerfully explain such improbabilities away, although over time elements of his meandering explanations radically changed. That shifting pattern also described the confessions. To experienced civil rights lawyers, one indication of a false confession is an evolving case narrative. If accumulating witness statements and confession transcripts keep realigning in parallel with the police's uncovering of new evidence, it suggests police are feeding information. In the Fields case, it wasn't just the different sources of the gun. The inciting event had been a street argument in Bobby's first confession, became a chance robbery in his second, and then, as details of Fields's financial transactions were belatedly understood by the investigators, the motive would rest as the targeting of someone known to possess a large sum of cash. Operating here were so many forces that could lead to a false confession, a mixture of shaky professional know-how, cocksure assumptions, vagueness instead of the nuance of pattern and the specificity of detail, all of it used to justify the decision not to pursue a likely suspect.

Bobby would say, "It's funny. Willdebee told me, 'This dude ain't the one who did the crime, but I don't care. We know Major did it.' The last time they grabbed me up, they sat in the interrogation room and said, 'Hah, Major's dead. We know who killed him, but we won't even look for who killed him. He did a favor for us.'" These strong accusations could never be proven, but Walter McCain had heard Willoughby tell him something similar about Bobby. Over the years, Bobby always insisted they happened, and as with all significant details of the case that Bobby readdressed across time, he remained consistent with what he said. "Major was dead, nobody to arrest," Bobby said of Willoughby. "Close this case with this man."

There was considerable difference between Bobby and Major in the risk they presented the community, but Bobby thought Willoughby's long career had gradually made him regard all Newhallville boys with the equalizing contempt James Baldwin once warned of when he wrote, "A black policeman could completely demolish you. He knew far more about you than a white policeman could and you were without defenses before this black brother in uniform whose entire reason for breathing seemed to be his hope to offer proof that, though he was black, he was not black like you." Willoughby once related to Newhallville on a family level, as Jim Ponteau and Gil Burton did. Now he was solving crimes with brisk, impersonal intuition. There it had been, dangling irresistible in the fluorescent light of the Box, another solve. To get it, Willoughby resorted to pursuit featuring the sinister behavior his solves were supposed to prevent. "I came to the conclusion he didn't care," Bobby said. "He's the most aggressive person I met in my life. I've met a lot of aggressive people. They thought I was another troublemaking kid in the neighborhood. I think that's just how they saw the neighborhood."

Chapter Ten

The Monday morning after Bobby's second confession, a prison transport vehicle known as the ice-cream truck took him, with about twenty handcuffed, shackled men, from the police lockup to a sally port beneath the New Haven County Courthouse. Everyone filed into a dim stone basement holding pen; lawyers who went underground to meet their clients said it was "like walking into the Dark Ages." There were vestiges of flooding, paint peeling like the rind of old tangerines, the cool walls were covered with graffiti inscribed by prisoners with their boot soles, the echo of slamming doors mixed with the chatter of marshals' radios. Once handcuffs were removed from frustrated people waiting together, fights erupted. The menu offering was the meal of the day—the meal of the day being bologna-and-cheese sandwiches every day.

Connecticut was then one of three states where Bobby, now at seventeen, given his crime, was automatically considered an adult. In the pen, he was the youngest, spindliest person, and was separated into a holding cell with three or four other younger people. "I'm in shock," he said. Years before, Grace had given Bobby a talk about avoiding prison, telling him, "Whatever you do, you don't go to High Court. That's where you get life." After a judge presented Bobby his charges, older prisoners warned him that now his case would be transferred across the street, to the judicial area District Court, where the more serious cases were arraigned. It came to Bobby that this was High Court. He thought, "What the hell's happening to me?" He still kept expecting a probation officer to turn up and rescue him. Instead, he was driven by bus to Cheshire and placed in the Manson Youth Institution, the state prison for males under twenty-one, where he became one of the country's approximately 48,000 incarcerated children. He didn't sleep all weekend.

The following Monday night, Bobby was in the District Court's bullpen. Here there were fewer people, everyone was kept fully cuffed, the quiet cells were solid cement and steel. Bobby could overhear men morosely discussing their cases, what they'd done, how much time they expected to get. He watched people led from their cell to "plead out" and be sentenced, and then return, "Guys coming back with sixty years or life, crying. Mostly Black guys, older guys from the neighborhood I knew." To Bobby, "it was mind-boggling." Eventually, a well-dressed white man came down to meet him. This was Larry Hopkins, a court-appointed special public defender who was being paid $75 an hour to represent Bobby.

Hopkins was a tall, good-looking man with a deep, resonant voice that gave him an imposing court presence. When Hopkins was the head public defender in Hartford, a lawyer named Kenneth Simon said, "I learned how to argue from him. A wonderful orator in front of the jury." Judges thought of him as a genuine person, willing to take the cases staff public defenders didn't want. In Bridgeport, where he was reputed to have won ten murder cases in a row, Hopkins was a legend. But in recent years, to colleagues Hopkins often seemed preoccupied, and his legal reputation was not for persuading juries but instead for guiding plea arrangements.

In his cell, Bobby had been realizing he'd made "a horrible mistake." When Hopkins met with him in a conference room at the District Court lockup, Bobby told Hopkins he was innocent, and "he said, 'I can't do nothing. You confessed.' I tried to convince him. He asked me why I confessed. I said, 'The people pressured me.' He said, 'It's hard to believe a guy trying to get the truth by doing something like that.'" Bobby's reaction was, "I agreed with him." This was not the level of outrage Bobby needed to exude if he hoped to make this lawyer in this moment overlook a signed murder confession and fight for him. Hopkins told Bobby the best he could do was try to arrange a favorable plea.

In her college dorm room, Shay received a telephone call from her sister, Melanie, who said, "Bobby got locked up. It's some dumb shit." Shay asked, "Well, what he do?" Melanie told her, "They said he killed the guy around the corner." Shay was incredulous: "What?! Bobby? How'd he kill somebody? Nah. Uh-uh. This is not Bobby."

She wrote Bobby a letter asking him what had happened, told him how worried she was. He was supposed to be visiting her at UConn, attending college parties with her. She posted it to Manson Youth. As the days passed and she heard nothing back, she began speculating. Maybe, Shay thought, somebody somehow forced Bobby into doing it. Or somebody was making him wear their crime. "Bobby was small," she thought. "Such a little boy. But Bobby and Kwame hung out at the 2-4 where they had no business being. The way they were got them caught up."

Bobby never received her letter. Shay assumed it had reached him, and that he didn't want to communicate. So she let him be.

Standing at the 2-4, Bobby had become accustomed to young people arriving back from prison asserting how "a bid ain't nothing." But now at Manson Youth, he saw it was all talk. Manson was named for a progressive former state corrections commissioner, but to Bobby, it was an overcrowded "out-of-control" place everyone called "gladiator school." Most people fought, because if you didn't, you'd go hungry and own nothing. Beds came with sheets and blankets, but Bobby had no pillow; he created his from clothes. Then, once the lights went out, around him strong people pressed their faces down. "All them dudes cry," Bobby said. "Not everybody, but plenty of people cry over their situation."

The blocks at Manson were called cottages, yet there was no mistaking rooms with a bunkbed and a toilet as anything but prison cells. Depressed, homesick kids were so lonely for companionship they stood on their toilet seats and called out to others, communicated through the vents near the floor. Bobby saw Manson as "people leaving and coming, like birth and death," and while he tried to put up a nonchalant front, "it was dark. No kid has hope that's going through a murder bid." Being at Manson "when I shouldn't have been there" was a routinely wretched experience. One day a boy Bobby liked was attacked. Bobby tried to intercede, somebody drew a knife, and Bobby had to watch.

At first, Bobby didn't attend classes because a murder case required an escort, and he was told the institution had nobody. He wore green clothing, designating him a security risk, and spent his days playing basketball, hands of spades, and crazy eights. Eventually, he worked a cleaning job and attended night classes: "It's gladiator school, but I stayed out of the way."

Bobby reached a low point at Manson when he learned his sister Shavonne had months before given birth to a stillborn child, and nobody from his family had thought to tell him. "Hasn't spoken to anyone from home," a social worker noted for his file. There was little to encourage him, nobody bringing pancakes and bacon in from home for him here.

Bobby never talked with Kwame, who'd been housed elsewhere. Manson was, however, well populated with boys Bobby knew from Newhallville. One was Jerome, there for his part in the murder of the thirteen-year-old girl. "We used to joke about Manson Youth was our high school reunion," Jerome said. "Everybody I went to school with was there. I took forty years. Plea deal. I was still around the same people as home. Still getting in trouble. Trouble makes time go by faster." Some young people there became incorrigible, lost concern for right and wrong. Jerome, however, eventually became a serious student in his cell. When he read Martin Luther King Jr., he recognized that while "violence doesn't solve anything, in Manson [nonviolence] wouldn't work. If you don't stand up for yourself there, you're food. People eat you."

People have always survived prisons by finding solidarity with those from the same communities. Manson brought previously beefing kids from New Haven's various neighborhoods together. They set aside their old conflicts because of the threat of strangers "repping" Hartford and Bridgeport. Jerome got to know a kid from Newhallville's rival New Haven neighborhood, the Tre, at Manson. In the streets, they'd shot at each other. Now here they were, shipwrecked basically forever. "We talked to each other," Jerome said. "Asked each other why do we shoot each other? We couldn't figure it out. Just because of what neighborhood we lived in we shot each other. And for what? Once you sit back, you see how stupid it is."

WHEN THE PROSECUTOR assigned to Bobby's case, James Clark, read the reports and transcripts, his reaction was, "Where you have a confession and [soon] another confession in court, it doesn't make you say, well, I better go back and look at all the files again." Clark offered Bobby a sentence of thirty-eight years, and Larry Hopkins's advice was that if Bobby didn't take the plea and was found guilty, Clark might exert a so-called "trial tax," seek a longer sentence, perhaps sixty years. Other variables seemed to contend against going to trial. Bobby had dark skin and, as Georgetown law professor and former prosecutor Paul Butler explained, "The blacker you look, the more time you get." But Bobby thought Hopkins was "crazy! He told me, 'Dude, take the time. I could be home at his age.' He said it six more times. And every time he said it, I'd look at him, like, 'Yo! He's old as dirt! Like, how can I come home his age?' And then I'm like, 'I just want to cry right now.'" Bobby was curious how old Hopkins was, but "I'm scared to ask him. But I decide to ask him. He's like, 'I'm fifty-five.' I'm like, 'Fifty-five! What I'm going to do there until fifty-five? No!' "

Nancy Gertner, a Harvard law professor and retired federal judge, referred to plea bargaining as Kabuki, because it had become a ritual theatre of justice. In 2007, there would be 81,210 criminal and DUI cases in Connecticut resolved by plea, and 190 by trial. It wasn't so much plea bargaining that was going on but rather sentence-bargaining, and some of the full-time public defenders in New Haven, including the chief, Thomas Ullmann, would look back and say that given Bobby's youth, lack of a criminal record, and the minimum twenty-five years without parole murder carried, Hopkins made a bad bargain for Bobby. (Because of what neuroscience research has concluded about adolescent brain development and impulse control, parole is now a possibility in Connecticut for people under eighteen convicted of murder.) But at the time, as the days passed, Hopkins worried that if Bobby didn't soon accept Clark's plea, the prosecutor would revise the terms upward.

Bobby's father, Tim-Buck II, was taking his son's predicament hard. Tim-Buck II hated the criminal justice system, hated the way he could be walking down the street, talking with a friend, and the police would pull up on him. He'd been to prison himself, knew how the streets were policed, and from the moment he learned Clarence Willoughby was involved, Tim-Buck II believed Bobby was in trouble. The parent with say in the matter was Bobby's mother, and Grace didn't want Bobby "to cop out" either. By July, when Hopkins repeatedly failed to convince Grace that Bobby should take his plea advice, Hopkins did what Bobby later decided was "something slick."

In adult court, if a defendant under eighteen wants to plead guilty, the court can appoint a guardian ad litem—a temporary legal guardian of the child's best interests, who may testify that the child is making an informed decision. Now Hopkins asked to be appointed Bobby's guardian ad litem so Bobby could accept Hopkins's advice rather than his mother's. "My mom said, 'You can't do that,' " Bobby recalled. "He did it anyway. My mom, she was not happy. Crying. Livid. I was confused. I'm like, I'm trying my best to handle this." Bobby had seen those weeping men who'd got sixty years; he felt he had to go with the person on his side who knew the system.

Under the high ceilings of the courtroom, the judge worked quickly. He acknowledged that Grace was present and disagreed with Hopkins's tactics. Once stated, this fact of troubling significance was then allowed to recede before the formal legal momentum of so much happening to Grace's son and nothing for her to do. The judge asked Bobby if he understood his guilty plea meant he was giving up the right to plead not guilty going forward. He said yes. Did anyone, the judge wanted to know, "force you or threaten you to plead guilty?" Bobby answered nobody had. Clark described the crime, for the record, as an incident involving three boys, and then once more Bobby accepted guilt that wasn't his. You had to be very broken to keep throwing your life away. "I was just trying to get it done," Bobby said. "I gave up."

Bobby was sentenced in October, days after his eighteenth birthday. In attendance were Pete Fields's daughter, Susan, Pete's nephew Floyd Hooks, and teenagers from Newhallville. Court hearings and trials were spectator events in New Haven for those who knew people involved in cases, making courtrooms perhaps the city's most representative cross-section. Looking at Bobby, Susan felt misgivings she could only partially explain. She'd heard about Major's gun and BlackJack's handprint, and had wondered ever since, "Why'd they overlook that? That's so weird." She'd hoped the sentencing would offer her closure, but sitting there, she found she was still "so upset." When Floyd Hooks read a Bible verse about finding inner truth, and extended to Bobby the Fields family's forgiveness, Hooks's impression, too, was, "I didn't think he did it. That's why I said what I said. That was [Pete] speaking."

In the sentencing session, Clark spoke of how commendable it was for someone to publicly admit his guilt. That Bobby had done so, Clark told the room, allowed "some possibility that when he gets out of jail he may be a productive citizen."

Then it was Hopkins's turn to speak, and the defense attorney began, "It's a tragic situation all the way around and, clearly, he's accepted . . ." As Bobby listened to the lawyer with whom "the longest I ever spent with him was five minutes," now describing his state of mind, Bobby was thinking, "I hate when men slack." Suddenly, from the spectator area a voice yelled, "Bobby didn't do it!" Everybody looked back. It was Bobby's friend Little Blue. The presiding judge, Richard Damiani, ordered silence. But Little Blue shouted, "This is crazy. He didn't do it." Judge Damiani was displeased with the outburst. He threatened Little Blue with prison, made him apologize, and ordered him to leave. "It hurt me," Little Blue remembered. "Everybody knew he didn't do it. It's all around the Ville who did it. Told me the system do that, they can fry anybody. All Bobby ever did was get high. He was known as an honest kid in every way. They wanted someone to pay. It was an old man. If it's us [dying] they wouldn't care. Everybody knew. The streets knew it, and if the streets knew it, the cops knew it."

When Little Blue departed, banging the door, Damiani sent court officers after him. Little Blue insisted Bobby was innocent, the bailiffs asked, "Who was it?" and Little Blue replied, "I ain't no snitch. I don't play that. Too dangerous. My friends do a lot of things I stay out of."

With order restored, Judge Damiani told Bobby he was "cowardly," and that was why he was now sending him to prison for "twice the number of years you've been on this earth." After spending over a year at Manson Youth, Bobby's length of sentence meant he would now move to the adult prison at Cheshire.

This result felt off the mark to Susan, and she was far from the only one. There were New Haven detectives and street cops convinced a perversion had taken place. For them to intervene with their opinions would violate unofficial police canons not so unlike Newhallville's street codes. But some of those police thought such professional orthodoxies invidious, and self-defeating for their work, because the distrustful community would turn away until Newhallville got full justice from them. As one detective said, "You don't think the neighborhood knows Bobby didn't do it?"

WHEN KWAME WAS assigned Diane Polan as his own court-appointed special public defender, Polan's assessment was "Kwame was just a bit luckier than Bobby. He got me!" During her 1960s New Jersey childhood, Polan had been given the nickname Cookie for being both smart and tough. As a teenager, Polan refused to stand for the national anthem at sporting events because society was so filled with bigotry. She came to New Haven in 1969 as a freshman in the first Yale class to admit women. Soon Polan was volunteering for the defense during the Black Panther murder trials, working on anti-poverty initiatives and Connecticut's first rape crisis hotline, before attending Yale law school. She prepared for the bar with her good friend Thomas Ullmann, and then joined New Haven's first feminist law firm. Polan was a single-mother social-justice warrior who raised her kids in a countercultural community of people who encouraged their children to play games of Brink's robbery and conscientious objector, and forbade cowboys and Indians. The younger women lawyers she was a professional example to, like Molly Arabolos, said, "Cookie Polan is a rock star. She comes in, and she's this little thing, but she's so fierce and so smart." Polan had a thriving practice, but "I have a deal with Tom," she said of Ullmann, the head public defender. "I take at least one murder a year."

Polan traveled out to Manson and met Kwame, who, Polan said, "barely spoke he was so traumatized by being there. He was traumatized as most adolescents in this situation would be traumatized—despondent." But Polan noticed that Kwame and his aunt separately told the story of what happened to them in the police department "fishbowl" with such consistency Polan thought they'd either have to be uncannily well rehearsed or were just truthful. So, for the court-appointed rate of $35 an hour, she hired a private investigator named John Hoda and asked him to approach the Pete Fields murder as though he was a detective newly assigned to the case.

Hoda had once been a police officer, and now lived to expose those who dishonored law enforcement. "Hoda has an agenda," Polan said. "He's a true believer, hoping and helping to uncover [police] corruption. I have no problem with people having an agenda. I have an agenda. I want to stop cops from violating people's civil rights." Of the white-haired, Dockers and V-neck-sweater-wearing Hoda's interviewing technique, Polan marveled, "Hoda's a white guy who is really good at it. It's amazing how much people in the hood talk to him." Hoda was so consumed with his desire to learn the truth, he walked into people's lives without inhibition, and once he got there, since it seemed he'd wait around indefinitely until people answered his questions, most did.

Polan gave him the four interrogation audiotapes Willoughby and Quinn recorded, and Hoda thought he knew what he was hearing. "Why didn't they take pictures of Bobby and Kwame and show them to all the street witnesses who were there?" he asked himself. "You know why? They knew those guys weren't there."

On West Ivy Street, Hoda found one of the murder witnesses, who was so skittish, this made him think she knew more than she'd said to police. Eventually, she told Hoda she couldn't say who the murderers were, but she knew Terry, Bobby, and Kwame, and it definitely wasn't them. Hoda was sure the witness was well aware of who'd done it but was too afraid to reveal their names. Next, Hoda talked with Fields's former girlfriend, Ella, and thought it unsurprising that she refused to put him in touch with her grandson, Spikes, who had "disappeared."

To Hoda, the case didn't seem complicated. The only people besides Fields who knew he would be on West Ivy Street at that precise moment, carrying a large sum of cash, were Ella and her grandson. Hoda's instinct for sharp dealing told him, as he said to Polan, "This is not a random opportunistic robbery." That gunshots from blocks away led Spikes to hide behind a dumpster instead of claiming his loan sounded suspicious to Hoda. Spikes wouldn't have known the shots came from the precise address he was bound for. More likely, Spikes had never intended to meet Fields. Hoda's theory had Spikes as "the bird dog" for the stickup kids he'd pointed Fields's way. According to Hoda's thinking, the dumpster was where they'd planned to divide the money. No charges were ever brought against Ella or her grandson in this case.

Clark eventually reduced Kwame's charges from felony murder to robbery, and the prosecutor offered Kwame a seven-year sentence in exchange for a guilty plea. If he turned it down and went to trial, Kwame risked serving thirty years in prison. Public defenders could describe absolutely innocent clients who insisted on pleading guilty for short sentences because they were so afraid of something going wrong at trial. When Polan presented his options to Kwame, he said, "I didn't do it. Do you believe me?" Polan told him she did.

Polan had become more convinced of Kwame's innocence than with any previous client, and before the trial, she repeatedly urged Clark to drop the case. Each time, he refused and Polan smoldered, "He thinks he's the white knight. Very liberal on social issues. Supports Planned Parenthood, UConn's women's teams before most people did that, equality for women. I fought with him—*You've got the wrong people.* He wouldn't budge. So arrogant." Then she added, "Jim Clark's a weasel prosecutor."

He was a little more than that. Clark went to Yale when Polan was there, in the time of demonstration and social change between 1968 and 1972, and then Clark worked restoring rare books before going to the University of California's Hastings College of Law in San Francisco, where he helped found a legal clinic for victims of domestic violence. Clark became a prosecutor "to try to give something to one victim at a time, in one case at a time," and saw himself as a defender of fear-harrowed communities like Newhallville, where "nearly everybody who is there is hardworking, trying to make it, decent people, but their neighborhood has somehow been taken over by a small group of thugs who make their lives horrible."

When the Fields murder case had come along, Clark was in his midfifties, a dedicated parent with the lean, taut face of the competitive triathlete. Some of the attributes of an endurance racer—preparation, discipline, eyes forever on the distant finish—Clark also brought to his work. He was a formidable litigator: of the roughly one hundred serious felony cases Clark tried, he said juries voted against him only three times. If you were a crime victim, this was who you wanted on your side.

One former prosecutor said that if Clark lacked anything, "it's his bedside manner. I always liked him. He's a wonderful guy. A community guy. He's just obnoxious." Another colleague thought even that was too kind. "I considered Jim Clark a goddamned pain in the ass," he said. "Jim was an extremely bright guy. Very aggressive—unbending. It could be a dangerous thing to want to win that bad. That's where mistakes get made. An obsessive belief you're doing God's work is more dangerous in a prosecutor than a defense lawyer. A prosecutor is in charge. Jim Clark was very dangerous because he was so good."

Preparing for Kwame's trial, Clark made a review of the literature relating to false confessions and was not impressed. "A lot of social science research sucks, and this is among it," he said. "Some is very enlightening, but they do not use the same criteria that real scientists use." For purposes of experiment, he believed it was impossible to simulate the high-pressure settings in which false confessions happened. A scholar whose work in this area Clark did consider "objective" was Brandon Garrett, now on the Duke law faculty. Garrett said it was possible to stage coercive interrogations, and when he read Clark's brief against allowing expert false confession testimony, Garrett considered Clark's arguments "dated."

As the trial approached, Clark had concluded, "I needed Bobby to convict Kwame." So Clark went out to Cheshire, accompanied by an inspector, Kevin Grenier. "I sat in a room with Bobby," Clark recalled, "and he confirmed that everything he said [in his confession] was true. Long after his conviction. It wasn't like there was anything I could do for him or any pressure that I put on him." But Grenier's typed summary of the meeting reports that Bobby was much more "ambiguous" than Clark recalled, and Bobby would also remember the day very differently from Clark. "The prosecutor came," he said. "James Clark and his assistant. They said, 'We need you to take the stand and tell us what you know about the situation. You've been convicted. It's not fair to let him get away with it.'" But, Bobby said, as they talked Grenier seemed dubious: "He told me, 'It doesn't feel like you all had anything to do with this.' I said, 'We didn't do it.' So, the assistant says, 'Why didn't you fight the conviction? You gave up?' I said, 'Kinda.' He said, 'Fight!'" Bobby's impression was "Clark couldn't believe this guy was trying to help me. Clark was so aggressive. [Grenier] balanced the atmosphere. He kept saying, 'It doesn't sit right.' He thought it was unbelievable, some guy tearing up the streets suddenly he lets you guys borrow his gun." Grenier later said of Bobby's account that although he could no longer remember their meeting, "[It] seems like something I would say." Clark remained convinced he had the right men: "In terms of Bobby's case, you got a guy who not only confesses but pleads guilty after advice of counsel, which could hardly be more confirmatory of his confession."

KWAME HAD SPENT his fifteenth and sixteenth birthdays waiting in prison for his trial. It began in late April 2008, at the county courthouse in New Haven. Soon, Terry testified, arriving from detention, where he was on unrelated charges. As he'd first told the police in 2006, he'd been at home when Willoughby and Quinn appeared and took him to the station in an unmarked car. There, after repeatedly maintaining, "I ain't had nothing to do with it," Terry said he'd given in because "they told me I would have a warrant for my arrest if I would have left without telling them nothin'."

Clark asked him, "And so then you just made up a story?"

Terry said that was it, exactly. Terry was never charged in the case.

When it was Bobby's turn, he came from prison, jumpsuited and shackled. People involved with the case thought Clark wanted him to testify regardless of what he said, because his confessions implicating Kwame were inadmissible under rules of evidence. But if Bobby did testify and deviated from anything crucial he'd told the police, Clark could argue for the inclusion of the confessions as conflicting documents. This exception existed largely because frightened witnesses too often took the stand and recanted what they'd told law enforcement. The truth now was Clark, Polan, and Kwame all had no idea what Bobby would say in court.

Bobby was eighteen; he'd been locked away for almost two years. Sunken down in his witness chair, everyone staring at him, Bobby himself "was surfing the room," noticing the bailiffs, court recorder, lawyers, prosecutors, judge, taking in how white the criminal justice system was. Only Kwame knew Bobby well enough to tell that he'd grown several inches since they'd been arrested. Nobody was there for Bobby. The judge told him to sit up straight.

That Bobby was so completely alone made him feel free. Imprisoned on a sentence he could not appeal, there was nothing at stake for him, nothing to gain or lose, nobody here to fear. He was also more mature. Bobby looked at Kwame and thought to himself, "Why should he suffer for these people who want to be spiteful? This is all bullshit." So, at first Bobby tried to put all the blame on himself. His responses to Clark's questions cast himself as the lone perpetrator of Pete Fields's murder, no Kwame, no Terry. When Bobby described his confrontation with Fields, Clark asked what he'd said to Fields. Bobby was unable to answer. Finally he replied, "What else a robber will say to somebody?" Then Bobby went ahead and offered up the stock stand-and-deliver of stickup kids: "I told him to run everything." How did Fields reply? Clark asked, and Bobby again didn't know what to say. To him, the prosecutor had become like Willoughby and Quinn, pushing him to invent plausible descriptions of what he hadn't done. Beyond his innocence, as he'd later say, Bobby hated being associated with something debased: "It was so gruesome, this vile crime." Instead of responding to Clark, Bobby announced, "I'm not about to go through this." Told by the judge he must, Bobby shook his head, "I ain't even shoot him, man." But, Clark pointed out, Bobby had confessed to doing exactly that. "A lie, come on." Bobby was publicly recanting his confession.

Bobby said later that in the safety of an open courtroom, "I suddenly realized at this moment I could say what I wanted to say." The inspector, Grenier, was there, and after their conversation at the prison, Bobby thought Grenier would expect him to speak up for himself, would be disappointed in Bobby if he didn't: "I felt like in his head it was, 'Why did this innocent guy go along with Clark?' "

Clark was asking, "Is it your testimony now to this jury that you were the only person there?" and Bobby answered, "I wasn't the only person there. *I* wasn't even there."

Since this flatly contradicted Bobby's confessions, Clark could now play the tapes. When Polan questioned Bobby about them, it all came out, how terrified he'd been in the airless interview room, that the detectives had ordered him first to confess, and then to amend his confession or "If I don't say nothin', I could go for the death penalty."

Clark asked Bobby why Kwame had suddenly become such a person of emphasis in his second confession. Bobby explained, "I was trying to keep him out of there, but I ended up putting him in there . . . and I made a mistake." Clark began to talk, but Polan said, "I don't think he finished," and the judge told Bobby to continue, which he did: "And now I realize I made a mistake cause I'm putting they life on the line, stopping they life 'cause of what I said, a mistake of what I said, and that's wrong and I apologize for putting him in that."

Polan cross-examined Bobby's reasons for creating so much fiction, and Bobby said that every time he couldn't answer a question, "He'll get mad," and "so I made up anything." Which detective had grown angry? Bobby was asked, and he replied, "The Black one." Asked if he knew who was really involved in the murder, he answered, "Everybody knows."

To Clark, Bobby's testimony was a performance disrespectful to Pete Fields's memory. Clark knew that trials can be a time of painful reckoning for a victim's family, and that doubt about a culprit interferes with overcoming grief and loss. "Jim Clark wanted Bobby and Kwame to go to jail and suffer," Susan said. "He truly believed Bobby and Kwame did it." But now she herself was watching young people who could have been her son claiming they'd been framed for her father's murder. She still couldn't get her head around falsely confessing to police, but she believed Bobby enough to feel doubt about what had happened. She wanted clarity and was getting the opposite. It was all, she thought, way too much.

Clark was aware that jurors also might have been swayed by Bobby, might even have found him to be sympathetic. In the courtroom, plain for all to see was what other prosecutors said of Clark; more than any of these competitive people, he did not like to lose. So now, with his case in peril, Clark ridiculed what Bobby had said about putting Kwame's life on the line as "your little apology." Then Clark asserted Bobby was in league with Polan, that Bobby had decided before the trial to "buy into whatever she was suggesting." Bobby and Polan had never met, and as his accusations noticeably angered Bobby, Clark repeated them twice more, chiding him in a tone that made Bobby feel mocked. Bobby responded, "I swear, man."

Bobby was thinking he'd outlined for Clark in Cheshire what had really happened, and had come here and testified voluntarily, at Clark's request. He'd got involved by trying to help and obey the police and had lost his freedom. Now because he wouldn't lie again for Clark, the prosecutor seemed to want to mutilate whatever self-respect Bobby had left. "I suddenly realized I had a platform," Bobby would explain. "And at this moment I could say what I wanted to say. The way he asked me things, the guy, he felt like a third detective, and it felt like the same thing again. He always over-talked me, interrupting every time." Bobby hoped people could "see how aggressive he was. Just like the detectives, and our parents are not around."

Clark told Bobby that from the beginning he'd been lying to obscure the fact he'd committed murder. Bobby recoiled: "Hey, don't. Yo, I didn't kill him. Stop saying that."

Back came Clark: "Wasn't that you who said that?"

Bobby looked Clark in the eye and said, "I'm telling you, I'm this close to hitting."

Clark moved quickly toward Bobby, close enough to feel the prosecutor's breathing on his face as Clark said, "Okay. I'm right here." It was an extraordinary moment. A prosecutor was baiting a shackled witness to fight. "We were all looking at him like he was from Mars," Hoda said. Both the judge, Bruce Thompson, and Polan began to intercede, but Clark told Bobby again, "I'm right here, sir. Go right ahead."

"Yo, I'm telling you," Bobby said, turning toward the judge for help. The judge barked "Mr. Clark!" He ordered Clark to back off, motioned a bailiff between them, and then he cleared the courtroom. "Clark *would* taunt somebody to act like a thug," Polan thought to herself with immense satisfaction. Clark later regretted it as "one of my worst moments in trial, in court." Every time Bobby thought back on the day, he was alternately amazed and amused by what had happened. "He couldn't break me," he joked. "So, he tried to beat me up."

When they resumed, Clark continued to press Bobby about the content of his confessions. "It's all from your imagination?" he asked Bobby sarcastically. "It ain't all from my imagination," Bobby replied. "The detectives was feeding me a lot of stuff. You act like you was there." As Clark tried to respond, Bobby then suggested how Clark, in effect, could have been there: "Tell them to put a camera every time they interrogate somebody." Clark was affronted. "At least twice on tape recorder you told the police that you were there!" Bobby was shaking his head. "You don't know what they be doing to us," he said. Clark began to interrupt again, but Bobby went ahead and explained, "Ain't nobody helping us."

Detective Quinn was called to testify. In an unruffled tone, Quinn denied he'd ever threatened Bobby or Kwame, but he acknowledged, "You can lie to them, yes." This exchange pleased Polan because, she said, "He basically admitted that they lied to the kids. Juries don't like it when cops lie just to get people to confess." When Quinn was asked if, in response to Bobby's explanation that he'd been at Visels during the murder, the detective had ever followed up by going to the store and checking out the alibi, Quinn said, "I don't recall doing it, no." When Polan asked how it was that Quinn convinced Bobby to completely change what he'd said in his first confession, and in a second confession implicate Kwame instead of Terry, Quinn said, "I didn't say anything to him." Polan looked at him with incredulity.

"That all came out of his mouth all by himself with no encouragement?" she asked. Quinn allowed, "We told him that the statement he gave us . . . wasn't as truthful as it could have been." Spattered as it was with mistakes about names, addresses, event sequences, and shoddy record-keeping, nobody would have considered Quinn's to be reassuring testimony. Clark himself was an assiduous person, and listening to Quinn must have been for him like someone scraping a butter knife across cement.

Willoughby did not testify before the jury. Instead he'd raised his right hand in a private session with the judge, asserting his Fifth Amendment rights. Willoughby was following the advice of his own lawyer, Norman Pattis. There was a vibration of irony in the extractor of confessions not required to say anything himself, and armed with such talented support. Years later, when an elderly Judge Thompson had forgotten almost every detail of the trial—"Did false confessions play a role?" he asked—what the judge did recall was Willoughby's dazzling lawyer, because "he's not forgettable when he's there to protect the witness." Pattis made a specialty of defending the vilified, and Willoughby by 2008 was that. If Willoughby had taken the stand, Polan would have introduced his police internal affairs file, a cauldron bubbling and boiling with allegations of Willoughby's fraudulent use of confidential informants and skimming the funds supposedly used to pay them. The last thing Clark wanted the jury to know was that Willoughby had been arrested in February and was being prosecuted for corruption by Clark's own office.

During the trial, Willoughby had come to court to learn whether he could take the fifth in private or if he'd have to do so before the jury. Julia Sykes was sitting on a bench, waiting to testify herself. These were dark times for Kwame's aunt. She'd spent the entire trial on that bench, either weeping or feeling like weeping because of what she believed she'd done to Kwame by telling him to give Willoughby what he wanted. Now Willoughby approached, and their eyes met for the first time since he'd arrested Kwame. "He walked up to me and said, 'Sorry and good luck.' I'll never forget it." What the detective might have been thinking, Sykes really couldn't imagine.

BlackJack also came to court, taking the fifth. His grandmother, Rose, who had helped raise both BlackJack and his cousin Major, did briefly testify. She was a beloved woman in Newhallville, locally known as grandmother to the entire neighborhood for her generosity to poor children. When Rose was asked by Polan about Major, at the mention of her dead grandson, she became emotional and said, "I've never gotten over him, please don't talk to me about him, please." What made her upset, Rose explained, was that

Major, too, had been murdered and "nobody" seemed to be investigating "his case." Rose said, "I don't talk about it, I don't complain about it, I just remain quietly. I don't know nothing. Please don't bother me about my grandson." When Polan pressed her, Rose lost composure. "I cannot take it," she said. "I loved my grandson; he was my heart. Please, don't, don't do it. Don't do it. He was my heart. I raised that child." The judge told her that she need answer only one more question "about your grandson who got shot." Then Polan asked Rose if BlackJack and Major were close. Rose said, "They were like brothers."

Also appearing for the defense was the porch witness who'd looked up from her book to see the crime unfold. She testified what she'd told Hoda, that neither Terry nor Kwame had been involved. The shorter and darker of the two attackers, she said, had been on the passenger side of Fields's car, where BlackJack's palm print had been discovered. Shorter and darker was the description of Bobby and, as it happened, of BlackJack. Fields, of course, had been shot from the driver's side. Testimony concluded on May 1, and the jury was instructed to begin deliberations the next morning, a Friday.

Friday trial verdicts are common because juries want their work to finish before the weekend. That same Friday, May 2, the jury's foreman passed a note to the judge. Hoda, the former police officer, said, "I've faced down guns, been married, [seen] the birth of my kids, combine them all that's the most nervous I've ever been." The verdict for Kwame was not guilty, and now Polan, for the only time in her thirty-five years as a tough-Cookie criminal lawyer, cried at work. According to Polan, Clark was not gracious afterward. He told her he was sure Kwame would soon be in trouble again. Polan worried the same, that although this ordeal was done, Kwame would leave it a young person who'd lived in poverty, around violence, without parents, pulverized with embittering experiences, and now was going home from a cell.

For kids like Little Blue, it seemed implicit that Kwame's trial was also Bobby's trial, since the evidence against them was the same. Little Blue said, "We wondered why, if Kwame got acquitted, they shouldn't have acquitted Bobby."

As for Bobby, on May 2, he was out in a prison yard filled with grown men as word circulated that "Kwame beat trial." In that moment, Bobby felt sudden hope. It had been cathartic, he recalled, for him to testify and finally "let the truth out." For two years, he'd been consumed by rage and depression. "I'm sitting there," he said, "time started to weigh on me as the years go by. When he got out I looked at it, it's easier for me. It's possible."

PART III

THE STICKUP KID AND THE INNOCENT BOY

Chapter Eleven

In 2006, a gray-bearded statistical engineer in Hartford named Ivan Kuzyk was asked to assist Connecticut and federal agencies in reducing the rampant youth gun violence of poor city neighborhoods. "Two hundred people in New Haven were getting shot every year," Kuzyk said. "The homicide rate's nothing compared to who's getting injured." Kuzyk's role was "to mine arrest data and see who to focus on," and as Kuzyk did his close study, one boy captured his attention. "He emerged like a comet on the scene," Kuzyk said of Major. "He wasn't the typical guy."

Major was smart, talented, beloved, and such a mysterious loner that long after he died, his name would hold a sacred quality for boys who never met him and be a word of dread to some who had and still hesitated to say it aloud.

His family came from the Pee Dee River farming region of South Carolina from which so many New Haven families traced their pre-Migration lineage, including Bobby's and the Fieldses'. Major's grandmother Rose arrived in New Haven in the early 1960s, just in time to become a straight-A high school senior. "My mother always said she'd never go back to the South," said Rose's second daughter, whom Major called Auntie. "The Promised Land—it was true."

Rose worked full-time, walked everywhere, and was dear to so many transplanted Carolinians, she became an unelected local representative—the community relative. After her husband died, Rose moved the family into Presidential Gardens, a subsidized housing complex built for working families in Newhallville, a few paces from the Mudhole. There was a self-contained, village-within-a-village feeling to Presidential Gardens. If somebody made honey biscuits, they might go ahead and bake enough for the whole complex.

Then the big factory jobs left and crack-cocaine money made for all-night revelry out on Winchester Avenue, with sightings of golden age rappers like Big Daddy Kane and Biz Markie. Rose's daughters, Gloria and Auntie, were part of the scene. Auntie had presence and personality, good-looking younger men were drawn to her, and she to them. "Boys!" she said. "Wooh! I liked boys that were bad. That was rough. All of them was handsome, now." Auntie's friend Goody said, "She had a lot of game! The gift of gab to get what she wanted. She might grate you if you didn't know her, but she's witty."

Auntie's sister, Gloria, went to school by day, worked at night, had a daughter, Kiki, and then Major. A daycare van driver considered Major impeccably well behaved and thought "he seemed special. A kid with something to give." Then Gloria began losing weight. "My sister was a mom," Auntie said. "Two kids. Major and Ki. She died. Major was five. Ki was seven."

Of the specifics Auntie said, "I don't know if the kids knew. I never sat down and had the conversation." Major's father was a quiet laborer, and when he received a cancer diagnosis, Major's cousin BlackJack's impression was, for Major, "that took more of a toll on him." Major's father recovered, but oncologists have seen over and over that all a young child understands about cancer is the fear of what the parent's illness might do to his life.

Auntie was a paralegal who, with her flair for argument, might have made an excellent lawyer. She faced the lower-income single mother's conundrum of staying at home with her children during the day and being criticized for accepting public assistance or going to work and being blamed for neglecting her kids. Bringing up her own and her sister's children, Auntie cooked big Southern-style meals, enrolled the four boys in youth sports, provided pets, restaurant outings, and Florida vacations. "They didn't have their father around," she said, "but those kids did not want for anything." The problem, Auntie believed, was that in Newhallville "there's really nothing for them kids to do," and when boys become adolescents, they desire their own way of being.

"We used to find old rifles, my friends and me, in the Winchester abandoned brick buildings," said BlackJack. "Some of them actually did work. Was a risk going in there. You could fall right through the floor." Like those dilapidated lofts, Presidential Gardens reflected the fallen times. "People sold and took drugs," said one mother who lived there. "There were guns, violence, shootouts, beefs with the Tre—it was our normal." The building units were set well off the street, offering drug dealers "run-through" toward the busy avenues to the front and the back. Amidst it all, neighborhood children came to visit Rose, who gave them treats, clothing, and heart-to-hearts. "I loved everything about that woman and she probably wouldn't even remember me," one kid said. But as for Rose's grandsons, "my uncle told me, don't be close to them."

Major dressed well, and girls were drawn to the tall, slim athlete with pooling almond eyes under high, arched eyebrows—"a little ladies' boy, curly hair, caps on all his teeth," one said fondly. But as another kid said, "The type of dudes he hung out with were the roughest kids in the neighborhood. You can tell they're gonna be monsters early on." Major was laid back, but there was within him the pulse of illicit activity, the ever-present potential for aggression. "He reminded me of Snoop," said one teacher. "Not loud, not crazy, but you know he's there with his experience of the edgy inner city, so you don't question his ability to act."

Major attended Urban Youth Middle School and had younger cousins there. When they became upset at school, only he could calm them down. To the principal, Milton Brown, Major was polite, gracious, and emanating stress. "He came in and did what you asked him to do until he couldn't take it, and you'd have to release him," Brown said. "He was very much someone who had a lot to give to society and no one to guide him. How dangerous he was, was conveyed to me." There were some overwrought days at Urban Youth when Major would end up in the school's refocus room with a young male faculty member who said, "He was crying. Out of anger. Pain cry. Frustration cry. In the refocus room he didn't hide anything. The missing of the parenting. A not-belonging feeling. He felt he was by himself. At what, thirteen? It's tremendous to have that acknowledgment. He saw the future. 'This is what I have. There's nothing better for me.' " James Gilligan, of Harvard, wrote in a 1996 reflection on American men who commit violence, that characteristic "is an unusually strong wish to be loved and taken care of, and unusually strong feelings of being inadequate and unlovable."

Violent people have typically first been exposed to danger. At fourteen, after police heard shots, Major was arrested two blocks from his grandmother's apartment, with two guns found among his football gear. Among the responding police was Dave Rivera, a police officer who'd known Major since he was small. Major explained to Rivera that he had the two guns because he was having "issues" on his half-mile walk to school. Kids wanted to hurt him, and school was the place where people knew they'd find him. Rivera said, "I remember him telling me, 'I have to do what I have to do to protect me. You can't protect me.' I'd tell him, 'Tell me who's doing whatever it is to you.' " But Major never would. Eventually, Rivera concluded "Major did some really bad things. Fear might have played a big role. His mindset was, I don't want to die. I'm gonna do what I have to do to survive out here." At some point a "switch flipped, and then it turned to he was committing homicides as he got a little older, if you want to call that older. A lot of people saw him as a cold-blooded killer. He didn't start off that way."

Major had been a fast, sure-tackling member of a nationally ranked youth football team, but to his family's regret, Major didn't play for Hillhouse High School. A story circulated that the coaches feared Major would be a "thug" influence on other players and cut him, but the coaches maintained this wasn't so, and Major told a youth coach he was close to, Reggie Lytle, it was his own decision. "We had several conversations," Lytle said. "Why did he want to quit? He felt that hanging out on the streets was more fun than going to practice."

By now, fear and loss in Major seemed to manifest as the desire to make others feel pain. Major became a notorious stickup kid around the city. His cousin and housemate BlackJack was also falling deep into the streets. Because they were neighborhood kids, always there, others had to get along with them. "We all hung out," one girl said. "They dressed really nice. They were teenagers into stealing cars and drugs and guns. They weren't teenagers going to the mall." When one boy ran into BlackJack in the park across from the high school, BlackJack pulled up his shirt, revealing a pistol. "Yeah, man," he said. "I'm never lacking. They'll never catch me slipping." Another day he sidled up to a different boy, who remembered, "I saw BlackJack and he's, 'What are you doing tonight? Want to go rob somebody?' I was like, 'No, got to get ready for work.' That's what he did for fun."

Many stickup kids prefer robbing drug dealers because they have money and won't call the police. But one evening, Major went alone up the hill, across Prospect Street, and down into an area where many Yale graduate students lived. Major was in the midst of robbing someone on the sidewalk when police arrived. Major took off, tossing his gun, but the police ran him down and recovered the weapon.

At the juvenile detention center, Major was placed in a cell. Turning his back to the door, Major began banging it with the heel of his shoe. The noise was deafening. The door was opened, and Major was asked to stop. "I ain't doing nothing you tell me to," he said, and tried to bullrush past. The policy with belligerent prisoners was to restrain them and, if necessary, apply handcuffs. After five minutes in cuffs, Major was asked if he'd like to talk with a counselor. He refused. Back in his cell, he began kicking the door again. The supervisor of the unit on duty that night was Goody, who decided he'd try to talk with the kid himself.

Looking at Major's file, Goody realized who Major was. "Look, man," he told Major. "I don't want to restrain you. I know your father. I know Auntie. My job might be here, but I come from the same place as you." Goody told Major that racism in the South and then drugs had broken his own father down, and that when he'd been a teenager, Goody wanted so badly to pay his own pain over his lost parent forward: "I contributed a lot of nonsense in my days." Goody was a tall, broad-shouldered man, with a round face that always looked grave, even on his most lighthearted days.

When Goody asked Major about his parents, "He told me about his mother and broke down crying. He wept and wept." Then Major muttered something dismissive about his crying, and Goody reassured him, saying, "You're right to cry. You're not a punk to cry. You're feeling something normal. You're hurting. Your mother's not here." Major told Goody that the loss of his mother had "messed up his whole world." As Goody listened, he thought Major was "traumatized" by the unexplained loss of his mother and the feeling of being unwanted. "He seemed so upset about her. The circumstances of her death. Never getting answers as to what happened to her. He said, 'It all stays with me.'" Growing up in a segregated neighborhood, exposed to violence, intense loss, and fear, these were some of the "adverse childhood experiences" that psychologists who studied crime said accumulated to put young people at risk for drug abuse and for crime. Unreconciled grief was the close cousin of shame, and as such shame festered, James Gilligan had found, it could become a driver of violence. Looking at Major made Goody think about so many other people he'd known in his neighborhood who'd found self-destructive forms of coping with feelings of being less. "Newhallville's generations of sadness," Goody said.

As they spoke, Goody noticed other qualities in Major, how he vividly expressed his inner life by shifting between the use of street language and common English, like a song with a contrasting bridge. What Major conveyed was how intolerable he was finding his feelings. Goody had a pretty clear idea of what it all meant: "Depression, man. Smart kid. Smart dude. But he was so angry, you could feel it. He felt he had nothing." It was easy for Goody to perceive how such a person might become lethal. When Goody proposed counseling to Major, "He was so against mental health." Goody told Major they could talk whenever he liked.

Until Major went home, he and Goody continued to have conversations. Goody soon knew that Major carried pistols and roamed the city on his bike, a BMX version of a highwayman on his horse. "Major was an enforcer," he said. "He wasn't looking to run; he was on and popping. From what I get, he was a shooter. That dude had no problem pulling the trigger. He admitted it." Goody asked Major if he'd thought of putting the guns down, and "I got the feeling he wanted to, but they were his tool for survival. His way of avoiding death was shooting at other people. He told me, I put down my guns, somebody's gonna shoot me." To Goody, "It was profound. What do you tell a kid like that? I was shocked by his desire to get out of the violence and his statement that he couldn't get out because he was in it too deep."

In 2005, Major's high school history instructor was Bill Garraty, a white retired suburban police officer who was new to teaching. During the school's homeless food drive, a student collected a milk crate full of cans. When Garraty praised him, the boy said, "I know what it's like. I lived in a car all last year." Garraty's classes were filled with children existing in such extreme ways they were too upset to learn. One boy told Garraty, "Everything you're telling me now is irrelevant to my life." Then Garraty began to notice a thin, neatly dressed kid who was very engaged. Garraty would be talking about the Civil War, and "Major would pipe up, 'Did you see the History Channel last night?' " after which Major would hold forth "about historical matters on his mind. He was making connections to prior knowledge, what we strive to get kids to do." Garraty believed, "he wanted me to know he was learning stuff and was academic, and he wanted the class to know it too."

One winter day, Auntie's young daughter, Andrea, saw Major come into the house with blood dripping from his left hand. When Andrea asked Major what had happened, his answer was cryptic: "He was on his way home from school. He put his hand up and got shot in the hand." Major stopped going to school.

Several weeks later, Major returned to history class, his hand still heavily bandaged. Garraty was relieved to see him, except—"What did you do to your hand?" Major said, "I'll tell you after." Following class, Major came up and said, "I was trying to sell a gun to this guy, and he tried to steal it from me. I grabbed it, and it went off in my hand." Garraty was thinking "Jesus Christ!" As a police officer, Garraty had been "a priest cop," someone people felt safe confiding in. The teacher just kept listening: "He explained to me he could get a new gun in a box and sell it. Here he was selling just a regular gun."

Periodically, Major would miss a week of school. During one of these intervals, Garraty sent a misbehaving boy out of his classroom. As the kid left, suddenly he dropped his bag, turned, put his fists up, and said, "Let's go." Garraty just looked at him, unwilling. The student nodded and said, "That's what I thought. You're a pussy." Two or three days later, Garraty was out in front of the school when a dark-colored pickup truck rolled to a stop and Major leapt from the passenger seat, came bounding up to Garraty, and said, "I heard a kid squared up with you and you didn't do shit." Garraty shrugged and told him, "What am I gonna do, lose my job over this kid?" In the streets, it was a matter of safety and self-respect that nobody should get anything over on you. Garraty watched Major understand that in Garraty's profession, it was overreacting to a slight that would ruin you. Major told his teacher, "I know you're right." After that, Garraty noticed the boy who'd challenged him never missed class, sat in the front row, and whenever Garraty met his eyes, a "sheepish" look covered the boy's face.

Major's high school Spanish teacher was a woman in her early twenties named Millette Núñez. Núñez was considered a great beauty, and every day students flirted with her. But, said Núñez, Major "chatted me up" in a novel way, by energetically describing for her a World War II documentary he'd watched on TV. She thought, "This kid's on it." After that, they had hallway conversations, some about Ken Burns films. Núñez knew Major "wasn't a saint. Was a stickup kid. Robbing people. He told me about guns." She didn't forgive hurting others, yet she could tell what a curious, receptive mind he had, and tried, she said, to help Major imagine a different future, even as she sensed he was like many of her students—"They can't think past today." A man who lived in Newhallville for years said of Major, "Ambition makes it twice as bad to be in a community where it's such a struggle to get out. If you're talented, you just look up that hill and you know what you have means success right over there. Then talent feels like a curse."

Major seemed then pointed in so many emotional directions he'd become a person living hour to hour, all voltage and vector, no plan, no rest. Núñez was well aware that self-medicating was how her students often tolerated their childhoods. "I remember him always being high," Núñez said. "All the time. A coping mechanism." Adults and teenagers around the neighborhood said that Major was heavily abusing a popular drug called wet. Wet could mean dipping a blunt into embalming fluid, and if PCP was added to the murk, a common sensation was brief euphoria. Alternatively, a PCP-spiked fluid could be drizzled on leaves of mint, parsley, or weed that were cooked and then packed into a blunt. The drug made the cooked leaves glisten—appear wet. "Major was always high on wet," a woman who knew him said. "Wet escalates."

At seventeen, Major wore braids pulled back from a russet complexion, and his almond eyes suggested sensitivity. He could be wry and sweet when teasing a girl about coming to school in mismatched shoes. He impressed high school classmates by having every answer in math, and with the many eclectic facts he knew cold. Major was a player with older girlfriends, and a teenager who went to the prom with a date, a chaperone, and balloons.

He doted on his younger cousin Andrea. "He used to do my hair in ponytails and up in a puff," she said. "He'd walk me to the school bus stop every day and wait with me. He'd meet me at the bus stop at the end of the day. He never missed." Major also cooked for her—"Anything I wanted. Pancakes. French fries. Chicken. It was good. He was loving. He was really quiet though." Much about her cousin seemed off-limits: "There's a side we never seen. We only seen the loving Major. Kind. Smile. Quiet." Still, by the summer of 2006, it was plain to Andrea that "he was suffering by his demeanor." Major always assured Andrea, "I'm okay. You don't have to worry about me."

But he was so far from okay. By that summer, Major had foundered into personal entropy. There was some kind of overload, a violent inner velocity; Major's life became a collapsing mine shaft, protections and supports falling away, dirt pouring down until nothing to see, no way to breathe, then a final snap and all became darkness.

ROMANO RATTI, THE police department's Newhallville district manager in 2006, was a burly, well-muscled white man who wore a trim goatee, had a deep smoker's voice, rode Harleys, and was, at heart, a community activist. Ratti considered Newhallville "the forgotten neighborhood," a disregard, he said, "I took personal." Using his salary, he paid for school supplies and children's parties, led a successful effort to install a splash pad beyond the basketball court on Ivy Street, took kids like Jerome fishing. "He really tried to keep us out of trouble," Jerome said.

While knocking on doors in an effort to know the families of the most at-risk kids in his district, Ratti became friends with Auntie and Rose, and he began having talks with Major. "Major," Ratti said, "you could tell, he had hidden demons. The death of his mother was huge for him. [Because] it was hidden, I could see where he'd be embarrassed or ashamed. I'd try to reason with him, 'Why don't you get a job? Get out of this bullshit?' Major would say, 'What else is there?' I'd say, 'You'll end up dead or in jail.' Major'd say, 'That's the way it is. It's the way it goes out in the streets.' He didn't know there were other options out there."

Major had no driver's license, and that summer of 2006, for Ratti, the sight of Major riding off from his grandmother's apartment on his BMX bike was unsettling. "Major was responsible for a lot of shootings," Ratti said. "But nobody'd tell on him because they were afraid of him or he was smart enough not to get involved in any evidence, until he robbed the old guy in the car."

In the drug game, people assumed roles and specialties. As one kid from Newhallville explained, "Everybody stays within their realm. You hustle, you a hustler. You a shooter, you a shooter. Hustlers need shooters, so let's work together, get this done. Survival tactic." And where there were violent intra-neighborhood beefs, being close to a known shooter-enforcer was a deterrent against getting run up on. There was also a distinction to be made within the job descriptions of gun kids, the difference between shooters and killers. Shooters shot to put their name out, to achieve a reputation. Killers aimed to murder.

Rabbit was a shooter. As a young teenager, he acquired his first gun, and "once I got one and started doing stuff, people gave me them. Nobody paid me to shoot. I did it for friends I grew up with. It was an unspoken thing. Something happens to a friend, I got to look out for them. I got your back. Major was doing it differently. He was getting paid." This meant, Romano Ratti explained, that "Major was independent. People hired him to do their dirty work. He ran alone."

Major was used by older criminals to commit murders for them. As a young man called Wonderboy said, "First kid Major shot, someone offered him four grand, and before he finished the offer, Major shot him and was, 'Where's my four G?' This got around, and people were, 'This dude is crazy.' It worked for him as a reputation. Major was known as a dangerous little dude. He walked around wearing clothes that made him look homeless and surprised his victims. He also shot from his bike, which meant zip over there, shoot, come back. Violence is normalized in his world because poverty is violent. Major's only the extreme version."

What was most alarming about Major was the volume of targets. Murderers rarely kill more than once. "He was uncommon," said Elbow of Read Street, "because he was putting in a lot of work. All he did was shoot." The New Haven homicide detective Martin Podsiad said there was morbid value in someone so willing to commit murder. "Human beings," Podsiad explained, "have an innate fear of killing another human being. Very few have the ability to walk up and kill somebody. I've met probably four in my career." This was true also of soldiers. In her book about death and the Civil War, *This Republic of Suffering*, historian Drew Gilpin Faust described the craving to be off duty, how soldiers especially hated the idea of sharpshooters because "they found the intentionality and personalism involved in picking out and picking off a single man highly disturbing." In the streets, those who could kill up close were doing so partly for practical reasons; it's difficult to put someone to death even when you shoot them.

Truth could do it, and Truth knew Major. "He got infatuated with the life," Truth said. "Where he came from, they glorify violence. People want recognition. It goes from carrying a gun to shooting at people to shooting people to killing people. As far as killing people, it happened rapidly. He went crazy. There's a you-don't-give-a-fuck-anymore. Shoot somebody, it's nothing." By going crazy, Truth meant the state of dissociation that made shooting to kill possible.

Major's signature was the .45 caliber pistol. When he left the house, he was routinely strapped with two .45's. All guns are intimidating—mayhem is the purpose—but there's no more frightening pistol than a .45. As Claude Brown wrote, "A .45 has a big hole. As a matter of fact, it's the biggest hole I've looked into . . . It would take your whole head off." Acquiring a street .45 was more difficult than buying other handguns, but for someone like Major, who sold guns and was himself becoming a freelance weapon, there were always people to keep him in supply.

So much will be forever unrevealed about the stealthy movements of a charismatic loner descending into a vortex of violence, how many people he injured but did not kill, how many murders he committed. If there can be consensus about irresolution it's that Major killed a small multitude. "I know four they say he shot," said one man who'd been around Newhallville with an ear to the streets all his life. "My understanding was he killed at least six people," said Major's teacher, the former police officer Bill Garraty. But neither really knew. "Most people [who kill] want to put that out there," said the man who'd heard about four murders, "but he was quiet about it. To survive this game, you have to move in silence." Others thought Major's operating logic suggested the opposite: becoming so notorious, others would leave him alone. A woman sat on her porch watching one day as Major put a gun to another boy's head. When his gun wouldn't fire, she heard Major say, "It's your lucky day." The woman believed he'd wanted her to hear that. A boy who met Major in elementary school saw Major as driven by street reputation: "I know kids doing stuff all their lives not in the spotlight. Major wanted the spotlight. He was famous. All the other kids feared him."

Around Newhallville, and to most police, it became accepted as absolute truth that Major committed three homicides in a matter of weeks during the summer of 2006. To this day the stories of these deaths exist in local memory as a grainy montage of macabre scenes that are passed around furtively as object lessons in neighborhood violence.

On the night of June 13, a boisterous crowd was drinking and dancing at a dim, windowless two-room neighborhood bar called the Ebony Lounge on the town line where Newhallville meets Hamden. Tucked in among houses, a church, and a daycare, the Ebony drew people across sleepy residential blocks into a sudden nighttime dominion of excitement.

Among those in the youthful crowd was a popular, slightly older neighborhood man known for his love of the hip-hop group Wu-Tang Clan. Major was there with friends not from the immediate neighborhood. The older man began wondering why outsiders were in "our bar," jovially "clowning" them. One person who put a lot of thought into what happened next said, "He supposed to be older dude: 'Listen to me!' Major didn't agree with that. Older dude wasn't even talking to Major. He was talking to somebody else, but Major felt disrespected. And it happens from there."

An argument began, the two were kicked out of the bar and sent into the dark, where happily milling people stood in the sidewalk glow of signage and cigarette tips. In the old days, people took it outside for a fair one. Now it was the era of harder feelings. You couldn't bring guns into the Ebony, which checked at the door, but it was assumed Major kept one hidden nearby. Someone went running around the corner. "Gotta go get his ratchet," a voice in the crowd warned. "Major was no fighter," said a detective. "Skinny guy. But he'd shoot you without remorse."

The older man left to meet up with his girlfriend. A car moved through the poorly lit streets, taking sharp turns, and then, still a short walk from the bar, a lone figure got out at the mid-block. People heard him say, "You think it's over." Major approached the older man, asked, "What's up now?" Then Major said, "Word to my sister," and created a blaze of sound and firelight.

A bar full of people had watched them argue. The next day, Major was out in the neighborhood, talking about his evening, which had the desired effect. Witnesses, according to detective Al Vazquez, "blatantly refused to participate in the investigation. They live in the neighborhood. Major has a reputation as a stone-cold killer." A young man told his uncle Major had also tried to shoot him near the Ebony, but Major's gun jammed. "Major was proud of what he was doing at the end," said a young woman who knew him. "He was getting clout. There wasn't shame there. He'd come to a point where he didn't have fear."

THREE DAYS LATER, Major agreed to be interviewed by detectives Racheal Cain and Herb Johnson, but only after he took Bill Garraty's history exam, which he told them he couldn't miss. That was a homicide-investigation first for the detectives. They drove him to school, but it was nearly another month before the police could test him with their questions. That day, down at the police station, Major would grow tearful, leaving the impression that he was afraid of dying. Johnson said, "It's sad to see. They sometimes feel they have to do these things out in the street to fit in or survive." By then there had been another killing.

According to police reports, on the night of July 12, a drug dealer named Spubbsy was driving with Major across the "Corridor"—busy roadways spanning New Haven's poorest neighborhoods, from Newhallville to the Hill. As investigators later concluded, they were hoping to meet with a young drug dealer from Fair Haven. He and his friend, a former star high school baseball pitcher, had recently taken over a Hill drug-selling business from a dealer who'd gone to prison. The Fair Haven drug dealer set up his sales rendezvous by cell phone and then completed the exchanges from cars. Spubbsy and his own associates had arranged to bring Major across the Corridor to execute a drug rip—robbing the Fair Haven drug dealers of their merchandise and their money. The deterrent effect might be to discourage them from returning, allowing the Hill drug dealers to further control the territory.

Police records detail how once the plotters were in the Hill, the Fair Haven dealers were contacted by "a fiend," whom they agreed to meet and sell an eightball—an eighth of an ounce of crack cocaine—for $100 from a gray Chevrolet Impala. The Fair Haven dealers picked up the "fiend," Major, who had a baseball cap pulled so low over his eyes, the brim nearly reached the bridge of his nose. Major settled into the Impala's right rear passenger seat. The Impala moved away from the curb and circled the dark block until Major told the driver to pull over near a corner, in front of a large multifamily house. Out across the intersection were ballfields. Major shot the former pitcher several times, hitting him in the back of his head, bullets passing through his skull and breaking his teeth, as well as piercing his arm, abdomen, and hip. Then the gun barrel moved to the Impala driver, Major announcing, "You know what it is." The driver thrust his hand up to protect his face just before .45-caliber bullets struck him in the arm as well as the face and neck. Major kept firing bullet after bullet as the driver tried to escape, but by now his leg was shattered, so he sprawled half in and half out of the car, screaming in agony. According to reports, Spubbsy appeared on the driver's side and discharged his own gun, after which he rooted in the Impala driver's pockets and removed $500 while Major was sifting through the former pitcher's clothes and finding more.

One boy who committed a robbery with Major said that by this time, "Major was crazy. Crazy, crazy. I would like to say it was drugs, but even when he was sober he'd say crazy stuff." It was never certain to police whether Major was hired to kill the Fair Haven drug dealers or if he took the opportunity to garnish robbery with execution.

Eleven days later, Clarence Willoughby and Ed Reynolds interviewed Major at the police station. No need for detectives to build rapport with this man: "I go straight to the shooting part," Major began. Major freely admitted he'd "jumped in the backseat" of the Impala, planning to buy crack for his friends. But once there, he counted the money supplied to him and realized "it was short." So, Major claimed, "I jumped out the car. Spubbsy is in the street. Let off a shot over the top of my head." The baseball star's head slumped off the head rest. As Major bailed and ran, he said in the police interview, he saw the Impala driver standing outside the car, where Spubbsy killed him. After placing Spubbsy up against the wall for the police, Major then nailed him to it, confirming his identity and that of an associate on a photo board the detectives showed him. Major concluded by assuring the police on tape they'd treated him "like a human being" during this interrogation.

Major's account was easily disproven by investigators, who identified the path of the gunshots as coming from the backseat, where they also found a lode of spent bullet casings. The position of the Impala driver's mangled body meant he'd been unable to flee the car. There were fingerprints at variance with Major's version, and much more, including witnesses. In the interview room with Major, Reynolds found it striking, "He was so matter-of-fact. I told my bosses, 'You need to authorize overtime. We need to get this guy off the street. This guy's a serial killer.'"

Nine days later, on August 1, on another quiet side street, outside another wide multifamily home, another man was shot with a .45 semiautomatic pointed inches from his ear: Pete Fields. About Fields's murder, young men deep in the streets began hearing that a planned holdup had become a homicide. "Major shot him because he was high," it was said.

With Major embroiled in so much violence, it seemed unlikely he would lend (or rent) out his .45 to anybody, let alone a neighborhood boy like Bobby, who wasn't a stickup kid, who had no experience using guns to commit crimes, who might entangle the weapon in events that could bring it back to Major. Such a difficult-to-believe story for both local young people and police fit a false stereotype about how things worked in poor neighborhoods: that people like Major were Rent-a-Centers anybody could approach and ask for a weapon. A Newhallville relative of Bobby's said with incredulity, "Major's a hit man. Why would he lend a gun to Bobby?! He wouldn't even hang out with Bobby. He's just a cornball to Major. He ain't nobody. He's just around."

SUMMER PASSED WITH detectives developing enough probable cause against Major for a judge to grant an arrest warrant. Up in Hartford, the analyst Ivan Kuzyk had decided that the man outside the Ebony Lounge, the Hill drug dealer, and Fields had all probably been murdered by Major. During those summer weeks, there were lurid rumors about Major. A young woman who grew up near Read Street heard "every time he killed somebody, he had a pair of Jordan sneakers and he marked their initials on them." Ratti noticed that around his district, "everybody was terrified. All the shootings he did where people didn't die are countless. I'd hear. People would tell me. But they wouldn't get involved. Can't blame them. They were afraid to be next."

Major's former football coach, Reggie Lytle, was working then in corrections, "and the inmates were telling me, 'This cat, Major, he's lost it. Murders.' I'd call Auntie. She'd say, 'He's on the run. He doesn't want to talk to anybody.' I'd try to reach out. When he finally went off, it got very difficult." The detective Racheal Cain visited Rose at Presidential Gardens and told her, "You've got to convince him to turn himself in, and if you don't, he'll be dead."

In late August, warrants were approved by prosecutors for the arrest of Major in both the Ebony Lounge and Hill drug murders, as well as single warrants for Spubbsy and an associate. On August 30, patrolling police officers spotted Major on Dixwell Avenue and approached, intending to arrest him. But the warrants were still unsigned by a judge, so they had to let Major go. At some point, Major was out with Auntie in her car, and as she drove they listened to the gospel singer Kirk Franklin's song "Imagine Me," about a troubled person reborn after letting go of old pain.

When they got back to Presidential Gardens, several family members were outside, and with them sat a young man. Auntie said, "Strange dude on the doorstep. We know everybody. Somebody not from the neighborhood sitting on the porch none of us know, you're suspicious." But the man was familiar to Major, and after they spoke, Major told his family he had to leave. Major's sister, Kiki, begged him not to go. BlackJack wanted to accompany his cousin, but Major waved him off.

On a seasonably warm August night, Major was swathed in clothing. He wore three bottom layers, including boxer shorts, thermal long underwear, and belted jeans, and four top layers beginning with a sleeveless white undershirt, a white T-shirt, a green T-shirt embossed with the image of a skull, and finally a black hooded sweatshirt. On his feet were two pairs of socks and Timberland boots. He'd grown the wispy beginnings of a mustache. Some shooters favored contrasting light and dark layers of clothes so that, after firing their gun, they could strip the outer layer and throw off police pursuit by looking different. An abundance of clothing with elastic waistbands also helped to both secure and disguise a handgun. Then there were people who felt psychologically armored by wearing many layers. Those who were sick or drug-addicted could feel cold even in sultry weather. Nobody knew for certain what Major's thinking was. In his waist was a Ruger semiautomatic .45, while in his right pocket he carried the black-and-silver Smith and Wesson .45 that had killed Pete Fields.

Major and the strange dude drove across the Corridor to the Hill and parked on residential Frank Street. They were about a mile from the site where the baseball star was shot, the spaces in between an archipelago of storefront churches and corner minimarts. Frank Street was narrow, nearly treeless, and densely packed with lusterless single and subdivided homes, the chipping masonry and faded porch additions dating back to a time when the air was filled with Italian baking and the toll of Catholic bells. Major got out of the strange dude's car and began walking down the sidewalk. Yale's medical school wasn't far off, just across the food desert, two minimarts away. It was past ten o'clock. Auntie believed the first shot went to the side of Major's head, which meant he hadn't been expecting anything, that whomever he was walking alongside had literally turned on him.

Major died facedown on the sidewalk, shot in the temple above his left ear, below the left ear in the cheek, in the back of his head, and in the left arm. When his body was turned over, the Ruger protruded from Major's waist like a stick shift. The Smith & Wesson was discovered in Major's pocket. Ever after, Major became the little assassin who died with two big guns on him. A story circulated that Major was clenching a pistol so fiercely his fingers had to be broken to remove it. This became the first of many apocryphal details from Major's end.

Of how people reacted across Newhallville, a young woman Major's age said, "The streets were relieved. The community was sad." A former drug dealer, Sere, said, "I think Major was the fucking devil." At Hillhouse High, Bill Garraty discovered his fellow teacher Millette Núñez weeping. "They shot Major," she told him. For a week, Núñez cried hard every day, and she found herself praying for Major to have peace, even though she wasn't religious. "Major," she said, "was one of those kids, you know they were doing something very, very wrong to be where they are, but you have to say what a beautiful human being this kid is to me." Garraty, meanwhile, was "stunned to discover he had a completely different life, involved in something so dark. He was so kind to me. I knew he was into things, but it was such a strange thing, this kid was one person, a coin flips, and he's this completely different person." The former police officer had to admit "the word 'love' cannot be excluded from my feelings about that kid."

Goody was now living in Maryland. He also pondered this "one dude off the street. It's eerie. I had thousands of conversations with kids. He stuck with me." Goody decided Major expressed the "constant anguish" of the neighborhood they both came from.

Major's murder was never solved, and his investigation file remains wax-paper thin. Nobody else was arrested in the July murder of the baseball star. "I was very unhappy they wouldn't prosecute the case," said the lead detective, Martin Dadio.

Anthony Campbell, who would, a decade later, become New Haven's second Black police chief, said nobody would help the police. While Major himself had readily given up other people during his talks with detectives, Campbell knew many law-abiding Black people from Newhallville considered it anathema to deal with law enforcement. Campbell believed this had direct lineage to the Jim Crow–era Black understanding of the police as the paramilitary division of a continually oppressive state. Yale Law School professor Monica Bell, a Black South Carolina native, referred to the national legacy of Black mistreatment by Southern lawmen like Bill Wolfe in Wolfton as "legal estrangement." She said, "There are good reasons for why people don't talk to police. Will the police care about you enough to protect you?" That the estrangement had enabled murderers, and created more Black crime victims, was the painful paradox making members of families, like Pete Fields's, Bobby's, and Major's who'd left the South to get away from such oppression, feel doubly let down by the country and its systems.

Major's funeral service was held at the Immanuel Missionary Baptist Church, Connecticut's oldest African American Baptist church. In the 1950s and 1960s, Immanuel Baptist was the best-dressed congregation in the city—a Sunday glory of hats and dresses. Toward century's end, as unemployment and poverty overtook working-class Black New Haven, Immanuel Baptist became known for its leadership's early support of those infected with HIV. This was done, at first, from the church basement out of discretion. In plenty of New Haven families, adding to the devastation of the disease was the secret burden of stigma.

The church's high exterior walls and long, slanting gable was a design its Black architect, Edward Cherry, who'd lived on Great Migration–era Read Street, meant to recall rural Black churches in the South. The vast interior ceiling made the church's pastor, Samuel T. Ross-Lee, think of the hull of that "big boat," the Old Ship of Zion, with passengers on board sailing across the sorrowful seas of life to a peaceful shore. On the day of Major's funeral, the worship area's one thousand seats filled, and more people eddied out on the sidewalk. Major's was a Newhallville family with a beloved matriarch, and many came to the funeral for Rose. Others were young people from Newhallville who talked about Major in death becoming "lovable again." Erik Clemons, a Black man who ran a job-training organization on the grounds of the former Winchester factory explained, "Not everyone goes to a funeral to lament. A product of slavery is this idea of forgiveness. Black people are the most forgiving people I know. So a funeral is a happening, and it's the idea of seeing him as a child, the activation of forgiveness in that."

Barbara Tinney, a family social worker in Newhallville, thought that the rituals of the funeral were especially important for young people, because Major's life reflected struggles affecting so many Newhallville children, the risk of how they were growing up. She described Newhallville as "swarming with the loss of people." But instead of the whole city considering itself in crisis, Tinney thought most from nearby white neighborhoods were likely oblivious to the carnage, reinforcing belief that "gun violence involving poor Black boys is not recognized as a loss." The procession of funerals in 2006 and since, she said, were recurrent expressions of grieving that themselves became traumatizing.

Romano Ratti attended Major's service. Then, to pay further homage, he went to the grave. There Ratti kept a respectful distance, until only one other person was left, a teenage boy. "I worried he was going to throw a gun into the hole," Ratti said. Instead, as Ratti watched, "he broke out crying."

There was a history, Claude Brown wrote, of "bad" Black men in the Jim Crow South "who didn't take shit" from anybody, especially "crackers," and ladies cried at the funerals of even the meanest ones. But the behavioral tech who'd known Major at Urban Youth Middle School saw Major in death less as a Stagger Lee folk hero than as a suffering young person who "wanted other people, subconsciously, to have some of the pain he had. Almost a vindication thing. When he went off the deep end, I'm pretty sure he had no remorse. But earlier he did have compassion. I saw him with the cousins."

To her grandchildren, Rose's advice was "let it be." But what the police officer Dave Rivera noticed was that the three male cousins Major grew up with now slid into violence. "It was kind of crazy," Rivera said, "how they all went down the wrong path. When Major died it affected the whole family." After it became apparent the police would never arrest anybody for his murder, there was neighborhood expectation that Major's cousins would avenge his killing themselves. It was likewise assumed that Major's murderers might make a preemptive move on the cousins.

A few months after Major's death, BlackJack ditched a Hi-Point semiautomatic pistol in an elementary-school classroom toy bin as he ran through the building, trying to elude police. Blackjack's own teachers had considered him to possess abundant personal potential. A favorite instructor thought him to be "a beautiful guy when you talk with him, charming and cool, but a double life." The officers eventually ran BlackJack down at the elementary school, and one later said, "Something happened to him. Seemed like every time we arrested him, he was in possession of a gun." The police consensus was BlackJack had begun "trying to fill the shoes of Major after he got killed." Kids in the neighborhood said he'd "lost his bodyguard."

BlackJack now lived a pattern of arrest, prison, release, and arrest, with his expanding record rife with descriptions of car chases and police standoffs. He was discovered by police in his grandmother's attic crawl space, buried in pink insulation, holding two guns, one of them cocked. At another point, with news alerts of BlackJack out in the city, armed, dangerous, and wanted by police for instigating shootings, BlackJack turned himself in. At the police station, he explained he was carrying weapons because he knew who'd killed Major and the perpetrators were afraid he'd tell. The police asked him, "Do you know who might be trying to shoot you?" to which he answered, "So many of them."

After one of BlackJack's arrests, a police officer who was processing him began asking personal questions. "I remember talking to him," the officer said. "He started tearing up. Took a lot for me not to get emotional. I felt his pain." BlackJack told the officer that "after my father had nothing to do with my mother, he had nothing to do with me." As he listened, the officer became convinced that "with all he did, he was acting out the hurt from his father."

Another day, across a prison table, BlackJack spoke gratefully of his mother, "She did what she can for us," and his grandmother, "the angel, backbone of the family." But BlackJack said he couldn't discuss his father: "My father just gone. Definitely I know my father, but I, I, no." Violence, he said, "led to my downfall. Seeing death at a young age." When asked about the Fields murder, BlackJack became tense. Feet precisely together, he seemed to close in upon himself, a fortified bunker, as he said, "I don't know nothing at all. From my understanding, people say the dude had confessed. I don't know nothing at all. I really don't know."

Chapter Twelve

Bobby was eighteen years old, five-foot-ten, 160 pounds, and still growing at the end of 2007, when he arrived at the Cheshire Correctional Institution, a high-security adult prison known to most current inmates as "Big Cheshire." Some corrections officers (COs) called it the Rock. Bobby's green Manson Youth prison clothes now became tan as he joined more than 1,300 men serving sentences for committing serious crimes. Bobby resented being sent to Big Cheshire for what another person had done, but it wasn't otherwise his nature to consider himself above anybody else. The prison would become to him "a big universe of people full of talents who don't know how to conduct themselves. A lot of people there, their stomach crawls when they hear about the harsh crimes others there commit. They're disgusted." His Big Cheshire was likewise a place populated by men repenting their worst moments. The contrite were, for the most part, people who would never injure a CO, hurt a fellow prisoner. Some were older men who struggled increasingly with things they'd done in their youth, a level of shame that affected those around them. That it was difficult to be your best self in prison was as true for prisoners as it was for COs. COs found their work levels beyond stressful. Seeing and hearing about so much misery, plenty felt what was termed vicarious trauma. Among them were COs who developed guilt they could leave and go home while those they were responsible could not.

Far more than, say, going off to college, prison was a difficult adjustment, and one where freshman prisoners oriented themselves—figuring out as non-swimmers how to survive the cold water of the deep end on their own.

The environment didn't ask people to grapple internally with the things they'd done to others; prison told them to follow rules. Big Cheshire was a hard-time experience regulated by a more than seventy-page booklet of "procedures" and further unstated restrictions that someone like Bobby learned in the course of his days. No bleach was allowed (thrown bleach could be blinding), and not permitted either was cooking oil (very flammable.) The wide prison corridors had painted stripes designating makeshift highway lanes where inmates could walk. Dunking was forbidden during basketball games. During visitation, touching was limited to a short hug and kiss at the start and end.

Cheshire had the day-to-day feel of a crowded city, without those urban compensations of anonymity and solitude. Bobby was lonely and never alone in prison. Outside his cell, there was always someone coming at him; inside the cell, sharing space with a cellmate or "cellie," as people said, meant he had no privacy. How many cubic feet of possessions Bobby could own, the percentage of wall area he was allowed to paper with photographs and decorations, whether the ceiling light was kept on, none of this was up to him. "We go to sleep, the light be blazing," Bobby said. "In the cell we created blindfolds."

The view out his window was walls, razor wire, a narrow patch of grass; from one cell he could see the outline of trees, pieces of the sky. Cheshire cell windows that faced over a shaft to other cell windows sometimes produced chess partners, people seeking reprieve from the plague of unshaped time by signaling their moves back and forth across the void. Bobby didn't play long-distance chess, but he did learn the game well enough to see that chess could free you by overtaking your mind. He also bench-pressed bunk beds: "It's hard, but it's a good workout."

In the dining hall, there were spoons and forks, but no knives. On holidays and Super Bowl Sunday, the dining hall offered meals that made the air savory—with roast turkey at Thanksgiving, roast beef at Christmas, and for the annual Black History Month meal in February, the halls were redolent with collard greens, mac 'n' cheese, corn bread, barbecued chicken, and rice pudding. "That's when the COs say, 'It smells so good we'll have to shake down the cells,'" Bobby said. Casual spite was, like the place itself, virtually inescapable. Bobby knew of one kid who tried to flee. He threw a mattress over a gate, climbed, and jumped, but the top of the gate was strung with barbed wire, which cut him up so badly, the kid bled until he passed out in the woods.

During the day, noise was constant, a discordant din of banging and yelling. Most people had TVs and CD players in their cells, which they were supposed to listen to with headphones, though some modified the headphones into speakers. Radios played without interruption, and were cranked up especially on Fridays when, with circadian regularity, people still felt the impulse to party. Dozens of cells were connected by vents, so, Bobby said, "You can hear everything. No privacy." There was the click, slam, clack of domino tiles, the thrum of urgent male conversation, and the intermittent sound of crying and screaming from "people on meds or who can't take the pain of being in prison. Day or night, both."

Every person to enter Big Cheshire heard right away how crucial it was to do your time, not let your time do you. The months passed so slowly, old heads counseled living in the present, keeping your eyes down, eliminating the very concept of "next." Bobby said, "You never mark your days in jail. You live in the day." Yet if you followed the football and basketball seasons, noticed the weather, kept track of your daily workouts, then ignoring the passage of time became impossible. Prison time was different, and made people different because, for most, there was never enough happening to make the hours beat faster. No hurry existed in prison. With personal reservoirs drained of new experiences, it was natural for people lying in bed to fall into memories until the reality snapped them back.

Outside their cells, everywhere men went, everything they did was recorded on camera except for "in the cut" out-of-view locations, like the supply closets. Without open windows, the Cheshire smell was inescapable, a rancid blend of laundry detergent with such a distinctive scent that, a prison official noted, it helped dogs track escapees, and the cortisol-odor of stress and depression—the sour heaviness of not wanting to be there. "Jail doesn't give you soap," Bobby said. "So, if you don't have family [to put money in your commissary account], you don't have soap." Like everything else, Cheshire's "horrible stink," Bobby said, eventually "became natural."

The prison laundry was such an erratic operation that white T-shirts routinely came back brownish, and Bobby took to washing clothes in his cell sink, as he sometimes also washed himself—the practice known as "birdbathing." You weren't allowed to hang your clothes up to dry from a line, because this might impede a CO's view of the room through the "Judas window" from outside the door, but you could drape them from your desk or your towel hook. The funky dampness of drying cloth added to the claustrophobia.

Other smells seeped into the day. Men MacGyvered cooking devices generically known as stingers by attaching stripped extension-cord wires to batteries that were kept separate by a wedge of toothbrush handle or cutlery, bound together and then submerged in a plastic container filled with salted water. A plastic bag holding cookstuffs was placed in the container. When the extension cord was plugged into a wall socket, the water heated up in the plastic container, and soon the hallways might smell briefly of recipes. Sometimes there were power outages, and Bobby thought they happened because so many people had stingers running. The lights would go out and it was "literal darkness" in there for thirteen hours, until the daylight seeped in through the window crevices.

Although the food lived down to repute, "a lot of people gain weight," Bobby said. "Jail you eat and sit there all day." Men talked of turning into dump trucks. The consensus favorite dining-hall meal was popcorn chicken; the least popular was a dish described even by prison officials as "some sort of meat." Bobby most hated Friday's fish dinner, a seafood surprise, which he sampled exactly once: "They'd put all this stuff together. Crunch everything up, serve it to you." Meals were for Bobby "a dangerous time," because many people came together, first in the chow line and then at table, where Bobby did his best to concentrate on his tan dining tray and not offend anyone. Looking down every day at his starch-laden meals, Bobby believed he was confronting society's expectations for him. Sometimes he'd notice beetles had burrowed in to share.

Across the history of prisons, people with resources have supplemented their meals. The Big Cheshire commissary did a brisk trade in corner-store fare, from Nutella to Velveeta. There were Doritos for days, and ramen as far as the eye could see. And just as the bodegas of Newhallville were notorious for using their area monopoly to make it expensive to be poor, Cheshire's mostly impoverished clientele was charged steep commissary prices: Bobby paid $3 for soap, lotion cost $5, it was 60 cents for an envelope, more than a dollar for a small bag of potato chips. An alternative was to buy his snacks from the prison entrepreneurs, who used commissary ingredients to make their own burritos, s'mores, cake, and coffee treats. Cheshire was big for honeybuns, which Bobby spread with peanut butter after a workout. How people at Big Cheshire ate suggested they were seeking to fill emptiness, craved flavor and portion, wanted more sweetness in their lives.

People had so little individual authority in prison that whatever they owned took on outsized value. A stolen or confiscated bottle of lotion was difficult to move past. For Bobby it was like walking the sidewalks of Newhallville again; he had always to be monitoring his surroundings through a distanced personal windshield. Curiosity was discouraged. Men took on nicknames like Skunk or Shotgun helping them to assume a prison identity that was either a reinvention or a shield. Most people didn't discuss their crimes; they became an artifact you never referred to because you wanted to believe it didn't happen, you wanted to move past it. Bobby knew what only a few had done. "I don't judge people," he said, and "I didn't ask. I only found out about people when people gossiped." Mass incarceration had created such a large prison pool, Bobby found it mostly produced a tolerant effect. "It's a cold place," he said, "but people don't slander each other. They chill and do their bid."

If someone seemed too intent on making whatever crime he'd committed not come up, it was natural to wonder if he'd done something especially aberrant. Sex-crime prisoners were the traditional prison pariahs, and at Big Cheshire, Bobby said, if that became known about you, "nobody deals with rapists. What if this was my child or my sister or my mother?" But "the worst thing to be in prison," he said, "was a snitch. Worse than a rapist or a pedophile. A pedophile is worse than a snitch, but a snitch is treated worse." A retired New Haven prosecutor concurred. "It's absolutely dangerous to be a snitch in prison," he said. "One method cops used with people there who wouldn't help them was is to say, 'Okay, we'll just spread it around the community you're a snitch.' "

For most people, all but a few prison days were mundane, but the deviating moments could change you forever. Sexual predation and physical violence were much rarer than in the prison mythology, but people were taken advantage of all the time; though if it wasn't your cellie's eye socket stove in with a hair clipper, you might or might not hear about it. When someone lost his chill, what ensued was "drama," the catchall for behavior born of living in a place designed to be where nobody wanted to be. Bobby saw enough to believe that "prison is all about drama. Attitude. People are frustrated sitting there all day constantly being told what to do, and they want to take it out on somebody." Drama was the overt malice of men setting fires, clogging toilets, throwing things, fighting over whose turn it was to use the pay telephones on which you could only call collect, over whether the dayroom TV would be channeled to sports, a movie, or a crime show. Those watching crime shows, Bobby said, might exclaim, "There's my flaw! That's how I got caught."

That so many people at Big Cheshire came there young could make prison feel like an epidemic of lost hope. Large numbers of the population were poor and undereducated and fatherless, and that was difficult for the older men, whether inmates or COs. The level of trauma in the place was acute. One Thanksgiving, Bobby said, "I saw a guy kill himself. He was across from me. He couldn't take jail. I was eighteen. His cellie was asleep. He took the sheet and hung himself. His cellie was screaming and screaming, so we woke up."

Most of Bobby's coming-of-age years were spent in Cell Number 39 of South Block 4 at Big Cheshire, the upstairs far-corner cell, a room of cinder block, concrete, steel, and incandescent light that was just long and wide enough that he could run in place to "keep the blood flowing." Cells were such tiny rooms, everything a person did happened right in front of his assigned cellie. This included using the toilet. Because men were always being transferred or released, Bobby eventually realized he'd accumulated more cellies than he could count. Bobby judged himself a good cellie: "People admired that I live clean. I was easy to get along with." Typically, the choice of the upper or lower bunk went to the person who'd already been living in the cell, but if an older man was assigned to Bobby's cell, Bobby always ceded him the lower bunk. With everyone, Bobby tried making the long view his rooming policy. If his cellie came back from a disappointing telephone conversation spoiling to take his troubles out on Bobby, "I'd just shut up and stay in my lane. No need to argue." He tolerated whistlers, hummers, snorers, pranksters, masturbators, inaccurate toilet-bowl aimers, people who wouldn't bathe. "You can never get used to the lack of privacy, sharing such a small space," Bobby said.

If you weren't a discreet person when you got to Big Cheshire, you learned to be. Partly because people were rarely alone, many learned to achieve distance in the presence of others. The detachment and the sheer number of hardships people had experienced could make prison seem like an intensely unsympathetic place where nobody wanted to hear about your pain. Bobby listened one day from his cell as a man with terminal cancer lay curled up on his cell floor, moaning, as others barked at him, "Man up. You'll live." It was advisable at Big Cheshire to be slow to reveal yourself to your cellie—and everybody else—for personal information could be used to your detriment. But eventually cellies might drop their mask. Collectively, Bobby's cellies revealed so much, they made him feel buffeted by their trauma. One cellie was M. He was eighteen, and when he moved in, Bobby, all of a couple years older, eyed him uneasily, wondering if "he was going to be out of control in the cell." It was near Christmas, and M. asked Bobby "Yo, we get Christmas trees in here?" When Bobby told him they didn't, M. cried.

M. had so much energy, he'd dance for hours, and because he was loose-limbed and inventive, Bobby was always appreciative of this entertainment. Prisons are incubators for new dances, people choreographing innovative ways to move in a narrow space. With time no object, they could spend hour after hour perfecting combinations and sequences before putting it all out there during rec, taking on challenges in impromptu dance slams, the best new dances eventually leaving the prison and, prisoners heard, becoming popular in the city clubs.

One morning, M. began dancing as he brushed his teeth with one hand and brushed his hair with the other. Soon, Bobby said, "He's so focused on his waves, he forgot he was brushing his teeth." Twenty minutes passed. Then twenty-five. Finally, Bobby said, "Yo, your teeth are going to fall out." Bobby knew what he was seeing. "He had seven years," Bobby said.

At times, M. would become beside himself about prison, and to Bobby he'd begin "rambling" about what he'd done to get there. One day, M. suddenly asked Bobby, "Yo, how much time you got?" Bobby told him, "Thirty-eight years." Startled, M. asked, "For what?" Bobby told him. Now M. was really worked up. "What!" he yelled. "Yo! They done put me in a cell with a murderer?" Bobby reassured M. he would never hurt him.

Bobby himself encountered a few men who seemed to take pleasure in telling him, with clinical detail, how they'd killed someone in a yard or an alleyway. "These dudes," he said, "are never coming home. All they do is talk about their crimes. They do it to scare people." Other murderers, who might be in on a lesser charge, needed to revisit and revisit those undiscovered slayings they'd done, and Bobby could hear their voices carrying through the vents. "You want to catch a murderer, just listen," Bobby said. "That's all they talk about."

Known murderers weren't generally shunned at Cheshire. The general attitude was shit happens in life, you had your reasons, your business, you are doing your time, it's not for me to pass sentence on you. Bobby's experience was that murderers were usually people who'd committed the crime only once, and judged themselves more harshly for it than anybody judged them. "If they killed someone," he said, "it haunts them. I had a cellie who shot his best friend in the head. Every night he'd yell, 'I'm sorry, I'm sorry, I didn't mean to.' You can't sleep through that. All he could see when he slept was his friend."

Suffused as it was with human extremes, prison began to affect Bobby's ability to concentrate. His memory had always been excellent, but he'd put something down in his cell, get distracted, and then he'd look, "and I couldn't find it." Worse was at night, when those firsthand stories of homicides crept into Bobby's dream life.

Lifting weights built the means of self-protection, and working out relieved stress. Some men kept extra-fit, exercising both because your routine was a way to have autonomy in a rule-bound life and also to be ready for the distant year when you'd reenter the world. "A lot of guys try to stay younger for later," Bobby said. Mortality pressed on people. Bobby himself began to feel "like the days was fading away." The evanescence made him think there was "no reason to be good." For a person with a strong ethical outlook, all this was head-on wreckage.

He became, he said, "angry. The whole time. I was furious to be in jail." His rage turned him fearless in a dangerous place. "People were telling me I was mad disrespectful. I'd take the basketball and fling it. *This dude's crazy!* Another day, I was watching a movie on TV, they went to change the channel to sports, I went bananas. Talking smack to ten dudes. They could have murdered me." The men let him be because "older guy who ran the day room grew up with my family and knew my story. It was me frustrated at being there. It got to me."

In his cell Bobby began to have magical daydreams, cooking up what he called "stupid" bargains such as, "If they didn't let me out after fifteen years, I thought when I did get out I'd go shoot all the people who did that to me." This was as natural as him being in church and having fantasies about a woman in the next pew, but to Bobby, sitting in prison and even just imagining himself committing butchery seemed to justify his presence there a little more. After a while, he changed course and made a decision to disengage from the prison experience.

He resolved he would be in Big Cheshire, but not of Big Cheshire. If they were all, in a way, just passing through, he would live as a visitor among the visitors. Having grown up in a crowded household, he knew how to withdraw in full view. He began during rec to stay in his cell. "I didn't come out and chill," he said. "I felt like I needed space from other people's problems. I used to hate the backbiting and backstabbing—it was horrible." He obeyed all regulations, but otherwise, for a time, Bobby was present but gone.

If there was glory for Bobby to be won at Big Cheshire, it was on a basketball court. Prison basketball games could attract crowds watching the full-court games, which to Bobby "felt like the NBA. We used to bang out!" He was still an excellent player, with a sweet crossover dribble, and late in tied games, people would shout, "Get Bobby the ball!" It brought him pleasure to take in how much opponents "hate when the ball's in my hands. All tied up the game on the line. They know I'm gonna score! They put two or three guys on me. They'd leave open the dude who couldn't play at all. I'd get him the ball and for some reason he'd always score." Bobby was still a kid; he wanted his victories to matter.

The basketball wasn't typically rougher than playground games, but like everything at prison, it carried risk. Frustration with prison built in people until they might suddenly take it out on an opponent. Playing basketball, Bobby injured a shoulder, a leg, and after a game in which he fouled someone from Hartford, the man came looking for Bobby with a knife. Other men intercepted him. People did "get stabbed up," Bobby said, and just like at Manson Youth, self-protection was preeminent for everybody, so the old New Haven neighborhood street rivalries here also reconstituted as defensive alliances against those from other cities. It was advisable at Big Cheshire to walk the lined corridors with an unrevealing face. Bobby's stone mask suggested both that he was not to be messed with and that he belonged—an ironic feat of assimilation, given that he didn't belong at all.

FOR MOST YOUNG people in prison, the great source of consolation is family. When you left for prison as a teenager, even as you aged, you remained in some respects a child, and you needed the consistent acceptance of someone stepping into the visiting room to gather you up right there, before everyone else, an act of public affection that said, *He may be in this desolate place, but he's dear to me, he's my boy, and he is cared about.* It was unspoken public testimony that let everybody know, including you, he still matters. This was all so tacitly agreed upon that the Department of Correction published a handbook that urged families to support their incarcerated relatives, with the first reason given that positive support reduced recidivism, made another offense seven times less likely. But a prisoner was dependent upon his family overcoming the inconvenience and expense of driving to the (for most) far-flung prison during visiting hours, and otherwise paying for collect calls despite the minimum $4 cost. Those who filled the cheerless Big Cheshire waiting room, waiting patiently for the unrushed COs in charge to finally look up from what they were doing and slide open the doors, were all making sacrifices to get there, and for some, that sacrifice was too much.

Bobby loved his mother, and his mother loved him, but she didn't go to see him. Grace visited Big Cheshire only three times in Bobby's first six years of prison, and she wrote him a single letter. Bobby's incarceration was a calamity for Grace following her mother's death. In combination, said one of Bobby's sisters, the losses led Grace to "shut down. You can get to her and it's a roadblock. My grandmother died. She wouldn't come to family functions. It seemed like she didn't care about Bobby, but she wasn't herself. It was grief." Grace was working, raising her large family by herself, suffered health problems, didn't own a car. Having her son now untethered from New Haven, more than a thirty-minute drive away, was, as Bobby himself said, "hard for her. Lots of kids."

After Yusef Salaam was interrogated alone by police, who lied to him about fingerprints, he was wrongfully convicted and sent to prison at age fifteen as one of the Central Park Five. Salaam said of his own mother that she "was in a worse prison than I was. Because she couldn't protect me, that was itself a trauma. What tools did she have to be prepared for that?" Grace was a good person struggling. That the road to Big Cheshire became an unpassable distance wasn't anything she was proud of. She knew there were those who faulted her, but in the interests of what seemed, to her, self-preservation, she simply couldn't go there. "I haven't seen him for a while," she said during Bobby's ninth Cheshire year. "It bothers me. I get so depressed every time I go." On some days, Bobby could understand that, for Grace, the idea of him in a prison was demolishing. "She felt she failed as a parent," he said. "She felt then she could never pick herself up. She felt the overlap of my grandmother dying in '05, me going to jail in '06, it was devastating to her." But Bobby was mostly left to imagine their relationship, and there were other times when he felt undone by his mother's absence. One year, he sent Grace a Mother's Day card. When he didn't hear back, he became convinced she'd torn it up. This wasn't true, but in the moment he went to black. The reason he had such bad information was that he was bearing the full weight of Big Cheshire all on his own.

Grace's partial solution to loving her missing son was to bestow kindnesses upon Bobby's friend Little Blue. "His mom's like my mother," Little Blue said. "She's [there] whenever I need anything. I just ask her. She fed me. I reminded her of him. She loved him. She missed him. But people's life go on."

For Bobby, the Big Cheshire days and months passed mostly without visitors. His oldest sister, Tonya, came, but very occasionally; she had a job and young children. His younger sisters didn't drive. Infrequently, a couple of them were given rides. Here a cousin, there an aunt, and eventually Bobby's sparse callers dwindled to none. "My family," Bobby said, "nobody was there for me. Until my grandfather stepped up. Granddad doesn't just abandon people. But nobody gave him information. I was a mystery for a while. I was gone." It was after five years, in 2011, that Granddad had made his way to Cheshire and questioned his grandson. Granddad said of the day, "He told me, 'Granddad, I'm innocent. I didn't do it.' I said, 'Why'd you confess?' He said, 'I'm thinking of my family. They told me I'd get probation and get to see my family again, and if I didn't, I'd never get out of jail. They give you sixty years, you'll never get out." After Granddad took that in, he visited every two or three months, began sending money to Bobby's commissary account, and, in his reserved way, Granddad fumed at Northern justice. As Granddad drove out to the prison in one of his Chevrolets, his grandson's life so far from what he'd imagined for his family when he left South Carolina, Granddad said he would think, "It never would have happened to a Yale student, especially with not having his parent there. I don't know how they let them get away with that."

In the cold months, Granddad didn't come either, and when spring arrived, he and Bobby followed an agreement not to criticize other family members. It was nearly backbreaking for Bobby to be forsaken in this way. Rare is the prisoner who doesn't idealize life on the outside. Bobby imagined his younger relatives shimmying in nightclubs, he imagined the birth of new babies, weekend outings and celebrations. The phrase "out of sight, out of mind" ran like a chyron under images he could only invent. "I didn't get pictures," he said. "I find kids were born a year or two later. How was I not told these things? Unbelievable. They moved on." He never wept, because he decided nothing at Cheshire would make him do that, but rage drenched him. "At times I'd go black in the cell," he said. "For all of them."

What made Bobby's predicament worse were the people around him who were the recipients of an abundance of prison plenty. "People get mail every day," he said. "People get boxes on top of boxes. People were overwhelmed with love." Bobby had one cellie whose family members showed up for daily visits. There were days when the mail came through his door and "Four or five pieces and nothing for you." He felt so hurt and so foolish. It made him wonder if there was mercy for him anywhere.

There was. Older men with prison nicknames like Chi-Town, Twist, Yellow, C-Love, and Italian bestowed upon Bobby small kindnesses that he would later believe saved him. "If it wasn't for dudes being nice to me," he said, "I'd have been so fucked-up. I wouldn't have had soap or a washcloth or stamps—nothing."

Eventually, Bobby also saved himself, earning commissary money by doing cleaning work as a tierman. For years he would work five hours a day, seven days a week, being paid fifteen cents an hour, and "I never missed."

Bobby's Cell 39 was considered a desirable space in the block, both because it had the best TV reception and, tucked away in the back, it was comparatively quiet. When COs began a tour of the block's cells, searching everyone's quarters for contraband, by the time they got to Bobby's corner they were usually too tired from lifting, digging, and combing for cell phones, drugs, and "pruno" (home-brew) to conduct more than a perfunctory shakedown of 39. To Bobby, the one virtue of living out his youth in a concrete cabinet was that it had a monastic effect. "Only in prison did I reflect on my ways," he said. There in Cell 39, Bobby began to go deeper, probing his life pursuit, trying to make sense of ending up as a convicted murderer all alone at Big Cheshire.

Prison didn't, as Bobby had worried, turn him into a brutish person. Since childhood he'd always possessed moral clarity even if at fisted moments, as a teenager, he did not act morally. He was an accurate observer who could see existence clear as it was experienced by other people, and his great consolation during those early years in prison became his sympathetic outlook. He watched the delivery of the brown paper bags filled with food and sundries from the commissary, saw some people consistently receive eight bags and others consistently get "nothing but air." He watched lonely men who had gone decades without a visitor or a letter. It made him decide he had the toughness to deal with days where "it's never up to me, not being able to live my life, my younger years passing by."

Bobby's habitual sheathing against pain was detachment. Initially at Big Cheshire, he'd tried to go blank and distant, and succeeded well enough that "I just, like, I forgot about everything." He would describe his early-years approach to his long sentence as an attempt to place such intense focus on the lived moment that he could abolish "all the old memories." But the past was tenacious, he found, and "it seem like memories always come back and that's the mind. It always plays back in your mind. Even when you're not anticipating on it. It's like you just sit there and your mind will take you back to your past. I used to be like, dang, I wonder what Shay doing. I wonder how is she living. I wonder who she with. I used to be curious about a lot of things. And I used to try to wipe it out."

It was wretched to think in isolation about people who, as far as Bobby knew, weren't thinking about him. But he found it was worse to isolate himself from what had been good in his life. Within his cell, gradually, over two years, Bobby allowed himself to savor small memories, such as how, by calling one pretty cousin Halle Berry, he'd earned the wrath of the others who all wished to be similarly nicknamed. It was a problem of principle that there in his cell, Bobby still couldn't resolve: "This one wanted to be Halle Berry too. You don't look like Halle Berry! So I gave them other names. They were offended. It was a lose-lose. They'd say, 'Call me Beyoncé!' You don't look like Beyoncé!"

Achieving the strength to reminisce even when he felt the people he was remembering had dropped him was an act of emotional courage almost inconceivable for someone who hadn't been in prison. That here he was, perpetually in the back-then, while they'd all gone on, was a gale to his face. But his affection was durable enough for him to persist. That was a pure definition of love, caring regardless of what caring was returned. Thinking back gave Bobby something in prison that was vital to the former traveler: his interior life was up to him.

Now that the past felt safe, he confronted the present, Bobby also feeling free to admit his disappointments. "I want to know what my family went through. What did I miss?" There were his sisters' graduations, Hank's wedding, the funeral of a close friend who was murdered, the birth of a niece. Chubby had been another grandfather to Bobby. The street rumors that Chubby had cost Bobby by saying something unconsidered remained there hanging, with no chance for Bobby to talk it all out with him. That meant Chubby was lost to him too. ("That was my boy," Chubby would say. "My heart goes out to him.") Bobby had last seen Serena when she was six. Now she, whose diapers he'd changed, was a teenager. As he knew, families are built of friction as much as affection. He didn't have the map of slights and grudges. It hurt, he admitted, to lose his prom and graduation. Bobby missed spontaneity, reaching for the telephone, deciding on a shower, opening the refrigerator just to peruse what was in there, walking down the block to look-see if Shay was around. "The experience of eighteen, nineteen, twenty. I did miss those things. And girls. Girls more than anything. Being with them. Having fun. Talking. Sex."

BACK IN NEW HAVEN, nobody's days improved without Bobby. For Bobby's sisters, growing up absent the attentions of their fathers, and then losing the big brother who had done his best to be a father to them, was pain over hardship. Stephanie had liked it that her brother protected her from neighborhood boys when she was young, and that he praised her for being a good student. He'd encouraged her to write poems and music, taught her dances; sometimes they wrote songs together in three-part harmony. Now, she recalled, "A sense of me left. There was no more full person. When he left I had no sense of anything. I stopped writing. I stopped dancing. I stopped a lot of things."

It was similar for Bobby's other sisters, like Kenya. "My brother told me I can achieve anything I want," she said. When Kenya graduated from high school, "I was upset. I wanted my brother front and center when I graduated. Instead, I had to tell him on a jail phone. My mother didn't make it. She had to go to work. It would make me feel better if my brother made it. It was hard when I see everybody else's older brother there. When I'm angry or upset, he's the person who can calm me down."

The promising lives of some of Bobby's favorite relatives foundered. People lost scholarships, fell into financial trouble. Various factions cleaved because you had to blame somebody for what had happened to Bobby. Of Chubby, one cousin said, "Nobody's embraced him since." Another cousin felt for what Chubby had lost and said, "Nobody holds it against him, what happened." As for Lion, he would walk out of the room if somebody brought up Bobby's name. "All he seen was me," he said. "I feel guilty inside my heart. I showed him that road." Lion's mother, Bobby's vivacious aunt Joy, became glum. As Granddad's wife, Aretha, a teacher and a minister, said, "The commonality was everybody was hurt."

What made Bobby's imprisonment a particular source of family despair was the feeling of being let down by the system, that the country was against you, that for boys growing up in Newhallville, such events were inevitable and that nobody could do anything about it. One of the cousins who earned and then lost a college scholarship while Bobby was away said, "It hurt me. I know it wasn't him. I cry thinking about it. Him sitting in jail for that long." Everybody felt, as Bobby's older cousin Quay said, "he's been dealt a raw hand." Some also agreed with Quay's belief that given the way Bobby had been growing up, "This was a blessing in disguise. He could have been dead.

That was just the reality. No, he wasn't doing anything, but the company you keep." Bobby's mother believed that, and so did Bobby's sister Shavonne, who said, "I feel like everybody in jail be doing better than they're doing out here if you're a man. He's in a better place in jail. No killing or shooting." New Haven police officers pointed out the numerous people Bobby grew up around who had either been arrested or shot. "You hang with a group of people, you get guilt by association—your name pops up," one officer said. "It may have actually saved him."

Bobby's close cousin Hank was the person who'd spent every day with Bobby in Newhallville, the mornings beginning with a six-a.m. pebble at the window and Bobby calling, "Hank, get up!" For years after Bobby went to prison, Hank cried about Bobby. But even then, he said, "It really didn't sink in until when I first got my car and I was just driving around. I'm looking at my passenger side, like, 'My boy's not here right now.' Anybody that ever got in that passenger seat, it still didn't feel the same." Hank disliked relatives rationalizing about Bobby. "Sometimes our family will say since he's in jail, better there than here," he said. "But it's not good for him to be in there. A prisoner he is. With the mind Bobby has, he needs to be free."

Hank had every reason himself to be cynical. With Bobby gone from Newhallville, Hank had been jumped on his way home from work by a group of guys, one holding a shotgun. They took his telephone, earrings, and bus pass. "My cash was in the sole of my sneakers," he said. "I'm surprised they didn't take them. Those sneakers were Jordans. Thank God they weren't worried about Jordans." Hank blamed the neighborhood for Bobby, the way "the twenty-four-hour store, Division Street, all these sections competing with each other" were signs of an abandoned community where people who weren't cared about grew careless. Hank cared. The image of Bobby in shackles, when "Bobby didn't do anything," he found so hurtful it motivated Hank. He wrote Bobby letters, telling him, "You have a life. You have to say what you have to say. I don't know if it's the code of the street, no snitching, but real life is passing you by." And Hank himself went, as he said, "undercover" for Bobby.

A year after Bobby had gone to prison, Hank had been married. Sometime later, he discovered by chance that members of his wife's family had witnessed the murder from their West Ivy Street porch. They'd been too terrified of BlackJack and Major to tell the police anything that would help Bobby, but Hank said of his relatives, "They knew it wasn't him." Hank was thrilled, believed something now could be done to repair the injustice. But every time he brought up Bobby with these relatives, the response was "I don't want to talk about it." Hank would persist, ask what they'd seen, but the others just became irritated, shut him down. So, Hank devised a plan. When he next visited, just before he arrived, he pressed Record on his telephone. Inside, he sat down, put the phone on a table. Then, casually, Hank mentioned Bobby. Nobody bit. But Hank was ready for that. He got up and left the room, sure they'd say something now, with the subject raised and him gone. But later, when he checked the phone, he discovered "Just dead silence." So, for a while, Hank refused to talk with any of them.

NOBODY CAN SAY how many innocent people there are in prison. During Bobby's ninth year in Big Cheshire, when there were 15,816 people in Connecticut prisons, Scott Semple, the correction commissioner at the time, said, "Through my interactions doing this twenty-seven years, starting as a corrections officer, I can count on one hand how many people told me they were innocent. It wasn't for me to judge." A writer who'd been locked up, Reginald Dwayne Betts, said, "Everybody knows who's innocent. Bobby's innocent. You can't fuck with Innocent Bobby. It's so rare, innocent almost becomes your nickname."

Samuel Gross said his comprehensive study of wrongfully convicted exonerates led him to estimate that slightly more than 2 percent of people held in American prisons are innocent, which would mean above 30,000 wrongfully convicted people sitting among an American prison population of 1,526,800. Public defenders typically think wrongful convictions are far more frequent than do prosecutors and people who work in law enforcement. New Haven's veteran chief public defender in 2006 was Thomas Ullmann, who believed that the wider driftnet of mass incarceration meant that while more guilty people were caught up and sent to prison, entangled among them in the mesh were tens of thousands of innocent people whose inadvertent capture was "the cost of doing business."

"When I first came here," Bobby said of Big Cheshire, "a lot of older guys from my neighborhood were yelling at me, 'Why you in here for something you didn't do?' Really concerned." As knowledge of Bobby's innocence spread, he said, "Seemed like everybody knew my situation." And it was consoling to him that "every day I hear, 'You're not even supposed to be here. You should be home now.' You got a lot of people from my neighborhood, my childhood say it." He felt increasingly that "people were so genuine and caring to me. They knew I didn't do it." This, he said, was true for many prison officials and for fellow prisoners. Others at Big Cheshire had experienced difficult interrogation sessions with Detective Willoughby, and when they'd approach Bobby and tell him they knew "*exactly* what I went through," that also was gratifying to him. Some in the block even bestowed upon Bobby a prison nickname, "They used to call me the Innocent Boy."

To be in such a place under false terms, said Karen Wolff, a lawyer and social worker who worked with exonerees at the Innocence Project in New York, led innocent people in prison to contend with tremendous resentment and anger. Every day they might perseverate over their lost freedom, why they should be missing weddings, anniversaries, funerals. It gnawed at them, Wolff said, unless they found ways to cope. Most did cope, some by becoming immersed in lawbooks, fighting to prove their innocence. Others accepted the consolations of fate or religion—resigning themselves to the prayerful certainty that God had a plan. Blaming a drug addiction or putting it on another person also got people by. But none of those explanations could have satisfied Bobby. There in Cell 39, he was determined to lay the fault at his own door.

Like most teenagers Bobby knew, he'd planned on getting a tattoo. Many people also got them in prison. Bobby still wanted a tattoo, but not a prison tattoo; he didn't think he should be marked by where he didn't belong. But if Bobby had a core value, it was in the messiness and imperfection of all people, his dislike of "when somebody depicts you as somebody you're not. Say two young kids end up in a confrontation and one dies. Because he's dead, all they say is great things. Not the flaws. Misfortunes. It's always the good aspects. You want the whole." Speaking the truth of who people were made the world seem less arbitrary. Bobby went to prison by being duped into lying. Yet even as he recognized, "I was a sixteen-year-old in there with [Willoughby]," there was also now an intense desire to be flawed enough to deserve prison. "I don't like to blame nobody for my situation," Bobby said. "I take full responsibility for not listening, doing things the way I wanted to."

As Bobby worked it through in his cell, to have made the choice of standing with the popular neighborhood figures in front of the 2-4 implicated him: "I put my own self there. I chose to be out there." That Bobby hadn't killed or held up anybody made no difference. "You become literally what the environment is," he decided. And even if "the lifestyle I was living wasn't something I was designed for," he considered himself culpable by association because he stood among them, acting the part: "I had to ad-lib with them." Just as he'd defended his teachers in the school classroom, in front of the 2-4 he'd intervened at times when trouble began, which suggested to him that he should have intervened every time. Instead, sometimes, he said, "I would sit there and watch people harming people and not stop it. The reason why I say I'm more responsible than anybody is because I know better." That one sixteen-year-old could never have changed the will of a crowd was irrelevant. The fault lay in the knowing better. Because he'd grown up in a neighborhood of high crime and heavy policing, Bobby was well aware that to "hang out" meant risking being "antagonized by police." Now, in prison, he convinced himself he had prison coming to him. "Me living out there, thinking I can get away with anything. Then to get knocked back on your feet. That's karma."

That Bobby should reconcile himself to prison through personal responsibility could seem absurd. But it was not uncommon for rape victims, for example, to blame themselves as a reassertion of self over the power that had been taken away from them. And to an older New Haven man Bobby met in prison, Scott Lewis, Bobby's solution was understandable. Lewis had been convicted of a 1990 murder he steadfastly insisted he didn't commit. His was an unlikely story about being set up by a corrupt police officer in league with mobsters, and almost nobody believed it. Lewis would serve nearly twenty years in prison, fighting his conviction every day, until his unlikely story turned out to be true. Lewis was set free in 2014. Lewis was pretty sure he knew why it meant so much to Bobby to blame himself for being sent to prison. It resolved what was otherwise chaos by imposing order, fulfilling the natural human craving for agency. "I don't think it's his fault," Lewis said, "but it's easier to accept when you admit your part. That you made decisions that gave them power to do to him what they did. You're no longer pointing fingers at everybody else. It's freeing to me and to Bobby. The truth really will set you free."

Chapter Thirteen

Missing suffused Big Cheshire. There were people from the city who missed the sound of emergency-vehicle sirens and the explosion of holiday fireworks. Country prisoners missed the insect-hum of night. Men missed women—"Females drive guys crazy in there," Bobby said. "These guys take thirsty to another level." Pornographic magazines were passed from cell to cell, and the "Spanish channel" was judged the best for masturbation because the newscasters and the women in advertisements wore such revealing clothing. For female COs, their days meant ceaseless calls of "How you doin'?" and men in cells reaching down to their pants at the sight of them. While sexual-assault policies were prominently posted, as far as Bobby knew, there was no sex slavery. What people who were never alone seemed to miss most was intimacy. They missed being partners and husbands, and those who took the missing hardest of all, it seemed to Bobby, were the fathers.

The cells were humid with fatherly pining and self-recrimination, especially at Thanksgiving and Christmas. "Away from their kids at holidays," Bobby said, "it's the most depressing times men go through in prison." Men distraught in the failures that had landed them apart from their children, whom they were letting down on these days everybody knew signified family. "These guys are hurting," Bobby said. "You had this guy literally go bald in front of me because he couldn't see his son."

Almost everybody Bobby knew at prison was Black. Almost every son whose background Bobby knew at prison had no father in his life. Almost every father, so far as Bobby knew, wasn't married. "We all come from the same broken system of broken homes," he said. The subject of absent African American fathers has long been controversial, especially since the *Moynihan Report* blamed a tangle of cultural pathology for the phenomenon of broken Black families rather than lack of life opportunity. Similarly, poverty has long been misjudged as something deserved rather than caused. During Bobby's early years in prison, what was growing ever clearer was the parallel relationship between the loss of jobs at factories like Winchester and the massive Black male prison population from postindustrial neighborhoods like Newhallville. Bobby never experienced the beautiful "How-do" Newhallville Pete Fields knew as a teenager. What Bobby saw in prison was the longing for its stability.

The desire at Big Cheshire to be a father and son was palpable. Half of America's prisoners have children under eighteen, and at Big Cheshire young Bobby became the object of attempted surrogate parenting from cellies and others he scarcely knew. These included "an older Spanish guy that swore he was my father." In his early years, Bobby encountered so many of his friends' fathers, it hit him one day that prison was where the missing Newhallville fathers were. In the middle of conversations he would realize, "Okay, that's your son? I went to school with your son!" Then he'd think, "That's how you meet people these days." Jerome said he'd discover his Newhallville friends' fathers at Big Cheshire, and it would intrigue him that, even though the friend hadn't grown up with his father, they had an identical sense of humor—"That's where he gets it from!" Plenty of sons followed their fathers into the system; Bobby even knew of father-and-son cellies. One son reunited with a father who'd been in prison for twenty years. Bobby watched them embracing, hugging, and crying, and considered it such a "tragic" way to follow your father's example, Bobby said he "felt bad just seeing it."

In this way, the Big Cheshire that Bobby knew mirrored Newhallville. Newhallville was closer to Big Cheshire than were most American city neighborhoods to the large prisons they filled, and there were so many people in prison from back home that, for Bobby, "It was like walking through my neighborhood. You look and everybody I grew up with is here. It's the lifestyle of the streets—you end up in the same place. I hated it. The bad equation. You think you've been taken out of it, and it keeps sending its reinforcements to you." There were no guns in prison, but the two places, to him, had the same energy: "Prison feels similar to hanging on the corner. You see nothing different except you won't get killed." Sociologist Andrew Papachristos, then at Yale, studied the patterns of violence in city neighborhoods, and he agreed with Bobby that the relationship between Newhallville and the prison was so fluid that, in effect, the neighborhood prepared its young people for prison. And even in prison, Papachristos said, "these guys are still out in the neighborhood, still in network. Prison, it's part of the neighborhood." A man in prison told Bobby, "The Ville eats its babies," and for Bobby the phrase was instantly indelible, for it said, "Anybody that grew up in the Ville grows up to be nothing. How sad it is that the whole neighborhood's incarcerated together."

When it came to relationships, prison's reputation was for Dear John letters, tidings of "Jody" gone with your woman while you were away, people outside resolving to grow distant from those they couldn't have anymore and would otherwise want too much. What Bobby saw, however, was that the happiest people in prison were the 10 percent who were married and those who had a committed partner. Just receiving love letters improved prison outcomes. "I used to watch guys' relationships when they were in jail," Bobby said. "They lived in bliss if they had a relationship compared with everybody else. It made them cope better."

One such person was part of the churn of people who flowed through Cell 39, a short, fit man with an air of leaderly calm named Jamaal Alexander. Bobby called his cellie Maaly, which he pronounced "Mawly." Maaly was from Hartford, more than ten years older than Bobby, had a wife who worked as a nurse, and children. Within himself Bobby might be gaining self-control, but what Maaly saw in the other bunk was a "little loose cannon." A committed autodidact, Maaly read history and business books. Bobby talked street, he listened to gangster rap unceasingly, and he read stacks of hood books, a genre of street-life thrillers with plots that depended on guns, cocaine, vendettas, side women, and people with a capacity for (or named) Hennessy. Rec hour would come, Bobby'd hurry out into the tier, and Maaly could hear a group of older dudes start working him again, winding Bobby up, talking greasy, teasing him for his big lips, putting down his favorite rappers, putting down people from Newhallville, putting down anything that meant anything to Bobby just to get him "mad with attitude." Eventually they'd have him again. Rec would end and Bobby'd come trudging back, wearing what Maaly began to think of as Bobby's bad-day-at-the-playground face. "He had a reputation he could be riled up," Maaly said. "He let people under his skin."

In the cell, Bobby would tear off his T-shirt, throw it down, poke out his lip, knock over his drinking cup—what Maaly called his post-rec "huffing and puffing." If Maaly asked what the problem was, Bobby was in such a state it took him a while to get out, "I'm just mad!" Once, while Maaly was cooking with a stinger, Bobby put his hand in the water and shocked himself. Maaly thought: "A kid upset without the means of dealing with it."

Maaly took his time sizing people up. He had come across many kinds in prison, some who turned out to be very different from his first impression. Maaly saw that Bobby "wasn't ever doing bad things. He followed the rules." Bobby didn't get disciplinary tickets, had no sharp needles of character, put on no airs. When he was cheerful, Bobby was likable and enthusiastic. When he was brooding and sullen, anybody could see that too. Maaly had been around grifters and connivers. There were plenty at Big Cheshire. What Bobby had, Maaly decided, was "a good heart." He decided to find out who the kid was.

Learning in any depth about your cellie without him knowing was difficult, but it could be done. Maaly made quiet inquiries about Bobby's "situation," and at the mention of Bobby's name, people from Newhallville would readily say, "That's the one up here for that shit he didn't do." This wasn't just New Haven people. To Maaly, it seemed, "everybody knew he got screwed." Maaly was sure that if so many prisoners had heard the story, officials must have too. "When everyone knows you made a mistake," he thought, "why didn't they try to fix that?" One day, carefully, he raised the subject with Bobby himself, and after Bobby told him about his experience, Maaly would look up from what he was reading, close his eyes, and think, *Thirty-eight years and he didn't do the crime*. To Maaly, Bobby's life was still "supposed to be smiles, happiness." Maaly understood that being a just-around kid in a neighborhood like Newhallville could mean, he said, "when you have nothing else to do, nobody else to love you, you do what everybody else is doing." There had once been stacks of hood books in Maaly's cell. He'd never lost his temper with Bobby, because "I was that same person."

Having decided that Bobby's sentence was more than anybody should carry alone, Maaly resolved to help him. Prison cells were close spaces, and time stretched endless, so if someone did open up in there, it could be momentous. With little prompting, Bobby did open up, and as Maaly listened, his sympathy deepened. "I understood he was just a kid crying out," Maaly said. "There's damage there. He was still a kid to me. I loved him because I believed he was innocent, and stuff he shared about his life, being out there, stuff with his mother. I believed he was broken. I thought, 'It ain't his fault.' "

A reason prisoners were reluctant confidants was that although pain was everywhere, acknowledging that in yourself betrayed weakness. And making yourself vulnerable by awakening personal demons in a cell could tilt a person. Prison was transient, people suddenly were just gone. You learned not to get too attached. But Maaly promised himself that in whatever time they had together, for Bobby he would do what he could.

So when Bobby returned in a state after another roasting out on the tier, Maaly would be waiting to scold him for bringing "nonsense" back into Cell 39. "I used to say the dumbest stuff," Bobby said. Maaly refused to hear any more about rappers or gun violence in New Haven. "I'd talk hard to him," Maaly said. "Why do you come in here with that? With my passion I talked firm. Clarity. I wanted him to know why I felt that way, and he grabbed that. He liked a lecture. I wasn't talking at him. I was talking to the kid."

When Bobby took up a hood book, Maaly scolded him for "reading trash about shooting in the street. I'd be like, 'You're reading *what*? About what we're trying to get *away* from?' " A reading list was created for Bobby consisting of what Maaly called "conscious books." That was inspirational literature on topics of self-improvement, such as Hill Harper's *Letters to a Young Brother* and James Allen's *As a Man Thinketh.* While Bobby read, Maaly would "just watch me read all day. For hours. He'd stare at me for nine straight hours. Tell me, 'Stay focused. Keep reading.' He was reading too. We used to sit there. My brain!" Sometimes Bobby would ask what a word meant, and Maaly would gesture to the thick Webster's dictionary on Bobby's desk and say, "No! Look it up!" Bobby thought, "He really tried to act like I was a kid. But he really pushed me. I needed that." When the last page was turned, Maaly would demand written book reports, along with the delivery of what he called statement speeches, about the content. Prison made people passive, Maaly thought, while what the world called for was self-reliance.

Maaly decreed formal reading and study hours, a division of cleaning assignments, and TV time. He taught Bobby to cook seasoned meat in a stinger, how to make baking dough from crackers and water, led fitness sessions of burpees and push-ups in the cell, and weight-lifting circuits out in the prison gym. Maaly introduced Bobby to Aretha Franklin and other R&B singers. When soul music made Maaly too sad about missing his family, he let Bobby cut it with hip-hop. In the cell, Maaly said, "everything between us was always mutual. That he didn't have much didn't matter. Show someone you love him in a place where there isn't a lot of love—he knew it was genuine. If he didn't have a clean T-shirt, I'd say, 'Take that,' and give him one."

Sometimes they'd stay up late watching a movie together. "When you're locked up," Maaly said, "you get a movie, you get to live life for an hour and a half. You see a married couple, it brings you back into the world. He's whispering to her, it brings you out there. You're watching yourself living that. Painful, but more wonderful."

Bobby did his best to reciprocate. During the hour when cell doors in the block were opened, Bobby knew Maaly would want to shower quickly so he'd have more telephone time with his wife. The problem was "the herd" surging to the showers. So, the door would pop and Bobby halfbacked it out of the cell, sprinting ahead to hold a shower for Maaly. On the telephone, Maaly began to talk with his wife about how crucial it was with their own kids not just to be with them but to really know them.

At first Bobby had refused to attend school in prison. He was one among many younger people with decades-long sentences who didn't see the point. "People don't try," he said. "Lack of hope. What can you do with what you learn? People give up. Shut down so much." Bobby wasn't making any efforts to advocate for his innocence, either, and when Maaly would encourage him to take initiative, Bobby would look stricken. Maaly thought that childhood and prison had left Bobby "almost destroyed." Maaly would exhort him, "*Do* something! Nobody going to try to help you. I know you gonna get out and you have to be prepared. What are you gonna do when the gates open [and] you done wasted mad time?"

One day, during Bobby's fourth prison year, telling a prison official that, more than anything, he wanted "to have an education," Bobby took what was for him the deep gulp of pursuing his GED. People who attended school in Big Cheshire were given $7 every two weeks toward their commissary spending. That incentive was bestowed because American prisons are filled with undereducated people. At intake in Connecticut adult prisons, the average level of education was below ninth grade, and the great predictor for recidivism is a lack of education. "The more education you get, the less likely you are to be involved in a trauma-related future incident," said Scott Semple. "Even people on the waiting list for a GED this is true for."

Living a few cells away on the tier from Bobby and Maaly was Troy Westberry, thirteen years older than Bobby, and serving sixty years. Westberry was watching Bobby with curiosity. "There was a dude in the block who didn't have anything," Westberry said. "Dude was an outcast. People didn't deal with him. Bobby would look out for him. Treat him as a friend. People wondered why." Westberry was referring to a short, slight man named Joey, among the handful of white men in the block. Joey was beginning work as a tierman, and Bobby had taken it upon himself to train him to clean floors and showers to standard. "He was a cool dude," Bobby said. "He ain't had nothing. No family." Besides the janitorial duties, a tierman responded to cell-requests for tissues, cleaning supplies, or cooking water. Around the tier, people tormented Joey with demands, then made fun of him when he came near. "Everybody mess with the dude," Bobby said. "People tried to run him over. I felt bad for him. I used to be going sick, tell people I'd smack them. So people would leave him alone. I used to be sitting talking to him, and out of nowhere he'd start crying. I'd think, 'I didn't ask for this.' But he was there on his own."

When Westberry found a way to ask Bobby about why he was so friendly to that guy, Bobby told him, "Doesn't matter. I treat [everyone] the same way." For Westberry, this was admirable, and he said the "cherry on top was [Joey] was white." Maaly told Bobby it was decent of him to stick up for Joey, but had Bobby noticed that once Joey's work shift was over, he'd invariably gravitate to his bullies for more abuse? "He's a glutton for pain," Maaly told Bobby. Prison was a hypermasculine space where submissive behavior wasn't respected. Some people at Big Cheshire thought white people were more accepting of prison, trusted the system, faulted themselves, and took their punishment meekly because they weren't part of a mass culture of discrimination. But whatever it was with Joey, Maaly said Joey had to "raise his shoulders," and learn to stand up for himself or prison wasn't going to work out for him.

One day, Bobby came back to the cell from class, and Maaly's belongings were gone. He'd been transferred out. Bobby began walking with Maaly's slow, deliberate gait, adopted Maaly's straight-up posture, took on Maaly's speaking inflections. He decided he was "sick of hip-hop" and began to listen to other forms of music, including the country and rock that were the preference of many COs. Bobby grew to like the bluesy, irreverent Irish singer Hozier, especially his song "Take Me to Church," an exuberant call to devotion at the altar of desire and acceptance. At night, in his bunk, Bobby overcame anxiety by rereading *As a Man Thinketh*. The book became like a blanket over a birdcage, his way of going to sleep. He read it through thirty times. Bobby had never known what brought Maaly to Big Cheshire. "I don't ask people what they did," he said. What Bobby cared about was that, as Maaly told him, "I wouldn't let you be young. I let you grow up around me."

IN THE PRISON classroom, Bobby's instructor for three hours a day was a married, middle-aged math-loving Black woman named Michelle Mouzon. Miss Mouzon, as Bobby always called her, said she "didn't look at my students as criminals. I treat them as a person who's here and we'll make the best of it." Mouzon liked math because math did not discriminate. "I try to tell the guys," she said, "you can handle math problems, it's like handling life. Here's a situation, figure it out." Nearly all of her students were young men of color, and she was aware that often, "I became a surrogate mother or sister. A woman they could relate to. Some of it is race. And I'm concerned about them."

Mouzon took in Bobby's "mannerisms." She thought he was "kind, polite, not rude or disrespectful. He came to class daily. Did his work. He was a fun and pleasurable student to have." As Bobby had at Urban Youth, when other students misbehaved, he chastised them. Mouzon assigned her classes weekly essays, and Bobby began writing about his upbringing, having no father at home, being raised by both his overwhelmed mother and his doting grandmother, even as he himself was caring for his younger sisters. Mouzon praised him for all this, and Bobby was quick to demur that he was no hero. "He used to tell me he didn't listen and acted out at home," she said. Mouzon found him so responsive, the teacher wondered what could have happened to make such a person end up at Big Cheshire.

Then one day, Miss Mouzon came upon an article in which Diane Polan discussed Kwame's and Bobby's case. As she read along, Mouzon became very upset. The rules of her job included strict student-teacher boundaries and limited her from discussing her students' legal circumstances with them. So Mouzon carried the article in her lunch bag every day as a talisman reminding her that life was complicated. "It was a hard thing to look at this kid and know he shouldn't be there," she said. "The most shocking thing to me, here's this kid, had almost forty years for something he didn't do, and he smiled as if he was outside. I'd say, 'Man, I don't know if I could do that.' "

At first Bobby struggled with reading comprehension. "Once he was taught how," Mouzon said, "he was fine. I don't know how much he'd done before." She learned about his low IQ-test grade, and his prison-entry evaluation as "barely literate," and also that his IQ had supposedly risen in prison.

She had read plenty about how intelligence tests failed to account for cultural bias, and all Bobby did was increase her skepticism. "I think he's a sponge—taking in everything, learning whatever you offer him," she said. "He never seemed as though there were challenges he couldn't handle." Bobby did well, she said, at algebra and geometry, and at certificate courses where he improved his writing.

The first time Bobby took his GED examination, it was just a few months after he enrolled in the class, and he wasn't ready. But early in 2012, he received his degree. Mouzon named him the class speaker for graduation, which Granddad and Bobby's big sister Tonya attended. In his remarks, Bobby told of feeling redeemed by the support of others he'd met at Cheshire. Listening to her brother speak ardent sentences, Tonya's reaction was, "I'm amazed. It's completely different. I didn't know he played chess."

Granddad said of Bobby as a boy, "He wasn't a good student. He's much better in jail. It's heartbreaking, but maybe it's a good thing. I'm not sure. He doesn't seem to be bitter. If there's an explanation, I don't know it except I think he's motivated by the fact he knows he's innocent." Granddad thought that Bobby had become again in prison the person he'd been as a little kid. "He smiles all the time. He always did. It's a glowing type of smile."

Once Bobby was no longer her student, Mouzon could speak candidly with him. She arranged a meeting and said, "I know your situation. You need to go and fight." At first Bobby said he "brushed it off. What's this lady talking about? Then the next day and the next day she was attacking me on it. I began to take heed. I'd thought once the case was closed it was closed. Basically, I thought I was doomed."

Among the elective educational and vocational programs on offer at Big Cheshire were two popular certificate courses in commercial cleaning. Maaly had told Bobby "the class will do you right," and now Bobby enrolled. Commercial cleaning explained how to walk into any kind of business, survey soiled carpeting, filthy tiles, or begrimed toilets, and know how to make it all inspector-grade immaculate. But this, Bobby soon decided, was only "a front" to lure people into class for a polishing of the self. "It was," Bobby said, "really about interpersonal skills, how to have a bright future in the world."

Commercial cleaning's star attraction was the instructor, Michael Bosco. Maaly said Bosco was a man who regarded prison as a lost country of young men from fatherless homes, "Someone who really cares, and a lot of them, they know nobody cares. They're bitter. They don't care. But somebody shows them that, and they take to it right away."

Bosco led a small, packed classroom, and he was made that way himself, "a short, passionate, caring Italian white guy," Bobby called him. Walking in from the gloom of another prison day to encounter the fervor of Bosco expounding on individual potential was the difference between water and wine. Bosco's belief was self-respect comes from work, people work harder at jobs that fulfill them, and the only way to get fulfilling work was to prepare for it. He offered advice for interviews, talked about nonverbal communication: "They say one thing, their face says another." He demonstrated how to exude confidence you didn't feel, explained why it was important to speak well, abandon self-pity, and pull up your pants. All this Bosco supported with the findings of sociologists and statisticians, and with much cussing and weeping. To Bobby, for whom clean sinks, belted trousers, and sincerity were next to godliness, it was all beautiful, the conscious books come alive, except for Bosco's actual godliness. "I paid him no mind when he talked about religion," Bobby said.

That "I question God," Bobby said, went back to his bike rides over Prospect Hill where adjoining neighborhoods offered such "distorted" life contrasts. Bobby wondered, "Why's he, the Almighty Powerful, allow it? Why do such a small amount of people have all the money to do what they want? If God knows about that, why he allow it? That make God look spiteful. How many are praying to get out of a situation and they're still in it, suffering, poor, broke, just getting by, scraping the plate." Bobby judged Bosco didn't mind that he was "a freethinker." Where was God, Bobby thought, when he was alone with Willoughby?

Bosco knew that his class often had a delayed effect. That's how it was for Bobby. "I only loved him after I left his class," Bobby said. "Everybody like Bosco after his class." Bobby completed both the elementary and advanced units of commercial cleaning, and received a commendation for outstanding achievement. One of Bobby's vows, if he ever got free, became to host a picnic for Bosco and Maaly.

THE WAY PEOPLE habitually came to terms with prison was by taking responsibility. Even if you thought the system was unfair, there was still justice in paying for the wrong you'd done. But having a sometimes-despondent young person in his midst who didn't deserve to be at Big Cheshire was troubling to Troy Westberry. Westberry took in how bewildered, uncared-for, and life-blasted Bobby seemed some days, and he also noticed Bobby trying to improve himself. Westberry already was predisposed to Bobby because of his kindness to the shunned Joey. Now Westberry resolved to help Bobby.

Westberry was stocky with a shaved head, a prizefighter's neck and torso, and a deferential manner. "Troy pays attention; he takes in a lot," Bobby said. "He lays back, allows you to explain your side first before he explains his." Westberry found a way to ask Bobby why he'd confessed to a crime he didn't commit. As Bobby told about his interrogations, Westberry listened, and he concluded there was "no explanation except he's a kid, he's a child." There were similarities in Bobby and Westberry, the straitened neighborhoods they'd come up in, the siblings they babysat, their love for basketball and now for books. Eventually they became such good friends that Bobby received permission to move into Cell 36, Westberry's cell.

Westberry could see how bleak feelings about his family would suddenly come over Bobby, and all his resolve for himself would burst like a pillow. Westberry thought that the care Bobby had given to his sisters was a remarkable thing for a boy to have done, and he wanted his friend to stop undermining it. Westberry told him, "It hurts. You do all these things for your family out there, and now they drop off the face of the earth." Cooking for and taking care of his sisters, Westberry said, meant "you have relationships with your sisters I never had." He urged Bobby, "Don't forsake those relationships. You can't place expectations on how you think people should be, because of what you would do. They're not you, and that's where disappointment comes. The person who gave birth to you and she's not there. I can't imagine. In the long run you'll have to forgive." Talking helped Bobby to consider that for some of his family members, perhaps visiting him at prison, confronting there what had happened to him, might just be too painful. "It kind of shattered a lot of people" was Bobby's eventual conclusion.

Because Westberry had found solace in religion, Bobby asked him to explain why he and others cared about the Bible so much. They began a Bible study together, with close readings. Their Bible conversations ranged into personal history, and they talked about their families' migrations from the South, all the aspiration, and then how many of these journeys had ended in unemployment and prison. "Used to be a lot of togetherness," Westberry said. "The Migration families started to be broken up, dysfunction creeped in. They think it's just normal. Me growing up, I recognize what I thought was normal was dysfunctional." The intensity of what they were talking about made them feel closer than friends. Bobby began calling Westberry

Big Bro, considered him "my big brother. But we used to play jokes: 'You my son. I birthed you.' "

As a reader of scripture, Westberry didn't consider Bobby to be any kind of saint, but he was perhaps a prison Job, an honest, hardworking soul tested and tested by life. And Bobby's response to these tests was to be harder on himself than the guilty were on themselves. "Shit is what it is," shooters would be saying about violence, while Innocent Bobby wanted to convince himself he deserved to be in prison. Westberry, like Maaly, felt uplift from helping Bobby. Bobby was the opportunity to achieve hope and dignity, a way forward to being better. Both men felt lucky that Bobby had been receptive to them, and they wanted him to have love.

Bobby and Westberry became members of a book group in the block that also included five others, their friends Black Rob, Ty, Great, Poe, and Jerome. They read James Baldwin's essays, Viktor Frankl's concentration-camp reflections *Man's Search for Meaning*, and Condoleezza Rice's memoir *Extraordinary Ordinary People*. They'd get together at a table outside Cell 12, for heated discussions. "It was coming from the heart," Bobby said. "But we would say some crazy stuff to each other, and then we'd apologize later." Black Rob was, Bobby said, "the biggest challenger of all of us. He's a shit-talker, but about books." At first this was "annoying," but the rest played basketball and it was decided Black Rob, who didn't, needed the competitive outlet. They all grew close in their conversations about issues like gun control, where "you'd have guys say it's essential for hunters and self-protection, and then you'd have guys saying it's not worth it, guns are killing people. You always had to argue both sides." This was difficult after completing Michelle Alexander's treatise on mass incarceration, *The New Jim Crow*, which they thought revealed a balance fallacy. "We discuss the Black recidivism rate," Bobby said. "We discuss 104 guys in the block, one white guy, and whites use way more drugs than Blacks."

There was the revelation of reading about yourself in the writings of others. Bobby came across this passage in Baldwin: "It is clearly much easier to drag some ignorant wretch to court and burden him with whatever crimes one likes than it is to undergo the inconvenience and possible danger of finding out what actually happened, and who is actually guilty. In my experience, the defenders of the public peace do not care who is guilty." Condoleezza Rice's memoirs left everyone holding the war in Iraq against her, except Bobby, who told them all, "I love her! Nothing nobody can say to me. I read her book two times. I traveled through her world. In Cheshire, people go crazy talking bad about her. She had a grandmother making her read books. She had an uncle making her read and study. Things I wish I had in my life."

It was likewise moving for Bobby to read how Frankl, separated from his wife, Tilly, not knowing whether she was even alive anymore, could imagine her warm smile, her encouraging eyes, and draw strength from feeling love for her. Bobby thought a lot about the ill-fitting shoes Frankl and other Auschwitz prisoners wore. Because the shoes could no longer be laced over their swollen feet, the shoes filled with snow and ice during forced walks. "That's scary," Bobby said. "The shoes. It's deep. I don't think I could have handled that. His experience was excruciating. He was going through pain that could never compare to me. Man searching for meaning—you really see yourself." Frankl had missed light switches, the sound of a ringing telephone, the feeling of solitude. Prison deformed time, it cost some men their pity for others. Was it so different to feel no sympathy for the pain of a man with cancer writhing in his cell than to look on with indifference as a concentration-camp doctor tweezered off a boy's frostbitten toes? Bobby said he was "impressed by the idea it was up to him to make himself happy wherever he was," even in prison. Frankl encouraged the reading group because he'd looked back on captivity as his crucial time of growth.

The seven reading-discussion men were envied by others in the block for being such a close community. They were sometimes referred to as the group, and were proud, Bobby said, of giving "our intellect to each other. We call it *building*." Sharing books brought the closest approximation of what members of the group had lacked in childhood: the supported growth of emotional and intellectual maturity. Reading in prison was intense because you were redrawing your picture of the world while surrounded by people who'd had such destabilizing experiences. Books for the reading group were a way into aspects of their inner lives they didn't otherwise bring up, and the group took such discoveries very seriously. When someone wasn't prepared for a discussion or was lazy in his thinking, there was censure. "If you don't know what you're talking about," Bobby said, "they'd square up and press you all day. So, everybody used to make sure they wasn't that person. We were awake until four in the morning getting ready. Everybody's eyes is bleeding, ready to sleep. Then, when we got together, we were so tired, talking slow."

They were eager to test all the vocabulary they were absorbing, but employing a prized new word was perilous. "If you say a word and none of us knew exactly what it was," Bobby said, "everybody would run to their cell and go grab their dictionary." And if it turned out a man had used language in error, they'd "clown" him. Vocabulary meant so much because it was aspirational, the premise that a new way of talking makes for a new you. Bobby noticed that "you start to get a new taste for learning. Now you're looking at everything differently. Now you're dying to hear each other's perspectives."

Of all the books read at Big Cheshire by people Bobby knew, Richard Wright's 1940 novel *Native Son* had the most profound effect. *Native Son* was the story of Bigger Thomas coming of age poor and Black in Chicago's South Side ghetto, circumstances he realizes have damned him to failure. Thomas's spirit-crushed response is crime. Bobby said it was a revelation for young Black men at Big Cheshire to read a passage about young Black men that said, "They had always robbed negroes. They felt that it was much easier and safer to rob their own people." To find pieces of yourself on the pages of a book was to see yourself anew. "*Native Son* touched so many people in Cheshire," Bobby said. "Everybody'd go read it and say, 'That's my story.' Everybody was reading it and going through their own identity. Everybody. When I had it, they're all, 'Let me get the book!'"

After Bigger Thomas murders two women and is arrested, he explains to his lawyer that he'd been "scared and mad" all his life until he began killing. He was finally "doing something." Asked, "What were you afraid of?" his response is "Everything." Bobby's interpretation was that segregation left Bigger so cut off from good in the country, he could freely express himself only through depravity. Bobby had known people like that. Treated without sympathy, shunted to the margins, they became utterly unsympathetic. Bobby said, "A lot of people are violent because of how they think other people see them, and because they feel rejected."

In Richard Wright's introduction there was this: "The boy will plead guilty one day then not guilty the next, according to the degree of pressure and persuasion that is brought to bear upon his frightened personality from one side or the other . . . So far removed are these practices from what the average American citizen encounters in his daily life that it takes a huge act of his imagination to believe that it is true."

Bobby also read *Black Boy*, Wright's memoir of his family's migration from the Deep South to the North. For Bobby, there was past as prologue in Wright's mother coming home from work in the evening to tell her fatherless children "that we must learn as soon as possible to take care of ourselves, to dress ourselves, to prepare our own food; that we must take upon ourselves the responsibility for the flat while she worked."

Bobby considered the most talented member of his reading group to be little Jerome from Newhallville, the boy Romano Ratti would take fishing. Bobby and Jerome had become close friends in prison. Jerome was serving his forty years for his part in the murder of the young girl killed by the stray bullet. She was a gifted hip-hop and jazz dancer, had been widely loved, was the favorite friend of one of Bobby's sisters, and Bobby said there were so many ripples pooling out from the cast stone of her death, it told how risky it was to be a child in their city. When Jerome was young his father was shot to death, and then, at ten, Jerome had nearly been murdered in North Carolina when the aunt he was sitting next to while watching TV was shot during a home invasion. Soon Jerome came up to Newhallville, where, Bobby said, "everybody loved Jerome." But out in the neighborhood, Jerome gravitated toward a group of street kids who hung out on a porch on Division Street, near Moe's Market, and he grew, he said, "infatuated with the lifestyle." Jerome acquired a gun that was "brand-new fresh out the box. Somebody on the street going to jail needed money for the commissary." Now, he said, "My identity was a shooter." He rarely hit anything because "I was a bad shooter. I was so little. Big gun. I couldn't shoot it."

At Big Cheshire, Bobby and Jerome were college-age study partners. That they wouldn't be released until they were in their fifties made both depressed. "When he came to prison, he struggled with it every day," Bobby said. "He couldn't bring himself up. Like me, when he's down he was down. He came in the month before me. We both were learning the world together. That made us tight. We lost everything at the same time."

Now Bobby believed he was watching in Jerome a second coming-of-age. "Out of anybody you talk to he'll be the realest," Bobby said. "He doesn't hide his faults or his mistakes. All he does is study all day. He be chopping books down." Thomas Ullmann, the New Haven public defender, said he and his colleagues had seen it "a lot with juveniles convicted as adults for serious crimes with long sentences. Their brains mature." Jerome's intelligence and imagination made him a prison legend among young people from New Haven. One said, "Jerome came to prison as a high school junior reading at a second-grade level. He's brilliant. Has an incredible ear and writes amazing music. He's an urban Mozart."

Even in his late twenties, Jerome still had the face of a high school student, and he said "when I was young, I looked at education as a weakness.

I never saw how education gives you tools for life. I thought for it you had to sound British. Back then it was this neighborhood versus this neighborhood. I talked about stuff I was doing all on one wavelength—violence."

At Big Cheshire, he had been admitted to Wesleyan University's prison education program and was thriving, studying linear equations, how to write essays, Greek drama. He received an A on a history paper and rewrote it anyway. On his own he read European fiction by Flaubert and Mary Shelley. "I read *Frankenstein*," he said. "I empathized with [the monster]. He wanted companionship. Someone to love him. I wanted love. I had something missing. When you learn new information it expands your heart. At home you can't see or know that. Everything's in such fast motion you don't know what a feeling is."

Jerome said one reason he and Bobby hadn't been close in Newhallville was that Bobby was a kid who would go home when trouble began, while Jerome stayed to shoot. He thought he and Bobby had different forms of intelligence. "Bobby's smart when it comes to human behavior," Jerome said. "He had an issue, he could discuss it, he didn't just explode. He cares a lot about people."

The members of the group were like a tiny circle of friends within the neighborhood that was the prison block. Because of what came up among them in conversations, Bobby began to watch public television in his cell, listen to Beethoven, jazz, Shakespeare plays on tape. When group members were excited about something, like Barack Obama's performance in a presidential debate or accounts of the Ferguson riots after the police shooting of Michael Brown, "We used to sit in the cell," Bobby said, "and we would try to call to a person outside the cell. But they won't hear it sometimes. So, I'd be pacing. Me and my cellie, we would pace back and forth in the cell, keep jotting things down, trying to find a way to get it out."

They developed interests in parts of life whose reality they could only imagine, such as fine dining. Westberry had been to restaurants in Hartford and remembered the menus. He described them for the others, slowly advancing down, describing how everything looked and tasted, from appetizers to dessert. "A lot of people did that," Bobby said. "We called it eating in our heads. I ate a whole Sunday dinner that my mom cooked. Cabbage, yams, mac 'n' cheese, cornbread—I baked a cake. I was the baker in the family. I was Betty Crocker!"

Another source of fantasy was automobiles. "In prison we all thought about cars," Bobby said. "The commercials you see on TV, everybody in jail's fascinated with cars, talk about getting their license. It's the point of real liberty. People have car magazines, pictures of cars on the wall of their cell, in photo albums. You got mechanics schooling you on all types of cars. You have your own car—ultimate freedom. Lifts you up and out. Best feeling ever. Period."

Bobby described his group elders as "These humongous guys, big as ever," telling him, "Do this! Do that! And it was great. I read because of them. I am the way I am because of them." His gratitude was effusive enough that others were skeptical, wondered if he thought he'd found Glory Land in prison. But the gratitude was to the people, not the place. To him, prison was "demoralizing and adds no sense of worth or value to your life. You're never encouraged or complimented, and you're around strangers who sometimes do crazy acts. But I feel like a lot of people who did do harm were giants to me. They admitted it, tried to correct themselves, do better. In such a harsh environment that's so negative and takes you out of your character, to make it out of there mentally stable, it's a struggle."

One person who agreed with Bobby was that other wrongfully convicted Cheshire prisoner Scott Lewis, who said, "People have the perception people come in there and people are piranhas who want to attack you. You have a good-people element who made bad decisions, and then you have vultures. You have a world inside a world, and Bobby ran into people whose second chance was giving him a second chance."

The men of the group offered Bobby the kind of support and encouragement he'd wanted all his life. "They pushed me the most," he said. "They've been pushing me and pushing me to do something with myself." The men told him he wasn't cursed. No matter how hopeless things seemed, eventually someone would realize what had happened. In the meantime, instead of succumbing to a forever adolescence, Bobby needed to become an adult. Slowly, fitfully, Bobby said, "they made me grow up." The older men persisted, he believed, "because of my story. Everybody."

PRISON DEPLETED. EVEN with the group's companionship, Bobby couldn't ever escape what he called the "hectic" of it. There was relentless interaction with other people living pressed right up against you, the rank odor, the whims of counts, searches, and lockdowns. It was like riding a bicycle over endless stones, Bobby's whole body absorbing the vibrating stress of holding course. For an introverted person, the need for retreat was intense, and even the group couldn't offer that. "The joint really hurts your heart," Bobby said.

At the concentration camp, Viktor Frankl believed the worst people to be around were the optimists, because their hope took him out of the focus he needed to endure the moment. Bobby's bête noire were the Big Cheshire pessimists who wrenched him from the places he went to on pages and in headphones, dragged him back to the reality of "those walls, that cell, them COs telling me what to do." There were people at Big Cheshire who, he said, liked to shove his innocence in his face, tell him, "I don't think you'll beat it. It won't happen for you. They don't care about you. You're Black. You this, you that." Frankl wanted to live in the present, but Bobby felt "stuck in the now. Because I was stuck in the now, I started to see my experience for what it was, and that made it hard to see myself ever released."

As his fifth year ended, Bobby had been increasingly discouraged. To a brief zenith and then pendulum-reversing way, way down, was how prison went for him, the tremendous effort to avoid depression. Bobby could feel that his hope "was gradually fading away, my optimism, my strength, my ability to stay strong and keep my head up every day. Because the longer you're in there, the more you lose hope and say, 'All right, this may never happen. This may be my reality.' So you become complacent with that." The majority of the men in prison who spent their days sleeping as much as possible and watching mindless TV programming hadn't always been that way. Some of them had once read novels and bench-pressed bunkbeds too. Bobby now wondered if lasting until 2044 might be more than he could do. "Facing thirty-eight years," he said, "I don't see how a person can maintain faith." He hoped he wouldn't, like so many, slide into inertia, stop caring.

During one of Bobby's grueling downward trajectories, word arrived of a visitor. It was a day Bobby, who hated drama, described with uncharacteristic flourish. He'd been sliding deep into misery and "Then," he said, suddenly "came Ken, the magic man."

PART IV

TRUE BELIEVER

Chapter Fourteen

Years later, thinking back to 2010, Ken Rosenthal could no longer remember how it was that he became Bobby's lawyer. Rosenthal was a wholehearted person, someone who occupied himself with legal projects so time-consuming, years of strenuous effort, that they rapidly became what he had always been doing and always would be doing. His moment-to-moment engagement in these cases was complete. He did not defer or avoid or postpone or procrastinate or run errands. When others temporized, he became impatient, might rail against these obstacles to his onward motion. For recreation, Rosenthal was a long-distance runner who, at age sixty-five, completed his third marathon in eighteen months. But more accurately, all of those running races, like his cases, were one single forever race. He didn't care about money, he didn't care about fame, he didn't care what he drove or ate or wore. He had no evident relationship to irons, dry cleaners, combs, fabric softener, or dinnertime. When he submitted to family summer vacations in rural Maine, it was understood that he would pack law books but not his swimsuit, and his days would be spent at the nearest library. Occasionally, there came a morning when he stayed away from the library. Then he could be found at the regional courthouse, observing. To children's birthday parties he brought the legal briefs he was drafting and sat on the couch penciling improvements amid hats and hooters. He almost always took on unwinnable cases, put in his all, and lost more than 90 percent of them. But against opposing lawyers with the most fearsome reputations, sometimes he won.

When Diane Polan learned, in May 2008, that Kwame had been acquitted, with the jury still in the room she'd said, "Now, Bobby." She meant "I wanted to do something for Bobby. Kwame won the lottery when he got me. Bobby didn't win the lottery." The evidence against the two was the same. Find Bobby new lawyers, she said, and "I proved their case for them."

With Polan's encouragement, a few days later Bobby's mother wrote a letter about Bobby to Karen Goodrow, the lawyer who ran the Connecticut Innocence Project in Hartford. Goodrow's was a new area of the law. Through most of the twentieth century, the typical prosecutor went to work convinced the profession sent no innocent people to prison, and the public had similar confidence in the judgment of juries. In 1989, however, the first American was released from prison and exonerated from his crime on the exculpatory basis of a new forensic detection technique: DNA profiling. In the ensuing twenty-five years, hundreds of people were similarly vindicated. But more than 90 percent of all cases lacked testable DNA potential, meaning there must be a considerable number of innocent people in prison without scientific means of proving it. Facing that was to confront an ethical abyss of unknown scale, and most people turned away.

Prosecutors, like the public at large, continued to regard prisons as the realm of the guilty with a rigidity that for Peter Neufeld, the cofounder of the original Innocence Project, the Dixmoor Five exemplified. This was a group of fourteen- to sixteen-year-old boys who, in 1991, were convicted of the rape and murder of a teenage girl in Chicago. Twenty years later, when DNA testing of the semen sample from the crime scene was belatedly matched to a recently paroled rapist, the prosecuting district attorney posited that the teenagers simply hadn't ejaculated; the paroled man was likely a necrophiliac who'd happened upon the corpse. "I almost got myself held in contempt," said Neufeld, who was representing one of the five in a post-conviction hearing. "I told the judge, I'm from New York, is necrophilia big here? Are zombies prevalent in Cook County? Psychologically, what happens is prosecutors feel their primary duty is not to seek justice and truth, it's to defend the conviction at all costs."

As in most murder cases, Pete Fields's crime scene yielded no DNA. Bobby couldn't appeal his conviction because he'd waived the possibility by pleading guilty. An incipient legal concept, freestanding "actual" innocence was, like a drug at the earliest stages of testing, more an enticing tiding than something likely to help. Instead, a more antiquated stratagem now came to Bobby's cause—personal connection. Connecticut was a small state with a kindred criminal justice community, so when Goodrow received Grace's letter with vouching from such a respected figure as Polan, she went ahead, had case-related documents gathered, and assembled a file. That took a year. Next, the Innocence Project searched for a lawyer willing to work essentially for nothing on a case with significant possibility of failure. Unable to find one, toward the end of 2010, Bobby was informed his file had been packed away. But just then Goodrow and Polan had a joint inspiration. They would urge their old friend Rosenthal to represent Bobby. Both thought him ideally "motivated" and "obsessed" for this kind of long-shot job. "Kenny," Goodrow said, with approval, "gives headaches."

Rosenthal grew up on a Connecticut chicken farm; neither of his parents had been to college. He attended Yale, but withdrew during his junior year to register Black voters in Mississippi. Then he went west, circulating through the Chicago chapter of Students for a Democratic Society, the Free Speech Movement at the University of California, and picking plums amid the effort to organize California farm workers. After college, he collected eggs for his father, taught elementary school, and held a job at an unemployment office, which led him to law school at the University of Connecticut. There he prepared for exams by reducing courses into summaries that fit onto one tiny slip of paper. When Rosenthal joined study groups, a classmate observed, "Ken didn't drink coffee. Only hot water."

Rosenthal was hired as a young commercial litigator at Wiggin and Dana, an old-line New Haven firm, where he had a walnut nameplate on his door. After four years before the mast, Rosenthal joined the Public Defender's Office and was rarely seen by his children until he burned out and returned to Wiggin and Dana. This established a career pattern in which Rosenthal over-devoted himself to the defense of the indigent until it became necessary to reenergize at a prominent firm where his wealthy clients at times became enraptured with their scruffy attorney. When invited to their summer homes, Rosenthal might show up in his year-round personal uniform of green wool hat and wool sweater with pens emerging like cattails through spacious holes at the breast. When his living room required a couch, he recovered one from the town dump. After his wife told him to become a more present father, he began making his children breakfast and lunch, and driving them to appointments. One daughter attended Hillhouse High in the 1990s, where she was one of four white children in a student body of one thousand. Her best high school friends lived in Newhallville, which meant for Rosenthal "I was driving down streets I never knew existed and I've lived here all my adult life. It's a world within the city, and it's not a very big city."

When the families of his daughter's friends had difficulties, Rosenthal acted as their lawyer, free of charge.

Once his children left home, Rosenthal became of-counsel for a succession of firms, which asked him to take a few cases in exchange for overhead, and otherwise allowed him to remain, he said, "separate," a lone legal rider. The arrangement let him follow what he considered his calling, defending poor men accused of crimes, and his life shaped to his work.

In 1988, Murray Colton was accused of a lurid New Haven crime known as "The Dimes Murder," in which a police informant had been stabbed 248 times around midnight, with a scatter of dimes left near her body, thought to be a reference to "dropping a dime" or informing on someone. Across ten dogged years of trials, mistrials, convictions, and appeals Rosenthal fought several prosecutors including the last, Jim Clark. Rosenthal eventually accused Clark of concealing exculpatory information by enabling a witness he knew to be dishonest, the opinion of Clark's chief investigator. The bad feeling between Rosenthal and Clark reached a pitch when Rosenthal succeeded in arranging something unprecedented in state judicial history: making Clark himself a witness and grilling him for thirty-five contentious hours about his conduct. "I put Jim Clark on the stand for eight days," Rosenthal exulted. "He couldn't stand being a witness. I ask him one question, he yells at the prosecutor, 'You should object to that!'" The *Hartford Courant* described the judge holding his head in his hands during the ceaseless "sniping and sarcasm." Only in 1998 was the case finally resolved, when Clark withdrew prosecution.

In 2010, Rosenthal's face was narrow, his dark, determined eyes hooded behind glasses, his hair silver and askew, and his resting expression a dismayed frown. His austere, single-minded approach to life meant he sang while washing dishes, but only one continuous note, D flat; and he bicycled to appointments to keep up his conditioning without sacrificing work time. When preparing cases, for maximum lawyerly efficiency, seven days a week Rosenthal worked until a few minutes before midnight. Should he grow hungry at his desk, Rosenthal kept apple slices in the drawer, and ate them no matter how brown they got. At midnight, behind his desk, he set down a thin blue rubber mat, then placed on it a pillow and a yellow sheet. He slept there until three, whereupon he resumed work. Some of Rosenthal's clients carried around photographs, not of their lawyer but his blue mat. When the COVID-19 pandemic closed his office, Rosenthal said, "It's a disadvantage.

I have to sleep in my bed." He was then seventy-five years old. None of this was self-abnegation. It was how he liked to be.

Goodrow arranged to meet Rosenthal at a coffee shop near Big Cheshire, and while she explained Bobby's case to him, Rosenthal felt a rising vocational excitement. As a young public defender, Rosenthal had "hoped for cases where people were wrongfully accused." Innocence as a conceptual matter was of such interest to him, he'd once designed a course on the subject and convinced Western New England University School of Law to let him teach it. The burden of proving actual innocence was so "ridiculously high" since the state had reorganized such claims, only one person he knew of had ever succeeded.

After they talked, Goodrow took Rosenthal to meet Bobby at the prison. Listening to Bobby recount his interrogations, Rosenthal had the impression of a "mild mannered" young man; there wasn't any of the accumulated outrage the lawyer had expected. But perhaps, Rosenthal thought, Bobby's experiences had made him frugal with what he told strangers. Afterward, Rosenthal said he was intrigued, and asked Goodrow for Bobby's file. A week passed, and Goodrow's office received an impatient communication that was then circulated in this way: "Email from attorney Rosenthal. He is anxious to begin work on Bobby. We are still looking for file."

It took a month to locate it. Paging through, Rosenthal felt exhilaration. "Every lawyer," he said, "has a handful of cases in his career where you know that they've got the wrong person." About his chances to help Bobby go free, Rosenthal was generally optimistic. Barack Obama was president, and with his administration had come a public conversation about mass incarceration. The country, Rosenthal thought, was rethinking its convictions. In early 2011, Rosenthal returned to visit Bobby and told him, "I know your situation and I am not going to stop until justice is done."

ROSENTHAL PREFERRED POST-CONVICTION law because it was the second draft of a case. Abundant information had been set forth and, all alone, he could probe for faults and divots of logic and rule. The Bobby documents contained so many pages that no person could absorb them right away. That was also as Rosenthal preferred. Good appellate lawyers read their dense files the way some people did James Joyce novels, the understanding deepening with the increasing familiarity of rereadings, each pass yielding new insights, a plan of defense slowly taking shape. The cache of police reports and other materials the prosecution had sent to Bobby's original lawyer, Larry Hopkins, Rosenthal deemed "a great file. An excellent file! He had it all there. He just hadn't touched it."

From Kwame's trial transcript Rosenthal had taken in something that forever formed his feeling about his new client. Reading the transcript, Rosenthal reached the moment when, on the witness stand, Bobby abruptly disavowed his two confessions, said he'd come to understand his "mistake," and apologized for placing Kwame in jeopardy. "I'm so moved by reading his testimony," Rosenthal said. "They bring him in to testify for the prosecution at Kwame's trial, and at this point he's got nothing to gain. He's been told by the cops everybody's going against you, that Kwame had given a statement implicating him. He comes into this courtroom, he has no lawyer. He has nobody. He's there alone. They ask him to review his statement on the stand. He says, 'I can't do that,' in a very street way. 'I can't do that. Words can ruin a person's life. I won't do it for you.' The kid has a stronger moral compass than all the judges and prosecutors and lawyers in the room. He's such a good person. And every time I think of that moment, it brings tears to my eyes."

Rosenthal saw no contradiction in that person lying to the police. He said that while the police "strongarm" methods were effective enough for extracting confessions even from seasoned criminals, they were disastrous with a young person who wanted to please. The kid was confronting large, experienced authority figures with all the power and a settled theory of the crime. Something had to give. "Scared innocent people falsely confess in part because they believe in the system and think it will prove them innocent by finding the true perpetrator," Rosenthal said. Just how misguided this whole process had been, Rosenthal thought, became evident earlier in the transcript from Kwame's trial, before Bobby had retracted his confession. Jim Clark asked Bobby to describe his attempt to rob Pete Fields, and Bobby set out to do that. He then proved incapable without Willoughby and Quinn to script it for him. "Clark tries to lead him through the story," said Rosenthal, "and when he gets to the point where he asks what's a robber supposed to do, he has no idea! It's ridiculous. It shows how difficult it is for him to make it up." Rosenthal believed that the Bobby who emerged from the documents was "a wonderful human being." Rosenthal's challenge now would be to convince other people of that. "When I tell people Bobby pled guilty, nobody believes he could be innocent," he said. "They don't want to hear it. Plus most people who plead guilty are guilty." But even there, the lawyer said, he'd defended people charged with crimes far more serious than what wrong they'd actually done.

Rosenthal decided he would begin on the grounds of procedural violation, by filing a petition for writ of habeas corpus. The petition would claim Bobby had been compelled to testify against himself through police-coerced false confessions, and that he'd been inadequately represented by Larry Hopkins. As Bobby had written down himself in the initial petition he'd filed pro-se through the Cheshire warden, "The police questioned me and a friend without our parents present. I was confused and I had never been in this situation. Not understanding what was going on I confessed to a crime I did not commit. I was sixteen."

Next, Rosenthal visited a cramped basement space a short walk from the courthouses in New Haven. This was Hopkins's law office. The two men sat together, Rosenthal asking about Bobby, Hopkins chain-smoking cigarettes. Hopkins confirmed Bobby had told him he was innocent, and that when Hopkins asked why he'd then confessed, Bobby had shrugged. As Rosenthal began to describe his intentions, Hopkins's face whitened and, said Rosenthal, "He says to me, 'Oh, Jesus, don't tell me this was an innocent person.' He was genuine. He's dealing with cases where 99 percent are guilty as sin." Polan had thought the same about Hopkins, that "It's not irrational for a lawyer to say to a client, 'You confessed. With your confession you could get sixty years. Take it. Take the plea.'" But there in the files was evidence of someone else's palm print on the murder victim's car window, a glaring forensic fact that, if pursued, could have lit up a trailhead positioning Hopkins to follow a path marked with such bright blazes as ballistics reports, witness testimony, criminal records, internal police files, all of it concluding where Polan had, that there was credibility to this client.

Every serious appeal means reinvolving people in something they've moved past. The private investigator on Kwame's case, John Hoda, had been working on a baseball novel, posting instructional videos dedicated to the art of interviewing, going about his private investigations, when there was Rosenthal on the phone asking, "You know the Herbert Fields case inside out?" Hoda replied, "Yeah." Rosenthal told him, "I'm doing Bobby's habeas," and Hoda's rejoinder was, "About fucking time!" Then Hoda said, "This is an open file on my desk. As long as somebody's fighting for Bobby, I'm in."

They met, and Hoda helped Rosenthal assess who would most credibly testify for Bobby at a habeas hearing. Then Hoda began traveling around

Newhallville, revisiting those he'd come to know when working on Kwame's case, including the crime witnesses. Most were unhappy to see him. "She's concerned about her safety," the investigator said of one young woman from West Ivy Street. "Nobody wants to be a witness in a murder case."

At Big Cheshire, meanwhile, Miss Mouzon had stayed in touch with Bobby, encouraging her former student to fight for his release. Now she was leaving Big Cheshire for a new job. "I called him down to my classroom. I told him. It's a large room. He walked to the other end. He came back. I said, 'Listen, you're getting out of here someday. This isn't your home. Be productive.'" Yet Bobby wondered what exactly anybody expected from him. He rarely saw Rosenthal, had no real conception of what the lawyer might be doing for him. And so Bobby shrugged and stayed in the prison moment.

Rosenthal had decided Bobby's case came down to police misconduct. For all of his time spent with the files, the lawyer could not understand why Willoughby and Quinn had landed on Bobby and Kwame as their suspects. It seemed bizarre to Rosenthal to have hung an entire case on two conflicting confessions, brushing away contradictions, avoiding verification. Rosenthal knew Willoughby had once owned a substantial reputation in the department. He also knew Willoughby claimed "a 100 percent solvability rate," a distinction previously unattained in the history of American city policing. Since the Fields case, in 2006, Willoughby had been investigated for corruption and was in retirement now, a diminished figure. Rosenthal wondered what during his career had changed for Willoughby. Across the city, others also wondered.

In 1998, the respected senior detective Jim Ponteau retired, and he and former chief Melvin Wearing both eventually moved back down to South Carolina, settling not in the old Plantersville plantation community where they'd grown up but in Georgetown proper. There they mostly lost contact with Willoughby. From afar they retained affection for the younger man they'd guided into investigative police work, were confident of their protégé's abilities, and dismissed anything contrary. "I don't believe most of the things I hear," Ponteau said. "I knew the kid. He was a heck of a uniformed officer who became a good detective. When you work in an area like that, some people won't like you." Wearing said, "Willoughby was great until we left. I don't know what happened after we left. Willoughby was the only detective going out there and kicking butt, arresting people. I don't want to say one bad word about Detective Willoughby. If he went bad after I left, I don't know."

Otha Buffaloe felt similarly about Willoughby. "He was a good cop," the pioneering Black detective said. "He investigated and followed up. That's what makes him—follow-up." Unlike the others, when Buffaloe heard rumors about underhanded activities, he sought out Willoughby and warned him to be careful. Yet Buffaloe continued to hear the rumors. "I was told about it so many times," he said. "I didn't want to believe it. But after I came across a couple of sources I knew would tell me the truth—it was happening. Unfortunate a good cop gets like that. It's like a drug dealer. Gets greedy, gets caught."

By August 2006, when Pete Fields was murdered, Willoughby was the highest-paid detective in a New Haven police department beset with turmoil. There were factions of stressed-out detectives who believed their supervisors were empowering shoddy police work and, feeling powerless to do anything about it, to calm their spirits they'd sink to their knees in department stairwells, linking arms and bowing in prayer. About investigations, they became watchful, tight-lipped, which meant there was no open exchange of case information. One group of young detectives sarcastically named themselves the "B Team," as a way of distinguishing themselves from Willoughby's "A Team" big boys. Rumors of federal agents investigating the department persisted, and there were honest cops who took gallows satisfaction as those they distrusted lost large amounts of weight. "It's the best diet," one of them said. Among the many disaffected members of the force was Willoughby himself, who said he was oppressed by "envy and jealousy. Probably 'cause I was solving the cases."

One March day in 2007, months after Willoughby and Quinn had solved the Fields murder by arresting Bobby and Kwame, the FBI sting finally came, and with it the astonishing spectacle of crime-scene caution tape inside a police station. The FBI revealed a New Haven police culture of bribery, evidence tampering, forgery, and misappropriated funds. Veteran officers were sent to prison. A new police command structure was put in place, with John Velleca charged with rebuilding the detective bureau. As just-appointed administrators looked through the file cabinets they, and prosecutors, were troubled by documentation in cases led by Detective Willoughby. An internal affairs investigation was ordered and, in February of 2008, Willoughby resigned just before he was charged with falsifying confidential informant reimbursement forms and paying thousands of dollars from department funds over to himself. When Willoughby was arrested, he proclaimed his perfect solve rate. "He was cocky as hell," one officer recalled. "He almost laughed at it. He pats his chest. One hundred percent! One hundred percent!"

By 2008, when the national homicide clearance rate fell to 63 percent, out in Los Angeles there was one homicide detective, David Lambkin, who was reputed, over a five-year period in the 1990s, to have achieved solve-rate perfection. But Lambkin himself said it wasn't true. Anybody who claimed 100 percent clearance, Lambkin thought, was "fishy." In New Haven, Archie Generoso, who spent forty-three years in law enforcement, and returned from retirement in 2012 to run the detective bureau, said of a purportedly perfect investigator, "He'd either be lying or he had one case."

To Willoughby's detractors in the police department, Willoughby was out of a black-hat Western—tall, smiling, and genial, with sleet behind the star on his chest. Most police do not publicly speak ill of colleagues. Here the many exceptions included a Black officer who worked closely with Willoughby for years, had considered him "an excellent investigator." But eventually that officer said he wouldn't work with Willoughby anymore. He didn't like to explain why except, he said, "We had a difference of philosophy." He mentioned that "there were disagreements in terms of the interview room." Among the few officers still willing to "ride with" Willoughby by the end of his career was the affable Michael Quinn. Because John Velleca regarded Michael Quinn as experienced at narcotics work, but less sure of "what he was doing" with homicide investigations, he said, "I could totally see him being susceptible to Willoughby. If you didn't know, you thought he was a superstar."

In late 2007, police internal affairs investigators had become suspicious of confidential informant payment vouchers Willoughby submitted that were not referenced in case reports. They traced $1,500 Willoughby had requested while investigating a homicide, and found the referenced informant's code number revealed no such person. When Willoughby here seemed cornered, he claimed that the informant was actually someone else, Willoughby's former brother-in-law and close traveling companion, the informant Speed Limit. This was the man who'd heard Walter McCain discussing Bobby at the Shop, and whom McCain saw speak with Quinn twice and receive $200 from Quinn. When internal affairs interviewed Speed Limit about the payment, his account contradicted Willoughby's version. After that interview concluded, a state inspector was to hold his own interview with Speed Limit. But in the hour between sessions, Speed Limit's story abruptly shifted. Cellphone records revealed Speed Limit had telephoned Willoughby during the recess. Willoughby later explained he'd hurried to Speed Limit's bedside and found Speed Limit had been confused, thought he was being asked about writing bad checks rather than police payment vouchers.

Internal affairs discovered Willoughby had submitted informant vouchers in three other recent murder cases that seemed not to substantiate the payments. One was $1,000 paid to the same out-of-state person from the shooting case, with the typed reason given: "individual provided this detective with information regarding the names of the person(s) responsible for the homicide of Herbert Fields. The results of this information led to the arrest of one Bobby for murder, and an arrest warrant for Kwame for murder." Willoughby later testified his Fields-related information also came from Speed Limit. Someone who knew both men said of Willoughby's investigations, "If anything came up, Speed Limit always said Willoughby gave it to him."

When Quinn was asked under oath if he'd ever used confidential informants in any homicide or a shooting investigation, Quinn replied, "Not that I remember." Quinn would, however, say in a deposition that he'd met Speed Limit "a bunch of times."

To represent him at his 2009 trial on multiple counts of larceny and forgery, Willoughby hired his celebrated defense attorney. Norman Pattis was a self-described "misanthrope," believed that too often people conflated innocence with virtue, and said, "I fight for unpopular people." Among the abhorred on his client list would be Alex Jones, the *InfoWars* radio host who thundered that the mass-shooting of Connecticut children at the Sandy Hook Elementary School was a hoax, leading to a lawsuit from appalled parents. During a 2022 stand-up comedy performance, Pattis first dared himself to "say the N-word," and then did so, with a Black woman seated in the first row a couple of feet away from him. Pattis said that he'd spent more than ten years in psychoanalysis attempting to fully understand "why I do what I do." The childhood memory of how intensely he'd fantasized about murdering his mother's abusive partner now led him to believe "we're all capable of everything." He also seemed to relish the theatre of lawyering. Pattis was well prepared, clever, and enjoyed juries, and they enjoyed him. For a time he'd been law partners with Cookie Polan, but they fell out and parted, probably, Pattis thought, because she was driven by political causes, while his was a near-literary interest in people as characters. Pattis owned a used bookstore, wore a graying ponytail, and could be at turns brazen and then puckishly disarming: "I'm a lone wolf. I'm a shark," he said of himself.

Defending Willoughby at trial, Pattis suggested that as an employee in a dysfunctional workplace, Willoughby had been savvy to create extra layers of diversionary protection to ensure confidentiality for his informants. "We were able to portray the New Haven Police Department as itself a suspect organization and made a lot of that FBI raid," Pattis said. "Our message was that Willoughby was a scapegoat, that New Haven was using him to avoid confronting darker truths in the department." This was, Pattis explained, "a misdirection strategy." Willoughby was acquitted of all charges.

Willoughby wanted to sue his police investigators and the city. Pattis refused to represent him. During the trial, the lawyer had asked the jury for a "reluctant" not-guilty verdict. He later said he believed there had been "probable cause" for arresting Willoughby. "He insisted on bringing that meritless lawsuit," Pattis said. "I moved on." Willoughby hired another lawyer, but the suit was quickly dismissed. Of Bobby's case, it seemed to Pattis a "reasonable" take that Willoughby coerced a confession because he truly believed Bobby had done the crime. "A good investigator's got to be charming," Pattis said. "Got to have a touch of sociopathy to manipulate a sixteen-year-old into his own undoing without leaving marks on his body."

In retirement Willoughby drove a black Mercedes and lived on his comfortable pension in the blue ranch house. Across subsequent years, confidentiality agreements would mean the public could not know how many millions of dollars were spent on the settling of lawsuits brought by those who claimed the detective had mistreated them.

One such man was a former Newhallville teenage drug dealer, Ernest Pagan, whom Willoughby interviewed as a suspect in a 2006 early Christmas Eve murder outside a bar. Pagan was the first to say he hadn't lived a blameless youth, but was no killer, and had since become a skilled carpenter, making a good living. Even the murder victim's fiancée had said Pagan wasn't at the bar that night in 2006. But Pagan would recall of his long interrogation weekend with Willoughby, "he made it abundantly clear he didn't really care who did it. He just wanted a face for the crime so he could close it." After Pagan refused to admit anything in the Box, his high bail meant Pagan spent over a year in prison awaiting trial. Then, Willoughby was arrested. At Pagan's trial, witnesses claimed that they'd been guided by Willoughby in making their statements, which they recanted. One witness testified, "Anytime he asked me a question, if I don't answer it, he stop the tape and tell me what to say and play it again." The witness added, "When I told them what I seen, they kept telling me I seen other stuff that I didn't see." Pagan was acquitted.

Pagan's lawyer had been Thomas Ullmann, and as Rosenthal investigated Bobby's case, he spoke with Ullmann, spoke with Willoughby's supervisor, spoke with other police officers. Rosenthal found it telling that when Willoughby and his partner interviewed witnesses, "The pattern of interrogation was [they] had a suspect they wanted them to give up, and they told them what to say. It's what Bobby says." Almost all this alleged pre-interview scripting by Willoughby had taken place unseen and unrecorded, behind closed interrogation-room doors where, Rosenthal conceded, "I have no idea what happened. But I think it happened."

Among the documents Rosenthal reviewed was the internal affairs report from the police department's Willoughby investigation. In it were excerpts from cases Willoughby worked in 2006, including the murder of the drug dealer in the Hill. Names were redacted, but Rosenthal noticed that the coding numbers of the guns used in the Fields and Hill murders were identical, meaning it was the same .45 later recovered from Major's dead body. This was a revelatory moment. Rosenthal could now be sure that Major possessed the gun that killed Fields shortly before the Fields murder and not long after it, which should have suggested to Willoughby, working on both cases, that Major was almost certainly the person who'd used it to kill Fields. That counted as newly discovered potentially exculpatory evidence, the classic marrow of a habeas petition. Hopkins (and Polan) hadn't been given the information, possibly violating Brady rules of evidence disclosure. Rosenthal amended his petition, writing that Willoughby's method "shocks the conscience" and "contravenes the fundamental principles of fair play."

That Willoughby worked two similar street murders committed with the same weapon, that he knew all about Major, and then chose to focus on Bobby infuriated Rosenthal. "Nobody connects the dots on Major," he thought, "because he'd died and nobody cares. You can't prosecute him, because he's dead." Or perhaps it was that the detectives had already extracted confessions from the wrong kids by the time the ballistics and handprint information came in, and suddenly making Major their suspect would have been too revealing of their methods. Criminal justice often meant making difficult decisions with imperfect information, but here the opposite had happened. The detectives had unnecessarily complicated a simple case. And, inverting the axis, they'd simplified complicated people. What Rosenthal now really wanted to see were the police files on Major.

Rosenthal was approaching seventy. He had office space under the third-floor eaves in the nineteenth-century turreted brick Queen Anne mansion belonging to the New Haven firm of Brenner, Saltzman & Wallman. Nobody else went up there, leaving Rosenthal to an "intense stage" of work. The blue mat came out at night, and otherwise time became no object.

He found himself thinking back to an old case. A Subway sandwich shop had been robbed, a man was identified as the culprit by a store employee. Then a person who'd committed a succession of robberies confessed to the Subway crime. The confession was convincing, but the employee still was sure she'd pointed out the correct robber. "There's a fixation we get," Rosenthal said. "Willoughby probably believes to this day he had the right person. He's so arrogant and unconcerned that he could have made a mistake. It's laziness and pressure. The mayor wants these murders solved. It's terrible there are so many murders in New Haven. We need them solved. They love Willoughby, until they don't."

ROSENTHAL WASN'T SPENDING a lot of time with Bobby. Rosenthal considered himself "a book person and an idea person, not a people person." He was caring, but scholastic in both his approach to work and his feeling for it. The law was for him a matter of ethics and theology, and he engaged with it in a clerical way, alone at his desk, a solo practitioner, personally of-counsel, immersed in the literature. It was characteristic of Rosenthal that he'd formed his high opinion of the client he was devoting himself to by reading a court transcript.

So it was to Bobby's advantage that among those Rosenthal hired to assist him with the case was a forensic psychologist named Alan Goldstein. False confessions were at the legal penumbra, a controversial niche, sketchily understood, attacked as scientifically squishy, and they were just rare enough that there were only a few people who claimed expertise. Goldstein was one. He had helped police departments to evaluate both job candidates and also the status of troubled officers, had worked for prosecutors and defense lawyers in the pretrial assessment of defendants. False confessions were, however, his professional passion. When Rosenthal asked for help analyzing Bobby's experience with the police, Goldstein went twice to Big Cheshire for interview sessions with Bobby, which convinced Goldstein this was an honest person who'd been derailed from telling the truth by police sure they had their man.

When Goldstein and Rosenthal debriefed at Rosenthal's office, there was a sudden power outage. Much of their work was done sitting on a staircase in the dim red glow of emergency-exit lighting, Rosenthal holding a flashlight as Goldstein explained his belief that Bobby had been let down by society and lacked, Goldstein said, "general knowledge. What you could learn through school, through academic experience, through culture." Bobby's bind was that these liabilities made him more suggestible to people who, meanwhile, overvalued their own perspicacity. "Police believe they can tell what the truth is better than others," Goldstein said. "But statistics say they are as a group worse than college students." Look, Goldstein told Rosenthal. He worked for police departments. He wasn't anti-police. Police needed to push at guilty criminals who insisted "It wasn't me." The issue came when an interaction became so unpleasant, so frightening, that an innocent person's judgment was eclipsed and it seemed better to say "I did it."

Rosenthal's solitary pursuit of Bobby's case brought him occasional moments of euphoria. One was the 2012 day he discovered *Convicting the Innocent*, written by Brandon Garrett, the law professor admired by Jim Clark. Garrett's book made a detailed study of the first 250 convicted people exonerated by DNA profiling, and included court transcripts from sixty-six court cases where police officers testified about what were later proven to be false confessions. *Convicting the Innocent* became Rosenthal's Gideon Bible, kept on his bedside table, and present with such frequency in his thoughts that when Rosenthal was speaking with somebody else, at any moment, without warning, Brandon Garrett might come bursting into the room. "Look what Brandon Garrett did with sixty-six cases!" Rosenthal would shout, non sequitur. "He quotes cop after cop who testifies and insists they didn't coerce confessions. They lie under oath time after time. It's outrageous! It's what everybody expects them to do. And the result is people like Bobby go to prison and nobody cares." Then he'd be rhapsodizing about Garrett's content analysis of police interrogations, his discoveries of police feeding crime details to innocent confessors, of confirmation and hindsight bias, his description of leading interview questions, of photographs slid across tables, of death penalty threats, of nonexistent fingerprints, of the tunnel vision that led to cases prematurely closed without any attempt at corroboration. Everything Bobby said had happened to him in the statement room Garrett had seen before. "It's all bullshit!" Rosenthal would sigh. "Thugs lying their way to get a confession and the Supreme Court said it's okay to lie about evidence that doesn't exist in order to induce a confession." After long minutes, Rosenthal would walk it halfway back. "They may think it's okay to step over the line to close the case, but it's not," he'd say. "These guys thought they were doing right. I don't have a devil's theory of anything. But policemen have tremendous power."

For all of his anger at police officers, Rosenthal was self-defined in opposition not to them, but to their supervisors. "These cops," he'd say, "the pressure to solve cases is intense." Because "it's tough to break people who are incorrigible criminals," he thought police overzealousness was inevitable, an old story. He became fond of referencing not only Garrett but also Agatha Christie's description of errant detectives who "conceive a certain theory and everything has to fit into that theory. If one little fact will not fit it, they throw it aside. But it is always the facts that will not fit in that are significant."

In the Fields murder case there were so many facts Rosenthal believed he'd never reconcile. He couldn't explain why the police had shaken and bent the case to implicate the shorter, darker-skinned Bobby as Fields's shooter when the best witnesses and the forensic evidence implicated the taller, lighter-skinned Major. Rosenthal still couldn't even be certain how the police had first come upon Bobby's name and why they never reconsidered once they suspected him. "They latched on to Bobby for some reason," he said. "It's unsophisticated, and it's a combination of 'we don't care' and 'we're arrogant.' It's not this case, it's not just New Haven, it's the country. The tragedy of these cases is the wrong guy goes to prison and they get away with it. Dangerous people are out there running around who should be in prison."

Police work was fraught with old, human problems, he thought, and a solution to them was someone to watch over police, to notice what conflicted, to unsettle the theory. That someone was intended to their department supervisors and, in particular, the prosecutor, whose responsibility was for both sides in criminal cases. Prosecutors had support staffs, investigators, laboratory testing, a full legal apparatus behind them, all because prosecutors were expected to independently evaluate crimes before they tried people. Right through to a verdict, the prosecutor had to remain sure of the defendant's guilt, and if the prosecutor developed doubts, it was unethical to keep pursuing the case. Yet it was often said of prosecutors that their job was to feel certainty where others might experience doubt. This was the "conviction psychology" that law professor George Felkenes warned of—a professional predisposition to regard defendants as guilty. As a judge once told Rosenthal, "If he didn't do this, he did something else." The reason Bobby was an ideal client for Rosenthal was that Bobby's case, he said, "wasn't about Bobby. It was about the integrity of the system."

Such grand purpose needed a windmill. For Rosenthal, that was Jim Clark. As Rosenthal worked alone, Bobby and Kwame's (and Murray Colton's) prosecutor became Rosenthal's anti–Brandon Garrett. "The problem with Jim is he has such a big ego," Rosenthal would jab. Then, swerving into another round at the heavy bag: "I don't pretend to understand what's driving him. His issues are very big issues because he's so confident." Clark, it seemed to Rosenthal, thought it would be disloyal to crime victims if he developed sympathy for the accused. No doubt Clark was effective; he pushed hard and usually won. Yet sometimes people were bulldozed.

Jim Clark was no longer involved in Bobby's case. He was not the prosecutor who would assess Bobby's habeas petition at the end of 2012. After twenty-seven years on the job, Clark didn't even work as a prosecutor anymore. In retirement, Clark was a professor for the U.S. military in Virginia, teaching graduate-level law students about sexual-assault policy and trial advocacy skills. Worthy and decent endeavors! And yet, as Rosenthal soldiered on with Bobby's case, there was a fever-dream quality to his declamations against Clark, an animating enmity that led him to hold even Clark's virtues against him. "Inflexible prosecutors can be a tremendous problem," Rosenthal would announce. "Jim Clark's the poster child. He shouldn't have been a prosecutor. He doesn't appreciate he can make a mistake. I understand defense lawyers are a pain in the ass. But these are people's lives. This should not be adversarial. We should protect the innocent." As he prepared for Bobby's habeas hearing, Rosenthal's tilting against the absent shade of Clark motivated him, even as he claimed, "I've never had a problem with Clark. I see him for what he is. True believer."

From Clark's end, all this was strident and perplexing. "Ken Rosenthal has had a negative impression of me for a very long time," Clark said, "and I don't know why that is. But Ken Rosenthal has an acerbic personality towards lots of people in authority, and he is one of the relatively few lawyers who makes a habit of attacking his opponents personally in court, which I find to be inappropriate and offensive, besides being irrelevant." Karen Goodrow, by now a judge, knew each man and observed, "I think they both have a passion the other might describe as a passion to a fault. As obsessed as Ken is, Jim's the same way. If you said to them, the two of you have similar personality traits, they'd flatly deny it." These two driven, long-distance Yale men of the countercultural time did have much in common, right down to Clark's own admiration for Brandon Garrett. And yet somehow the same received information had taken them to opposite sides.

CONNECTICUT'S HABEAS HEARINGS were held at Superior Court in the small village of Rockville, northeast of Hartford. Rockville was at enough distance from the state's urban centers where most criminal cases originated that there was also the atmosphere of legal remove. When Rosenthal arrived to advocate for Bobby late in 2012, everyone else seemed to him to be used to working with one another, and he soon had the feeling of intruding on a family gathering, a court with its own habeas culture.

The presiding judge, John Newson, was a relatively young Black former New Haven public defender, in his second year on the bench. In a state where most of the judiciary and other leading figures in the criminal justice system were white men, Newson might have seemed to the defense an ideal audience for Bobby. He was an engaged, curious person who'd seen firsthand the city's "stark" demarcations, had himself represented clients who promised him they didn't commit a crime, but then refused to risk a trial and instead pled guilty. But former defense lawyers typically made for tougher judges than former prosecutors—thought to be a consequence of representing many guilty people.

When Rosenthal arrived at the court, he was summoned to the judge's chambers with the prosecutors Adrienne Maciulewski and David Clifton, who'd been assigned to present the state's position. There Rosenthal listened to the judge "chew me out" for what Newson considered the disrespectful tone of Rosenthal's pretrial motions and requests. "After that," said Rosenthal, "whenever we went into his chambers he was seething."

Nobody contested that Rosenthal was an excellent lawyer, but his tendency to steep himself in his cases, expanding on every theme, carried over to the courtroom where his style of speaking in blocks of dense text where a single trenchant phrase might have done, as he himself said, sometimes "wore out" other people. "There was," said one judge, "the danger of going in too many directions when one direction was sufficient for the jury." The judge thought that Rosenthal was admirably self-critical, well aware of who he was, and that his courtroom approach was thus intentional—a matter of personal principle from somebody who understood that in a system where so many people were just going along, disruption was essential. "He's not big on social cues," the judge said. "Doesn't know when to shut up when he's aggravating a judge or witness. He's single-minded in his resolve. He thinks he's doing the right thing. A true believer. He makes people crazy, but he's a hero because that's what it takes to save a poor kid."

In the large, windowless Rockville basement courtroom, Rosenthal argued that Bobby's lawyer, Hopkins, had done no investigation, and reasons for that failure were the prosecution's failure to inform Hopkins of potentially exculpatory evidence implicating Major and BlackJack, and Willoughby being under investigation for corruption in cases including Bobby's. Hopkins himself testified in Rockville he would have proceeded very differently had Clark sent him this information. In response, the prosecution found it telling that Bobby had told Hopkins so meekly that he was innocent and then only "shrugged his shoulders" after Hopkins asked him why he'd confessed. Rosenthal explained that Bobby's meek nature was exactly the quality that had made him capitulate to an aggressive police interrogator.

Willoughby had taken the fifth instead of testifying in Kwame's trial, but one day, in the back of the Rockville courtroom, Rosenthal was surprised to notice a striking man. "He wore an impeccable suit and tie," Rosenthal said. "He looked like a movie star when he came in. He was an imposing, authoritative witness. A very believable guy. But anybody but a prosecutor will tell you, cops are trained to lie." Willoughby raised his right hand and then testified he'd overcome "three aneurisms. Not one aneurism. Three. The average person woulda died from one." His answer to questions was a variation of "I don't remember none of that stuff." Beyond providing Willoughby with what Rosenthal considered "an excuse that allows him not to answer anything," it had a vitiating effect that this handsome, suffering man here in front of everyone seemed so different from the defense portrait of a brutal behind-closed-doors detective.

Conflict developed between lawyer and judge. At times, Newson seemed harsh to Bobby's side as he told Rosenthal, "Counsel, you're done," told him to "sit down and stop objecting," and lectured him on being "professional." At one point, Rosenthal finally asked Newson, "Why is Your Honor shouting at me?" At another juncture, the judge suddenly stood, left the bench for long minutes, then returned to warn Rosenthal that he would have sent him to have lunch down in the lockup with Bobby except that a judge should never punish a client for a lawyer's conduct. The New Haven *Independent* described Rosenthal's increasingly "convoluted" and "flustered" attempts to make his case in contrast to the "crisply efficient" ways of Maciulewski. Alan Goldstein came to Rockville to testify, and the psychologist later said, "What struck me there was tremendous tension between the lawyer Ken Rosenthal and the judge. The judge appeared to me to have his back up." Half the courtroom's spectator area was filled with members of Bobby's family. Among the contingent was Granddad, who said, "The judge seemed like he wasn't interested in anything Ken had to say. That upset me. Everybody in there felt that way except the prosecutor, of course."

The state dealt with eight hundred to nine hundred habeas cases annually; Clifton himself handled four a month. To Rosenthal, while most were "frivolous, nothing-to-lose" gestures, in his mind, here was the real opportunity for all of them to help a truly innocent person. But so far as the prosecution knew, Maciulewski later said, Rosenthal's "working every angle, wouldn't take no for an answer" was simply how Rosenthal approached all cases. Going into the hearing, Maciulewski had no idea that Rosenthal thought this was the rare habeas case that merited special review for "real innocence."

In October 2013, Newson issued his opinion, writing that procedural rules had been followed, that what had been "devastating" to Bobby's defense had not been Hopkins, but Bobby's confessions and his subsequent failures to guide the hand of his lawyer. Newson later said that from the bench he'd "fascinated" with the question of whether a person who'd made a "straight guilty plea" could legally reverse course and claim "actual innocence," and had debated the matter with colleagues. In the end, Newson decided that by voluntarily making a guilty plea Bobby "waived" the future right to prove his actual innocence. Newson also thought no compelling-enough new evidence had materialized to suggest innocence. The judge wrote that he was untroubled by "inconsistencies," which he explained were in the nature of most criminal cases.

In Bobby's block at the prison, when Newson's ruling came through, its subduing effect on Bobby's future was such, said Troy Westberry, "You had some people who doubted he would go home. They read his decision: Man, they shot everything down. Judge rubber-stamped it."

Chapter Fifteen

Following the habeas hearing, Rosenthal took measure. He'd been working on Bobby's case for three years without result or payment beyond an occasional $75 hourly state allotment. Something had to change. What he decided was to work harder. By the end of the following year, Rosenthal said, "I did nothing but Bobby." He became a high-speed train on dedicated track, a man so completely pointed in the one direction that during telephone conversations, talking with people about the case, there was no interrupting him as he explained and decried. If the call was disconnected, return calls went straight to voicemail, making it possible to imagine Rosenthal out there, unaware, goading himself on in his fatalistic way: "The system doesn't want to review these things. There's always some reason not to review unless there's DNA." But if the system had low gears, they were shifting. In 2013, of the record eighty-seven Americans who were exonerated, fifteen had pled guilty, and only eighteen were DNA cases.

What now changed for Bobby had again to do with Connecticut's insular legal community, how as one judge said, "across the state, everybody knows everybody." In early March 2015, Rosenthal attended a seminar on wrongful conviction, exoneration, and compensation held at the University of Connecticut's law school in Hartford, where one of the speakers was Kevin Kane, Connecticut's chief state's attorney—the top prosecutor. Kane was now in his seventies, and with his flushed red face, unflinching eyes, thick white hair, and bristling mustache, he had the throwback, *L.A. Confidential* mien of a formidable lawman. Which he was; he'd been a prosecutor for more than forty years. Yet people thought Kane to be open-minded and receptive to untraditional ideas. When Latino citizens in East Haven complained of racial profiling by the police department, Kane attended a church community meeting, listened in tears as people told of their experiences, and then, when he was asked to speak, Kane began by apologizing. His office had solicited tips on unsolved murders by printing-up decks of "cold case" playing cards with the details of homicides on them and making them the only playing cards sold in the state's prisons. Kane also changed state policy so that all police interrogations related to serious crimes would be videotaped.

The Hartford wrongful-conviction seminar Rosenthal attended came two days before the Justice Department released its report on the Ferguson police department. During his remarks Kane said that he believed systemic change was in the air, and in the public interest. There followed discussion of how unfair many African Americans considered the system to be, and how prosecutors were themselves undermined in their work by wrongful convictions. "I agree we are too adversarial," Kane said. All this inspired a member of the audience in a well-worn sweater to stand and offer what began as questions about post-conviction appeals, and then meandered into a jeremiad against police interrogations. After some time, the man chastised himself, saying, "I'm babbling on and on because I'm exercised about this." It was Rosenthal. But as he spoke, Kane was thinking, "I always knew of Ken. His questions were good questions." After the session, Kane asked Rosenthal to write him a letter describing his concerns.

A month later, Rosenthal attended another public symposium, on police transparency, at Gateway Community College in New Haven. Again Kane was on the panel, as was New Haven's police chief, Dean Esserman. Again Rosenthal rose to ask a question that became a screed, this time on how adversarial post-conviction review was, prosecutors fighting to sustain convictions, not fairly reevaluating cases. Again Kane was taken with Rosenthal's critique. Again afterward, said Kane, "I told him to write me a letter." Rosenthal also spoke with Chief Esserman, who invited him to "come see me" at the police department.

This was surprising. Police departments were typically so pressed with new crimes they were reluctant to revisit settled cases, perhaps especially one presented by a lawyer claiming mistakes had been made because of police malfeasance. But since taking the position in 2011, the NYU Law School–educated Esserman was a chief who, in staff meetings, told subordinates that "police are the community and the community are the police."

He was quoting from the nine policing principles that had guided Sir Robert Peel's creation of modern policing with London's Metropolitan force, in 1829—the belief you couldn't cure disorder without public respect and cooperation. Esserman and Kane agreed a high volume of cases made mistakes inevitable, and not acknowledging them damaged public trust in police and prosecutors.

That Kane and Esserman were willing to admit such fallibility was rare. In New York, at the Innocence Project, Peter Neufeld said he thought often about "how difficult it is for law enforcement people to acknowledge error. We have detectives who say about DNA, it's fine to convict people, I use it all the time, but it's not as reliable to clear people. That's how they reconcile [convicted] people who turn out to be not guilty."

Then, as Rosenthal's mail slot was suddenly filling with these invitations from important leaders, he heard related news from an old colleague from Wiggin and Dana, Darcy McGraw, now at the state Innocence Project. McGraw had been discussing post-conviction cases for potential review with Leonard Boyle, Kane's deputy. Boyle was a former East Hartford police officer who, as a federal prosecutor, became known for the vigor with which he'd pursued relationships between police and organized crime figures, like Whitey Bulger. McGraw told Rosenthal that when she'd briefed Boyle about Bobby, Boyle too had been "interested." A feature of the case that attracted Boyle, she said, was Bobby's plea. Pleas were so final they curtained off all mistakes—implied there never were mistakes.

Before Rosenthal acted on any of this, on an early April evening in 2015, he met with twelve members of Bobby's family at his latest office, giving them an appeal update, telling them of the police chief saying to him, "If there's somebody who's innocent I'm interested and concerned." Afterward, he walked everyone out. Standing on the dark sidewalk, watching the family disperse, some making U-turns back in the direction of Newhallville, Rosenthal said, "Bobby really loves his family. So that's how Willoughby got him. He told him if he didn't confess, he'd never see his family again. And now he's never seen his family again."

During the next week, Rosenthal wrote his letters to Kane, Boyle, and Esserman, the first installments of what soon became a one-way correspondence, single spaced missives that went on at novella length, with additional entreaty made via tabs and exhibits. Letters urging that a criminal conviction be reconsidered have a quality of madness, the beseeching of an unrequited heart, because it's so difficult to convince someone who's decided against you and moved on to relent, feel a different way, give you another chance.

But Rosenthal was also doing the novelist's work, making the object of his emotional concern the object of theirs, and his many pages affected readers. In late April, Rosenthal met with Esserman and two of his deputies, including Generoso, now the assistant chief in charge of detectives. Esserman found Rosenthal to be "a true believer," but also credible. Esserman was well aware of BlackJack and, by extension and repute, Major. After meeting with Rosenthal and receiving his request for Major's case files, Generoso studied them and, for impartiality's sake, Generoso also asked the state's attorney's office to separately review the Fields investigation.

Rosenthal didn't know what Generoso was doing, and so the lawyer continued to busy lawmen's letterboxes with his frustration. By early May, Rosenthal said he was "in an angry, impatient state." He wrote again to Boyle and judged it "not an accommodating letter." Then more Rosenthal commentary toward Esserman. Letter upon letter, though even as Rosenthal sealed the envelopes he said, "They're so damn long nobody's gonna read them."

Dina Fisher read them. Fisher was a lawyer working for the chief state's attorney's Cold Case Unit, pursuing unsolved murders of prolonged duration. It was she Boyle assigned to review the integrity of Bobby's case. Fisher wasn't sure why she was chosen, except that "I was just a different sort of person. I had a different set of eyes." Fisher had studied art at Brown University and, even as she worked as a lawyer, for years she audited classes at the Yale School of Art to improve her skill at painting figurative portraits, to improve how she saw.

It took weeks for Fisher to assess all the correspondence from Rosenthal, by now a layer-cake of paper, as well as police crime and internal affairs reports. Fisher's analysis diverged from Judge Newson's. She thought flimsy initiating evidence had led to confessions riddled with inconsistent facts, suggesting to her they had been conducted under duress. Willoughby's basic integrity troubled her, as did what the confession transcripts led her to adduce about Willoughby's and Quinn's approach to interviewing. She was baffled by their failure to follow up the potentially exculpatory forensic evidence as well as their reluctance to show photographs of Major and BlackJack to the crime witnesses from West Ivy Street. She grew skeptical that any criminal connection between Major and Bobby had ever existed, and told Boyle that the numerous felonies committed by BlackJack since the murder "bothered me a great deal." What she was reading changed Fisher as a person: "It shattered my innocence, the lying that goes on and is permitted."

In the middle of June 2015, Rosenthal was invited to another meeting, this time at New Haven state's attorney Michael Dearington's downtown New Haven office, along with Boyle and Kane. In Connecticut, prosecutorial authority belonged to the state's attorneys presiding over the thirteen judicial districts, a network of fiefdoms that traced back to the 1600s. Nothing could happen for Bobby without Dearington's approval. During the meeting, the three prosecutors were keenly interested in the line of murders linked to Major's gun, and in BlackJack's palm print. That Pete Fields didn't live in Newhallville told them he was unlikely to have been the victim of a chance street encounter. Like Rosenthal, the prosecutors thought it a case that hadn't been complicated until detectives complicated it.

June became July, and away from all this government discussion, Rosenthal was brow-furrowed, weary, rasping, puce-faced, an Eeyore beset. "Yeah, they're reinvestigating," he said in his it's-all-for-naught way.

At the end of the month, Rosenthal was invited to Kane's office in Rocky Hill, a Connecticut River bedroom community outside Hartford. There Boyle told Rosenthal they were granting him permission to see Major's police files. Then Boyle slid a document across the table to Rosenthal, explaining this was "something else you're entitled to have." It was a confidential informant reimbursement voucher from the Fields case made out and signed by Det. Michael Quinn. It was also signed and dated by a supervisor, Billy White, who was no longer with the department because he'd been arrested and imprisoned after the FBI undercover operation found he'd stolen money. On this Fields voucher, Quinn had written, "Informant was paid $100 for providing this detective with the name of a suspect that shot and killed a man on West Ivy Street on 8/1/06. This information resulted in the arrest of this suspect Bobby for the murder of Herbert Fields." Rosenthal looked up at Boyle, not understanding the significance. "Look at the date," Boyle told him. "Look at the complaint number." The voucher's submission date, signed August 11 by both Quinn and White, was chronologically impossible, because that was four days before Bobby was first questioned, and more than a month preceding his arrest. The case number also did not correspond to the Fields murder. Clearly legible on one side of the document was that Quinn had first put in for $200, crossed it out, and cut the sum in half. No informant was mentioned in Quinn's case report. Willoughby's own case-voucher had claimed paying for the same information. Quinn had told internal affairs he'd never once used informants investigating shootings or murders. This document defined newly discovered evidence.

"A good prosecutor is Len Boyle," Rosenthal crowed back in New Haven. "He's somebody who's not emotionally invested in his own righteousness. His personality is the right personality for a prosecutor." He thought Boyle probably liked working up in quiet Rocky Hill, that it provided a vantage to survey with clarity. Rosenthal dipped his shoulder and said, "They have the power to free Bobby tomorrow. If they don't let him out, I'll fight three years! Five years to get him out! I won't be surprised if they say no."

Rosenthal was an older white man devoted to a young Black man in prison, and yet through it all Bobby never thought Rosenthal became a self-serving rescuer, validating himself by helping somebody else, never suffered from any white-savior complex. "You can't stop Ken from being good," Bobby would say. "Color has nothing to do with it. People kill for somebody like that. Somebody to take over as your protector when you're in your toughest spot."

Rosenthal was unsentimental, less a do-gooder than a crusader all in on the cause. What Rosenthal wanted from Bobby's case was not love or recognition or a plaque for the office wall. He wanted Bobby to be free, and the police to be better the next time a Bobby came along. After all this, Rosenthal still thought of Bobby as another person he represented, and he treated him that way. "He's a wonderful client," Rosenthal said one day at the end of the summer of 2015. "Clearly one of the best I've ever had. Never complaining. Never hassles me. Maybe to a fault. Nice for me. But what gets me going is all about the big issues. It's the opportunity to fight abuse of power. I'm not a social worker. Once Bobby's out, I've done what I can do. Helping him after that, that's not me."

When Rosenthal received, at last, Major's police file, to Rosenthal this wasn't quite DNA, but he considered it several solid tiles in "an evidentiary mosaic" of Bobby's innocence, including sordid accounts of murders, some collected by Willoughby and Quinn themselves. That Quinn had been one of the detectives working the Ebony Lounge murder meant he and Willoughby, in combination, had participated in all three murder investigations involving Major from June 2006. Yet somehow the detectives had not been impressed that the murders had similar patterns of method, people shot in the head area at point-blank range by someone who'd then fled initially on foot. The eyewitness accounts naming Major in the first two murders matched the descriptions of Field's killer. Rosenthal was surer than ever the detectives had somehow become prematurely convinced Bobby was the murderer, which made them unable to value any information that didn't implicate Bobby. This was confirmation bias coupled with tunnel vision and at the end of the tunnel was catastrophe—and old poetry. "Oh, what a tangled web we weave, when first we practice to deceive!" Rosenthal recited. "That's Walter Scott," he said.

Rosenthal posited a reason Quinn hadn't pursued the forensic evidence linking Major and BlackJack to the case might be that by then he'd already locked himself in to Bobby by creating the $100 voucher. "It's a phony, fabricated document," Rosenthal cried. "Sloppy. Probably pre-dated." He was sitting in his office, wearing a T-shirt, bicycle shorts, and brown laced dress shoes. His voice was at an indignant pitch, high even for him, as he said, "I trust Julia Sykes about what happened in that interrogation room much more than I trust Michael Quinn. What's Quinn gonna say? 'I committed a felony'?"

Something else Rosenthal discovered in Major's file was BlackJack explaining that, after Major was murdered and the case went unsolved, he'd taken to storing a .45 at his grandmother's house out of fear, "because I knew everything that happened."

In a different sort of way, now so did Kane, Boyle, Esserman, and Dearington. They were the guardians of the system, and Rosenthal had provided a shock to it.

Chapter Sixteen

On September 1, 2015, New Haven was warm with scattered clouds, the back-to-school time of new beginning. Rosenthal was spending the morning dragooned into babysitting grandchildren with his wife, his feet in the backyard, his mind on his next moves, which included "subpoena everybody!" He couldn't wait to get across a conference-room table and question Jim Clark again. Rosenthal's telephone rang. It was Leonard Boyle on the line. There'd been a motion to set aside judgment. The state was freeing Bobby from custody. Rosenthal and his wife clasped hands and began dancing around the yard as the grandchildren watched.

Rosenthal headed for his car. This was a black 2006 Hyundai that he habitually left parked under a fruit tree. Sap and tree-fall had stained the roof and hood. It looked awful, but it ran fine. Rosenthal got in and began driving out to Big Cheshire to tell Bobby the news. Near the prison, however, he pulled off the road and stopped at the same coffee shop where Karen Goodrow had first told him about Bobby nearly two thousand days earlier. Rosenthal's shoes were untied, his belt was forgotten out on the car seat, his undershirt hung untucked below an equally liberated striped Oxford-cloth shirt that had only one button fastened. Rosenthal ordered his victory meal—hot tea (no milk, no sugar) and a salad (no dressing).

Something in Rosenthal needed to move away from the moment. So he reached for a familiar comfort and took up the subject of Jim Clark. "Cookie talked at length with him trying to get him to drop Kwame's case," Rosenthal said. More raillery about the power of prosecutors ensued, concluding with speculation that embedded in the prosecutor's refusal to change his mind about Kwame and Bobby was the wishful rationalizer in all of us: the need to believe the police get it right; the need to believe doctors know how to take care of us. Why wouldn't people see clear that perfection was not human, that injustice was everywhere? Rosenthal sighed. "I'm really glad they did it. I'm appreciative. But I certainly don't want to say the system worked. Boyle did the right thing. A lot of prosecutors wouldn't." True humanity was the pursuit of better in a fallen world.

He began the salad, then put down his fork to savor professional delicacies: Kwame refusing a plea offer of seven years, risking thirty years, to clear his name; Polan declaring at the verdict, "Now Bobby." Rosenthal completed this impromptu valedictory by allowing that after all the days and nights committed to Bobby's freedom, now it felt "a little anticlimactic. Ask any lawyer after a trial. You put your heart and soul into something and then it's over."

Bobby didn't know it was over. Minutes passed in the coffee shop as Rosenthal lingered. Something momentous had happened for Bobby and Rosenthal seemed in no rush to tell him. In his triumphal moment he was lugubrious, anxious about Bobby, worried about Bobby's future. "He'll have to readjust to the crazy world we live in," Rosenthal said. "It's occurred to me that for all the bad things about prison, certain things in life are taken care of. You don't have to make money. You want a job, you have a job. Everything's structured. As my daughter said when she graduated college, 'It's doomsday! Now I have to support myself.'" And how much greater the challenge when leaving behind not the quad with a diploma at age twenty-two, but a cell block where you'd matriculated at sixteen. Rosenthal said, "He's been away nine years. There's a big difference between sitting in jail thinking about what you're going to do, and the reality when you get out." He hoped Bobby wasn't a believer in happily ever after.

Rosenthal had wanted to arrive at Big Cheshire in an optimistic frame for Bobby. It was past time to get over there. "Maybe I've got to be more of a social worker," he said. And then, cheered suddenly by the realization that it was not over, that there was work for Bobby yet to be done, Rosenthal walked out to the parking lot, threaded his belt, tucked in his shirts.

At the prison metal detector, when the presiding CO learned what Rosenthal had come to do, the CO became excited. You didn't hear about something like this every day. Rosenthal passed through electronic sliding gates and doors to the windowless cinder-block prison meeting room with its blue and white plastic chairs and the small, circular brown table across which he and Bobby had been talking since 2010. Bobby entered in a tan jumpsuit and white sneakers. Rosenthal said, "Hi, Bobby. They're setting you free."

Nobody can imagine themselves confessing to a murder they didn't commit. Everyone can imagine the ecstasy of suddenly being told they're free after doing nine years in prison for a murder they didn't commit. But Bobby only seemed numb. It was that his mind had instantly gone forward in time, to telling the people in his study group that he was leaving while they must remain. "You serious?" he finally said to Rosenthal.

With that, Rosenthal launched lengthily into how the release would unfold, filling in the time until, at last, Bobby caught up with him, came around, and said, "I can't contain myself. This is the best gift ever!" Rosenthal said instantly this was no gift. "You deserve it. It's been a long time coming. It's always good for people to be reminded that just because the police arrest someone doesn't mean they're guilty. There's been a lot of that lately in this country." And, Rosenthal told him, their work was unfinished, because Bobby was owed "compensation" for his lost years. "It's a complicated, interesting part of the law!"

Rosenthal said it would be Friday or Monday before Bobby was released. "I've been patient this long," Bobby said. He was five inches taller and thirty-five pounds heavier than when he'd been arrested as a high school teenager. But to Rosenthal, from the day he'd first met Bobby in 2010, Bobby "was always the same."

Growing up as he had, of course Bobby didn't believe in happily ever after. He thought aloud about what the coming months would bring. "That's the scary part," he said. "It's hard to fathom." So, Rosenthal told Bobby about his daughter and doomsday. Bobby said, "I was just talking to my mother this morning about how much I hate to be stuck and dependent on other people. Now I get the challenge. This is awesome. I can't believe it."

Back out in the foyer, the excited corrections officer had some belated counsel for Rosenthal. "Tell him don't tell anybody," the CO said. "They'll be jealous and want to fight him." As Rosenthal left the building, over his shoulder came a postscript: "Tell him don't come back to see me."

Bobby had returned to his cell and found Troy Westberry sitting on his bed. "I've been exonerated," Bobby told his cellie. Westberry shot into the air, hugging Bobby and crying, "That's what I'm talkin' about! That's what I'm talkin' about!" His reaction meant that now Bobby, too, could fully embrace the moment. Bobby declared he would never sleep another night in prison. To make sure, he removed all the sheets and the mattress from his bed.

Then, as was prison tradition, he presented his possessions to others, his CDs and CD player, the TV cable converter box, the TV itself, his books. He traded his new sneakers for a man's older pair. Such unregistered gifting was a violation. Bobby had still never received a prison disciplinary ticket.

Bobby stayed up all of Tuesday night and all of Wednesday night. On Thursday evening, he was a report on the evening news and, Bobby said, "Everybody was so happy." COs congratulated him by saying, "Mr. Famous Guy going home!" Bobby had a sudden worry that having his face on the news would cause the authorities to reconsider.

Bobby's former Urban Youth teacher, Dyane Rizzo, watched the newscast and wept because, "Very honestly, I didn't believe he did it. There was just something special about him." Addie Wardlaw, also from Urban Youth, said, "People will say it's hope. I heard lots of stories like Bobby's. Of course I did. One judge asked a kid if he had any remorse, and the kid didn't know what remorse was and he said, 'No, sir.' And the judge sentenced him."

Through Bobby's final Big Cheshire night, Westberry kept him company. The friends made a pie of meat and beans and chips, cooked in a chip bag that was eventually kept heated in an oven built of clothes and blankets. It was what Bobby called a "sounds bad/tastes good" prison last supper. Westberry advised Bobby to remain aware of who'd been there for him when he was "down and out," and to trust only them. Then Westberry warned, "You can't expect everything out there to be how it was nine years ago."

At 4:40 Friday morning, as Bobby was led from the block, he saw all the faces pressed to all the doors, watching him leave. He had a memory of childhood, when friends' families had moved from New Haven to the South, how abandoned he'd felt, them on to better places while he was left behind. Now "I was the one who was leaving. I looked at everybody's face congratulating me."

BOBBY'S COUSIN HANK'S wife was shaking Hank from a sound sleep, "Get up! Bobby's here!" Was Bobby downstairs? "No! He's at the court!" Hank threw on the first pants he could reach, yesterday's dirty work clothing, drove downtown, and parked in the only spot he could find near the courthouse, an illegal space. "Don't you owe taxes?" his wife asked, worried the city would tow their car. "Yeah," Hank replied, "but if they take this car, so what?" They sprinted for the courthouse. Cousins Benji and Johnny were also parking. Nine years before, they had shared clothes with Bobby, and everything else. Since then, Hank, Benji, and Johnny had always told one another, "Next time we all chill we're going to be old men with canes!" Now the three wondered how large Bobby would be, whether his lower lip would still be too big.

The ice-cream truck brought Bobby to the federal courthouse bullpen. He was warned to watch his back so a jealous person didn't come at him down there. At ten o'clock, still in prison clothes, he was escorted to the wood-paneled Courtroom 6-A. Bobby sat down and looked out from a protective slouch. Seated in benches arranged like church pews, here was his family at last. He saw Granddad in pressed tailoring, Grace wearing Roman sandals. Several girls had on T-shirts imprinted JUSTICE FOR MY BROTHER, and several more wore tops emblazoned JUSTICE FOR MY COUSIN. All those faces Bobby hadn't seen in nine years told him "life been carrying on." The rows were mostly filled by women. An entire generation of men—fathers and uncles—was not there. Was this a happy day, bittersweet, or one of sadness? There, as so often happened with families, feelings divided.

Also occupying benches were Rosenthal, in a stained khaki suit, Hoda the investigator, Darcy McGraw and her staff, Dina Fisher down from Hartford. Some of Bobby's friends had come, including Bounce, who still worked at Visels. Said Bounce of that ordinary evening in New Haven nine years back when Bobby had been at the store while two blocks away an elderly gentleman was murdered, "I just can't remember." Aunt Joy said, "Sure I remember that day. I was at work." They were all taking off work. For Hank, that meant a day away from two jobs. Just outside the door lingered Kwame. Courtrooms, he said, were places he no longer would enter.

Judge Patrick J. Clifford, a red tie under his robe, began the proceeding. Clifford's grandparents had met and lived in Irish Newhallville. Calling it "a tragic case," Clifford asked everyone to "hold their emotions." Cousin Johnny was looking at Bobby and noticing, "Yo, he grew into his lip. Wow!" Cousin Hank was looking at Bobby and noticing, "He got tall. Everybody done left me! We all used to be the same height."

Rosenthal moved for the case to be dismissed, and Dearington did not object. Pete Fields's daughter, Susan, wearing a white blouse with a floral burst of red and lavender, stood and described her anger and confusion after Kwame was acquitted and Bobby remained in prison. She said she'd now finally found some redemption. "I'm really happy for Bobby," Susan said. She hoped he would have a good life, be as fine a grown man as her father had been.

Rosenthal, speaking at length, concluded by saying, "It was a privilege to represent him." Darcy McGraw stood and praised Rosenthal, who "really threw himself into the case. He left no stone unturned." The judge allowed, "He has a reputation for doing that." There was the feel of a graduation as the judge announced, "Dismissal is entered. Good luck, sir." Outside the door, Kwame was recalling how Bobby had come from prison to testify at his trial. "He was right there with me that day," Kwame said. "He was my best friend."

Somebody in the family gave Bobby a pair of jeans and a white T-shirt. They fit like billowing flags because nobody knew his correct size. Bobby walked outside the building and looked up at the sky. Newsmen were gathered. Bobby told the press he'd never again eat ramen noodles or another chip. Grace handed him packages of Reese's Peanut Butter Cups, his favorite childhood treat. With all these people showing up for him after so many years alone and away, Bobby felt as though he was performing to meet a public expectation of his gratitude. He existed outside of the experience, somewhere still in emotional transit from Cheshire to New Haven, up in the air between resentment and relief. Rosenthal hosted everybody for a catered lunch at his office, where Bobby said, "I always knew I was a good person." Then he left to play basketball at the park with his cousins.

PART V

REENTRY

Chapter Seventeen

In 1975, the national prison population had been 240,593, but by the time Bobby was sentenced, in 2007, he was one among 2,310,300 people living locked up in America. Now, seven years later, when Bobby's release sent him, joining 650,000 others, out of the block and back into free society, mass incarceration had created an inevitable mass reentry.

Reentry was an enormous problem Americans tended to know very little about. It meant the changeover time of the formerly incarcerated rejoining the community, a process that left most lost in transition. Within three years of their release, two-thirds of former prisoners were rearrested. After five years, the number rose to three-quarters. For those like Bobby, who'd spent nine years in prison, the recidivism rate was 83 percent. One hundred released prisoners returned every month to New Haven, where a judge, grimly assessing the justice system's approach to reentry, said, "If we were a corporation, we'd be out of business."

The fallow educations, the lack of good jobs, poverty, abuse, and the violence of home and neighborhood that had helped many into handcuffs were scarcely addressed during their prison years. Instead, prison time so often was wasted time. Then came reentry, with people confronting the urgent adult priority of finding work that would pay for housing, food, clothing, and health care. But almost all left prison without a viable vocational skill or the basic concepts of professional etiquette: how to follow through, how to accept criticism. People in prison had no models of those who'd been inside and then succeeded in changing their lives, because by definition success didn't come back there. Prisoners had instead learned to shower in their underwear, to refrain from looking others in the eye, to live their unfulfilled days as people related to time before the age of clocks.

Neighborhoods like Newhallville promised so little support, reentry slang called going back to them "returning to the crackhouse." At Big Cheshire, Bobby and Westberry knew plenty of men who dreaded living again where they'd grown up because, they said, there was nothing awaiting them except poverty, old neighborhood beefs, and the memory of whatever had happened there to derail them. Bobby didn't want to live in Newhallville, and Westberry said, "I don't want to go back to my town either."

For the recently released, pinioned out on the lean flank of the city, the days pressed with the existential wish to be younger. Many aspects of reentry had not even achieved vocabulary, such as the lack of a word for years lost to prison. In reentry support groups, men talked of their anxiety, depression, and lack of sleep, said things like "I've never been proud of myself for anything" and "Nobody ever praised me for anything."

Such people needed luck, a break. Typically they got the opposite. Fear and resentment of those released from prison meant rules and circumstances canting so heavily toward protecting society, the fear accomplished what it sought to guard against. In Connecticut, a felony record exposed a person to 625 so-called collateral consequences upon prison release, restrictions on housing, student loans, and forms of employment like being a barber, electrician, or plumber—professions it might have made sense to license in prison, since the proven means of ensuring that former inmates didn't commit more crimes was steady work. With no professional network, a person returning to postindustrial Newhallville from prison was expected to get a job through his personal industry and reformed character. "You fucked up, now fix yourself," went the thinking. Yet for finding salaried employment with a criminal record in the absence of connections, said one New Haven former inmate, "there's almost no hope." Even for the most highly motivated former prisoners, advice for job seeking began with "good pair of shoes," because you were going to walk so much pavement. At New Haven's Transitions Clinic, where Yale affiliates offered medical care to people recently released from prison, the program calculated 87 percent unemployment among the population it served. As a result, Bobby had met plenty of drug dealers in prison who had vowed to leave the game, but once released, after months of applying for jobs and being rejected, gave up and resumed what they knew.

The reentering people most likely to go back to prison were, like Bobby, poor Black city men. As sociologist Devah Pager wrote, they were in all ways "marked," assumed to be criminals, which led to arrest, which burdened them with a record, which meant nobody would hire them, which meant churn. Black men with no criminal record had a more difficult time being hired than white men who'd been convicted of a felony. That left people Bobby knew purposeless and adrift, describing "a black cloud over New Haven." Some called their city "Nevah Win"—which was New Haven spelt backwards phonetically. It was an American problem and a historical problem. During Reconstruction a former enslaved person had warned that by denying Black men the self-sufficiency of career training, the nation was creating an inevitable mass industry: "He ought to have made a brickmason out of me, for as sure as Negroes go to prison for stealing they will have to build a prison reaching five miles out on the prairie to hold them all."

A WEEK AFTER his release, Bobby appeared drawn with fatigue, strain tightening the bones in his face, a weight burdening his movements, the way men of his grandfather's generation on their return from Vietnam had seemed heavy when walking the streets of Newhallville. Lack of sleep had faded the color from Bobby's eyes, and there was a dull, burnt-tissue-paper pallor to his skin, as though prison had slow-cooked him with the oven timer set to 78,576 hours. American men age two years for every year spent in prison. Bobby was soon to turn twenty-six. His adult life was defined by prison. He had no college degree, no profession, and no worldly job experience. Half the time those who knew him wondered what would become of him, and half the time they debated what Bobby might have been.

In prison, Bobby's focus had been the vanishing point, and his imagination ran riot with plans for all he would do when he got out. He dreamed of walking through the gate, telling nobody, and striking out alone, a voyager to "somewhere else." Rosenthal noticed this, said, "I get the sense that he's done well in prison, had an intellectual awakening. That's nice, but it's the opposite of dealing with the realities of life. Will he be in a place to figure out what to do now?"

Bobby left prison without money or possessions. The $20 a month he earned cleaning the tiers he'd always spent on soap and envelopes. In New Haven, he found that his childhood belongings had disappeared in the course of his mother's changes of address. "I have nothing," he said.

Most people who reemerged from prison moved in with a female relative, as now did Bobby. His cousin Quay was a recently divorced nurse and mental health counselor with three children living on the first floor of a three-family house on Atwater Street in Fair Haven, across the city from Newhallville. Quay gave Bobby her daughter's bedroom, the daughter now sharing Quay's. "That's my cousin," Quay said of hosting Bobby. "He needed somewhere to go." Quay was a perceptive, mature, warmhearted mom—a religious woman who'd thought a lot about the daily getting through of life. Bobby's sister Shavonne had a floor in the Atwater house, as did another favorite cousin. Bobby was grateful to Quay for taking him in, and determined to leave a small footprint—not impose. "Guys who come out of jail," he said, "can overstay, try to run the household. I'm not that kind of person."

He sought to contribute right away by regularly cleaning Quay's entire house, helping Quay's three children with their homework, and also becoming a family personal trainer, supervising Quay and other cousins in a circuit of squats, lunges, and sprints at a nearby park. Cleaning, workouts, and study were activities that had filled his prison days, and yet doing them at Atwater felt completely different. He was, in some ways, like an exchange student, come home with something new to share. After prison, what Bobby most wanted was to shed prison. His happiest times were spent alone in Quay's house, headphones on, listening to Kendrick Lamar and J. Cole. "Atwater's a great place," he enthused. "So positive. From upstairs all the way downstairs. My sister to my cousins. They're showing me so much love." As the first days passed, years disappeared from Bobby's face.

Bobby remained in close touch with Rosenthal, who checked in all the time. "If not for him, I wouldn't have my life," Bobby said of his lawyer. "He's so genuine, so dedicated. He told me, 'By the time I'm done with you, I know you're going home.' He lived up to it. I wish Ken was my father. What Ken did was how a father should love his child." Bobby didn't say such things to Rosenthal. They were alike in finding it more comfortable to speak well of others out of their hearing.

A few days after Bobby's release, he and Rosenthal sat in an auditorium at the Yale University Art Gallery, where onstage, as part of a conference on race and arrest patterns, a panel was discussing prison reentry. Those who came back to New Haven were said to be mostly "without direction, without hope." Afterward, men who'd been in prison approached Bobby to tell him, "You're gonna have some challenges." He was warned how violent "those young bloods" were getting, so he'd best "be careful out there." But it was Bobby's first time inside a Yale building, and rather than look over his shoulder, he admired the gleaming rooms filled with valuable objects. "I am loving this," he said. "I was never exposed to these environments." Rosenthal, however, was nonplussed by what he'd heard from the panelists. "How's he going to live?" Rosenthal fretted. "He needs help, even if he doesn't recognize it."

On a weekend night not long after his release from prison, as Bobby's cousins and sisters dressed to go dancing, he waved off their invitations to join until, finally, he was persuaded. Once at the club, he saw boisterous groups of people passing through the entrance and decided to remain out in the car. Eventually, Bobby asked a cousin to drive him back to Atwater because "I felt like I wasn't ready." When his cousin Johnny took him to a party of college students, Bobby "hated it."

On the weekend, Bobby preferred going roller skating and trampoline jumping with Quay and her two adolescent sons. Quay seemed to have an instinctive understanding of how Bobby's life, interrupted at sixteen, now made him simultaneously an adult and a teenager. She hadn't given him a house key, instead making sure that if he went out, there were people at home to let him in. Some of his excursions consisted of taking daytime walks in the city. One afternoon, he crossed the sun-splashed Yale campus, past neo-Gothic buildings and students recumbent on lawns with books. "It's so beautiful here," Bobby said. "I love being here. All these people making something of themselves, getting educated. I love seeing this. I've only seen it in the movies. Nobody in my neighborhood wanted to go to college, even thought about it. Except girls. And people'd say, 'Why do you want to do that?'" Approaching Yale's School of Music, he realized he'd passed it once before. "We were chased by cops on this street," he recalled. "Must have been seventy of us on bicycles. Coming back from a party."

Walking around downtown, Bobby encountered people he knew who, invariably, offered him reentry advice. It could sound like wisdom being extended at the behest of a concerned collective. "Bobby!" a skinny man in a tie and creased slacks called out from a busy corner. "Dude, we are so happy you're out. We're all so glad." Turning to Bobby's companion, the man said, "Everybody knew he didn't do it. Of course he didn't do it." Then the man warned Bobby to "keep hanging out with the right people." After the man departed, Bobby said, "I used to like that guy and look up to him until I found out he was doing crack." A few blocks away, a young man with whom Bobby had played basketball at Urban Youth seemed to have been waiting for Bobby to show up because, without even a greeting, he said, "Bobby, you have been blessed by God. But it can happen again so easily. Be careful." Passing through Newhallville on the way to a party with Cousin Johnny, Bobby had briefly seen his father: "He's yelling at me, telling me to get out of the area." These admonitions, seemingly from all sides, were unwelcome to someone who'd just got clear of COs. "I hate it when people tell me what to do, tell me how to live my life," Bobby said. "My mom and them are trying to tell me now to stay safe. That's fine, but when they tell me not to talk to people they don't like, I hate that. I don't bother nobody. I don't judge. I stay away from all the drama."

Not quite. Passing through Newhallville one day, Bobby recognized some older guys outside the 2-4 and paused to say hello. Standing with the older guys was a young teenager, who suddenly spoke up, asking if Bobby was out of prison because "you snitch?" A gun was displayed. Bobby told the kid, "If you think I'm a snitch, go ahead, shoot me now." In the aftermath, Bobby said he wasn't afraid for himself but for the kid because the older guys had been that indignant on Bobby's behalf.

Bobby's story was well known in the Newhallville streets. "He got caught up in something he had nothing to do with," said one young man. "He went through that because he didn't want to be a snitch. He went the way he was raised. Bobby wasn't in the game. Came off the porch late. He played ball, girls. But he was held to a neighborhood standard. We don't tell." The hard gradations of the rules also meant Pete Fields's killer wouldn't be blamed for allowing Bobby to go to prison for him. "It's an environment where you're a casualty, like a death," the man said. "We don't care who goes down for your crime. [Bobby] should never have been in the area."

That was even truer now, said Stacy Spell, the retired detective from Newhallville who now directed Project Longevity, working with youth at risk for violence. Spell thought Bobby would have lonely periods until his community broadened beyond those he'd known in childhood. But even so, he said, Bobby had to separate, and Bobby knew it.

As the month turned to October, Bobby was shivering outdoors; after all those years stored inside, he chilled easily. The high hopes his release had sparked were likewise already subsiding, and he began regularly to describe himself as "overwhelmed." Everybody expected visits. Many of his cousins were driving now, and each, it seemed, wanted to pick him up, take him around, make up for lost time. Granddad hoped to work with him on practical skills like driving and banking. Quay expected him to go to church with her. A woman offered to hire him to help with the industrial cleanup of an old armory, good news except the job site turned out to be filthy with rust, mildew, mold, and the strong odor of urine. After nine innocent years in prison, Bobby thought he at least deserved work that wasn't degrading. But Rosenthal knew about the job, and Bobby didn't want him thinking he believed himself too good for anything that paid.

When Bobby had gone away, some of those around him still listened to boomboxes and spoke into receivers attached to coiled cords. A person walking along the sidewalk talking to himself in public now meant something very different from what it had suggested in 2006. Bobby had no idea that the way to draw water in a public sink was to hold your hand beneath the remote faucet and wait. He felt now a little as Eartha Kitt had, arriving in New York from Wolfton, confronting a toilet and a radio, having no idea what they were.

The world was full of such changes, an accumulating disorientation, and the single biggest of them concerned bright little rectangles. Everywhere Bobby went, everyone's head was bent in magnetic thrall. "I feel people are so distracted," he said. "I just came home and not one person made eye contact! They're just looking at their phones." Most disconcerting to him was that phones made public and private seem unboundaried. Words like "Facebook" and "Instagram" felt almost threatening. Social media's collective function, so far as Bobby could tell, was to create drama. Avoiding drama had required so much energy in prison, and to find the open air crackling with it made him feel vulnerable. Yet, when the Connecticut Innocence Project gave him a small reentry grant, he bought himself an iPhone 6, which he then used to photograph another purchase, so he could share with others that he was wearing a fresh pair of dove-gray Air Jordan sneakers.

It was said by New Haven reentry workers that incarcerated people made a tenth of the decisions they did outside. Bobby was beyond glad to decide for himself when he would take a shower, for how long he would linger under the warm spray before he applied powder and maybe cologne. But beyond the Atwater transom, Bobby's days did not achieve habitual rhythms. He had "no idea" what a successful working adult did all day. He couldn't operate a computer on his own, had never written a check, had never paid a bill, had never used a bank, had never scheduled appointments or canceled them. He didn't own a personal ID. There was the constant sensation of lacking necessary information. "Seems like everything vibrates too fast," he said.

For those who went into prison when they were young and reemerged a significant number of years later, everything seemed to exist to make you feel stupid. It was common for people in Bobby's position to be unnerved by how to cross busy streets, the new bus routes and schedules to learn. The bus-stop designs themselves could look different, and there were reentering men who walked right past them and then were late to appointments because they hadn't known where to stand. Some soon refused to leave home, remaining out of fear of further humiliation.

Unlearning prison behavior could also be challenging. If you'd spent years turning your head to put your ear to the open slot in your cell door so you could hear what people in nearby cells were saying to you, turning your head became how you listened. But others didn't know that prison had conditioned you; they thought you'd lost your hearing, and so they began speaking louder. The amount of salt in prison cooking meant it was usual to complete a prison term with higher blood pressure. When Bobby felt bewildered by the "too many choices" available to him on menus, was knocked back by which brand of barbecue sauce to select at the supermarket, this, too, was typical. "At the grocery," he said, "I remember what I used to eat, but I haven't eaten it in so long; I'm confused and conflicted and there's way more than what I saw back then."

People who left prison were calibrated to the age they'd been when they entered prison. Those, like Bobby, who'd gone to prison in their teens, usually still wanted to dress in youthful fashions, listen to pop music, and eat fast food, to be, as one person put it, "all stuck in what they were then." Most had unresolved emotional consequences of whatever adversities they'd encountered that had led them to prison. And the common impulse was to somehow make up for lost years. "You feel like you don't have time," one former prisoner said. "But it's the one thing you have."

A MONTH OUT of prison, Bobby had become "discouraged about jobs." He made haphazard forays to other people's computers, where he didn't know what to search: "I never had a job before." When he did finally locate an application, he had no idea how to describe himself to sufficient advantage that he might appeal to a potential employer.

As the weeks went by, this lack of progress began to concern Rosenthal. "He needs structure," the lawyer said. "Like all of us. Work's so important. Your identity is wrapped up in your value to society, as opposed to sitting around doing nothing." Bobby knew others were impatient with his progress, thought he should "Get over it! Strap up!" "My grandfather wants me to achieve," he said. His mother was telling him, "Get focused. Move on. Don't live in the past."

Prison had cost Bobby the years when middle-class Americans his age were expected to complete childhood, sort out who they hoped to be, and make their way into adulthood. Pete Fields's sister, Katie-Jean, was following Bobby's progress from afar, and she grew concerned enough she called a nephew who worked in a Florida prison. It turned out to be a conversation "that curled my hair. My nephew said, Katie-Jean, they came in as young boys and they stopped growing. There are ninety-year-olds acting like sixteen-year-olds." Bobby's sister Stephanie understood her brother's problem: "He wants his life back. All the things he missed, was taken from him. He wants to go be adventurous, he wants to be a kid again. Yet he also wants to grow up. He's sixteen and also thirty-six."

With this chasm of years to vault, what was really occupying Bobby in his new Jordans were things seizing the attention of teenagers. Texts and calls flowed in and out of his phone more or less ceaselessly. He hoped now to get a tattoo, meet young women, and to accomplish that rite of grown-up passage for sixteen-year-old Americans—"I want to drive," he said. "I want to have my license. That's one of my biggest goals I'm fixed on. Cars are freedom. Pick up and go."

As for women, even as family members were warning him to take it slow, opportunities were presenting themselves. The weeks went by, further softening Bobby's features, and he now resembled the endearing young person others had remembered in his absence. On good days, he emanated warmth and jovial spirits, and he was handsome in a way that everywhere he went, young women tried to talk with him. Virility was inevitably complicated for former prisoners, and it was common for them to seek out someone they'd known before to help soothe the anxiety associated with having sex after years of celibacy. One night, Bobby went roller skating with some cousins and encountered a former girlfriend, Leylea, who walked up to him and astonished him by saying, "You were bad the way you treated me. But we were young. So I forgive you." Then she informed him, "You were supposed to be the father of my first baby." Bobby wasn't sure how to take that. He talked often about not wanting children until he could afford to support them, and when he was given condoms during a visit to the health center, he worried that free condoms might be cheaply made, prone to breakage. Yet now Bobby was finding ways to bring conversations back to Leylea, talking about how being with her recaptured some of the way he'd felt before prison.

In mid-October, a month and a half after his release, Bobby awakened at seven a.m., excited. He put on his nicest jeans, a Chicago White Sox baseball cap, a mist of cologne, and left the Atwater house, declaring, "I'm ready to go and find my future." In prison, caps hadn't been allowed, so wearing one for job-hunting was the logic of inverted stigma. Bobby had a ride, but contemplating a job inevitably raised the issue of how he would get himself to work until he had his driver's license. He said, maybe Leylea could take him.

Bobby had no job-hunting plan, except to "go downtown," saying "as long as you have a good attitude, it all is going to fall into place." Yet a downtown New Haven with blocks of family-owned businesses in need of responsive employees was a Kodachrome memory. Now there were mostly discount chains staffed by people answerable to an office in a distant state. Near the Yale campus were more upscale chains, food and clothing concerns whose lack of distinctive local character seemed the point. This was familiar commercial reassurance for students and parents who worried about New Haven's dangerous reputation. What Bobby wanted was a caring, self-made boss with old-fashioned expectations of Bobby's performance, someone who would prize Bobby's energy and good intentions and guide him into becoming a trusted employee, a protégé, a community-minded future homeowner.

When Bobby's cousin Hank had been a teenager, he'd had a good experience working for the large home improvements chain store Home Depot on Dixwell Avenue in Hamden. Improvement! DIY! These described what Bobby sought for himself. With his destination decided, Bobby said, "Scary a little bit now that we're going. Pressure's on now." The Home Depot parking lot was filled with customers, cars, and empty shopping carts. Bobby parted these obstacles, passed under the store's battlement of an orange sign, and walked in. There he met a woman working at the customer service counter who said she was a retired high school principal. She told Bobby all job applications had to be filled out online and sent to the company's Atlanta headquarters. Bobby sat down at a careers kiosk near a soft drinks refrigerator and began work on the application. After Bobby overheard someone refer to the eventual recipient of his application as the Man in Atlanta, he began doing the same.

Bobby was asked to create identifying passwords. He chose his childhood dog's name. As for his preferred salary, he wrote "whatever is fair," which was rejected. He needed to propose an amount. He thought, after all he'd been through, that a million dollars sounded right. Several employees had now taken interest in Bobby, were hoping for him. They recommended he ask for $10, which was a typical entry-level hourly wage. Another onlooking employee told Bobby, "That's the hardest thing to do, get your first job. Everybody wants to see what you've done." The challenge in 2015 of explaining why someone his age had graduated from high school in 2012 and had remained unemployed since made Bobby feel panicky. He telephoned Rosenthal, who offered to draft a letter of explanation for Bobby to attach. Bobby himself wrote, "I had an extraordinary experience. I'm trying to move on." And then he created a link to a newspaper article detailing his release. Asked whether he had a criminal record, he checked the "No" box. "This is fun!" he said as he typed. For special recognitions he'd received, he considered and then said, "I think everybody thought I was special in jail." His phone, meanwhile, shuddered with the usual heavy text and call volume, and he ignored all the incoming.

There were seventy-two multiple-choice questions for Bobby now to answer. Traveling through them, Bobby engaged with queries about his relationship to laws and rules, whether he believed others had good intentions, how he'd respond if he observed a fellow employee stealing or if a struggling colleague repeatedly asked him for help completing tasks. Inevitably, each question was first read through the lens of the place Bobby had just emerged from, and then reconsidered from the Man in Atlanta's point of view. To a question asking if Bobby agreed he should show persons of authority respect, he whispered, "Certain persons of authority," but then he strongly agreed that respect for authority figures was warranted. "I want to meet this guy in Atlanta," Bobby said. "This guy's very interesting."

Completing the application took two hours. As Bobby left the store, employees wished him luck, encouraged him to be persistent, to keep calling and expressing enthusiasm. In the car, he said, "It felt good to be able to put cleared of all charges. Not too many people can say that."

SINCE GETTING OUT of prison, Bobby hadn't met up with Kwame. Until they were arrested in 2006, Kwame had been, as Bobby always said, "the brother I never had." They still had yet to speak with each other about Bobby's testimony. Since Kwame's acquittal, with Bobby in prison, around Newhallville Kwame received insinuations he'd somehow sold out his best friend. "They were close," said Bobby's sister Stephanie. "I saw Kwame a couple of times.

What the police did had a big effect. Everybody looked at Kwame, 'How'd you do that to somebody you're close to? Why are you here and he's in jail?' "

One prison evening in 2013, Bobby had been watching the news, and suddenly there was Kwame. That morning, Kwame had been picked up in a car driven by a friend. The car had been stolen in Canada. Police eventually found Kwame and his friend hiding in a house. Kwame's guardian aunt, Julia Sykes, said that Kwame had telephoned her, horrified because he didn't know the car was stolen. He'd just accepted a ride from his friend.

Kwame received probation for trespassing, and Sykes worried about him. She said he'd qualified for both his driver's license and a fork-lift operator's license, lived with his girlfriend and their child in an apartment not far from Presidential Gardens. But "he's at the corner," Sykes said. "He didn't completely turn it." She thought Manson had changed him as a person.

Kwame and Bobby were forever bonded by their tribulations, and with both now free, Bobby wanted finally to discuss it all with Kwame, even as he understood that Kwame was reluctant. "Our relationship is kind of strange," Bobby said in October. "We haven't talked. The only day I saw him was the day I got out. He wants me to call him, but he's scared. He doesn't like talking about stuff like that."

Bobby was taken to visit New York, where he rode his first subway, reveled in the city's blood buzz of sensations. Each fresh experience made him want to have others. Yet he would propose these ambitions, like tasting wine, in ways that revealed how hesitant embarking on anything new made him. His way of telling Rosenthal how much he wanted a job was explaining the fear of becoming "that guy roaming around." So Rosenthal encouraged him: Being "turned down for lots of jobs" happened to everyone. "Looking for a job is *No, No, No, No, No, Yes!* You have to keep trying." After Bobby left, Rosenthal recalled his comments about not being a social worker. "Well," he said, "I've gotten more involved."

Bobby and Kwame at last got together, and Kwame immediately brought up Bobby's testimony at his trial. "He kept thanking me," Bobby said. "He thought I was going to tell them he should be in jail with me. That I wanted some vengeance." Bobby sought to reassure Kwame. "He thinks my family is extremely mad at him," Bobby said. "I told him it doesn't matter what they think. They're not in this friendship."

As they spoke, Kwame had grown relieved. "Good energy," Bobby said. "He kept telling me, 'We was young!' " Going forward, Bobby said they had vowed to "try to leave the situation in the past. I feel like it's gonna bring us closer because we both ended up at the same side of the truth." It immensely pleased Bobby to discover "we still had our love for each other."

They soon met up again at a diner, intending to address what had happened to them with the police, for the purpose of forever putting it behind them. Like Bobby, Kwame was much taller than in 2006, when he'd been fourteen. Otherwise, he was still slim, his sleepy eyes were melancholy, and his voice was flattened of inflection. He no longer had braids, but he wore what he and Bobby had dressed in as kids, a white T-shirt, jeans, unblemished Nike high-tops. Among the tattoos along Kwame's lean arms was one emphasizing his allegiance to the 2-4. They sat down and, taking a breath, Kwame and Bobby went back there.

"You came out of Visels," Kwame ventured. "I was coming out of the 2-4 across the street. I had a Dutch. We was gonna go smoke. Crazy, man." Kwame described for Bobby his lengthy struggle to convince the detectives that the fingerprint on Pete Fields's car "wasn't mine." He was aware that the detectives must have known it wasn't his. He made clear how embittering that had been. Kwame described for Bobby the moment when Detective Willoughby played a tape of Bobby implicating him. "I knew the situation. Never hated," Kwame said. But with Willoughby laughing and telling him, "C'mon man. He already gave you up. Just tell me what happened," Kwame hadn't known what to do: "I'm just like, *man*! I'm *stuck* and I don't believe it. This is not real. I know I didn't do nothing. I should be straight. My aunt's telling me, and here he imitated Sykes's voice, 'Just tell them what they want to hear.' He was asking me questions with the tape on. Were you doing this and that? I finally said, 'Yeah.' I was crying. He asked, did I rob him? Was I near the car? I came to my senses and said no. They looked at each other and cut the tape off."

Kwame thought nothing good had come of the experience. "I have an inmate number I'm not supposed to have, I'll have the rest of my life. Every time I'm pulled over by the police, that thing pops up. They say I have to tell them about it when I don't." These police stops Kwame accepted as the normal course of life. "They pull me over just doing their job," he said. But being sent to Manson had splintered him. "I couldn't graduate from middle school," he said. "When I came back I had to adapt to the world. I have a lot of trust issues. I don't trust a lot of people." Kwame told Bobby he was happy he was back, and that he'd prayed for him. As he said "happy," it was striking how unhappy he seemed.

Bobby, Johnny, and Hank met up for Bobby's first ever taste of wine.

Hank and Johnny had been in jubilant spirits around their cousin ever since he'd been returned to them. Their sense of lost time was such they couldn't spend enough hours reconnecting with Bobby, riding around with him, listening to music, teasing him about Leylea, referring to her as "wifey," teaching him about his iPhone. For this evening's festivities, there was a bottle of red wine and a bottle of white, along with provisional containers of root beer and lemonade, in case Bobby and Johnny hated wine. Hank explained to the others that wine was to be sipped, not thrown back like a shot. "It'll sneak up on you," Hank warned. Bobby sipped some of the red. His expression made everyone laugh. "It's good, though," Bobby said. Soon he was drinking root beer.

Both Hank and Johnny kept exclaiming about how well-spoken Bobby had become. "Just watching him come home and be so intelligent and pick up on so much in there," Hank shook his head. A toast was raised with wine and root beer. Then Bobby was telling his cousins about his prison reading group, and proposing they create a weekly book club of their own. Hank, the busiest of them with one wife, two jobs, and three children, said he was down to "get my read on," as long as they also agreed to discuss any unfamiliar words they came across. "This feels like a Christmas Day now!" Bobby exclaimed. The glee all around was how much they'd missed one another.

When the others told Bobby a cousin had become a police officer, Bobby said he couldn't decide what was more surprising, Hank with three kids or the cousin a cop. None could recall happy experiences with the police. Since they'd been small, they remembered the police were there to suspect them, order them to "get out" of public spaces. Before police officers even met them, they attempted to take their photographs. When they asked why the camera, the officer's reply was "in case something happens." An effect of such assumptions on the cousins was to sow doubt about every interaction with police across one's life. You never knew if you were being treated as everyone was or differently because of your race.

Johnny said he'd been wanting to ask Bobby something about prison. Bobby said Johnny could ask him whatever he liked. "Yo," Johnny said. "Did you cry at all when you was in jail?" When people who hadn't been to prison thought about it, they assumed it reduced all but the hardest people. In his cell, Bobby used to try to make himself cry, produced facial contortions that were noticed by his cellies, all to no avail. Bobby shook his head. "No," he said. "I never cried."

Johnny nodded. This was his confirmation. He'd run into someone who'd been at Cheshire with Bobby. Johnny reported, "The dude, he told me, 'Yo, your cousin, he's something else, man. The whole time, he was just smiling.' " Bobby was smiling now, the smile they used to call the cheese. Hank, too, was grinning. "That smile's still the same," he said looking over at Bobby. "His smile's still the same."

ADVICE FOR BOBBY came daily, much of it in refrain, people trying to guide him along. At his former teacher Miss Mouzon's suggestion, he visited her husband, Darien, who worked at Easter Seals, directing a grant-funded initiative to help New Haven residents returning from prison avoid going back. Darien was handsome, with an appealing, accepting presence. Bobby sat down and told Darien, "I was so young when I went to jail, I'm not really sure what I'm good at." Just then, the door flung open and into the meeting ambled William "Juneboy" Outlaw. This was potentially awkward. It had been a young relative of Outlaw's, Sway, who had supposedly given Bobby's name to the police in 2006. Outlaw was now a massive man of well over three hundred pounds, with an outgoing personality to match. Since leaving federal prison, Outlaw had been exerting his considerable influence as both a reentry support coordinator and a counselor to at-risk youth, a so-called violence interrupter. Part of what made Outlaw very effective was that he mixed charm, intelligence, and an intimidating propensity for getting fearlessly to the point. Immediately, he took over the meeting.

"You might know Sway," he said, looking Bobby right in the eye.

"Yeah, I definitely do," Bobby replied, laughing a little uneasily. It was difficult to say what Outlaw's purpose was. Bobby already knew the reality, that everything in New Haven was close and entangled.

"He be doing good. He's working," and Outlaw named Sway's sales position. Perhaps the point was that you couldn't escape your past, but you could move on, as Sway had.

"All right," Bobby said.

"Full benefits. So, he's working." That finished with, Outlaw told Bobby he needed more education, a source of income, and "you got to think about when you was little what you always wanted to be. Just think about what you really want to do, and you got to do it."

Bobby proposed that he might like to join the maintenance staff at Yale. With that, Outlaw was off, explaining all about Yale and its "power," detailing how "City Hall" should help Bobby leverage a position at Yale because he'd "sat all those years for something you didn't do." He told Bobby to be careful around women, take his time, "get to know a person."

Darien spoke up, echoing Outlaw about not getting involved with women "till you're ready." Bobby said nothing about Leylea.

Outlaw informed Bobby that he was using him as an object lesson with young men so they'd understand how, just by being around in Newhallville, "you can get caught up" with the police. He paused, appraised Bobby, and said, "five-eleven, short haircut, dark skin." Bobby nodded. Outlaw said, "I'll ride right through the Ville right now and load my car with fifty of them, same description."

Within two days of the Outlaw meeting, Bobby said, "I did some thinking and realize I need to slow down. Need to stick to priorities. I told Leylea we should be friends and nothing more. I'm not ready for that. With thinking about school, looking for a job, trying to be situated, it's too complicated to try and be in a relationship." He'd begun sleeping through the night, and believed life to be achieving regularity, though he expected calm would not be possible until he had a job.

To help with the immediate costs of rent, food, and clothing, Rosenthal thought Bobby should apply for an interest-free reentry "bridge" loan from the Connecticut Innocence Project. So, one morning at the end of October, Bobby put on a new blue knit hat with white snowflakes and a new watch so large and round it brought to mind a cup and saucer. Prison had made him dislike being too conscious of time, but he said, "Hank gave it to me for my birthday, and so I want him to see me wearing it." He had turned twenty-six. Out he went to discuss finances with Rosenthal.

Their plan had been working up the budget for a loan application. The problem was that neither Bobby nor Rosenthal knew anything about day-to-day living costs. They drifted around the question of what Bobby might spend on meals in a month until, feeling marooned, they called Quay, who patiently and expertly broke it all down—not simply food, rent, and a winter coat but the difference between what a gas bill cost in winter and summer, to smaller expenditures such as haircuts, coins for the laundromat, a session at the roller rink.

When an older friend accompanied Bobby to an appointment, she proposed dropping Bobby off while she parked, and panic slashed his face. "I could be a little timid, maybe," he admitted. "I don't want to get shut down."

Everywhere, Bobby drew back. He stopped exercising. He ate too much fast food and Halloween candy, and then almost nothing for a week. His blood pressure soared. Quay found out and took him to the hospital. “My heart rate’s fluctuating,” he reported afterward. “I need to calm down.” Yet Bobby kept melting weight and muscle, unable to finish meals, not even a ham sandwich. He returned to the hospital, where he was found to have intestinal problems related to anxiety. From the hospital Bobby texted around photographs of his intake bracelet, grateful to these diagnoses for lending legitimacy to his stressful time.

Rosenthal had become “a little concerned. He doesn’t have any money. He feels pressure from everybody. It’s a harder transition than I realized it would be.” Karen Wolff, the social worker at the Innocence Project in New York, said common among exonerees was that so much in them needed mending, and there was nobody to supervise the repairs. Quay, for instance, was the picture of a nurturing person. But Quay worked almost fifty-five hours a week. Meanwhile, Bobby noticed Quay’s adolescent son DaDa was becoming “fascinated” by the streets. During one of their Atwater video game competitions, Bobby sat DaDa back from the PlayStation and offered himself as a warning.

Bobby hoped to move on from Fair Haven because, he said, “It’s not as dangerous as Newhallville, but there are a lot of people into the streets, and I don’t want to be around that.” Bobby also imagined that his presence at Atwater as an unemployed, able-bodied male might not sit well with those around him who had jobs and responsibilities. “I hate irking people, getting on people’s nerves,” Bobby said.

A letter arrived from Westberry describing how prisoners had watched Bobby walk from court a free man on the TV news. “The block was going sick,” Westberry wrote, choosing a favorite Bobby phrase for jubilation. Westberry offered encouragement: “It’s too many people behind you for you to fail. Everyone is rooting for you.” He said, “I’m very interested in how people are going to respond to you not being the same person,” and told Bobby that from now on he was no longer Bobby, but Robert, a non-prison form of reference. “I love you kid,” Westberry said. “I made a pie in memory of you.” It seemed a long time since Bobby had left Cheshire, and yet what Westberry couldn’t know was that Bobby was still half-there with him.

SHAY’S OLDER SISTER, Melanie, learned of Bobby’s release, tracked down his telephone number, and left him repeated messages until he finally called Melanie back. They arranged to meet up, and were sitting in Melanie’s car, outside her grandmother's house on Willis Street, when Bobby heard "Oh my God! You're grown now!" At his window was Shay. Shay! Bobby's great childhood crush. *Shay!* The woman Bobby had spent three thousand days in prison thinking about. They hugged tightly without speaking for two full minutes—"a good nine-year hug," as Shay put it. When Shay had last set eyes on Bobby, he was spindly and not quite her height. Now he was "Hulkamania! You got tall! At least your lip's still on the floor!" Bobby was laughing as she zoomed off to an appointment in her black car. Melanie had propped her phone on the dashboard, and Bobby saw a text come in: "OH MY GOD MELANIE! I want him Melanie!"

Night after night Bobby and Shay stayed up until seven in the morning, "reminiscing." Of Bobby going to prison, Shay said, "I thought that you just wanted to take the rap for somebody. Like, people don't snitch around in the hood and I ain't telling." Bobby gently corrected her: "I think the reason why I took the time is because that was my only good option."

Shay drove a black Chrysler 300 a relative had passed on to her, and she had named the car Darla, or in full "My Delectable Darling." To Shay, Darla was "a powerful luxury cruiser that could turn into some fast stuff." Shay enlivened life in a way that made Bobby say what everybody thought: "There's nobody like Shay." She was cheerful in such an original way that she shone, her face alight with personality, just as Bobby remembered.

At college Shay had taken mostly sociology and women's studies courses—"I didn't know I was a feminist till I went to UConn!"—and participated in campus singing groups. "It's so awesome up there," she told Bobby. "It's like a whole different life. It's like its own little city." Black students were, she explained, "six percent up there. Not many of us. So we'd congregate together. When Obama won in 2008, Confederate flags came out. The police had to escort us." College had been the highlight of Shay's life. But Shay had been married, which she said had cut her financial aid so much she'd left college a year's worth of credits short of a diploma. The marriage hadn't taken, and now here she was, a divorced home health worker, back in the Ville.

Along with religion, music was still at the center of Shay's days. She sang in a gospel chorus that performed in regional churches, and in her free time listened to the singers her grandmother had introduced her to: Teddy Pendergrass, James Brown, Al Green, and their favorite, Otis Redding. "Everything my grandmother played had that old-school vibe," Shay said. "And she took me back to the world she grew up in. Music takes me somewhere else."

Soon Shay was driving with Bobby on forays beyond New Haven, including to her singing performances. "It was so flash!" Bobby enthused after the first one, in Bridgeport. Shay wouldn't have it. Bobby was, she said, "perpetrating fraud" with this contrived enthusiasm. At the church, while everybody was "getting what they need, really catching the spirit, laid out on the floor," Bobby'd texted her from his pew, "Why doesn't God talk to me the way he talks to you?" Shay told him, "If you're gonna love me, you need to love God."

Bobby's view of a higher power was, "There's something out there. But I don't believe you do this, you go to heaven. I believe Jesus was a human being who reached a more loving plateau than others—a better model of who we could be." His Bible study with Westberry hadn't dissuaded his feeling that faith was often a salve for poor Black people's disappointments, a way of putting up with unfairness instead of confronting it. "I disagree with the whole foundation," Bobby said. "I believe it's misogynist. Goes against women's rights. I know it provides structure for people—if they didn't have God, where would they look to? But it stagnates people too."

Shay's response was what*ever* about Bobby's opinions. "He needs to buckle down," she said. "He wants to keep a woman, he got to have a job. There's religion!" But her affection for him was unmistakable. "He's trying to catch up all at once," she said sympathetically.

Around Shay, the staccato gusto of Bobby's laugh was now heard with frequency, as were those favored Bobby expressions of confident enthusiasm, "I already know! I already know!" and "Of course!" Shay and he, Bobby said, "seems like we picked up where we left off." Bobby spent a glad Thanksgiving with Shay and her family and had "a blast! I chilled!"

Now he was aspiring to his own apartment, with Shay, though he had no salary to pay for it. Even though his days were far from full of obligations, his instinct was to pare away. He dissolved the cousins' book club after one meeting about James Baldwin. That seemed a symbolic gesture, something he could do to express the urgency of his purpose. "Reading's not hard," he said, "but I have to study for the driver's test. It's overwhelming."

Bobby applied for food stamps—a household contribution he could make—and then was offering to babysit. Not long afterward, Quay gave him an Atwater house key of his own.

One day Bobby's phone buzzed. It was Home Depot calling him in for an interview. Bobby borrowed some dress shoes, a belt, and put on a "button-front" shirt for his 2:00 p.m. appointment. Bobby preferred to arrive early, and when, at 1:30, he couldn't find his wallet, stricken horror crossed his face. He arrived at 1:58 for his first ever job interview. Jogging through the door he confronted Christmas music over the PA, a massive holiday display of poinsettia, a store special on waterproof shower speakers—and an old friend from Willis Street, now working at the Home Depot. She enveloped him in a hug and guided him to the manager's office. "He's such a good kid," she said. "He just got caught up in something he had nothing to do with. He really deserves this." They hadn't seen each other since 2006, and Bobby seemed thrown to have encountered a face from the past. He'd wanted to think about only the interview, to be his best new self.

The interview began, and almost immediately the manager told Bobby he could not be hired because he'd lied on his application. He had a serious criminal record. Bobby explained why this wasn't true. The manager left the room and returned to say Bobby was right. He told Bobby he was sorry for what he'd been through. The man had photographs of his own family displayed and was kind. He asked Bobby questions about his willingness to follow instructions. He explained that the store was interviewing several people and would make a part-time hire in January. The job for which Bobby had answered seventy-two multiple-choice questions, the job for which he was now in fierce competition, turned out to be supervisor of shopping-cart collection in the parking lot. The simplicity of the task contrasted with how badly Bobby wanted it. He wanted in such an unalloyed way that the idea of this person committing brutal daylight violence seemed more inconceivable than ever. But Bobby would never hear from the Home Depot again.

IN DECEMBER, MISS MOUZON's husband, Darien, arranged for Bobby to interview for a position with Easter Seals at a warehouse on the North Haven industrial corridor. First there was a job application to fill out, two different forms asking up front if the applicant had ever been convicted of a crime. This was a puzzle. Bobby had been convicted, but then the conviction had been retracted. The letter of truth was "yes," but the truth was grounded in falsehood. He decided the safe way to go was to leave it blank and explain at the interview.

In the drafty, metal-roofed, windowless warehouse, employees pushed wheeled bins stuffed with donated items to be sold by the pound. What

Bobby called an "old-people-clothes smell" pervaded as a straggle of shoppers moved among plastic Christmas trees with drooping limbs, tube-era TVs, upright exercise bikes with spoked wheels, pilled sweaters, broken toys, country music CDs from the 1990s. Shay had come along, and in the forlorn surroundings she spotted a lounging chair she thought might work in her and Bobby's future apartment.

Shay was also an optimistic scout for Christmas gifts. Christmas was familiar to Shay as that make-it-through time of year when, she said, convention around Newhallville stipulated "skip[ping] out for the holidays. Take your bills money for gifts. You make arrangements in January. Get caught up in February. This is a lot of people. You either sacrifice on the cable or sell your food stamps. Do anything to get by." The Christmas season, she thought, put people down, because it imposed societal expectations of joy they couldn't live up to. January was a sigh of relief.

An energetic woman led Bobby away for his interview. He emerged jubilant, with a job offer. He seemed far happier even than on the day, three and a half months before, when Rosenthal had come to Big Cheshire bearing news. "I feel great," Bobby exulted. "No, it ain't the best job, but it's a job. I'm going to pull through and do what I got to do."

It was decided to celebrate with cheesesteaks from an upscale market. Shay wanted Bobby to stay in his creased interview jeans, buttonfront shirt, and tie, but he declared it now a "sweats day" and changed. As he settled the clothes into Darla's trunk, Shay said, "Bobby spreads out," widening her eyes.

Cars were a mutual enthusiasm for Bobby and Shay, and on the drive, they looked out the window and commented on them. "Oh! that's a nice car," Shay said about a luxury sedan.

"I want a two-door," Bobby replied.

Shay told him, "Bobby, no. We're supposed to have kids. Who you, going to have a two-door?" At the mention of children, Bobby made a joke about "men could get their tubes tied."

All of December, Bobby and Shay were travelers together. "I'm never around," he said happily. "Shay and I get in Darla and go to Meriden. Go to Hartford. She'll go sing. Then we'll go out to eat." Another day, they drove to a town outside New York, parked, and took the commuter train on into the city for Shay to get her hair done. They arrived in Harlem not long after four in the afternoon, without an appointment. Shay had said this was no problem, and she was right. Shay wore her silk bonnet and carried a bag full of hair to be woven into extensions. At the train station, as they alighted, the sight of Shay's bonnet and bag attracted beauty shop representatives—people Bobby called "hair hustlers." A deal was soon struck. Shay then spent nearly seven hours in the chair. Bobby didn't mind. He liked being away from New Haven. He read part of a money-management book; he sent a teenage cousin a stream of joking texts describing the beauty shop scene: "Real African ladies! Nice shapes! I love the motherland!" He also made food runs. "I was savaging!" he said. "I'd get up and go to Popeye's. Come back. Go get a donut at Dunkin'. Come back. Go to Friday's. Come back. Make myself feel good and killing myself—all the junk we eat."

Back in New Haven, Bobby lay in bed planning his January moves. Some nights he never closed his eyes. "I don't feel sleepy," he enthused. "I can't wait for New Year. I'm so motivated. Get my job. Get focused. Get started with school. Start my journey. I want to live! Wake up to my girl every day! I'm ready. I'm so ready to start my journey." Looking back, Bobby assessed his first four months of freedom as "cruising just to get a feel."

Right before New Year, Bobby and Shay began their apartment hunting. Bobby hoped for a space with access to the basement so, if he couldn't sleep, he'd be able to go down below and dribble a basketball in the dark. With the soothing tempo of a basketball, he said, "I can calm down my nerves a lot." They drove around New Haven and surrounding towns, looking at available rentals. Everything cost so much it stung them. When they arrived at Willis Street, where Shay's grandmother still lived, Bobby said, "I hate Willis." Shay wanted to know why instead he didn't hate West Ivy Street. "I hate Willis because that's where my life changed," Bobby said. "I don't hate West Ivy because I wasn't on West Ivy that day."

What they'd seen, and what Craigslist offered, told them they'd have to wait for their own apartment. Besides the problem of cash flow, it didn't help that while Bobby was in prison, someone had "stolen" Bobby's Social Security number and ruined his credit rating. His credit history, his employment history, his rent-paying history: there was no helpful history.

The housing setback involved only the imagination. Nothing had been ventured except hope. As Bobby and Shay took in what had happened, they felt foolish for going even a short distance into an area it seemed wasn't their world. Shay made a joke that "I'm his cellie now," and said they would share their frustrations together. Bobby said that no part of this time could match the frustrations of prison. "Anything out here is better than being in there," he declared. "So I would deal with ten times the pain out here than to go in there for one day and suffer." Bobby had recently told Shay he hadn't been in a serious argument in all his prison years. In moments like this, she could see how that was possible. When he felt troubled in mind, he fell back upon the long view.

Shay, meanwhile, had lately been "in her feelings," said she might quit singing. She'd been a member of three groups, and all the commitment was sapping her pleasure. Singing relied on full-hearted emotion. But Bobby seemed unruffled by Shay's mood, and she praised him: "He's extremely patient with me. And I'm not that patient, but I gotta learn in 2016 to have patience."

They were two young people still getting to know one another. What was emerging as their great issue of compatibility was whether a very religious person like Shay could coexist with Bobby's skeptical, secular outlook. "It's hard," she said. "'Cause as a couple you wanna be on one accord. I just hope he converts."

"That will never happen, though," Bobby said instantly. He loved her, but he wasn't going to mislead her. Besides, if his morals followed those the Good Book preached, did it matter that he refused to attend church services?

Shay talked of her grandmother, who'd raised her. "My grandma is the pillar. She went to church, we went to church. Some people don't have the structure of religion. But if I didn't go, I couldn't do anything else. I'd feel empty. I would like for us to be on one accord, but I don't knock him." She reconsidered. "I do knock him, but I'm trying not to knock him in 2016."

Bobby pointed out that his granddad and Aretha were different in this way, but they had an admirable marriage, respecting each other's beliefs and preferences.

"But she would love to have him right by her side!" said Shay.

"And he *is* right by her side," Bobby said.

"You supposed to have the same mindset!" Shay insisted.

"And we do have the mindset. It's just that people make things complicated. They make situations complicated."

"I feel like prison helped you and it ruined you," Shay said sadly. "You read all that, but you had no experience to put what you read into practice."

"I don't have no problem with church," Bobby said again. "Me and Troy went through the Bible twice. I don't have a problem with what people believe in."

"I really be bothered," Shay said. His equanimity could itself be frustrating, because it made her feel wrong for wanting what she was already disappointed not to be getting. In such moments, it seemed possible that their potential for a great love might not make it. Such an attractive, outgoing woman as Shay would have the chance to date plenty of men who were committed churchgoers, but Shay knew it might be difficult to find somebody who felt life as deeply as Bobby. "Bobby had me on the brink of tears sometimes," she said. "I'll be like, you know what, let me just relax."

As the year ended, after he got into bed Bobby's mind raced with wakefulness as he again searched for some kind of reason why his nine years in prison had been deserved. Him being to blame might justify all that was making his present so difficult.

Finally, one morning, Bobby said to Shay, "Just hanging around made me a person of interest." It was a significant moment; he was explaining himself to her. "Living that certain lifestyle, you have to be ready for the ramifications. Even if you did nothing." And now came what he'd worked out: that everything had actually turned out for the best, that prison had saved Bobby from a worse fate. "For me, personally," he told Shay, "I feel like I had to go through that. Like, I had to feel the struggle. I had to feel the pain. I had to feel alone, to really just to tap into my flaws and see what I was doing wrong." Just recently, he'd told her that anything was better than being in prison. But prison, he now clarified, "slowed me down. It calmed my anger down. It helped me, basically, empathize with people more. I'm well-educated more." He'd do all nine years over, he said, because "it's about the people that I met that helped me change, the people I met that encouraged me to do better. I didn't get that out here."

Shay wasn't having it. "But in Cheshire," she said, "your environment was the same people!"

No, Bobby told her. The change was leaving Newhallville. "Cheshire brought me out of an environment that I needed to get out of," he said. "I needed to be introduced to people other than my environment, because I was stuck in it." Soon he was informing her, "I wanted to be gangsta. I wanted to be out there shooting. I wanted a name for myself." All of this was news to Shay, who'd known him as an easygoing kid who played sports and would "go to parties and try to meet girls!" But Bobby's point appeared to be that hardness was so valued, even a kid like him at least imagined living the life. Cheshire made him understand more was possible. "To me," he said, "the American dream growing up, that was a lot of money, cars, and girls. Now I have to find out what it is. What I could tell you now would be someone else's dream."

"You wouldn't have known that if you didn't go to Cheshire?" Shay asked, baffled.

Then he was backtracking, admitting he'd been exaggerating his past interest in the streets as a way of coming to a peace with his false confessions. "Because it was stupid," he said helplessly. "That's why I point out my flaws. I don't point at them to make it seem like I'm this evil type of person." But it was true that prison had removed him from the neighborhood. "You realize different things when you're not in that culture," he said. "And that's what jail did to me. That's why I say I would do it again. Because even though I was going through pain and suffering, I had some of the greatest moments of my life that I wish I could just rewind." He was not, he said, "a saint," he didn't want to be flawless, he didn't want to be a victim. He wanted to overcome.

Reuben Miller, a University of Chicago professor who volunteered as a chaplain at Chicago's Cook County Jail, found Bobby familiar: "Every week I meet people who are making sense of their lives. Either it's 'I deserved it, I was a bad guy,' or it's 'It worked out for my own good.' Black people can't get jobs, are used to being mistreated. So they reconcile it. 'My suffering has a purpose.'"

Who Bobby was after prison he showed in his lack of rancor, his desire for a terrible experience to have elevated him, his refusal to blame anybody else for his current circumstances. Holding himself accountable allowed him to make meaning out of a horrible experience that otherwise made no sense. It also permitted him to see those he'd grown up around, like Major, with more sympathy than he extended to himself. "Dudes on the streets," Bobby said, "I think you gotta understand them, how they got out there, what's happened to them."

Chapter Eighteen

Bobby was impatient for his better life. In prison his recurrent dream was being released, telling nobody, and striking out for "somewhere else." The anticlimax of freedom was being stuck in the city, no feeling of release. Lying sleepless in bed, he reprimanded himself for lack of progress: "I'm not putting in enough effort. I'm too lazy. I feel like I'm inhibited by my fear of failure, my fear of feeling stupid. I don't think I'm stupid. To suddenly be free by someone's good deed, coming out here it's a whole different reality I'm in as an adult." To him, his freedom was justice, not anything he'd accomplished. He wanted accomplishments.

The solution, he decided, was not to begin working at Easter Seals, but to "start fresh." In his early teens, he'd visited both Savannah and Atlanta with his uncle Mikey, and now Georgia beckoned. "It's a better outlook, more opportunities," Bobby thought. "You got kids having better jobs. Atlanta has a Black middle class. A lot of Black-owned businesses." In New Haven, the class structure was such that if you were Black, there was the common assumption that you were downtrodden. Bobby said upward mobility was so unusual for someone from "the hood" like him, that such people were known in New Haven as "cornballs" and "weirdos." "I want to be a weirdo!" he said. "Smart as hell, got my life together, multifaceted, treat my spouse with utmost respect. That's what they call a weirdo!"

But first Bobby imagined testing himself alone against the American grain. Books and films were full of such journeys of deliverance, the *Invisible Man* who went "moving into the unknown," the boys in *Stand by Me* who "knew exactly who we were and exactly where we were going." When real people joined movements, they were sent for, joined a lurching wagon train, sailed in steerage, rode the railroad, lashed the furniture to the car roof. These destinations meant the helping hand of leads and connections, neither of which Bobby had in Savannah.

What Bobby did possess was a small network of men in Connecticut who shared his experience of wrongful conviction and were as worried about what was happening to him as Bobby was worried about himself. Bobby had known Stefon Morant at Big Cheshire, and he'd also met Morant's codefendant, Scott Lewis. The pair were there because of the rogue New Haven detective who'd falsely implicated them in a double-murder. At prison, Lewis pursued his own innocence for nearly twenty years until, with end-game help from lawyers and law students, he prevailed. Morant, meanwhile, had the same evidence against him, but not such effective counsel. After Lewis went home, Morant's lawyer encouraged him to accept release with his sentence reduced to time served, meaning that, unlike Lewis, Morant retained his convictions. Morant and Lewis were old enough to be Bobby's father, and when the men now contacted Bobby, they told him that they were concerned and wanted to talk. It was to be "kind of an intervention," as Bobby described it. "They want to get personal."

Lewis was a natural entrepreneur, neat, pressed, and driven. Since leaving prison, he sold vacuum cleaners, then real estate, was soon to earn his broker's license. The field was attractive to Lewis, he said, because he intended to build a company and also help formerly incarcerated people find housing. With his felony record, Morant worked as a flag man, collected garbage, and eventually as a counselor in halfway houses and at clinics. He was bighearted and empathic, had love for Bobby, and Bobby for him.

Lewis and Morant met up with Bobby, and, Lewis recounted, "He said, 'Scott, I'm losing it.' I thought, Here's a guy who needs help and he's genuine about wanting it. It was important to get that guy an apartment. I know how important it is to have a place of peace."

A month before, Lewis had been invited to speak at Yale's Jewish leadership society, a cultural and civics salon founded by law students, including Cory Booker, and a New Haven businessman named Shmully Hecht, whose real-estate company, Pike International, was one of New Haven's largest property owners: Hecht rented out among the most and least expensive apartments in the city. After Lewis told his story at the salon that night, said Hecht, "There's tears in the room. People are going out of their mind." Hecht offered Lewis a job on the spot, explaining, "Society owes Scott Lewis a debt."

Hearing how Bobby was struggling, Lewis decided to approach Hecht: "I thought, this is how I see if the guy really wants to help someone put his life back together." To his boss Lewis proposed finding Bobby his own Pike-owned apartment, and he told Hecht, "I want no commission and I will make sure he pays his rent. I guaranteed him!"

Hecht and Lewis got together with Bobby the next morning, which was Martin Luther King Jr. Day, and, said Hecht, "I meet him and you want to hug him. Tragic, tragic story."

Soon they were all in a car heading for the west edge of the city, where Hecht owned an apartment complex that had a rental billboard out front asking, LOOKING FOR A NEW LOVE? Inside the geode-like, bruised brick buildings, there were shiny new granite counters, burnished hardwood floors, and modern fixtures. The rent on a basement studio was $950. Hecht cut it to $700. Then he asked Bobby what kind of work he'd done. Bobby told him cleaning. Hecht wanted to know what Bobby *liked* to do. When Bobby said, "I like to work with my hands," Hecht said, "Come with me."

Back at the Pike offices, Hecht assembled his senior staff and told them, "Bobby went to prison for nine years for a crime he didn't commit. In the spirit of King and this day, this will be the most important thing we do." Pointing to a carpenter, Hecht told Bobby, "He'll teach you a trade. Now you have a job." Everyone hugged up. Then Hecht headed for the back office: "I tell the guy at the back to sign the lease and underwrite him. He's employed! Hours later I get a call: 'Boss, this guy's got a murder conviction. On record.' I said, 'Yes. Keep reading.' Oh. Overturned."

Bobby was ecstatic. He planned to move into New Love with Shay as soon as they saved up for furniture. "It's quiet," he enthused. "And it's only the beginning."

Bobby began work two days later, painting and laying tile. Of his supervisor, Bobby said, "He shows me what to do and he's genuine. He told me, 'I don't expect you to be perfect.'" A few mornings later, Bobby was called in to sign his lease and was given keys. "I forgot to brush my teeth and wash my face," he said. "I just went. I was so happy!" After work, he and Shay brought a mattress over to what they were already calling "the crib," and "I blasted J. Cole and cleaned up. I was thinking, Nobody will mess up this house besides Shay and me. In the morning, I woke up with a new energy. The greatest sleep of my life."

The next day was Saturday, and looking up through the basement window, all Bobby and Shay could see was snow blowing around the glass. And yet through the blizzard came Rosenthal with a table, household items, and blankets. Rosenthal's retired secretary sent a bed frame, a dresser, and cooking equipment. Hank delivered a box spring. Aunts Faith and Joy offered dishes. Bobby's mother brought kitchen staples. Once these magi left, Bobby got to work organizing the apartment. "I did it like I do in jail," he said. "I turn on the music and try to set up everything at once."

IT WAS SOON apparent that Bobby's supervisor had no time to teach him a trade. Bobby was placed on a demo crew, stripping down apartments for renovation. Using a long metal bar to remove ceramic floor tiles was, Bobby said, "the hardest work I've ever done."

In February, Bobby received his first paycheck, which he deposited in his new bank account. That weekend, using food stamp money, he and Shay filled the refrigerator, the freezer, and the pantry "to the rim." Bobby had also bought a PlayStation 4 video game console. After Shay cooked steak and onions with yellow rice and broccoli, Bobby stayed up until six in the morning, "mobbing" games while doing the laundry down the hall.

Life still felt uncertain. Bobby's first check bounced. When a week passed with no replacement, Bobby inquired, and Pike's accountant spread his hands: checks sometimes bounced. As a result, Bobby's new bank account was frozen, meaning now he could not access his Innocence Project stipend money. Bobby was frustrated, but "I just want to keep it civilized," he said. "That's the man I'm renting from."

Making it all more challenging, Shay and Darla were at the gas station when another driver plowed into Shay's beloved black Chrysler, totaling it. With the insurance money, Shay replaced Darla with a used green Ford Explorer, an SUV she named Samuel Green, after the singer Sam Cooke. But Darla had really sent Shay, while Samuel Green was just "the truck."

Another week passed with Bobby still unpaid, his bank account still frozen. Finally, Bobby was ushered to Hecht's office, the accountant was also there, as well as a property manager. The accountant said again, "Unfortunately, checks sometimes bounce." Hecht asked Bobby sharply, "Do you want to work?" Bobby said yes. Would Bobby clean? Bobby would clean. Bobby tried to explain he couldn't get to work if he had no money for bus fare. He had no way of paying his rent if the check didn't clear. A different expression crossed Hecht's face, as though he was suddenly understanding how limited Bobby's resources were. "The rent," Hecht said. "Don't worry about the rent. That's our last concern."

Soon the accountant was back with a check for Bobby's second pay period. Hecht began explaining to Bobby about the portion he would need to hold back for taxes, but then Hecht saw the amount of the check, how low it was. Hecht now hastily explained to the others Bobby had been in prison for a murder "he didn't do," and that, as a result, he didn't yet drive, so he couldn't easily travel from site to site. He asked the property manager if there was a location for Bobby to report to every day. Indeed, there were recently vacated low-income apartments in a nearby neighborhood that needed cleaning and painting. Hecht asked the accountant how much Pike was paying Bobby. The answer was $12.50 an hour, meaning that if Bobby worked fifty-two weeks of forty hours, Bobby would earn $26,000. Hecht told Bobby the expectation was he'd soon be making much more. The property manager gave Bobby his cell number. Told him to call anytime.

At Bobby's bank, a sympathetic young woman with the promising first name of Lendia explained to Bobby that a letter on Pike letterhead was still needed because "if there's the slightest bit of suspicion about account activity, they close the account." Bobby was thinking, "People like to sit me in a room and disappear." He meant they wanted to help so long as the helping required no real effort. "They know I don't know things," he said. "I don't want to argue with anybody. I've been through enough. It's not about the check bouncing. It's all the runaround afterwards." It took another two weeks before Bobby received his first check.

The apartments Bobby was sent to clean out had moldy rugs, toxic growth in the bathroom tile grout, refrigerator rot, piles of trash, abandoned clothing stinking of urine. As Bobby entered, insects and rats scattered. The complex was located in New Haven's Tre neighborhood. Because Bobby came from Newhallville, the longstanding feud with the Tre worried him. "When I was growing up, people shot people in the leg," he said. "Now they shoot people in the head." He imagined being at the bus stop, someone exclaiming, "He's from the Ville. That's that old dude, Bobby."

SHAY WAS TEACHING Bobby to drive Samuel Green, and one night he drove them all the way back from New York, where they'd gone for supper at a

Greenwich Village barbecue joint. If a police officer pulled Bobby over, they agreed, he would explain he was driving because Shay had too much to drink. Driving Bobby considered his right, something he would have long ago been licensed to do if his life had not been interrupted. He didn't often break a rule, and didn't consider himself to be doing so now. His grandmother, who first taught him the basics of driving, had told him that commanding the open road was an expression of his freedom.

Good times with Shay meant a lot because it cast him down how many "lives is ruined" among the people he most cared about. The woe all around him also made Bobby prize the day his mother rented out the basketball court at the Y, where she staged a birthday party for Bobby's two-year-old twin sisters. The party was carefully planned and beautifully executed, from the bounce house, sno-cones, popcorn, cotton candy, and kid tattoo stations right down to the shining, glittering "princess" table centerpieces Grace had designed and made herself. Many family members and friends attended the event, which was so convivial one of the twins' young guests asked, "Why don't I have more cousins?" That remark pleased Bobby immensely—he craved everyone getting along. It also delighted him when people praised Grace's centerpieces. In this way, Bobby was like the writer Alice Walker, the youngest of eight children, who'd watched her "overworked" laborer mother use what free time she had to create "ambitious gardens," noticing that "it is only when my mother is working in her flowers that she is radiant." Grace made centerpieces for all family occasions, was adept at finding themes that reflected the interests of the celebrant. Bobby kept photographs of her work on his telephone and would produce them proudly. He believed his mother had true creativity, thought the centerpieces helped reveal her finest self, and he wished she'd go into business. It saddened him to think she'd probably never try.

Bobby sought to be there for his family. He did other people's laundry and, with Shay, provided rides in Samuel Green, delivered groceries, chaperoned at a school dance, helped his mother with many "missions," gave a piece of his just-acquired furniture away to a bereft relative because "she's trying." One weekend, when Shay was on a singing trip, Bobby invited nephews and his brother to bring their pillows over for a sleepover. "They were young or not born when I went away," he said. "It's a chance to spend some time with them." But the nephews didn't come. He heard there'd been a dispute. "Everybody's hurting," Bobby said in March. "Nobody's talking. I try to explain I've been there nine years. I seen the worst struggles—people dying to be with their family."

Listening to Bobby, Shay would sigh and say, "He genuinely loves them."

"My love for them is vague," he'd retort.

"From my perspective," Shay said, "Bobby's hurt. Not holding malice, but they left him so long."

"They weren't in my life when I did nine years," he'd agree, a blue note falling in his voice.

"Bobby tips a lot from feelings," Shay said. "One day, from I love them all to fuck 'em all."

That Shay liked Bobby's family, and they liked Shay, made it easier for her to support him in these moments. His family wasn't loaded for Shay. Together they placed a gift-shop sign on their bookshelf that made them both smile: "If You Met My Family You Would Understand."

But Bobby and Shay were increasingly confronting their own incompatibilities. At first disagreements were jovial, like couples in the romantic comedies they both liked to watch. But the studio was a small space, and aggravations grew. Bobby was fine with stacking clothing, while Shay thought, Why won't he fold each piece and put it all away? She considered it "frivolous" for Bobby to buy a game system when they were both marginally employed. If they were going to spend on entertainment, Shay would have enjoyed going dancing. Bobby, in turn, wished Shay to be tolerant about how much was new to him, rather than calling him "a handful" so often. "He don't think I have patience," Shay said one day. "Which I really don't. But I'm trying."

A serious point of conflict was exposed after Bobby attended one of Shay's rehearsals. Members of her group had critiqued the singing of someone who wasn't there, and afterward Bobby expressed outrage at this "backbiting" and "bashing" of their friend. "I think you should protect people when they're not around," he said. Then, another day, Bobby went along with the group to see a performance out of state. They traveled by carpool, and in Bobby and Shay's car, a discussion began about a woman riding in a different vehicle. When somebody declared, "She can't sing," Bobby spoke up, "Why don't you say it to her when you're with her?" Shay made clear she didn't think it was Bobby's place to chide her colleagues for gossiping, and that made Bobby so angry, he slapped the back of the car seat in front of him. Later, he was still seething. "They'll say, 'You don't know her!' I want to know why can't they be the strong one?"

Shay didn't understand. To her "gossip" was people processing their lives. When Bobby called her "frivolous," she was hurt, and she said, "I'll bust out, 'Why are you with me?'"

But gossip meant something more ominous to Bobby. "I spend a lot of time thinking about this," he said. "A lot of time." Gossip was rumors. Gossip was danger. Gossip had put Bobby into the prison slipstream. "When somebody being talked about, I feel like I'm being talked about," he'd say. Gossip was the world ambushing him. "Honestly," he said, "every day I wake up and I feel like just disappearing from everybody. I wish I could start fresh, new name, identity, everything. I just be wanting to just eradicate my existence and just start over with a new one. Every day I feel disgusted by the stuff I see. This is something I've been longing for, for a while, and now that I have it, it's not what I thought or what I expected it to be."

Increasingly, Bobby did separate himself. "I don't want anger and bitterness," he'd say. "I want to appreciate the world. I do my best to be nice to people. But I'm not around. I'm doing my own thing with Shay, and I find it hard to deal with Shay sometimes."

Shay would pipe up, "I'm doing better, right?!" Then she'd sigh, "But I think sometimes you should be alone for a while. We got together when you were out, what, two months. I'm still dealing with Cheshire Bobby."

"What's Cheshire Bobby?" he asked.

"Readjusting," she said. "Getting used to things. Bobby'll shut down, get quiet, won't say anything all day long. That's a problem."

"For nine years that's how I coped."

"Not my fault, not your fault you had to do nine years. I'm dealing with your nine years."

"I can go without."

"Bobby can be without me and that's hard for me," she said, looking upset. "Simple for him. Complex for me. And that's what Cheshire did to him."

IN THE SPRING, Bobby decided he belonged to the Facebook generation, began posting and quickly felt rewarded. "I do get sad in this world because I see all the things I missed," he reflected. "People getting married, having kids. I told Shay I didn't want the Facebook. I thought it was a world of slander. It's just life." Then he discovered that details of his case were being discussed online by Newhallville young people. Ten years after the Fields murder, the legacy among those with direct knowledge of the crime was they didn't talk about what had happened on West Ivy Street because, Bobby said, "People get harmed. Nobody scared of murderers in my neighborhood. They're more scared of the label 'snitch.' The label carries long. You snitch, a crew member or a relative might retaliate." Despite the fact that he hadn't ever named others, even after he'd been falsely named himself, Bobby sensed people "aren't too sure about me. A lot of people think I snitched my way out, gave somebody up." When Bobby encountered witnesses to the murder or those who'd seen him that day, some apologized for not speaking out to defend him with the truth, told him how threatened they'd felt. Others acted as though they didn't recognize him. It's hard to be at your best when you're very scared.

Bobby was still clothing himself by "recycling the same three pairs of sweatpants," but there was neighborhood gossip that he'd become wealthy and carried a thick wallet. "I don't feel safe out here," he said. "Anybody'll tell you that type of money, you can't live in this environment. They'll kill you for it. They don't want to see you enjoy life, because they suffer. It's, 'If I can make you suffer as me, that's what I do.'" These "crabs-in-a-barrel" forebodings made him miss the safety of prison. "Honestly, no lie, I be feeling sometimes I'm better off in there."

Bobby reached out to his old cellie, Maaly, about his "slump." Telling Bobby, "I know what you're going through," Maaly said that the muted colors of the prison interior, although intended to calm a person, actually dulled him so, upon release, the brightness was blinding.

On any day when he could again be a traveler, moving around, interacting with people, Bobby was at his most optimistic. He wanted his life to permanently open up. Across the difficult first year, the former boy on a bike now made earning his driver's license his top priority.

Back when Bobby turned sixteen, his driver's license wasn't for him a defining American moment—or even on his mind. "Somebody could always come and get you," he said. "Or buses. Or your friend's mom or dad. We'd all pile in." Growing up in a disenfranchised community, many sixteen-year-olds from Newhallville didn't pursue their licenses. Glen Worthy, the Newhallville native who was principal at Hillhouse High, said, "When it comes up with kids, they say, 'Hush, Mr. Worthy, I don't want to talk about that now.' Mostly, they can't afford it." Beyond the hundreds of dollars it cost to become licensed, many families owned no vehicle, making it impossible to secure a car in which to learn to drive, and then to reach the Department of Motor Vehicles, which was out in Hamden. There was also the reluctance to fail sometimes felt by kids who'd already endured many defeats. Shay, who'd described getting a license as "extra stuff," had been twenty-one and away at college when she finally got hers. She said that for Newhallville kids, there was no driver's-ed class offered at Hillhouse, and no way of getting to the high school in Hamden, where such courses were held.

Perhaps a license wasn't even necessary. Bobby's mother and father hadn't, so far as he knew, ever had licenses. Across the state, an estimated more than 20 percent of African American drivers were operating cars without driver's licenses. (Nationally, 20 percent of Black households owned no car, in contrast to 6.5 percent of whites.) That a "lot of people where I'm from ride around without licenses," Bobby said, was a practice known to many in Newhallville as riding or driving "dirty." Dirty was versatile slang, with many applications. Shay said everybody she knew growing up was "dirty somehow. Suspended license, no license, no insurance, car taxes. Let my insurance lapse because it was either phone bill or insurance. Food or insurance. Which would you rather pay? Car insurance, it was 'Let me pray. This is a lot of people.' And you have to drive to make money at your job. So you take a chance." Studies had found that insurance companies charged higher rates in predominantly Black zip codes, that Blacks were not infrequently charged more for purchasing the same-value cars.

For those emerging from prison, there were added complications with driver's licenses. Some reentrants were resistant, suspecting the license as a form of system surveillance, a means of harassment by law enforcement. There were also those who, while in prison, had craved the autonomy and independence of driving, maybe even subscribed to car magazines, but shared the reentry experience of Scott Lewis, who said "coming out of a correctional facility it's almost impossible to get an ID. People want to be valid, but it's so hard to get."

Bobby was determined. He talked about the driver's license as his golden fleece, said to him it "means the world," because "when I have my license I can get a job outside New Haven, where it is safer." Bobby's desire was to be upstanding, not someone who resorted to driving dirty, who remained unlicensed because he'd been in prison. Bobby's grandmother had called driving "freedom" when she'd taught him as a boy, and Bobby thought having the license would now finally make him feel liberated.

Bobby's cousin Quay helped him to get the formal process started with a learner's permit. She and Granddad gave him a few driving lessons, then Shay took over. They had glorious times together out on the road. Shay loved to drive and he did too. Four months after his release from prison, Shay helped Bobby enroll in an eight-hour accredited course on safe driving practices, where he sat in the back row of the classroom, behind all the teenagers, and enjoyed learning about the potential on-road dangers of a messy car, about how passenger weight distribution affects turning radius. After completing the course came the qualifying tests, first written, then road.

Bobby went to the DMV in Hamden to take his written examination, and by the time he got to the DMV, he was visibly shaking. The atmosphere at the squat brick DMV building didn't help. With its uniformed guards, stale smell, the dulled faces of all the people standing by, the DMV could have been a correctional institution. Bobby began his test, and soon a question about skids slid him so far off course that he became rattled—rushed through the remaining questions just so he could get out of that room, get out of that building. He failed the test by one point. Afterward he could barely speak, he was so crushed.

He'd been through worse, which here helped. A day after the test he allowed, "I failed by one. I was nervous. I didn't know what to expect. Uncertainty makes me nervous." Test-taking was a new skill for Bobby. He found the failure made him want this more than ever. "I was mad at myself," he said. "I'm not anymore."

The next available test date in Bobby's part of the state was at the Cheshire DMV, in mid-April. He could have waited a few days more and gone to a closer Connecticut town, one where he hadn't been incarcerated, but he was eager to defeat the test and, besides, Bobby felt no need to avoid Cheshire; his time there was someone else's mistake. He began studying the manual "hard."

On his second written-test day, Bobby arrived at a coffee shop in Cheshire three hours before his appointment time, and prepared like an athlete. He hydrated with water, ate a banana, and limbered up with practice tests. He wanted a victory in Cheshire. He'd all but memorized the manual, but these practice tests asked for knowledge of the specifics of tire alignment and teen curfews, areas outside the manual's coverage. What was up with these non-manual-related questions? When Bobby answered one incorrectly, he jumped up, nearly knocking the table over.

On the way to the DMV, Bobby passed a deep-umber brick building with Ionic porch columns, a cupola, high church windows—what could have been the campus of a small New England college but for sunlight glinting off spools of blade-sharp wire atop the walls. Bobby was seeing Big Cheshire for the first time since he'd left it in September. A long drive curved down through a grassy, tree-shaded lawn toward the street, and past the line of trees came a silver pickup truck, its bed full of head-shaven Black men in prison tans. "I know all those guys," Bobby said. They were trustees, prisoners whose good behavior had won them the privilege of working jobs outside the walls. Despite having been the rare man not to receive one single ticket for a minor disciplinary infraction, Bobby was never made a trustee because at the time his sentence made him ineligible. Waiting at a stoplight, Bobby said, "This is the way we went for my habeas. I'd see that intersection and think of all the people driving to their jobs. I'd think, I got to get out of that prison."

The Cheshire DMV was a much smaller building than Hamden and had the hospitable ambience of a national park welcome center. As he went in, Bobby was making nervous jokes and saying, "I'm not nervous! I'm not failing! I got this." His twenty-six-year-old face contrasted with the rosy-white teenagers who were arriving with their parents for the test. As the woman at the front desk signed him in, she took a practiced glance and said, "You'll do fine." Then she advised Bobby, "Take your time." Once registered, Bobby disappeared down a hallway.

Forty minutes later he emerged, arms raised, roaring, high-fiving, cheesing. His test score had been nearly perfect. There had been several questions identical to those on the practice test. "It seemed like all the answers were popping out!" he said, speaking in a joyous rush. "I'm suped! I'm turnt! I'm ecstatic! So supe!" From the car, he made calls, left voice messages. Passing the prison again, he brought up Detective Willoughby. "I don't bear him any grudges," Bobby said. "It's not in my heart to do that. People can do wrong things and it doesn't make me hate them. I'm just letting people be who they are."

Bobby would have to wait three months before taking his road test, in mid-July. Deferring his wishes he knew how to do, and he was so steadfast about license preparation it seemed worrisome to think what would happen when there was no longer the upcoming road test to organize his life. He enjoyed practicing with Shay, she warning, "It's no more smooth-sailing church drivers today; don't let anybody break your flow." Which was not to say Bobby wanted the process to last. "I can taste it," he said. "When I pass, I'm gonna cry. You'll see tears."

The day before the road test, in July 2016, Bobby drove around the city, practicing what he judged were his weaknesses. He reminded himself to check his mirrors every five seconds, to note the speed limit, to place his hands six hours apart on the wheel. Near the 2-4, he said, "we were sitting there when they pulled me off the porch and arrested me. It was raining." Then he beeped a greeting, explaining, "That was Kwame and them."

Kwame's group was out there every day. Bobby drove so well, you could forget he was practicing. Then, when he made a small error, forgetting to signal for a lane change, his hands trembled from wanting something so much.

The next day the weather was hot, bright, and clear. Hours before the 1:30 examination time, Bobby was behind the wheel, not far from the Hamden DMV, practicing parallel parking and nailing each attempt. In prison, he recalled, "We used to sit there and see guys in nice cars on TV, in car advertisements, we'd visualize it. We used to say we all are going to go legit." Bobby reminded himself to use his directional signals. He said he was fully "confident." He said, "I know how to drive. My grandmother taught me, but Shay brought it back to me." Arriving at the DMV, Bobby recalled his visits there with his grandmother. "I can't remember exactly the age, but my grandmother was like, 'You gotta come with me to the DMV, 'cause you gotta get used to it.' "

After all the waiting, everything happened very fast. A large, graying white man in sunglasses, a blue agency-issue polo shirt, and blue khakis approached Bobby. The man looked like a country-boy state trooper, and it turned out Bobby's examiner was a retired suburban police officer. He asked Bobby to get into the driver's seat. To turn on the car's ignition. To use his turn indicators, first the right, then the left. To press the brake pedal. As the car crept out of the parking lot, Bobby signaled left, and something in the air lifted.

The road test lasted less than ten minutes. "Perfect," the examiner said as they got out of the car. Then he corrected himself. "One minor mistake." Bobby had unnecessarily signaled at a sharp curve. A subtle expression crossed Bobby's face. The instructor said, "Not a major mistake. Very good!" He sent Bobby inside to claim his license. On his way out of the DMV, Bobby said, "Aw man! I'm so happy. I dreamed about this before I came home, and I made it possible, and I'm not even a year home yet. I'm just looking forward to all my good accomplishments." It was a big American moment, which Bobby acknowledged saying, "I'm happy to be joining the team. I did it. I'm a licensed driver." With an impish smile, he added, "Now I get to say to my family, 'If you need me, just holla at me, I'll *think* about giving you a ride!' "

ON HIS GOOD days, Bobby would call people on the telephone and make pronouncements. They might begin: "This is the day of true commitment for the comeback of Bobby!" Then he would name his ambitions. Owning a car came first because a car made everything else possible: finding a better job; attending school; going on trips; getting to the gym. Bobby thought he should have a nice car after missing out on so much. Acuras were "cool" and "smooth," a "spaceship." But Acuras were expensive. How was he going to buy an Acura without first finding that better job?

On too many days Bobby was "miserable." It was the inconsolable realization that in his life there was too little to care about in the way he wanted to care. "My driver's license don't mean anything," he said. He still yearned for "that spark" of fulfilling work, but "I have no clue what to do," he said sadly. And then he began to speak a threnody that brooded beyond himself to the laments of generations. "They talk about they let me free," he said. "I don't feel free. I don't know this world. Everything is new. It's like I'm out here, but I'm not."

His relationship to his employer, Pike, was increasingly informal. By summer, Bobby rarely went, except in occasional spurts when there was assured work. Meanwhile, he filled out application after application for entry-level positions at chain restaurants like Red Lobster and Friendly's and TGI Friday's, and inevitably received communications back that began, "After careful consideration . . ." A relative put him in touch with a woman at Olive Garden, and the connection yielded a group interview with two other applicants. "It went great," Bobby enthused afterward. A call back was promised "soon." The possibility of this work lifted him; "Everything going great," he said. But then, soon enough, the woman wouldn't take his calls, and Bobby thought stopping by inadvisable, because "I don't want to harass anybody." Days later, he learned the two applicants he'd interviewed with had been hired, which injured his feelings. "I don't want to work there anymore anyway," he said proudly.

He applied to a restaurant-supply business for a position stocking meat. He was not hired.

Another connection led to a job interview with a commercial cleaning company in the Tribe neighborhood, not far from Newhallville. Bobby had the same safety concerns about the Tribe as he did the Tre, but a job mattered more. So, Bobby put on a white dress shirt, black pants, black Vans sneakers, and set off to another interview that went well. He was offered twenty hours of work per week cleaning medical offices and promised additional hours soon. Then, the day before Bobby was to start, he was told his job had been given to two other people.

Bobby wore an invisible scarlet *P* everyone could see, with the prison experience he was trying to overcome defining him for others. When anyone went online, they never read past the one word. "Murder," Bobby said. "Murder still, *still* sticks above my head. No matter how innocent I am, certain people won't believe it." He had limited education and work history, no hookup, and while he kept applying himself, he began to feel desperate. His stipend was soon to end. "I gotta start buying clothes," he said. "I have no clothes. I want to get a car. I want to do everything right. I feel like I be stuck in a rut. You see people living their life. I want to be that. But how do I get there?"

Bobby had been innocent, he was an interesting and loyal guy, and yet had been collected into the cohort of young Black men who'd done time, a notoriety employers found so threatening they couldn't be trusted to work. "I was thinking yesterday I'm ready to get away from everybody," Bobby said toward the end of the year. "Feels like I'm still in prison."

To worsen the struggle, like so many men who came out of prison, Bobby discovered his health had permanently suffered there. There were night sweats, sharp chest pains, migraines, a lack of appetite. Most days he could get down only a single meal. Sometimes he ate only two bites of food. He wasn't overweight, and so without the twenty-five pounds of muscle he'd lost in his nine months in New Haven, he appeared wan and sucked-in. Back in late winter, he'd gone to the emergency room at Yale–New Haven Hospital. The admitting line was long. All the people in it were Black. "Everybody I know uses the hospital as your doctor," Bobby said. "They use Yale–New Haven because they feel your survival is more likely because of Yale. As young kids, we take that into account. We seen so many people get shot, and it's always after the ambulance pulls up, 'What hospital they take him to?' If it's not Yale, it's 'My brother gonna die.'" The man in front of Bobby in line wandered off. When the admitting nurse asked, "Who's next?" Bobby pointed to the wandering man. The nurse said, "Thank you, sir, for being honest."

Bobby was seen by a physician assistant who asked, "What's going on today?" Bobby described his headaches, chest and stomach pain, waking up in the night drenched with sweat. "It's been hard for me to eat for a very long time," he said. He explained about having been in prison. She asked him more about himself, drew him out, and then said, "It's not unusual for somebody with the experiences you've had not to be eating, feeling slight anxiety from the past. After what you've been through, it might not be unusual for you to be depressed. You don't know what it feels like to be anxious because you've never been not anxious."

As she measured Bobby's blood pressure, Bobby noticeably tensed his foot, arm, and neck. The meter passed 140, and the physician assistant told him, "Honey, you can relax." It was uncanny. As soon as she said it, the blood pressure began dropping. Bobby's heart rate was monitored, and as the numbers on the panel fluctuated between the 30s and the 70s, the PA said in wonder, "It's as though he has a pacer, but there's no pacer." Bobby said, "This has been going on since I came home. I never had no heart problem like this." Soon he was attached to an EKG and an IV drip. "I hate being in this position," he said. "I feel vulnerable. All my power is taken." When Bobby's bloodwork came back normal and he was assured he was suffering only from stress and needed rest, he lightened.

Across the year, Bobby's insomnia and headaches continued, and he often seemed despondent. When Shay was out, he turned off the lights and sat in the dark, face-in-hands by himself. "I can't read," he said. "I can't work out. I don't know what it is." He'd return to the hospital, receive confirmation that his health was poor, and feel relieved at least people would realize he wasn't loafing, that he truly wasn't well. "It's one of the most difficult transitions ever," he said. Across the spring and summer, Bobby craved his first anniversary of the release from prison. September 4 passing would, he thought, as with divorces and deaths, make a difference.

Bobby also grew intensely homesick for prison. "I miss the guys in jail the most," he'd say, and then he'd list names, "Troy, Jerome, Ty, the Great One, Black Rob. I miss them all." These were the people who'd "stayed on" him, treating him with humanity when he was most down. "My interactions out here don't feel like our interactions in there," he'd said in the spring. "We were always trying to pick each other up." From his basement, he recalled the predictable structure of prison days, the pleasure of the fiercely contested basketball games, and he thought nostalgically of Big Cheshire as his refuge.

But Bobby didn't want to go back to prison, and he feared doing anything that might return him there. He believed he was having such trouble adjusting precisely because prison trounced people. If, as he'd heard, there were men who got themselves arrested because they couldn't survive outside, these were rare exceptions. "I haven't met anyone who said he wanted to stay," said Scott Semple, the former correction commissioner.

Bobby usually took care not to confide his troubles in Rosenthal. Yet if ever he did let on, Rosenthal's response was "Why don't you tell me these things?" Rosenthal himself was grieving. His friend Diane Polan, Kwame's lawyer, had died recently, at sixty-five, of a rare and virulent form of cancer. To the end, Rosenthal said, Polan had been "unrelenting," winning acquittals in her last four cases. Rosenthal wanted to be that way for Bobby. "I don't know how to get Bobby a job," he said. "But I have to try harder." He looked into finding Bobby a suitable therapist, and soon Bobby was seeing a Black CSW who'd once worked in corrections. "I love her," Bobby said after an early session. "She's straightforward. Holds nothing back." What the therapist decided was there wasn't going to be any easy solution to Bobby's troubles. The grief and strain stretching back had accumulated to the extent he now suffered from what could be called post-prison stress disorder.

That summer, Bobby and Shay broke up. Bobby was more aware than anyone that there was nobody like Shay, that she had the rare ability to collect observations into expressive language that enlivened everything around her. Speaking of an adaptable person, Shay might say, "She got that changing-faces thing going on." But since Shay and Bobby had moved in together, too often her needs and desires seemed unfulfilled. Bobby worried that by being with him, Shay, too, was becoming depressed. Bobby felt in himself such deficits of worldly experience, and Shay could see for herself what she wanted, commitment to a family, was unthinkable to him. "Those things do scare me," he said. "I don't feel like I want to raise another kid. Taking care of my sisters was enough. I believe kids are beautiful and unique, but I don't think they're for everybody. Not for me, at least." He imagined fathering a little boy, soon to go astray as a teenager, "wilding, don't listen." Look at Quay's son. DaDa was a promising student, a gifted athlete, and yet he seemed drawn ever more to the streets. "You'd think with what happened to me . . ." Bobby said, shaking his head.

After they broke up, Bobby and Shay lived together as roommates. She was one of the few people he trusted with the fullness of his feelings. And something in Shay now seemed to relax, and she became more sympathetic to Bobby than she'd been when she felt let down by him as his girlfriend. He, too, was kinder with her. They encouraged each other, were solicitous and caring in the way of old, dear friends who'd been through a lot together. When Bobby felt unhappy, Shay now could see that he simply didn't have the resources to overcome it. He was at a point where his means were so small.

IN THE AFTERMATH of his decision to release Bobby from prison, Michael Dearington, New Haven's supervising prosecutor, readily admitted the case had unsettled him. The white-haired Dearington wore white shirts, wire-rimmed glasses, and quiet neckties. Dearington said he found it "distressing to be part of a system where we have people like Willoughby. Most cops are honest, decent people." The case, he said, increased his foreboding: "I often think how many people are in jail now who are innocent. One is a cause for concern. I wonder how many where there isn't DNA evidence. Realistically, we know there has to be a percentage." Another former prosecutor, now a judge, assessed the case and said, "I was a prosecutor who didn't believe you could confess to something you didn't do. Now I do."

One day near the courthouses in downtown New Haven, Rosenthal encountered Jim Clark. The former prosecutor told Rosenthal he'd been conducting training sessions with police departments, helping investigators to avoid deciding prematurely what had happened in cases, to avoid fixating on a theory of a crime and keep their minds open. Clark was likewise urging detectives to stay neutral in the interrogation room, to question people in search of information, not for confirmation of a settled narrative. Then, later, another New Haven criminal defense lawyer told him that that Clark "had gone out of his way" to help her successfully conclude a wrongful conviction case. Rosenthal was so impressed by what Clark was doing he decided his own theory of Clark had been premature. "He's very low-key these days," Rosenthal reported of Clark. "He's not a prosecutor anymore. He's for victims."

Clark had founded a Connecticut organization offering free legal support to victims of violence. From his desk, in a small exurban office park, in the aftermath of Bobby's release Clark's reflection on the case was "If I screwed up, I'm unhappy about it. You also have the reality I prosecuted [Kwame] on essentially the same evidence." He meant he'd acted as best he could, given what he knew. That he stood by all the convictions he'd won, he said, "doesn't mean that I'm necessarily right. It means that I've done my very best to make sure that I didn't prosecute people who didn't do it. But we all have errors in our world, so I wouldn't ever assert that, and it's one of the reasons I have never believed that the death penalty was an appropriate punishment."

Assessing his nearly thirty years as a prosecutor, Clark said he considered himself to have been prepared, well organized, logical, adept at connecting with juries. If he faulted himself, he said, it was "I don't think that I have a great imagination." Cookie Polan had agreed with all of that. Clark, to her, was like most intelligent, caring people; embedded in his virtue was his weakness. When it came to crime victims, Polan had believed so sincere was Clark's compassion, and so resolute his determination, it made him unable to conceive of Kwame and Bobby as victims themselves. Clark was a worthy opponent, she thought, but the inability to see these two cases clear had been a failure of the imagination.

When he met up with Clark, Rosenthal had been spending long days and evenings completing the claim he would file for Bobby with the state of Connecticut seeking compensation for Bobby's wrongful imprisonment. If there was compensation awarded, Rosenthal told Bobby, he didn't plan to take his own full share. "I'm not doing this for the money," Rosenthal said. "I've come to like lawyering more than I ever have before." Rosenthal said he'd always been fine with Jim Clark, never had a problem with him.

In late December, with Bobby's stipend about to lapse, Shmully Hecht called and offered to put him back on the job at Pike with a new supervisor. "I'm happy," Bobby said. "Ready to start the New Year fresh." Looking back, he said, "First year's the hardest. I'm optimistic for this year." He had to hurry. He was helping his mother move again. Her new home was on West Ivy Street, but the prospect of visiting Grace at the very point of the city that was the source of the trouble in his life, Bobby said was of no concern to him. "I don't care," he said. "That doesn't bother me. Honestly, I'm happy my mother finally has a good space to live in." He was looking forward.

Chapter Nineteen

There were men and women who left prison and flourished afterward, received Ivy League degrees, built profitable businesses. These were the quasars of reentry, spectacular, luminous, celestial exceptions that helped create the myth any young person could go to prison, separate from family, from school, from training, employment, and community, then depart prison with only the person they were to recommend them and make their fortune in America. All of it giving others license to say if the young person didn't reach the apex, went instead adrift in their twenties, the failure was on them.

For typical young people entering prison from poor city neighborhoods, they'd been scratched and torn by life on the outside, and then inside they accumulated more lacerating experiences. Prison took away a person's prime. It kept you young even as you aged, a perpetual first act. Reentry followed, and coming out bewildered was how it went. The lack of preparation and purpose Bobby felt, his understanding that nowhere was he needed, all this made him a reentry everyman.

Some people could conceal their disappointments, but not Bobby. He didn't flaunt his troubles, yet when it came to expressing his feelings, Bobby had no guile. "I hate depending on people," Bobby said that February. In him was the transparent emotional truth of reentry. As a year of mishaps came falling down hard on him like hail, it would get to the point where people were either frowning in disbelief or comparing Bobby to Job, suffering innocently as everything was taken away.

Not everything. People became devoted to Bobby, and all he had to give them was the person he was.

Resuming work at Pike in January, Bobby joined another demolition team. "I know I have to go in there with a better mindset," he said. "The project is fascinating. You can see through where the walls were." He didn't own steel-toe boots, and after eight hours of swinging a sledge, he came home with sneakers coated in drywall dust. One day, those working a floor below Bobby looked up to see his sneakered foot dangling, like a chandelier.

Bobby's latest supervisor was a recently hired man up from New York named Sol. "You know," Bobby said, "he's a slim guy, he's got this funny purple tie, he's got a yarmulke on, and he's got blond hair, and he's got glasses that look like sunglasses. And he walks very briskly and he seems like a very efficient all-business sort of man. And I didn't know what to expect from him at all. The first thing I wouldn't have said about him was that he was open." But Sol knew about Bobby from Hecht, and it turned out that as he drove around New Haven in his car, Sol was preoccupied with this employee he'd been handed. Sol determined he would design a workday that took into account Bobby's past.

Every morning, Sol met with Bobby, gave him an address and keys, and sent him off. Then Bobby could check in throughout the day. Sol considered it to be "a pleasure working with him, especially knowing everything that's going on behind. He continuously calls me and he's like, 'Okay, what am I doing today? Okay, I'm about to finish. I'm going to go to lunch, but what am I doing after lunch?' So right now he's working with a mop and a pail. And when it requires something a little bit more, with electric tools and things like that, it's around other people that are there. I understand the situation. I have the whole entire picture. And I understand that things can happen, not because he wants to, because, unfortunately, that's what he went through."

Bobby appreciated Sol—"he always try to understand"—and in the spring, when Bobby was relieved of filling out time slips and placed on the payroll, he rejoiced, "I'm official! Pay official taxes on it too." But transportation remained a problem; you couldn't take mops, brooms, and buckets on the city bus. While Shay still dropped him off and picked him up, she couldn't shuttle Bobby from site to site. And to someone for whom cleanliness was so important, the nature of the work was antithetical, like asking a vegetarian to work for a butcher.

SHAY AND BOBBY were still sharing the studio as roommates, Bobby paying the bills, when in February, Bobby attended a game night at Hank's house. Another guest was one of Hank's wife's cousins, a composed young woman named Rhonda. During the gathering, Bobby and Rhonda debated the legalization of marijuana, and as "the great conversation" unfolded, a warm, breathless feeling came over Bobby; stars filled his sky. Returning home, perhaps he told Shay he wanted to start seeing somebody else. Perhaps he merely intended to tell Shay this. Perhaps only he was fully aware of his and Shay's earlier breakup and the couple's revised status as friends. Shay was the person who'd set up Bobby's Facebook account for him, and Shay now discovered that "some girl" had written to Bobby, "Everybody says you like me. True?" Then Shay saw that Bobby did not reply "Shay's home cooking for me right now" but typed instead, "I do like you."

Shay was livid. Shay didn't know Rhonda, but she knew something about her. Rhonda had been on West Ivy Street the evening Pete Fields was killed, and although she was aware of what had happened, she'd declined to tell investigators that Bobby hadn't been involved. She was among those Hank had tried cajoling into speaking up back when Bobby was still in prison. "These people didn't even come to court for him!" Shay said, and that burned her up for Bobby. That he'd date someone who so profoundly hadn't done right by him left Shay "insulted" for herself.

Bobby and Shay talked and set a two-month deadline for her to move out. But with each passing hour, Shay was more upset by Bobby, right over there, unable to hide being in the first infatuated throes: "He's texting her. Sending kissy faces!" If Bobby wasn't going to hold off, neither would Shay. "I was taking shots at him," she reported. "He was barking back at me. I was in my feelings about him and the way he did it. It was just very abrupt, I should say."

After four days, Shay decided to "make room for the new girl" and return to her childhood space up in her grandmother's Willis Street attic. Bobby helped her pack, and Shay took breaks to walk over every inch of the apartment floor so that "any girl comes through here will feel my wrath! Praised the Lord all through there!" They loaded up Samuel Green, and then Bobby hugged Shay as she wept. "Shay, it will not be hard," he said. "You will be okay." Shay told him, "Bobby, breakups *are* hard." Bobby felt "bad that it happened. She's hurt by it." After Shay was gone, he asked for a day off from work to plan how to get there now that Shay would not be available to drive him. The bus felt too risky.

Bobby hoped to remain friends with Shay, but she took to herself, thinking everything through. She had been with Bobby every day for nearly a year and a half and recognized "it all did happen so fast with us. He just want to live a little. Like experience stuff on his own, I guess." Of the clumsy way he'd broken up with her, she concluded, "I don't think he knew how to do it. So, it hurt me. But then I realize he didn't know. He's twenty-seven, but he's eighteen out here in the mind." For herself, Shay regretted "the drama," and, as always, she owned herself. "He hates drama, and I probably caused some."

Bobby enjoyed dating Rhonda. He admired her for working long, steady hours as a medical technician, and also for being a devoted mother to her daughter. Rhonda was good to Bobby. When she brought takeout from Popeye's over to the apartment after work and then watched him eat, it was her concern for his happiness that filled him up. He'd always wanted someone to watch over him. Nor did she rush him to make commitments to her. Bobby began to sleep more easily. Quay, among other family members, was dismayed that Bobby was dating someone who'd refused to help an innocent person. But Bobby said he understood how "scared" Rhonda and her family had been. Bobby saw Newhallville as a place where fear could register as a higher ethical principle.

The resonance of that swept in when friends at Big Cheshire heard a rumor that Bobby had been shot. The idea seemed senseless; what harm had Bobby ever caused anyone? Was some guy messing with his friends for sport? In the illogic were unsettling truths: the emotional proximity of the prison to city life, the long tail of the unsolved crime, the free-floating resentments of generational poverty, the danger of false rumors. Bobby felt buried in ill portent. "Everybody thinks I have money," he said. In recent years, Connecticut's claims commissioner had awarded millions of post-prison dollars to a handful of wrongfully convicted men as compensation for their years unjustly served. In federal court settlements, Scott Lewis and a few others had received prodigious sums of money after filing civil rights lawsuits. All Bobby had come into was the small Innocence Project stipend and a modest loan for housing. Yet Bobby feared Pete Fields's fate happening to him, Bobby returning to where he'd grown up and getting shot because of loose talk about what he supposedly had in his wallet. "Everybody keeps warning me, 'Watch out for this dude, watch out for that one.'"

Visiting Rhonda brought Bobby regularly back to Newhallville, and visiting the neighborhood disheartened him further. He detected "no energy, no love, perpetually a negative vibe sucking the life out of people. Somebody asked me, 'Do you watch *The Walking Dead*?' I said not on TV, but I do when I go outside." He didn't blame Newhallville. He blamed those with the authority to improve Newhallville, those with budgets and line items who never, ever made it a priority. Bobby asked, "What perpetuates this? What made it happen? What could make it thrive? What is the purpose of politics if not to fix it?"

Looking around him, Bobby compared the present disarray of those he'd grown up with in Newhallville with people he'd known from his grandmother's Hamden neighborhood: "All those guys went on to do great things with their lives. People from Hamden tell me, 'How did this happen to you?' But there the kids were all part of a house life. They had moms and dads. They didn't tolerate nothing. The New Haven kids I was hanging out with were so caught up and confined to that environment that they don't see outside of that."

Sometimes it seemed Bobby must be exaggerating the dangers of Newhallville. Yet Hank said he only drove around the neighborhood and "wouldn't feel comfortable walking there like I used to." When kids told police officer Scott Shumway the Ville was "Beirut," as Mayor DeStefano had once described it, Shumway shook his head. He'd been active-duty military and said this was "far" from what "a war-torn country" was like. But then Shumway, pointing out Newhallville's attractive housing but low property values, asked, "Would you pay for a neighborhood where the kids could get shot when they're in the yard playing?" Leonard Jahad, who counseled young people at risk for violence, said he didn't think Bobby himself was in personal danger there, though the reasoning Jahad offered was grim: "Everybody his age is either dead, has a long jail term, or they changed their lives."

THREE WEEKS AFTER Bobby's breakup with Shay, a heavy quilt of snow fell over the city, and Bobby remained alone in his apartment, feeling personally buried. This was the first time he'd been all on his own. He stopped eating and sleeping and communicating. He kept the lights off, remained submerged in the basement dark, unable to get up, to turn on the sink, wash a dish, or watch TV. He was overtaken by memories of prison—murder stories, shakedowns, screams. A wish for death came over him. Four silent snowbound days and nights passed.

On the fifth day, Bobby walked outside to go to the hospital. The sun's glare off the pristine white banks blinded him. During the ride, he was still silent until, near the hospital, the car passed a convenience store, and Bobby said, "Somebody got shot in there."

At Yale–New Haven Hospital, his caretakers took note of his severe anxiety, high blood pressure, and low heart rate, and they urged him to stay, but Bobby wanted to return to the apartment and tunnel back in. With his skin pulled taut, he looked again as he had when he came out of prison, had lost his lustrous glow.

Bobby brooded about his family. He loved them "to death," but "I conditioned myself to not care about them for so long that it's become a natural feeling and second nature to me." It frustrated Bobby that he could not simply forgive and move past. He didn't want to hate. And when his telephone rang and his mother needed his help, off he went. Two days later he was making fun of himself for how he whiplashed between emotions. It was the first time he'd laughed in two weeks.

Not having a car remained a substantial problem. Bobby's predicament recalled the spatial mismatch theory developed in the 1960s by social scientists who watched American job growth leave for the suburbs while poor, mostly Black men were stranded back in the cities, unable to drive to where the work was. It was also that, as a man from Newhallville said, "Having no car demeans you. You're always in need, and anywhere outside your neighborhood's a faraway place."

Then Scott Lewis told Bobby about a way to buy his own car. From people at the Innocence Project in New York, Lewis had learned about companies that offered what was known as pre-settlement funding. These were cash advances against future awards related to legal cases. If the plaintiff lost his lawsuit and received no damages, he didn't have to pay the advance back. But if he did receive official compensation, he'd be obligated to return all he'd borrowed from the company, along with serious interest. The interest resembled the terms of the prison economy. In prison, people were accustomed to paying high exchange rates against whatever they borrowed from the guy running a little store out of his cell. You couldn't divide a cup of instant ramen into fractions, so if you borrowed one cup, you paid the guy two back. Lewis had borrowed funds and paid back much more. Bobby, too, was intrigued.

Litigation financing was an industry still new enough that it was scarcely regulated. People with capital, some supplied by large hedge funds, assessed lawsuits and compensation claims, and if they deemed one promising, they "invested" in the case. The industry was resistant to the term "loan"—the potential realm of usury. It was expensive for smaller or individual plaintiffs to bring suit against corporate or institutional defendants with their in-house counsel. Litigation financing evened the field, bought the time such cases took to resolve. But to some, like civil-rights lawyer Jonathan Moore, who'd represented Central Park Five defendants and the family of Eric Garner, who had died after being choked by a New York police officer, it was offensive to charge a gouging rate of interest so that poor people who'd suffered social injustice could survive as their case slowly made its way through the courts.

Wrongful conviction suits involving exonerees seemed to offer "investors" little actual risk, since exonerees almost always received some kind of award. Lit-financing companies required their potential "partners" to send over the details of their cases. That necessarily meant the involvement of the "partner's" lawyer. There Richard Supple, a specialist in legal professional ethics, saw risks for lawyers in divulging their yet-to-be argued case strategies. Supple further noted that lawyers could feel complicated advising impoverished clients against deals with such high back-end interest.

After spending almost half his life in prison, Scott Lewis's impatient priority had been founding a business. A company named USClaims evaluated Lewis's civil-rights lawsuit and informed him they'd be glad to send him a substantial check. In a *Vermont Law Review* article, a law professor named Julia H. McLaughlin had scrutinized USClaims and described them acidly as inveigling clients to potentially "mortgage their future economic security." Lewis agreed with McLaughlin that "the interest rates are usurious. But I didn't care. I needed to accomplish things. I borrowed a million bucks. I paid back $1.4 [million], because I settled my case in a year and a half. To me, all that mattered was non-recourse. I needed resources. I had dreams I wanted to accomplish." Lewis's advice to Bobby was, "Get enough to be comfortable while you wait."

Indisputable was that Bobby needed a car to reach work, and a non-recourse loan from USClaims could buy him one. He'd decided he wanted that Acura, and was happy to buy it secondhand. A particular feature Bobby liked was the push-button starter. Keys got lost, somehow always led to problems. Such a car would probably cost around $15,000—not cheap, but hardly what many Americans, devoid of context, would consider a lavish car purchase. Bobby lived in a basement studio. His closet contained empty hangers. When he dined out on a date, it was at modest chain restaurants. If anyone should have a car he enjoyed, why not Bobby? Yes, the lit-financing interest was exorbitant, but Bobby didn't just need a car. Bobby needed sources of optimistic forward motion.

All this was why, one morning in late March, accompanied by a cousin, Bobby visited Rosenthal at his office to discuss a lit-financing loan. Rosenthal's instinct was not to. He found it troubling that USClaims's interest schedule meant Bobby could easily find himself owing USClaims 100 percent on what they sent him. Here, potentially, was the position Richard Supple had warned about. Rosenthal was a white lawyer with a secure income telling a poor Black client wearing sweatpants glazed by frequent wear how to think about money.

As Rosenthal pushed back, Bobby became upset. "You doubtin' me. Your lack of trust in me is disappointing to me."

"He's not doubtin' you, bro," Bobby's cousin said. "He wants you to be smart."

"I'm concerned you think a car's a magic help," Rosenthal said.

"It's a big help," Bobby told him. "I don't have the support of my family. I'm basically by myself, Ken." Rapidly, Bobby grew emotional. "My cousin can vouch. I'm on my own."

"All the more reason to be careful. You're talking a $15,000 car. That is crazy! I've never bought a $15,000 car."

Suddenly Rosenthal was yet another parental figure trying to win a disagreement about supposed extravagance by describing how it had been for him. The old "when I was your age" move had never convinced anyone, at least until they themself became a parent, and it didn't convince Bobby. He said, "I'm searching for a car that will last me. I don't want a cheap car like people get and it breaks down. I'm depressed in the place I live. I have no clothes. I have nothing. I'm basically September 4, 2015. Pike owns eight hundred apartments. I go to one for fifteen minutes. Then to another. I can't go on the bus with my equipment."

"Honestly," the cousin said, "all jobs need a car." As if to emphasize his point, he got up, fingered his keys, said goodbye, and left for work.

Bobby and Rosenthal continued the discussion, with Bobby growing more indignant while Rosenthal stayed unflappable. There behind his desk, Rosenthal seemed less and less a lawyer than that older-generation relative taking the dadly long view. Then the lawyer did something unexpected. He shifted, began advancing Bobby's position. Rosenthal said it was tacit, with Bobby's credit rating, no conventional bank would give him a car loan.

Setting aside whatever Connecticut's claims commissioner might or might not award Bobby, a federal civil-rights lawsuit would take a long time to resolve, years of motions. Opposition lawyers would "know that people in your position need money and they will offer less because they know you'll be tempted to take it. An outfit like this allows you to hold out for a bigger return. They believe in your lawsuit enough to give you the ability to invest in your future."

When Rosenthal said "believe," the word went through Bobby like an injection, and he relaxed. The money didn't just mean a car to Bobby, it meant someone had faith in him—enough faith to invest in his life.

After all that, it turned out Rosenthal had already spoken for Bobby with USClaims, to a "savvy" and "fast-talking" woman there, and she'd agreed to advance Bobby money. "She was very responsive," Rosenthal told Bobby. "She made the decision in about three hours." The financing company was so skilled at valuing cases, the woman had told Rosenthal that only 8 percent of the cases USClaims invested in went bad. Since she'd explained a large hedge fund was backing them he said now, "they have money. Nothing but money." If the percentages went with Bobby, he would be awarded a judgment and USClaims would end up with some of it. For the first six months, Bobby's obligation was 16 percent interest on what he was advanced. Then the number would grow by 16 percent every six months, to a maximum of a 100 percent interest debt, again contingent upon Bobby being successfully compensated. So, should Bobby accept $35,000, in three years his debt to USClaims would become $70,000.

Rosenthal told Bobby, "You sound like you know what you want to do." Then, again, he prodded Bobby to "get a cheap car. I've never had a new car in my life."

Bobby now relented. "I know I don't have to spend $15,000 on a car. I can spend $7,000 or $8,000. But I don't have furniture. I have no clothes."

The lawyer said, "If you want the money, you'll get the money. I just want to be sure you understand the cost." Then he observed, "Your cousin seems like a good support."

"He just got stabbed last weekend," Bobby said. "He just broke up with his girlfriend. He's basically homeless."

Rosenthal heard Bobby to be saying Rosenthal wasn't always right. "Bobby, I'm not criticizing you," Rosenthal said. "I'm understanding of how difficult it is for you. But in life experience you're just getting out of high school. The concern is not doing something you regret. It's not bad to have advice from people. I'm giving you my thoughts. But I won't stop you. I will sign the dotted line. The money you'll pay them will be out the door."

"I'm fine with that," Bobby said.

Bobby decided on taking nowhere near the maximum he could have asked for. He put in only for money up front to buy the car and then modest payments to use for rent that would be paid out monthly across the year. Once the application was done, Rosenthal said, "I've never seen you so assertive. I was happy. You were very determined. When we first met, you were very passive. I like it that you speak up for yourself."

After Bobby left, Rosenthal said, "A car gives you independence, even your identity. So why not? He has money coming to him. He's waited long enough. I'm concerned he's trying to do too much all at once. These things he wants, he's entitled to want. I hope it works out."

Right away, Bobby and Hank searched local car sites on the web, reviewing secondhand Acuras. A white Acura on the lot of a popular, high-volume used car dealer out in Naugatuck spoke to Bobby. The car had 46,000 miles on it, cost $13,895, and had a push-button starter. They drove off to Naugatuck for an Acura viewing. After a test drive, Bobby said he loved it, that the car was him. He went home to arrange partial financing.

Old folks in Bobby's life had begun debating Bobby's Acura among themselves. Heads bent together recalling extra shifts taken, nights worked to purchase a Dodge Dart with their sister. Saving up for that Dodge meant having no money for toothpaste and chewing a stick of wood instead. One woman began praying every day that Bobby wouldn't buy the Acura.

Returning to Naugatuck, Bobby looked out at verdant rolling suburbs and farmland. "I definitely want to live out in the environment like this," he said. He sighed. "Every time I'm in this type of environment I feel sad for my environment." Near Naugatuck, Bobby announced, "I'm getting nervous."

Bobby arrived to a sales floor dense with people drinking complimentary coffee, milling about the desks, scenting a discount. Bobby's white salesman had salt-and-pepper hair, sleeve tattoos, and, after Bobby handed over his pay stubs for the financing application, the brusque manner of someone accustomed to facing down exaggeration. The salesman asked Bobby to provide further verification. When he then mentioned more fees, Bobby's face looked the way it had when Rosenthal seemed to doubt him. He was out the door, past the Acura, back on the road for New Haven.

From the car, Bobby telephoned Stefon Morant. Morant had been a prison car maven, reading magazines and catalogues, checking prices, keeping up. Now Morant was working as a reentry counselor at a halfway house in Waterbury. He drove a shiny black pickup truck and had just bought his first house. After Bobby explained his trouble, Morant told Bobby, "We're going to my guy."

That was lanky Marvin Henderson, a Black man who'd been selling cars for nearly forty years. Henderson came to his dealership in a blue suit, a paisley tie, and a barbered mustache, and had many clients in New Haven's African American community. Morant's work had taught him that reentering people who'd been in prison for a long time had a tendency to rush the big things. When Bobby mentioned to Morant he might be in love with his girlfriend, Morant widened his eyes. "You *just* met her! Slow down. You don't know her yet." Morant urged Bobby to be similarly deliberate about buying a car. A car was an enormous purchase, and very personal. To find not just any car but a match, Bobby should first let Henderson know something about himself. So, when they met up with Henderson, Bobby described Granddad's love for Chevrolets. Morant explained about Bobby's case. Henderson nodded along. He was the opposite of a fast-talking car salesman. They walked the lot. On the car Bobby liked best, Henderson offered a price several thousand dollars south of the Acura line. Morant's phone soon captured a photograph of Bobby waving from the driver's seat of a forest-green 2014 Chevrolet Cruze. "Marvin treated him like a man," Morant said with satisfaction. Bobby spoke of the Cruze as "the greatest purchase I've made in my life."

SINCE BREAKING UP with him, Shay had realized, "I had the hardest job with Bobby. He was fresh out of Cheshire. I had my faults. We all had faults. But I went through it with him. Up at night, him depressed and don't want to tell nobody he's depressed. Or him reliving Cheshire moments. I remember one time touching him and he was "Hoooo!!!" I went through his PTSD. Cheshire was a lot, and he couldn't shake it. And I still feel like he's dealing with some Cheshire aspects."

After a month, Shay decided, "I know Bobby loves me. I know Bobby cares about me. He's had a hard time and he doesn't know what to do." She believed "I was his refuge. And if he called me today, 'Shay, this is what I need,' if my car was running, I would bring it. So I don't hold malice towards him. I just didn't like the way he hurt me. I feel like he'll know better next time what to do in a relationship because he was with me." For herself, Shay cared too much about Bobby just to cut him loose. He would always be "Bobby from Willis Street" to her.

As soon as Shay decided she and Bobby could be friends, they spoke every day. They'd also text, checking in to see how the other was. One day, Bobby thanked her, saying, "You taught me a whole lot." Shay replied, "I know you taught me a whole lot, too. I will never deal with anyone just straight out of jail again."

Shay wished for Bobby that he could "stop beating himself up about work." She admired his ethic, understood his impatience with the situation at Pike, but thought, "He got to realize this is just a step, like a starter job. I don't have my dream job yet." Living back in her childhood neighborhood had Shay remembering the feeling of returning to Newhallville from college. "I was like geesh, this is really how everybody still is here. I could come home Thanksgiving weekend, it's a shootout. Ain't no shoot out at UConn. When you go away and come back, that's when you really could see what was wrong." Shay had "loved" college and regretted not having her degree. "I was really close," she said. The promise of college for Shay had been that it would lift her up and away. Her inability to complete her degree had stakes for her, and for her family, that were far more dire than for a middle-class student taking a semester off. Because Shay couldn't afford to go back, the earning power and work opportunity a degree confers had disappeared. That Shay had reveled in college, and that UConn had, in a sense, broken up with her, was still confusing and very painful.

Shay thought there was an essential belief among Americans who'd never lived in a struggling neighborhood that the address spoke to all you desired out of life. Shay knew Newhallville's history as an aspirational family community where historical restrictions on what jobs Blacks could hold, and how much they could earn, had left people lastingly resourceful. One side-hustling woman did hair in her front room. Another baked and sold cakes. Every other Friday, the lady who lived over there made up fish or barbecue dinners for takeout. There was a frozen "icy" lady, and a penny-candy lady who did her trade through a first-floor window. The "car wash man" operated out of his driveway. The "extreme coupon lady" bought detergent, deodorant, and toothbrushes with coupon discounts and sold them at a profit. That guy was a shade-tree mechanic. Those people would come to you carrying a bucket loaded with all the equipment they needed to detail your car. What Shay and others applauded in all of these unofficial ventures was the imagination involved, the shrewd way poor people who felt excluded from grander opportunity could navigate tight economic times.

Yet when Shay passed the 2-4, she agreed with what Scott Shumway had said about Newhallville, thought "none of it looks like what it was supposed to live up to. You do not want to move over here." Shay felt conflicted about elders, like her grandmother, whose impulse was to patiently wait until the neighborhood they'd invested their lives in revived.

For Shay, it was difficult to see how that would happen. "People in the same spot," she said. "Seemed like people just couldn't get ahead." Shay regarded the violence and the police presence in Newhallville similarly, as symptoms of segregation. "People know nothing outside of New Haven," she said. "I feel like people often get stuck here, caught up in the hype." Shay's suspicion was that all those out there who believed you were where you came from had no idea how hard it was to leave. Perhaps, Shay thought, such people were themselves part of a status quo conditioned to believe people who were poor deserved it. With college a train in the distance, she said, "I don't miss the work, I miss UConn."

Shay said she herself was not stuck, and would have already left town to seek her fortune. "But my grandma's alive. Otherwise I would be gone. I'm a pretty girl. Not hard to go!" Instead, she soon met Corey, "a little church boy. He's a drummer. Sings and works at the church."

Driving offered Bobby perspective on the city, and his conclusions were similar to Shay's. "I was on the highway last night, thinking what a beautiful highway," he said. "The beautiful signs. The intellect it takes to make a world. And I wondered why the people that created that world are not from my world. Our environment would be beautiful if we had the same kind of education." The only person from his growing up who'd gone to college was Shay, and as for work, he said, "Somebody here must have a good job, but I haven't heard."

Driving his Cruze, within short weeks several times patrol cars had signaled Bobby for stops when he knew he hadn't done anything wrong. He'd roll down his window, and some officers made no pretense. "Cops know me," he said. " 'Hey, Bobby. How you doing? Staying out of trouble?' "

Kwame wasn't. "Kwame can't stay off the corner," explained one police officer. Kwame had a girlfriend and a child, and the police officer said that with a young mouth to feed, "Kwame deals enough to get by." Once Bobby gave Kwame a ride, and a cruiser immediately pulled them over. Looking through Bobby's driver's-side window, the officer asked, "You taking him on a little drug run?"

Bobby believed the way Kwame had been treated by the police at fourteen had turned him into a person of concern to them. "I want to help him," Bobby said of his friend. "I worry about him, that he's susceptible because of our experience." If the goal really was criminal justice, Bobby thought the police ought to be helping Kwame, not harrying him. Bobby was as aware as a person could be of how humiliating and intimidating it felt to submit before police officers. "Black America's getting shot," he said. "I feel passionate every day. I just don't usually say it." When Kwame was later imprisoned for selling drugs to an undercover operative and for gun possession, Bobby considered this wish fulfillment by the system. "They ruined Kwame" was also Shay's opinion. "No mom. Bobby was a kid. Kwame was a kid-kid."

For Bobby, with a new girlfriend, a new car, and sometimes the new girlfriend driving the new car while Bobby drove hers, there was spring giddiness. One day, Bobby was "just playing around. Just joking," and mentioned marriage to Rhonda, but she did not find this stuff amusing, told him pointedly to "stop playing." He was contrite. He'd heard Morant's advice about patience. Yet running beneath the surface was believing he'd probably lost a big life ambition to prison, the possibility of having a fiftieth wedding anniversary.

Early in June, Bobby was driving along busy Orange Street in New Haven, and as he passed through an intersection, an older woman ran a stop sign and hit the Cruze flush in the side. The heavy impact spun the car around, knocking off a rear wheel. Bobby and Rhonda were taken by ambulance to the hospital, and while Bobby had neck and side pain, the real damage was to the totaled Cruze. "It seems like nothing ever goes right," Bobby said. "I'm so messed up now I don't know what to think about stuff anymore." A day later he felt better. Following his most challenging moments, what Bobby dependably said was not that life was taunting him but, "I'm all right. I'll get over it. You know how it go with me and tragedy. I be mad for a second."

Sometimes at Pike, all the handyman assignments involved skilled carpentry, leaving Bobby on an office bench, waiting for work. He could have still billed for the waiting time, as others did, but Bobby refused. "I need a trade," he said with a sigh. Life seemed to be offering him a surfeit of lessons in the value of bearing up. Bobby knew that what had befallen him in recent years might have crushed many people. No part of him believed all the good times were past and gone. What he thought was how much that

Cruze had meant to him. "Everybody talks about missing the car," he said. "Everybody loved that car. They were happy I had that car. Sad I had to take that loss. It just happens too much. I used to think it was natural. Now it's like I'm still paying for something. I don't like to point out these things. Seems like I'm complaining. I hope it pays off like Job. Better farm. Better farm animals. Triple what he lost."

At lunchtime on the Friday of July Fourth weekend, Bobby went to discuss having no car again with Rosenthal, who was just getting to the eating of his breakfast, a bowl of cereal with water. Rosenthal listened and told Bobby, "I have a car. It was in this little accident. So I bought my cousin's car. You can use the other car in the meantime. You can have it. I'll give it to you."

Then Rosenthal told Bobby more about this black Hyundai Sonata, the car he kept under the fruit tree. "It has 150,000 miles on it. I've never had a problem with it." Noticing perhaps a skeptical shadow, Rosenthal said, "I know you like a nice-looking car, and it doesn't look fancy. I haven't taken care of it. It has a dent. But it'll save you from having to buy another car right away." A call came in to Rosenthal. It was a health-care job Bobby had applied for, checking Bobby's references. Rosenthal walked into the hallway. But Bobby could still hear as Rosenthal said, "He's an excellent person, very conscientious, who is well-meaning and hardworking. He's really considerate of others, and very aware of what it takes to take care of people."

The unfancy Sonata was dappled with dents, a smear of sap, rust, earth, and the vestiges of a sideswipe. Bobby said, "I know a guy who will clean that all up nice." Then he began singing along with Jay-Z, "*Even when we win, we gon' lose.*"

In the subsequent months, someone tried to break into Bobby's apartment, and then twice into his car. The new job hadn't been as advertised, so Bobby was still eddying at Pike. Each time, Bobby was mad for a second. He was remarkably forgiving of Rhonda's relative who'd witnessed Pete Fields's murder from her porch. "She told me, 'It's crazy—we know you didn't do it,'" Bobby said. "'We saw them run up on the guy.' Everybody knows who did it, but we talk about it and still don't say his name. That's a legacy of its own that's not going anywhere."

IN ALL THIS was the way life grinds you, with little indignities after big. At meals, lately Bobby could get down only ramen noodles—the prison food he'd promised he would never taste again. When Bobby had insomnia, he might get out of bed at two or three in the morning and clean his apartment. He wanted rest. People suggested sleeping pills. But he had grown up around too many "fiends" and wouldn't take them. From what he'd seen in Newhallville, Bobby's belief about drugs was that they medicated the inequities. Drug use was what happened, he said, when people were mistreated and told to get over it. "It gives you a temporary fake relief," he said. "You forget about the outside world."

Bobby himself smoked weed, but for a long time, he didn't talk about why. He called his depression instead "stress," and as he explained, "lot of times, if I'm stressed, I don't tell nobody I'm stressing. I feel like when I tell people that I'm stressing, then people add onto my stress by telling me they're also stressed, and it's like filling up a balloon with a bunch of adversities and stress and it's just going to explode eventually." It was as though he'd held everything inside until he was released from prison, and now, two years later, he couldn't personally release, leaving him to manage what he held in or else rupture. The rest Bobby wanted was a rest from being Bobby. Others worried he was indulging his suffering. "I don't even know who he is," his mother said.

Reuben Miller, the Chicago professor who did volunteer prison work, had a term, "learning to languish," for what happened to people in the months and years after prison. Bobby agreed that prison had made him "lethargic." Yet lethargy was one way to describe someone who often felt anxious and worn out, someone who couldn't eat or sleep, talked of having no energy, feeling empty, muddy bricks for feet. At this time Bobby, who had believed in prison he should not be marked by the experience, now acquired a tattoo. It depicted a clock set to nine, the prison years now literally imprinted, his bid written into him.

Bobby was a soldier back from the campaigns besieged by interior trip wires, unable to shake where he'd been, what he'd seen. Prison was most present in him when he slept. He had nightmares of the lurid murders people who'd committed them had described. Over and over he dreamed of stabbings, pools of thick blood. A faceless assailant wanted to shoot Bobby, was coming hard down the dream hallway toward him. He'd wake up, his sheets and blankets soaked in sweat. Always on the lookout, the most Bobby could sleep without waking was two hours. When Rhonda visited, so as not to wake her, he went outside to his car and sat inside by himself, sometimes for hours.

Among all the upsetting events, to have been out of prison this long and still not be further along was most upsetting. A likely explanation was that reliving his traumatic experiences over and over was affecting Bobby's biology. Catherine Panter-Brick, a Yale anthropologist, studied stress and resilience in children and adolescents growing up in profoundly difficult circumstances such as war, displacement, social marginalization, and homelessness, by tracking their cortisol levels over time to create a biological stress diary. She learned that while most young people living with chronic stress show normal cortisol levels, some will be unable to regulate cortisol production. The young people with these problematic stress profiles will either maintain very high cortisol levels (being always on vigilant alert) or very low cortisol levels (a flat profile that signals being unengaged and unable to respond, probably as a way to cope with overload, and one that is problematic because the body is not able to take on otherwise routine demands).

During the second September since his release, Bobby decided to speak with a clinical social worker whose specialty was childhood trauma and exposure to violence. The social worker's book-lined office had a view out beyond downtown, revealing the natural beauty surrounding the small city. The social worker had graying hair, glasses, and a direct manner. They began to talk, and Bobby didn't spare her the details. He said his typical day now was "Get up in the morning. Sit in the dark for hours. I don't deal with my family because when I went in, my family wasn't with me. I feel everything vanished."

"The physical things you're describing, that's an anxiety response," the social worker said. "Like what happens to your body when you're in danger."

Bobby could tell right away she not only believed him, she had experience with what he was telling her about. He liked that he couldn't surprise her, that his difficulties existed in a known realm. "I can have good days," he said. "The majority of my time is depression."

"I'm not surprised you're depressed," she said. "You've had a lot of bad things happen."

She asked him, "How'd you get your job?"

"Through a friend," he said. "I think they felt sorry for me."

"How do you think people get into Yale?" she replied. Then she offered to see him, at no cost, through the year.

BOBBY FRETTED ABOUT Shay. With her intelligence, emotional maturity, and imagination, that her life wasn't ascending, he said, made him "feel bad every time I think about it." Shay was feeling just as worried about Bobby.

She tried to encourage him. "I tell him, 'I pray for you. Keep your head up. Keep on pushing. You're two years home. Soon it'll be three. Do stuff. Go to an open gym. Find a rec team.'" Her belief remained "he needs time for himself. He left me. A couple of days later he's with another girl. He's doing high school stuff. He has to go through the motions. But he doesn't want to go through the motions. He feels he should be past it. But he's gotta fall the way we all did."

When Bobby and Rhonda broke up there were tears, the hope of friendship in the future. Bobby now admitted he'd rushed into the relationship and needed time alone. Then, with a sly look, he added, "If I'm alone it just frees me up to make another bad decision!"

One afternoon, Bobby was giving a cousin a ride from school, and as he met up with her on the crowded sidewalk, somehow he dropped his wallet, which was packed with cash to pay his phone bill and for gas. By the time Bobby noticed, went back, and picked the wallet up, all the cash had been removed. Then Bobby missed an appointment with his new therapist and didn't let her know. The therapist's impression was similar to Shay's: "The problem is he needs a parent. And at twenty-eight years old, that's just not possible."

A MONTH LATER, Bobby and Rosenthal went north to Hartford for Bobby's hearing with Connecticut's claims commissioner. It was a chilly fall day, but Bobby wore only a white short-sleeved dress shirt to go with black trousers. Rosenthal had on a suit with a sweater underneath, and he brought along the work of years—armfuls of accordion legal files, large cardboard charts, binders, folders, thick documents, yellow pads filled with his handwriting. In Hartford, Bobby passed through a concrete streetscape of government buildings and parking garages, and then took an elevator up to a windowless courtroom with low ceilings and a conference table. Preparing to make his presentation, Rosenthal set up a boxy Toshiba laptop, which somehow was the computing equivalent of the Sonata. "This is a dinosaur," he said, "but it has great speakers!" He'd recorded and edited interviews to go along with slides. Among the others also on hand in the room were Bobby's new therapist and Granddad. In brown trousers, a brown dress shirt, and black dress shoes, Granddad was as immaculate as he kept his cars. He'd come not to testify but to bear witness, to be sure no officer of justice messed again with his grandson.

The state said it wasn't contesting that Bobby deserved compensation. So, the proceedings amounted to helping the claims commissioner, a white lawyer and former high school English teacher named Christy Scott, decide how much was fair. Scott wore a red cardigan, had glasses down on the tip of her nose, and a friendly, informal demeanor. Instead of sitting up at the judicial bench, she joined the others around the conference table. Rosenthal began describing "the egregiousness of what happened here." He summarized the events of the case, Bobby's captivity, and subsequent travails. What seemed to affect Scott most was the photograph Rosenthal displayed of Bobby at sixteen. People sometimes said Bobby should have known to ask the police whether he was being detained or was free to go, that he should have refused to speak to detectives unless there was an attorney present. In the photograph was a cup-eared, small-faced boy who scarcely resembled the solidly built man approaching thirty sitting quietly over there. Every high school English teacher knows William Blake's description of innocence: "he is meek and he is mild, he became a little child."

Bobby's therapist told the commissioner she believed life-blasting experiences had been "encoded" within Bobby. As a result, she explained, Bobby was reliving his bad moments rather than remembering them. His hyperarousal to danger meant he was always attuned to threats, making sleeping, eating, romance, trust, and focus all tenuous. He'd now lost thirty-five pounds since prison. Still, she said, Bobby remained an open and honest person, someone the state should compensate for what had been done to him while also considering any award as investment in his promise.

When it was Bobby's turn to answer questions from Scott, he told her of his hopes for having an education, a career, and a wife. "I'm sorry for the terrible thing that happened to you," Scott said. "It's not something society is proud of." Her decision would come within months.

ON AN EARLY-JANUARY weekend in 2018, Bobby and some cousins went seven miles out east of the city to the seaside town of Branford, visiting "the big area where the rich people got boats and mansions." They chose it because, he said, "that's the spot to hang out, clear your mind." It was like Prospect Street when he was a kid. Life was peaceful there, nothing to fear. You could just be. Down at the shore in the depths of winter, Bobby said, "I lost my phone. It slipped out of my pocket. Fell in the water."

In the places Bobby had been, people paid hypervigilant attention to personal safety, and became used to losing things. Prison had been the place of lost years, and when Bobby left Big Cheshire for home, he took his losses with him. Back in New Haven, the losses accumulated, all of it lengthening the disaster of his lost youth. Maybe it was better not to get too attached. One night, Bobby walked outside and discovered the Sonata, too, was gone.

Granddad had a younger brother, Brock, whom members of the family compared with the charming and enigmatic character Tommy on the old Fox sitcom *Martin*. If you saw Uncle Brock, it was without warning—and good things usually happened. When word of all Bobby's trouble with cars reached Uncle Brock, he showed up, said, "Get in," took Bobby to Milford, and watched the dealer sell him a six-year-old silver-gray Honda Accord. "Love it," Bobby said. "Roomy. Kind of huge!" Bobby fitted out his car with seven different buttons of Febreze air-freshener because, "I like nice smells!"

Where the Cruze had crumpled so easily, the Accord seemed "built to take a hit. Accords last a long time, and you see them everywhere. Everybody has one everywhere I look." But as one of Bobby's Black male New Haven contemporaries pointed out, Accords had their own liability. The man said that at one time, people in the game were known to drive "a car so nice everybody knows they're selling drugs." So now, instead of Mercedes, "the most visible dealers" all drove Hondas. As a result, Accords had become "the car fit a description" vehicles, the line local Black men said police routinely laid on them during traffic stops.

Then Bobby enlisted Scott Lewis to help convince Rosenthal to sign off on another infusion of USClaims money. This time Bobby wanted a sum large enough he could finally leave New Haven, rent somewhere else offering "new scenery, the good peace of mind." He had Branford in mind. At Rosenthal's office, Lewis proposed Bobby buy a three-family home, live on one floor, and use the rental income from the apartments to cover his mortgage. Rosenthal wasn't sure Bobby was ready to be a landlord. Bobby wasn't either. He looked at Rosenthal and said with a smile, "Scott's crazy!" After Rosenthal agreed to another advance, he said, "What I like about Bobby is he knows who he's not. He's figuring out who he is."

Lewis helped Bobby find a two-bedroom duplex apartment not far from the Long Island Sound in Branford. "The apartment is way bigger to me than a car," Bobby said. He'd become increasingly afraid someone would shoot him for money he didn't possess, for snitching he hadn't done. "New Haven's tricky," he explained. "When the majority don't have, people start to hate." For the rest of the month, Bobby talked about how "excited I am to move out of New Haven." Rosenthal was glad for him, but cautious: "He'll be in a new place, but it's the same old him."

But not just him. Bobby had grown closer to his cousin Tee, Johnny's younger sister, a composed woman just past twenty and, as Bobby always said, an old soul. Tee was interning as a medical assistant, following along in the family healthcare tradition. Bobby invited her to use the second bedroom as his roommate. On a late-January morning snowy enough that schools were closed, Bobby, in a gray sweatshirt, and Tee, in lavender sneakers, hurried out to Branford, where they met up with Lewis and the realtor to walk through the apartment before signing the lease.

Lewis and the realtor, a white woman, arrived swathed in boots, heavy coats, and thick sweaters. The realtor explained that the apartment owners were choosing to rent to Bobby even though they knew he'd been in prison because one worked in corrections and believed "everybody needs a break." A family with four children had been the previous tenants. Bobby's welcome note from the owners lay on a counter beneath a cabinet that was missing two doors. Paint was chipped; the baseboards were dingy and scuffed. As Lewis busily wrote down and photographed all the imperfections, the realtor told Bobby he'd inevitably find more "little flaws." Bobby had offered to pay the full year's rent up front.

With everything settled, Lewis gazed out the window and appraised: "Nice little view!" The apartment complex could have been a condominium development near a ski area. The cars in the parking lot were tarped in snow, beyond them was a line of pines, and then the enormous, somber ocean. "You'll look out one day and it's all sparkling like the curvature of the earth," the realtor said. She handed Bobby his keys, and he shook them like chimes.

As she and Lewis were leaving, the realtor abruptly offered Bobby directions to a nearby park where he could play basketball. Then she turned to Tee, touched her braids, and told her, "You have beautiful hair."

After a long, awkward moment, with Bobby and Tee just standing there, Bobby said of the apartment, "I'm going to appreciate it."

"I hope you're very happy here," the realtor told him.

"He's gonna have to be," Lewis said briskly. "This is a long way from New Haven."

Bobby went upstairs. Watching him, Tee said, "I'm so excited and it's not even my place!" She knew evidence of their slovenly predecessors would immediately disappear, because "Bobby sets things up very nice." Tee hoped living anonymously out by the shore would be soothing for her cousin. She understood how unsafe he'd begun to feel near a community where people sometimes claimed "we don't count that as noise, shots fired." When Tee's family had lived elsewhere, days had been uneventful, and then "we moved to Newhallville, and everything changed." Beyond the sirens and gunshots, Tee said, being there had meant "nobody thinks you'll make it."

Some felt that way about Bobby. Not Tee. She sympathized with his inability to understand why he still lacked direction and purpose. In *Manchild in the Promised Land*, Claude Brown's solution to his similar problems was "I decided to move, I was trying to get away from the fear." And that was what Bobby had now done.

THE DUPLEX'S ROOMS were soon immaculate, the TV framed with diplomas from certificate programs at Cheshire, a vase filled with a spray of branches. The dining table was permanently set for four. On the love seat, a pillow announced, THIS IS MY HAPPY PLACE. Bobby appeared relaxed there. His only complaint was that the family living above him seemed to do a lot of jumping. He talked of someday buying a quiet home, of looking out a window at his wife working in the garden. But this he deemed a long way off. "I love being free," he said.

When Bobby drove into New Haven, because where else did he know, the police kept pulling him over. Once his car was searched by the K-9 unit. Another time, he'd been ticketed for speeding, though he knew he hadn't exceeded the posted limit. Every story he could tell about the New Haven police, he said, had the same moral: "Stay out of New Haven."

But it wasn't the police who upset Bobby most. He was ever-consumed by the dread of others being after him. When he rasped that aloud to Lewis, Lewis said, "Trouble finds you when you're not busy." Another New Haven man who knew Bobby said Bobby's greatest danger was not shooters but fear. Once you were exposed to the nearby presence of gun violence, it contaminated you by association and you worried all the time; it felt safer to worry. Stefon Morant thought, "Bobby's mentally in danger."

One evening, Bobby drove into New Haven to attend a film screening held at a local music school's auditorium. The film was a documentary about Henry Green, a young Black contemporary of Bobby's from Newhallville, entitled *I Am Shakespeare*. Green had been a teenager living two New Haven lives in 2009, as both a talented student actor who'd played the role of Tybalt, Romeo's violent rival, in a New Haven Shakespeare summer stock production of *Romeo and Juliet,* and as a real-life participant in Newhallville street violence, nicknamed Renegade. Green proved a lucid narrator of his childhood, describing the humiliations of growing up without enough food or clothing, his resentment of people up across Prospect Street living life to the fullest, of how Yale students enraged him with their happy faces and excellent wardrobes. Daily in Newhallville, Green said, a teenage boy was presented with the choice of making people fear him or of being a victim. When he played Tybalt, it was natural for him to inhabit someone who located his own dignity through aggression.

As the film continued, Green told how neighborhood violence was messing his mind up. The fear made it impossible to focus in school or on anything else. Green described looking a gun in the eye as he contemplated suicide, of his hope that somebody would just shoot him and be done with it. As Green spoke, Bobby began moving around uneasily in his seat. Then Green was recalling a winter night, heading home through Newhallville from the bus stop. He was confronted by four young men wearing hoodies and ski masks—stickup kid commandos. In his seat, Bobby was making small noises. The youngest of the four put the muzzle of a silver handgun against Green's stomach. Green knew that if he refused to give up his belongings, the kid would be obligated to pull the trigger. With the others watching, if the kid didn't shoot Green, he'd lose his street reputation, ensure his own victimhood. These were the circumstances that some speculated had led Major to shoot Pete Fields. Bobby said, "I'm uncomfortable," and got to his feet. He knew the handgun was about to tear Green apart. Over the years, doctors saved Green with many surgeries. Green studied psychology, became a social worker helping children, married his best friend. But then he'd died, of complications, eight years after being shot.

Out in the lobby, Bobby was too shaken to leave. He began talking about how Newhallville's sidewalks were layered for young people with the impressions of those who'd been beaten and shot there. "Every day you go down the street and have a mental picture of all the tragedies," Bobby said. "It's completely terrifying in Newhallville, and that's all your parents can afford. You got so many people dying. The shocking reality, it takes a toll. I know that guy. I know who he is. I had to travel back through my whole experience as a child to remember."

THREE MONTHS AFTER moving to Branford, Bobby's electricity was cut off with notice that he'd need to send in $800 for service to resume. How could this bill be? Bobby was sure "I been keeping up," and $800 approached what plenty of small apartment renters remitted annually for electricity. When Bobby called the company for explanation, he was placed on hold, where he remained for hours, knees pressed together. He waited and he waited, sitting there in the dark, his cell phone battery charge percentage slowly draining. The impotent feeling became existential. Bobby's life was forever on hold, nothing certain about it except the uncertainty of awaiting a better future that never came, because he lacked the power.

During such moments, those who cared about Bobby found it easy to imagine all the worst-case ways he could go, fateful possibilities, the headwinds of inability and inexperience propelling him without funds, without groceries, into oblivion and abyss, sleeping under bridges.

Morant, Lewis, and Rosenthal were never going to let that happen. They loved Bobby as the person who, even when he was by himself without a lamp, thought of those who had it darker than he did. Part of Bobby's charm was that he had no pretext, was openhearted without ever trying to seem openhearted. Morant believed what would unlock life for Bobby was more living. How many college kids had called home with an unexpected utility bill? The way Bobby would learn to manage money was making mistakes. "Bobby's doing what I did when I first came home," Morant said. "He's trying to catch up to something you can't catch up to. I went to prison in 1994. I'm still trying to get out of 1994. The world changed. I didn't have credit or debit cards. In prison, I used to tell myself, 'When I go home, I'm not turning right until the light turns. Then I come home to right on red.'"

Morant, Lewis, and Bobby all knew how prison conditioned passivity. If you weren't asserting yourself in the prison ecosystem by running a little shop out of your cell, telling your study group what books to read, weren't claiming some independence by hopping the chow line a second time—known as "beating the deuce"—you might emerge helpless to provide for yourself. "Even Scott," Bobby said, "he gives out so much energy, but he has to fight those twenty years every day." Bobby worried that the "fight," combined with how hard Lewis pushed himself to succeed, "was killing Scott."

A day after he lost his electricity, Bobby paid the bill. Hours later, he was still waiting for his lights to be switched back on. He remained mystified how the charges had been so high. But he didn't doubt that he was at fault. Losing light was, he said, "For me a way to learn responsibility. I'm used to my mind drifting off. That's how we were in there." Over and over, year following year, he achieved the same revelations, the redundancy of revelations itself eventually a revelation.

Bobby's life was short on stirring events, and those occurrences that did happen were often interior. What Bobby wanted, he said, was "to be a different me." He hoped for a career, no great expectations, just something fulfilling for the straightforward person he was. At present, he had no prospects. Branford had become a waystation, somewhere to reset. Looking forward, Bobby scanned the region for a place that personified the self-reliant existence he craved, as though he could finally absorb it by geographic location. Considering the state's employment demographics, such osmosis wasn't such a bad assumption. "I like the environment of Milford," Bobby proposed, mentioning the town Uncle Brock had taken him to buy the Accord. "Everybody goes to work. It's a working environment. Active. Industrious."

People who knew Bobby heard he'd moved to Georgia, journeyed off into the New South with its New Economy, a migration to a new him. The new places college and work took people were how many found in their lives what Bobby wanted: close community, a wife, a safe home with a garden—which he called "The Destination." For now, he was like the young men of his grandfather's generation in lonesome-whistle country towns, who used to watch the daily goods train pass by and think about going where the boxcars went. "The little clean town of Milford!" Bobby said brightly. "Spotless. I love it. Never can be too clean for me."

PART VI

AMERICAN DREAMS

Chapter Twenty

For many years, a highlight of summer in Newhallville was the annual round-robin playground basketball tournament held across several weekends on the pale-green concrete court in the park next to Lincoln-Bassett Elementary School. The tournament featured teams made up from the best players in the city. Crowds lined up five rows deep, people peering through fencing links that left such minimal out-of-bounds space, the spectators were part of the play.

In the hot, humid summer of 2018, as Bobby settled into his new apartment out in Branford, he would have liked to attend, but he was gone to ground, avoiding the tournament, and so were most people. In recent days, there had been a chain reaction of shootings in Newhallville, and social media was aflame with threats of more. Social media threads could achieve such traction; they subsumed any other explanation in the confluence of possible factors besides gun violence for why people weren't showing up at a basketball tournament. "Praying for my city," people wrote. Downtown, in the fourth-floor police operations room, department commanders charted gunshot exchanges, tracing the interconnection of victims and weapons.

Despite the fear, in late July the pale-green court was again a Newhallville public performance space, and before a sparse crowd, basketball teams began playing for pride on six consecutive Sundays. Most players wore Jordans and bright-colored T-shirts sometimes emblazoned with the names of sponsoring local businesses and then embellished by players who used Sharpies to add a basketball moniker, such as "Kyrie." One team brought with them an extra shirt with "RIP" written on it. While that team played, they looped the shirt through the fencing like a prayer flag, in memory of a former teammate. A longtime neighborhood resident, Rodney Williams, who owned a construction business, said that this was also a more general way of "showing love" for the many "people that died from Newhallville."

Beyond the court was a greensward set up with large grills that made the sweltering air fragrant with cooking meats, enlivening the other sounds and the smells of the tournament—the whack of a ball propelled through rimmed metal, ice-cream-truck bells, skilled trash talk, the sweetness of weed and body lotion, courtside tunes that competed with the downbeats from twenty car audio systems, the PA announcer rejoicing over notable rejections. It was so atmospheric everything seemed almost usual. The sidewalk foot traffic was also lively, if thin. One kid made the scene in a white T-shirt that proclaimed HAVING FUN ISN'T HARD WHEN YOU HAVE A LIBRARY CARD. He didn't actually own library privileges but said young ladies liked the shirt. When Tim-Buck II came along, you could hear him stopping to counsel some hustlers, "Not how I'd play it."

The police were also there. A muscular white lieutenant in a Red Sox ballcap moved through the crowd, offering free chilled drinks he'd paid for himself. Everyone recognized Karl Jacobson, and those who knew him liked him for being one of those heart-on-his-sleeve cops in it to make a difference.

As the tournament weeks progressed, the crowds stayed small. The police tended to park their cruisers beyond the court on narrow, tree-shaded Ivy Street, and most officers clustered there. One said, "For years we always have thirty or forty cops in the park. And somebody gets shot anyway. It's 'I've got a beef with you and I know you're gonna be there because everybody's there.'"

Into this tensed neighborhood moment, steps from where Bobby, Kwame, and Terry had all lived, on the last Sunday in July, arrived the street outreach worker William "Juneboy" Outlaw, with a lawn chair, which he set down facing the court from right smack in the middle of the sidewalk along Shelton Avenue, his address long ago, as his own youthful street days were beginning. Here in the heat, Outlaw was resplendent, his great bodily girth set off handsomely by a crisp checked shirt, designer sunglasses, and a gold tooth. Sherman Malone, a leader of the antiviolence organization Outlaw worked for, said of him, "You can't succeed in the criminal world without real skills. But it's very hard for us to find people who are not still entranced with their skills. William isn't. But William's like a politician."

Sure enough, the lawn chair became a congressional office, attracting a procession of seekers and supplicants. Among them was a young man in his late teens with a dark-blue sleeveless shirt and strain all over his face. Sleeveless wanted Outlaw to know that another kid, notably small and swaggering, whom he named, had stolen his purple bicycle. Both were from the housing project three blocks away. When Sleeveless briefly left his bike unlocked outside his apartment, Swagger had ridden off on it. Sleeveless seemed both subdued and yet holding within him a deep anger to be without his bike and reduced to pressing his case to Outlaw. Kids in Newhallville, Outlaw would say later, have so little that what they do own matters too much to them. One crucial thing the bike meant to Sleeveless: it was his means of periscoping trouble in the near distance and evading it.

As Outlaw and Sleeveless were talking, Swagger came into view, swooping down Shelton on Sleeveless's bike. Spotting Sleeveless, he banged a right and disappeared along Brewster Street, toward Dixwell. Sleeveless turned back to Outlaw and said in a flat voice that he either wanted his bike back or Swagger owed him eighty bucks. Outlaw told Sleeveless the bike would be returned if it was really his, but was it? He hadn't stolen it himself, had he? No, it wasn't a stolie, Sleeveless said. His cousin had given it to him three years ago. Sleeveless didn't want any beef. He didn't want anything at all, except his bike. Sleeveless looked far beyond tired, like the oldest teenager in history. The furrow in his brow was a two-month ditch. Would Outlaw help, he asked, effort emanating. Outlaw would help. Sleeveless closed his eyes and took a breath. He opened his eyes and blinked them for the first time since he'd arrived.

Outlaw telephoned Kermit Carolina, the popular neighborhood native who'd been the Hillhouse principal and was now in charge of Youth Stat, a city government organization that partnered with assorted social-service and law-enforcement agencies, identifying and working with the most at-risk kids in the school system. The stories Carolina's cell-phone contacts list could tell were so tragic, people wondered how he retained his well-known bonhomie. Within minutes, Carolina arrived at Outlaw's chair, clad in dapper black workout gear—he was also a former state-championship-winning Hillhouse basketball coach. In no time, Carolina and Outlaw had communicated with Swagger about Sleeveless's bike, which Swagger agreed to return in exchange for a $10 "finder's fee" he negotiated from Outlaw. Then, almost right away, here came Swagger, lean, diminutive, cocksure, and strutting. Everything about Swagger advertised what was true; that he had friends with guns. To look at him was to confront Sleeveless's just-around predicament—

and Bobby's and Henry Green's. You had to prove yourself so many times to those who tried you, and it never, ever stopped.

The two peace negotiators pulled Swagger aside and talked to him vigorously. The agreement was brokered, the $10 paid over, and then Outlaw said sternly to Swagger, "That's the end of this. Stops here. I don't want to hear anything more." He looked meaningfully at Swagger, and told him, "I gave you twenty last week." He meant that crime paid, but not forever. Only now did Swagger quite leisurely depart, and then return minutes later with the bike. It was a simple mountain-bike model, and not, in fact, purple, but red with uneven streaks of blue spray-painted over portions of the red. Both coats of color had sustained abundant scrapes and scratches, and the frame tubing was well buffered with use. A thick chain with lock was coiled around the seat post. Swagger walked off without looking at Sleeveless. Sleeveless had never looked at him. Once Swagger was gone, Sleeveless hopped on his bike and rode away. As he did, Outlaw and Carolina simultaneously yelled to him to use that chain from now on. Sleeveless called back that the chain wouldn't work because he couldn't unlock it from the seat post.

Outlaw and Carolina agreed that the second coat of spray paint probably did mark the bike as a stolie. They had pessimism about Swagger. He was close to another neighborhood kid whose ascendant street reputation had won him the nickname Little BlackJack. Everything Outlaw and Carolina knew about Swagger made them very worried for Sleeveless. In this time when handguns had become widely accessible to young people, and an accepted way among them of settling arguments, beefs that ended in death had begun over much less. With Swagger living in his apartment complex, how was Sleeveless going to navigate his day-to-day? Neither Outlaw nor Carolina could in any way promise Sleeveless his well-being. Was he now in peril for snitching to them about his bike? Or was being paid to "return" a bike he'd stolen a sufficient victory for Swagger that Sleeveless's possible breach of street code could be overlooked? Could Swagger have scammed with Sleeveless to play Outlaw for some cash? Unlikely. But Outlaw and Carolina never estimated the ingenuity of teenagers. It was likewise easy for the two violence interrupters to imagine Sleeveless becoming so cornered by menace, he might acquire a gun himself, and try to take out Swagger, which would solve Sleeveless's problem and also armor him with a street reputation. Sleeveless didn't seem like that kind of kid at all, but you never knew how thermal pressure in the cannister of only bad choices could transform someone into a shooter. Getting the gun would be the easy part for Sleeveless; one could be arranged at a price not much more than the value of a beat-up mountain bike.

The 2018 basketball tournament ended without any shootings, but plenty of young Newhallville people were routinely "terrified," as one fifteen-year-old described himself in 2020. That was three years after a just-around friend of his was shot on a Newhallville sidewalk for what reason the fifteen-year-old still didn't know. Now a cousin had been shot. And now again a man down the block. The fifteen-year-old said he'd solved his personal terror by acquiring "protection." For his other pocket, he was saving up for a cell phone. Except his terror didn't seem solved. The combination of a few shootings and widespread discussion of violence heightened the fear affecting everyone.

Near the court lived the Black journalist Babz Rawls-Ivy, who'd been brought up in 1960s Newhallville. She'd recently returned because "Newhallville is so vibrant. I love sitting on my porch watching young Black kids walking their dog. Black people hand in hand walking down the block. Roller-skaters. Moms and dads with their little kids." Rawls-Ivy's own children were grown-up now and, she said, that had made the timing right for her to return. "I wouldn't raise kids here," she said sadly. "It's too hard to be a working mother with keeping your arms around them. There's so much danger."

An *American Journal of Public Health* study had found New Haven's violence "disproportionately occurs in communities experiencing social and economic inequities, including residential racial segregation and concentrated poverty." Residents like Rawls-Ivy wondered how people could occupy the same zip code, share the same alderman and police substation, and not feel compelled to do something about an adjoining neighborhood where there was just one park for kids, who were too scared of getting shot to use it.

People existed who did care, who were spending their lives thinking about preventing neighborhood gun violence. Those who collectively, as an institution, had been thinking the longest in New Haven were the police, the outside officials who came most regularly to Newhallville. And just as neighborhoods were not monoliths, neither were police departments. A New Haven chief from the late 1960s, James Ahern, had regarded his work through a sociological lens. Ahern published a book, *Police in Trouble*, in which he linked crime reduction with giving poor men "a feeling of identity" and "meaningful jobs." Two decades after Ahern's time came the crack epidemic, and regressive policing policies like the "beatdown posse" of officers who came bursting out of unmarked vans to "tune up" sidewalk drug dealers. A staggering 106 murders between 1989 and 1991 soon led Chief Nick Pastore, with help from his assistant chief, Dean Esserman, to bring "community policing" to New Haven. Pastore, who as a young patrolman filled Oak Street–area parking meters out of his own pocket instead of placing tickets on windshields, argued that "mean-spirited policing leads to mean streets," and urged his officers to immerse themselves in the character of their districts, knowing people on personal terms. That way, when violence did arise, the community would want to help.

Violence declined while Pastore was in command. But following Pastore's departure, violent crime rose during Bobby's teenage years. The corruption scandal that had enveloped Willoughby and others coincided with murder by handgun becoming, according to police, the leading cause of death for young Black and Latino men in "gun-wavin' New Haven."

In 2011, 34 people were killed, almost all Black men, and 268 people were shot, leaving Mayor DeStefano brooding about how "we lost our way" with policing. On a flight to Washington, DeStefano became absorbed in a new book, *Don't Shoot*, which argued for proactive policing that focused on identifying the few individuals most prone to violence in neighborhoods and deterring them before they shot people—or were shot themselves. In *Don't Shoot*, the mayor confronted a description of his own city as having "a terrible reputation for youth violence." DeStefano's plane landed, he walked through the airport terminal, and encountered Nick Pastore's former deputy, Esserman. The chance meeting again changed New Haven policing when DeStefano offered Esserman the job of chief.

In Newhallville, most believed the neighborhood was simultaneously under- and over-policed, Shay among them. The preferable relationship, she thought, was the police should understand Newhallville by engaging residents. "A lot of the cops here are from outside neighborhoods, so they don't really know what goes on in the neighborhood," she said. "The beat walkers have no idea what they're walking through." She thought "they should be more a part of the community. Like you know how people have to take a citizenship test. They need to take a community test."

Esserman was with her. The son of a New York family doctor who made house calls from Harlem to SoHo, Esserman believed police should have a similar outlook as "family cops." Under him, New Haven became the only department in the country, he said, where all academy graduates walked the beat for their first year of service. Aware that the high rate of unsolved murders in poor Black communities had convinced residents the police didn't care about them, making them uncooperative with police, leading to more murders, the chief established a cold case unit. He regarded successful reentry from prison as crime prevention and arranged meet-and-greets hosted by the police for every resident returning from incarceration. Esserman asked his officers to take into consideration the financial circumstances of rule violators and gave the discretion not to impose tickets and fines upon poor people. Instead of solve rates and arrest totals, he prioritized tight cases against those who were the primary drivers of violent crime.

Policing was a little like professional baseball—a tradition-bound American institution suddenly attracting both sophisticated data analysis and leaders with Ivy League degrees. The Dartmouth-educated Esserman instituted CompStat, the use of shared data and information by law-enforcement partners to oppose crime. Jack Maple, with inspiration from George Kelling, was generally credited with its conception, yet well before Kelling, the basic CompStat idea was right there in James Ahern's book about New Haven. Under Esserman, every week the New Haven police department hosted fourth-floor meetings attended by members of law enforcement from surrounding towns, state and federal agencies, from community and social service organizations, from schools, hospitals, and the courts. Leads relating to specific crimes were discussed in relation to emerging trends and patterns of crime. Everybody could weigh in on how to keep violence from ruining a basketball tournament that was dear to a neighborhood.

The Newhallville street cop most extolled by Esserman was a Black military veteran in his fifties with a pencil-thin mustache named Robert Hayden. "We solve half our crimes because of his cell phone," the chief said. He meant Hayden knew so many people that when a crime took place, he could examine sidewalk video, recognize those who'd been nearby, consult with them, and develop suspects. Hayden liked to arrive suddenly for his conversations, defeating lookouts by driving in the wrong direction down one-way streets, threading his way on foot through backyards, jumping fences, abruptly appearing from alleys and driveways to shout his signature greeting, "What's up, Mah," and his signature question: "Do you have any drugs or weapons?" Hayden could tell whose pants were suddenly sagging in a way that suggested firearm acquisition, was relentless in his pursuits, and made more arrests and recovered more illegal firearms than any officer.

This made Hayden a source of ambivalence around Newhallville, where he was derisively known as "Uncle." There were "Fuck Hayden" tags spray-painted on building walls, and grandmothers whose opinion was "he didn't figure out how to step it down." Hayden said he was unbothered: "One woman told me, 'I hate you, but I know if you're here my son won't get shot.'" Driving around Newhallville, he could point out a drug dealer of whom Hayden said, "He put a $20,000 hit on me." Kids in the game, he said, had created a system that told them which cops worked their shifts when. Hayden thought of himself as protecting the peaceful majority whose lives were disrupted by the problem few.

Yet Hayden also had sympathy for gun-carrying, street-corner men. Hayden was the unequivocal enemy of violence, but "everything else, we can talk about it." He knew a teenager who carried a shotgun. "The parents were always yelling at me, 'Why are you bothering my son?'" Hayden said. "But they eventually realized it's not personal. I can arrest you today and buy you a soda tomorrow and sit down and drink it with you." When the man found a job and began driving to work, Hayden knew he didn't have a driver's license, but never ticketed him. Scott Shumway had adopted similar methods. "I'm not one for doing motor-vehicle enforcement in this neighborhood unless for a reason—we're looking for somebody," Shumway said. "I understand that registration, insurance, making it to the DMV—it's expensive. So it's a vicious cycle. You need money, but you need to go to work to get it."

Under Esserman, the number of shootings and homicides in New Haven plummeted. Following Michael Brown's 2014 death at the hands of a Ferguson, Missouri, police officer, the head of the Department of Justice's Civil Rights Division in the Obama administration, Vanita Gupta, said that New Haven was a "model" for community policing.

"Model" was a charged word in this city. Within police departments, lieutenants are typically beloved, while the chief is rarely popular. Plenty of veteran New Haven police officers chafed about Esserman, sniped that he wasn't a true cop but a prosecutor who'd never made an arrest. But among people in New Haven's Black neighborhoods, Esserman was praised. One of the city's leading civil rights lawyers, Michael Jefferson, approved "because a lot of police officers didn't. Told me he didn't care about being liked. He held folks accountable. And he understood racism. He got it." Older women from Newhallville were grateful to the chief for freely distributing his cell-phone number, said even if you called him in the middle of the night, "he made it happen." The chief was also popular with academics, like Yale's Andrew Papachristos, who considered such "forward thinking" rare in a police chief. Esserman and Tracey Meares, the first Black woman tenured at Yale Law School, had long conversations about her research, which found what civilians most want is their dignity, the chance to tell their side, to feel confidence that the police are fair and listen in a caring way. Papachristos discussed with Esserman his data about the network nature of neighborhood violence in American cities, but Papachristos was also vexed about Esserman's propensity for "inexplicable" acts of self-destructive behavior. Esserman had a temper, and in 2016, when he'd too often lost it in public, a five-year crime decline was no match for the outcry that he resign, which he did.

By then, what had happened to Bobby with Willoughby and Quinn was considered, by police department leaders, of "a different time." The department now worked with violence interrupters like Stacy Spell of Project Longevity. This organization used David Kennedy's ideas about proactive policing, and part of Spell's job was offering in-person "custom notifications" to those identified in New Haven as most at risk for violent crime. If they renounced guns, they'd be offered community support; if not, they'd be the focus of police attention.

"We're gonna *warn* them?" was Karl Jacobson's reaction. Jacobson was the burly white cop from the basketball tournament. As an award-winning member of gun-violence suppression units, he'd been used to policies like "flooding the area," which meant rolling into neighborhoods after a shooting, shutting everything down. When Jacobson was told by Black people in Newhallville, "It's unfair about jobs, it's unfair about living conditions," his reaction had been "I'm a local cop. I'm not the government." Jacobson said Project Longevity's approach made him understand that when he walked through a door, he was "hated" for embodying every white bureaucrat who'd come by with checklists and threats. Now when he met members of Newhallville families who'd been there since the 1950s, he admired their homes, told them that he cared about the neighborhood, wished he'd grown up in such a close-knit place. He began to relish helping Newhallville kids get their driver's licenses, took prom-night photographs, arranged visits to job fairs. He decided, "I love body cameras. Holds us accountable." Around Newhallville, Jacobson said, "I tell them I didn't sign up to decimate a section of society. Mandatory minimums. I used to think they're great. Now they're ridiculous." In 2018, when Jacobson made a gun arrest in the middle of Newhallville, something surprising happened to him. People began clapping.

Violence interrupters and better policing policies helped New Haven follow the American trend with sharp statistical reductions in rates of shooting in the pre-COVID years. The Connecticut violent-crime analyst Ivan Kuzyk said part of the explanation was open-air drug markets had mostly given way to more discreet cell-phone dealing: "hit men and robbers like Major don't have the flow of cash that sustained the gun culture." But there remained two Americas. Connecticut was a small, wealthy state, yet violent crime in New Haven remained well beyond the national average, and three times higher than the typical city of its size. Kuzyk said Black men who lived "socially and economically isolated" in poor, unstable postindustrial communities within cities like New Haven, Hartford, and Bridgeport still had good reason to fear. "Connecticut shouldn't have three such violent cities," Kuzyk said. He thought often about a Black Hartford teenager he'd met who, at age seventeen, convinced a police officer to buy him a bulletproof vest, which then became part of his underwear—what he put on every morning above his briefs when he got dressed. "There's no white kids living in a community where they feel they need to put on a bulletproof vest every day," Kuzyk said. Fear of gunshots smashed and smashed at some people until they were so emotionally worn down, they imploded. "Criminals are largely created by alienation," Kuzyk thought. Such violence-induced depression was rarely treated, so Kuzyk said that even if sent to prison, men completed their sentences as "traumatized young people returning to the same place that traumatized them."

Kuzyk was programmatic, an engineer seeking to describe troubled human systems. One way he'd tried to explain modern gun violence was by thinking about Major. Even after Bobby was arrested for the murder of Pete Fields, Kuzyk's impulse from his desk in Hartford still was still to consider this a Major crime. Kuzyk had never met Major, didn't know anybody who had, but there in his data was what Kuzyk considered the personification of the shocking number of young Black men being shot in Connecticut's postindustrial city neighborhoods.

Kuzyk agreed with scholars who found that American gun violence mostly involves adults but usually has its roots in adverse childhoods. An expert in patterns of trauma would notice that a child who lost his mother in the way Major did might well lose a sense of security, might feel unwanted by parents who weren't there to raise him, by the society that didn't respect his personal promise and instead exposed him to gunfire, leading him, with his ready access to guns, to punish in return. Comparing Newhallville with "Belfast during the occupation," Kuzyk said that while young men like Major weren't Catholic political guerrillas in balaclavas, they had a similar desire for belonging, a need to feel included in something significant. Kuzyk linked the racialized disparities in neighborhood opportunity with racialized disparities in violence.

The only solution Kuzyk could imagine for the disadvantages he saw in Connecticut's cities was what had first brought aspiring people to them: well-paying jobs. The factories of Hartford had lifted Kuzyk's own immigrant family. In the vacuum of a postindustrial solution, violence was now an intergenerational inheritance, people without hope connected by bright orbits of gunfire. Major's feeling for history interested Kuzyk. He thought Major would have understood himself to have lived in a way that revealed his postindustrial neighborhood's devastation. The problem in making the overcoming of adversity such an American virtue was that, in Major's world, almost nobody could do it.

Long after his death, in the Newhallville streets Major's reputation lived. Kuzyk thought this mystique expressed the plight of many people who felt excluded by society and its systems. "In a way," Kuzyk said, "the attention Major got was very similar to Depression-era gangsters. Dillinger, Pretty Boy Floyd. Major was kind of like that. Someone who emerged as something special. How many teenagers in New Haven do people still remember? A lot of people in the criminal justice system are unimpressive people. Major was a star. His problem, and the problem for a lot of kids, is the stage he can star on is small. And how he becomes a star is his tragedy. There's a half-life on reputation. It's a wonder to me there aren't more Majors."

SINCE 2006, BOBBY, of course, had heard a lot about Major. Bobby and Major had important virtues in common, their fatherly roles in their families, the person who could calm distraught younger household members, the one their grandmothers considered "my heart," the student who defended their teachers, those in whom teachers saw unusual personal potential. But they were two very different boys on bikes. Bobby hadn't known Major well, but he had compassion for him. Terrible events happened, intertwining children in a form of violent empathy. It was as though Major had become Bobby's secret sharer, Bobby sensing in his neighbor "so much pain. Major was a great dude. Major been going through a lot of things his whole life." Bobby's conclusion was "at the end of the day he felt adult despair too early."

Plenty of social scientists rejected the idea of causal connection between violence and inequality, but Bobby thought the lives of Major, Green, and so many others he'd known suggested one existed. Living in privation and fear and yet so close to all, it seemed, a kid could want, in some people encouraged a homicidal hopelessness that made violence more viable: "Being from the rusty, dirty neighborhood, and then mansions, and we're struggling, it adds a level of anger." As the inequality got worse in New Haven, Bobby believed, the shooting was "only gonna get worse."

It made intuitive sense that, in a country that placed great emphasis on economic aspiration, those who felt they had no legitimate means of achieving their American dreams would feel intense frustration and shame. Someone who thought that was Dean Esserman's successor, New Haven's second African American police chief, Anthony Campbell. Campbell was from Harlem. His mother was a Riker's Island corrections officer; his father sold drugs and was in and out of prison. When Campbell became the first member of his family to attend college, he joined the Yale class of 1995. One reason Campbell was later well suited to New Haven as its police chief was that, from personal experience, he understood the city in terms of opportunity and its shadow: "When you can walk three minutes, make a right and see nothing but wealth and security and well-being, happiness, people with future outlooks hopeful and bright, and you're looking over your shoulder because you might be harmed, you worry about eating, rent, that wealth becomes a magnifying glass that takes any light and turns it into a laser beam that cuts you to the core: 'They don't care. They're right there, they *have* to notice, and they don't care.' Becomes 'I got to do what I got to do.'"

By now there were researchers documenting, as one New Haven study did, a relationship between rates of violence and "socioeconomic inequalities between neighborhoods." The Canadian evolutionary psychologists Margo Wilson and Martin Daly found that the Gini Index of inequality was a surprisingly good predictor of homicide rates. Homicide rates, Daly said, had always been highest in segregated American ghettos where for poor, uneducated men, whether Irish, Italian, or Black, violence was a rational and relational decision—a means of demonstrating freedom and agency for those alienated from the mainstream with little ability to change their circumstances. If within your community it was a gun that could most empower you, that would make some people more willing to shoot.

For several years, Andrew Papachristos and Tracey Meares taught Yale courses on the study of city neighborhoods, gun violence, and policing, and worked in collaboration with city residents, advising Esserman, Campbell, and other New Haven police on how to reduce shooting in this city. When Papachristos returned to his hometown of Chicago to teach at Northwestern University, he thought back on the years he'd spent in New Haven in relation to subsequent criminal-justice reform movements, like defunding American police departments. Papachristos could in theory support plenty of alternative means of performing community-related roles that police were not really trained for. The job requirements for police had always shifted; early American police responsibilities included lighting streetlamps, street sweeping, and serving food to the poor in soup kitchens. But Papachristos wasn't yet sure anybody but professionally trained "preventionists," whether called police or something else, could be charged with protecting neighborhoods from violence. Intervention really worked, and trusted community members like Jahad, Spell, Carmon, Outlaw, and Carolina could make a difference. But they couldn't be available to deescalate the thousands of small moments in a summer day that might potentially blaze into gunshots. And if you ceded the whole role to untrained amateurs from the community, Papachristos feared you might get perversions of justice—might get George Zimmerman, who was on neighborhood-watch when he killed Trayvon Martin. Papachristos understood that with bad policing, you got Bobby, creating a devastating lack of trust in neighborhoods, increasing the sense of disenfranchisement. He knew that improving policing techniques was vitally important.

Yet to Papachristos, and many others, the biggest policing problem in communities like Newhallville was the entrenched inequity of the system. Policing was a responsive profession. By the time people attracted the attentions of Willoughby, Hayden, Shumway, or Jacobson, they were already in some form of crisis. "Unless you change the big stuff," Papachristos said, "nothing really changes. Unless you change the network, the same problems get inherited. The police can't and shouldn't fix schools and jobs and poverty."

Chapter Twenty-One

What could be done about the grim medley of inequities in housing, education, healthcare, jobs, and every other root cause that added up to the disproportionate violence in segregated neighborhoods was a great, enduring American dilemma. As a matter of both economic scale and intellectual challenge, finding solutions to such an urgent national issue seemed to call out for the resources of a great, enduring American institution. In New Haven, that meant Yale University. The challenge was that Yale had long considered the problems of the city to be none of its business.

There was no starker illustration of the have-and-have-not nature of New Haven than the elite university enclosed by Black poverty. Yale's origins as what is now called a tax-exempt nonprofit educational institution were of a time when offering support to the college was, as the legislature held just before the American Revolution, "Of the greatest Publick importance." Yale then was, in effect, a public school—a poor local institution that offered educations to future local leaders and also advanced social and scientific work of direct practical value to the community. (In 1761, every lawyer in New Haven had been to Yale.) The college flourished because the city population, and the state's General Assembly, forgave or paid its debts, granted easements, offered large financial subsidies, did not send tax bills. In 1831, meanwhile, an effort to open a college for Blacks met with mob resistance. A New Haven newspaper described the "ruinous" effect it would have upon "public morals." The *Boston Courier* blamed "apprehension of giving offense to the Southern patrons of Yale College."

In 1933, a residential college named for the slavery champion, South Carolina politician John Calhoun, opened replete with stained-glass windows depicting enslaved people working in the cotton fields and shackled at Calhoun's feet.

As the century progressed, Yale's wrought-iron gates to courtyards and quadrangles, high stone walls, and sunken moats suggested a neo-Gothic garrison fending off New Haven. Since the early nineteenth century Yale had regularly absorbed public contumely about neglecting and depleting New Haven. The city's numerous town-gown riots had as incitements and features grave-robbing by medical students and a large brass cannon aimed by locals at the campus walls. It was perhaps telling that, in 1894, Yale had created the country's first campus police force. In the 1930s, Mayor John Murphy became so incensed at what the erosion of the tax base was doing to his budget, he accused Yale of "eating into the vitals of the city." In the 1960s, Yale political scientist Robert Dahl said the strained coexistence defined New Haven as "a city where rancor between town and gown is never far below the surface."

The relative distance between Yale and New Haven sometimes was crossed by violence. Between 1985 and 1995, there was so much larceny and robbery on Yale property that *USA Today* called it the country's most dangerous campus. The 1991 murder of a student led Yale to modernize security. Experienced New Haven police officers were recruited to Yale's force for higher wages. Meanwhile, some of Yale's Black students made a habit of wearing attire inscribed with the word "Yale" around campus so the police wouldn't keep confronting them.

Yale did not in any significant way attempt to apply its resources to understanding and addressing the unemployment, dropout rates, poverty, hunger, and youth violence in besieged city areas, like Newhallville, where people around the age of undergraduates were killed in numbers year after year. To critics who contended the university's prospering was interconnected with its New Haven history, meaning Yale should "do more," the quiet response was that Yale's mission was education, research, and creating new ideas, and that much of Yale's money was directed—had been raised for specific goals and, accordingly, was air-locked with restrictions and terms. It was also noted that New Haven's poverty contrasted with wealthy surrounding towns, which relied on city institutions and services but paid no New Haven taxes. Another belief was that a once-thriving manufacturing town fallen on hard times was lucky to be affixed to the compelling ornament it was subsidizing. A commonly heard shorthand for this was "Without Yale, New

Haven is Bridgeport." The modern Yale administrator who over the decades had taken the greatest formal interest in Newhallville was Henry "Sam" Chauncey Jr., a white descendant of the first Yale graduate who kept a painting of the Yale bulldog on his living-room wall. Chauncey said, "The problem is that everybody at Yale lives in a world that denies the existence of the real world that is around them." His belief was "Yale always acted like the manor on the hill." Only in 2017, the year after Corey Menafee, a Black dishwasher, smashed the Calhoun College "slave window" with a broomstick, saying it was "degrading" to work under, leading to national opprobrium, did the university deem Calhoun's legacy in fundamental conflict with the university mission and rename it Grace Hopper College.

These views (and attitudes) were not Yale's alone. "All town-gown relationships are unhappy, each in their own way," said Steven Conn, an urban historian at Miami (Ohio) University. Prestigious universities alongside impoverished communities had become an American phenomenon, from Baltimore to Durham to Palo Alto to Chicago, where, in 1958, Lawrence Kimpton, chancellor of the University of Chicago, said, "It is not possible to operate and maintain a great university in a deteriorating or slum neighborhood." Beginning in the 1980s, admitted a former Harvard dean, "the view was keep the neighborhood at arm's length."

In postindustrial New Haven, the city often lacked the resources to meet its basic costs. New Haven's 2020 municipal budget was under $600 million. Yale's operating budget was more than $4 billion, sometimes at surplus. Back in the 1990s, Yale had agreed to make voluntary payments instead of taxes, and spokespeople could reliably list bountiful other contributions, like funding scholarships for locals. But New Haven's white mayor Justin Elicker, who had two Yale degrees, winced at the public relations. As an alderman, he'd watched aghast as the city met a budget shortfall by selling four actual street blocks to Yale for $3 million. By his calculation, property exemptions saved Yale more than $146 million a year. When, in 2021, Yale's endowment value passed $42 billion, Yale agreed to pay over to the city an additional $52 million over the next six years and seed $5 million during that period toward a new Center For Inclusive Growth at Yale's business school. In return, Yale was ceded control of another street block. Thomas Piketty, in his 2013 book *Capital in the Twenty-First Century*, compared tax-free endowments like Yale's to inherited wealth, noting how contrary this was to the stated spirit of American education, which was promoting social mobility.

Yale was the dominant feature of New Haven's landscape, and in Newhallville, everything Yale did was regarded through a smolder of suspicion, the detectable resentment of those who had no agency confronting an institution whose power they could scarcely fathom but profoundly felt. As one of Bobby's friends said, "You don't have to pay taxes, but the poor people still have to." When Bobby first encountered the Yale campus on his bicycle, the discovery of this new world was what he hated about New Haven, that there was no flow between communities. Shay wondered what it said about Yale, that the university had prospered beyond anybody's imagination in a city that was an American exemplar of concentrated inequity. Inevitably, the worst was imagined of Yale's motives. Bobby's friend Little Blue explained his point of view by taking out his telephone and placing it on a table next to a plate. "It's like this," he said. "Newhallville's the slums, and I never heard of them doing anything for Newhallville." Little Blue said that juxtaposition had led him to commit serious crimes as a high school kid. "Any way you can get it, you gotta get it," he said. "If they won't help you, gotta go on the block."

These were old American problems, old American divisions, and they created old American feelings. In 1854, Herman Melville had written in "Poor Man's Pudding and Rich Man's Crumbs" of how the American poor "suffer more in mind than the poor of any other people in the world" because of "the smarting distinction between their ideal of universal equality and their grindstone experience of the practical misery and infamy of poverty." Problems persist when those who can address them don't. W.E.B. Du Bois had warned, back in 1903, that racial inequity was a risk because "whether you like it or not, the millions are here, and here they will remain. If you do not lift them up, they will pull you down." The Kerner Commission in 1968 considered two separate, unequal Americas to be "the major unfinished business of the nation," and called for funding on "unprecedented levels." Well-intended people still now felt trapped by historical duration and the Mars-landing immensity of the task.

ONE EXPLANATION FOR why colleges remained disengaged from the poor, segregated neighborhoods in their midst was a lack of personal experience with them. Most faculty came from white echelons of elsewhere and felt a part of the institution, not the town. It wasn't until 1988 that Yale College tenured an African American woman, art historian Sylvia Ardyn Boone. Tracey Meares's appointment at the law school came nineteen years after that. As more people of color achieved positions of influence in universities, some began asking why a university's priority shouldn't be to uplift the chronically disadvantaged. At Yale, the senior vice president of Human Resources at Yale–New Haven Hospital was Kevin Myatt, an executive who, as a child had come from his home in the South for summertime visits with a favorite uncle who lived on the Newhallville line, among the first Black homeowners in Highwood. "When I drive through Newhallville, my heart hurts," Myatt said. "We need to help it grow." In an increasingly restive time, for a nonprofit institution to hoard resources in a poor city also seemed untenable public ethics. Sam Chauncey thought eventually endowments of wealthy private universities would be taxed, but only after "a huge court battle that will last years."

Why wait? Deans said that certainly money could be raised for community development, but such an initiative required a case being made within the educational mission. Yet Yale wasn't just a wealthy, prestigious institution. Yale was, to the country, the shining example of significant research accomplishment, at the forefront of the nation's pandemic response, creating the rapid COVID-19 saliva test, developing wastewater testing, and supplying the government with prominent emergency public-health officials. And what was postindustrial poverty if not a great national problem, exactly the sort of pursuit universities existed to engage with. Big institutions don't often change out of guilt. But would not a robust dedication to postindustrial studies, examining the structures that shape communities—everything from economic inequality to job creation to violence to the interplay of history—fall not only within the great university's capability but also within its own enlightened self-interest? Deindustrialization, wrote Columbia University's Nobel laureate economist Edmund Phelps, meant "markedly fewer lead the good life." Postindustrial urban inequality with its global ramifications was too big a problem for small neighborhood organizations to solve, too big a problem for mayors with lean budgets, daily governance, and two-year terms. So was gun violence. As the COVID year of 2020 brought the largest ever American recorded increase in homicides, New Haven's murders and shootings increased 50 percent. The next year, shootings slightly declined, but murders rose again. In his 2021 State of New Haven Address, Elicker said "most people in our city do not feel safe from violence."

Newhallville's interactive experience with Yale as a research institution had often meant participating in academic studies. When Bobby saw a city bus with an advertisement on its side that offered $365 OR MORE TO THOSE WHO EXPERIENCE DEPRESSION he was quick to note, "That's a Yale study. They want to use us like guinea pigs. I am not their guinea pig." His reaction spoke to a long American history of appropriation and exploitation. People in Newhallville were quick to mention the Tuskegee syphilis study. The belief that researchers dating back to slavery cared more about their work than any rights or feelings of poor Black individuals created fear, even now, that Black people would be snatched off the street for use in racialized experiments. Katie-Jean Fields once had a sister living in an apartment two blocks from the campus. The Fields siblings joked that when the sister went out at night, "she needed to be careful because otherwise Yale would grab her up to do research on her." With public health, as with policing, the simple desire was to be treated with care and respect. "I'm tired of being studied," said Diane Brown, a Black librarian who grew up in Newhallville. "And once I talk to them, they don't come back."

Judith Rodin did go back. Rodin grew up in the middle-class Jewish and Catholic neighborhood of West Philadelphia, not far from the campus of the University of Pennsylvania. She went to Penn and, in 1972, became a behavioral psychologist at Yale, where she rose to be provost. During her time in New Haven, she was robbed near Prospect Street and said, "I felt exposed to crime. I felt the unsafe part, but also how amazingly interesting New Haven was." Rodin likewise saw how "the architecture of Yale is so closed to the city." Rodin was turned down for Yale's presidency because, as a member of the search committee told the *New York Times*, "Judy scared them." Instead, in 1994, Rodin became the first woman named permanent president of an Ivy League university when she took lead of her alma mater in Philadelphia.

Returning to West Philadelphia, failed businesses and crack dealers made Rodin "horrified by how much" her bustling childhood neighborhood "had changed." Right before she began as Penn president, a grad student was shot and killed by local teenagers. Rodin said hers were "typical responses" consistent with what she'd seen done at Yale: "We hunkered down and tried to protect ourselves." This had included directing students where not to walk in the city.

In 1996, after a Penn bioresearcher was stabbed to death, Black student leaders asked Rodin to introduce external student IDs so "that way other students wouldn't cross the street and would know they were Penn students." She found this "shocking" and felt "heartbreak." Rodin believed, as she later wrote in a book, *The University and Urban Revival*, that Penn's growth and expansion had "created a university island rather than an energetic, viable university city." Now, Rodin decided, "we were going to do something radically different."

With support from Penn's board, in 1998 she embraced the "prospect of taking the lead in redeveloping a distressed neighborhood that disliked us and of assuming an unprecedented level of financial and social risk." Meeting with skeptical Black politicians who challenged her, saying, "What do *you* know?" She replied, "I grew up here."

The ensuing West Philadelphia Initiatives relied on financing from the university and recommendations from Penn faculty in close consultation with the community. Rodin authorized spending over $100 million on buying the land for and then constructing a new K–8 public school and upgrading old ones, work that partnered Penn's Graduate School of Education with parents, teachers, and city officials. Wharton School of Business faculty helped develop employee training and jobs. To create affordable housing, Penn bought and renovated homes and resold them in the community. One new retail venture unpaved a parking lot and put up a fresh grocery shop. The School of Design addressed greenery and street lighting. Rodin disliked the way Penn's walls "closed out" the neighborhood, so building facades were opened to the street.

For Penn, the results were incremental, steady, and significant, including an "appreciably" declining security budget. Since academic researchers had traditionally not regarded the problems of their neighbors as suitable scholarly pursuits, notable were the 250 Penn courses from thirty departments and eleven of the university's twelve schools with applied Philadelphia elements. The area of West Philadelphia near Penn, with its fine public schools, craft breweries, and bicycle and coffee shops, became a place professional people who enjoyed city life now wanted to live.

Rochelle Nichols-Solomon, a longtime West Philadelphia Black resident and community activist, said, "Judith Rodin gets credit, but there's no silver bullet in how change happens." New solutions meant new problems. The booming real-estate market displaced longtime Black residents from the school zone near Penn to lower-resource areas of the neighborhood with inferior schools. Ira Harkavy, who'd directed Penn's Netter Center for Community Partnerships since its founding in 1992, said this "relative deprivation" was an indication that "the urban crisis remains all these years later unsolved," and now "had been highlighted by COVID."

As the public health crisis spread in early 2020, the federal government left every American state and municipality to invent its own initial policies and protocols. In New Haven, Mayor Elicker reached out for advice from

Nathaniel Raymond, a Yale professor whose expertise was global disaster response. He'd worked on genocide in Sudan, massacres in Afghanistan, in Mississippi after Hurricane Katrina. Evaluating Elicker's predicament, Raymond saw an understaffed manager limited by an insufficient budget, "trying to do it all, looking at data, not sleeping. He was so alone." Meanwhile, Yale was converting its gym into a temporary hospital with world-class testing and care. When Elicker asked if city emergency first responders could sleep in dormitories, Yale refused. After this became public, Yale belatedly offered rooms, deepening the perception of people like Raymond that Yale cared about bad national press, not about the city. "Yale never expressed any concern about New Haven," he said.

Among Raymond's grad students were active and former military, most from special forces divisions like the Green Berets, Ranger Airborne, Night Stalkers, and also the CIA. Soon Raymond organized them into a secret volunteer COVID-response unit for the city, available to Elicker's chief legislative aide, Kevin Alvarez. Each area of need, from PPE tracking to paycheck protection, was also staffed by Yale undergraduates. The city neighborhood beset by disproportionate infection and death was Newhallville. Residents, Raymond said, "had essential jobs and had to put bread on the table. They lived in multigenerational, multifamily dwellings. And they weren't isolating." He advised Elicker to focus resources on the neighborhood. Two years later, praising the mayor's COVID engagement, Raymond said, "He led."

Many other individuals, from city employees to Yale epidemiologists, performed critical individual roles, with the result that New Haven early on accomplished one of the fastest "crush curve" COVID case declines among American cities. When CNN interviewed Elicker, Raymond and the students were all watching the broadcast, and afterward held an impromptu Zoom celebration. The professor said some of the joy was, "these kids were flawless. And they couldn't talk about it. But we didn't want credit. We wanted a change in the town-gown relationship. We wanted New Haven to know we are of New Haven and for New Haven."

EDWARD BOUCHET'S FATHER came to New Haven in 1824, from South Carolina as the enslaved "body servant" of a Yale student. In 1876, Bouchet became the first Black American to earn a doctorate, a PhD in physics from Yale. Elected to Phi Beta Kappa, he sought work as a professor, but no university would hire him. Bouchet worked as a teacher of "colored youth." It has never been that children living in larger New Haven could not excel. It has always been a question of opportunity.

The New Haven people who see up close how the dangers and difficulties of neighborhood inequity affect children are other children, local heirs to Bobby, Shay, and Major, like Coral Ortiz. Ortiz gave the 2017 valedictorian's speech at the Hillhouse High School commencement on the football field, just off Newhallville's Sherman Parkway. In her graduation cap and gown, Ortiz was a slight figure beneath a white mortarboard she had strewn with colorful fabric flowers, and her voice rose with the occasion. Ortiz described the day as "an act of defiance to those who said we could not," and she told of going through high school steadily aware of the contempt others in the city felt for her and her classmates. They were, Ortiz said, dismissed as mostly low-income and first-generation children of color presumed to be without academic promise, defined by poverty, bound for prison rather than college. She told of how her classmates had been denied textbooks and computers, had watched their friends get shot while political leaders "refuse to address gun violence." In spite of these conditions, she said that across the past six years, the Hillhouse graduation rate had risen from 51 percent to 91 percent. "We've had it harder than most people," Ortiz said. "Despite this inequality, we beat the odds."

Ortiz had served as student representative to the city's board of education, and she brought to meetings the perspective of someone attending a school that provided her with AP packets to work through on her own instead of AP classes. In a city where the public schools were 86 percent non-white, the students in gifted-and-talented programs were almost 40 percent white. Black students, on average, were 2.5 grades behind whites and more than three times as likely to be suspended.

Yale law professor Monica Bell explained a consequence of going through high school years in the ways Ortiz described in her speech was "leveled aspirations" with no "entitlement to dream." In a coup for Hillhouse, Ortiz and her classmates Amber Green and Bryanna Moore were each admitted to Yale. As they contemplated their freshman year at the Ivy League college four minutes away from their school, Green recalled how during high school, "I thought of it as the gorgeous castle and I was a peasant." Ortiz noticed that she, Green, and Moore all had parents who were either educators or people deeply invested in education. Moore said that she and her two friends had also succeeded in ways similar to how at first Shay had, by finding workarounds for what their homes and school couldn't offer them, like a college counselor.

When Ortiz said that by graduating, "We beat the odds," she knew how temporary a truth this could be. People had warned Ortiz her studies at Yale would be much more challenging than at Hillhouse, but the opposite turned out to be true. Hillhouse provided no calculus teacher or calculus textbook, and so, she said, "I taught myself." At Yale, she found "libraries with millions of books," and not only professors but also tutors and abundant academic support. She was one mile east of where she'd come from, but the difference between her two New Havens struck Ortiz as "extreme." Right away, at the welcome reception for incoming freshmen, she was astonished by how "super wealthy" Yale seemed: "There were multiple forks. Serving people carried platters of lobsters. Steak. And there were all these ice sculptures." Dormitories had their own movie theaters and pottery studios. In summertime, her classmates could find vacation internships that paid them $15,000. Ortiz was grateful for her opportunities at Yale but, looking around, she said, "The big takeaway I've had is Yale and other elite universities are part of the problem, not solving it. They only get a couple of kids from inner-city schools. And in classrooms, honestly it's draining for me, and probably for Amber and Bryanna, to be the ones always offering them an understanding of the community around them. These might be future leaders. Yale should teach them how most people live."

Chapter Twenty-Two

Trying to establish a footing after you left prison could make anybody feel doubt, and for Bobby, nearly three years after leaving Big Cheshire, the challenge still often seemed impossible. In 2018, he was less resolving things than waiting them out. Since November, he'd known he would receive some form of financial compensation from the Connecticut claims commissioner for his years in a state prison as an innocent man. Bobby had no idea how much money he'd be granted or when he'd be told, and the unknown had become one more impediment to moving ahead. Without quite intending so, he'd been living for his future reward, time slipping out with the tide.

Rosenthal had heard that the commissioner's decision might be imminent, worrying Bobby that everything was about to get "more intense." People already begrudged him "the place I live, the car I drive." He was "nervous" the news would attract envy and maybe bring harm. "You can't get nothing past nobody out here," he said. "Hard for people to see someone in a better situation. Crazy, crazy world. A lot of people think I'm vulnerable now."

Bobby knew about lottery winners and NFL players from poor families who were broke in short years. Afterward, it could be difficult to find sympathy. That they'd been left with nothing meant only being back where they'd been before. Bobby wanted no part of returning to empty pockets. His intention was to invest most of whatever he received. To strengthen his resolve, Bobby began exercising more. As for women—"I'm dating myself, driving solo." He said he was counting on the money to buy him time to educate himself. These days, after his bills were paid, by the end of each month Bobby could barely afford parking meters.

Putting a worth on nine years was challenging. As the lawyer for four of the five members of the Central Park Five when they became plaintiffs in a lawsuit against New York City, Jonathan Moore had negotiated a $40 million settlement. Moore thought back wages was the least of what his clients had been owed as "young people who haven't been able to establish themselves, lost the time in life to form relationships, stand on their own two feet, interactions with family. You can't replace that. But you have to put a value on that."

Bobby's nine years represented a full interval of a person's life, especially a younger person. In photographs taken across nine years, faces transformed, clothing fell out of fashion, the color cast and tone of the photographs themselves became dated. There was also negative memory, the void of all a person never heard, never saw, never felt. It was as impossible to imagine all those moments that hadn't been as it was to turn back calendars and datebooks. The way Granddad worked on his Chevrolets, what Rosenthal put into his cases, they were expressions of self because of the continuity across years. Bobby had missed out on having a young sweetheart on Valentine's Day. He'd missed out on *not* having a young sweetheart on Valentine's Day. He'd missed out on learning from mistakes. He'd missed out on watching somebody else keep making the same mistake over and over. He'd missed out on the deepening of things. No wonder, even as he sought a new life, the old one kept calling him back.

Jonathan Moore said he believed the best way to value wrongful prison time was to ask how much a person would pay "not to spend a year in federal prison." Sitting on the couch at the apartment one day, Bobby took up the question with his cousin Tee. She wrinkled her face and inverted Moore's proposal, saying she'd take $50 million to spend a year in federal prison "as long as they deck out my cell." Bobby laughed and said it wouldn't be prison if they did that. Then he told her, "Not even fifty million would make me go back."

In mid-September, Bobby could say, "I got a check." In her judgment, the claims commissioner, Christy Scott, wrote that "powerful evidence" troubled her about the impact of prison on Bobby's youth. She described Bobby's sufferings, all the missed years of development, education, and relationships, concluded that he'd been inhibited from "an independent sense of identity." In making her financial calculations, Scott agreed that the various amounts of money Rosenthal had requested for Bobby's loss of liberty, lost enjoyment, lost earnings, and lost reputation were all reasonably assessed, but she deemed the sum proposed as just redress for Bobby's suffering to be too low. There, Scott had given Bobby more than he'd asked for.

In closing Scott wrote, "The claimant has suffered an injury the pain of which is unfathomable and which will be with him in some form or another for the rest of his life. No apology can make what happened to him right. As a member of the society that allowed its law enforcement system to go wrong and inflict this wound on him, I nevertheless would like to give him an apology that I feel from a very deep place. If I had the power to unmake this injustice, I most assuredly would. Instead, I have implemented the law enacted by the Connecticut General Assembly in the manner I believe it was intended to be used—to bring a modicum of justice and comfort to an otherwise irremediable injury."

Though nothing like the Central Park amount, after his loans were repaid, the remainder could cover Bobby's next nine years, and possibly more. In addition, he'd been awarded "life restoration" money directed for costs related to deficits in his health, education, and career training. Bobby seemed most enthused about this smaller fund. That gesture made his compensation seem not just a payout and a washing of hands but an active investment by the system in him as a worthwhile person with a destiny he was yet to fulfill.

When Rosenthal received the news, it pleased him how affected Scott had been by Bobby's case. As for the money, he urged Bobby to consider "how not to let it ruin your life." Bobby agreed, declaring, "That money's for my future family." He was abrim with courses he hoped to enroll in, including carpentry, so he wouldn't need to hire anybody to work on his future house, as well as economics, finance, and psychology. Bobby's first visit to the bank with his new account balance had been an entirely happy experience. After completing his business, as Bobby prepared to leave the bank it began raining heavily. A banker insisted he take her umbrella. That was what he wanted out of society, basic protection against life's downpours.

Money didn't appear to change anything about Bobby. When his mother had to be at work and needed someone to watch the littles, Bobby did it. His younger brother came out for a stay in Branford to give the boy a break from "all those girls," and Bobby taught him how to do the laundry and then neatly fold it. His initial purchases were, for the most part, practical. Bobby threw out the frayed wardrobe he'd worn for three years, replacing it with sweats, ballcaps, a matte-black Patagonia jacket, clothes that he liked but weren't flashy. He was sensitive to those who might look him over and say, "You got it! You fresh every day! You got money! Bobby's *too*!" His one great extravagance was purchasing a gray BMW. "I always wanted nice cars," he said. "A lot of people in jail think about it. We see cars promoted on TV and get caught in the fantasy of freedom. And it feels great, me sending pictures to Troy and Jerome. They get the chance to live through it, and they say it motivates them." Elijah Anderson could understand all that. "My dad used to drive really nice cars," the Black Yale sociologist said. "Brand-new Oldsmobile 98s. He would do it on a workingman's salary. He loved it because he felt so free in that big fancy car. People feel equal as everybody else if you're out there in a nice car."

Money also bought problems that were as old as coin. Like Frederick Douglass, whose fame, wrote his biographer David Blight, made Douglass "the target of never-ending requests for money," Bobby was left with the option of being lauded, if he said yes, or instantly resented. Douglass's financial decisions gutted his spirits while reducing his debit and credit, and similarly, Bobby's compensation stressed his relationships. That fall, Bobby found that "almost everybody asks for money. They pull me aside, catch me at an awkward moment." Most of the people he knew hadn't much, and while it was clear to him he couldn't try to save everybody without soon sinking himself, he saw that, if allowed, others would pluck him of money until "I'm naked with no clothes." But if Bobby saved only himself, he was not himself.

Worthy causes appeared unlimited. Bobby's voicemail recorded an oratorio of disasters. Other people's creditors were also regularly in touch. In none of these solicitations did anybody acknowledge that the money had come to Bobby because horrible things had happened to him, nor did those who'd abandoned him to years in prison without a visit, a commissary infusion, or a letter now regard those lapses as any brake. They took their shots anyway, made their petitions, offered up their ideas for schemes and ventures. Abner Louima, who'd received compensation after being tortured by New York City police, would respond to tugs at his own purse by saying, "I'm sorry. I don't deal in cash." Bobby didn't know quite what to say, and so "I just listen and don't respond." It helped that Granddad took him aside and counseled resolve. "My grandfather told me don't be trying to take care of people. They'll keep driving you crazy."

Bobby attempted to be magnanimous in ways that felt true to him.

From the world he wanted connection, and his family was his front line. In November he rented out a hall so that everyone could have Thanksgiving together. Close relatives, like sisters, whom he judged to be in urgent need, he helped. He gave the most by far to Grace, to pay off all her unpaid bills. The hope that generosity would bring mother and son closer instead became more evidence of how far apart nine years sometimes took them. Soon, Bobby learned, to his incredulity, that instead of attending to her liabilities she, who didn't have a license, didn't drive, bought a car for her boyfriend to drive for her, which the boyfriend then totaled. She also bought the boyfriend clothes. Why Grace did this, Bobby had "no idea." He didn't speak with his mother for "a long time." Grace avoided the Thanksgiving, but a huge contingent turned out, and Bobby was glad that everyone sat down and ate together. Some people might have found it thrilling to suddenly have a powerful role in the family, but Bobby's way was to park the BMW a considerable distance from the rented hall so as to place nothing in anybody's face.

One person who appreciated how thoughtfully Bobby was handling the sensitivities of this moment, and his impulse to protect others, including even those who'd failed to protect him, was Uncle Mikey. "Family members ask me if I've seen Bobby's new car, and he ain't giving us shit," Uncle Mikey said. "I tell them, nobody came to see him, nobody put money on his books. You can't be mad now." To Bobby, Mikey proposed, "Nobody was there for you. Now everybody has their hand out. I'd take the money and get far away from Connecticut."

For the time being, Bobby was glad to be in the well-mannered town of Branford. "Wherever you go," he said, "people always hold the door for you. So polite." He liked his neighbors, who did borrowing-of-sugar-level favors for him, as he did for them, and he felt a safe distance from the city. Late in the year he said, "Branford's the best decision of my life. Lot of the stuff I used to think about don't bother me no more."

Mostly, he kept to himself. He helped Tee to earn her driver's license, paying her fees and transporting her to her driving and safety courses. Once she passed her tests, Bobby gave her his Honda. He admired how hard Tee worked at caring for the elderly, that she was a perfect roommate. Of the living relationship, he said, "I can help for a while. She needs to make her own way." As for himself, he said, "the dream is solitude."

IN 2017, ROSENTHAL had also filed a federal civil-rights lawsuit for Bobby against the city of New Haven, as well as detectives Willoughby, Quinn, and their supervisors, charging that police malfeasance had led to Bobby's wrongful arrest, conviction, and imprisonment. Bobby knew from Scott Lewis how effective the lawyers were at Neufeld, Scheck & Brustin, the Innocence Project–derived law firm famed for trying plaintiff's wrongful conviction cases. Bobby asked Rosenthal if he would work with them on the civil-rights suit, and this was arranged. Rosenthal was the local co-counsel, part of the team, but no longer in charge. If this felt to him like a sudden case of bigfooting after all his years walking alone with Bobby, Rosenthal didn't reveal it. He admired the specialty firm's history of social justice–oriented litigation, as he did the abilities of those he always referred to as "Bobby's New York lawyers." The new lawyers appreciated, of course, that Rosenthal wasn't territorial, spoke of the "commitment" the solo practitioner had brought to their client. As a practical matter, Rosenthal offered the team the benefits of his years of immersion in the case, doing whatever was asked of him. This included providing use of the large conference room at his firm in New Haven.

Late in 2018, it was time for the retired detective Michael Quinn to be deposed in the conference room. The space was crowded with lawyers and their assistants, as well as the court reporter, a videographer, and Bobby. He hadn't seen Quinn since his final interrogation. Bobby said he was there because his lawyers "told me to show up." The thinking was that with whatever Quinn testified, now he would, in effect, be addressing Bobby. "My lawyer was like, 'Listen, stand here and still say my client's guilty,'" Bobby said. "That's a huge accusation."

Bobby's New York attorney handling most of the depositions was Emma Freudenberger, tall, poised, and polished as a dueling saber, with abundant experience revealing misconduct in police departments and at crime labs. As a law student, she'd been the editor of *A Jailhouse Lawyer's Manual*, a nearly 1,400-page Blackstone for prisoners. When she'd deposed Bobby, she saw that his answers were consistent with what he'd been saying since Kwame's trial. Freudenberger consulted with a Yale forensic psychiatrist who told her it wouldn't have been possible for Bobby to commit a crime as a child and then lie about it in the same consistently detailed way for twelve years. One doctor met Bobby and told Freudenberger afterward, "You could see the kid inside the adult trying to navigate the stark psychological coercion of 'Say you did it and you go home, or you get the death penalty.'" Freudenberger herself thought Bobby was "still trying to figure out what happened to him." For her, his case "wasn't pure business to me, because he was a kid. I almost wanted to be his mom. Partly because of prison, you can still see the kid in there." With Quinn now to be deposed, Freudenberger and others worried it would be upsetting for Bobby to confront the detective again.

Bobby sat himself away from the long wooden conference table, tucked against the wall alongside staff members from the law firm. Quinn wore a black long-sleeve T-shirt and a black vest. When he answered Freudenberger's questions, Bobby's impression was "he looked like a middle-aged white guy. He wasn't rough or anything. He didn't seem embarrassed about nothing." Quinn referred to Pete Fields's Chrysler as a "ghetto Bentley," said he hadn't reviewed any documents for this session, said, "My mother always told me to tell the truth," said that when news of Bobby's release arrived at his door, it took him a day and then he was past it. Quinn denied he'd ever threatened Bobby or fed him case details. Of BlackJack's failure to provide information to confirm his Bridgeport alibi against the palm print and other evidence potentially implicating him in a murder, Quinn said blithely, "He just didn't want to talk about it." Bobby would have liked that option. He admired Freudenberger's technician's methods, was grateful that when Quinn said something about how Bobby had signed his missing pre-interview notes or about the confidential informant who'd allegedly named Bobby, he now had in this room with him a fencer who calmly sliced back, proposing that Quinn was "completely" making things up. "This guy's crazy," Bobby said. "He still believes I'm the right guy. But my lawyers kept catching him in lies."

Hours into the deposition, Freudenberger placed in front of Quinn the problematic voucher Leonard Boyle had given Rosenthal on which Quinn requested reimbursement for $100 he'd paid a confidential informant in mid-August 2006, whose help, Quinn wrote, led him to arrest Bobby over a month later for Pete Fields's murder. As Quinn sought to explain how a document signed, dated, and submitted in August could pay for information related to a September event, and why nothing about it appeared in case reports, Quinn's face lost color and his explanations faded and curled. Reviewing the voucher, he said he could tell someone else had filled out some portions, because "It's not my horrible writing." He'd probably written August because it had been "back-dated." That the incorrect case number was on the form had not been intentional but would be a "mistake." Quinn explained the $100 was probably not paid to a confidential informant but actually had been for the "throwing-around money" Quinn distributed in August to prostitutes and drug addicts throughout Newhallville in search of tips. Yet, Quinn said, "I would never write it's throwing-around money," which would have violated department protocol, so he'd referenced the $100 as confidential-informant money, an expedient way of recouping his funds. Since he'd earlier told Freudenberger the throwing-around money hadn't led anywhere, writing it led to Bobby's arrest was untrue. Well, Quinn reflected, perhaps the voucher referred to money he'd paid to an actual informant, "the old man" who ran the card game. That was Walter McCain. "He's telling a lie," McCain would later say. "He paid me nothing. He paid Speed Limit $200." To Freudenberger, Quinn testified he didn't know Speed Limit's actual name, what he looked like, or how much Speed Limit himself was paid because "that was Clarence's informant." But earlier Quinn said he'd met Speed Limit "a bunch of times." This was a difficult man to forget. Speed Limit was so-called because of his 6'5" height. Eventually, Quinn said to Freudenberger, "the whole thing was a mess," and he admitted, "It looks unusual if you weren't part of the workings of the police department." Quinn never explained why the crucial case-breaking informer of Bobby's name was not mentioned anywhere in his case reports, as was policy.

"It's pure bullshit," assessed a detective from the time, who was fond of Quinn but not of his relationship with Willoughby. "They were so inept, so dirty." A second detective dismissed Quinn's various explanations, "You don't just give money to people." Other police officers, who all liked Quinn and "never would have guessed that of Mike Quinn" shrugged and said, as one did with knowing sorrow, "He got caught up in it."

AFTER QUINN'S DEPOSITION, Bobby said, "It was kind of cool. I wasn't upset. It was funny when he kept saying I was the guy who murdered Herbert Fields. I didn't get no flashes. He tried to make eye contact with me a lot. I felt it gave me the power." Shrugging, Bobby said, "I felt normal. I was prepared for it. People are affected by trauma differently." When it was time for the second detective to be deposed, however, Bobby said, "I won't go to Willdebee. I mean Willoughby. For some reason I can never say his name right."

Retired detective Clarence Willoughby had been through his own sufferings since Bobby had gone to prison. He'd lost his lawsuit against the city, in 2009 he had suffered multiple brain aneurysms, and after one burst he spent forty-two days in a medically induced coma. Some people took this as justice, said the big player had got his. In 2013, Bobby had watched Willoughby make his limited appearance at the habeas hearing, an experience that made Bobby sure Willoughby's reaction to Bobby's release would be "I had three aneurysms! I can't remember nothing! But when he testified, I saw his face. It wasn't a face of 'I don't remember that.' It was a face of remembering. I read the nonverbals."

Willoughby would now put on a tailored gray suit and, in his own deposition with Freudenberger, take personal stock, saying, "I thought I was the best. You gotta have that confidence." And then, "I had it one time. I lack it now." He was insistent he had followed correct police procedure and Bobby was guilty. But Willoughby's testimony contained egregious errors: "I only interviewed Bobby one time." When explanations were sometimes inconsistent with his previous testimony, a word Willoughby fell back on was "misspoke." Occasionally he asked Freudenberger to define words she used. One was "coercive."

The account of the Fields case Willoughby now gave began in August 2006, with him "home in my backyard minding my business," when Speed Limit stopped by the house to tell him about Bobby. Willoughby said Speed Limit's nickname spoke to exaggeration: Speed Limit was actually six-three.

Freudenberger reviewed Bobby's confessions, and Willoughby repeatedly offered testimony that conflicted with the detectives' reports from 2006: that Bobby chose Fields because he routinely carried large sums of money; that Fields was known to Bobby as "a loan shark in that area." But here was evolving case narrative, for in the first confession Fields is someone Bobby's cousin fought with and then in the second a random robbery target, an "old man" Bobby had never heard of. He and the others wanted to rob this stranger because "our pockets was dry." As to the murder weapon, Willoughby explained Bobby armed himself by renting a gun from Major for "$200 or $300." There's nothing in the confessions about rental, only that Major loaned the gun. As for why information about this alleged renting of the gun wasn't documented by police, Willoughby said that Quinn wrote up the reports and "Quinn probably wasn't in the room when I asked [Bobby]." That he'd "overlooked" including such details in the record, Willoughby testified, "wasn't important to me. At that time. We already got a confession." Freudenberger stared at him in wonder, asked what could be more important in a murder case than documenting the motive and the source of the murder weapon.

Of his interrogation methods, Willoughby said, "I didn't know about any rules." He judged his style mellow: "I never had to yell at nobody." Of the probation gambit, however, he averred, "Might have used that one before." Had he used it with Bobby? First he said "probably." Then he didn't remember. Then he said, "Bobby ain't that dumb" to fall for such a ploy. Willoughby said he "probably did" make written record of the pre-interviews, but "I don't know what I did with my notes." He didn't recall BlackJack, couldn't remember anything about a palm print, hadn't been aware anybody suspected Major of the murder. Belatedly, it turned out "I didn't ask" Bobby about why he chose Fields because "everybody knew" Fields carried large amounts of money. Then, when Freudenberger repeatedly pressed him, Willoughby suddenly, volte-face, said Bobby had told him he knew about Fields's money.

Freudenberger's reaction afterward was "there is something weirdly magnetic and compelling about Willoughby." She considered him deeply untruthful. Later, at a settlement mediation session, Bobby did see the former detective. "I don't know what Willoughby was thinking," Bobby said. "He was smirking." The whole case was that way for Bobby. These many years after somebody killed Pete Fields, Bobby still didn't know why "of all the people in my neighborhood" Willoughby and Quinn had persisted in blaming him.

SINCE BOBBY'S RELEASE in 2015, Clarence Willoughby had continued living in his well-ordered, modest blue house with gleaming wood floors, African and religious art on the walls and his black Mercedes S550 in the driveway. By the end of 2016, gone was the springy way the tall, lean man moved through the city that had led people to nickname him Horsy. At the neck there was a large tracheotomy scar. Still in late middle age, turned-out in a blue dress sweatsuit, a blue-and-white striped polo shirt, running shoes, with a Yankees baseball cap shading a kempt boulevardier's mustache, Willoughby remained youthful and very handsome. He seemed at peace, even unguarded, as he explained, "You know, I had three aneurysms. Three or four of 'em. My whole memory got erased they say."

Yet soon he said, "Yeah, yeah, I remember Bobby. See, some cases I still remember. That case is one I definitely remember because he confessed." What Willoughby remembered, and how he explained what he remembered, Willoughby related through a helix of conversation, looping through descriptions of his methods, case detail, and thoughts on people involved, all of it told in an amiable, conversational way. He was calm, never defensive, and yet he was an immovable force, a steadfast man who didn't just believe—he knew.

"You gotta be careful up in Newhallville," he explained. "Now, family is family up there. And they took to me like I was family, you hear me? I can go anywhere, walk anyplace, and get information, where other guys couldn't do that, you know. I know the streets, and they didn't. The police department didn't understand the working of the streets." Willoughby's knowledge and access, he said, meant "I didn't have to go out there and look for people. I just call you up, you come in here, and I did most of my work from home most of the time. I could pick up my phone and call any of these guys. They would come get in their car or get over here, come here and tell me, you know what I mean? Any of the bad guys in the neighborhood. Any of 'em. Pick 'em, you know?" This unusual method of performing detective work, he said, was possible because he was on his honor. "They have no problem with it, 'cause they trusted me. I used to tell people, my word was my bond. And if it should fail, you can take my life. That's that jail talk, you know. I dealt with a lot of people who been to jail." Crimes were solved here at Willoughby's blue house, where criminals would tell Willoughby, he said, who their accomplices had been. "Most of my information came from somebody who was there with you," he said. "You know, one of your friends." He trusted these informants. "I had a different rapport with guys in the street, you know. They confide in me. They didn't do something, they say, 'Well, I didn't do it.' And I kind of believe 'em, you know?"

The murder of Fields, he said, amounted to "they probably went to rob the guy and didn't expect to shoot him, you know. That's all. Robbery went bad. That ain't the first time a robbery went bad up there." Of Bobby and Kwame, Willoughby's impression, shared by nobody else, was "They lived in the neighborhood. They was all over. Them guys are terrorizing."

The retired detective thought of confessions as recombinant of guilt because, "Why would you confess to something if you didn't do it?" That people wouldn't ever behave in this counterintuitive way made the process immune to error. "I would never lock up the wrong guy," he said. "If a guy tell you he did it, he did it, you know?" As to the possibility that Kwame or Bobby had been frightened, he shook his head. "Oh, no. They couldn't be scared of me." Their descriptions of his assorted threats, including the death penalty and his assertions that he had indisputable evidence against them, such as their fingerprints, Willoughby said, "I don't remember that.

But I remember you could use trickery and deception back then." There was no risk to employing swervy tactics because "I don't think nobody gonna say they killed somebody if they didn't do it. You gotta be crazy. I know one thing, I wouldn't confess to nothing if I didn't do it." Willoughby had hoped people would confess. Then his work was done. He saw no subsequent need for independent checking: "If you tell me you did it, that's even easier for me. Now, my job is not to prove that you didn't do it, if you tell me you did it already, you know?"

Willoughby also remembered Major, and said, "He was no angel." He told of a different murder Major had committed, and then Willoughby spoke about Major in ways sometimes inconsistent with the procedures (and the certitude) the detective had just described. "He one of those guys I used to be able to call up on the phone. He come and see me. Yeah, he killed people. I know he probably did it, but I'm just saying—you gotta look at this—one guy can't be all them places at one time. You just can't do it. It's impossible. But if he did something, he'd tell you he did it, you know?" But then, it turned out, Major had never visited the blue house. "Me and Major would meet in the street somewhere. I know Major. He would tell me. See, they don't realize I talked to him. It's not in the reports anywhere. And Bobby told me he rent the gun from Major. Major and Bobby was friends. People don't know that. They were best friends. Good friends. He was good enough to go over to his house and rent a gun from him and give him a couple hundred dollars cause he gonna do a robbery. But see, the police department and the courts are so naïve to that. They don't understand how the streets work. There's a whole different ball game in the street you know? You might have a gun that got four, five bodies on it."

Willoughby's claim that he'd omitted such central case information from his department reports was consistent with the way he set himself apart from the methods of colleagues. To Willoughby, it all came down to Major being the convenient means for detectives of inferior ability to solve murders: "When you don't have the skill level, you blame him for everything. That's the easy way out." The acquittals of Kwame and Ernest Pagan, and Bobby's release, Willoughby said happened because he himself had been "wrongly accused" of corruption. At court hearings, he had been forced to plead the fifth so defense attorneys wouldn't force him to discuss his serious legal troubles, and "That's why all those people got out of jail. They got a gift from me. If I could have testified, they all would not have got off, 'cause I could explain that stuff to them. How they get the gun and all that. I know how that works 'cause I was part of that. Pagan, he'd be still in jail. Bobby, they'd still be in jail. 'Cause I'm the only one could explain that stuff. 'Cause they didn't know. They don't understand how the inner city works. I'm from there. I knew it. I knew how it worked." A truth in this was juries did tend to believe police testimony. But another was Willoughby had testified at Bobby's habeas hearing, where he told the judge he couldn't remember details he was now addressing.

Willoughby said he never bore grudges or had agonies of the mind about past cases. It was all fated; what would be would be. "I don't sit around and think about stuff like that anymore, you know?" Willoughby said. "I tell 'em, 'God evens everything out in the end. God will take care of them,' you know? If they did it, they did it. If they didn't do it, they didn't do it, you know?" To be here in Willoughby's company, hearing about Major's willingness to admit his own sins, hearing that Bobby and Major were best friends, hearing that Kwame and Bobby had terrorized Newhallville, hearing the detective describe his own street omniscience, all of it was disquieting. He offered the possibility that "they didn't do it," and yet said he believed the confessions with such dedication that error was impossible. He'd got it right. If others saw the case at variance, nothing more Willoughby could do. "I got no ill will against Bobby," he said. "He did what he's supposed to do. He took his thing and fought it and he won. I'm glad he's out. He's a good guy. I wish him the best."

Then Willoughby said, "You can't just do something and not tell nobody. See, that's why people get caught in this town. They tell somebody what they did. Ask him. Tell him Willoughby said, 'Who did you tell beside him that you did it?' " When Bobby heard about this, he spread his hands. "That dude is too funny. He thinks it's a game."

EARLY IN 2020, BlackJack was released from prison, and New Haven law enforcement took careful notice. Prison was a relative force field where most people did their time, bided their bids, sometimes were even collegial to those they bore beef, and then a few came out and settled old scores. People from Newhallville said BlackJack had "done so much dirt" he could never leave all the harm behind. For him, moving around Newhallville was going to be such a high-resolution existence it would be as though he'd acquired a watermark unmistakable for all to see. And the danger would not only be from those who already had it in for him, but also the next nervy young person for whom BlackJack could be the source of a spotlessly bad reputation. BlackJack's mother, in Georgia, thought BlackJack should get out of town, and so did Stacy Spell, whose business card said "Longevity." "BlackJack should leave," Spell said. "Make a deal with probation. Go. BlackJack stays here, BlackJack's going to get shot. People will be coming for him. Old beefs don't get forgotten." As proof, Spell could point to a home on Read Street where a young person with too many enemies had lived. Repeated sprays of gunfire turned the face of the house to "Swiss cheese" because "everybody was after him."

Bobby was perfectly capable of resentment. It bothered him no end that Scott Lewis had been exonerated and was "in glory" while Stefon Morant somehow retained his felony record for the same crime. But across the fourteen years since Bobby was arrested for killing Pete Fields, Bobby never expressed any public enmity for BlackJack, as he hadn't for Major. He didn't mention or discuss them at all, except to express sympathetic fellow-feeling.

By the following August, BlackJack had moved South. The number of fatal and non-fatal shootings in New Haven had then already surpassed the totals from the entire previous year, and illegal guns had been confiscated by police in what the current chief, Otoniel Reyes, considered "staggering numbers" for so small a city. That making guns had once been what sustained Newhallville was such a powerful irony it seemed to hold deeper truths. Among the phrases people used for shooting somebody was "putting in work." The classic street handgun of this day was the 9mm, and everywhere nines were so busy, bullets had become hard to acquire, even for police departments, like New Haven's, which used them as service weapons. Bobby's cousin Quay's view of the gunfire was "It's worse than when Bobby and Major were around." She described angry young men with guns committed to vendetta and vengeance, willing to shoot merely because someone else's attitude was "*too*." Better than most, Quay knew about such boys. One of them was her eighteen-year-old son, DaDa, the cousin Bobby had tried to mentor when the family took him in on Atwater Street right after his release from Big Cheshire.

In the middle of a February afternoon in 2020, Quay was cooking chicken and broccoli for dinner when DaDa received a telephone call from a good friend. DaDa told his mother, "I'll be right back." They were living in a different house, out near busy Route 80, where DaDa played guitar, babysat, and cooked for his siblings. Out in the city, DaDa was an excellent quarterback, went to nursing homes to pray for the elderly. With his dimpled, mischievous smile, soft cheeks, and impish eyes here was the heart-dropping picture of an adorable teenage boy. But since Bobby's months with the family when Bobby had taken in that DaDa seemed to want others to see something harder in him, DaDa began to be arrested, once for riding in a stolen vehicle. "He didn't steal a car," his mother said, "but he was sure in it." Another day, Quay saw what she first thought was a baseball bat on the couch. It was a sawed-off shotgun. She turned the weapon and DaDa in to the police. "It's called tough love," Quay said.

Completely committed to her children as she was, Quay had no idea why DaDa was behaving this way, except that DaDa was an unafraid person in a small community saturated with fear: "He had a name in the streets—D-Honcho. Somebody's bothering you, they'd call D-Honcho and he was coming." Quay was "scared" for him, believed her son lived around such prevalent violence that, to save him, she needed "help" from somebody with authority or DaDa would "be a statistic."

That February afternoon, DaDa didn't come back for chicken and broccoli. He walked in the front door of a neighboring home. Quay was told five other young people were in the room, and an adult woman. A boy raised a gun and shot DaDa five times. It was a close space, and yet only one person was hit. Stacy Spell said, "Shooting him five times—that's an execution."

Quay was a widely admired person, a clear-thinking, hardworking, caring woman of faith, and there was abundant sympathy. People reassured her that as a parent, she "did an excellent job. But I feel I must have gone wrong somewhere. I lost my son." At a candlelight vigil memorializing DaDa, she looked out at a throng of unhappy young people in distressed jeans and sneakers, and asked them all to spare their own families her "unbearable, indescribable pain." The police had little to offer this mother. Nobody would cooperate with them. Quay said, "people want you to talk when it's their family. But when it's yours, nobody says anything, nobody sees anything. You need to help. They can't do an investigation without us helping them. They're not magicians." Bobby predicted, "New Haven's gonna be tense for a while."

Bobby himself was visited again by an old tension he was tired of feeling. That these premature deaths were distinctive lives pummeled into similarity by unexplained acts of violence was too disturbing. He sounded numb talking about DaDa. "This boy," Bobby said. "I'm a little shook up. Nobody in my family died in a while." After word had spread from phone to phone within his family that DaDa was in an ambulance, Bobby avoided the ritualized visit to the emergency room. "I couldn't go to the hospital," he said. "I don't like situations like that."

That day, Bobby had been in a classroom. He'd finally returned to school, taking a microeconomics course at Southern Connecticut State University. But the murder flung him down. It seemed incredible to Bobby that for kids like DaDa, coming of age *still* meant getting caught up, that his cousin's generation wasn't going off to college, marrying, receiving promotions at work, buying houses. Someone who knew Bobby said, "It's as if everybody still eats SpaghettiOs and drinks bug juice. Still kids murdering kids over nothing." After DaDa's death, Bobby ceased attending the economics class.

Some loving, mourning mothers of boys with guns received remorseful prison calls from sons who only there realized "I have wasted my life." For mothers, like Quay, each new day was grief that surged, ebbed, and surged back, an ocean of grief that salted every morning with the fresh sting of an experience impossible to get used to. Eight months after DaDa died, Bobby said of Quay, "She's going through a lot." So much that Quay obtained a pistol permit, and "I carry because of fear." Then she began to pack her home. Quay believed that with "change, New Haven could be something awesome." But for her remaining two children, the New Haven daughter of a migrant from South Carolina decided, "I have to get out of this town. Otherwise, I'll lose the only son I have left. So I'm going to a community I don't know."

Nobody liked to dwell on the tragedies that overtook promising young men. People wanted instead to rejoice in memories of them as endearing children, to find solace by doing whatever they could to make beauty out of the bleak. The murals, candles, sneakers on a wire, vigils, photographs clustered in places of honor, and flowers in churches were a collective vitrine expressing love and esteem. They also held the city's sorrow over generations of murders.

When Stacy Spell thought about the violence, the retired detective from Newhallville said he was like Bobby: it was impossible for him to walk his old neighborhood without experiencing it as a city topography of loss and death. Spell knew all the fatal Newhallville doorways, vestibules, and driveways, and they had become memorials in his memory. When the rare Yale student was killed on East Rock Road or Nicoll Street, national news coverage meant people across the country heard all about it. Down in the Ville, over the decades most homicides received brief notices in the city's newspapers. The lack of personal information made the Newhallville deceased unspecific people, forever unknown. For some who lived outside Newhallville, the crimes ran together, reinforcing preconceived ideas. But for Spell and other "sons of Newhallville," as he put it, the specter of the neighborhood dead was "overwhelming."

In the killing rage young people felt, there was, Spell believed, a commemorative effect. If what was mourned on East Rock Road was youthful promise, here the lament was never having had a chance. It was a question of mattering, that no crime mattered more than murder, that murder could happen for what seemed like casual reasons, but to believe it could ever be normalized was to mistake its crestfallen effect on a community. "When I was a kid in the Ville," Spell said, "walking down the street, going to get my father an orange soda, going to Staten's pool hall because he liked the hot peanuts, there was no question of safety. Now there's not a corner where I don't think, Archie died here. Dolphin died here. Tyrick Keyes died here. The list goes on." To Spell, whose pleasure was reading books about the past, none of this was anything new. For generations stretching back in poor Black neighborhoods from Cuthbert, Georgia, to Fort Scott, Kansas, the names of dear friends shot to death were crucial words in the repetitions of violent history that Spell once hoped the country had finally moved beyond.

SINCE 2015, THE 2006 death of Pete Fields had been one more unsolved New Haven murder. People who were familiar with the case believed there was unlikely to be another arrest, because any defense attorney would say, "Well, you had the same evidence and yet you prosecuted Bobby." Most people thought of the murder as Major's crime, and he, too, was the victim of a shooting that also seemed unlikely ever to be solved. Historian Heather Ann Thompson found what criminologists also believed: that if a murderer has since been killed, related open cases that are left behind become far less appealing to prosecutors.

There was recency bias with murders. As the months passed, memories and bloodstains faded, people involved passed away, and cases lost their urgency as bright new red-ball murders were committed. A lawyer within Innocence Project circles said that in nearly half the wrongful conviction cases the Innocence Project worked on, they could with certainty identify the actual perpetrator, but the police almost never arrested the person. "The reason," the man said, "is that the police and the prosecutor shot their wad the first time. They rarely go back because it's too much work. They don't have the emotional zeal they had the first time they prosecuted an innocent person."

In Connecticut, a cold-case task force was led by a respected Waterbury prosecutor, Patrick Griffin, until he replaced Michael Dearington as New Haven's state's attorney in 2016. Griffin said that while it was true that "cold cases become colder over time," sometimes surprising things happened. People left the street life, wanted to get awful things they'd seen off their chest: "No homicide is ever closed. There's always hope." But during COVID-19, the city's streets were mostly too hot for cold cases. A preponderance of the terrifying gunfire Stacy Spell referred to as "spraying and praying" led to a New Haven murder count that, by the 2020 summer, had already surpassed the previous year's total. In 2021, the murder increase repeated, rising to twenty-five, with only three arrests made. That 12 percent solve rate was far below Connecticut cities like Hartford, which had a smaller population and sixty-eight detectives to New Haven's thirty-eight. Unlike New Haven, Hartford had invested in a network of public street cameras. (In 2022, money was budgeted for cameras and more detective promotions in New Haven. While non-fatal shootings increased, the shooting task force's solves and gun-related arrests showed early improvement.) Across the nation, police shootings of Black citizens and ensuing "defund" demonstrations coincided in New Haven with destabilizing leadership changes, all leading to tenuous police legitimacy and low officer morale. The killing of "George Floyd erupted everything and cooperation went extremely downhill," said one investigator. Pandemic-related stress and uncertainty were thought to have provoked domestic violence and old beefs. Guns were evermore available.

As far as Thomas Hargrove was concerned, it all added up to "New Haven is a good place to get away with murder." A former Scripps Howard News Service investigative journalist, Hargrove had the calm, deliberative manner of a somewhat solitary white-haired man who walked eight miles every day. While a reporter, Hargrove had used his facility with computers to achieve statistical insight into such subjects as sudden infant death syndrome, Social Security, and serial killers. That final interest led Hargrove, in retirement, to found the nonprofit Murder Accountability Project. He'd been horrified to discover that the 1960s murder clearance rate of over 90 percent had since descended to near 60 percent. So Hargrove built a database with every murder in the United States, and he armed it with algorithms that would enable searching for patterns in American homicides. The American story Hargrove read in the data confirmed what Ivan Kuzyk and Stacy Spell saw locally, that "Black murders are many, many times more likely to go unsolved than the murders of whites."

To look across the industrialized West was to see in other countries no such disparity in murders and clearances by police. Murders were comparatively rare in Scandinavia and Great Britain, and those few murders were almost all solved. In a typical year, all of Canada, a country of 38 million people, had roughly as many murders as Chicago. American homicide detectives were not inherently less able. This suggested to Hargrove that "the failure to solve homicides is a failure of will by local leaders." The American explanation for recent declining clearance rates included those factors speculated in New Haven. But across time, the repercussions of police illegitimacy meant that even the most diligent and caring police couldn't solve major crimes when communities were disinclined to help them. Rosenthal thought the same: "It's so hard to be a police officer. The rules run up against the nature of what they do on the street." In some places, when an upstanding seventy-year-old man was killed on the sidewalk or an eighteen-year-old boy was shot in a crowded room, the city council mobilized a campaign to knock on every door within a mile radius of the crime, ordinary people from across the city showing up to ask, "Did you see anything?" people saying to their neighbors, "There's no need to live in fear," people imploring those they lived among, "Please help, the next victim could be you or me."

AFTER PETE FIELDS's death, his children had felt sure the anguish of losing their father would never go away. "I'll tell you one thing," Susan said, "murder ruins a family." As the years passed, at unpredicted moments she'd suddenly believe she'd just heard the "clankety-clank" of her father closing his recliner after watching *The Man Who Shot Liberty Valance* before bedtime. Her brother Peter, meanwhile, found the lack of resolution in the case so upsetting he labored not to think about it. Since his father's death, Peter's health hadn't been good, first a heart attack, then a stroke. As for their cousin Floyd Hooks, because of his closeness to his uncle, he had inherited all of his cowboy hats, and when Floyd wore one, he was mistaken for Pete.

In that little confusion, Susan believed, was again the problem, a failure to appreciate people's individuality. Willoughby, she thought, heard a street legend about the culprit in her father's death, and the legend became fact when Willoughby hastily went with it. "It's like they wanted to hurry up and blame somebody," she said. "Find somebody. A Black man. They didn't care about the victim, an older Black man. They just wanted to close the case. I think they overlooked so much. I don't get how they let that poor boy go to jail. I wish he never pleaded guilty. It didn't help. It made matters worse for him and for me." The irresolution of the case was painful to Susan—"I get no closure." Newhallville had been her family's community. Like Quay, she imagined all the people who could have helped solve a murder and said nothing. "How could a secret like that stay a secret?" she asked. "Many people know it."

Sometimes, it appeared the world was too full of silence. Down in South Carolina, the old Fields family homeplace in recent years had been used as somebody's hunting reserve and then, again, money had changed hands and it was owned by a company that developed golf courses. The patrolman Bill Wolfe was dead, as was his son Billy, but a nephew, Albert Wolfe, remained an Orangeburg accountant, now in his seventies. Albert Wolfe was locally respected among Black people as a fine person, and also as someone who understood about the relationship between South Carolina's racial history and the land. But Albert Wolfe had never heard anything of the Fields's property confiscation, which would have taken place before he was born. He didn't deny the possibility, he said, since "things like that could happen. I don't really know." Nobody else would know either, he guessed, becausc "all the relatives are gone."

Living a full day's drive away from the former family homeplace was Pete's younger sister Katie-Jean. Of her brother, she said that, in 2006, he'd believed he was making progress in reclaiming for the family the 190 acres. "When he died, he'd told us he was working with Billy Wolfe, the son of the highway patrol," she said. "Pete died, and then Billy Wolfe died. The land belongs to God. We took care of it for a while."

Katie-Jean continued to pray every day for Bobby, to think hard about him. She said about Bobby's boyhood that "he was born into a job, this having to take care of the other kids when he should have been outside playing. That's an abandonment of childhood, of his innocence." Because Katie-Jean didn't actually know Bobby, he existed for her as a half-lit figure, an innocent boy whose boyhood, inflected as it was with gun violence, spoke for the experience of many boys. "This is a tragedy in America for young Black males," she said. "I'm a retired Black teacher. I see it all the time." She herself had "two sons and two grandsons. I live with that anxiety constantly—would they be caught in the wrong place and the wrong time by the wrong people." Nor did she hold bitterness toward Major, and she felt for Auntie, who herself noted that had Major been arrested, it would still be possible for her to visit him. "I don't think most babies are born violent, born to be mean, born to be hateful," Katie-Jean said. "Their environment shapes them. I could see that happening to my twenty-one-year-old grandson who's pre-med now. I do have sympathy. Oh my God, yes. I'm the mother of boys."

For Katie-Jean, these worries for her sons' and grandsons' safety were intertwined with fear of police officers. "I'm seventy-five years old," she said. "And ever since I've known life, as long as Black people are killing Black people, law enforcement people are satisfied. Intellectually, we know Black men are not valued. We're born and learn quickly to be afraid. We live with underlying fear all the time."

As her brother Pete had been, Katie-Jean was devoted to family and immersed in family. She had dozens of relatives still in Connecticut, but since her brother had been shot there, Katie-Jean avoided the state. Her older sister Nina lived up there, and when Katie-Jean spoke with Nina by telephone, which was at least five times a week, they always talked about their brother. Nina had been six years older than Pete, and Katie-Jean said, "She was his sentry, watching him. He hated it!" Nina was a curious and intelligent person, Katie-Jean thought, and Pete was sufficiently interesting to satisfy her. "She loved him so," Katie-Jean said. "We talk like Pete's still alive." They would tell their brother how angry they were with him for going to the Mudhole in his shiny car, even as both would always conclude, "Well, he was going there to help people."

Pete's daughter, Susan, had remained in North Haven for years after her father died, but being in Connecticut felt like a bad winter that never brought spring. James Baldwin could have been writing down Susan's thoughts when one of his characters said, "The menfolk, they die, and it's over for them, but we women, we have to keep on living and try to forget." With both her parents and a brother dead, Susan found that "things changed after they passed. Things changed. Holidays aren't the same. They were so festive. I took it for granted. You wake up and realize, 'Look what I miss now.'" Eventually, she migrated across the country, to California. "I decided to get out of Connecticut and make a change," she said in Los Angeles. "Made me very much happier. A new start. Me coming to California, his death is part of why I'm here. I needed a different place. That was horrific for me. I remember that day as clear as today. I saw him sitting in his recliner looking at westerns. So many years gone by, I still hurt. But your life has to go on. What can I do? It was my dad and I think of the good things. He tried to raise his family well, take care of that. It's sad. He took care of me. I wanted to take care of him." When Susan became ill with multiple forms of cancer in 2020, she returned to New Haven, where she died.

EPILOGUE

Prospects

Some men went into prison young as boys, came out later, and believed they had to speed up their lives. Wanting a legacy and feeling fated, they got the first woman they met pregnant. Then they landed in shelters or became addicted or made terrible decisions and were sent back to prison. Others didn't do those things, found it within themselves to persevere. Bobby's reentry mistakes were many, but they happened on a scale, and afterward he did not repeat them. He sensed a satisfying future, even if he could not yet define it. To others he gave what he could, and he remained close to those who valued his kindness. He avoided annihilation and existed, always, for those who knew him, as a decent, upstanding man, or as kids he grew up with would say, a citizen.

Bobby's life changed out in the shoreline suburbs and it didn't. "Racism in the North is subliminal," he said one day. "A lot of subliminals. I walk into a restaurant, everybody gets quiet." In the first months after he purchased the BMW, Bobby was pulled over seven times by police cruisers. Patrol would spot him, reverse course, and he'd hear a siren. Once, cars with flashing cherry tops came at him from two directions, four officers, their hands on their guns, ordering him and Shay's "little church boy" boyfriend, Corey, out of the car's front seats, patting them down. Bobby's provocation was that his car windows were tinted. Since the Jim Crow South, window tinting became a practice among Black drivers who wished to deflect attention from white police who might be offended by Black car ownership. Now it was like an illegal turn, a gateway means for some police to trawl for criminal behavior. The police asked Bobby how he could afford the coupe. He told them, "google me." After they did, he received apologies and "I can't believe that happened to you, Mr. Bobby!"

Soon, Bobby bought another Honda. Now he blended better. "Nobody can see me," he said. "I'm a ghost." The Honda also felt truer to the unobtrusive person he was. "I feel good in that Honda," he said. "The other goes too fast and gas costs too much." Bobby used the money that he had been paid in legal compensation to buy these cars but did not consider that money a source of fulfillment. This was redress, reparation, something owed. The money also brought with it constant reminders of where he came from. "Some days," Bobby said, "I set the phone down on the dresser, it rings all day. Family, friends, people from prison, people I just met. Everybody wants money, money, money. I'm hearing the needs of a community. But it's not my fault. I didn't put people in this position."

Bobby visited his old cellmate and mentor Troy Westberry at Big Cheshire, and even toured the prison's new True Unit for young offenders of promise, an experiment he applauded because it would "help them to do better" upon release. But for Bobby, returning to Big Cheshire came at a personal cost. "Going back," he said after one visit, "ugh. Bittersweet. You instantly can't forget the trauma it caused you. And thinking about the people there still struggling. Brought back a lot." He tried hard to stifle those feelings, to go for Westberry and for Jerome, but he had to admit, "Sometimes I get near there and turn around. Brings up stuff. And the [corrections] people, when I get there, they say things to me. 'Oh, he was here.' Gets to me." In *Convicting the Innocent*, a seminal study of wrongful conviction, Edwin M. Borchard found that an "essentially irreparable injury" was done to an innocent person by convicting him.

Westberry urged Bobby to move far away. Start fresh. And Bobby had the old desire to be elsewhere. So, in 2019, thirteen years after going to prison for a crime he didn't commit, the former traveler who'd come to know New Haven by bicycle got into his fast car and drove "back South" where the flag of slavery times had recently been removed from the South Carolina state house. He looked at the land in South Carolina, which he found to have "a depressing vibe. So big and lonely. Just horses standing out there. Takes forever to get through and parts of it are so dark." Bobby out there was a deep-sea fisherman in Dakota. Not a match; wouldn't do.

Instead, Bobby came back and bought a house in an old New England town. To visiting family, he was generous on his terms. He'd treat younger cousins to outings for bowling, skating, go-kart riding, take them to the movies and to dinner, host all comers for Thanksgiving and Christmas. From afar, he thought sympathetically about his mother, worried that her struggles might be rooted in experiences from growing up that "she'll never tell anybody about." He became closer to older relatives, like Aunt Faith, who never asked anybody for anything, worked and walked through the day with a personal consistency Bobby admired.

For some family elders, like his uncle June, Bobby was a cautionary tale. "I told my son about this," Uncle June said. "He was hanging out with some other young boys, smoking weed, going to parties, places he shouldn't be. I told him, 'You can't do this. You got to go to college or get a job. Keep yourself motivated. It only takes one thing. Look what happened to Bobby.' " Then Uncle June said, "I'm dying to see Bobby. I haven't seen him in years."

Bobby was never going to be *too*. His own struggles had given him the clarity of mind to "want opportunity for others. I would love to see people prosper." When Stefon Morant became the first person in Connecticut pardoned on grounds of actual innocence, members of the pardon board cried, but nobody was happier for Morant than Bobby.

People dear to Bobby were Shay and her now-fiancé, Corey. They could tease him, lighten him, make Bobby laugh and laugh. After Shay's grandmother died, Bobby invited Shay and Corey to come stay with him for a while. Shay found, "Bobby is still the same Bobby, still wears Crocs and sweats every day." When Corey and Shay married, Bobby was the best man.

Bobby also gave a cousin from South Carolina a bedroom. There were no jobs for the cousin to find in the rural area outside Florence, and when the cousin spoke of how generous Bobby was to reprise the old tradition of those in the North hosting Southern migrants, Bobby didn't say anything, but he glowed.

They all liked to watch movies together, sometimes sharing a bowl of banana pudding Shay made using her grandmother's recipe. They took in *When They See Us*, Ava DuVernay's miniseries based on the experiences of the Central Park Five. Everybody had seemed to be talking about it, and Bobby was curious. But as the boys were coerced on the screen, Bobby became as upset as anybody had ever seen him, even more than at the Henry Green film. "You watched his face and you saw the pain resurfacing," said Corey. "You saw what he went through." Yelling, "Cut this off!" Bobby burst into tears, as he'd never done in prison, and bolted from the room. But later he forced himself to get through it. "Bobby was a kid," Shay said afterward.

TAKING RESPONSIBILITY FOR an evil he didn't commit was a decision Bobby would spend years trying to understand in himself. He would talk about his confession as a rune, a text of cryptic ambiguity into which he could still hear so many profound things that had been in play. "I was listening to the tape the other day," he said one afternoon, "thinking how deep and intimate it was." Bobby's life, all he'd seen and done, had been reduced into his ownership of a single moment that didn't happen. In the course of his confession, he'd been attempting to understand what was wanted rather than what was real. It didn't cross his mind he'd just been fleeced of his own story. A coerced false confession could be considered a metaphor for how Bobby grew up. He had no agency. He'd become who somebody else expected him to be.

Sworn falsehood forever altered Bobby's life but, he said, "I'm the same truthful person." For all of it, Bobby wasn't someone who believed in modern movements for police abolition for the same reasons Quay was opposed—because "the Ville would suffer. It's so violent. We just need better cops." By *better* he meant police who knew how to protect people like him.

Protecting people meant police, prosecutors, judges, lawyers, and parole officials regarding them as individuals. Mass incarceration was the depersonalizing of crime and punishment, not knowing "the circumstances," as Bobby said. He meant that the aspiration of prison should be to help people there become their better selves. At the moment, he wished prison on "nobody. It's just not a place for reform. It's a place of torture."

The day before he turned thirty, Bobby said, "I don't get a thrill out of birthdays anymore. Jail took it out of me." What did he want to be when he grew up? His neighborhood, his education, prison, none of it had prepared him to know. There was a positive world out there that he aspired to be part of, a world he'd always defined by describing a well-dressed, well-educated young man going off to work every day and then staying home on the weekend, at the head of a full table, helping the kids learn how to be. Happily ever after, the American dream, both meant being grateful for the peace you'd found and kissing the envelopes you sent to others.

Nobody, certainly not Bobby, wanted to be defined by injustice, by oppression, by being exploited, by martyrdom. Shay and Bobby both liked to talk about the need to "finesse the world," which was a way of describing operating from a position of experience. Innocence was such an admired virtue, the pure and unblemished, but like everything else, innocence had its dark side. It could get you into so much trouble.

Slowly, Bobby got to know all his new neighbors. Everybody owned licensed guns for their protection, and everybody, he joked, was also Betty Crocker. After he'd moved in, they all baked Bobby muffins and brought them over. A good neighbor was something to be. Bobby outfitted his home with security cameras. He qualified for a gun license, took target-shooting lessons, became a skilled marksman, and he began to raise pit-bull puppies. First he had two dogs. Then a third, a fourth, and a fifth. "They will be the sweetest girls in the world," he said, and he gave them dog first names like Charm and Snow, as well as his own surname, to make them feel like family. Around the house, they were referred to as "the kids."

The dream was solitude. The dream was coming from places he hadn't been to yet. The reality was that away, safe, out in the quiet, Bobby loved sleeping with the windows open.

ACKNOWLEDGMENTS

At the very beginning, David Remnick and Willing Davidson of *The New Yorker* told me to go off and see what I could learn about my hometown. I felt lucky to have their engaged encouragement, as I was to have that of David Haglund.

To investigate this project early on, I received a grant from First Look Media, where I thank Sam Champtaloup, Erin May O'Rourke, Adam Pincus, and especially the thoughtful, far-seeing Eric Bates. After almost six years of work, I received a project-sustaining grant from Art for Justice, a completely inspiring organization founded by Agnes Gund, in partnership with the Ford Foundation, that seeks to end mass incarceration through fine art and literature. Thanks to Le Anne Alexander, Agnes Gund, Helena Huang, Sue Simon, and the motivating fellowship of the wondrous A4J community. At the very end, when I hadn't been paid in over two years, the Community Foundation for Greater New Haven gave me what they called a "small grant." It meant so much to me. Thanks to Will Ginsberg and Denise Canning.

My agent, David McCormick, and Bridget McCarthy have offered all the support a person could ask. McCormick long worked as an editor, making me fortunate to have the benefit of such a clear critical mind sitting above such a large heart. I also thank Cheryl Kenn, Sylvie Rabineau, and Jay Roach.

Editing a book during the unruly waters of a pandemic is no joke. Deep appreciation to the magnificent Matt Weiland for his faith, patience, and his skillful, demanding piloting of this large vessel to harbor. Huneeya Siddiqui was my coast guard. Rachelle "Ace" Mandik is a copyeditor whose work sings. "Philly" Don Rifkin always has the good word.

I am blessed in my friends who encouraged and fortified me across the eight years. For offering me particular help, counsel, advice, and guidance with this project, I am grateful to Elizabeth Alexander, Emily Bazelon, Terese Betts, Ted Conover, Ingrid Ellen, James Forman Jr., Jonathan Franzen, Miriam Gohara, Andrei Harwell, Tom Hjelm, Maya Jasanoff, Titus Kaphar, Michael Kaplan, Adrian Nicole LeBlanc, Marcus McFerren, Tracey Meares, Tom Powers, Sarah Ruhl, Susan Sawyer, Vijay Seshadri, Erica Spatz, Jeff Turner, Clifton Watson, and Colson Whitehead.

Among those I am indebted to for reading and criticizing drafts or draft portions of the manuscript are Dwayne Betts, William Brown, Ingrid Ellen, Roland Fasano, James Forman Jr., Andrei Harwell, Ivan Kuzyk, Maya Jasanoff, Michael Jefferson, Daniel Markowitz, David McCormick, Andy Papachristos, Kaari Pitkin, Clifton Watson, and Colson Whitehead. The time, care, and attention my friend Adrian Nicole LeBlanc gave to reading every chapter, and then to discussing them, was among the most generous things anybody's ever done for me.

Much appreciation to Titus Kaphar for all of our conversations through the years, including talking over the book cover with me and then allowing me to use his haunting, evocative painting *Forced out of frame*, 2016. The image was inspired by police car dash-cam video footage and is painted in tar on wood panel.

During the course of writing this book, people from New Haven I knew died. I join so many others in mourning the passing of the beloved Otha Buffaloe, Vanessa Tyson Bromell, Sherman Malone, Kevin Mills, DaDa Myers, Fred Parris, Diane Polan, Vincent Scully, Rosa Smith, Thomas Ullmann, and Cynthia Watson.

It's heartbreaking to me that after spending so many hours across so many years discussing her late father's life and community, the bright, effortlessly loving, and frank Susan Troxler will never read this book.

I first met Roland Fasano as a child. I feel fortunate to have shared so much time with him during his last years, talking about criminal justice in Connecticut; he was endlessly forthcoming in his shrewd, compassionate assessments, which people say is just the way he was as a judge.

I cherish the conversations my brilliant friend Randall Kenan and I had across the decades, and now the memory of his beautiful, gentle spirit.

Some days I miss the thirty years of talking with Dan Frank so much I don't know what to do.

Larry Harris, Greg Lyss, and Jamie Wright have been my dear, constant friends since I met them when we were all still kids.

Dwayne Betts and I spoke at least once a day about our work and lives during the course of this project. Along the way, he read the full draft twice. I can't adequately express what it meant to have a friend whose belief in what I was trying to do, and whose commitment to thinking it through with me in all its many complications, sorrows, and hopes, made the ring of the telephone something always to look forward to.

The best part of my life is my wife, Kaari Pitkin, and our children, Bea and Ozzie.

A NOTE ON SOURCES

In some ways this book began during my New Haven childhood in the mid-1960s, '70s, and early '80s. New Haven was then, as it is now, a city of neighborhoods, a remarkably diverse place with often segregated racial and ethnic distribution. Children tended to stay in their own areas. It was, therefore, my good fortune to attend two public elementary schools that drew from several communities, including Newhallville, and to play a lot of baseball. I spent my days on fields in almost every New Haven neighborhood, got to know kids and their families from across the city. My family lived on the first floor of a rented two-family house; I had a single, schoolteacher mother who'd worry aloud at night out on the fold-out couch: "How am I going to make it through the month?" My father lived in another state, sometimes wandered the streets, was in and out of institutions. A signal revelation of my childhood came in the years I played baseball on Bowen Field, which is adjacent to Hillhouse High School, more or less in Newhallville. There I met boys from families whose evident struggles providing for their basic needs were so much more pressing than my own. After I grew up and left New Haven, when I'd return to visit my mom I saw that nothing much was really changing for the economic better in Newhallville, even as nearby Yale University and its surroundings grew conspicuously more prosperous.

I moved back to New Haven with my family in 2012, planning to try to write about the city as it reflected postindustrial American issues of long standing. To begin interviews, I'd tell the person I was meeting a version of what I've described above about myself. I would have interviewed the entire city if I could have. But I settled for speaking with some 500 people (most listed below). I always tried to make clear that my job was to be considerate, neutral, objective, and observational, that I couldn't be anybody's advocate, and I had to represent, as best as I could, all points of view. One of the many reasons to speak with so many people is that life is complicated and there's no absolute validity, but there is accuracy in description, representation, and fact. When I'd ask for advice and criticism at the end of interviews, people emphasized the need for blunt accuracy. "It is what it is," they'd remind me. About the fact that I am white, I was struck by something a friend told me: "Why is it always up to Black people to talk about these problems? Black people want white people to engage. Black people are tired. Your job is to tell this as a citizen."

Some writers working on projects involving specific neighborhoods or communities describe "hanging out." I didn't hang out. I didn't ever go anywhere without an appointment to meet up with someone or without a stated purpose—to attend something happening, like a playground basketball tournament, that I wanted to see or watch. I met just about everybody through somebody else, receiving introductions from a person who vouched. The ensuing conversations took place in homes, police stations and substations, law offices, cars, parks, on porches, sidewalks, schools, hospitals, fast-food restaurants, diners, sandwich shops, bars, courthouses, government buildings, car dealerships, prisons, and detention facilities. In Newhallville I was sometimes mistaken for a police officer or a government agency employee. Discussions then might follow about everything from cars to eyeglasses to policing to jobs, jobs, jobs. The desire for well-paying, interesting work was/is palpable.

Early on, I met with people in a haphazard fashion, trying to find my way. Then the telephone rang one day and everything changed. It was the lawyer Ken Rosenthal, calling to introduce himself. Rosenthal told me he'd heard about me, and that he had a client whose experience might inform what he'd been told I was doing. He then spoke at some length about Bobby's "case," concluding by asking would I like to hear more? That was how, on a snowy Sunday, up on the third floor in the eaves of an otherwise empty law office, I found myself looking through boxes of documents related to the legal history of Bobby's supposed role in the murder of Herbert Fields Jr. Soon enough I met Bobby in prison, met friends, relations, and acquaintances, met members of the Fields family, began hearing a lot about Major.

There have been many accounts of Black Americans and poverty. But there remain so many poor, Black, postindustrial neighborhoods in American cities, a disturbing fact. For the people I was spending time with, the subject seemed anything but overconsidered. This is one of the ways New Haven remains what it has long been, a representative U.S. city, compact and yet complex enough that it reveals other places. As Michael Jefferson, a Black New Haven lawyer who grew up in the Bronx, once said to me, "In school, in biology, they gave you a microscope and you could zoom in. That was New Haven for me. New York's too big. New Haven was the microscope for me on Black life, on American life."

At the project's end, my belief was in the need for a neighborhood's problems to be embraced by the greater city and its surroundings as collective problems, taken on especially by its leading institutions. Similarly, I came to feel just as strongly that solving and preventing homicides was not just a police obligation but the collective business of the city. If the broader community took homicide personally to the point of full, all-in priority collaboration, doing anything it could to help solve and prevent these tragic crimes, there would be far fewer of them.

It's sometimes said of nonfiction writers that their readers are affected to the degree to which the writers are transformed by their work. The great documentary filmmaker Frederick Wiseman once said during a public talk that ultimately his relationship to his film subjects becomes one of love.

Then there's hate. You can't write about Jim Crow South Carolina, or white-flight New Haven, without encountering use of the N-word. How or whether to print it is more complicated than a simple matter of accuracy. I think if you can do something to reduce a source of pain for others, soften its consumption, you should. On the other hand, I've been taught that revising or avoiding ugly history condemns societies to repeat it, that bad history has a way of enduring if it isn't directly engaged with. Thinking about this from his home in Newhallville, the Black artist Winfred Rembert concluded it's an ugly, sordid, mean word, but no substitute carries the same effect of a term devised only to humiliate and degrade others. I asked for advice from numerous people I know, including friends and figures in the book, and there was no consensus. Some thought that quoting the slur was appropriate, and that eliding it would undermine the historical intent and impact of the term. Others considered writing it out in full to be gratuitous. Ultimately, I decided that the word was so offensive I didn't want to write it out in full. So I didn't.

This is as much or more a book concerned with class as it is with race. As a middle-class person writing about those who were often impoverished, there was frequently the desire to help in tangible ways. Here I struggled, but I saw that if the project was to remain transparently objective in its descriptions of fact and feeling, I had to follow the common standard of journalistic ethics, which holds that a writer may not bestow gifts or make other gestures that would compromise their impartiality. I understand the principle, agree that a writer can easily intrude upon and distort the reality of what they seek to describe. Likewise, a writer who makes gestures can create false expectations of how they will portray a subject. When I took people's time, of course I paid for the meals we shared and expenses incurred. I gave people rides. A lot of what being a writer offers you is access to information. When I heard about job openings, I told those I knew who were looking. Bobby fully supported my desire to write about him as he was, for his experiences to offer insight into those of others, and he didn't ask me to do anything beyond my job.

A subject who suffered as much as Bobby could be made very vulnerable by such a project, and I hoped an honest assessment wouldn't cause him more trouble. As the project neared its end, I took this up not only with Bobby but with his cousin Quay, Ken Rosenthal, and others who were closest to him, asking how to square such concerns with telling the full story. They all agreed with Bobby's friend and mentor, Stefon Morant, who said not to worry about Bobby in these respects because "he's a very open-book person." He always said he thought people should be known to others as they are.

In my experience, Frederick Wiseman is right about writers and subjects. Over time, I came to care deeply about Bobby. I also cared very much about other people I came to know well, like Katie-Jean Fields and Susan Troxler. I reviled the brutal actions Major was accused of and the unimaginable ongoing pain suffered by the families of victims. But I could see why those who loved Major so much had such feelings; society failed him as a child. One young person I met in a prison told me, "I am making myself vulnerable [because] it's good to shed light on the situation, what went wrong with a kid like me, a kid like Major. He grew up in a crazy environment."

For a person who'd grown up seeing and exposed to so much, including many forms of neglect, there was always a clear integrity about Bobby that led others to shake their heads and call him a good dude, a good guy. This project would have been impossible if I was spending so much time with someone less likable, less forthright, less goodhearted. Among Bobby's many personal virtues are his ability to inhabit other people's points of view and his rare recall of the feelings of childhood. He was committed from the first, telling me, "Before I get ahead of myself, I want you to know you can ask me anything." He always said I should just tell the truth. "Is what it is," he'd say. "What happened, happened." I can't count how many times we spoke across the years, beginning in the prison, and then in homes, at diners and restaurants, in cars, in lines and waiting rooms, by telephone, out and about. "Kind of disturbing to go over it all," he said in one of our first conversations, but he always did. "I see what it takes," he told me. I know I tested his patience as I endlessly confirmed details about aspects of life he'd rather move past, and I appreciate his forbearance every time I yet again opened a notebook.

In addition to the countless conversations with Bobby, this book relied on interviews and conversations with those some-500 other people across eight years. All spoken words in the book were either said in my presence, were recounted by people who were there, or appear printed in legal documents such as police reports, court transcripts, or depositions. There is no satisfied consensus about the legal cases and social issues this book engages with. In each matter, I tried to reach an informed, independent understanding of what happened, and then chose representative voices to explain it. Those interviews and discussions, listed below, were supplemented by written correspondence and both primary and secondary source documentation. Particularly significant were public legal documents that I received either through official requests, or from lawyers or others whose clients granted written permission to share both materials and memories. One of them, Dr. Alan Goldstein, wanted it specifically mentioned that he was given permission to talk with me by Ken Rosenthal and by Bobby. These documents include court, deposition, and interview transcripts, legal exhibits, legal applications, discovery files, motions and briefs, New Haven Police Department reports, New Haven Public School records, Connecticut Department of Correction records, and legal correspondence. I listened many times to the recordings of Bobby's two taped interviews with the New Haven Police Department, including listening to them in his presence and then discussing them with him. Susan Troxler shared with me records from her father's life documenting his military service, his real estate transactions, and other aspects of his day-to-day. Almost everyone I contacted for an interview granted my request. Exceptions included Det. Michael Quinn, former chief Francisco Ortiz, and Bobby's first lawyer, Lawrence Hopkins; I spoke with several people who knew and worked with each of them. There were also family members and associates of those involved in unsolved crimes who, when I approached them, wanted "nothing to do with it." I spoke with many law-enforcement professionals, scholars, and academics, with educators, public servants, business owners, community members, and community activists.

It would be impossible to explain what had happened to and in Newhallville, and so many neighborhoods across the country, if I didn't always write with accurate factual specificity. I tried to do so fairly, avoiding the sentimental and reductive, but with compassion.

The following sent me helpful correspondence, for which I thank them.

Mark Abraham, Thomas Abt, Joan Acocella, Kevin Alvarez, Elizabeth Alexander, Carol Anderson, Elijah Anderson, anonymous Newhallville residents, anonymous police officers, Molly Arabolos, Ms. Auntie, Kyle Bagwell, Edward Ball, Andrius Banevicius, Jack Bass, Eric Bates, Kyle Baudoin, Emily Bazelon, Lara Bazelon, Randall Beach, Monica Bell, Dirk Bergemann, Miriam Berkman, Dwayne Betts, Mr. Bobby, Victor Bolden, Leah P. Boustan, John Bradley, Francis Bremer, William Brown, Nick Brustin, Cynthia Burns, Ken Burns, Sarah Burns, Mark Buyck, Racheal Cain, Colin Caplan, Lincoln Caplan, Paul Cates, Joan Cavanagh, Sam Chauncey, Kathy Chetkovich, James Clark, Lizabeth Cohen, Odell Cohens Sr., James Comer, Steven Conn, Ted Conover, Miles Corwin, Mr. Crossover, Lisa Dadio, Martin Dadio, Martin Daly, Willing Davidson, Robert Dawidoff, Michael Dearington, Michael

DeLand, Matthew Delmont, Tim Devine, Angel Diggs, Jack A. Dougherty, Kevin Doyle, Waverly Duck, John Durham, Thomas Easley, Judith Edersheim, Sheila Edmonds, Arthur Edwards, Mr. Elbow, Justin Elicker, Ingrid Ellen, David T. Ellwood, Gwen Evans, Donna Fasano, Roland Fasano, Drew Gilpin Faust, Katie-Jean Fields, Bill Fisher, Dina Fisher, Emily Forman, James Forman Jr., Emma Freudenberger, Brandon Garrett, Norman Garrick, Craig Gauthier, Heather Gerken, Glenda Gilmore, William Ginsberg, Miriam Gohara, David Goldblum, Alan F. Goldstein, Brian Goldstein, Douglas Gollin, Aaron Goode, Karen Goodrow, Mr. Goody, Colin Gordon, D. Gorton, Amber Green, Robert Greenberg, Anthony Griego, Joseph Greelish, Harlan Greene, Samuel R. Gross, Kathleen Gunning, Kathleen Hagearty, Steven Hahn, Deborah Hare, Thomas Hargrove, Ira Harkavy, Catherine Hartley, Andrei Harwell, Patricia Helliger, Jack Hitt, John Hoda, Floyd Hooks, Andy Horowitz, Lisa Howorth, Patrick Hynes, Maya Jasanoff, Jacqueline Jones, Jimmy Jones, Laquivia Jones, Ms. Aunt Joy, Andrew Kahrl, Titus Kaphar, David Keenan, Randall Kenan, Thomas A. Kinney, Ivan Kuzyk, Roger Lane, Shirley Lawrence, Adrian Nicole LeBlanc, Samuel T. Ross-Lee, Nicholas Lemann, Jill Leovy, Mr. Lion, Lisa Lowe, L'Heureux Lewis-McCoy, Julian Loose, Tappy Lynn, Reggie Lytle, Sherman Malone, James Marshall, Karen Martucci, David Maurrasse, Deirdre McCloskey, Darcy McGraw, Julia McLaughlin, Christian McNamara, Tracey Meares, Beth Merkin, Reuben J. Miller, Marlene Miller-Pratt, John Monk, Raymond Monk Jr., Barbara Morgan, Peter Neufeld, Rochelle Nichols-Solomon, Vivian Nixon, Patrick Norton, Millette Núñez, Jerry Oates, Coral Ortiz, James Pagan, Jim Paley, Catherine Panter-Brick, Andrew Papachristos, John Pitkin, Kaari Pitkin, Diane Polan, Maya Polan, Nancy Pollak, Sally Pollak, Arthur Pope, Eric Powell, Thomas Powers, Dandara Ramos, Nathaniel Raymond, Dorothy Robinson, Homer Robinson, Karen Roles, Dale R. Rosengarten, Kenneth Rosenthal, Kim Rossmo, Henry Rosovsky, Leah Rosovsky, Randolph Roth, Richard Rothstein, Elihu Rubin, Adrienne Maciulewski Russo, Paul Sabin, Inga Saffron, Wendy Samberg, H. Lee Sarokin, Jessica Santos, Judith Schiff, Vincent Schiraldi, Daniel Scully, John David Scully, Vincent Scully, Scott Semple, Ernest Shaw, Brian Sibley, Charles Siebert, Jennifer Skiba, David E. E. Sloane, Michael Smith, Jill Marie Snyder, Asali Solomon, Robert Solomon, Anthony Sorrentino, Stacy Spell, John Stallard, Jason Stanley, Alexander Star, Stephanie Steiker, Justin Steil, Mr. Stennett, Ellie Stewart, Fred Strebeigh, Ed Surato, Jeanette Sykes, Cynthia Teixeira, Alan B. Thorne, Jessica Trounstine, Susan Troxler, Jeffrey Turner, Thomas Ullmann, Al Vazquez, John Velleca, Roger Waldinger, Holly Wasilewski, Clifton Watson, Anna Weesner, Shirley West, Jim Whitney, Jonathan Wiener, Christopher Wigren, Michael Wishnie, John Witt, Amy Wrzesniewski, Allyn Wright, John Yinger, Virginia Young, Travis Zadeh, and Loren Ziff.

In the course of writing this book, I spoke with the following people, some of them many times. I'm very grateful for their time.

Shafiq Abdussabur, Doreen Abubakar, Mark Abraham, Thomas Abt, Elizabeth Alexander, Jamaal Alexander, Kevin Alvarez, Elijah Anderson, Lora Rae Anderson, Ms. Andrea, anonymous Newhallville residents, anonymous police officers, anonymous university employees, Molly Arabolos, Ms. Aretha, Janet Arterton, Ms. Auntie, Mr. B., Isabelle Baccus, Andrius Banevicius, Eric Barbarito, Daryel Barros, Mark Barros, Jack Bass, Kyle Baudoin, Jarrad Beck, Monica Bell, Mr. Benji, Miriam Berkman, Ernie Bertothy, Doug Bethea, Dwayne Betts, Mr. BlackJack, Charles Blango, Teasie Blasingame, Eric Blinderman, Earl Bloodworth, Noah Bloom, Mr. Bobby, Victor Bolden, Mr. Bounce, Leah P. Boustan, Michael Bowe, Sarah Boyd, Leonard Boyle, John Bradley, Kendra Bradner, Diane Brown, Milton Brown, Sam Brown, Verneda D. Brown, William Brown, Janet Brown-Clayton, Kahlila L.

Brown-Dean, Joe Bruckmann, Nick Brustin, Otha Buffaloe, Cynthia Burns, Sarah Burns, Gilbert Burton, Charles Butler, Tony Butler, Mark Buyck, Racheal Cain, Marc Calafiore, Anthony Campbell, Marlene Cannady, Christine Carey, Chaz Carman, Kermit Carolina, Paul Cates, Joan Cavanagh, Thomas Chadwick, Letitia Charles, Henry "Sam" Chauncey, Edward Cherry, Mr. Chubby, Renee Cimino, Allie Cislo, James Clark, Erik Clemons, Patrick Clifford, David Clifton, Odell Cohens Sr., James Comer, Steven Conn, Mr. Corey, Mr. Country Boy, Forrest Crawford, Orlando Crespo, Mr. Crossover, Lisa Dadio, Martin Dadio, Martin Daly, Malcolm Davis, Ron Davis, Michael Dearington, Joe Dease Jr., Michael DeLand, John DeStefano, Margie DeVane, Frankie Devins, Frankie Devins, Fiona Doherty, Gary Dos Reis, William Dow, Kevin Doyle, Young Dude, John Durham, Tom Dyer, William Dyson, Thomas Easley, Judith Edersheim, Beulah Edge, Douglas Edge, Sheila Thorne Edmonds, Alfreda Edwards, Arthur Edwards, Kim Edwards, Mr. Elbow, John Eldan, Justin Elicker, Ingrid Ellen, Harvey Elwood Jr., Dean Esserman, Harley Etienne, Ms. Aunt Faith, Justin Farmer, Roland Fasano, Drew Gilpin Faust, Peter Fields, Herbert "Hubert" Fields, Katie-Jean Fields, Monroe Fields, Xavier Fields, Bill Fisher, Dina Fisher, William Fisher Jr., Emily Forman, James Forman Jr., Ian Frazier, Mr. Fred, Emma Freudenberger, Ms. Aunt Fun, Edmund Funaro Sr., Charlie Gargano, Bill Garraty, Brandon Garrett, Norman Garrick, Gary Gates, Craig Gauthier, John Geanakoplos, Mr. Gene, Achilles Generoso, Heather Gerken, Ruth Wilson Gilmore, Miriam Gohara, David Goldberg, Jim Goldberg, Alan Goldstein, Brian Goldstein, Aaron Goode, Karen Goodrow, Mr. Goody, Ms. Grace, Paul Graham, Mr. Granddad, Betsy Grauer, Amber Green, Eric Green, Robert Greenberg, Kevin Grenier, Anthony Griego, Patrick Griffin, Samuel Gross, Kathleen Gunning, Jake Halpern, Mike Hanis, Mr. Hank, Deborah Hare, Thomas Hargrove, Ira Harkavy, Donald Harrison, Rose Hart, Dan Hartnett, Andrei Harwell, Robert Hayden, Shmully Hecht, Marvin Henderson, Barbara Hill, Jack Hitt, John Hoda, Floyd Hooks, Roberta Hoskie, Daniel Hunt, Patrick Hynes, Karl Jacobson, Leonard Jahad, Gerald Jaynes, Pamela Jaynez, Michael Jefferson, Mr. Jerome, Ms. Joanne, Mr. Joey, Mr. Johnny, Belle Johnson, Dorothy Johnson, Herb Johnson, Juliet Johnson, James Jones, Jimmy Jones, Laquivia Jones, Nancy Jordan, Ms. Aunt Joy, Mr. Uncle June, Ms. K., Kevin Kane, Titus Kaphar, Michael Kaplan, David Keenan, Randall Kenan, Ms. Kenya, Thomas Kinney, Ivan Kuzyk, Mr. Kwame, David Lambkin, Mike Lawlor, Shirley Lawrence, Ms. Lawrie, Adrian Nicole LeBlanc, Sally Lee, Tara Lee, Nicholas Lemann, Mr. LeRoy, Ron Lewis, Scott Lewis, Sol Lipschitz, Mr. Lion, Mr. Little Blue, Larry Livingston, Margaret Logue, Carrie Lytle, Reggie Lytle, Shanti Madison, Sherman Malone, Darien Manning, James Manship, Peter Markle, Daniel Markovits, Karen Martucci, David Maurrasse, Randy McAllister, Walter McCain, Tom McCormick, Darcy McGraw, Jabril McKoy, Kym McKoy, Nasrullah McKoy, Robert Mclaurin, Tracey Meares, Beth Merkin, Jeffrey Alker Meyer, Kenneth Middleton, Mr. Uncle Mikey, Reuben J. Miller, Marlene Miller-Pratt, Jason Minardi, Monika Mittelholzer, Bryanna Moore, Kim Morant, Stefon Morant, Donald Morris, Ned Moundsman, Michelle Mouzon, Senora Mumford, O'Donovan Murphy, Kevin Myatt, Dontae Myers, Ms. Nana, Frank Nasti, Ms. Neena, Peter Neufeld, James Newman, John Newson, Rochelle Nichols-Solomon, Ms. Nora, Patrick Norton, Millette Núñez, Kevin Nursick, Jerry Oates, James O'Brien, Craig O'Connell, Mr. Old Dude, Mark O'Neil, Coral Ortiz, William Outlaw, Anthony Pagan, Ernest Pagan, James Pagan, Rosemary Paine, Jim Paley, Andrew Papachristos, Amy Parmenter, Emma Parris, Fred Parris, Nicholas Pastore, James Patterson, Norman Pattis, Ken Paul, Gloria Perkins, Harry Perkins, John Pfaff, Yvonne R. Philpot, Richard Phipps, Maureen Platt, Martin Podsiad, Diane Polan, James Ponteau, Arthur Pope, Eric Powell, Thomas Powers, Marlene Miller Pratt, Gwen Prowse, Mr. Pruitt, Ms.

Pruitt, Lisa Puglisi, Elnora Pullen, Joe Pullen, John Purmont, Mr. Quiz, Mr. Rabbit, Douglas Rae, B. L. Ramirez, Romano Ratti, Babz Rawls-Ivy, Lucas Rayliss, Nathaniel Raymond, Sean F. Reardon, Thaddeus Reddish, Ms. Reesha, Sean Reeves, Larry Reid, Patsy Rembert, Ms. Cousin Renfroe, Mr. Granddad Renfroe, Ms. Grandma Renfroe, Edward Reynolds, Ms. Rhonda, Arnold Rice, Dave Rivera, Kishwar Rizvi, Dyane Rizzo, Judith Rodin, Jane Rosenstadt, Alice Rosenthal, Kenneth Rosenthal, Henry Rosovsky, Samuel T. Ross-Lee, Kim Rossmo, Randolph Roth, Elihu Rubin, Norris Russell, Adrienne Maciulewski Russo, Jessica Sager, Yusef Salaam, Wendy Samberg, H. Lee Sarokin, Jo Schaller, Judith Schiff, Vincent Scully, Scott Semple, Mr. Sere, Ms. Serena, Bruce Shapiro, Kitt Shapiro, Patrick Sharkey, Ms. Sharon, Herb Sharp, Ms. Shavonne, Ernest Shaw, Ms. Shay, Ms. Sherice, Scott Shumway, Brian Sibley, Dave Simon, David Simon, Kenneth Simon, Jennifer Skiba, David E. E. Sloane, Michael Smith, Ron Smith, Rosa Smith, Zanniece Smith, Jill Marie Snyder, Asali Solomon, Robert Solomon, Ms. Sparky, Stacy Spell, Mr. Stennett, Ms. Stephanie, Scott Stevenson, Jason Stiel, Ted Stingley, Mr. SugarBear, Richard Supple, Reggie Sutton, Jeanette Sykes, Julia Sykes, John Sylvia, Amy Tang, Ms. Tonya, Margo Taylor, Reuben Taylor, Ms. Tee, Demethra Telford, Cynthia Teixeira, Bruce Thompson, Alan Thorne, Robert Thorne Jr., Barbara Tinney, Mr. Cousin Tomboy, Jessica Trounstine, Susan Troxler, True Unit Mentee, True Unit Mentor, Mr. The Truth, Thomas Ullmann, Ms. Valerie, Bessel van der Kolk, Al Vazquez, John Velleca, Emily Wang, Addie Wardlaw, Holly Wasilewski, Clifton Watson, Cynthia Watson, Melvin Wearing, Vesla Weaver, Anna Weesner, Shirley West, Troy Westberry, Christopher Wigren, Donnell William, Allen Williams, Doug Williams, Hazel Williams, James Williams, Maurice Williams, Rodney Williams, Clarence Willoughby, Mike Wishnie, John Witt, Albert Wolfe, Karen Wolff, Mr. Wonderboy, Glen Worthy, Allyn Wright, Ms. Wright, Amy Wrzesniewski, Michael Wuchek, Virginia Young, Mr. Young Dude.

I am grateful for the use of and research assistance from the following institutions, libraries, and archives:

Buffalo Bill Center of the West, McCracken Research Library (Winchester archives), with thanks to Karen Roles.
Carriage Museum of America.
Connecticut Trust for Historic Preservation, with thanks to Christopher Wigren.
College of Charleston, Addlestone Library, with thanks to Harlan Greene.
Eli Whitney Museum, with thanks to William Brown.
Florence County Museum.
Lillian Goldman Law Library, Yale University.
Museum of Connecticut History—Connecticut State Library.
National Association of Real Estate Brokers—NAREB.
Netter Center for Community Partnerships, University of Pennsylvania, with thanks to Ira Harkavy.
New Haven Free Public Library.
New Haven Museum, Whitney Library, with special thanks to Ed Surato and also to Frances Skelton.
New Haven Register, with thanks to Angel Diggs.
Orangeburg County Historical Society, with thanks to Eric Powell.
Southern Connecticut State University (the John DeStefano Papers).
Texas Tech University, Southwest Collection/Special Collections Library, with thanks to James Marshall.

West Haven Historical Society with thanks to John Purmont.

Yale University Department Manuscripts and Archives, with thanks to Judith Schiff.

I spent a year attending the sessions of the Federal Reentry Court held in the New Haven courtroom of Judge Jeffrey Alker Meyer. Thanks to Judge Meyer and to Carly Levinson, Nicholas Lombard, Emma Sokoloff-Rubin, Holly Wasilewski, and Chana Zuckier.

Lev Cohen, Anita Diggs, Michael Falero, Amber Green, Valerie Maczak, and Patricia Milardo offered different forms of help at crucial moments. Jock Reynolds brought sustenance. Kate Tuttle and Kevin Young left a light on for me in Georgia, as Anna Weesner did in Philadelphia. Jonathan Wiener and Ginger Young made two research trips possible by taking care of the children. On those days, and whenever else Kaari Pitkin joined me for interviews or events, everything was better.

Creating the narrative involved parsing multiple confessions, depositions, and the testimony of many people whose accounts sometimes shifted over time. Then there was what they told me. Because it was challenging to describe what truly (or falsely) went on at any given moment, I felt fortunate that, at the end, Dan Greene put his calm, meticulous gaze to everything. Naturally, any mistakes of fact, or errors of tone or interpretation or judgment, are mine alone.

Mark Abraham and his organization DataHaven gave me a great deal of patient assistance. I'm especially grateful for DataHaven's community index, for reports on relative equity, neighborhoods, missing men, health, violent crimes, and for *Mapping Inequality*, an excellent report on local redlining.

I attended community outreach events hosted by Project Longevity, where I am indebted to Stacy Spell for our many conversations about gun violence and policing. Addressing those same broad subjects, Leonard Jahad of the Connecticut Violence Intervention Program couldn't have been more generous with his time. Chaz Carmon of Ice the Beef was just as welcoming.

The New Haven Police Department, especially Chiefs Dean Esserman and Anthony Campbell, helped me to speak with dozens of past and present officers about their work.

I interviewed people held in Connecticut prisons, always with their prior granted permission. I'm very grateful to the Connecticut Department of Correction as well as the individual wardens at the Cheshire and MacDougall-Walker prisons for making this possible, most especially Andrius Banevicius, Karen Martucci, Scott Semple, and the department's fine sociologist, Patrick Hynes. Then-Commissioner Semple allowed me to regularly visit Bobby while he was incarcerated at the Cheshire Correctional Facility, including making quick arrangements with the warden, Scott Erfe, so that I could be present when Ken Rosenthal informed Bobby that he was being released. At different times, I was fortunate that two scholars immersed in the study of neighborhood violence, Tracey Meares and Andrew Papachristos, separately accompanied me to interviews with people held in Connecticut prisons.

BIBLIOGRAPHY

For this project, I read anything I could that seemed to have practical or thematic bearing on the subjects and topics I was engaging with. These books and articles helped me to become informed and to ask better questions, to study and even test the broader application of what I was learning on anecdotal levels, from described experience, and within small sample sizes. If someone recommended it, I read it.

The problems described in this book are not new; they are old American problems, historic world problems; they are problems of choices, intentions, and environment, and have to do with the precariousness of so many lives for so many generations that writers have been vexing over and then describing, in different ways, almost since there have been books. Generation after generation, writers are driven to describing children in poverty, the complexity in attempting to improve as a people, the futile impossibility of fixing anything at a remove—especially when the physical and emotional gulfs between people are themselves the source of so much damage.

It's sometimes dispiriting how much of today exists in accounts of the past. Fyodor Dostoevsky, working from personal experience of Siberian captivity in *Notes from a Dead House,* captured enduring truths about the interior lives and behaviors of people in prisons, telling how men came to hate others just because they shared the same dismal predicament inside and out: "We're beaten folk, they used to say, we're all beaten up inside; that's why we shout in our sleep." Being sent off to prison, Anton Chekhov said in *Sakhalin Island,* further reduced and degraded beaten people's health and morals. "Our intellectual classes have been repeating the phrase that every criminal is a product of society," he wrote, "but how indifferent they are to this product!" The truest description I've ever read of a coerced confession, virtually impossible to document in real time for obvious reasons, can be found in Richard Wright's *The Man Who Lived Underground,* written eighty years ago but only recently published. Aggressive and deceptive police interrogation techniques are now increasingly on the minds of judges like Steven Ecker of the Connecticut Supreme Court, whose impassioned partial dissent in *State of Connecticut v. Bobby Griffin* has significantly influenced the thinking of lower courts.

When we use the word "classic" in relation to a book, what we can mean is that it speaks to its time, and to our time. As I worked on this project, I read a number of books that engaged with the complex subject of how we think about others, how our lives exist in relation to the communities around us. Toni Morrison's novels are immersed in problems of race and class, but also how people endure—or don't. The juxtaposition of those who suffer with those who suffer less is a worldly dilemma, and in distant countries and foreign cultures we can still see New Haven, still see ourselves. The fiction and nonfiction, for example, of Charles Dickens, writing about childhood, criminal justice, and prisons, and that of Virginia Woolf, deeply engages with inequality by imbuing facts with imagination to create truths of life that remind us of our shared humanity. In *The Common Reader*, Woolf instructs the writer to "face the fact of other existences, grapple with the mechanism of external things . . . report the speeches of men and women who existed independently of herself." The exceptional books I thought about the most during this project were James Baldwin's *Collected Essays* and Claude Brown's *Manchild in the Promised Land*. It's the triumph and tragedy of such masterpieces that they should feel so contemporary. They make me sure that, though our lives contain multitudes of individual experience, in our virtues and our deficiencies, we are those who came before us, and we are our children, partners in the thousands of years of mankind living out the universal struggle that, for a fortunate few, bends toward freedom, fulfillment, and love.

BOOKS

Abdussabur, Shafiq R. F. *A Black Man's Guide to Law Enforcement in America*. Tucson, AZ: Wheatmark, 2010.

Abramsky, Sasha. *The American Way of Poverty*. New York: Nation Books, 2013.

Abt, Thomas. *Bleeding Out*. New York: Basic Books, 2019.

Adero, Malaika, ed. *Up South*. New York: The New Press, 1993.

Adler, William M. *Land of Opportunity*. New York: The Atlantic Monthly Press, 1995.

Agee, James. *Let Us Now Praise Famous Men*. New York: The Library of America, 2005.

Ahern, James F. *Police in Trouble*. New York: Hawthorn Books, 1972.

Alexander, Elizabeth. *The Trayvon Generation*. New York: Grand Central Publishing, 2022.

Alexander, Karl, Doris Entwisle, and Linda Olson. *The Long Shadow*. New York: Russell Sage Foundation, 2014.

Alexander, Michelle. *The New Jim Crow*. New York: The New Press, 2010.

Alexievich, Svetlana. *Secondhand Time*. New York: Random House, 2016.

Allis, Marguerite. *Water over the Dam*. New York: G. P. Putnam's Sons, 1947.

Ammon, Francesca Russelo. *Bulldozer*. New Haven: Yale University Press, 2016.

Anderson, Elijah. *Code of the Street*. New York: W. W. Norton & Company, 1999.

———. *The Cosmopolitan Canopy*. New York: W. W. Norton & Company, 2011.

———. *A Place on the Corner*, Chicago: The University of Chicago Press, 2003.

———. *Streetwise*. Chicago: The University of Chicago Press, 1990.

Anderson, Carol. *White Rage*. New York: Bloomsbury, 2016.

Applebaum, Anne. *Gulag*. New York: Doubleday, 2003.

Aurelius, Marcus. *The Meditations of Marcus Aurelius*. Translated by George Long for the Harvard Classics. New York: P. F. Collier & Son, 1965.

Baldwin, Davarian L. *In the Shadow of the Ivory Tower*. New York: Bold Type Books, 2021.

Baldwin, James. *Collected Essays*. New York: The Library of America, 1998.

———. *The Evidence of Things Not Seen*. New York: Holt, Rinehart, and Winston, 1985.

———. *Go Tell It on the Mountain*. New York: Vintage Books, 1952.
———. *Later Novels*. New York: The Library of America, 2015.
Baldwin, Simeon. *Theophilus Eaton*. New Haven: New Haven Colony Historical Society, 1907.
Ball, Edward. *Slaves in the Family*. New York: Farrar, Straus and Giroux, 1998.
Baraka, Amiri. *Blues People*. New York: William Morrow, 1999.
Barber, Charles. *Citizen Outlaw*. New York: Ecco, 2019.
Barr, Mary. *Friends Disappear*. Chicago: The University of Chicago Press, 2014.
Bass, Paul, and Douglas W. Rae. *Murder in the Model City*. New York: Basic Books, 2006.
Bauer, Shane. *American Prison*. New York: Penguin Press, 2018.
Bay, Mia. *Traveling Black*. Cambridge: The Belknap Press, 2021.
Bazelon, Emily. *Charged*. New York: Random House, 2019.
Beatty, Paul. *The Sellout*. New York: Farrar, Straus and Giroux, 2015.
Beauregard, Robert A. *Voices of Decline*. New York: Routledge, 2003.
Becker, Howard. *Outsiders*. New York: The Free Press, 1963.
———. *What About Mozart? What About Murder?* Chicago: The University of Chicago Press, 2014.
Beckert, Sven. *Empire of Cotton*. New York: Vintage Books, 2014.
Benson, Lee, Ira Harkavy, et al. *Knowledge for Social Change*. Philadelphia: Temple University Press, 2017.
Berlin, Isaiah. *Russian Thinkers*. New York: Penguin Books, 1978.
Bernstein, Nell. *Burning Down the House*. New York: The New Press, 2014.
Betts, Dwayne. *A Question of Freedom*. New York: Avery, 2009.
Betts, Reginald Dwayne. *Bastards of the Reagan Era*. New York: Four Way Books, 2015.
———. *Felon*. New York: W. W. Norton & Company, 2019.
———. *Shahid Reads His Own Palm*. Farmington, ME: Alice James Books, 2010.
Bishop, J. Leander. *History of American Manufactures. Vol 3*. Philadelphia. Edward Young & Co. 1868. (Reprint Augustus Kelley 1966.)
Black, Timothy. *When a Heart Turns Rock Solid*. New York: Vintage Books, 2009.
Blackmon, Douglas A. *Slavery by Another Name*. New York: Anchor Books, 2008.
Blight, David. *Frederick Douglass*. New York: Simon & Schuster, 2018.
———. *Race and Reunion*, Cambridge: The Belknap Press, 2001.
Bloom, Amy, ed. *New Haven Noir*, Brooklyn: Akashic Books, 2017.
Boo, Katherine. *Behind The Beautiful Forevers*. New York: Random House, 2012.
Borchard, Edwin M. *Convicting the Innocent*. New Haven: Yale University Press, 1932.
Boustan, Leah Platt. *Competition in the Promised Land*. Princeton: Princeton University Press, 2017.
Braly, Malcolm. *False Starts*. Eureka, California: Stark House Press, 2016.
———. *On the Yard*. New York: New York Review Books, 2002.
Braman, Donald. *Doing Time on the Outside*. Ann Arbor: University of Michigan Press, 2004.
Branch, Taylor. *At Canaan's Edge*. New York: Simon & Schuster, 2006.
Bremer, Francis J. *Building a New Jerusalem*. New Haven: Yale University Press, 2012.
Brooks, Richard R. W., and Carol M. Rose. *Saving the Neighborhood*. Cambridge: Harvard University Press, 2013.
Brown, Claude. *The Children of Ham*. New York: Stein and Day, 1976.
———. *Manchild in the Promised Land*. New York: Touchstone, 2012.
Brown, Elizabeth Mills. *New Haven: A Guide to Architecture and Urban Design*. New Haven: Yale University Press, 1976.

Brown, Otis Jr. *How Did We Get Here?* New Haven: self-published, 2015.
———. *Things We Don't Talk About.* New Haven: self-published, 2017.
Buckley, William F. *God & Man at Yale.* Washington, DC: Regnery Publishing, Inc., 1986.
Burgess, Anthony. *A Clockwork Orange.* New York: W. W. Norton & Company, 1962.
Burns, Sarah. *The Central Park Five.* New York: Vintage Books, 2011.
Burton, Charles Wesley. *Living Conditions Among Negroes in the Ninth Ward.* New Haven: New Haven Civic Federation, 1912–1919.
Burton, Susan, and Cari Lynn. *Becoming Ms. Burton.* New York: The New Press, 2017.
Butler, Paul. *Choke Hold.* New York: The New Press, 2017.
Butterfield, Fox. *All God's Children.* New York: Alfred A. Knopf, 1995.
———. *In My Father's House.* New York: Alfred A. Knopf, 2018.
Camp, Jordan, and Christina Heatherton. *Policing the Planet.* New York: Verso, 2016.
Canada, Geoffrey. *Fist Stick Knife Gun.* Boston: Beacon Press, 1995.
Caro, Robert. *Master of the Senate.* New York: Alfred A. Knopf, 2002.
———. *The Passage of Power.* New York: Alfred A. Knopf, 2012.
Cash, W. J. *The Mind of the South.* New York: Alfred A. Knopf, 1941.
Cavanagh, Joan. *Our Community at Winchester.* New Haven: Great New Haven Labor History Association, 2020.
Chauncey, Henry "Sam," John T. Hill, and Thomas Strong. *May Day at Yale 1970.* Westport, CT: Prospecta Press, 2016.
Chekhov, Anton. *Sakhalin Island.* Richmond, U.K.: Alma Classics, 2019.
Cherlin, Andrew J. *Labor's Love Lost.* New York: Russell Sage Foundation, 2014.
Christie, Agatha. *Death on the Nile.* New York: HarperCollins, 2011.
Clark, Kenneth B. *Dark Ghetto.* New York: Harper & Row, 1965.
Clifton, Lucille. *Blessing the Boats.* Rochester, New York: BOA Editions, Ltd., 2000.
Coates, Ta-Nehisi. *The Beautiful Struggle.* New York: Spiegel & Grau, 2009.
———. *Between the World and Me.* New York: Spiegel & Grau, 2015.
———. *We Were Eight Years in Power.* New York: One World, 2017.
Cohen, Lizabeth. *A Consumer's Republic.* New York: Vintage Books, 2003.
———. *Saving America's Cities.* New York: Farrar, Straus and Giroux, 2019.
Coles, Robert. *Farewell to the South.* Boston: Little, Brown and Company, 1972.
———. *The South Goes North.* Boston: Little, Brown and Company, 1967.
Colley, Linda. *The Gun, the Ship, and the Pen.* New York: Liveright Publishing Company, 2021.
Collins, Randall. *Violence.* Princeton: Princeton University Press, 2008.
Comer, James. *Maggie's American Dream.* New York: New American Library, 1988.
Connor, Myles J. Jr., with Jenny Siler. *The Art of the Heist.* New York: HarperCollins, 2009.
Conover, Ted. *Newjack.* New York: Random House, 2000.
Contreras, Randol. *The Stickup Kids.* Berkeley: University of California Press, 2013.
Cook, G.&D. *G.&D. Cook & Co.'s Illustrated Catalogue of Carriages and Special Business Advertiser.* New York: Dover Publications, Inc., 1970.
Corwin, Miles. *Homicide Special.* New York: Henry Holt and Company, 2003.
Cox, Alexandra. *Trapped in a Vice.* New Brunswick: Rutgers University Press, 2017.
Crawford, Lacy. *Notes on a Silencing.* New York: Little, Brown and Company, 2020.
Cronon, William. *Changes in the Land.* New York: Hill and Wang, 1983.
———. *Nature's Metropolis.* New York: W. W. Norton & Company, 1991.
Currie, Elliott. *Confronting Crime.* New York: Pantheon Books, 1985.

———. *A Peculiar Indifference*. New York: Metropolitan Books, 2020.
Dahl, Robert A. *Who Governs*. New Haven: Yale University Press, 2005.
Dailey, Jane. *The Age of Jim Crow*. New York: W. W. Norton & Company, 2009.
Daly, Martin. *Killing the Competition*. New Brunswick, NJ: Transaction Publishers, 2016.
Daly, Martin, and Margo Wilson. *Homicide*. New York: Aldine de Gruyter, 1988.
Danticat, Edwidge. *The Art of Death*. Minneapolis: Graywolf Press, 2017.
Davis, Allison, Burleigh B. Gardner, and Mary R. Gardner. *Deep South*. Columbia: University of South Carolina Press, 2009.
Davis, David Brion. *Homicide in American Fiction 1798–1860*. Ithaca: Cornell University Press, 1957.
Davis, Mike. *City of Quartz*. New York: Verso, 2018.
De Tocqueville, Alexis. *Democracy in America*. New York: Harper & Row, 1969.
DeCarava, Roy, and Langston Hughes. *The Sweet Flypaper of Life*. New York: First Print Press, 2018.
Delbanco, Andrew. *Melville: His World and Work*. New York: Alfred A. Knopf, 2005.
Delmont, Matthew F. *Why Busing Failed*. Oakland: University of California Press, 2016.
DeLuca, Stefanie, Susan Clampet-Lundquist, and Kathryn Edin. *Coming of Age in the Other America*. New York: Russell Sage Foundation, 2016.
Denby, David. *Lit Up*. New York: Henry Holt and Company, 2016.
Desmond, Matthew. *Evicted*. New York: Crown Publishers, 2016.
Dexter, Franklin B. *Sketch of the Life and Writings of John Davenport*. New Haven: New Haven Colony Historical Society, 1877.
Dickens, Charles. *American Notes*. New York: Thomas Nelson and Sons, 1904.
———. *David Copperfield*. London: Collins, 1972.
———. *Great Expectations*. New York: Penguin Books, 1980.
———. *Our Mutual Friend*. New York: Penguin Books, 1971.
Didion, Joan. *After Henry ("Sentimental Journeys")*. New York: Vintage Books, 1992.
Domhoff, G. William. *Who Really Rules?* Santa Monica, CA: Goodyear Publishing Company, Inc., 1978.
Donaldson, Greg. *The Ville*. New York: Ticknor & Fields, 1993.
Dostoevsky, Fyodor. *Crime and Punishment*. New York: Vintage Books, 1993.
———. *Notes from a Dead House*. New York: Vintage Classics, 2015.
Dougherty, Sean Thomas. *The Second of Sorrow*. Rochester, NY: BOA Editions, Ltd., 2018.
Douglas, Geoffrey. *Dead Opposite*. New York: Henry Holt and Company, 1995.
Drake, St. Clair, and Horace R. Cayton. *Black Metropolis: A Study of Negro Life in a Northern City*. Chicago: University of Chicago Press, 1970.
Dubber, Markus Dirk. *The Police Power*. New York: Columbia University Press, 2005.
Du Bois, W.E.B. *The Philadelphia Negro*. Philadelphia: University of Pennsylvania Press, 1996.
———. *Writings*. New York: The Library of America, 1986.
Dulaney, W. Marvin. *Black Police in America*. Bloomington: Indiana University Press, 1996.
Duneier, Mitchell. *Ghetto*. New York: Farrar, Straus and Giroux, 2016.
———. *Sidewalk*. New York: Farrar, Straus and Giroux, 1999.
Dunne, John Gregory. *Regards*. New York: Thunder's Mouth Press, 2006.
East, Michael. *Beyond Hope*. West Conshohocken, PA: Infinity Publishing, 2009.
Eberstadt, Nicholas. *Men Without Work*. West Conshohocken, PA: Templeton Press, 2016.
Eggers, Dave, and Lola Vollen, eds. *Surviving Justice*. New York: Verso, 2017.

Ellen, Ingrid Gould. *Sharing America's Neighborhoods*. Cambridge: Harvard University Press, 2000.
Elliott, Andrea. *Invisible Child*. New York: Random House, 2021.
Ellison, Ralph. *Invisible Man*. New York: Random House, 1952.
———. *Shadow and Act*. New York: Vintage International, 1964.
Estes, Eleanor. *The Moffats*. New York: Harcourt, Brace & World, Inc., 1941.
———. *Rufus M*. New York: Harcourt, Inc., 1943.
Etienne, Harley F. *Pushing Back the Gates*. Philadelphia: Temple University Press, 2012.
Fader, Jamie J. *Falling Back*. New Brunswick: Rutgers University Press, 2013.
Fanon, Franz. *Black Skin, White Masks*. New York: Grove Press, 2008.
Farley, Reynolds, and Walter R. Allen. *The Color Line and the Quality of Life in America*. New York: Oxford University Press, 1989.
Fassin, Didier. *Enforcing Order*. Malden, MA: Polity Press, 2013.
———. *Prison Worlds*. Malden, MA: Polity Press, 2017.
Faust, Drew Gilpin. *This Republic of Suffering*. New York: Alfred A. Knopf, 2008.
Fernandez-Kelly, Patricia. *The Hero's Fight*. Princeton: Princeton University Press, 2015.
Fielding-Singh, Priya. *How The Other Half Eats*. New York: Little, Brown Spark, 2021.
Fields, M.K.J. *The Fields of Purple*. Kindle Direct Publishing, 2019.
———. *My Time Has Come and Gone*. Self-published, 2009.
Finnegan, William. *Cold New World*. New York: Random House, 1998.
Fisher, Ronald P., and R. Edward Geiselman. *Memory-Enhancing Techniques for Investigative Interviewing*. Springfield, IL: Charles C. Thomas, 1992.
Fiss, Owen. *A Way Out*. Princeton: Princeton University Press, 2003.
Fitzgerald, Sally, ed. *The Habit of Being*. New York: Farrar, Straus and Giroux, 1979.
Flaubert, Gustave. *Sentimental Education*. New York: Penguin Books, 1964.
Florida, Richard. *The New Urban Crisis*. New York: Basic Books, 2017.
Foner, Eric. *Reconstruction*. New York: Harper Perennial, 2014.
Forman, James. *Locking Up Our Own*. New York: Farrar, Straus and Giroux, 2017.
Fosdick, Raymond B. *American Police Systems*. New York: The Century Company, 1920.
Frank, Jerome, and Barbara Frank. *Not Guilty*. Garden City, New York: Doubleday & Company, Inc., 1957.
Frankl, Viktor E. *Man's Search for Meaning*. Boston: Beacon Press, 2006.
Franklin, H. Bruce, ed. *Prison Writing in 20th Century America*. New York: Penguin Books, 1998.
Freund, David M. P. *Colored Property*. Chicago: University of Chicago Press, 2007.
Gaines, Ernest J. *The Autobiography of Miss Jane Pittman*. New York: Dial Press, 1971.
Garb, Margaret. *City of American Dreams*. Chicago: University of Chicago Press, 2005.
Garrett, Brandon L. *Convicting the Innocent*. Cambridge: Harvard University Press, 2011.
Gattis, Ryan. *All Involved*. New York: Ecco, 2015.
Genovese, Eugene D. *Roll Jordan Roll*. New York: Vintage Books, 1974.
George, Henry. *Progress and Poverty*. New York: Robert Schalkenbach Foundation, 1929.
Gerald, Casey. *There Will Be No Miracles Here*. New York: Riverhead Books, 2018.
Gershman, Bennett. *Prosecutorial Misconduct*. Eagan, MN: Westlaw, 2015.
Glazer, Nathan, and Daniel Patrick Moynihan. *Beyond the Melting Pot*. Cambridge: The M.I.T. Press, 1963.
Goffman, Alice. *On the Run*. Chicago: The University of Chicago Press, 2014.
Goldberg, Carey, ed. *Inside New Haven's Neighborhoods*. New Haven: George E. Platt, 1982.

Goldberg, Jim, and Donovan Wylie. *Candy/A Good and Spacious Land*. New Haven: Yale University Art Gallery, 2017.
Goldstein, Amy. *Janesville*. New York: Simon & Schuster, 2017.
Gonnerman, Jennifer. *Life on the Outside*. New York: Farrar, Straus and Giroux, 2004.
Gordon, Colin. *Mapping Decline*. Philadelphia: University of Pennsylvania Press, 2008.
Gordon, Robert J. *The Rise and Fall of American Growth*. Princeton: Princeton University Press, 2016.
Goree, Thomas. *Some Features of Prison Control in the South. Proceedings of the Annual Congress of the National Prison Association of the United States (held at Austin, Texas, December 1897)*. Pittsburgh: Shaw Brothers, 1898.
Gottesdiener, Laura. *A Dream Foreclosed*. Westfield, NJ: Zuccoti Park Press, 2013.
Gould, Jonathan. *Otis Redding*. New York: Crown Archetype, 2017.
Grandin, Greg. *The End of the Myth*. New York: Metropolitan Books, 2019.
Grant, Robert. B. *The Black Man Comes to the City*. Chicago: Nelson-Hall Company, 1972.
Gregory, James N. *The Southern Diaspora*. Chapel Hill: The University of North Carolina Press, 2005.
Griffin, Farah Jasmine. *"Who Set You Flowin'?"* New York: Oxford University Press, 1995.
Griswold, Eliza. *Amity and Prosperity*. New York: Picador, 2018.
Grossman, James R. *Land of Hope*. Chicago: The University of Chicago Press, 1989.
Gwaltney, John Langston. *Drylongso*. New York: The New Press, 1993.
Haag, Pamela. *The Gunning of America*. New York: Basic Books, 2016.
Hacker, Andrew. *Two Nations*. New York: Scribner, 2003.
Hahn, Stephen. *A Nation Under Our Feet*. Cambridge: Harvard University Press, 2003.
Hakutani, Yoshinobu, ed. *Theodore Dreiser's Uncollected Magazine Articles 1897–1902*. Newark: University of Delaware Press, 2003.
Halpern, Jake. *Bad Paper*. New York: Picador, 2015.
Hamper, Ben. *Rivethead*. New York: Warner Books, 1986.
Handlin, Oscar, ed. *Children of the Uprooted*. New York: George Braziller, 1966.
Harcourt, Bernard E. *Language of the Gun*. Chicago: The University of Chicago Press, 2006.
Harding, David J. *Living the Drama*. Chicago: University of Chicago Press, 2010.
Hare, Deborah. *The Things They Carried*. Self-published, 2019.
Hare, Deborah, and Dru Nadler. *HomeBoys*. New Haven: Advocate Press, 1993.
Harrington, Michael. *The Other America*. Baltimore: Penguin Books, 1962.
Harris, Dianne. *Little White Houses*. Minneapolis: University of Minnesota Press, 2012.
Hartman, Saidiya. *Wayward Lives Beautiful Experiments*. New York: W. W. Norton & Company, 2019.
Hayden, Robert. *Collected Poems*. New York: Liveright Publishing, 1985.
Haynes, George Edmund. *The Negro at Work in New York City*. New York: Columbia University Press, 1912.
Heaney, Christopher. *Cradle of Gold*. New York: Palgrave Macmillan, 2010.
Heaney, Seamus. *North*. London: Faber & Faber, 1975.
Hegel, Richard. *Carriages from New Haven*. Hamden, CT: Archon Books, 1974.
Helper, Rose. *Racial Policies and Practices of Real Estate Brokers*. Minneapolis: University of Minnesota Press, 1969.
Hemphill, J. C. *Men of Mark in South Carolina*. Washington, DC: Men of Mark Publishing Company, 1909.

Hicks, Frederick C. *William Howard Taft, Yale Professor of Law and New Haven Citizen.* New Haven: Yale University Press, 1945.

Hinton, Elizabeth. *America on Fire.* New York: Liveright Publishing, 2021.

———. *The Making of Mass Incarceration in America.* Cambridge: Harvard University Press, 2016.

Hirsch, Arnold R. *Making the Second Ghetto.* Chicago: University of Chicago Press, 1983.

Hobbs, Jeff. *The Short and Tragic Life of Robert Peace.* New York: Scribner, 2014.

Hochschild, Arlie Russell. *Strangers in Their Own Land.* New York: The New Press, 2016.

Hochschild, Jennifer L. *Facing Up to the American Dream.* Princeton: Princeton University Press, 1995.

Homberger, Eric. *Scenes from the Life of a City.* New Haven: Yale University Press, 1994.

Hornstein, Harold, ed. *New Haven Celebrates the Bicentennial.* New Haven: New Haven Bicentennial Commission, 1976.

Hounshell, David. *From the American System to Mass Production.* Baltimore: Johns Hopkins University Press, 1984.

Hughes, Langston. *Selected Poems.* New York: Vintage Books, 1990.

Hyde, Lewis. *A Primer for Forgetting.* New York: Farrar, Straus and Giroux, 2019.

Ingraham, Prentiss. *Buffalo Bill and the Cattle Thieves.* New York: Street & Smith, 1908.

Isenberg, Nancy. *White Trash.* New York: Viking, 2016.

Jackson, Kenneth T. *Crabgrass Frontier.* New York: Oxford University Press, 1985.

Jackson, Mandi Isaacs. *Model City Blues.* Philadelphia: Temple University Press, 2008.

Jackson, Mitchell S. *The Residue Years.* New York: Bloomsbury, 2013.

———. *Survival Math.* New York: Scribner, 2019.

Jacobs, Jane. *The Death and Life of Great American Cities.* New York: Vintage Books, 1989.

———. *The Economy of Cities.* New York: Random House, 1969.

Jefferson, Margo. *Negroland.* New York: Vintage Books, 2015.

Jentleson, Barbara C. *Better Together.* New York: Teachers College Press, 2011.

Johnson, C. W. *Heart's Desire.* Hamden, CT: Inner Quest, 2012.

———. *Splintered.* Hamden, CT: Inner Quest, 2005.

Johnson, Daniel M., and Rex R. Campbell. *Black Migration in America.* Durham: Duke University Press, 1981.

Johnson, Matt. *Loving Day.* New York: Spiegel & Grau, 2015.

Johnson, Owen. *Stover at Yale.* New York: Collier Books, 1968.

Johnson, Rucker C., and Alexander Nazaryan. *Children of the Dream.* New York: Basic Books, 2019.

Jones, Jacqueline. *American Work.* New York: W. W. Norton & Company, 1998.

Joyner, Charles. *Down by the Riverside.* Urbana: University of Illinois Press, 1984.

Kahrl, Andrew W. *Free the Beaches.* New Haven: Yale University Press, 2018.

Kathrada, Ahmed. *Letters from Robben Island.* East Lansing: Michigan State University Press, 1999.

Katz, Jack. *Seductions of Crime.* New York: Basic Books, 1988.

Keefe, Patrick Radden. *Say Nothing.* New York: Doubleday, 2019.

Kelley, Brooks Mather. *Yale.* New Haven: Yale University Press 1974.

Kempowski, Walter. *All for Nothing.* New York: New York Review Books, 2006.

Kenan, Randall. *Walking on Water.* New York: Alfred A. Knopf, 1999.

Kendi, Ibram X. *Stamped from the Beginning.* New York: Nation Books, 2016.

Kennedy, David M. *Don't Shoot.* New York: Bloomsbury, 2011.

Kennedy, Randall. *Race, Crime, and the Law*. New York: Pantheon Books, 1997.
Kernan, Alvin. *In Plato's Cave*. New Haven: Yale University Press, 1999.
Kerner Commission. *Report of the National Advisory Commission on Civil Disorders*. New York: Bantam Books, 1968.
Kersten, Andrew E. *Race, Jobs, and the War*. Champaign: University of Illinois Press, 2007.
Kidder, Tracy. *Home Town*. New York: Pocket Books, 1999.
King, Gilbert. *Devil in the Grove*. New York: HarperPerennial, 2012.
Kinney, Thomas. *The Carriage Trade*. Baltimore: Johns Hopkins University Press, 2004.
Kitt, Eartha. *Alone with Me*. Chicago: H. Regnery Co., 1976.
———. *Confessions of a Sex Kitten*. London: Barricade Books, 1989.
Klockars, Carl. *Thinking About Police*. New York: McGraw-Hill, 1983.
Koestler, Arthur. *Darkness at Noon*. New York: Bantam Books, 1986.
Kohler-Hausmann, Issa. *Misdemeanorland*. Princeton: Princeton University Press, 2018.
Kotlowitz, Alex. *An American Summer*. New York: Doubleday, 2019.
———. *There Are No Children Here*. New York: Doubleday, 1991.
Kozol, Jonathan. *Amazing Grace*. New York: Harper Perennial, 1995.
———. *Rachel and Her Children*. New York: Fawcett Books, 1988.
———. *Savage Inequalities*. New York: Harper Perennial, 1991.
Lane, Roger. *Murder in America*. Columbus: Ohio State University Press, 1997.
Lareau, Annnette. *Unequal Childhoods*. Berkeley: University of California Press, 2003.
Latzer, Barry. *The Rise and Fall of Violent Crime in America*. New York: Encounter Books, 2016.
Laub, John H., and Robert J. Sampson. *Shared Beginnings, Divergent Lives*. Cambridge: Harvard University Press, 2003.
Laurence, Peter. *Becoming Jane Jacobs*. Philadelphia: University of Pennsylvania Press, 2016.
Lavalle, Victor. *The Changeling*. New York: Spiegel & Grau, 2017.
Laymon, Kiese. *Heavy*. New York: Scribner, 2018.
LeBlanc, Adrian Nicole. *Random Family*. New York: Scribner, 2003.
Leeming, David Adams. *James Baldwin*. New York: Alfred A. Knopf, 1994.
Leeney, Robert J. *Elms, Arms & Ivy*. Montgomery: Community Communications, Inc, 2000.
Lemann, Nicholas. *The Promised Land*. New York: Alfred A. Knopf, 1991.
Leovy, Jill. *Ghettoside*. New York: Spiegel & Grau, 2015.
Lepore, Jill. *These Truths*. New York: W. W. Norton & Company, 2018.
Lerman, Amy E., and Vesla M. Weaver. *Arresting Citizenship*. Chicago: The University of Chicago Press, 2014.
Leveritt, Maria. *Devil's Knot*. New York: Atria Books, 2002.
Lewis, Oscar. *La Vida*. New York: Random House, 1966.
Lewis-McCoy, L'Heureux. *Inequality in the Promised Land*. Palo Alto: Stanford University Press, 2014.
Liebow, Elliot. *Tally's Corner*. Lanham, MD: Rowman & Littlefield, 2003.
Lingeman, Richard. *Theodore Dreiser*. New York: G. P. Putnam's Sons, 1986.
Lipsitz, George. *The Possessive Investment in Whiteness*. Philadelphia: Temple University Press, 1998.
Little, Gregory L., and Kenneth D. Robinson. *How to Escape Your Prison*. Memphis: Eagle Wing Books, 1989.
Litwack, Leon F. *Been in the Storm So Long*. New York: Vintage Books, 1979.

———. *Trouble in Mind*. New York: Vintage Books, 1998.
Loewen, James W. *Sundown Towns*. New York: Touchstone, 2006.
London, Jack. *John Barleycorn*. Mineola, NY: Dover Publications, Inc., 2018.
Lowe, Jeanne R. *Cities in a Race with Time*. New York: Random House, 1968.
Lukas, J. Anthony. *Common Ground*. New York: Alfred A. Knopf, 1985.
Lynch, Kevin. *The Image of the City*. Cambridge: The M.I.T. Press, 1960.
Macdonald, Ross. *The Doomsters*. New York: Vintage Books, 1958.
MacFarquhar, Larissa. *Strangers Drowning*. New York: Penguin Books, 2015.
MacLeod, Jay. *Aint No Makin' It*. Boulder, CO: Westview Press, 1987.
Malcolm, Andrew H. *Final Harvest*. New York: Signet Books, 1986.
Malcolm X. *The Autobiography of Malcolm X*. New York: Ballantine Books, 1965.
Manning, Peter K., and John Van Maanen, eds. *Policing*. Santa Monica: Goodyear Publishing Company, 1978.
Markovits, Daniel. *The Meritocracy Trap*. New York: Penguin Books, 2019.
Marks, Carole. *Farewell—We're Good and Gone*. Bloomington: Indiana University Press, 1989.
Massey, Douglas S., and Nancy A. Denton. *American Apartheid*. Cambridge: Harvard University Press, 1993.
Matusow, Allen J. *The Unraveling of America*. New York, Harper & Row, 1984.
Maurrasse, David J. *Beyond the Campus*. New York: Routledge, 2001.
Mawby, R. I. *Burglary*. Portland, Oregon: Willan Publishing, 2001.
Maynard, Preston, and Marjorie B. Noyes, eds. *Carriages & Clocks, Corsets & Locks*. Lebanon, New Hampshire: University Press of New England, 2004.
McBride, James. *The Color of Water*. New York: Riverhead Books, 1996.
Mehta, Suketu. *Maximum City: Bombay Lost and Found*. New York: Vintage Books, 2004.
Merton, Robert. *Social Theory and Social Structure*. New York: The Free Press, 1968.
Messner, Steven F., and Richard Rosenfeld. *Crime and the American Dream*. Belmont, CA.: Thomson Learning, 2001.
Meyer, Philipp. *American Rust*. New York: Spiegel & Grau, 2010.
Middleton, Earl W., with Joy W. Barnes. *Knowing Who I Am*. Columbia: The University of South Carolina Press, 2008.
Miles, Tiya. *All That She Carried*. New York: Random House, 2021.
Miller, Adam David. *Ticket to Exile*. Berkeley: BayTree Books, 2007.
Miller, Reuben Jonathan. *Halfway Home*. New York: Little, Brown and Company, 2021.
Miller, William Ian. *Humiliation*. Ithaca: Cornell University Press, 1993.
Miller, William Lee. *The Fifteenth Ward and the Great Society*. Cambridge: The Riverside Press, 1966.
Mirsky, Jeannette, and Allan Nevins. *The World of Eli Whitney*. New York: The Macmillan Company, 1952.
Mitchell, James. *The Dynamics of Neighborhood Change*. Washington, DC: Office of Policy and Development Research of U.S. Department of Housing and Urban Development, 1975.
Montross, Christine. *Waiting for an Echo*. New York: Penguin Press, 2020.
Morris, Norval, and David J. Rothman, eds. *The Oxford History of the Prison*. New York: Oxford University Press, 1998.
Morrison, Toni. *The Bluest Eye*. New York: Vintage Books, 1970.
———. *Jazz*. New York: Alfred A. Knopf, 1992.
———. *Song of Solomon*. New York: Vintage Books, 1977.

Moskos, Peter. *Cop in the Hood.* Princeton: Princeton University Press, 2008.
Muhammad, Khalil Gibran. *The Condemnation of Blackness.* Cambridge: Harvard University Press, 2010.
Mumford, Lewis. *The City in History.* New York: Harcourt, Inc., 1989.
———. *Sticks and Stones.* New York: Dover Publications, Inc., 1955.
Murch, Donna Jean. *Living for the City.* Chapel Hill: The University of North Carolina Press, 2010.
Murphy, Chris. *The Violence Inside Us.* New York: Random House, 2020.
Murray, Albert. *The Omni-Americans.* New York: The Library of America, 2020.
Musto, David F. *The American Disease.* New York: Oxford University Press, 1999.
Myrdal, Gunnar. *An American Dilemma.* New York: Harper & Brothers, 1944.
Newman, Katherine S. *No Shame in My Game.* New York: Vintage Books, 2000.
Noah, Trevor. *Born a Crime.* New York: Spiegel & Grau, 2016.
O'Connell, Craig S. *Up from the Ville.* Self-published, 2020.
O'Connor, Flannery. *Collected Works.* New York: The Library of America, 1988.
Ogbu, John U. *Black American Students in an Affluent Suburb.* New York: Routledge, 2003.
Olmsted, Frederick Law. *The Cotton Kingdom.* New York: Da Capo Press, 1996.
Olmsted, Frederick Law, and Cass Gilbert. *A Plan for New Haven (1910).* San Antonio: Trinity University Press, 2012.
Onyebuchi, Tochi. *Goliath.* New York: Tordoctcom, 2022.
Osofsky, Glibert. *Harlem.* Chicago: Ivan R. Dee, Inc., 1996.
Osterweis, Rollin G. *Three Centuries of New Haven, 1638–1938.* New Haven: Yale University Press, 1953.
Ovington, Mary White. *Black and White Sat Down Together.* New York: The Feminist Press, 1995.
Packer, George. *The Unwinding.* New York: Farrar, Straus and Giroux, 2013.
Pager, Devah. *Marked.* Chicago: The University of Chicago Press, 2007.
Painter, Nell Irvin. *Exodusters.* New York: W. W. Norton Publishers, Inc., 1976.
Parker, Karen F. *Unequal Crime Decline.* New York: New York University Press, 2008.
Parks, Gordon. *A Choice of Weapons.* St. Paul, MN: Minnesota Historical Society Press, 2010.
———. *Voices in the Mirror.* New York: Nan A. Talese, Doubleday, 1990.
Patterson, James T. *Grand Expectations.* New York: Oxford University Press, 1996.
Pattillo, Mary. *Black Picket Fences.* Chicago: The University of Chicago Press, 1999.
Patton, Sharon F. *African-American Art.* New York: Oxford University Press, 1998.
Pellegrino, Robert L. *I See Color.* New Haven: Design Monsters, 2015.
Pepper, Art, and Laurie Pepper. *Straight Life.* New York: Da Capo Press, 1994.
Perkinson, Robert. *Texas Tough.* New York: Picador, 2010.
Perry, Andre, Jonathan Rothwell, and David Harshbarger. *The Devaluation of Assets in Black Neighborhoods.* Washington, DC: Brookings Institution, 2018.
Peterson, Ruth D., and Lauren J. Krivo. *Divergent Social Worlds.* New York: Russell Sage Foundation, 2010.
Petry, Ann. *The Street.* New York: Houghton Mifflin, 1946.
Pfaff, John F. *Locked In.* New York: Basic Books, 2017.
Phillips, Brian. *Impossible Owls.* New York: Farrar, Straus and Giroux, 2018.
Pietila, Antero. *Not in My Neighborhood.* Chicago: Ivan R. Dee, 2010.
Piketty, Thomas. *Capital in the Twenty-First Century.* Cambridge: Harvard University Press, 2014.
Pinker, Steven. *The Better Angels of Our Nature.* New York: Penguin Books, 2011.

Pinkney, Darryl. *Busted in New York*. New York: Farrar, Straus and Giroux, 2019.
Pope, Arthur. *Carry Me Back*. Charleston, SC: CreateSpace Independent Publishing, 2015.
Powell, Adam Clayton Jr. *Adam by Adam*. New York: Kensington Publishing Group, 1971.
Powledge, Fred. *Model City*. New York: Simon & Schuster, 1970.
Proto, Neil Thomas. *Fearless*. Albany: State University of New York Press, 2020.
Puchner, Martin. *The Language of Thieves*. New York: W. W. Norton & Company, 2020.
Putnam, Robert. *Bowling Alone*. New York: Simon & Schuster, 2000.
———. *Our Kids*. New York: Simon & Schuster, 2015.
Putnam, Robert D., with Shaylyn Romney Garrett. *The Upswing*. New York: Simon & Schuster, 2020.
Rae, Douglas W. *City*. New Haven: Yale University Press, 2003.
Rankine, Claudia. *Citizen*. Minneapolis: Graywolf Press, 2014.
Raper, Arthur F. *Preface to Peasantry*. Columbia: University of South Carolina Press, 2005.
Raper, Arthur F., and Ira De Augustine Reid. *Sharecroppers All*. Chapel Hill: The University of North Carolina Press, 1941.
Redfield, Robert. *The Little Community and Peasant Society and Culture*. Chicago: The University of Chicago Press, 1960.
Reed, Austin. *The Life and Adventures of a Haunted Convict*. New York: Random House, 2016.
Rembert, Winfred, with Erin I. Kelly. *Chasing Me to My Grave*. New York: Bloomsbury Publishing, 2021.
Reymont, Wladyslaw. *The Peasants*. New York: Alfred A. Knopf, 1924.
Ribowsky, Mark. *Dreams to Remember*. New York: Liveright Publishing, 2015.
Rich, John A. *Wrong Place, Wrong Time*. Baltimore: The Johns Hopkins University Press, 2009.
Rideau, Wilbert. *In the Place of Justice*. New York: Vintage Books, 2010.
Riis, Jacob. *How the Other Half Lives*. New York: Hill and Wang, 1957.
Rios, Victor M. *Punished*. New York: New York University Press, 2011.
Robinson, Eugene. *Disintegration*. New York: Doubleday, 2010.
Rodin, Judith. *The University & Urban Revival*. Philadelphia: University of Pennsylvania Press, 2007.
Rose, Jonathan F. P. *The Well-Tempered City*. New York: Harper Wave, 2016.
Rosengarten, Theodore. *All God's Dangers*. New York: Alfred A. Knopf, 1975.
Roth, Randolph. *American Homicide*. Cambridge: The Belknap Press, 2009.
Rothman, Adam. *Beyond Freedom's Reach*. Cambridge: Harvard University Press, 2015.
Rothstein, Richard. *The Color of Law*. New York: Liveright, 2017.
Rubinstein, Jonathan. *City Police*. New York: Farrar, Straus and Giroux, 1973.
Rybczynski, Witold. *Makeshift Metropolis*. New York: Scribner, 2010.
Salaam, Yusef, *Better, Not Bitter*. New York: Grand Central Publishing, 2021.
Sample, Albert Race. *Racehoss*. New York: Ballantine Books, 1984.
Sampson, Robert J. *Great American City*. Chicago: The University of Chicago Press, 2012.
Sampson, Robert J., and John H. Laub. *Crime in the Making*. Cambridge: Harvard University Press, 1993.
Satter, Beryl. *Family Properties*. New York: Metropolitan Books, 2009.
Saunders, Ernest. *The Autobiography of a Dual American*. New Haven: Advocate Press, 1979.
Scott, John Anthony. *Settlers on the Eastern Shore, 1607–1750*. New York: Alfred A. Knopf, 1967.

Scully, Vincent, Catherine Lynn, Erik Vogt, and Paul Goldberger. *Yale in New Haven*. New Haven: Yale University Press, 2004.

Sellers, Bakari. *My Vanishing Country*. New York: Amistad, 2020.

Sered, Danielle. *Until We Reckon*. New York: The New Press, 2019.

Shapiro, James. *Shakespeare in a Divided America*. New York: Penguin Press, 2020.

Sharkey, Patrick. *Stuck in Place*. Chicago: The University of Chicago Press, 2013.

———. *Uneasy Peace*. New York: W. W. Norton & Company, Inc., 2018.

Shedd, Carla. *Unequal City*. New York: Russell Sage Foundation, 2015.

Sherman, William Tecumseh. *Memoirs of General W. T. Sherman*. New York: The Library of America, 1990.

Shuler, Jack. *Blood & Bone*. Columbia: University of South Carolina Press, 2012.

Shulman, Alix Kates, and Honor Moore, eds. *Women's Liberation!* New York: The Library of America, 2021. (Anthology includes Johnnie Tillmon's "Welfare Is a Women's Issue" and Alice Walker's "In Search of Our Mother's Gardens.")

Shumway, Floyd, and Richard Hegel, eds. *New Haven*. Woodland Hills, CA: Windsor Publications, Inc., 1981.

Simon, David. *Homicide*. New York: Picador, 2006.

Simon, David, and Edward Burns. *The Corner*. New York: Broadway Books, 1997.

Simpson, Brooks D., ed. *Reconstruction*. New York: The Library of America, 2018.

Singer, Merrill. *Something Dangerous*. Long Grove, Illinois: Waveland Press, Inc., 2006.

Skloot, Rebecca. *The Immortal Life of Henrietta Lacks*. New York: Broadway Books, 2010.

Sletcher, Michael. *New Haven*. Charleston, SC: Arcadia Publishing, 2004.

Smith, Caroline. *Our City*. San Francisco: Blurb Books, 2017.

Smith, Caroline, and Elizabeth Larkin. *New Haven and Yale*. San Francisco: Blurb Books, 2019.

Smith, Clint. *How The Word Is Passed*. New York: Little, Brown and Company, 2021.

Snyder, Jill Marie. *Dear Mary, Dear Luther*. Bloomington, IN: AuthorHouse, 2015.

Solzhenitsyn, Alexander. *One Day in the Life of Ivan Denisovich*. New York: Bantam Books, 1963.

Sorin, Gretchen. *Driving While Black*. New York: Liveright Publishing, 2020.

Souljah, Sister. *No Disrespect*. New York: Vintage Books, 1994.

Spear, Allan H. *Black Chicago*. Chicago: The University of Chicago Press, 1967.

Speth, James Gustave. *Angels by the River*. White River Junction, VT: Chelsea Green Publishing, 2014.

St. Germain, Jim, with Jon Sternfeld. *A Stone of Hope*. New York: HarperCollins Publishers, 2017.

Stack, Carol. *All Our Kin*. New York: Basic Books, 1974.

———. *Call to Home*. New York: Basic Books, 1996.

Stampp, Kenneth M. *The Era of Reconstruction*. New York: Vintage Books, 1965.

———. *The Peculiar Institution*. New York: Vintage Books, 1956.

Stevens, Wallace. *The Palm at the End of the Mind*. New York: Vintage Books, 1972.

Stevenson, Bryan. *Just Mercy*. New York: Spiegel & Grau, 2014.

Stewart, Daniel Y. *Black New Haven: 1920–1977*. New Haven: Advocate Press, 1977.

———. *The Dan Stewart Story*. New Haven: self-published, 1980.

———. *New Haven Black History*. New Haven: self-published, 1978.

Stewart, George R. *Names on the Land*. New York: New York Review of Books, 2008.

Stuntz, William J. *The Collapse of American Criminal Justice*. Cambridge: Harvard University Press, 2011.

Suddler, Carl. *Presumed Criminal*. New York: New York University Press, 2019.

Sugrue, Thomas. *The Origins of the Urban Crisis*. Princeton: Princeton University Press, 2005.

———. *Sweet Land of Liberty*. New York: Random House, 2008.

Suskind, Ron. *A Hope in the Unseen*. New York: Broadway Books, 2005.

Suttles, Gerald D. *The Social Order of the Slum*. Chicago: The University of Chicago Press, 1968.

Talbott, Allan R. *The Mayor's Game*. New York: Praeger Publishers, 1967.

Taub, Richard P., D. Garth Taylor, and Jan D. Dunha. *Paths of Neighborhood Change*. Chicago: The University of Chicago Press, 1984.

Taylor, Candacy. *Overground Railroad*. New York: Abrams Press, 2020.

Taylor, Craig. *New Yorkers*. New York: W. W. Norton & Company, 2021.

Taylor, Keeanga-Yamahtta. *Race for Profit*. Chapel Hill: The University of North Carolina Press, 2019

Teaford, Jon C. *The Twentieth Century American City*. Baltimore: Johns Hopkins University Press, 1993.

Terry, Wallace. *Bloods*. New York: Ballantine Books, 1984.

Thompson, Heather Ann. *Blood in the Water*. New York: Pantheon Books, 2016.

Thompson, John, with Jesse Washington. *I Came As a Shadow*. New York: Henry Holt And Company, 2020.

Trainum, James L. *How the Police Generate False Confessions*. Lanham, MD: Rowman & Littlefield, 2016.

Travis, Jeremy. *But They All Come Back*. Washington, DC: The Urban Institute Press, 2005.

Trevelyan, Laura. *Winchester*. New Haven: Yale University Press, 2016

Trillin, Calvin. *Killings*. New York: Random House, 2018.

Trounstine, Jessica. *Segregation by Design*. New York: Cambridge University Press, 2018.

Turgenev, Ivan. *Fathers and Sons*. New York: Penguin Books, 1984.

Turner, Patricia A. *I Heard It Through the Grapevine*. Berkeley: University of California Press, 1993.

Tyler, Tom R. *Why People Obey the Law*. Princeton: Princeton University Press, 2006.

Van der Kolk, Bessel. *The Body Keeps Score*. New York: Penguin Books, 2014.

Vance, J. D. *Hillbilly Elegy*. New York: Harper Collins, 2016.

Vargas, Robert. *Wounded City*. New York: Oxford University Press, 2016.

Venkatesh, Sudhir. *Gang Leader for a Day*. New York: Penguin Books, 2008.

———. *Off the Books*. Cambridge: Harvard University Press, 2006.

Venter, Sahm, ed. *The Prison Letters of Nelson Mandela*. New York: W. W. Norton & Company, 2018.

Vergara, Camilo Jose. *American Ruins*. New York: The Monacelli Press, 1999.

———. *The New American Ghetto*. New Brunswick: Rutgers University Press, 1997.

Vuong, Ocean. *On Earth We're Briefly Gorgeous*. New York: Penguin Press, 2019.

Wacquant, Loic. *Punishing the Poor*. Durham: Duke University Press, 2009.

Waldinger, Roger. *Still the Promised City?* Cambridge: Harvard University Press, 1996.

Ward, Jesmyn, ed. *The Fire This Time*. New York: Scribner, 2016.

Warner, Robert Austin. *New Haven Negroes*. New York: Arno Press, 1969.

Warren, Robert Penn. *The Legacy of the Civil War*. Lincoln: University of Nebraska Press, 1998.

Warshauer, Matthew. *Connecticut in the American Civil War*. Middletown: Wesleyan University Press, 2011.

Weaver, Robert C. *Dilemmas of Urban America*. Cambridge: Harvard University Press, 1965.
Western, Bruce. *Homeward*. New York: Russell Sage Foundation, 2018.
———. *Punishment and Inequality in America*. New York: Russell Sage Foundation, 2006.
White, Richard. *The Republic for Which It Stands*. New York: Oxford University Press, 2017.
Whyte, William Foote. *Street Corner Society*. Chicago: The University of Chicago Press, 1993.
Whyte, William H. *The Social Life of Small Urban Spaces*. New York: Project for Public Spaces, 1980.
Wideman, John Edgar. *Brothers and Keepers*. Boston: Houghton Mifflin Company, 2005.
Wilkerson, Isabel. *Caste*. New York: Random House, 2020.
———. *The Warmth of Other Suns*. New York: Vintage Books, 2010.
Williams, Thomas Chatterton. *Losing My Cool*. New York: Penguin Books, 2010.
Williams, Yohuru. *Black Politics/White Power*. St. James, NY: Brandywine Press, 2000.
Williamson, Harold. *Winchester*. Washington, DC: Combat Forces Press, 1952.
Willis, Paul. *Learning to Labor*. New York: Columbia University Press, 1977.
Wilson, August. *King Hedley II*. New York: Theatre Communications Group, 2005.
Wilson, Edward O. *Genesis*. New York: Liveright Publishing Company, 2019.
Wilson, James Q. *Thinking About Crime*. New York: Basic Books, 1975.
Wilson, R. L. *Winchester*. New York: Random House, 1991.
Wilson, William Julius. *The Truly Disadvantaged*. Chicago: The University of Chicago Press, 2012.
———. *When Work Disappears*. New York: Alfred A. Knopf, 1997.
Wirth, Louis. *The Ghetto*. New Brunswick, NJ: Transaction Publishers, 1998.
Wolfinger, Raymond. *The Politics of Progress*. Englewood Cliffs, NJ: Prentice-Hall, Inc., 1974.
Woolf, Virginia. *The Common Reader*. New York: Harcourt Inc., 1984.
———. *To the Lighthouse*. New York: Mariner Books, 1981.
———. *The Waves*. Ware, Hertfordshire: Wordsworth Editions Limited, 2000.
Woodard, Colin. *American Nations*. New York: Penguin Books, 2011.
Woodward, C. Vann. *The Strange Career of Jim Crow*. New York: Oxford University Press, 1974.
Woodward, C. Vann, ed. *Mary Chesnut's Civil War*. New Haven: Yale University Press, 1981.
Wright, Richard. *Black Boy*. New York: Harper & Row, 1966.
———. *The Man Who Lived Underground*. New York: Library of America, 2021.
———. *Native Son*. New York: Harper & Row, 1966.
———. *12 Million Black Voices*. New York: Basic Books, 2008.
Yinger, John. *Closed Doors, Opportunities Lost*. New York: Russell Sage Foundation, 1995.
Young, Kevin. *Bunk*. Minneapolis: Graywolf Press, 2018.
Zeldin, Theodore. *An Intimate History of Humanity*. New York: HarperCollins, 1995.
Zimbardo, Philip. *The Lucifer Effect*. New York: Random House, 2007.
Zoellner, Tom. *The National Road*. Berkeley, CA: Counterpoint, 2020.
Zorbaugh, Harvey Warren. *The Gold Coast and the Slum*. Chicago: The University of Chicago Press, 1976.

ARTICLES

I read many back issues of and kept up with relevant contemporary coverage in the following publications.

Connecticut Magazine
Connecticut Mirror
Connecticut Post
Daily Nutmeg
Hartford Courant
New Haven Independent
New Haven Register
New York Review of Books
New York Times
ProPublica
The Atlantic
The New Yorker
Yale Daily News

I have particular admiration for the reporting of the *New Haven Independent*, an online newspaper with a dedicated and rigorous staff who cover issues and experiences across the entire city.

My research was informed by reading back issues of the following publications:

Kurumi.com
New Journal (at Yale)
New West
OZY.com
Daily Pennsylvanian
Post and Courier (Charleston, South Carolina)
Times and Democrat (Orangeburg, South Carolina)

Specific articles that particularly informed the project include:

Aaronson, Daniel, Daniel A. Hartley, and Bhashkar Mazumder. "The Effects of the 1930's HOLC 'Redlining Maps.'" FRB of Chicago working paper, August 2020.

Alexander, J. Trent, Christine Lieibbrand, Catherine Massey, and Stewart Tolnay. "Second-Generation Outcomes of the Great Migration." *Demography* (2017).

Als, Hilton. "The Enemy Within." *The New Yorker*, February 9, 1998.

Ananat, Elizabeth Oltmans. "The Wrong Side(s) of the Tracks." *American Economic Journal* (April 2011).

Anderson, Elijah. "The White Space." *Sociology of Race and Ethnicity* (January 2015).

Archer, John. "Puritan Town Planning in New Haven." *Journal of the Society of Architectural Historians* (May 1975).

Asbury, Bret D. "Anti-Snitching Norms and Community Loyalty," *Oregon Law Review* 89, no. 4 (2011).

Asher, Jeff, Ben Horwitz, and Toni Markovic. "Why Does Louisiana Consistently Lead the Nation in Murders?" *New York Times*, February 15, 2021.

Badger, Emily. "Have You Ever Seen Someone Be Killed?" *New York Times*, May 25, 2018.

Badger, Emily, and Christopher Ingraham. "The Striking Power of Poverty to Turn Young Boys into Jobless Men." *Washington Post*, January 29, 2016.

Baldwin, James. "Interview." *The Paris Review* 91 (Spring 1984).

———. "Letter from a Region in My Mind." *The New Yorker,* November 17, 1962.

Banks, Ralph Richard. "An End to the Class vs. Race Debate." *New York Times,* March 21, 2018.

Bell, Daniel. "Crime as an American Way of Life." *The Antioch Review* (Summer 1953).

Bell, Monica C. "Black Security and the Conundrum of Policing." *Just Security,* July 15, 2020.

———. "Legal Estrangement: A Concept for These Times." *Footnotes* 48, no 4 (July–August, 2020).

———. "Police Reform and the Dismantling of Legal Estrangement." *The Yale Law Journal* (2017).

———. "Safety, Friendship and Dreams." *Harvard Civil Rights–Civil Liberties Law Review* (2019).

Bellafante, Ginia. "Have Urban Universities Done Enough for the Neighborhoods Around Them?" *New York Times,* December 10, 2021.

Black, Dan A., Seth G. Sanders, Evan Taylor, and Lowell Taylor. "The Impact of the Great Migration on Mortality of African Americans." *American Economic Review* (February 2015).

Blau, Judith R., and Peter M. Blau. "The Cost of Inequality." *American Sociological Review* 47 (February 1982).

Blow, Charles. "Officers' Race Matters Less Than You Think." *New York Times,* March 26, 2015.

Boo, Katherine. "The Marriage Cure." *The New Yorker,* August 18, 2003.

Bosman, Julie, and Monica Davey. "3 Officers Acquitted of Covering Up for Colleague in Laquan McDonald Killing." *New York Times,* January 17, 2019.

Brayne, Sarah. "Big Data Surveillance: The Case of Policing." *American Sociological Review* (August 2017).

———. "Surveillance and System Avoidance: Criminal Justice Contact and Institutional Attachment." *American Sociological Review* (April 2014).

Burnett-Zeigler, Inger E. "Young Black People Are Killing Themselves." *New York Times,* December 16, 2019.

Caniglia, John. "What Cities Can Learn from New Haven's Fight to Rein in Gang Violence." Cleveland.Com, March 24, 2016.

Chalfin, Aaron, and Justin McCrary. "Are U.S. Cities Under Policed?" *Review of Economics and Statistics* (March 2018).

Chein, Jason, et al. "Peers Increase Adolescent Risk Taking by Enhancing Activity in the Brain's Reward Circuitry." *Developmental Science* (2011).

Chetty, Raj. "The Impacts of Neighborhood on Economic Opportunity." Brookings Institution.

Chetty, Raj, and Nathaniel Hendren. "The Impacts of Neighborhoods on Intergenerational Mobility." *The Quarterly Journal of Economics* (August 2018).

Chetty, Raj, Nathaniel Hendren, and Lawrence Katz. "The Effects of Exposure to Better Neighborhoods on Children." *American Economic Review* (April, 2016).

Chetty, Raj, Nathaniel Hendren, Patrick Kline, and Emmanuel Saez. "Where Is the Land of Opportunity? The Geography of Intergenerational Mobility in the United States." *The Quarterly Journal of Economics* (November 2014).

Chlebowski, Susan, and Cecilia Leonard. "The Forensic and Legal Implications of Water, Wet or Fry." *The Journal of the American Academy of Psychiatry and Law* (April 2012).

Coates, Ta-Nehisi. "The Black Family in the Age of Incarceration." *The Atlantic*, September 15, 2015.

Cole, Teju. "A Chronicle of Life and Pain in Upstate New York." *New York Times Magazine*, November 21, 2018.

Connecticut Circle Magazine, May 1938.

Connecticut Magazine. "Rating the Towns." November 2015.

Cook, Philip J., Jens Ludwig, Suhir Venkatesh, and Anthony A. Braga. "Underground Gun Markets." *The Economic Journal* (November 2007).

Cook, Philip J., Susan T. Parker, and Harold A. Pollack. "Sources of Guns to Dangerous People: What We Learn By Asking Them." *Preventive Medicine* (October, 2015).

Cowan, Alison Leigh. "Income Gap in Connecticut Is Growing Fastest, Study Finds." *New York Times*, April 9, 2008.

Cromartie, John, and Carol B. Stack. "Reinterpretation of Black Return and Nonreturn Migration to the South 1975–1980." *Geographical Review* 79, no. 3 (July 1989).

Cross, Christina. "The Myth of the Two Parent Home." *New York Times*, December 9, 2019.

———. "Racial/Ethnic Differences in the Association Between Family Structure and Children's Education." *Journal of Marriage and Family* (December 2019).

Davey, Monica. "Police 'Code of Silence' on Trial After Murder by Chicago Officer." *New York Times*, December 3, 2018.

Davidoff, Paul. "Advocacy and Pluralism in Planning." *Journal of the American Institute of Planners* (1965).

Davidson, Justin. "New Studies Say Gentrification Doesn't Really Force Out Low-Income Residents." *New York Magazine*, August 5, 2019.

Delbanco, Andrew. "Our Universities: The Outrageous Reality." *New York Review of Books*, July 9, 2015.

Dixon, Ken. "Whites-Only Rules Still Surface in Connecticut Property Records." *The Middletown Press*, March 1, 2020.

Dobrow, Joe. "A Farewell to Arms: Winchester Repeating Arms Company and New Haven, Connecticut." *Journal of the New Haven Colony Historical Society* (Spring 1993).

Driskell, Jay. "An Atlas of Self Reliance: The Negro Motorist's Green Book (1937–1964)." Smithsonian Museum Natural History Blog, July 30, 2015.

Drizin, Steven A., and Richard A. Leo. "The Problem of False Confessions in the Post-DNA World." *North Carolina Law Review* 82 (2005).

Dwyer, Jim. "Ex-Officer Off Tough Beat Seeks to Free the Innocent." *New York Times*, June 10, 2001.

———. "No Way Out." *New York Times*, June 23, 2002.

Ebony. The White Problem in America (special issue), August 1965.

Ellickson, Robert. "The Zoning Strait-Jacket: Evidence from The Silicon Valley, Greater New Haven, and Greater Austin." Stanford Law School, Workshop Draft.

Elorza, Jorge O. "Absentee Landlords, Rent Control and Healthy Gentrification: A Policy Proposal to Deconcentrate the Poor in Urban America." *Journal of Law and Public Policy* (2007).

Equal Justice Initiative. "Black Youth Five Times More Likely Than White Youth to Be Incarcerated." September 9, 2017.

Felkenes, George T. "The Prosecutor: A Look at Reality." *Southwestern University Law Review* 98, no. 110 (1975).

Fields, Gary, and John R. Emshwiller. "Putting Police Officers Back on the Beat." *Wall Street Journal*, March 12, 2015.

Finnegan, William. "The Blue Wall." *The New Yorker*, August 3 & 10, 2020.

———. "Out There I and II." *The New Yorker*, September 10 and 17, 1990.

Ford, Ben. "The Cruttendon Carriage Works: The Development and Decline of Carriage Production in New Haven, Connecticut." *Industrial Archeology* 38 (2012).

Forman, James Jr. "Racial Critiques of Mass Incarceration: Beyond the New Jim Crow," *New York University Law Review*, February 26, 2012.

Friedersdorf, Conor. "New Haven's Top Cop: 'You Don't Know Us Anymore.'" *The Atlantic*, November 19, 2015.

Garrett, Brandon. "Contaminated Confessions Revisited." *Virginia Law Review* (2015).

———. "The Substance of False Confessions." *Stanford Law Review* (2010).

Gates, Henry Louis Jr. "The Truth Behind 'Forty Acres and a Mule.'" *The Root*, 2013.

Gelb, Adam, and Jacob Denney. "National Prison Rate Continues to Decline Amid Sentencing, Reentry Reform." The Pew Charitable Trusts, January 16, 2018.

Gertner, Nancy. Letter to the editor. *New York Review of Books*, January 8, 2015.

Gibson, Lydialyle. "Color and Incarceration." *Harvard Magazine*, September–October 2019.

Gilmore, Ruth Wilson. "Race, Prisons and War: Scenes from the History of US Violence." *Socialist Register*, 2009.

Goldman, Joanne Abel. "From Carriage Shop to Carriage Factory." In *Nineteenth Century Carriages: Their Manufacture, Decoration and Use*. The Museum of Stony Brook, 1987.

Goldstein, Brian. "Planning's End? Urban Renewal in New Haven." *Journal of Urban History* (May 2011).

Gootman, Elissa. "New Haven and Yale." *New York Times*, February 18, 2001.

Grabar, Henry. "Trouble in America's Country Club." *Slate*, June 2, 2017.

Green, Erica L., and Annie Waldman. "You Are Still Black: Charlottesville's Racial Divide Hinders Students." *New York Times*, October 16, 2018.

Greenblatt, Stephen. "If You Prick Us." *The New Yorker*, June 10 and 17, 2017.

Greenwood, Peter W. "The Rand Criminal Investigation Study: Its Findings and Impacts to Date." The Rand Corporation, July 1979.

Grim, Valerie. "African American Landlords in the Rural South." *Agricultural History* (Spring 1998).

Groeger, Lena V., Annie Waldman, and David Eads. "Miseducation." ProPublica, October 16, 2018.

Gross, Samuel R. "Lost Lives, Miscarriages of Justice in Capital Cases." *Law and Contemporary Problems* (1998).

Gross, Samuel R., Kristin Jacoby, Daniel Matheson, and Nicholas Montgomery. "Exonerations in the United States 1989 Through 2003." *The Journal of Criminal Law and Criminology* (2005).

Gross, Samuel R., Barbara O'Brien, Chen Hu, and Edward H. Kennedy. "Rate of False Conviction of Criminal Defendants Who Are Sentenced to Death." *Proceedings of the National Academy of Sciences of the United States* (May 20, 2014).

Groves, Allison K., Linda M. Niccolai, Danya E. Keene, et al. "Housing Instability and HIV Risk: Expanding Our Understanding of the Impact of Eviction and Other Landlord-Related Forced Moves." *Aids and Behavior Journal* (June 2021).

Gurwitt, Rob. "The Death of a Neighborhood." *Mother Jones*, September/October 2000.

Gutting, Gary. "I'm for Affirmative Action Can You Change My Mind." *New York Times*, December 10, 2018.

Hager, Eli. "The Seismic Change in Police Interrogations." The Marshall Project, March 7, 2017.

Hall, Peter Dobkin. "East Rock: Facts, Artifacts and Memories." *Journal of the New Haven Colony Historical Society* (Spring 2002).

Halpern, Jake. "The Cop." *The New Yorker*, August 3, 2015.

Hammer, Langdon. "Shadows Walking." *Los Angeles Review of Books*, July 3, 2021.

Hannah-Jones, Nikole. "Choosing a School for My Daughter in a Segregated City." *New York Times Magazine*, June 9, 2016.

Hannah-Jones, Nikole, et al. "The 1619 Project." *New York Times Magazine* (special issue), August 14, 2019.

Harris, Adam. "The Burden of Being 'On Point.'" *The Atlantic*, April 26, 2021.

Hartley, Catherine A., and Leah H. Somerville. "The Neuroscience of Adolescent Decision Making." Department of Health and Human Services author manuscript, 2016.

Haughney, Christine, and Janet Roberts. "Connecticut Foreclosure Crisis Appears to Be Worsening." *New York Times*, May 17, 2009.

Hauser, Philip M. "Demographic Factors in the Integration of the Negro." *Daedalus* 94, Fall 1965.

Henning, Emil H. III. "From Temple Mount to New Haven Green." Ezekiel's Temple, blog post, 2018.

Henry Hooker & Co. of New Haven CT. "A History of an Important Carriage Building Firm." *The Carriage Journal* (Spring 1984).

Herszenhorn, David. "Rich States, Poor Cities and Mighty Suburbs." *New York Times*, August 19, 2001.

Hoffman, Chris. "Defender of the Despised." *Connecticut Magazine*, March 2020.

Holmes, Natalie, and Alan Berube. "City and Metropolitan Inequality on the Rise Driven by Declining Income." Brookings Institution, January 2016.

Horowitch, Rose. "Pandemic Heightens Town-Gown Tensions." *Yale Daily News*, March 29, 2021.

Hughes, Langston. "Down Under in Harlem." *New Republic*, March 27, 1944.

Hwang, Jackelyn, and Lei Ding. "Gentrification and Residential Mobility in Philadelphia." *Regional Science and Urban Economics*, November 2016.

———. "Unequal Displacement: Gentrification, Racial Stratification, and Residential Destinations in Philadelphia." *American Journal of Sociology* 126, no. 2 (November 2020).

Jekel, James F. and David F. Allen. "Trends in Drug Abuse in the Mid-1980s." *The Yale Journal of Biology and Medicine* 60 (1987).

Johnson, Cherise. "Interview: G Herbo Opens Up." HipHopDX, February 2020.

Johnson, Doria Dee. "100 Years After Lynching, S. C. Historical Marker to Pay Tribute to Murdered Patriarch." *The Undefeated*, October 2016.

Johnson, John S. "Why Negroes Drive Cadillacs." *Ebony*, September 1949.

Johnson, Nicholas. "Negroes and the Gun: A Winchester 'In Every Black Home.'" *Washington Post*, January 29, 2014.

Johnson, Rucker C. "Long-Run Impacts of School Desegregation & Quality on Adult Attainments." National Bureau of Economic Research, January 2011 and 2015.

Kaba, Mariame. "Stopping the Causes of Violence." *The Socialist Worker* (2013).

Kalven, Jamie. "Code of Silence" (four-part series). *The Intercept*, October 6, 2016.

Karakatsanis, Alec. "Why 'Crime' Isn't the Question and Police Aren't the Answer." *The Atlantic*, August 2020.

Kassin, Saul M. "False Confessions: Causes, Consequences, and Implications for Reform." *Current Directions in Psychological Science* (2008).

———. "False Confessions: Cause, Consequences, and Implications for Reform." *Policy Insights from the Behavioral and Brain Sciences* (2014).

———. "The Psychology of Confessions." *Annual Review of Law and Social Science* (2008).

Kassin, Saul, et al. "Police-Induced Confessions: Risk Factors and Recommendations." *Law and Human Behavior* (2009).

———. "Police Interviewing and Interrogation." *Law and Human Behavior* (2007).

Kassin, Saul M., and Katherine Kiechel. "The Social Psychology of False Confessions." *Psychological Science* (1996).

Kaufman, Dan. "The End of The Line." *New York Times Magazine*, May 5, 2019.

Kelling, George L., and James Q. Wilson. "Broken Windows." *The Atlantic Monthly*, March 1982.

Kolko, Jed. "Normal America Is Not a Small Town of White People." *FiveThirtyEight*, April 2016.

Kraus, Michael W. "How Fair Is American Society?" *Yale Insights*, September 2017.

Krivo, Lauren J., and Ruth D. Peterson. "Extremely Disadvantaged Neighborhoods and Urban Crime." *Social Forces* 75, no. 2 (December 1996).

Langbein, John H. "Torture and Plea Bargaining." The William Crosskey Lecture in Legal History, University of Chicago Law School, October 19, 1978.

"The Largest Carriage Mart in the World." *Harness and Carriage Journal* 14 (August 20, 1870).

Lennon, John J. "There Is No Name for This Thing You Become." *Poetry*, November 2019.

Lepore, Jill. "The Long Blue Line." *The New Yorker*, July 20, 2020.

———. "Sirens in the Night." *The New Yorker*, May 21, 2018.

Lewis, Katherine Reynolds. "One Ohio School's Quest to Rethink Bad Behavior." *The Atlantic*, May 8, 2018.

Lopez, German. "We Don't Need Mass Incarceration to Keep People Safe." *Vox*, January 16, 2018.

Love, David. "From 15 Million Acres to 1 Million: How Black People Lost Their Land." *Atlanta Black Star*, June 30, 2017.

MacFarquhar, Larissa. "Our Town." *The New Yorker*, November 13, 2017.

MacGillis, Alec. "What Philadelphia Reveals About America's Homicide Surge." ProPublica, July 30, 2021.

Magee, Lauren A., J. Dennis Fortenberry, Wanzhu Tu, and Sarah E. Wiehe. "Neighborhood Variation in Unsolved Homicides." *Injury Epidemiology* (December 1, 2020).

MainLine Today. "Doctor Death." July 7, 2008.

Marti, Douglas. "Fence Is Not Neighborly in a Suburb of Cleveland." *New York Times*, June 27, 1987.

McGuffin, David. "In Canada, Gun Violence Is a Growing Problem for Toronto." NPR, January 3, 2020.

McIntyre, Douglas A., and Michael B. Sauter. "The Ten Most Dangerous Cities in America." *The Atlantic*, May 2011.

McLaughlin, Julia H. "Litigation Funding." *Vermont Law Review* (2007).

Meares, Tracey L. "The Path Forward: Improving the Dynamics of Community Police Relationships to Achieve Effective Law Enforcement Policies." *Columbia Law Review* 117, no. 5 (2017).

———. "Policing and Procedural Justice." *Northwestern University Law Review* (2017).

Meares, Tracey L., and Tom R. Tyler. "The First Step Is Figuring Out What Police Are For." *The Atlantic*, August 2020.

Meisner, Jason, and Annie Sweeney. "Case Spotlights Code of Silence." *Chicago Tribune*, December 17, 2015.

Miller, Claire Cain. "Class Differences in Child-Rearing Are on the Rise." *New York Times*, December 17, 2015.

Miller, Ivor. "If It Hasn't Been One of Color: An Interview with Roy DeCarava." *Callalo* (Autumn 1990).

Miller, Reuben Jonathan, and Forrest Stuart. "Carceral Citizenship." *Theoretical Criminology* (October 2017).

Mooallem, Jon. "You Just Got Out of Prison: Now What?" *New York Times Magazine*, July 16, 2015.

Mullen, Arthur. "Town-Gown Riots Bane of New Haven." Roger Sherman House (blog), November 4, 2019, Rogershermanhouse.com.

Nettles, Arionne. "Black Mothers Are the Real Experts on the Toll of Gun Violence." *New York Times*, May 7, 2021.

New England Historical Society. "The Secret History of New England's Sundown Towns." Online. Undated, without byline, but acknowledges the research of James Loewen.

New York Times. "The Best and Worst Places to Grow Up." May 4, 2015.

New York Times (editorial). "Connecticut's Second-Chance Society." January 4, 2016.

———. "Governor Weicker's Bully Bugle Call." January 8, 1993.

———. "New Haven's Problems and Promise." December 17, 2006.

———. "Rich Get Richer, Poor Get Poorer: Unfortunately, the Tale of the Two Connecticuts Continues." April 25, 2002.

Nola.com. "Why Does New Orleans Have More Murders Than Similar Cities?" May 11, 2018.

Orfield, Gary, with Ee Jongyeon. "Connecticut School Integration." The UCLA Civil Rights Project, 2015.

Papachristos, Andrew. "Murder by Structure." *American Journal of Sociology* (July 2009).

———. "Small World of Murder." *Chicago Sun-Times*, January 16, 2011.

Papachristos, Andrew, Noli Brazil, and Tony Cheng. "Understanding the Crime Gap: Violence and Inequality in an American City." *City and Community* 17 (2018).

Payne, Charles M., and Mariame Kaba. "So Much Reform So Little Change: Building-Level Obstacles in Urban School Reform." *Social Policy* (2007).

Payne, H. Morse. "The Ordering of Towns: Massachusetts Bay Colony 17th Century Land Strategy." *NEARA Journal* 36, no. 1 (2007).

Peterson, Ruth D., and Lauren J. Krivo. "Macrostructural Analyses of Race, Ethnicity and Violent Crime." *Annual Review of Sociology* (2005).

Phelps, Edmund. "What Is Wrong with the West's Economics?" *New York Review of Books*, August 13, 2015.

Porter, Michael. "The Competitive Advantage of the Inner City." *Harvard Business Review* (May/June 1995).

Presser, Lizzie. "Their Family Bought Land One Generation After Slavery." ProPublica, July 15, 2019.

Purnell, Derecka. "How I Became a Police Abolitionist." *The Atlantic*, July 2020.

Ramos, Dandara de Oliveira, Maria Lucia Seidl-de-Moura, and Luciana Fontes Pessoa. "Achievement Goals of Youngsters in Rio de Janeiro in Different Contexts." *Paideia* (September–December 2013).

Reardon, Sean F., Demetra Kalogrides, and Ken Shores. "The Geography of Racial and Ethnic Score Gaps." The Stanford Center For Education Policy Analysis, April 2016.

Redlich, Allison D., and Gail S. Goodman. "Taking Responsibility for an Act Not Committed." *Law and Human Behavior* (2003).

Reznikoff, Charles. "New Haven: The Jewish Community." *Commentary* (November 1947).

Ridolfi, Kathleen M., Tiffany M. Joslyn, and Todd H. Fries. "Material Indifference: How Courts Are Impeding Fair Disclosure in Criminal Cases." *Santa Clara Law Digital Commons* (2014).

Roberts, Janet, and Elizabeth Stanton. "A Long Road Back After Exoneration, and Justice Is Slow to Make Amends." *New York Times*, November 25, 2007.

Rohrlich, Ted, and Frederic N. Tulsky. "Not All L.A. Murder Cases Are Equal." *Los Angeles Times*, December 3, 1996.

Rosenthal, Kenneth. "Prosecutor Misconduct, Convictions and Double Jeopardy." *Temple Law Review* 71, no. 4 (Winter 1998).

Ross, Colin. "The Myth of Dangerous Dixwell." *Yale Daily News*. February 15, 2012.

Rossmo, D. Kim, and Jocelyn M. Pollock. "Confirmation Bias and Other Systemic Causes of Wrongful Convictions." *Northeastern University Law Review* 11, no. 2.

Sampson, Robert J., and Dawn Jeglum Bartusch. "Legal Cynicism and (subcultural?) Tolerance of Deviance: The Neighborhood Context of Racial Differences." *Law and Society Review* 32, no. 4 (1998).

Santilli, Alycia, et al. "Bridging the Response to Mass Shootings and Urban Violence." *American Journal of Public Health* (March 2017).

Sarata, Phil. "North Native Eartha Kitt: From Tears to Triumph." *The Times and Democrat* (Orangeburg), December 27, 2008.

Sawyer, Wendy, and Peter Wagner. "Mass Incarceration: The Whole Pie." *Prison Policy Initiative* (March 2019).

Schweninger, Loren. "A Vanishing Breed: Black Farm Owners in the South." *Agricultural History* (Summer 1989).

Sedgwick, John. "The Last Boola-Boola." *GQ*, April 1994.

Seigel, Steven M. "Community Benefits Agreements in a Union City." *The Urban Lawyer* (2014).

Shaw, Jonathan. "He Has Made the World a Safer Place." *Harvard Magazine*, June 2018.

Shertzer, Allison, and Randall P. Walsh. "Racial Sorting and the Emergence of Segregation in American Cities." National Bureau of Economic Research, 2016, 2018.

Shufro, Cathy. "Everyday Justice." *Yale Alumni Magazine*, January–February 2018.

Shuval, Kerem, et al. "I Live by Shooting Hill." *Journal of Health Care for the Poor and Underserved* (February 2012).

Sills, Charlotte B. "The Early New Haven Carriage Builders Were True Craftsmen." *Connecticut Circle Magazine, May, 1938.*

Simon, Ruth. "The Company of Second Chances." *The Wall Street Journal*, January 25, 2020.

Sloane, David E. E., ed. "Nineteenth-Century American Industry and Culture." Eli Whitney Issue, *Essays in Arts and Sciences*, University of New Haven, West Haven, CT, vol. 10, no. 2, March 1982. See especially contributions by James R. Krut, Merrill Lindsay, Rollin G. Osterweis, and David E. E. Sloane.

Solomon, Robert A. "Building a Segregated City." *Saint Louis University Public Law Review* (1997).

Sorrentino, Anthony. "Philadelphia's Universal City." *International Society of City and Regional Planning Journal*, Review 11, 2016.

South, Eugenia C. "To Combat Gun Violence, Clean Up the Neighborhood." *New York Times*, October 8, 2021.

Srinivasan, Sujata. "Deep Roots Drive Newhallville Stakeholders to Advance Neighborhood Equality." Connecticut Health I-Team, August 2, 2021.

Staples, Brent. "Traveling While Black." *New York Times*, January 25, 2019.

Stark, Evan. "Wealth of a City Should be Measured in People." *New York Times*, January 11, 1987.

Starr, Douglas. "The Interview." *The New Yorker*, December 1, 2013.

———. "Juan Rivera and the Dangers of Coercive Interrogation." *The New Yorker*, May 22, 2015.

Stoddard, Sarah A., Susan J. Henly, Renee E. Sieving, and John Bolland. "Social Connections, Trajectories of Hopelessness, and Serious Violence in Impoverished Urban Youth." *Journal of Youth and Adolescence* 40, no. 3 (2011).

Sullivan, Thomas P., and Maurice Possley. "The Chronic Failure to Discipline Prosecutors for Misconduct." *Journal of Criminal Law and Criminology* 105, no. 4 (2015).

Surowiecki, James. "Why the Rich Are So Much Richer." *New York Review of Books*, September 24, 2016.

Thompson, Derek. "What on Earth Is Wrong with Connecticut?" *The Atlantic*, July 5, 2017.

Torralva, Krista. "New Haven Police's Approach Aids Children of Violence." *Corpus Christi Caller Times*, February 27, 2016.

Travis, Jeremy, Ronald Davis, and Sarah Lawrence. "Exploring the Role of the Police in Prisoner Reentry." U.S. Department of Justice, July 2012.

Wacquant, Loic. "Prisoner Reentry as Myth and Ceremony." *Dialectical Anthropology*, (December 2010).

———. "Relocating Gentrification: The Working Class, Science, and the State in Recent Urban Research." *International Journal of Urban and Regional Research* (March 2008).

Westfall, Sammy. "Crime Is Decreasing: Rhetoric or Reality?" *Yale Daily News*, April 10, 2019.

Wilkinson, Richard. "Why Is Violence More Common Where Inequality Is Greater?" *Annals of the New York Academy of Science* (2004).

Woodhouse, Kellie. "Widening Wealth Gap." *Inside Higher Ed*, May 21, 2015.

Wray, Caroline. "The Thing About Winter." *The New Journal* (February 2017).

REPORTS, STUDIES, AND PAPERS

Adger, Petisia M. "2005 Analyses of Homicides & Non-Fatal Shootings in the City of New Haven." New Haven Department of Police Service Planning & Research Division, 2006.

Bernstein, H. William. "From Paris to New Haven." Yale University History Department senior essay, 2018.

Black Census Project, conducted by the Black Futures Lab.

Bloom, Matthew. "A Disintegration of Morale: The Failure to Organize Black Workers at Winchester During World War II." Calhoun College thesis, Yale University, 2005.

Caplan, Colin. National Register of Historic Places Winchester District nomination (Western Division).

Census Bureau, Harvard University, Brown University, The Opportunity Atlas.

Codish, K. D. *The New Haven Police Academy: Putting One Sacred Cow Out to Pasture*. New Haven: City of New Haven, 1996.

DeStefano, John. Materials from the papers in the Southern Connecticut State University archive, 2006.

Donaldson, Sarah. "After de facto." History thesis, Yale College, 2001.

Elicker, Justin. Mayor's "Messages" to New Haven residents, 2019–2021.

Ellickson, Robert C. "The Zoning Strait-Jacket." Paper delivered at Law and Economics Seminar, Stanford Law School, November 15, 2018.

Ellis-West, Shirley, and Sherman Malone. "We Just Kept Walking Towards It." The Girls Experience with Violence Project, 2008–10.

Fox, Nathan A., Charles A. Nelson, and Charles H. Zeanah. "The Effects of Psychological Deprivation in Attachment." Department of Health and Human Services author manuscript, 2018.

Geanakoplos, Constantin. "Reclaiming the Mill River District." Yale University thesis, 2015.

Geller, William A. "Police Videotaping of Suspect Interrogations and Confessions." A Report to the National Institute of Justice, 1992.

Gould, Eric D. "Torn Apart? The Impact of Manufacturing Employment Decline on Black and White Americans." IZA Discussion Papers, No. 11614, Institute of Labor Economics, Bonn.

Hansmann, Henry. "Why Are Colleges and Universities Exempt from Taxes?" Paper given at the National Center on Philanthropy and Law, October 2013.

Harlem Community Justice Center, Upper Manhattan Reentry Task Force. "Starting Off on the Right Foot: A Needs Assessment of Reentry in Upper Manhattan," 2007.

Horowitz, Andy. "The Rise and Fall of Carriage Making in New Haven." Hopkins School AP History term paper, 1998.

King, Martin Luther Jr. "The Other America." Lecture given at Grosse Pointe (Michigan) High School, March 14, 1968.

Kraus, Michael W., with Julian M. Rucker and Jennifer A. Richeson. "Americans Misperceive Racial Economic Equality." *Proceedings of the National Academy of Sciences*, September 2017.

Loether, Paul, and John Herzan. National Register of Historic Places Winchester District nomination (Eastern Division).

Loether, Paul, and Dorothea Penar. New Haven Historic Resources Inventory, The New Haven Preservation Trust, June 1983.

Mandujano, Gabriel, and Mark Mills. Penn/Wash Cycle Case Study. The Netter Center, University of Pennsylvania, Draft Paper.

Miller, Meredith Sawyer. "Residential Planning Areas for New Haven." December 1961.

National Inventory of Collateral Consequences of Conviction.

New Haven City Directories, J. H. Benham, Price and Lee.

New Haven Family Alliance, with Robert Wood Johnson Clinical Scholars. "Understanding Youth Violence in New Haven." Yale School of Medicine, 2009.

New Haven Redevelopment Agency Report 1973–1974.

New Haven Revenue Commission Report, 1985.

Newhallville Safe Neighborhood Initiative. A Proposal Submitted to the United States Department of Justice, May 2014.

Notes on Embalming Fluid from the Connecticut Clearinghouse (Connecticut Center for Prevention, Wellness and Recovery), 2002.

Palmer, Stuart H. "The Role of the Real Estate Agent." Doctoral dissertation, Yale University, 1955.

Policy Link and USC Equity Research Institute, National Equity Atlas.

Report of the New Haven Revenue Commission, February 4, 1985.

St. Ronan-Edgehill Historic District, Study Report, New Haven, 2008.

Seaberry, Camille. "Connecticut Data Story: Housing Segregation in Greater New Haven." DataHaven, May 2018.

Shaw, Ernest. "The Face of a Black Town." Independent study paper, Southern Connecticut State College, 1972.

———. "From Williamsburg to New Haven." Master's thesis, University of Connecticut, School of Social Work, 1975.

The Shenachie, volumes 1 and 2, 1989–90. Newsletter of the Connecticut Irish-American Historical Society.

Skerritt, Mary Louise. "New Haven Neighborhood Change, 1960–1970." Master's thesis, Southern Connecticut State College.

Stuart, Bryan, and Evan Taylor. "Migration Networks and Location Decisions." Working paper, The George Washington University Institute for International Economic Policy, 2017.

Suber, Avery C. (ed. Kate Tuttle). "Taking the Wheel: Consumerism and the Consequences of Black Automobile Ownership in the Jim Crow South." The Georgia Civil Rights Cold Cases Project at Emory University.

State of Connecticut v. Bobby Griffin, July 22, 2021.

Teaching Guides on New Haven history and neighborhoods sponsored by Yale–New Haven Teachers' Institute, written by Clarence Roberts, Cynthia Roberts, and Carolyn Smith, 1978–2020.

Violent Crime Working Group, Council on Criminal Justice, Bulletins.

Watson, Clifton. "Making a New Haven: Post World War II Black Migration, Historical Memory, Community Building and Activism in the Late Twentieth Century." Fordham University doctoral dissertation, 2015.

Wood, Alan. "Correlating Violence and Socio-Economic Inequality: An Empirical Analysis." World Organization Against Torture (OMCT), Draft 2006.

Wolfe et al. v. Wolfe et al. Supreme Court of South Carolina, November 4, 1949.

FILM AND TELEVISION

Burns, Ken, Sarah Burns, and David McMahon. *The Central Park Five*, 2012.

Christopherson, Scott, and Brad Barber. *Peace Officer*, 2015.

Dest, Steven. *I Am Shakespeare: The Henry Green Story*, 2017.

Duvernay, Ava. *13th*, 2016.

———. *When They See Us*, 2019.

Ford, Yance. *Strong Island*, 2017.

Lowe, Richard, and Martin Torgoff. *Planet Rock: The Story of Hip-Hop and the Crack Generation*, 2012.

Jacobson, Kristi. *Solitary*, 2016.
James, Steve. *The Interrupters*, 2011.
Nadel, Matt. *120 Years*, 2018.
Peck, Raoul. I *Am Not Your Negro*, 2016.
Rothstein, Hale. "Please Don't Feed the Animals." *Black-ish*, Season 4, Episode 7, 2017.
Sanders, Jessica. *After Innocence*, 2005.

PODCASTS

Hazel, Mycah. "Last Witness: The Kerner Commission." *Radio Diaries*, 2021.
Joffe-Walt, Chana. "Three Miles." *This American Life* (550), March 2015.
Letson, Al. "Mississippi Goddam." *Reveal*, 2021.
Lutton, Linda. *The View from Room 205*, WBEZ, Chicago, January 2017.
Maron, Marc. *WTF*, episodes 698 (David Simon, 2016); 1012 (Brené Brown, 2019); 1083 (Brittany Howard, 2019).
Poor, Nigel, Rahsaan Thomas, Antwan Williams, and Earlonne Woods. *EarHustle*, 2017–2021.
Roberts, Russ. *EconTalk*, episodes March 30, 2015 (David Skarbek), and March 9, 2020 (Richard Davies.)
Rodriquez, Melissa, with Joe Richman and Sarah Kate Kramer. "Melissa's Diary, Revisited." *Radio Diaries*, 2013.
Wright, Kai, Karen Frillmann, Kaari Pitkin, et al. *Caught*, WNYC, 2019.

EXHIBITIONS

Cavanagh, Joan, dir. *Our Community at Winchester*. An exhibit produced by the Greater New Haven Labor History Association, 2020.
Greenberg, Robert. *Lost in New Haven*. A permanent collection exhibit, New Haven, CT.
Larned, Emily. *Police Others as You Would Have Others Police You*. An exhibition created and curated by Frank Mitchell, at ArtSpace, New Haven, 2020.

MISCELLANEOUS SOURCES

Alvin A. Mermin Collection on family relocation for the New Haven Housing Authority/Redevelopment Agency from 1958–1966.
The Amistad Committee: Dugdale, Antony, J. J. Fueser, and J. Celso de Castro Alves. "Yale, Slavery & Abolition."
Burford Capital, company website discussion of litigation funding.
CTN Wrongful Conviction Seminar, University of Connecticut Law School.
Diversitykids.org.
Family and Friends Handbook, Connecticut Department of Correction, 2013.
Newhallville maps, land, and home inventories in the collection of the Whitney Library.
Newhavenmuseum.org.
The Open File. Blog on prosecutorial misconduct and accountability.
Peterkin, Brent. "Questioning Answers." Manchester High School TEDx talk, April 2017.
Policing Post-Ferguson. Conference sponsored by the Justice Collaboratory Yale University, April 2015.
Reid.com.

Robert Solomon shared his interviews with George Edwards, Hugh Price, Warren Kimbro, and Sophie Turner, New Haven, 2011.
Rogershermanhouse.com.
Ron Wilmore, 2009, Yale Class of 1965 Speech.
Sanborn Insurance Maps of New Haven.
Slavenorth.com.
State of Connecticut Historic Resources Inventory.